CONTENTS

THE SECRET AGENT

I

Mr Verloc, going out in the morning, left his shop nominally in charge of his brother-in-law. It could be done, because there was very little business at any time, and practically none at all before the evening. Mr Verloc cared but little about his ostensible business. And, moreover, his wife was in charge of his brother-in-law.

The shop was small, and so was the house. It was one of those grimy brick houses which existed in large quantities before the era of reconstruction dawned upon London. The shop was a square box of a place, with the front glazed in small panes. In the daytime the door remained closed; in the evening it stood discreetly but suspiciously ajar.

The window contained photographs of more or less undressed dancing girls; nondescript packages in wrappers like patent medicines; closed yellow paper envelopes, very flimsy, and marked two-and-six in heavy black figures; a few numbers of ancient French comic publications hung across a string as if to dry; a dingy blue china bowl, a casket of black wood, bottles of marking ink, and rubber stamps; a few books, with titles hinting at impropriety; a few apparently old copies of obscure newspapers, badly printed, with titles like *The Torch*, *The Gong*—rousing titles. And the two gas jets inside the panes were always turned low, either for economy's sake or for the sake of the customers.

These customers were either very young men, who hung about the window for a time before slipping in suddenly; or men of a more mature age, but looking generally as if they were not in funds. Some of that last kind had the collars of their overcoats turned right up to their moustaches, and traces of mud on the bottom of their nether garments, which had the appearance of being much worn and not very valuable. And the legs inside them did not, as a general rule, seem of much account either. With their hands plunged deep in the side pockets of their coats, they dodged in sideways, one shoulder first, as if afraid to start the bell going.

The bell, hung on the door by means of a curved ribbon of steel, was difficult to circumvent. It was hopelessly cracked; but of an evening, at the slightest provocation, it clattered behind the customer with impudent virulence.

It clattered; and at that signal, through the dusty glass door behind the painted deal counter, Mr Verloc would issue hastily from the parlour at the back. His eyes were naturally heavy; he had an air of having wallowed, fully dressed, all day on an unmade bed. Another man would have felt such an appearance a distinct disadvantage. In a commercial transaction of the retail order much depends on the seller's engaging and amiable aspect. But Mr Verloc knew his business, and remained undisturbed by any sort of æsthetic doubt about his appearance. With a firm, steady-eyed impudence, which seemed to hold back the threat of some abominable menace, he would proceed to sell over the counter some object looking obviously and scandalously not worth the money which passed in the transaction: a small cardboard box with apparently nothing inside, for instance, or one of those carefully closed yellow flimsy envelopes, or a soiled volume in paper covers with a promising title. Now and then it happened that one of the faded, yellow dancing girls would get sold to an amateur, as though she had been alive and young.

Sometimes it was Mrs Verloc who would appear at the call of the cracked bell. Winnie Verloc was a young woman with a full bust, in a tight bodice, and with broad hips. Her hair was very tidy. Steady-eyed like her husband, she preserved an air of unfathomable indifference behind the rampart of the counter. Then the customer of comparatively tender years would get suddenly disconcerted at having to deal with a woman, and with rage in his heart would proffer a request for a bottle of marking ink, retail value sixpence (price in Verloc's shop one-and-sixpence), which, once outside, he would drop stealthily into the gutter.

The evening visitors—the men with collars turned up and soft hats rammed down—nodded familiarly to Mrs Verloc, and with a muttered greeting, lifted up the flap at the end of the counter in order to pass into the back parlour, which gave access to a passage and to a steep flight of stairs. The door of the shop was the only means of entrance to the house in which Mr Verloc carried on his business of a seller of shady wares, exercised his vocation of a protector of society, and cultivated his domestic virtues. These last were pronounced. He was thoroughly domesticated. Neither his spiritual, nor his mental, nor his physical needs were of the kind to take him much abroad. He found at home the ease of his body and the peace of his conscience, together with Mrs Verloc's wifely attentions and Mrs Verloc's mother's deferential regard.

Winnie's mother was a stout, wheezy woman, with a large brown face. She wore a black wig under a white cap. Her swollen legs rendered her inactive. She considered herself to be of French descent, which might have been true; and after a good many years of married life with a licensed victualler of the more common sort, she provided for the years of widowhood by letting furnished apartments for gentlemen near Vauxhall Bridge Road in a square once of some splendour and still included in the district of Belgravia. This topographical fact was of some advantage in advertising her rooms; but the patrons of the worthy widow were not exactly of the fashionable kind. Such as they were, her daughter Winnie helped to look after them. Traces of the French descent which the widow boasted of were apparent in Winnie too. They were apparent in the extremely neat and artistic arrangement of her glossy dark hair. Winnie had also other charms: her youth; her full, rounded form; her clear complexion; the provocation of her unfathomable reserve, which never went so far as to prevent conversation, carried on on the lodgers' part with animation, and on hers with an equable amiability. It must be that Mr Verloc was susceptible to these fascinations. Mr Verloc was an intermittent patron. He came and went without any very apparent reason. He generally arrived in London (like the influenza) from the Continent, only he arrived unheralded by the Press; and his visitations set in with great severity. He breakfasted in bed, and remained wallowing there with an air of quiet enjoyment till noon every day—and sometimes even to a later hour. But when he went out he seemed to experience a great difficulty in finding his way back to his temporary home in the Belgravian square. He left it late, and returned to it early—as early as three or four in the morning; and on waking up at ten addressed Winnie, bringing in the breakfast tray, with jocular, exhausted civility, in the hoarse, failing tones of a man who had been talking vehemently for many hours together. His prominent, heavy-lidded eyes rolled sideways amorously and languidly, the bedclothes were pulled up to his chin, and his dark smooth moustache covered his thick lips capable of much honeyed banter.

In Winnie's mother's opinion Mr Verloc was a very nice gentleman. From her life's experience gathered in various "business houses" the good woman had taken into her retirement an ideal of gentlemanliness as exhibited by the patrons of private-saloon bars. Mr Verloc approached that ideal; he attained it, in fact.

"Of course, we'll take over your furniture, mother," Winnie had remarked.

The lodging-house was to be given up. It seems it would not answer to carry it on. It would have been too much trouble for Mr Verloc. It would not have been convenient for his other business. What his business was he did not say; but after his engagement to Winnie he took the trouble to get up before noon, and descending the basement stairs, make himself pleasant to Winnie's mother in the breakfast-room downstairs where she had her motionless being. He stroked the cat, poked the fire, had his lunch served to him there. He left its slightly stuffy cosiness with evident reluctance, but, all the same, remained out till the night was far advanced. He never offered to take Winnie to theatres, as such a nice gentleman ought to have done. His evenings were occupied. His work was in a way political, he told Winnie once. She would have, he warned her, to be very nice to his political friends.

And with her straight, unfathomable glance she answered that she would be so, of course.

How much more he told her as to his occupation it was impossible for Winnie's mother to discover. The married couple took her over with the furniture. The mean aspect of the shop surprised her. The change from the Belgravian square to the narrow street in Soho affected her legs adversely. They became of an enormous size. On the other hand, she experienced a complete relief from material cares. Her son-in-law's heavy good nature inspired her with a sense of absolute safety. Her daughter's future was obviously assured, and even as to her son Stevie she need have no anxiety. She had not been able to conceal from herself that he was a terrible encumbrance, that poor Stevie. But in view of Winnie's fondness for her delicate brother, and of Mr Verloc's kind and generous disposition, she felt that the poor boy was pretty safe in this rough world. And in her heart of hearts she was not perhaps displeased that the Verlocs had no children. As that circumstance seemed perfectly indifferent to Mr Verloc, and as Winnie found an object of quasi-maternal affection in her brother, perhaps this was just as well for poor Stevie.

For he was difficult to dispose of, that boy. He was delicate and, in a frail way, good-looking too, except for the vacant droop of his lower lip. Under our excellent system of compulsory education he had learned to read and write, notwithstanding the unfavourable aspect of the lower lip. But as errand-boy he did not turn out a great success. He forgot his messages; he was easily diverted from the straight path of duty by the attractions of stray cats and dogs, which he followed down narrow alleys into unsavoury courts; by the comedies of the streets, which he contemplated open-mouthed, to the detriment of his employer's interests; or by the dramas of fallen horses, whose pathos and violence induced him sometimes to shriek piercingly in a crowd, which disliked to be disturbed by sounds of distress in its quiet enjoyment of the national spectacle. When led away by a grave and protecting policeman, it would often become apparent that poor Stevie had forgotten his address—at least for a time. A brusque question caused him to stutter to the point of suffocation. When startled by anything perplexing he used to squint horribly. However, he never had any fits (which was encouraging); and before the natural outbursts of impatience on the part of his father he could always, in his childhood's days, run for protection behind the short skirts of his sister Winnie. On the other hand, he might have been suspected of hiding a fund of reckless naughtiness. When he had reached the age of fourteen a friend of his late father, an agent for a foreign preserved milk firm, having given him an opening as office-boy, he was discovered one foggy afternoon, in his chief's absence, busy letting off fireworks on the staircase. He touched off in quick succession a set of fierce rockets, angry catherine wheels, loudly exploding squibs—and the matter might have turned out very serious. An awful panic spread through the whole building. Wild-eyed, choking clerks stampeded through the passages full of smoke, silk hats and elderly business men could be seen rolling independently down the stairs. Stevie did not seem to derive any personal gratification from what he had done. His motives for this stroke of originality were difficult to discover. It was only later on that Winnie obtained from him a misty and confused confession. It seems that two other office-boys in the building had worked upon his feelings by tales of injustice and oppression till they had wrought his compassion to the pitch of that frenzy. But his father's friend, of course, dismissed him summarily as likely to ruin his business. After that altruistic exploit Stevie was put to help wash the dishes in the basement kitchen, and to black the boots of the gentlemen patronising the Belgravian mansion. There was obviously no future in such work. The gentlemen tipped him a shilling now and then. Mr Verloc showed himself the most generous of lodgers. But altogether all that did not amount to much either in the way of gain or prospects; so that when Winnie announced her engagement to Mr Verloc her mother could not help wondering, with a sigh and a glance towards the scullery, what would become of poor Stephen now.

It appeared that Mr Verloc was ready to take him over together with his wife's mother and with the furniture, which was the whole visible fortune of the family. Mr Verloc gathered everything as it came to his broad, good-natured breast. The furniture was disposed to the best advantage all over the house, but Mrs Verloc's mother was confined to two back rooms on the first floor. The luckless Stevie slept in one of them. By this time a growth of thin fluffy hair had come to blur, like a golden mist, the sharp line of his small lower jaw. He helped his sister with blind love and docility in her household duties. Mr Verloc thought that some occupation would be good for him. His spare time he occupied by drawing circles with compass and pencil on a piece of paper. He applied himself to that pastime with great industry, with his elbows spread out and bowed low over the kitchen table. Through the open door of the parlour at the back of the shop Winnie, his sister, glanced at him from time to time with maternal vigilance.

2

SUCH WAS THE HOUSE, the household, and the business Mr Verloc left behind him on his way westward at the hour of half-past ten in the morning. It was unusually early for him; his whole person exhaled the charm of almost dewy freshness; he wore his blue cloth overcoat unbuttoned; his boots were shiny; his cheeks, freshly shaven, had a sort of gloss; and even his heavy-lidded eyes, refreshed by a night of peaceful slumber, sent out glances of comparative alertness. Through the park railings these glances beheld men and women riding in the Row, couples cantering past harmoniously, others advancing sedately at a walk, loitering groups of three or four, solitary horsemen looking unsociable, and solitary women followed at a long distance by a groom with a cockade to his hat and a leather belt over his tight-fitting coat. Carriages went bowling by, mostly two-horse broughams, with here and there a victoria with the skin of some wild beast inside and a woman's face and hat emerging above the folded hood. And a peculiarly London sun—against which nothing could be said except that it looked bloodshot—glorified all this by its stare. It hung at a moderate elevation above Hyde Park Corner with an air of punctual and benign vigilance. The very pavement under Mr Verloc's feet had an old-gold tinge in that diffused light, in which neither wall, nor tree, nor beast, nor man cast a shadow. Mr Verloc was going westward through a town without shadows in an atmosphere of powdered old gold. There were red, coppery gleams on the roofs of houses, on the corners of walls, on the panels of carriages, on the very coats of the horses, and on the broad back of Mr Verloc's overcoat, where they produced a dull effect of rustiness. But Mr Verloc was not in the least conscious of having got rusty. He surveyed through the park railings the evidences of the town's opulence and luxury with an approving eye. All these people had to be protected. Protection is the first necessity of opulence and luxury. They had to be protected; and their horses, carriages, houses, servants had to be protected; and the source of their wealth had to be protected in the heart of the city and the heart of the country; the whole social order favourable to their hygienic idleness had to be protected against the shallow enviousness of unhygienic labour. It had to—and Mr Verloc would have rubbed his hands with satisfaction had he not been constitutionally averse from every superfluous exertion. His idleness was not hygienic, but it suited him very well. He was in a manner devoted to it with a sort of inert fanaticism, or perhaps rather with a fanatical inertness. Born of industrious parents for a life of toil, he had embraced indolence from an impulse as profound as inexplicable and as imperious as the impulse which directs a man's preference for one particular woman in a given thousand. He was too lazy even for a mere demagogue, for a workman orator, for a leader of labour. It was too much trouble. He required a more perfect form of ease; or it might have been that he was the victim of a philosophical unbelief in the effectiveness of every human effort. Such a form of indolence requires, implies, a certain amount of intelligence. Mr Verloc was not devoid of intelligence —and at the notion of a menaced social order he would perhaps have winked to himself if there had not been an effort to make in that sign of scepticism. His big, prominent eyes were not well adapted to winking. They were rather of the sort that closes solemnly in slumber with majestic effect.

Undemonstrative and burly in a fat-pig style, Mr Verloc, without either rubbing his hands with satisfaction or winking sceptically at his thoughts, proceeded on his way. He trod the pavement heavily with his shiny boots, and his general get-up was that of a well-to-do mechanic in business for himself. He might have been anything from a picture-frame maker to a lock-smith; an employer of labour in a small way. But there was also about him an indescribable air which no mechanic could have acquired in the practice of his handicraft however dishonestly exercised: the air common to men who live on the vices, the follies, or the baser fears of mankind; the air of moral nihilism common to keepers of gambling hells and disorderly houses; to private detectives and inquiry agents; to drink sellers and, I should say, to the sellers of invigorating electric belts and to the inventors of patent medicines. But of that last I am not sure, not having carried my investigations so far into the depths. For all I know, the expression of these last may be perfectly diabolic. I shouldn't be surprised. What I want to affirm is that Mr Verloc's expression was by no means diabolic.

Before reaching Knightsbridge, Mr Verloc took a turn to the left out of the busy main thoroughfare, uproarious with the traffic of swaying omnibuses and trotting vans, in the almost silent, swift flow of hansoms. Under his hat, worn with a slight backward tilt, his hair had been carefully brushed into respectful sleekness; for his business was with an Embassy. And Mr Verloc, steady like a rock—a soft kind of rock—marched now along a street which could with every propriety be described as private. In its breadth, emptiness, and extent it had the majesty of inorganic nature, of matter that never dies. The only reminder of mortality was a doctor's brougham arrested in august solitude close to the curbstone. The polished knockers of the doors gleamed as far as the eye could reach, the clean windows shone with a dark opaque lustre. And all was still. But a milk cart rattled noisily across the distant perspective; a butcher boy, driving with the noble recklessness of a charioteer at Olympic Games, dashed round the corner sitting high above a pair of red wheels. A guilty-looking cat issuing from under the stones ran for a while in front of Mr Verloc, then dived into another basement; and a thick police constable, looking a stranger to every emotion, as if he too were part of inorganic nature, surging apparently out of a lamp-post, took not the slightest notice of Mr Verloc. With a turn to the left Mr Verloc pursued his way along a narrow street by the side of a yellow wall which, for some inscrutable reason, had No. 1 Chesham Square written on it in black letters. Chesham Square was at least sixty yards away, and Mr Verloc, cosmopolitan enough not to be deceived by London's topographical mysteries, held on steadily, without a sign of surprise or indignation. At last, with business-like persistency, he reached the Square, and made diagonally for the number 10. This belonged to an imposing carriage gate in a high, clean wall between two houses, of which one rationally enough bore the number 9 and the other was numbered 37; but the fact that this last belonged to Porthill Street, a street well known in the neighbourhood, was proclaimed by an inscription placed above the ground-floor windows by whatever highly efficient authority is charged with the duty of keeping track of London's strayed houses. Why powers are not asked of Parliament (a short act would do) for compelling those edifices to return where they belong is one of the mysteries of municipal administration. Mr Verloc did not trouble his head about it, his mission in life being the protection of the social mechanism, not its perfectionment or even its criticism.

It was so early that the porter of the Embassy issued hurriedly out of his lodge still struggling with the left sleeve of his livery coat. His waistcoat was red, and he wore knee-breeches, but his aspect was flustered. Mr Verloc, aware of the rush on his flank, drove it off by simply holding out an envelope stamped with the arms of the Embassy, and passed on. He produced the same talisman also to the footman who opened the door, and stood back to let him enter the hall.

A clear fire burned in a tall fireplace, and an elderly man standing with his back to it, in evening dress and with a chain round his neck, glanced up from the newspaper he was holding spread out in both hands before his calm and severe face. He didn't move; but another lackey, in brown trousers and claw-hammer coat edged with thin yellow cord, approaching Mr Verloc listened to the murmur of his name, and turning round on his heel in silence, began to walk, without looking back once. Mr Verloc, thus led along a ground-floor passage to the left of the great carpeted staircase, was suddenly motioned to enter a quite small room furnished with a heavy writing-table and a few chairs. The servant shut the door, and Mr Verloc remained alone. He did not take a seat. With his hat and stick held in one hand he glanced about, passing his other podgy hand over his uncovered sleek head.

Another door opened noiselessly, and Mr Verloc immobilising his glance in that direction saw at first only black clothes, the bald top of a head, and a drooping dark grey whisker on each side of a pair of wrinkled hands. The person who had entered was holding a batch of papers before his eyes and walked up to the table with a rather mincing step, turning the papers over the while. Privy Councillor Wurmt, Chancelier d'Ambassade, was rather short-sighted. This meritorious official laying the papers on the table, disclosed a face of pasty complexion and of melancholy ugliness surrounded by a lot of fine, long dark grey hairs, barred heavily by thick and bushy eyebrows. He put on a black-framed pince-nez upon a blunt and shapeless nose, and seemed struck by Mr Verloc's appearance. Under the enormous eyebrows his weak eyes blinked pathetically through the glasses.

He made no sign of greeting; neither did Mr Verloc, who certainly knew his place; but a subtle change about the general outlines of his shoulders and back suggested a slight bending of Mr Verloc's spine under the vast surface of his overcoat. The effect was of unobtrusive deference.

"I have here some of your reports," said the bureaucrat in an unexpectedly soft and weary voice, and pressing the tip of his forefinger on the papers with force. He paused; and Mr Verloc, who had recognised his own handwriting very well, waited in an almost breathless silence. "We are not very satisfied with the attitude of the police here," the other continued, with every appearance of mental fatigue.

The shoulders of Mr Verloc, without actually moving, suggested a shrug. And for the first time since he left his home that morning his lips opened.

"Every country has its police," he said philosophically. But as the official of the Embassy went on blinking at him steadily he felt constrained to add: "Allow me to observe that I have no means of action upon the police here."

"What is desired," said the man of papers, "is the occurrence of something definite which should stimulate their vigilance. That is within your province—is it not so?"

Mr Verloc made no answer except by a sigh, which escaped him involuntarily, for instantly he tried to give his face a cheerful expression. The official blinked doubtfully, as if affected by the dim light of the room. He repeated vaguely.

"The vigilance of the police—and the severity of the magistrates. The general leniency of the judicial procedure here, and the utter absence of all repressive measures, are a scandal to Europe. What is wished for just now is the accentuation of the unrest—of the fermentation which undoubtedly exists—"

"Undoubtedly, undoubtedly," broke in Mr Verloc in a deep deferential bass of an oratorical quality, so utterly different from the tone in which he had spoken before that his interlocutor remained profoundly surprised. "It exists to a dangerous degree. My reports for the last twelve months make it sufficiently clear."

"Your reports for the last twelve months," State Councillor Wurmt began in his gentle and dispassionate tone, "have been read by me. I failed to discover why you wrote them at all."

A sad silence reigned for a time. Mr Verloc seemed to have swallowed his tongue, and the other gazed at the papers on the table fixedly. At last he gave them a slight push.

"The state of affairs you expose there is assumed to exist as the first condition of your employment. What is required at present is not writing, but the bringing to light of a distinct, significant fact—I would almost say of an alarming fact."

"I need not say that all my endeavours shall be directed to that end," Mr Verloc said, with convinced modulations in his conversational husky tone. But the sense of being blinked at watchfully behind the blind glitter of these eye-glasses on the other side of the table disconcerted him. He stopped short with a gesture of absolute devotion. The useful, hard-working, if obscure member of the Embassy had an air of being impressed by some newly-born thought.

"You are very corpulent," he said.

This observation, really of a psychological nature, and advanced with the modest hesitation of an officeman more familiar with ink and paper than with the requirements of active life, stung Mr Verloc in the manner of a rude personal remark. He stepped back a pace.

"Eh? What were you pleased to say?" he exclaimed, with husky resentment.

The Chancelier d'Ambassade entrusted with the conduct of this interview seemed to find it too much for him.

"I think," he said, "that you had better see Mr Vladimir. Yes, decidedly I think you ought to see Mr Vladimir. Be good enough to wait here," he added, and went out with mincing steps.

At once Mr Verloc passed his hand over his hair. A slight perspiration had broken out on his forehead. He let the air escape from his pursed-up lips like a man blowing at a spoonful of hot soup. But when the servant in brown appeared at the door silently, Mr Verloc had not moved an inch from the place he had occupied throughout the interview. He had remained motionless, as if feeling himself surrounded by pitfalls.

He walked along a passage lighted by a lonely gas-jet, then up a flight of winding stairs, and through a glazed and cheerful corridor on the first floor. The footman threw open a door, and stood aside. The feet of Mr Verloc felt a thick carpet. The room was large, with three windows; and a young man with a shaven, big face, sitting in a roomy arm-chair before a vast mahogany writing-table, said in French to the Chancelier d'Ambassade, who was going out with the papers in his hand:

"You are quite right, mon cher. He's fat—the animal."

Mr Vladimir, First Secretary, had a drawing-room reputation as an agreeable and entertaining man. He was something of a favourite in society. His wit consisted in discovering droll connections between incongruous ideas; and when talking in that strain he sat well forward of his seat, with his left hand raised, as if exhibiting his funny demonstrations between the thumb and forefinger, while his round and clean-shaven face wore an expression of merry perplexity.

But there was no trace of merriment or perplexity in the way he looked at Mr Verloc. Lying far back in the deep arm-chair, with squarely spread elbows, and throwing one leg over a thick knee, he had with his smooth and rosy countenance the air of a preternaturally thriving baby that will not stand nonsense from anybody.

"You understand French, I suppose?" he said.

Mr Verloc stated huskily that he did. His whole vast bulk had a forward inclination. He stood on the carpet in the middle of the room, clutching his hat and stick in one hand; the other hung lifelessly by his side. He muttered unobtrusively somewhere deep down in his throat something about having done his military service in the French artillery. At once, with contemptuous perversity, Mr Vladimir changed the language, and began to speak idiomatic English without the slightest trace of a foreign accent.

"Ah! Yes. Of course. Let's see. How much did you get for obtaining the design of the improved breech-block of their new field-gun?"

"Five years' rigorous confinement in a fortress," Mr Verloc answered unexpectedly, but without any sign of feeling.

"You got off easily," was Mr Vladimir's comment. "And, anyhow, it served you right for letting yourself get caught. What made you go in for that sort of thing—eh?"

Mr Verloc's husky conversational voice was heard speaking of youth, of a fatal infatuation for an unworthy—

"Aha! Cherchez la femme," Mr Vladimir deigned to interrupt, unbending, but without affability; there was, on the contrary, a touch of grimness in his condescension. "How long have you been employed by the Embassy here?" he asked.

"Ever since the time of the late Baron Stott-Wartenheim," Mr Verloc answered in subdued tones, and protruding his lips sadly, in sign of sorrow for the deceased diplomat. The First Secretary observed this play of physiognomy steadily.

"Ah! ever since. Well! What have you got to say for yourself?" he asked sharply.

Mr Verloc answered with some surprise that he was not aware of having anything special to say. He had been summoned by a letter—And he plunged his hand busily into the side pocket of his overcoat, but before the mocking, cynical watchfulness of Mr Vladimir, concluded to leave it there.

"Bah!" said that latter. "What do you mean by getting out of condition like this? You haven't got even the physique of your profession. You—a member of a starving proletariat—never! You—a desperate socialist or anarchist—which is it?"

"Anarchist," stated Mr Verloc in a deadened tone.

"Bosh!" went on Mr Vladimir, without raising his voice. "You startled old Wurmt himself. You wouldn't deceive an idiot. They all are that by-the-by, but you seem to me simply impossible. So you began your connection with us by stealing the French gun designs. And you got yourself caught. That must have been very disagreeable to our Government. You don't seem to be very smart."

Mr Verloc tried to exculpate himself huskily.

"As I've had occasion to observe before, a fatal infatuation for an unworthy—"

Mr Vladimir raised a large white, plump hand. "Ah, yes. The unlucky attachment—of your youth. She got hold of the money, and then sold you to the police—eh?"

The doleful change in Mr Verloc's physiognomy, the momentary drooping of his whole person, confessed that such was the regrettable case. Mr Vladimir's hand clasped the ankle reposing on his knee. The sock was of dark blue silk.

"You see, that was not very clever of you. Perhaps you are too susceptible."

Mr Verloc intimated in a throaty, veiled murmur that he was no longer young.

"Oh! That's a failing which age does not cure," Mr Vladimir remarked, with sinister familiarity. "But no! You are too fat for that. You could not have come to look like this if you had been at all susceptible. I'll tell you what I think is the matter: you are a lazy fellow. How long have you been drawing pay from this Embassy?"

"Eleven years," was the answer, after a moment of sulky hesitation. "I've been charged with several missions to London while His Excellency Baron Stott-Wartenheim was still Ambassador in Paris. Then by his Excellency's instructions I settled down in London. I am English."

"You are! Are you? Eh?"

"A natural-born British subject," Mr Verloc said stolidly. "But my father was French, and so—"

"Never mind explaining," interrupted the other. "I daresay you could have been legally a Marshal of France and a Member of Parliament in England—and then, indeed, you would have been of some use to our Embassy."

This flight of fancy provoked something like a faint smile on Mr Verloc's face. Mr Vladimir retained an imperturbable gravity.

"But, as I've said, you are a lazy fellow; you don't use your opportunities. In the time of Baron Stott-Wartenheim we had a lot of soft-headed people running this Embassy. They caused fellows of your sort to form a false conception of the nature of a secret service fund. It is my business to correct this misapprehension by telling you what the secret service is not. It is not a philanthropic institution. I've had you called here on purpose to tell you this."

Mr Vladimir observed the forced expression of bewilderment on Verloc's face, and smiled sarcastically.

"I see that you understand me perfectly. I daresay you are intelligent enough for your work. What we want now is activity—activity."

On repeating this last word Mr Vladimir laid a long white forefinger on the edge of the desk. Every trace of huskiness disappeared from Verloc's voice. The nape of his gross neck became crimson above the velvet collar of his overcoat. His lips quivered before they came widely open.

"If you'll only be good enough to look up my record," he boomed out in his great, clear oratorical bass, "you'll see I gave a warning only three months ago, on the occasion of the Grand Duke Romuald's visit to Paris, which was telegraphed from here to the French police, and—"

"Tut, tut!" broke out Mr Vladimir, with a frowning grimace. "The French police had no use for your warning. Don't roar like this. What the devil do you mean?"

With a note of proud humility Mr Verloc apologised for forgetting himself. His voice,—famous for years at open-air meetings and at workmen's assemblies in large halls, had contributed, he said, to his reputation of a good and trustworthy comrade. It was, therefore, a part of his usefulness. It had inspired confidence in his principles. "I was always put up to speak by the leaders at a critical moment," Mr Verloc declared, with obvious satisfaction. There was no uproar above which he could not make himself heard, he added; and suddenly he made a demonstration.

"Allow me," he said. With lowered forehead, without looking up, swiftly and ponderously he crossed the room to one of the French windows. As if giving way to an uncontrollable impulse, he opened it a little. Mr Vladimir, jumping up amazed from the depths of the arm-chair, looked over his shoulder; and below, across the courtyard of the Embassy, well beyond the open gate, could be seen the broad back of a policeman watching idly the gorgeous perambulator of a wealthy baby being wheeled in state across the Square.

"Constable!" said Mr Verloc, with no more effort than if he were whispering; and Mr Vladimir burst into a laugh on seeing the policeman spin round as if prodded by a sharp instrument. Mr Verloc shut the window quietly, and returned to the middle of the room.

"With a voice like that," he said, putting on the husky conversational pedal, "I was naturally trusted. And I knew what to say, too."

Mr Vladimir, arranging his cravat, observed him in the glass over the mantelpiece.

"I daresay you have the social revolutionary jargon by heart well enough," he said contemptuously. "Vox et. . . You haven't ever studied Latin—have you?"

"No," growled Mr Verloc. "You did not expect me to know it. I belong to the million. Who knows Latin? Only a few hundred imbeciles who aren't fit to take care of themselves."

For some thirty seconds longer Mr Vladimir studied in the mirror the fleshy profile, the gross bulk, of the man behind him. And at the same time he had the advantage of seeing his own face, clean-shaved and round, rosy about the gills, and with the thin sensitive lips formed exactly for the utterance of those delicate witticisms which had made him such a favourite in the very highest society. Then he turned, and advanced into the room with such determination that the very ends of his quaintly old-fashioned bow necktie seemed to bristle with unspeakable menaces. The movement was so swift and fierce that Mr Verloc, casting an oblique glance, quailed inwardly.

"Aha! You dare be impudent," Mr Vladimir began, with an amazingly guttural intonation not only utterly un-English, but absolutely un-European, and startling even to Mr Verloc's experience of cosmopolitan slums. "You dare! Well, I am going to speak plain English to you. Voice won't do. We have no use for your voice. We don't want a voice. We want facts—startling facts—damn you," he added, with a sort of ferocious discretion, right into Mr Verloc's face.

"Don't you try to come over me with your Hyperborean manners," Mr Verloc defended himself huskily, looking at the carpet. At this his interlocutor, smiling mockingly above the bristling bow of his necktie, switched the conversation into French.

"You give yourself for an 'agent provocateur.' The proper business of an 'agent provocateur' is to provoke. As far as I can judge from your record kept here, you have done nothing to earn your money for the last three years."

"Nothing!" exclaimed Verloc, stirring not a limb, and not raising his eyes, but with the note of sincere feeling in his tone. "I have several times prevented what might have been—"

"There is a proverb in this country which says prevention is better than cure," interrupted Mr Vladimir, throwing himself into the arm-chair. "It is stupid in a general way. There is no end to prevention. But it is characteristic. They dislike finality in this country. Don't you be too English. And in this particular instance, don't be absurd. The evil is already here. We don't want prevention—we want cure."

He paused, turned to the desk, and turning over some papers lying there, spoke in a changed business-like tone, without looking at Mr Verloc.

"You know, of course, of the International Conference assembled in Milan?"

Mr Verloc intimated hoarsely that he was in the habit of reading the daily papers. To a further question his answer was that, of course, he understood what he read. At this Mr Vladimir, smiling faintly at the documents he was still scanning one after another, murmured "As long as it is not written in Latin, I suppose."

"Or Chinese," added Mr Verloc stolidly.

"H'm. Some of your revolutionary friends' effusions are written in a *charabia* every bit as incomprehensible as Chinese—" Mr Vladimir let fall disdainfully a grey sheet of printed matter. "What are all these leaflets headed F. P., with a hammer, pen, and torch crossed? What does it mean, this F. P.?" Mr Verloc approached the imposing writing-table.

"The Future of the Proletariat. It's a society," he explained, standing ponderously by the side of the arm-chair, "not anarchist in principle, but open to all shades of revolutionary opinion."

"Are you in it?"

"One of the Vice-Presidents," Mr Verloc breathed out heavily; and the First Secretary of the Embassy raised his head to look at him.

"Then you ought to be ashamed of yourself," he said incisively. "Isn't your society capable of anything else but printing this prophetic bosh in blunt type on this filthy paper eh? Why don't you do something? Look here. I've this matter in hand now, and I tell you plainly that you will have to earn your money. The good old Stott-Wartenheim times are over. No work, no pay."

Mr Verloc felt a queer sensation of faintness in his stout legs. He stepped back one pace, and blew his nose loudly.

He was, in truth, startled and alarmed. The rusty London sunshine struggling clear of the London mist shed a lukewarm brightness into the First Secretary's private room; and in the silence Mr Verloc heard against a window-pane the faint buzzing of a fly—his first fly of the year—heralding better than any number of swallows the approach of spring. The useless fussing of that tiny energetic organism affected unpleasantly this big man threatened in his indolence.

In the pause Mr Vladimir formulated in his mind a series of disparaging remarks concerning Mr Verloc's face and figure. The fellow was unexpectedly vulgar, heavy, and impudently unintelligent. He looked uncommonly like a master plumber come to present his bill. The First Secretary of the Embassy, from his occasional excursions into the field of American humour, had formed a special notion of that class of mechanic as the embodiment of fraudulent laziness and incompetency.

This was then the famous and trusty secret agent, so secret that he was never designated otherwise but by the symbol [delta] in the late Baron Stott-Wartenheim's official, semi-official, and confidential correspondence; the celebrated agent [delta], whose warnings had the power to change the schemes and the dates of royal, imperial, grand ducal journeys, and sometimes caused them to be put off altogether! This fellow! And Mr Vladimir indulged mentally in an enormous and derisive fit of merriment, partly at his own astonishment, which he judged naive, but mostly at the expense of the universally regretted Baron Stott-Wartenheim. His late Excellency, whom the august favour of his Imperial master had imposed as Ambassador upon several reluctant Ministers of Foreign Affairs, had enjoyed in his lifetime a fame for an owlish, pessimistic gullibility. His Excellency had the social revolution on the brain. He imagined himself to be a diplomatist set apart by a special dispensation to watch the end of diplomacy, and pretty nearly the end of the world, in a horrid democratic upheaval. His prophetic and doleful despatches had been for years the joke of Foreign Offices. He was said to have exclaimed on his deathbed (visited by his Imperial friend and master): "Unhappy Europe! Thou shalt perish by the moral insanity of thy children!" He was fated to be the victim of the first humbugging rascal that came along, thought Mr Vladimir, smiling vaguely at Mr Verloc.

"You ought to venerate the memory of Baron Stott-Wartenheim," he exclaimed suddenly.

The lowered physiognomy of Mr Verloc expressed a sombre and weary annoyance.

"Permit me to observe to you," he said, "that I came here because I was summoned by a peremptory letter. I have been here only twice before in the last eleven years, and certainly never at eleven in the morning. It isn't very wise to call me up like this. There is just a chance of being seen. And that would be no joke for me."

Mr Vladimir shrugged his shoulders.

"It would destroy my usefulness," continued the other hotly.

"That's your affair," murmured Mr Vladimir, with soft brutality. "When you cease to be useful you shall cease to be employed. Yes. Right off. Cut short. You shall—" Mr Vladimir, frowning, paused, at a loss for a sufficiently idiomatic expression, and instantly brightened up, with a grin of beautifully white teeth. "You shall be chucked," he brought out ferociously.

Once more Mr Verloc had to react with all the force of his will against that sensation of faintness running down one's legs which once upon a time had inspired some poor devil with the felicitous expression: "My heart went down into my boots." Mr Verloc, aware of the sensation, raised his head bravely.

Mr Vladimir bore the look of heavy inquiry with perfect serenity.

"What we want is to administer a tonic to the Conference in Milan," he said airily. "Its deliberations upon international action for the suppression of political crime don't seem to get anywhere. England lags. This country is absurd with its sentimental regard for individual liberty. It's intolerable to think that all your friends have got only to come over to—"

"In that way I have them all under my eye," Mr Verloc interrupted huskily.

"It would be much more to the point to have them all under lock and key. England must be brought into line. The imbecile bourgeoisie of this country make themselves the accomplices of the very people whose aim is to drive them out of their houses to starve in ditches. And they have the political power still, if they only had the sense to use it for their preservation. I suppose you agree that the middle classes are stupid?"

Mr Verloc agreed hoarsely.

"They are."

"They have no imagination. They are blinded by an idiotic vanity. What they want just now is a jolly good scare. This is the psychological moment to set your friends to work. I have had you called here to develop to you my idea."

And Mr Vladimir developed his idea from on high, with scorn and condescension, displaying at the same time an amount of ignorance as to the real aims, thoughts, and methods of the revolutionary world which filled the silent Mr Verloc with inward consternation. He confounded causes with effects more than was excusable; the most distinguished propagandists with impulsive bomb throwers; assumed organisation where in the nature of things it could not exist; spoke of the social revolutionary party one moment as of a perfectly disciplined army, where the word of chiefs was supreme, and at another as if it had been the loosest association of desperate brigands that ever camped in a mountain gorge. Once Mr Verloc had opened his mouth for a protest, but the raising of a shapely, large white hand arrested him. Very soon he became too appalled to even try to protest. He listened in a stillness of dread which resembled the immobility of profound attention.

"A series of outrages," Mr Vladimir continued calmly, "executed here in this country; not only *planned* here—that would not do—they would not mind. Your friends could set half the Continent on fire without influencing the public opinion here in favour of a universal repressive legislation. They will not look outside their backyard here."

Mr Verloc cleared his throat, but his heart failed him, and he said nothing.

"These outrages need not be especially sanguinary," Mr Vladimir went on, as if delivering a scientific lecture, "but they must be sufficiently startling—effective. Let them be directed against buildings, for instance. What is the fetish of the hour that all the bourgeoisie recognise—eh, Mr Verloc?"

Mr Verloc opened his hands and shrugged his shoulders slightly.

"You are too lazy to think," was Mr Vladimir's comment upon that gesture. "Pay attention to what I say. The fetish of to-day is neither royalty nor religion. Therefore the palace and the church should be left alone. You understand what I mean, Mr Verloc?"

The dismay and the scorn of Mr Verloc found vent in an attempt at levity.

"Perfectly. But what of the Embassies? A series of attacks on the various Embassies," he began; but he could not withstand the cold, watchful stare of the First Secretary.

"You can be facetious, I see," the latter observed carelessly. "That's all right. It may enliven your oratory at socialistic congresses. But this room is no place for it. It would be infinitely safer for you to follow carefully what I am saying. As you are being called upon to furnish facts instead of cock-and-bull stories, you had better try to make your profit off what I am taking the trouble to explain to you. The sacrosanct fetish of to-day is science. Why don't you get some of your friends to go for that wooden-faced panjandrum—eh? Is it not part of these institutions which must be swept away before the F. P. comes along?"

Mr Verloc said nothing. He was afraid to open his lips lest a groan should escape him.

"This is what you should try for. An attempt upon a crowned head or on a president is sensational enough in a way, but not so much as it used to be. It has entered into the general conception of the existence of all chiefs of state. It's almost conventional—especially since so many presidents have been assassinated. Now let us take an outrage upon—say a church. Horrible enough at first sight, no doubt, and yet not so effective as a person of an ordinary mind might think. No matter how revolutionary and anarchist in inception, there would be fools enough to give such an outrage the character of a religious manifestation. And that would detract from the especial alarming significance we wish to give to the act. A murderous attempt on a restaurant or a theatre would suffer in the same way from the suggestion of non-political passion: the exasperation of a hungry man, an act of social revenge. All this is used up; it is no longer instructive as an object lesson in revolutionary anarchism. Every newspaper has ready-made phrases to explain such manifestations away. I am about to give you the philosophy of bomb throwing from my point of view; from the point of view you pretend to have been serving for the last eleven years. I will try not to talk above your head. The sensibilities of the class you are attacking are soon blunted. Property seems to them an indestructible thing. You can't count upon their emotions either of pity or fear for very long. A bomb outrage to have any influence on public opinion now must go beyond the intention of vengeance or terrorism. It must be purely destructive. It must be that, and only that, beyond the faintest suspicion of any other object. You anarchists should make it clear that you are perfectly determined to make a clean sweep of the whole social creation. But how to get that appallingly absurd notion into the heads of the middle classes so that there should be no mistake? That's the question. By directing your blows at something outside the ordinary passions of humanity is the answer. Of course, there is art. A bomb in the National Gallery would make some noise. But it would not be serious enough. Art has never been their fetish. It's like breaking a few back windows in a man's house; whereas, if you want to make him really sit up, you must try at least to raise the roof. There would be some screaming of course, but from whom? Artists—art critics and such like—people of no account. Nobody minds what they say. But there is learning—science. Any imbecile that has got an income believes in that. He does not know why, but he believes it matters somehow. It is the sacrosanct fetish. All the damned professors are radicals at heart. Let them know that their great panjandrum has got to go too, to make room for the Future of the Proletariat. A howl from all these intellectual idiots is bound to help forward the labours of the Milan Conference. They will be writing to the papers. Their indignation would be above suspicion, no material interests being openly at stake, and it will alarm every selfishness of the class which should be impressed. They believe that in some mysterious way science is at the source of their material prosperity. They do. And the absurd ferocity of such a demonstration will affect them more profoundly than the mangling of a whole street—or theatre—full of their own kind. To that last they can always say: 'Oh! it's mere class hate.' But what is one to say to an act of destructive ferocity so absurd as to be incomprehensible, inexplicable, almost unthinkable; in fact, mad? Madness alone is truly terrifying, inasmuch as you cannot placate it either by threats, persuasion, or bribes. Moreover, I am a civilised man. I would never dream of directing you to organise a mere butchery, even if I expected the best results from it. But I wouldn't expect from a butchery the result I want. Murder is always with us. It is almost an institution. The demonstration must be against learning—science. But not every science will do. The attack must have all the shocking senselessness of gratuitous blasphemy. Since bombs are your means of expression, it would be really telling if one could throw a bomb into pure mathematics. But that is impossible. I have been trying to educate you; I have expounded to you the higher philosophy of your usefulness, and suggested to you some serviceable arguments. The practical application of my teaching interests *you* mostly. But from the moment I have undertaken to interview you I have also given some attention to the practical aspect of the question. What do you think of having a go at astronomy?"

For sometime already Mr Verloc's immobility by the side of the arm-chair resembled a state of collapsed coma—a sort of passive insensibility interrupted by slight convulsive starts, such as may be observed in the domestic dog having a nightmare on the hearthrug. And it was in an uneasy doglike growl that he repeated the word:

"Astronomy."

He had not recovered thoroughly as yet from that state of bewilderment brought about by the effort to follow Mr Vladimir's rapid incisive utterance. It had overcome his power of assimilation. It had made him angry. This anger was complicated by incredulity. And suddenly it dawned upon him that all this was an elaborate joke. Mr Vladimir exhibited his white teeth in a smile, with dimples on his round, full face posed with a complacent inclination above the bristling bow of his neck-tie. The favourite of intelligent society women had assumed his drawing-room attitude accompanying the delivery of delicate witticisms. Sitting well forward, his white hand upraised, he seemed to hold delicately between his thumb and forefinger the subtlety of his suggestion.

"There could be nothing better. Such an outrage combines the greatest possible regard for humanity with the most alarming display of ferocious imbecility. I defy the ingenuity of journalists to persuade their public that any given member of the proletariat can have a personal grievance against astronomy. Starvation itself could hardly be dragged in there—

eh? And there are other advantages. The whole civilised world has heard of Greenwich. The very boot-blacks in the basement of Charing Cross Station know something of it. See?"

The features of Mr Vladimir, so well known in the best society by their humorous urbanity, beamed with cynical self-satisfaction, which would have astonished the intelligent women his wit entertained so exquisitely. "Yes," he continued, with a contemptuous smile, "the blowing up of the first meridian is bound to raise a howl of execration."

"A difficult business," Mr Verloc mumbled, feeling that this was the only safe thing to say.

"What is the matter? Haven't you the whole gang under your hand? The very pick of the basket? That old terrorist Yundt is here. I see him walking about Piccadilly in his green havelock almost every day. And Michaelis, the ticket-of-leave apostle—you don't mean to say you don't know where he is? Because if you don't, I can tell you," Mr Vladimir went on menacingly. "If you imagine that you are the only one on the secret fund list, you are mistaken."

This perfectly gratuitous suggestion caused Mr Verloc to shuffle his feet slightly.

"And the whole Lausanne lot—eh? Haven't they been flocking over here at the first hint of the Milan Conference? This is an absurd country."

"It will cost money," Mr Verloc said, by a sort of instinct.

"That cock won't fight," Mr Vladimir retorted, with an amazingly genuine English accent. "You'll get your screw every month, and no more till something happens. And if nothing happens very soon you won't get even that. What's your ostensible occupation? What are you supposed to live by?"

"I keep a shop," answered Mr Verloc.

"A shop! What sort of shop?"

"Stationery, newspapers. My wife—"

"Your what?" interrupted Mr Vladimir in his guttural Central Asian tones.

"My wife." Mr Verloc raised his husky voice slightly. "I am married."

"That be damned for a yarn," exclaimed the other in unfeigned astonishment. "Married! And you a professed anarchist, too! What is this confounded nonsense? But I suppose it's merely a manner of speaking. Anarchists don't marry. It's well known. They can't. It would be apostasy."

"My wife isn't one," Mr Verloc mumbled sulkily. "Moreover, it's no concern of yours."

"Oh yes, it is," snapped Mr Vladimir. "I am beginning to be convinced that you are not at all the man for the work you've been employed on. Why, you must have discredited yourself completely in your own world by your marriage. Couldn't you have managed without? This is your virtuous attachment—eh? What with one sort of attachment and another you are doing away with your usefulness."

Mr Verloc, puffing out his cheeks, let the air escape violently, and that was all. He had armed himself with patience. It was not to be tried much longer. The First Secretary became suddenly very curt, detached, final.

"You may go now," he said. "A dynamite outrage must be provoked. I give you a month. The sittings of the Conference are suspended. Before it reassembles again something must have happened here, or your connection with us ceases."

He changed the note once more with an unprincipled versatility.

"Think over my philosophy, Mr—Mr—Verloc," he said, with a sort of chaffing condescension, waving his hand towards the door. "Go for the first meridian. You don't know the middle classes as well as I do. Their sensibilities are jaded. The first meridian. Nothing better, and nothing easier, I should think."

He had got up, and with his thin sensitive lips twitching humorously, watched in the glass over the mantelpiece Mr Verloc backing out of the room heavily, hat and stick in hand. The door closed.

The footman in trousers, appearing suddenly in the corridor, let Mr Verloc another way out and through a small door in the corner of the courtyard. The porter standing at the gate ignored his exit completely; and Mr Verloc retraced the path of his morning's pilgrimage as if in a dream—an angry dream. This detachment from the material world was so complete that, though the mortal envelope of Mr Verloc had not hastened unduly along the streets, that part of him to which it would be unwarrantably rude to refuse immortality, found itself at the shop door all at once, as if borne from west to east on the wings of a great wind. He walked straight behind the counter, and sat down on a wooden chair that stood there. No one appeared to disturb his solitude. Stevie, put into a green baize apron, was now sweeping and dusting upstairs, intent and conscientious, as though he were playing at it; and Mrs Verloc, warned in the kitchen by the clatter of the cracked bell, had merely come to the glazed door of the parlour, and putting the curtain aside a little, had peered into the dim shop. Seeing her husband sitting there shadowy and bulky, with his hat tilted far back on his head, she had at once returned to her stove. An hour or more later she took the green baize apron off her brother Stevie, and instructed him to wash his hands and face in the peremptory tone she had used in that connection for fifteen years or so—ever since she had, in fact, ceased to attend to the boy's hands and face herself. She spared presently a glance away from her dishing-up for the inspection of that face and those hands which Stevie, approaching the kitchen table, offered for her approval with an air of self-assurance hiding a perpetual residue of anxiety. Formerly the anger of the father was the supremely effective sanction of these rites, but Mr Verloc's placidity in domestic life would have made all mention of anger incredible even to poor Stevie's nervousness. The theory was that Mr Verloc would have been inexpressibly pained and shocked by any deficiency of cleanliness at meal times. Winnie after the death of her father found considerable consolation in the feeling that she need no longer tremble for poor Stevie. She could not bear to see the boy hurt. It maddened her. As a little girl she had often faced with blazing eyes the irascible licensed victualler in defence of her brother. Nothing now in Mrs Verloc's appearance could lead one to suppose that she was capable of a passionate demonstration.

She finished her dishing-up. The table was laid in the parlour. Going to the foot of the stairs, she screamed out "Mother!" Then opening the glazed door leading to the shop, she said quietly "Adolf!" Mr Verloc had not changed his position; he had not apparently stirred a limb for an hour and a half. He got up heavily, and came to his dinner in his overcoat and with his hat on, without uttering a word. His silence in itself had nothing startlingly unusual in this household, hidden in the shades of the sordid street seldom touched by the sun, behind the dim shop with its wares of disreputable rubbish. Only that day Mr Verloc's taciturnity was so obviously thoughtful that the two women were impressed by it. They sat silent themselves, keeping a watchful eye on poor Stevie, lest he should break out into one of his fits of loquacity. He faced Mr Verloc across the table, and remained very good and quiet, staring vacantly. The endeavour to keep him from making himself objectionable in any way to the master of the house put no inconsiderable anxiety into these two women's lives. "That boy," as they alluded to him softly between themselves, had been a source of that sort of anxiety almost from the very day of his birth. The late licensed victualler's humiliation at having such a very peculiar boy for a son manifested itself by a propensity to brutal treatment; for he was a person of fine sensibilities, and his sufferings as a man and a father were perfectly genuine. Afterwards Stevie had to be kept from making himself a nuisance to the single gentlemen lodgers, who are themselves a queer lot, and are easily aggrieved. And there was always the anxiety of his mere existence to face. Visions of a workhouse infirmary for her child had haunted the old woman in the basement breakfast-room of the decayed Belgravian house. "If you had not found such a good husband, my dear," she used to say to her daughter, "I don't know what would have become of that poor boy."

Mr Verloc extended as much recognition to Stevie as a man not particularly fond of animals may give to his wife's beloved cat; and this recognition, benevolent and perfunctory, was essentially of the same quality. Both women admitted to themselves that not much more could be reasonably expected. It was enough to earn for Mr Verloc the old woman's reverential gratitude. In the early days, made sceptical by the trials of friendless life, she used sometimes to ask anxiously: "You don't think, my dear, that Mr Verloc is getting tired of seeing Stevie about?" To this Winnie replied habitually by a slight toss of her head. Once, however, she retorted, with a rather grim pertness: "He'll have to get tired of me first." A long silence ensued. The mother, with her feet propped up on a stool, seemed to be trying to get to the bottom of that answer, whose feminine profundity had struck her all of a heap. She had never really understood why Winnie had married Mr Verloc. It was very sensible of her, and evidently had turned out for the best, but her girl might have naturally hoped to find somebody of a more suitable age. There had been a steady young fellow, only son of a butcher in the next street, helping his father in business, with whom Winnie had been walking out with obvious gusto. He was dependent on his father, it is true; but the business was good, and his prospects excellent. He took her girl to the theatre on several evenings. Then just as she began to dread to hear of their engagement (for what could she have done with that big house alone, with Stevie on her hands), that romance came to an abrupt end, and Winnie went about looking very dull. But Mr Verloc, turning up providentially to occupy the first-floor front bedroom, there had been no more question of the young butcher. It was clearly providential.

3

" . . . All idealisation makes life poorer. To beautify it is to take away its character of complexity—it is to destroy it. Leave that to the moralists, my boy. History is made by men, but they do not make it in their heads. The ideas that are born in their consciousness play an insignificant part in the march of events. History is dominated and determined by the tool and the production—by the force of economic conditions. Capitalism has made socialism, and the laws made by the capitalism for the protection of property are responsible for anarchism. No one can tell what form the social organisation may take in the future. Then why indulge in prophetic phantasies? At best they can only interpret the mind of the prophet, and can have no objective value. Leave that pastime to the moralists, my boy."

Michaelis, the ticket-of-leave apostle, was speaking in an even voice, a voice that wheezed as if deadened and oppressed by the layer of fat on his chest. He had come out of a highly hygienic prison round like a tub, with an enormous stomach and distended cheeks of a pale, semi-transparent complexion, as though for fifteen years the servants of an outraged society had made a point of stuffing him with fattening foods in a damp and lightless cellar. And ever since he had never managed to get his weight down as much as an ounce.

It was said that for three seasons running a very wealthy old lady had sent him for a cure to Marienbad—where he was about to share the public curiosity once with a crowned head—but the police on that occasion ordered him to leave within twelve hours. His martyrdom was continued by forbidding him all access to the healing waters. But he was resigned now.

With his elbow presenting no appearance of a joint, but more like a bend in a dummy's limb, thrown over the back of a chair, he leaned forward slightly over his short and enormous thighs to spit into the grate.

"Yes! I had the time to think things out a little," he added without emphasis. "Society has given me plenty of time for meditation."

On the other side of the fireplace, in the horse-hair arm-chair where Mrs Verloc's mother was generally privileged to sit, Karl Yundt giggled grimly, with a faint black grimace of a toothless mouth. The terrorist, as he called himself, was old and bald, with a narrow, snow-white wisp of a goatee hanging limply from his chin. An extraordinary expression of underhand malevolence survived in his extinguished eyes. When he rose painfully the thrusting forward of a skinny groping hand deformed by gouty swellings suggested the effort of a moribund murderer summoning all his remaining strength for a last stab. He leaned on a thick stick, which trembled under his other hand.

"I have always dreamed," he mouthed fiercely, "of a band of men absolute in their resolve to discard all scruples in the choice of means, strong enough to give themselves frankly the name of destroyers, and free from the taint of that resigned pessimism which rots the world. No pity for anything on earth, including themselves, and death enlisted for good and all in the service of humanity—that's what I would have liked to see."

His little bald head quivered, imparting a comical vibration to the wisp of white goatee. His enunciation would have been almost totally unintelligible to a stranger. His worn-out passion, resembling in its impotent fierceness the excitement of a senile sensualist, was badly served by a dried throat and toothless gums which seemed to catch the tip of his tongue. Mr Verloc, established in the corner of the sofa at the other end of the room, emitted two hearty grunts of assent.

The old terrorist turned slowly his head on his skinny neck from side to side.

"And I could never get as many as three such men together. So much for your rotten pessimism," he snarled at Michaelis, who uncrossed his thick legs, similar to bolsters, and slid his feet abruptly under his chair in sign of exasperation.

He a pessimist! Preposterous! He cried out that the charge was outrageous. He was so far from pessimism that he saw already the end of all private property coming along logically, unavoidably, by the mere development of its inherent viciousness. The possessors of property had not only to face the awakened proletariat, but they had also to fight amongst themselves. Yes. Struggle, warfare, was the condition of private ownership. It was fatal. Ah! he did not depend upon emotional excitement to keep up his belief, no declamations, no anger, no visions of blood-red flags waving, or metaphorical lurid suns of vengeance rising above the horizon of a doomed society. Not he! Cold reason, he boasted, was the basis of his optimism. Yes, optimism—

His laborious wheezing stopped, then, after a gasp or two, he added:

"Don't you think that, if I had not been the optimist I am, I could not have found in fifteen years some means to cut my throat? And, in the last instance, there were always the walls of my cell to dash my head against."

The shortness of breath took all fire, all animation out of his voice; his great, pale cheeks hung like filled pouches, motionless, without a quiver; but in his blue eyes, narrowed as if peering, there was the same look of confident shrewdness, a little crazy in its fixity, they must have had while the indomitable optimist sat thinking at night in his cell. Before him, Karl Yundt remained standing, one wing of his faded greenish havelock thrown back cavalierly over his shoulder. Seated in front of the fireplace, Comrade Ossipon, ex-medical student, the principal writer of the F. P. leaflets, stretched out his robust legs, keeping the soles of his boots turned up to the glow in the grate. A bush of crinkly yellow hair topped his red, freckled face, with a flattened nose and prominent mouth cast in the rough mould of the negro type. His almond-shaped eyes leered languidly over the high cheek-bones. He wore a grey flannel shirt, the loose ends of a black silk tie hung down the buttoned breast of his serge coat; and his head resting on the back of his chair, his throat largely exposed, he raised to his lips a cigarette in a long wooden tube, puffing jets of smoke straight up at the ceiling.

Michaelis pursued his idea—*the* idea of his solitary reclusion—the thought vouchsafed to his captivity and growing like a faith revealed in visions. He talked to himself, indifferent to the sympathy or hostility of his hearers, indifferent indeed to their presence, from the habit he had acquired of thinking aloud hopefully in the solitude of the four whitewashed walls of his cell, in the sepulchral silence of the great blind pile of bricks near a river, sinister and ugly like a colossal mortuary for the socially drowned.

He was no good in discussion, not because any amount of argument could shake his faith, but because the mere fact of hearing another voice disconcerted him painfully, confusing his thoughts at once—these thoughts that for so many years, in a mental solitude more barren than a waterless desert, no living voice had ever combatted, commented, or approved.

No one interrupted him now, and he made again the confession of his faith, mastering him irresistible and complete like an act of grace: the secret of fate discovered in the material side of life; the economic condition of the world responsible for the past and shaping the future; the source of all history, of all ideas, guiding the mental development of mankind and the very impulses of their passion—

A harsh laugh from Comrade Ossipon cut the tirade dead short in a sudden faltering of the tongue and a bewildered unsteadiness of the apostle's mildly exalted eyes. He closed them slowly for a moment, as if to collect his routed thoughts. A silence fell; but what with the two gas-jets over the table and the glowing grate the little parlour behind Mr Verloc's shop had become frightfully hot. Mr Verloc, getting off the sofa with ponderous reluctance, opened the door leading into the kitchen to get more air, and thus disclosed the innocent Stevie, seated very good and quiet at a deal table, drawing circles, circles, circles; innumerable circles, concentric, eccentric; a coruscating whirl of circles that by their tangled multitude of repeated curves, uniformity of form, and confusion of intersecting lines suggested a rendering of cosmic chaos, the symbolism of a mad art attempting the inconceivable. The artist never turned his head; and in all his soul's application to the task his back quivered, his thin neck, sunk into a deep hollow at the base of the skull, seemed ready to snap.

Mr Verloc, after a grunt of disapproving surprise, returned to the sofa. Alexander Ossipon got up, tall in his threadbare blue serge suit under the low ceiling, shook off the stiffness of long immobility, and strolled away into the kitchen (down two steps) to look over Stevie's shoulder. He came back, pronouncing oracularly: "Very good. Very characteristic, perfectly typical."

"What's very good?" grunted inquiringly Mr Verloc, settled again in the corner of the sofa. The other explained his meaning negligently, with a shade of condescension and a toss of his head towards the kitchen:

"Typical of this form of degeneracy—these drawings, I mean."

"You would call that lad a degenerate, would you?" mumbled Mr Verloc.

Comrade Alexander Ossipon—nicknamed the Doctor, ex-medical student without a degree; afterwards wandering lecturer to working-men's associations upon the socialistic aspects of hygiene; author of a popular quasi-medical study (in the form of a cheap pamphlet seized promptly by the police) entitled "The Corroding Vices of the Middle Classes"; special delegate of the more or less mysterious Red Committee, together with Karl Yundt and Michaelis for the work of literary propaganda—turned upon the obscure familiar of at least two Embassies that glance of insufferable, hopelessly dense sufficiency which nothing but the frequentation of science can give to the dulness of common mortals.

"That's what he may be called scientifically. Very good type too, altogether, of that sort of degenerate. It's enough to glance at the lobes of his ears. If you read Lombroso—"

Mr Verloc, moody and spread largely on the sofa, continued to look down the row of his waistcoat buttons; but his cheeks became tinged by a faint blush. Of late even the merest derivative of the word science (a term in itself inoffensive and of indefinite meaning) had the curious power of evoking a definitely offensive mental vision of Mr Vladimir, in his body as he lived, with an almost supernatural clearness. And this phenomenon, deserving justly to be classed amongst the marvels of science, induced in Mr Verloc an emotional state of dread and exasperation tending to express itself in violent swearing. But he said nothing. It was Karl Yundt who was heard, implacable to his last breath.

"Lombroso is an ass."

Comrade Ossipon met the shock of this blasphemy by an awful, vacant stare. And the other, his extinguished eyes without gleams blackening the deep shadows under the great, bony forehead, mumbled, catching the tip of his tongue between his lips at every second word as though he were chewing it angrily:

"Did you ever see such an idiot? For him the criminal is the prisoner. Simple, is it not? What about those who shut him up there—forced him in there? Exactly. Forced him in there. And what is crime? Does he know that, this imbecile who has made his way in this world of gorged fools by looking at the ears and teeth of a lot of poor, luckless devils? Teeth and ears mark the criminal? Do they? And what about the law that marks him still better—the pretty branding instrument invented by the overfed to protect themselves against the hungry? Red-hot applications on their vile skins—hey? Can't you smell and hear from here the thick hide of the people burn and sizzle? That's how criminals are made for your Lombrosos to write their silly stuff about."

The knob of his stick and his legs shook together with passion, whilst the trunk, draped in the wings of the havelock, preserved his historic attitude of defiance. He seemed to sniff the tainted air of social cruelty, to strain his ear for its atrocious sounds. There was an extraordinary force of suggestion in this posturing. The all but moribund veteran of dynamite wars had been a great actor in his time—actor on platforms, in secret assemblies, in private interviews. The famous terrorist had never in his life raised personally as much as his little finger against the social edifice. He was no man of action; he was not even an orator of torrential eloquence, sweeping the masses along in the rushing noise and foam of a great enthusiasm. With a more subtle intention, he took the part of an insolent and venomous evoker of sinister impulses which lurk in the blind envy and exasperated vanity of ignorance, in the suffering and misery of poverty, in all the hopeful and noble illusions of righteous anger, pity, and revolt. The shadow of his evil gift clung to him yet like the smell of a deadly drug in an old vial of poison, emptied now, useless, ready to be thrown away upon the rubbish-heap of things that had served their time.

Michaelis, the ticket-of-leave apostle, smiled vaguely with his glued lips; his pasty moon face drooped under the weight of melancholy assent. He had been a prisoner himself. His own skin had sizzled under the red-hot brand, he murmured softly. But Comrade Ossipon, nicknamed the Doctor, had got over the shock by that time.

"You don't understand," he began disdainfully, but stopped short, intimidated by the dead blackness of the cavernous eyes in the face turned slowly towards him with a blind stare, as if guided only by the sound. He gave the discussion up, with a slight shrug of the shoulders.

Stevie, accustomed to move about disregarded, had got up from the kitchen table, carrying off his drawing to bed with him. He had reached the parlour door in time to receive in full the shock of Karl Yundt's eloquent imagery. The sheet of paper covered with circles dropped out of his fingers, and he remained staring at the old terrorist, as if rooted suddenly to the spot by his morbid horror and dread of physical pain. Stevie knew very well that hot iron applied to one's skin hurt very much. His scared eyes blazed with indignation: it would hurt terribly. His mouth dropped open.

Michaelis by staring unwinkingly at the fire had regained that sentiment of isolation necessary for the continuity of his thought. His optimism had begun to flow from his lips. He saw Capitalism doomed in its cradle, born with the poison of the principle of competition in its system. The great capitalists devouring the little capitalists, concentrating the power and the tools of production in great masses, perfecting industrial processes, and in the madness of self-aggrandisement only preparing, organising, enriching, making ready the lawful inheritance of the suffering proletariat. Michaelis pronounced the great word "Patience"—and his clear blue glance, raised to the low ceiling of Mr Verloc's parlour, had a character of seraphic trustfulness. In the doorway Stevie, calmed, seemed sunk in hebetude.

Comrade Ossipon's face twitched with exasperation.

"Then it's no use doing anything—no use whatever."

"I don't say that," protested Michaelis gently. His vision of truth had grown so intense that the sound of a strange voice failed to rout it this time. He continued to look down at the red coals. Preparation for the future was necessary, and he was willing to admit that the great change would perhaps come in the upheaval of a revolution. But he argued that revolutionary propaganda was a delicate work of high conscience. It was the education of the masters of the world. It should be as careful as the education given to kings. He would have it advance its tenets cautiously, even timidly, in our ignorance of the effect that may be produced by any given economic change upon the happiness, the morals, the intellect, the history of mankind. For history is made with tools, not with ideas; and everything is changed by economic conditions—art, philosophy, love, virtue—truth itself!

The coals in the grate settled down with a slight crash; and Michaelis, the hermit of visions in the desert of a penitentiary, got up impetuously. Round like a distended balloon, he opened his short, thick arms, as if in a pathetically hopeless attempt to embrace and hug to his breast a self-regenerated universe. He gasped with ardour.

"The future is as certain as the past—slavery, feudalism, individualism, collectivism. This is the statement of a law, not an empty prophecy."

The disdainful pout of Comrade Ossipon's thick lips accentuated the negro type of his face.

"Nonsense," he said calmly enough. "There is no law and no certainty. The teaching propaganda be hanged. What the people knows does not matter, were its knowledge ever so accurate. The only thing that matters to us is the emotional state of the masses. Without emotion there is no action."

He paused, then added with modest firmness:

"I am speaking now to you scientifically—scientifically—Eh? What did you say, Verloc?"

"Nothing," growled from the sofa Mr Verloc, who, provoked by the abhorrent sound, had merely muttered a "Damn."

The venomous spluttering of the old terrorist without teeth was heard.

"Do you know how I would call the nature of the present economic conditions? I would call it cannibalistic. That's what it is! They are nourishing their greed on the quivering flesh and the warm blood of the people—nothing else."

Stevie swallowed the terrifying statement with an audible gulp, and at once, as though it had been swift poison, sank limply in a sitting posture on the steps of the kitchen door.

Michaelis gave no sign of having heard anything. His lips seemed glued together for good; not a quiver passed over his heavy cheeks. With troubled eyes he looked for his round, hard hat, and put it on his round head. His round and obese body seemed to float low between the chairs under the sharp elbow of Karl Yundt. The old terrorist, raising an uncertain and clawlike hand, gave a swaggering tilt to a black felt sombrero shading the hollows and ridges of his wasted face. He got in motion slowly, striking the floor with his stick at every step. It was rather an affair to get him out of the house because, now and then, he would stop, as if to think, and did not offer to move again till impelled forward by Michaelis. The gentle apostle grasped his arm with brotherly care; and behind them, his hands in his pockets, the robust Ossipon yawned vaguely. A blue cap with a patent leather peak set well at the back of his yellow bush of hair gave him the aspect of a Norwegian sailor bored with the world after a thundering spree. Mr Verloc saw his guests off the premises, attending them bareheaded, his heavy overcoat hanging open, his eyes on the ground.

He closed the door behind their backs with restrained violence, turned the key, shot the bolt. He was not satisfied with his friends. In the light of Mr Vladimir's philosophy of bomb throwing they appeared hopelessly futile. The part of Mr Verloc in revolutionary politics having been to observe, he could not all at once, either in his own home or in larger assemblies, take the initiative of action. He had to be cautious. Moved by the just indignation of a man well over forty, menaced in what is dearest to him—his repose and his security—he asked himself scornfully what else could have been expected from such a lot, this Karl Yundt, this Michaelis—this Ossipon.

Pausing in his intention to turn off the gas burning in the middle of the shop, Mr Verloc descended into the abyss of moral reflections. With the insight of a kindred temperament he pronounced his verdict. A lazy lot—this Karl Yundt, nursed by a blear-eyed old woman, a woman he had years ago enticed away from a friend, and afterwards had tried more than once to shake off into the gutter. Jolly lucky for Yundt that she had persisted in coming up time after time, or else there would have been no one now to help him out of the 'bus by the Green Park railings, where that spectre took its constitutional crawl every fine morning. When that indomitable snarling old witch died the swaggering spectre would have to vanish too—there would be an end to fiery Karl Yundt. And Mr Verloc's morality was offended also by the optimism of Michaelis, annexed by his wealthy old lady, who had taken lately to sending him to a cottage she had in the country. The ex-prisoner could moon about the shady lanes for days together in a delicious and humanitarian idleness. As to Ossipon, that beggar was sure to want for nothing as long as there were silly girls with savings-bank books in the world. And Mr Verloc, temperamentally identical with his associates, drew fine distinctions in his mind on the strength of insignificant differences. He drew them with a certain complacency, because the instinct of conventional respectability was strong within him, being only overcome by his dislike of all kinds of recognised labour—a temperamental defect which he shared with a large proportion of revolutionary reformers of a given social state. For obviously one does not revolt against the advantages and opportunities of that state, but against the price which must be paid for the same in the coin of accepted morality, self-restraint, and toil. The majority of revolutionists are the enemies of discipline and fatigue mostly. There are natures too, to whose sense of justice the price exacted looms up monstrously enormous, odious, oppressive, worrying, humiliating, extortionate, intolerable. Those are the fanatics. The remaining portion of social rebels is accounted for by vanity, the mother of all noble and vile illusions, the companion of poets, reformers, charlatans, prophets, and incendiaries.

Lost for a whole minute in the abyss of meditation, Mr Verloc did not reach the depth of these abstract considerations. Perhaps he was not able. In any case he had not the time. He was pulled up painfully by the sudden recollection of Mr Vladimir, another of his associates, whom in virtue of subtle moral affinities he was capable of judging correctly. He considered him as dangerous. A shade of envy crept into his thoughts. Loafing was all very well for these fellows, who knew not Mr Vladimir, and had women to fall back upon; whereas he had a woman to provide for—

At this point, by a simple association of ideas, Mr Verloc was brought face to face with the necessity of going to bed some time or other that evening. Then why not go now—at once? He sighed. The necessity was not so normally pleasurable as it ought to have been for a man of his age and temperament. He dreaded the demon of sleeplessness, which he felt had marked him for its own. He raised his arm, and turned off the flaring gas-jet above his head.

A bright band of light fell through the parlour door into the part of the shop behind the counter. It enabled Mr Verloc to ascertain at a glance the number of silver coins in the till. These were but few; and for the first time since he opened his shop he took a commercial survey of its value. This survey was unfavourable. He had gone into trade for no commercial reasons. He had been guided in the selection of this peculiar line of business by an instinctive leaning towards shady transactions, where money is picked up easily. Moreover, it did not take him out of his own sphere—the sphere which is watched by the police. On the contrary, it gave him a publicly confessed standing in that sphere, and as Mr Verloc had unconfessed relations which made him familiar with yet careless of the police, there was a distinct advantage in such a situation. But as a means of livelihood it was by itself insufficient.

He took the cash-box out of the drawer, and turning to leave the shop, became aware that Stevie was still downstairs.

What on earth is he doing there? Mr Verloc asked himself. What's the meaning of these antics? He looked dubiously at his brother-in-law, but he did not ask him for information. Mr Verloc's intercourse with Stevie was limited to the casual mutter of a morning, after breakfast, "My boots," and even that was more a communication at large of a need than a direct order or request. Mr Verloc perceived with some surprise that he did not know really what to say to Stevie. He stood still in the middle of the parlour, and looked into the kitchen in silence. Nor yet did he know what would happen if he did say anything. And this appeared very queer to Mr Verloc in view of the fact, borne upon him suddenly, that he had to provide for this fellow too. He had never given a moment's thought till then to that aspect of Stevie's existence.

Positively he did not know how to speak to the lad. He watched him gesticulating and murmuring in the kitchen. Stevie prowled round the table like an excited animal in a cage. A tentative "Hadn't you better go to bed now?" produced no effect whatever; and Mr Verloc, abandoning the stony contemplation of his brother-in-law's behaviour, crossed the parlour wearily, cash-box in hand. The cause of the general lassitude he felt while climbing the stairs being purely mental, he became alarmed by its inexplicable character. He hoped he was not sickening for anything. He stopped on the dark landing to examine his sensations. But a slight and continuous sound of snoring pervading the obscurity interfered with their clearness. The sound came from his mother-in-law's room. Another one to provide for, he thought—and on this thought walked into the bedroom.

Mrs Verloc had fallen asleep with the lamp (no gas was laid upstairs) turned up full on the table by the side of the bed. The light thrown down by the shade fell dazzlingly on the white pillow sunk by the weight of her head reposing with closed eyes and dark hair done up in several plaits for the night. She woke up with the sound of her name in her ears, and saw her husband standing over her.

"Winnie! Winnie!"

At first she did not stir, lying very quiet and looking at the cash-box in Mr Verloc's hand. But when she understood that her brother was "capering all over the place downstairs" she swung out in one sudden movement on to the edge of the bed. Her bare feet, as if poked through the bottom of an unadorned, sleeved calico sack buttoned tightly at neck and wrists, felt over the rug for the slippers while she looked upward into her husband's face.

"I don't know how to manage him," Mr Verloc explained peevishly. "Won't do to leave him downstairs alone with the lights."

She said nothing, glided across the room swiftly, and the door closed upon her white form.

Mr Verloc deposited the cash-box on the night table, and began the operation of undressing by flinging his overcoat on to a distant chair. His coat and waistcoat followed. He walked about the room in his stockinged feet, and his burly figure, with the hands worrying nervously at his throat, passed and repassed across the long strip of looking-glass in the door of his wife's wardrobe. Then after slipping his braces off his shoulders he pulled up violently the venetian blind, and leaned his forehead against the cold window-pane—a fragile film of glass stretched between him and the enormity of cold, black, wet, muddy, inhospitable accumulation of bricks, slates, and stones, things in themselves unlovely and unfriendly to man.

Mr Verloc felt the latent unfriendliness of all out of doors with a force approaching to positive bodily anguish. There is no occupation that fails a man more completely than that of a secret agent of police. It's like your horse suddenly falling dead under you in the midst of an uninhabited and thirsty plain. The comparison occurred to Mr Verloc because he had sat astride various army horses in his time, and had now the sensation of an incipient fall. The prospect was as black as the window-pane against which he was leaning his forehead. And suddenly the face of Mr Vladimir, clean-shaved and witty, appeared enhaloed in the glow of its rosy complexion like a sort of pink seal, impressed on the fatal darkness.

This luminous and mutilated vision was so ghastly physically that Mr Verloc started away from the window, letting down the venetian blind with a great rattle. Discomposed and speechless with the apprehension of more such visions, he beheld his wife re-enter the room and get into bed in a calm business-like manner which made him feel hopelessly lonely in the world. Mrs Verloc expressed her surprise at seeing him up yet.

"I don't feel very well," he muttered, passing his hands over his moist brow.

"Giddiness?"

"Yes. Not at all well."

Mrs Verloc, with all the placidity of an experienced wife, expressed a confident opinion as to the cause, and suggested the usual remedies; but her husband, rooted in the middle of the room, shook his lowered head sadly.

"You'll catch cold standing there," she observed.

Mr Verloc made an effort, finished undressing, and got into bed. Down below in the quiet, narrow street measured footsteps approached the house, then died away unhurried and firm, as if the passer-by had started to pace out all eternity, from gas-lamp to gas-lamp in a night without end; and the drowsy ticking of the old clock on the landing became distinctly audible in the bedroom.

Mrs Verloc, on her back, and staring at the ceiling, made a remark.

"Takings very small to-day."

Mr Verloc, in the same position, cleared his throat as if for an important statement, but merely inquired:

"Did you turn off the gas downstairs?"

"Yes; I did," answered Mrs Verloc conscientiously. "That poor boy is in a very excited state to-night," she murmured, after a pause which lasted for three ticks of the clock.

Mr Verloc cared nothing for Stevie's excitement, but he felt horribly wakeful, and dreaded facing the darkness and silence that would follow the extinguishing of the lamp. This dread led him to make the remark that Stevie had disregarded his suggestion to go to bed. Mrs Verloc, falling into the trap, started to demonstrate at length to her husband that this was not "impudence" of any sort, but simply "excitement." There was no young man of his age in London more willing and docile than Stephen, she affirmed; none more affectionate and ready to please, and even useful, as long as people did not upset his poor head. Mrs Verloc, turning towards her recumbent husband, raised herself on her elbow, and hung over him in her anxiety that he should believe Stevie to be a useful member of the family. That ardour of protecting compassion exalted morbidly in her childhood by the misery of another child tinged her sallow cheeks with a faint dusky blush, made her big eyes gleam under the dark lids. Mrs Verloc then looked younger; she looked as young as Winnie used to look, and much more animated than the Winnie of the Belgravian mansion days had ever allowed herself to appear to gentlemen lodgers. Mr Verloc's anxieties had prevented him from attaching any sense to what his wife was saying. It was as if her voice were talking on the other side of a very thick wall. It was her aspect that recalled him to himself.

He appreciated this woman, and the sentiment of this appreciation, stirred by a display of something resembling emotion, only added another pang to his mental anguish. When her voice ceased he moved uneasily, and said:

"I haven't been feeling well for the last few days."

He might have meant this as an opening to a complete confidence; but Mrs Verloc laid her head on the pillow again, and staring upward, went on:

"That boy hears too much of what is talked about here. If I had known they were coming to-night I would have seen to it that he went to bed at the same time I did. He was out of his mind with something he overheard about eating people's flesh and drinking blood. What's the good of talking like that?"

There was a note of indignant scorn in her voice. Mr Verloc was fully responsive now.

"Ask Karl Yundt," he growled savagely.

Mrs Verloc, with great decision, pronounced Karl Yundt "a disgusting old man." She declared openly her affection for Michaelis. Of the robust Ossipon, in whose presence she always felt uneasy behind an attitude of stony reserve, she said nothing whatever. And continuing to talk of that brother, who had been for so many years an object of care and fears:

"He isn't fit to hear what's said here. He believes it's all true. He knows no better. He gets into his passions over it."

Mr Verloc made no comment.

"He glared at me, as if he didn't know who I was, when I went downstairs. His heart was going like a hammer. He can't help being excitable. I woke mother up, and asked her to sit with him till he went to sleep. It isn't his fault. He's no trouble when he's left alone."

Mr Verloc made no comment.

"I wish he had never been to school," Mrs Verloc began again brusquely. "He's always taking away those newspapers from the window to read. He gets a red face poring over them. We don't get rid of a dozen numbers in a month. They only take up room in the front window. And Mr Ossipon brings every week a pile of these F. P. tracts to sell at a halfpenny each. I wouldn't give a halfpenny for the whole lot. It's silly reading—that's what it is. There's no sale for it. The other day Stevie got hold of one, and there was a story in it of a German soldier officer tearing half-off the ear of a recruit, and nothing was done to him for it. The brute! I couldn't do anything with Stevie that afternoon. The story was enough, too, to make one's blood boil. But what's the use of printing things like that? We aren't German slaves here, thank God. It's not our business—is it?"

Mr Verloc made no reply.

"I had to take the carving knife from the boy," Mrs Verloc continued, a little sleepily now. "He was shouting and stamping and sobbing. He can't stand the notion of any cruelty. He would have stuck that officer like a pig if he had seen him then. It's true, too! Some people don't deserve much mercy." Mrs Verloc's voice ceased, and the expression of her motionless eyes became more and more contemplative and veiled during the long pause. "Comfortable, dear?" she asked in a faint, far-away voice. "Shall I put out the light now?"

The dreary conviction that there was no sleep for him held Mr Verloc mute and hopelessly inert in his fear of darkness. He made a great effort.

"Yes. Put it out," he said at last in a hollow tone.

4

MOST OF THE thirty or so little tables covered by red cloths with a white design stood ranged at right angles to the deep brown wainscoting of the underground hall. Bronze chandeliers with many globes depended from the low, slightly vaulted ceiling, and the fresco paintings ran flat and dull all round the walls without windows, representing scenes of the chase and of outdoor revelry in mediæval costumes. Varlets in green jerkins brandished hunting knives and raised on high tankards of foaming beer.

"Unless I am very much mistaken, you are the man who would know the inside of this confounded affair," said the robust Ossipon, leaning over, his elbows far out on the table and his feet tucked back completely under his chair. His eyes stared with wild eagerness.

An upright semi-grand piano near the door, flanked by two palms in pots, executed suddenly all by itself a valse tune with aggressive virtuosity. The din it raised was deafening. When it ceased, as abruptly as it had started, the be-spectacled, dingy little man who faced Ossipon behind a heavy glass mug full of beer emitted calmly what had the sound of a general proposition.

"In principle what one of us may or may not know as to any given fact can't be a matter for inquiry to the others."

"Certainly not," Comrade Ossipon agreed in a quiet undertone. "In principle."

With his big florid face held between his hands he continued to stare hard, while the dingy little man in spectacles coolly took a drink of beer and stood the glass mug back on the table. His flat, large ears departed widely from the sides of his skull, which looked frail enough for Ossipon to crush between thumb and forefinger; the dome of the forehead seemed to rest on the rim of the spectacles; the flat cheeks, of a greasy, unhealthy complexion, were merely smudged by the miserable poverty of a thin dark whisker. The lamentable inferiority of the whole physique was made ludicrous by the supremely self-confident bearing of the individual. His speech was curt, and he had a particularly impressive manner of keeping silent.

Ossipon spoke again from between his hands in a mutter.

"Have you been out much to-day?"

"No. I stayed in bed all the morning," answered the other. "Why?"

"Oh! Nothing," said Ossipon, gazing earnestly and quivering inwardly with the desire to find out something, but obviously intimidated by the little man's overwhelming air of unconcern. When talking with this comrade—which happened but rarely—the big Ossipon suffered from a sense of moral and even physical insignificance. However, he ventured another question. "Did you walk down here?"

"No; omnibus," the little man answered readily enough. He lived far away in Islington, in a small house down a shabby street, littered with straw and dirty paper, where out of school hours a troop of assorted children ran and squabbled with a shrill, joyless, rowdy clamour. His single back room, remarkable for having an extremely large cupboard, he rented furnished from two elderly spinsters, dressmakers in a humble way with a clientele of servant girls mostly. He had a heavy padlock put on the cupboard, but otherwise he was a model lodger, giving no trouble, and requiring practically no attendance. His oddities were that he insisted on being present when his room was being swept, and that when he went out he locked his door, and took the key away with him.

Ossipon had a vision of these round black-rimmed spectacles progressing along the streets on the top of an omnibus, their self-confident glitter falling here and there on the walls of houses or lowered upon the heads of the unconscious stream of people on the pavements. The ghost of a sickly smile altered the set of Ossipon's thick lips at the thought of the walls nodding, of people running for life at the sight of those spectacles. If they had only known! What a panic! He murmured interrogatively: "Been sitting long here?"

"An hour or more," answered the other negligently, and took a pull at the dark beer. All his movements—the way he grasped the mug, the act of drinking, the way he set the heavy glass down and folded his arms—had a firmness, an assured precision which made the big and muscular Ossipon, leaning forward with staring eyes and protruding lips, look the picture of eager indecision.

"An hour," he said. "Then it may be you haven't heard yet the news I've heard just now —in the street. Have you?"

The little man shook his head negatively the least bit. But as he gave no indication of curiosity Ossipon ventured to add that he had heard it just outside the place. A newspaper boy had yelled the thing under his very nose, and not being prepared for anything of that sort, he was very much startled and upset. He had to come in there with a dry mouth. "I never thought of finding you here," he added, murmuring steadily, with his elbows planted on the table.

"I come here sometimes," said the other, preserving his provoking coolness of demeanour.

"It's wonderful that you of all people should have heard nothing of it," the big Ossipon continued. His eyelids snapped nervously upon the shining eyes. "You of all people," he repeated tentatively. This obvious restraint argued an incredible and inexplicable timidity of the big fellow before the calm little man, who again lifted the glass mug, drank, and put it down with brusque and assured movements. And that was all.

Ossipon after waiting for something, word or sign, that did not come, made an effort to assume a sort of indifference.

"Do you," he said, deadening his voice still more, "give your stuff to anybody who's up to asking you for it?"

"My absolute rule is never to refuse anybody—as long as I have a pinch by me," answered the little man with decision.

"That's a principle?" commented Ossipon.

"It's a principle."

"And you think it's sound?"

The large round spectacles, which gave a look of staring self-confidence to the sallow face, confronted Ossipon like sleepless, unwinking orbs flashing a cold fire.

"Perfectly. Always. Under every circumstance. What could stop me? Why should I not? Why should I think twice about it?"

Ossipon gasped, as it were, discreetly.

"Do you mean to say you would hand it over to a 'teck' if one came to ask you for your wares?"

The other smiled faintly.

"Let them come and try it on, and you will see," he said. "They know me, but I know also every one of them. They won't come near me—not they."

His thin livid lips snapped together firmly. Ossipon began to argue.

"But they could send someone—rig a plant on you. Don't you see? Get the stuff from you in that way, and then arrest you with the proof in their hands."

"Proof of what? Dealing in explosives without a licence perhaps." This was meant for a contemptuous jeer, though the expression of the thin, sickly face remained unchanged, and the utterance was negligent. "I don't think there's one of them anxious to make that arrest. I don't think they could get one of them to apply for a warrant. I mean one of the best. Not one."

"Why?" Ossipon asked.

"Because they know very well I take care never to part with the last handful of my wares. I've it always by me." He touched the breast of his coat lightly. "In a thick glass flask," he added.

"So I have been told," said Ossipon, with a shade of wonder in his voice. "But I didn't know if—"

"They know," interrupted the little man crisply, leaning against the straight chair back, which rose higher than his fragile head. "I shall never be arrested. The game isn't good enough for any policeman of them all. To deal with a man like me you require sheer, naked, inglorious heroism." Again his lips closed with a self-confident snap. Ossipon repressed a movement of impatience.

"Or recklessness—or simply ignorance," he retorted. "They've only to get somebody for the job who does not know you carry enough stuff in your pocket to blow yourself and everything within sixty yards of you to pieces."

"I never affirmed I could not be eliminated," rejoined the other. "But that wouldn't be an arrest. Moreover, it's not so easy as it looks."

"Bah!" Ossipon contradicted. "Don't be too sure of that. What's to prevent half-a-dozen of them jumping upon you from behind in the street? With your arms pinned to your sides you could do nothing—could you?"

"Yes; I could. I am seldom out in the streets after dark," said the little man impassively, "and never very late. I walk always with my right hand closed round the india-rubber ball which I have in my trouser pocket. The pressing of this ball actuates a detonator inside the flask I carry in my pocket. It's the principle of the pneumatic instantaneous shutter for a camera lens. The tube leads up—"

With a swift disclosing gesture he gave Ossipon a glimpse of an india-rubber tube, resembling a slender brown worm, issuing from the armhole of his waistcoat and plunging into the inner breast pocket of his jacket. His clothes, of a nondescript brown mixture, were threadbare and marked with stains, dusty in the folds, with ragged button-holes.

"The detonator is partly mechanical, partly chemical," he explained, with casual condescension.

"It is instantaneous, of course?" murmured Ossipon, with a slight shudder.

"Far from it," confessed the other, with a reluctance which seemed to twist his mouth dolorously. "A full twenty seconds must elapse from the moment I press the ball till the explosion takes place."

"Phew!" whistled Ossipon, completely appalled. "Twenty seconds! Horrors! You mean to say that you could face that? I should go crazy—"

"Wouldn't matter if you did. Of course, it's the weak point of this special system, which is only for my own use. The worst is that the manner of exploding is always the weak point with us. I am trying to invent a detonator that would adjust itself to all conditions of action, and even to unexpected changes of conditions. A variable and yet perfectly precise mechanism. A really intelligent detonator."

"Twenty seconds," muttered Ossipon again. "Ough! And then—"

With a slight turn of the head the glitter of the spectacles seemed to gauge the size of the beer saloon in the basement of the renowned Silenus Restaurant.

"Nobody in this room could hope to escape," was the verdict of that survey. "Nor yet this couple going up the stairs now."

The piano at the foot of the staircase clanged through a mazurka with brazen impetuosity, as though a vulgar and impudent ghost were showing off. The keys sank and rose mysteriously. Then all became still. For a moment Ossipon imagined the overlighted place changed into a dreadful black hole belching horrible fumes choked with ghastly rubbish of smashed brickwork and mutilated corpses. He had such a distinct perception of ruin and death that he shuddered again. The other observed, with an air of calm sufficiency:

"In the last instance it is character alone that makes for one's safety. There are very few people in the world whose character is as well established as mine."

"I wonder how you managed it," growled Ossipon.

"Force of personality," said the other, without raising his voice; and coming from the mouth of that obviously miserable organism the assertion caused the robust Ossipon to bite his lower lip. "Force of personality," he repeated, with ostentatious calm. "I have the means to make myself deadly, but that by itself, you understand, is absolutely nothing in the way of protection. What is effective is the belief those people have in my will to use the means. That's their impression. It is absolute. Therefore I am deadly."

"There are individuals of character amongst that lot too," muttered Ossipon ominously.

"Possibly. But it is a matter of degree obviously, since, for instance, I am not impressed by them. Therefore they are inferior. They cannot be otherwise. Their character is built upon conventional morality. It leans on the social order. Mine stands free from everything artificial. They are bound in all sorts of conventions. They depend on life, which, in this connection, is a historical fact surrounded by all sorts of restraints and considerations, a complex organised fact open to attack at every point; whereas I depend on death, which knows no restraint and cannot be attacked. My superiority is evident."

"This is a transcendental way of putting it," said Ossipon, watching the cold glitter of the round spectacles. "I've heard Karl Yundt say much the same thing not very long ago."

"Karl Yundt," mumbled the other contemptuously, "the delegate of the International Red Committee, has been a posturing shadow all his life. There are three of you delegates, aren't there? I won't define the other two, as you are one of them. But what you say means nothing. You are the worthy delegates for revolutionary propaganda, but the trouble is not only that you are as unable to think independently as any respectable grocer or journalist of them all, but that you have no character whatever."

Ossipon could not restrain a start of indignation.

"But what do you want from us?" he exclaimed in a deadened voice. "What is it you are after yourself?"

"A perfect detonator," was the peremptory answer. "What are you making that face for? You see, you can't even bear the mention of something conclusive."

"I am not making a face," growled the annoyed Ossipon bearishly.

"You revolutionists," the other continued, with leisurely self-confidence, "are the slaves of the social convention, which is afraid of you; slaves of it as much as the very police that stands up in the defence of that convention. Clearly you are, since you want to revolutionise it. It governs your thought, of course, and your action too, and thus neither your thought nor your action can ever be conclusive." He paused, tranquil, with that air of close, endless silence, then almost immediately went on. "You are not a bit better than the forces arrayed against you—than the police, for instance. The other day I came suddenly upon Chief Inspector Heat at the corner of Tottenham Court Road. He looked at me very steadily. But I did not look at him. Why should I give him more than a glance? He was thinking of many things—of his superiors, of his reputation, of the law courts, of his salary, of newspapers—of a hundred things. But I was thinking of my perfect detonator only. He meant nothing to me. He was as insignificant as—I can't call to mind anything insignificant enough to compare him with—except Karl Yundt perhaps. Like to like. The terrorist and the policeman both come from the same basket. Revolution, legality—counter moves in the same game; forms of idleness at bottom identical. He plays his little game—so do you propagandists. But I don't play; I work fourteen hours a day, and go hungry sometimes. My experiments cost money now and again, and then I must do without food for a day or two. You're looking at my beer. Yes. I have had two glasses already, and shall have another presently. This is a little holiday, and I celebrate it alone. Why not? I've the grit to work alone, quite alone, absolutely alone. I've worked alone for years."

Ossipon's face had turned dusky red.

"At the perfect detonator—eh?" he sneered, very low.

"Yes," retorted the other. "It is a good definition. You couldn't find anything half so precise to define the nature of your activity with all your committees and delegations. It is I who am the true propagandist."

"We won't discuss that point," said Ossipon, with an air of rising above personal considerations. "I am afraid I'll have to spoil your holiday for you, though. There's a man blown up in Greenwich Park this morning."

"How do you know?"

"They have been yelling the news in the streets since two o'clock. I bought the paper, and just ran in here. Then I saw you sitting at this table. I've got it in my pocket now."

He pulled the newspaper out. It was a good-sized rosy sheet, as if flushed by the warmth of its own convictions, which were optimistic. He scanned the pages rapidly.

"Ah! Here it is. Bomb in Greenwich Park. There isn't much so far. Half-past eleven. Foggy morning. Effects of explosion felt as far as Romney Road and Park Place. Enormous hole in the ground under a tree filled with smashed roots and broken branches. All round fragments of a man's body blown to pieces. That's all. The rest's mere newspaper gup. No doubt a wicked attempt to blow up the Observatory, they say. H'm. That's hardly credible."

He looked at the paper for a while longer in silence, then passed it to the other, who after gazing abstractedly at the print laid it down without comment.

It was Ossipon who spoke first—still resentful.

"The fragments of only *one* man, you note. Ergo: blew *himself* up. That spoils your day off for you—don't it? Were you expecting that sort of move? I hadn't the slightest idea—not the ghost of a notion of anything of the sort being planned to come off here—in this country. Under the present circumstances it's nothing short of criminal."

The little man lifted his thin black eyebrows with dispassionate scorn.

"Criminal! What is that? What *is* crime? What can be the meaning of such an assertion?"

"How am I to express myself? One must use the current words," said Ossipon impatiently. "The meaning of this assertion is that this business may affect our position very adversely in this country. Isn't that crime enough for you? I am convinced you have been giving away some of your stuff lately."

Ossipon stared hard. The other, without flinching, lowered and raised his head slowly.

"You have!" burst out the editor of the F. P. leaflets in an intense whisper. "No! And are you really handing it over at large like this, for the asking, to the first fool that comes along?"

"Just so! The condemned social order has not been built up on paper and ink, and I don't fancy that a combination of paper and ink will ever put an end to it, whatever you may think. Yes, I would give the stuff with both hands to every man, woman, or fool that likes to come along. I know what you are thinking about. But I am not taking my cue from the Red Committee. I would see you all hounded out of here, or arrested—or beheaded for that matter—without turning a hair. What happens to us as individuals is not of the least consequence."

He spoke carelessly, without heat, almost without feeling, and Ossipon, secretly much affected, tried to copy this detachment.

"If the police here knew their business they would shoot you full of holes with revolvers, or else try to sand-bag you from behind in broad daylight."

The little man seemed already to have considered that point of view in his dispassionate self-confident manner.

"Yes," he assented with the utmost readiness. "But for that they would have to face their own institutions. Do you see? That requires uncommon grit. Grit of a special kind."

Ossipon blinked.

"I fancy that's exactly what would happen to you if you were to set up your laboratory in the States. They don't stand on ceremony with their institutions there."

"I am not likely to go and see. Otherwise your remark is just," admitted the other. "They have more character over there, and their character is essentially anarchistic. Fertile ground for us, the States—very good ground. The great Republic has the root of the destructive matter in her. The collective temperament is lawless. Excellent. They may shoot us down, but—"

"You are too transcendental for me," growled Ossipon, with moody concern.

"Logical," protested the other. "There are several kinds of logic. This is the enlightened kind. America is all right. It is this country that is dangerous, with her idealistic conception of legality. The social spirit of this people is wrapped up in scrupulous prejudices, and that is fatal to our work. You talk of England being our only refuge! So much the worse. Capua! What do we want with refuges? Here you talk, print, plot, and do nothing. I daresay it's very convenient for such Karl Yundts."

He shrugged his shoulders slightly, then added with the same leisurely assurance: "To break up the superstition and worship of legality should be our aim. Nothing would please me more than to see Inspector Heat and his likes take to shooting us down in broad daylight with the approval of the public. Half our battle would be won then; the disintegration of the old morality would have set in in its very temple. That is what you ought to aim at. But you revolutionists will never understand that. You plan the future, you lose yourselves in reveries of economical systems derived from what is; whereas what's wanted is a clean sweep and a clear start for a new conception of life. That sort of future will take care of itself if you will only make room for it. Therefore I would shovel my stuff in heaps at the corners of the streets if I had enough for that; and as I haven't, I do my best by perfecting a really dependable detonator."

Ossipon, who had been mentally swimming in deep waters, seized upon the last word as if it were a saving plank.

"Yes. Your detonators. I shouldn't wonder if it weren't one of your detonators that made a clean sweep of the man in the park."

A shade of vexation darkened the determined sallow face confronting Ossipon.

"My difficulty consists precisely in experimenting practically with the various kinds. They must be tried after all. Besides—"

Ossipon interrupted.

"Who could that fellow be? I assure you that we in London had no knowledge—Couldn't you describe the person you gave the stuff to?"

The other turned his spectacles upon Ossipon like a pair of searchlights.

"Describe him," he repeated slowly. "I don't think there can be the slightest objection now. I will describe him to you in one word—Verloc."

Ossipon, whom curiosity had lifted a few inches off his seat, dropped back, as if hit in the face.

"Verloc! Impossible."

The self-possessed little man nodded slightly once.

"Yes. He's the person. You can't say that in this case I was giving my stuff to the first fool that came along. He was a prominent member of the group as far as I understand."

"Yes," said Ossipon. "Prominent. No, not exactly. He was the centre for general intelligence, and usually received comrades coming over here. More useful than important. Man of no ideas. Years ago he used to speak at meetings—in France, I believe. Not very well, though. He was trusted by such men as Latorre, Moser and all that old lot. The only talent he showed really was his ability to elude the attentions of the police somehow. Here, for instance, he did not seem to be looked after very closely. He was regularly married, you know. I suppose it's with her money that he started that shop. Seemed to make it pay, too."

Ossipon paused abruptly, muttered to himself "I wonder what that woman will do now?" and fell into thought.

The other waited with ostentatious indifference. His parentage was obscure, and he was generally known only by his nickname of Professor. His title to that designation consisted in his having been once assistant demonstrator in chemistry at some technical institute. He quarrelled with the authorities upon a question of unfair treatment. Afterwards he obtained a post in the laboratory of a manufactory of dyes. There too he had been treated with revolting injustice. His struggles, his privations, his hard work to raise himself in the social scale, had filled him with such an exalted conviction of his merits that it was extremely difficult for the world to treat him with justice—the standard of that notion depending so much upon the patience of the individual. The Professor had genius, but lacked the great social virtue of resignation.

"Intellectually a nonentity," Ossipon pronounced aloud, abandoning suddenly the inward contemplation of Mrs Verloc's bereaved person and business. "Quite an ordinary personality. You are wrong in not keeping more in touch with the comrades, Professor," he added in a reproving tone. "Did he say anything to you—give you some idea of his intentions? I hadn't seen him for a month. It seems impossible that he should be gone."

"He told me it was going to be a demonstration against a building," said the Professor. "I had to know that much to prepare the missile. I pointed out to him that I had hardly a sufficient quantity for a completely destructive result, but he pressed me very earnestly to do my best. As he wanted something that could be carried openly in the hand, I proposed to make use of an old one-gallon copal varnish can I happened to have by me. He was pleased at the idea. It gave me some trouble, because I had to cut out the bottom first and solder it on again afterwards. When prepared for use, the can enclosed a wide-mouthed, well-corked jar of thick glass packed around with some wet clay and containing sixteen ounces of X2 green powder. The detonator was connected with the screw top of the can. It was ingenious—a combination of time and shock. I explained the system to him. It was a thin tube of tin enclosing a—"

Ossipon's attention had wandered.

"What do you think has happened?" he interrupted.

"Can't tell. Screwed the top on tight, which would make the connection, and then forgot the time. It was set for twenty minutes. On the other hand, the time contact being made, a sharp shock would bring about the explosion at once. He either ran the time too close, or simply let the thing fall. The contact was made all right—that's clear to me at any rate. The system's worked perfectly. And yet you would think that a common fool in a hurry would be much more likely to forget to make the contact altogether. I was worrying myself about that sort of failure mostly. But there are more kinds of fools than one can guard against. You can't expect a detonator to be absolutely fool-proof."

He beckoned to a waiter. Ossipon sat rigid, with the abstracted gaze of mental travail. After the man had gone away with the money he roused himself, with an air of profound dissatisfaction.

"It's extremely unpleasant for me," he mused. "Karl has been in bed with bronchitis for a week. There's an even chance that he will never get up again. Michaelis's luxuriating in the country somewhere. A fashionable publisher has offered him five hundred pounds for a book. It will be a ghastly failure. He has lost the habit of consecutive thinking in prison, you know."

The Professor on his feet, now buttoning his coat, looked about him with perfect indifference.

"What are you going to do?" asked Ossipon wearily. He dreaded the blame of the Central Red Committee, a body which had no permanent place of abode, and of whose membership he was not exactly informed. If this affair eventuated in the stoppage of the modest subsidy allotted to the publication of the F. P. pamphlets, then indeed he would have to regret Verloc's inexplicable folly.

"Solidarity with the extremest form of action is one thing, and silly recklessness is another," he said, with a sort of moody brutality. "I don't know what came to Verloc. There's some mystery there. However, he's gone. You may take it as you like, but under the circumstances the only policy for the militant revolutionary group is to disclaim all connection with this damned freak of yours. How to make the disclaimer convincing enough is what bothers me."

The little man on his feet, buttoned up and ready to go, was no taller than the seated Ossipon. He levelled his spectacles at the latter's face point-blank.

"You might ask the police for a testimonial of good conduct. They know where every one of you slept last night. Perhaps if you asked them they would consent to publish some sort of official statement."

"No doubt they are aware well enough that we had nothing to do with this," mumbled Ossipon bitterly. "What they will say is another thing." He remained thoughtful, disregarding the short, owlish, shabby figure standing by his side. "I must lay hands on Michaelis at once, and get him to speak from his heart at one of our gatherings. The public has a sort of sentimental regard for that fellow. His name is known. And I am in touch with a few reporters on the big dailies. What he would say would be utter bosh, but he has a turn of talk that makes it go down all the same."

"Like treacle," interjected the Professor, rather low, keeping an impassive expression.

The perplexed Ossipon went on communing with himself half audibly, after the manner of a man reflecting in perfect solitude.

"Confounded ass! To leave such an imbecile business on my hands. And I don't even know if—"

He sat with compressed lips. The idea of going for news straight to the shop lacked charm. His notion was that Verloc's shop might have been turned already into a police trap. They will be bound to make some arrests, he thought, with something resembling virtuous indignation, for the even tenor of his revolutionary life was menaced by no fault of his. And yet unless he went there he ran the risk of remaining in ignorance of what perhaps it would be very material for him to know. Then he reflected that, if the man in the park had been so very much blown to pieces as the evening papers said, he could not have been identified. And if so, the police could have no special reason for watching Verloc's shop more closely than any other place known to be frequented by marked anarchists—no more reason, in fact, than for watching the doors of the Silenus. There would be a lot of watching all round, no matter where he went. Still—

"I wonder what I had better do now?" he muttered, taking counsel with himself.

A rasping voice at his elbow said, with sedate scorn:

"Fasten yourself upon the woman for all she's worth."

After uttering these words the Professor walked away from the table. Ossipon, whom that piece of insight had taken unawares, gave one ineffectual start, and remained still, with a helpless gaze, as though nailed fast to the seat of his chair. The lonely piano, without as much as a music stool to help it, struck a few chords courageously, and beginning a selection of national airs, played him out at last to the tune of "Blue Bells of Scotland." The painfully detached notes grew faint behind his back while he went slowly upstairs, across the hall, and into the street.

In front of the great doorway a dismal row of newspaper sellers standing clear of the pavement dealt out their wares from the gutter. It was a raw, gloomy day of the early spring; and the grimy sky, the mud of the streets, the rags of the dirty men, harmonised excellently with the eruption of the damp, rubbishy sheets of paper soiled with printers' ink. The posters, maculated with filth, garnished like tapestry the sweep of the curbstone. The trade in afternoon papers was brisk, yet, in comparison with the swift, constant march of foot traffic, the effect was of indifference, of a disregarded distribution. Ossipon looked hurriedly both ways before stepping out into the cross-currents, but the Professor was already out of sight.

5

THE PROFESSOR HAD TURNED into a street to the left, and walked along, with his head carried rigidly erect, in a crowd whose every individual almost overtopped his stunted stature. It was vain to pretend to himself that he was not disappointed. But that was mere feeling; the stoicism of his thought could not be disturbed by this or any other failure. Next time, or the time after next, a telling stroke would be delivered—something really startling—a blow fit to open the first crack in the imposing front of the great edifice of legal conceptions sheltering the atrocious injustice of society. Of humble origin, and with an appearance really so mean as to stand in the way of his considerable natural abilities, his imagination had been fired early by the tales of men rising from the depths of poverty to positions of authority and affluence. The extreme, almost ascetic purity of his thought, combined with an astounding ignorance of worldly conditions, had set before him a goal of power and prestige to be attained without the medium of arts, graces, tact, wealth—by sheer weight of merit alone. On that view he considered himself entitled to undisputed success. His father, a delicate dark enthusiast with a sloping forehead, had been an itinerant and rousing preacher of some obscure but rigid Christian sect—a man supremely confident in the privileges of his righteousness. In the son, individualist by temperament, once the science of colleges had replaced thoroughly the faith of conventicles, this moral attitude translated itself into a frenzied puritanism of ambition. He nursed it as something secularly holy. To see it thwarted opened his eyes to the true nature of the world, whose morality was artificial, corrupt, and blasphemous. The way of even the most justifiable revolutions is prepared by personal impulses disguised into creeds. The Professor's indignation found in itself a final cause that absolved him from the sin of turning to destruction as the agent of his ambition. To destroy public faith in legality was the imperfect formula of his pedantic fanaticism; but the subconscious conviction that the framework of an established social order cannot be effectually shattered except by some form of collective or individual violence was precise and correct. He was a moral agent—that was settled in his mind. By exercising his agency with ruthless defiance he procured for himself the appearances of power and personal prestige. That was undeniable to his vengeful bitterness. It pacified its unrest; and in their own way the most ardent of revolutionaries are perhaps doing no more but seeking for peace in common with the rest of mankind—the peace of soothed vanity, of satisfied appetites, or perhaps of appeased conscience.

Lost in the crowd, miserable and undersized, he meditated confidently on his power, keeping his hand in the left pocket of his trousers, grasping lightly the india-rubber ball, the supreme guarantee of his sinister freedom; but after a while he became disagreeably affected by the sight of the roadway thronged with vehicles and of the pavement crowded with men and women. He was in a long, straight street, peopled by a mere fraction of an immense multitude; but all round him, on and on, even to the limits of the horizon hidden by the enormous piles of bricks, he felt the mass of mankind mighty in its numbers. They swarmed numerous like locusts, industrious like ants, thoughtless like a natural force, pushing on blind and orderly and absorbed, impervious to sentiment, to logic, to terror too perhaps.

That was the form of doubt he feared most. Impervious to fear! Often while walking abroad, when he happened also to come out of himself, he had such moments of dreadful and sane mistrust of mankind. What if nothing could move them? Such moments come to all men whose ambition aims at a direct grasp upon humanity—to artists, politicians, thinkers, reformers, or saints. A despicable emotional state this, against which solitude fortifies a superior character; and with severe exultation the Professor thought of the refuge of his room, with its padlocked cupboard, lost in a wilderness of poor houses, the hermitage of the perfect anarchist. In order to reach sooner the point where he could take his omnibus, he turned brusquely out of the populous street into a narrow and dusky alley paved with flagstones. On one side the low brick houses had in their dusty windows the sightless, moribund look of incurable decay—empty shells awaiting demolition. From the other side life had not departed wholly as yet. Facing the only gas-lamp yawned the cavern of a second-hand furniture dealer, where, deep in the gloom of a sort of narrow avenue winding through a bizarre forest of wardrobes, with an undergrowth tangle of table legs, a tall pier-glass glimmered like a pool of water in a wood. An unhappy, homeless couch, accompanied by two unrelated chairs, stood in the open. The only human being making use of the alley besides the Professor, coming stalwart and erect from the opposite direction, checked his swinging pace suddenly.

"Hallo!" he said, and stood a little on one side watchfully.

The Professor had already stopped, with a ready half turn which brought his shoulders very near the other wall. His right hand fell lightly on the back of the outcast couch, the left remained purposefully plunged deep in the trousers pocket, and the roundness of the heavy rimmed spectacles imparted an owlish character to his moody, unperturbed face.

It was like a meeting in a side corridor of a mansion full of life. The stalwart man was buttoned up in a dark overcoat, and carried an umbrella. His hat, tilted back, uncovered a good deal of forehead, which appeared very white in the dusk. In the dark patches of the orbits the eyeballs glimmered piercingly. Long, drooping moustaches, the colour of ripe corn, framed with their points the square block of his shaved chin.

"I am not looking for you," he said curtly.

The Professor did not stir an inch. The blended noises of the enormous town sank down to an inarticulate low murmur. Chief Inspector Heat of the Special Crimes Department changed his tone.

"Not in a hurry to get home?" he asked, with mocking simplicity.

The unwholesome-looking little moral agent of destruction exulted silently in the possession of personal prestige, keeping in check this man armed with the defensive mandate of a menaced society. More fortunate than Caligula, who wished that the Roman

Senate had only one head for the better satisfaction of his cruel lust, he beheld in that one man all the forces he had set at defiance: the force of law, property, oppression, and injustice. He beheld all his enemies, and fearlessly confronted them all in a supreme satisfaction of his vanity. They stood perplexed before him as if before a dreadful portent. He gloated inwardly over the chance of this meeting affirming his superiority over all the multitude of mankind.

It was in reality a chance meeting. Chief Inspector Heat had had a disagreeably busy day since his department received the first telegram from Greenwich a little before eleven in the morning. First of all, the fact of the outrage being attempted less than a week after he had assured a high official that no outbreak of anarchist activity was to be apprehended was sufficiently annoying. If he ever thought himself safe in making a statement, it was then. He had made that statement with infinite satisfaction to himself, because it was clear that the high official desired greatly to hear that very thing. He had affirmed that nothing of the sort could even be thought of without the department being aware of it within twenty-four hours; and he had spoken thus in his consciousness of being the great expert of his department. He had gone even so far as to utter words which true wisdom would have kept back. But Chief Inspector Heat was not very wise—at least not truly so. True wisdom, which is not certain of anything in this world of contradictions, would have prevented him from attaining his present position. It would have alarmed his superiors, and done away with his chances of promotion. His promotion had been very rapid.

"There isn't one of them, sir, that we couldn't lay our hands on at any time of night and day. We know what each of them is doing hour by hour," he had declared. And the high official had deigned to smile. This was so obviously the right thing to say for an officer of Chief Inspector Heat's reputation that it was perfectly delightful. The high official believed the declaration, which chimed in with his idea of the fitness of things. His wisdom was of an official kind, or else he might have reflected upon a matter not of theory but of experience that in the close-woven stuff of relations between conspirator and police there occur unexpected solutions of continuity, sudden holes in space and time. A given anarchist may be watched inch by inch and minute by minute, but a moment always comes when somehow all sight and touch of him are lost for a few hours, during which something (generally an explosion) more or less deplorable does happen. But the high official, carried away by his sense of the fitness of things, had smiled, and now the recollection of that smile was very annoying to Chief Inspector Heat, principal expert in anarchist procedure.

This was not the only circumstance whose recollection depressed the usual serenity of the eminent specialist. There was another dating back only to that very morning. The thought that when called urgently to his Assistant Commissioner's private room he had been unable to conceal his astonishment was distinctly vexing. His instinct of a successful man had taught him long ago that, as a general rule, a reputation is built on manner as much as on achievement. And he felt that his manner when confronted with the telegram had not been impressive. He had opened his eyes widely, and had exclaimed "Impossible!" exposing himself thereby to the unanswerable retort of a finger-tip laid forcibly on the telegram which the Assistant Commissioner, after reading it aloud, had flung on the desk. To be crushed, as it were, under the tip of a forefinger was an unpleasant experience. Very damaging, too! Furthermore, Chief Inspector Heat was conscious of not having mended matters by allowing himself to express a conviction.

"One thing I can tell you at once: none of our lot had anything to do with this."

He was strong in his integrity of a good detective, but he saw now that an impenetrably attentive reserve towards this incident would have served his reputation better. On the other hand, he admitted to himself that it was difficult to preserve one's reputation if rank outsiders were going to take a hand in the business. Outsiders are the bane of the police as of other professions. The tone of the Assistant Commissioner's remarks had been sour enough to set one's teeth on edge.

And since breakfast Chief Inspector Heat had not managed to get anything to eat.

Starting immediately to begin his investigation on the spot, he had swallowed a good deal of raw, unwholesome fog in the park. Then he had walked over to the hospital; and when the investigation in Greenwich was concluded at last he had lost his inclination for food. Not accustomed, as the doctors are, to examine closely the mangled remains of human beings, he had been shocked by the sight disclosed to his view when a waterproof sheet had been lifted off a table in a certain apartment of the hospital.

Another waterproof sheet was spread over that table in the manner of a table-cloth, with the corners turned up over a sort of mound—a heap of rags, scorched and bloodstained, half concealing what might have been an accumulation of raw material for a cannibal feast. It required considerable firmness of mind not to recoil before that sight. Chief Inspector Heat, an efficient officer of his department, stood his ground, but for a whole minute he did not advance. A local constable in uniform cast a sidelong glance, and said, with stolid simplicity:

"He's all there. Every bit of him. It was a job."

He had been the first man on the spot after the explosion. He mentioned the fact again. He had seen something like a heavy flash of lightning in the fog. At that time he was standing at the door of the King William Street Lodge talking to the keeper. The concussion made him tingle all over. He ran between the trees towards the Observatory. "As fast as my legs would carry me," he repeated twice.

Chief Inspector Heat, bending forward over the table in a gingerly and horrified manner, let him run on. The hospital porter and another man turned down the corners of the cloth, and stepped aside. The Chief Inspector's eyes searched the gruesome detail of that heap of mixed things, which seemed to have been collected in shambles and rag shops.

"You used a shovel," he remarked, observing a sprinkling of small gravel, tiny brown bits of bark, and particles of splintered wood as fine as needles.

"Had to in one place," said the stolid constable. "I sent a keeper to fetch a spade. When he heard me scraping the ground with it he leaned his forehead against a tree, and was as sick as a dog."

The Chief Inspector, stooping guardedly over the table, fought down the unpleasant sensation in his throat. The shattering violence of destruction which had made of that body a heap of nameless fragments affected his feelings with a sense of ruthless cruelty, though his reason told him the effect must have been as swift as a flash of lightning. The man, whoever he was, had died instantaneously; and yet it seemed impossible to believe that a human body could have reached that state of disintegration without passing through the pangs of inconceivable agony. No physiologist, and still less of a metaphysician, Chief Inspector Heat rose by the force of sympathy, which is a form of fear, above the vulgar conception of time. Instantaneous! He remembered all he had ever read in popular publications of long and terrifying dreams dreamed in the instant of waking; of the whole past life lived with frightful intensity by a drowning man as his doomed head bobs up, streaming, for the last time. The inexplicable mysteries of conscious existence beset Chief Inspector Heat till he evolved a horrible notion that ages of atrocious pain and mental torture could be contained between two successive winks of an eye. And meantime the Chief Inspector went on, peering at the table with a calm face and the slightly anxious attention of an indigent customer bending over what may be called the by-products of a butcher's shop with a view to an inexpensive

Sunday dinner. All the time his trained faculties of an excellent investigator, who scorns no chance of information, followed the self-satisfied, disjointed loquacity of the constable.

"A fair-haired fellow," the last observed in a placid tone, and paused. "The old woman who spoke to the sergeant noticed a fair-haired fellow coming out of Maze Hill Station." He paused. "And he was a fair-haired fellow. She noticed two men coming out of the station after the uptrain had gone on," he continued slowly. "She couldn't tell if they were together. She took no particular notice of the big one, but the other was a fair, slight chap, carrying a tin varnish can in one hand." The constable ceased.

"Know the woman?" muttered the Chief Inspector, with his eyes fixed on the table, and a vague notion in his mind of an inquest to be held presently upon a person likely to remain for ever unknown.

"Yes. She's housekeeper to a retired publican, and attends the chapel in Park Place sometimes," the constable uttered weightily, and paused, with another oblique glance at the table.

Then suddenly: "Well, here he is—all of him I could see. Fair. Slight—slight enough. Look at that foot there. I picked up the legs first, one after another. He was that scattered you didn't know where to begin."

The constable paused; the least flicker of an innocent self-laudatory smile invested his round face with an infantile expression.

"Stumbled," he announced positively. "I stumbled once myself, and pitched on my head too, while running up. Them roots do stick out all about the place. Stumbled against the root of a tree and fell, and that thing he was carrying must have gone off right under his chest, I expect."

The echo of the words "Person unknown" repeating itself in his inner consciousness bothered the Chief Inspector considerably. He would have liked to trace this affair back to its mysterious origin for his own information. He was professionally curious. Before the public he would have liked to vindicate the efficiency of his department by establishing the identity of that man. He was a loyal servant. That, however, appeared impossible. The first term of the problem was unreadable—lacked all suggestion but that of atrocious cruelty.

Overcoming his physical repugnance, Chief Inspector Heat stretched out his hand without conviction for the salving of his conscience, and took up the least soiled of the rags. It was a narrow strip of velvet with a larger triangular piece of dark blue cloth hanging from it. He held it up to his eyes; and the police constable spoke.

"Velvet collar. Funny the old woman should have noticed the velvet collar. Dark blue overcoat with a velvet collar, she has told us. He was the chap she saw, and no mistake. And here he is all complete, velvet collar and all. I don't think I missed a single piece as big as a postage stamp."

At this point the trained faculties of the Chief Inspector ceased to hear the voice of the constable. He moved to one of the windows for better light. His face, averted from the room, expressed a startled intense interest while he examined closely the triangular piece of broad-cloth. By a sudden jerk he detached it, and *only* after stuffing it into his pocket turned round to the room, and flung the velvet collar back on the table—

"Cover up," he directed the attendants curtly, without another look, and, saluted by the constable, carried off his spoil hastily.

A convenient train whirled him up to town, alone and pondering deeply, in a third-class compartment. That singed piece of cloth was incredibly valuable, and he could not defend himself from astonishment at the casual manner it had come into his possession. It was as if Fate had thrust that clue into his hands. And after the manner of the average man, whose ambition is to command events, he began to mistrust such a gratuitous and accidental success—just because it seemed forced upon him. The practical value of success depends not a little on the way you look at it. But Fate looks at nothing. It has no discretion. He no longer considered it eminently desirable all round to establish publicly the identity of the man who had blown himself up that morning with such horrible completeness. But he was not certain of the view his department would take. A department is to those it employs a complex personality with ideas and even fads of its own. It depends on the loyal devotion of its servants, and the devoted loyalty of trusted servants is associated with a certain amount of affectionate contempt, which keeps it sweet, as it were. By a benevolent provision of Nature no man is a hero to his valet, or else the heroes would have to brush their own clothes. Likewise no department appears perfectly wise to the intimacy of its workers. A department does not know so much as some of its servants. Being a dispassionate organism, it can never be perfectly informed. It would not be good for its efficiency to know too much. Chief Inspector Heat got out of the train in a state of thoughtfulness entirely untainted with disloyalty, but not quite free of that jealous mistrust which so often springs on the ground of perfect devotion, whether to women or to institutions.

It was in this mental disposition, physically very empty, but still nauseated by what he had seen, that he had come upon the Professor. Under these conditions which make for irascibility in a sound, normal man, this meeting was specially unwelcome to Chief Inspector Heat. He had not been thinking of the Professor; he had not been thinking of any individual anarchist at all. The complexion of that case had somehow forced upon him the general idea of the absurdity of things human, which in the abstract is sufficiently annoying to an unphilosophical temperament, and in concrete instances becomes exasperating beyond endurance. At the beginning of his career Chief Inspector Heat had been concerned with the more energetic forms of thieving. He had gained his spurs in that sphere, and naturally enough had kept for it, after his promotion to another department, a feeling not very far removed from affection. Thieving was not a sheer absurdity. It was a form of human industry, perverse indeed, but still an industry exercised in an industrious world; it was work undertaken for the same reason as the work in potteries, in coal mines, in fields, in tool-grinding shops. It was labour, whose practical difference from the other forms of labour consisted in the nature of its risk, which did not lie in ankylosis, or lead poisoning, or fire-damp, or gritty dust, but in what may be briefly defined in its own special phraseology as "Seven years hard." Chief Inspector Heat was, of course, not insensible to the gravity of moral differences. But neither were the thieves he had been looking after. They submitted to the severe sanctions of a morality familiar to Chief Inspector Heat with a certain resignation.

They were his fellow-citizens gone wrong because of imperfect education, Chief Inspector Heat believed; but allowing for that difference, he could understand the mind of a burglar, because, as a matter of fact, the mind and the instincts of a burglar are of the same kind as the mind and the instincts of a police officer. Both recognise the same conventions, and have a working knowledge of each other's methods and of the routine of their respective trades. They understand each other, which is advantageous to both, and establishes a sort of amenity in their relations. Products of the same machine, one classed as useful and the other as noxious, they take the machine for granted in different ways, but with a seriousness essentially the same. The mind of Chief Inspector Heat was inaccessible to ideas of revolt. But his thieves were not rebels. His bodily vigour, his cool inflexible manner, his courage and his fairness, had secured for him much respect and some adulation in the sphere of his early successes. He had felt himself revered and admired. And Chief Inspector Heat, arrested within six paces of the anarchist nick-named the Professor, gave a thought of regret to the world of thieves—sane, without morbid ideals, working by routine, respectful of constituted authorities, free from all taint of hate and despair.

After paying this tribute to what is normal in the constitution of society (for the idea of thieving appeared to his instinct as normal as the idea of property), Chief Inspector Heat felt very angry with himself for having stopped, for having spoken, for having taken that way at all on the ground of it being a short cut from the station to the headquarters. And he spoke again in his big authoritative voice, which, being moderated, had a threatening character.

"You are not wanted, I tell you," he repeated.

The anarchist did not stir. An inward laugh of derision uncovered not only his teeth but his gums as well, shook him all over, without the slightest sound. Chief Inspector Heat was led to add, against his better judgment:

"Not yet. When I want you I will know where to find you."

Those were perfectly proper words, within the tradition and suitable to his character of a police officer addressing one of his special flock. But the reception they got departed from tradition and propriety. It was outrageous. The stunted, weakly figure before him spoke at last.

"I've no doubt the papers would give you an obituary notice then. You know best what that would be worth to you. I should think you can imagine easily the sort of stuff that would be printed. But you may be exposed to the unpleasantness of being buried together with me, though I suppose your friends would make an effort to sort us out as much as possible."

With all his healthy contempt for the spirit dictating such speeches, the atrocious allusiveness of the words had its effect on Chief Inspector Heat. He had too much insight, and too much exact information as well, to dismiss them as rot. The dusk of this narrow lane took on a sinister tint from the dark, frail little figure, its back to the wall, and speaking with a weak, self-confident voice. To the vigorous, tenacious vitality of the Chief Inspector, the physical wretchedness of that being, so obviously not fit to live, was ominous; for it seemed to him that if he had the misfortune to be such a miserable object he would not have cared how soon he died. Life had such a strong hold upon him that a fresh wave of nausea broke out in slight perspiration upon his brow. The murmur of town life, the subdued rumble of wheels in the two invisible streets to the right and left, came through the curve of the sordid lane to his ears with a precious familiarity and an appealing sweetness. He was human. But Chief Inspector Heat was also a man, and he could not let such words pass.

"All this is good to frighten children with," he said. "I'll have you yet."

It was very well said, without scorn, with an almost austere quietness.

"Doubtless," was the answer; "but there's no time like the present, believe me. For a man of real convictions this is a fine opportunity of self-sacrifice. You may not find another so favourable, so humane. There isn't even a cat near us, and these condemned old houses would make a good heap of bricks where you stand. You'll never get me at so little cost to life and property, which you are paid to protect."

"You don't know who you're speaking to," said Chief Inspector Heat firmly. "If I were to lay my hands on you now I would be no better than yourself."

"Ah! The game!'

"You may be sure our side will win in the end. It may yet be necessary to make people believe that some of you ought to be shot at sight like mad dogs. Then that will be the game. But I'll be damned if I know what yours is. I don't believe you know yourselves. You'll never get anything by it."

"Meantime it's you who get something from it—so far. And you get it easily, too. I won't speak of your salary, but haven't you made your name simply by not understanding what we are after?"

"What are you after, then?" asked Chief Inspector Heat, with scornful haste, like a man in a hurry who perceives he is wasting his time.

The perfect anarchist answered by a smile which did not part his thin colourless lips; and the celebrated Chief Inspector felt a sense of superiority which induced him to raise a warning finger.

"Give it up—whatever it is," he said in an admonishing tone, but not so kindly as if he were condescending to give good advice to a cracksman of repute. "Give it up. You'll find we are too many for you."

The fixed smile on the Professor's lips wavered, as if the mocking spirit within had lost its assurance. Chief Inspector Heat went on:

"Don't you believe me eh? Well, you've only got to look about you. We are. And anyway, you're not doing it well. You're always making a mess of it. Why, if the thieves didn't know their work better they would starve."

The hint of an invincible multitude behind that man's back roused a sombre indignation in the breast of the Professor. He smiled no longer his enigmatic and mocking smile. The resisting power of numbers, the unattackable stolidity of a great multitude, was the haunting fear of his sinister loneliness. His lips trembled for some time before he managed to say in a strangled voice:

"I am doing my work better than you're doing yours."

"That'll do now," interrupted Chief Inspector Heat hurriedly; and the Professor laughed right out this time. While still laughing he moved on; but he did not laugh long. It was a sad-faced, miserable little man who emerged from the narrow passage into the bustle of the broad thoroughfare. He walked with the nerveless gait of a tramp going on, still going on, indifferent to rain or sun in a sinister detachment from the aspects of sky and earth. Chief Inspector Heat, on the other hand, after watching him for a while, stepped out with the purposeful briskness of a man disregarding indeed the inclemencies of the weather, but conscious of having an authorised mission on this earth and the moral support of his kind. All the inhabitants of the immense town, the population of the whole country, and even the teeming millions struggling upon the planet, were with him—down to the very thieves and mendicants. Yes, the thieves themselves were sure to be with him in his present work. The consciousness of universal support in his general activity heartened him to grapple with the particular problem.

The problem immediately before the Chief Inspector was that of managing the Assistant Commissioner of his department, his immediate superior. This is the perennial problem of trusty and loyal servants; anarchism gave it its particular complexion, but nothing more. Truth to say, Chief Inspector Heat thought but little of anarchism. He did not attach undue importance to it, and could never bring himself to consider it seriously. It had more the character of disorderly conduct; disorderly without the human excuse of drunkenness, which at any rate implies good feeling and an amiable leaning towards festivity. As criminals, anarchists were distinctly no class—no class at all. And recalling the Professor, Chief Inspector Heat, without checking his swinging pace, muttered through his teeth:

"Lunatic."

Catching thieves was another matter altogether. It had that quality of seriousness belonging to every form of open sport where the best man wins under perfectly comprehensible rules. There were no rules for dealing with anarchists. And that was distasteful to the Chief Inspector. It was all foolishness, but that foolishness excited the public mind, affected persons in high places, and touched upon international relations. A hard, merciless contempt settled rigidly on the Chief Inspector's face as he walked on. His mind ran over all the anarchists of his flock. Not one of them had half the spunk of this or that burglar he had known. Not half—not one-tenth.

At headquarters the Chief Inspector was admitted at once to the Assistant Commissioner's private room. He found him, pen in hand, bent over a great table bestrewn with papers, as if worshipping an enormous double inkstand of bronze and crystal. Speaking tubes resembling snakes were tied by the heads to the back of the Assistant Commissioner's wooden arm-chair, and their gaping mouths seemed ready to bite his elbows. And in this attitude he raised only his eyes, whose lids were darker than his face and very much creased. The reports had come in: every anarchist had been exactly accounted for.

After saying this he lowered his eyes, signed rapidly two single sheets of paper, and only then laid down his pen, and sat well back, directing an inquiring gaze at his renowned subordinate. The Chief Inspector stood it well, deferential but inscrutable.

"I daresay you were right," said the Assistant Commissioner, "in telling me at first that the London anarchists had nothing to do with this. I quite appreciate the excellent watch kept on them by your men. On the other hand, this, for the public, does not amount to more than a confession of ignorance."

The Assistant Commissioner's delivery was leisurely, as it were cautious. His thought seemed to rest poised on a word before passing to another, as though words had been the stepping-stones for his intellect picking its way across the waters of error. "Unless you have brought something useful from Greenwich," he added.

The Chief Inspector began at once the account of his investigation in a clear matter-of-fact manner. His superior turning his chair a little, and crossing his thin legs, leaned sideways on his elbow, with one hand shading his eyes. His listening attitude had a sort of angular and sorrowful grace. Gleams as of highly burnished silver played on the sides of his ebony black head when he inclined it slowly at the end.

Chief Inspector Heat waited with the appearance of turning over in his mind all he had just said, but, as a matter of fact, considering the advisability of saying something more. The Assistant Commissioner cut his hesitation short.

"You believe there were two men?" he asked, without uncovering his eyes.

The Chief Inspector thought it more than probable. In his opinion, the two men had parted from each other within a hundred yards from the Observatory walls. He explained also how the other man could have got out of the park speedily without being observed. The fog, though not very dense, was in his favour. He seemed to have escorted the other to the spot, and then to have left him there to do the job single-handed. Taking the time those two were seen coming out of Maze Hill Station by the old woman, and the time when the explosion was heard, the Chief Inspector thought that the other man might have been actually at the Greenwich Park Station, ready to catch the next train up, at the moment his comrade was destroying himself so thoroughly.

"Very thoroughly—eh?" murmured the Assistant Commissioner from under the shadow of his hand.

The Chief Inspector in a few vigorous words described the aspect of the remains. "The coroner's jury will have a treat," he added grimly.

The Assistant Commissioner uncovered his eyes.

"We shall have nothing to tell them," he remarked languidly.

He looked up, and for a time watched the markedly non-committal attitude of his Chief

Inspector. His nature was one that is not easily accessible to illusions. He knew that a department is at the mercy of its subordinate officers, who have their own conceptions of loyalty. His career had begun in a tropical colony. He had liked his work there. It was police work. He had been very successful in tracking and breaking up certain nefarious secret societies amongst the natives. Then he took his long leave, and got married rather impulsively. It was a good match from a worldly point of view, but his wife formed an unfavourable opinion of the colonial climate on hearsay evidence. On the other hand, she had influential connections. It was an excellent match. But he did not like the work he had to do now. He felt himself dependent on too many subordinates and too many masters. The near presence of that strange emotional phenomenon called public opinion weighed upon his spirits, and alarmed him by its irrational nature. No doubt that from ignorance he exaggerated to himself its power for good and evil—especially for evil; and the rough east winds of the English spring (which agreed with his wife) augmented his general mistrust of men's motives and of the efficiency of their organisation. The futility of office work especially appalled him on those days so trying to his sensitive liver.

He got up, unfolding himself to his full height, and with a heaviness of step remarkable in so slender a man, moved across the room to the window. The panes streamed with rain, and the short street he looked down into lay wet and empty, as if swept clear suddenly by a great flood. It was a very trying day, choked in raw fog to begin with, and now drowned in cold rain. The flickering, blurred flames of gas-lamps seemed to be dissolving in a watery atmosphere. And the lofty pretensions of a mankind oppressed by the miserable indignities of the weather appeared as a colossal and hopeless vanity deserving of scorn, wonder, and compassion.

"Horrible, horrible!" thought the Assistant Commissioner to himself, with his face near the window-pane. "We have been having this sort of thing now for ten days; no, a fortnight —a fortnight." He ceased to think completely for a time. That utter stillness of his brain lasted about three seconds. Then he said perfunctorily: "You have set inquiries on foot for tracing that other man up and down the line?"

He had no doubt that everything needful had been done. Chief Inspector Heat knew, of course, thoroughly the business of man-hunting. And these were the routine steps, too, that would be taken as a matter of course by the merest beginner. A few inquiries amongst the ticket collectors and the porters of the two small railway stations would give additional details as to the appearance of the two men; the inspection of the collected tickets would show at once where they came from that morning. It was elementary, and could not have been neglected. Accordingly the Chief Inspector answered that all this had been done directly the old woman had come forward with her deposition. And he mentioned the name of a station. "That's where they came from, sir," he went on. "The porter who took the tickets at Maze Hill remembers two chaps answering to the description passing the barrier. They seemed to him two respectable working men of a superior sort—sign painters or house decorators. The big man got out of a third-class compartment backward, with a bright tin can in his hand. On the platform he gave it to carry to the fair young fellow who followed him. All this agrees exactly with what the old woman told the police sergeant in Greenwich."

The Assistant Commissioner, still with his face turned to the window, expressed his doubt as to these two men having had anything to do with the outrage. All this theory rested upon the utterances of an old charwoman who had been nearly knocked down by a man in a hurry. Not a very substantial authority indeed, unless on the ground of sudden inspiration, which was hardly tenable.

"Frankly now, could she have been really inspired?" he queried, with grave irony, keeping his back to the room, as if entranced by the contemplation of the town's colossal forms half lost in the night. He did not even look round when he heard the mutter of the word "Providential" from the principal subordinate of his department, whose name, printed sometimes in the papers, was familiar to the great public as that of one of its zealous and hard-working protectors. Chief Inspector Heat raised his voice a little.

"Strips and bits of bright tin were quite visible to me," he said. "That's a pretty good corroboration."

"And these men came from that little country station," the Assistant Commissioner mused aloud, wondering. He was told that such was the name on two tickets out of three given up out of that train at Maze Hill. The third person who got out was a hawker from Gravesend well known to the porters. The Chief Inspector imparted that information in a tone of finality with some ill humour, as loyal servants will do in the consciousness of their fidelity and with the sense of the value of their loyal exertions. And still the Assistant Commissioner did not turn away from the darkness outside, as vast as a sea.

"Two foreign anarchists coming from that place," he said, apparently to the window-pane. "It's rather unaccountable."'

"Yes, sir. But it would be still more unaccountable if that Michaelis weren't staying in a cottage in the neighbourhood."

At the sound of that name, falling unexpectedly into this annoying affair, the Assistant Commissioner dismissed brusquely the vague remembrance of his daily whist party at his club. It was the most comforting habit of his life, in a mainly successful display of his skill without the assistance of any subordinate. He entered his club to play from five to seven, before going home to dinner, forgetting for those two hours whatever was distasteful in his life, as though the game were a beneficent drug for allaying the pangs of moral discontent. His partners were the gloomily humorous editor of a celebrated magazine; a silent, elderly barrister with malicious little eyes; and a highly martial, simple-minded old Colonel with nervous brown hands. They were his club acquaintances merely. He never met them elsewhere except at the card-table. But they all seemed to approach the game in the spirit of co-sufferers, as if it were indeed a drug against the secret ills of existence; and every day as the sun declined over the countless roofs of the town, a mellow, pleasurable impatience, resembling the impulse of a sure and profound friendship, lightened his professional labours. And now this pleasurable sensation went out of him with something resembling a physical shock, and was replaced by a special kind of interest in his work of social protection—an improper sort of interest, which may be defined best as a sudden and alert mistrust of the weapon in his hand.

6

THE LADY PATRONESS OF MICHAELIS, the ticket-of-leave apostle of humanitarian hopes, was one of the most influential and distinguished connections of the Assistant Commissioner's wife, whom she called Annie, and treated still rather as a not very wise and utterly inexperienced young girl. But she had consented to accept him on a friendly footing, which was by no means the case with all of his wife's influential connections. Married young and splendidly at some remote epoch of the past, she had had for a time a close view of great affairs and even of some great men. She herself was a great lady. Old now in the number of her years, she had that sort of exceptional temperament which defies time with scornful disregard, as if it were a rather vulgar convention submitted to by the mass of inferior mankind. Many other conventions easier to set aside, alas! failed to obtain her recognition, also on temperamental grounds—either because they bored her, or else because they stood in the way of her scorns and sympathies. Admiration was a sentiment unknown to her (it was one of the secret griefs of her most noble husband against her)—first, as always more or less tainted with mediocrity, and next as being in a way an admission of inferiority. And both were frankly inconceivable to her nature. To be fearlessly outspoken in her opinions came easily to her, since she judged solely from the standpoint of her social position. She was equally untrammelled in her actions; and as her tactfulness proceeded from genuine humanity, her bodily vigour remained remarkable and her superiority was serene and cordial, three generations had admired her infinitely, and the last she was likely to see had pronounced her a wonderful woman. Meantime intelligent, with a sort of lofty simplicity, and curious at heart, but not like many women merely of social gossip, she amused her age by attracting within her ken through the power of her great, almost historical, social prestige everything that rose above the dead level of mankind, lawfully or unlawfully, by position, wit, audacity, fortune or misfortune. Royal Highnesses, artists, men of science, young statesmen, and charlatans of all ages and conditions, who, unsubstantial and light, bobbing up like corks, show best the direction of the surface currents, had been welcomed in that house, listened to, penetrated, understood, appraised, for her own edification. In her own words, she liked to watch what the world was coming to. And as she had a practical mind her judgment of men and things, though based on special prejudices, was seldom totally wrong, and almost never wrong-headed. Her drawing-room was probably the only place in the wide world where an Assistant Commissioner of Police could meet a convict liberated on a ticket-of-leave on other than professional and official ground. Who had brought Michaelis there one afternoon the Assistant Commissioner did not remember very well. He had a notion it must have been a certain Member of Parliament of illustrious parentage and unconventional sympathies, which were the standing joke of the comic papers. The notabilities and even the simple notorieties of the day brought each other freely to that temple of an old woman's not ignoble curiosity. You never could guess whom you were likely to come upon being received in semi-privacy within the faded blue silk and gilt frame screen, making a cosy nook for a couch and a few arm-chairs in the great drawing-room, with its hum of voices and the groups of people seated or standing in the light of six tall windows.

Michaelis had been the object of a revulsion of popular sentiment, the same sentiment which years ago had applauded the ferocity of the life sentence passed upon him for complicity in a rather mad attempt to rescue some prisoners from a police van. The plan of the conspirators had been to shoot down the horses and overpower the escort. Unfortunately, one of the police constables got shot too. He left a wife and three small children, and the death of that man aroused through the length and breadth of a realm for whose defence, welfare, and glory men die every day as matter of duty, an outburst of furious indignation, of a raging implacable pity for the victim. Three ring-leaders got hanged. Michaelis, young and slim, locksmith by trade, and great frequenter of evening schools, did not even know that anybody had been killed, his part with a few others being to force open the door at the back of the special conveyance. When arrested he had a bunch of skeleton keys in one pocket, a heavy chisel in another, and a short crowbar in his hand: neither more nor less than a burglar. But no burglar would have received such a heavy sentence. The death of the constable had made him miserable at heart, but the failure of the plot also. He did not conceal either of these sentiments from his empanelled countrymen, and that sort of compunction appeared shockingly imperfect to the crammed court. The judge on passing sentence commented feelingly upon the depravity and callousness of the young prisoner.

That made the groundless fame of his condemnation; the fame of his release was made for him on no better grounds by people who wished to exploit the sentimental aspect of his imprisonment either for purposes of their own or for no intelligible purpose. He let them do so in the innocence of his heart and the simplicity of his mind. Nothing that happened to him individually had any importance. He was like those saintly men whose personality is lost in the contemplation of their faith. His ideas were not in the nature of convictions. They were inaccessible to reasoning. They formed in all their contradictions and obscurities an invincible and humanitarian creed, which he confessed rather than preached, with an obstinate gentleness, a smile of pacific assurance on his lips, and his candid blue eyes cast down because the sight of faces troubled his inspiration developed in solitude. In that characteristic attitude, pathetic in his grotesque and incurable obesity which he had to drag like a galley slave's bullet to the end of his days, the Assistant Commissioner of Police beheld the ticket-of-leave apostle filling a privileged arm-chair within the screen. He sat there by the head of the old lady's couch, mild-voiced and quiet, with no more self-consciousness than a very small child, and with something of a child's charm—the appealing charm of trustfulness. Confident of the future, whose secret ways had been revealed to him within the four walls of a well-known penitentiary, he had no reason to look with suspicion upon anybody. If he could not give the great and curious lady a very definite idea as to what the world was coming to, he had managed without effort to impress her by his unembittered faith, by the sterling quality of his optimism.

A certain simplicity of thought is common to serene souls at both ends of the social scale. The great lady was simple in her own way. His views and beliefs had nothing in them to shock or startle her, since she judged them from the standpoint of her lofty position. Indeed, her sympathies were easily accessible to a man of that sort. She was not an exploiting capitalist herself; she was, as it were, above the play of economic conditions. And she had a great capacity of pity for the more obvious forms of common human miseries, precisely because she was such a complete stranger to them that she had to translate her conception into terms of mental suffering before she could grasp the notion of their cruelty. The Assistant Commissioner remembered very well the conversation between these two. He had listened in silence. It was something as exciting in a way, and even touching in its foredoomed futility, as the efforts at moral intercourse between the inhabitants of remote planets. But this grotesque incarnation of humanitarian passion appealed somehow, to one's imagination. At last Michaelis rose, and taking the great lady's extended hand, shook it, retained it for a moment in his great cushioned palm with unembarrassed friendliness, and turned upon the semi-private nook of the drawing-room his back, vast and square, and as if distended under the short tweed jacket. Glancing about in serene benevolence, he waddled along to the distant door between the knots of other visitors. The murmur of conversations paused on his passage. He smiled innocently at a tall, brilliant girl, whose eyes met his accidentally, and went out unconscious of the glances following him across the room. Michaelis' first appearance in the world was a success—a success of esteem unmarred by a single murmur of derision. The interrupted conversations were resumed in their proper tone, grave or light. Only a well-set-up, long-limbed, active-looking man of forty talking with two ladies near a window remarked aloud, with an unexpected depth of feeling: "Eighteen stone, I should say, and not five foot six. Poor fellow! It's terrible —terrible."

The lady of the house, gazing absently at the Assistant Commissioner, left alone with her on the private side of the screen, seemed to be rearranging her mental impressions behind her thoughtful immobility of a handsome old face. Men with grey moustaches and full, healthy, vaguely smiling countenances approached, circling round the screen; two mature women with a matronly air of gracious resolution; a clean-shaved individual with sunken cheeks, and dangling a gold-mounted eyeglass on a broad black ribbon with an old-world, dandified effect. A silence deferential, but full of reserves, reigned for a moment, and then the great lady exclaimed, not with resentment, but with a sort of protesting indignation:

"And that officially is supposed to be a revolutionist! What nonsense." She looked hard at the Assistant Commissioner, who murmured apologetically:

"Not a dangerous one perhaps."

"Not dangerous—I should think not indeed. He is a mere believer. It's the temperament of a saint," declared the great lady in a firm tone. "And they kept him shut up for twenty years. One shudders at the stupidity of it. And now they have let him out everybody belonging to him is gone away somewhere or dead. His parents are dead; the girl he was to marry has died while he was in prison; he has lost the skill necessary for his manual occupation. He told me all this himself with the sweetest patience; but then, he said, he had had plenty of time to think out things for himself. A pretty compensation! If that's the stuff revolutionists are made of some of us may well go on their knees to them," she continued in a slightly bantering voice, while the banal society smiles hardened on the worldly faces turned towards her with conventional deference. "The poor creature is obviously no longer in a position to take care of himself. Somebody will have to look after him a little."

"He should be recommended to follow a treatment of some sort," the soldierly voice of the active-looking man was heard advising earnestly from a distance. He was in the pink of condition for his age, and even the texture of his long frock coat had a character of elastic soundness, as if it were a living tissue. "The man is virtually a cripple," he added with unmistakable feeling.

Other voices, as if glad of the opening, murmured hasty compassion. "Quite startling," "Monstrous," "Most painful to see." The lank man, with the eyeglass on a broad ribbon, pronounced mincingly the word "Grotesque," whose justness was appreciated by those standing near him. They smiled at each other.

The Assistant Commissioner had expressed no opinion either then or later, his position making it impossible for him to ventilate any independent view of a ticket-of-leave convict. But, in truth, he shared the view of his wife's friend and patron that Michaelis was a humanitarian sentimentalist, a little mad, but upon the whole incapable of hurting a fly intentionally. So when that name cropped up suddenly in this vexing bomb affair he realised all the danger of it for the ticket-of-leave apostle, and his mind reverted at once to the old lady's well-established infatuation. Her arbitrary kindness would not brook patiently any interference with Michaelis' freedom. It was a deep, calm, convinced infatuation. She had not only felt him to be inoffensive, but she had said so, which last by a confusion of her absolutist mind became a sort of incontrovertible demonstration. It was as if the monstrosity of the man, with his candid infant's eyes and a fat angelic smile, had fascinated her. She had come to believe almost his theory of the future, since it was not repugnant to her prejudices. She disliked the new element of plutocracy in the social compound, and industrialism as a method of human development appeared to her singularly repulsive in its mechanical and unfeeling character. The humanitarian hopes of the mild Michaelis tended not towards utter destruction, but merely towards the complete economic ruin of the system. And she did not really see where was the moral harm of it. It would do away with all the multitude of the "parvenus," whom she disliked and mistrusted, not because they had arrived anywhere (she denied that), but because of their profound unintelligence of the world, which was the primary cause of the crudity of their perceptions and the aridity of their hearts. With the annihilation of all capital they would vanish too; but universal ruin (providing it was universal, as it was revealed to Michaelis) would leave the social values untouched. The disappearance of the last piece of money could not affect people of position. She could not conceive how it could affect her position, for instance. She had developed these discoveries to the Assistant Commissioner with all the serene fearlessness of an old woman who had escaped the blight of indifference. He had made for himself the rule to receive everything of that sort in a silence which he took care from policy and inclination not to make offensive. He had an affection for the aged disciple of Michaelis, a complex sentiment depending a little on her prestige, on her personality, but most of all on the instinct of flattered gratitude. He felt himself really liked in her house. She was kindness personified. And she was practically wise too, after the manner of experienced women. She made his married life much easier than it would have been without her generously full recognition of his rights as Annie's husband. Her influence upon his wife, a woman devoured by all sorts of small selfishnesses, small envies, small jealousies, was excellent. Unfortunately, both her kindness and her wisdom were of unreasonable complexion, distinctly feminine, and difficult to deal with. She remained a perfect woman all along her full tale of years, and not as some of them do become—a sort of slippery, pestilential old man in petticoats. And it was as of a woman that he thought of her—the specially choice incarnation of the feminine, wherein is recruited the tender, ingenuous, and fierce bodyguard for all sorts of men who talk under the influence of an emotion, true or fraudulent; for preachers, seers, prophets, or reformers.

Appreciating the distinguished and good friend of his wife, and himself, in that way, the Assistant Commissioner became alarmed at the convict Michaelis' possible fate. Once arrested on suspicion of being in some way, however remote, a party to this outrage, the man could hardly escape being sent back to finish his sentence at least. And that would kill him; he would never come out alive. The Assistant Commissioner made a reflection extremely unbecoming his official position without being really creditable to his humanity.

"If the fellow is laid hold of again," he thought, "she will never forgive me."

The frankness of such a secretly outspoken thought could not go without some derisive self-criticism. No man engaged in a work he does not like can preserve many saving illusions about himself. The distaste, the absence of glamour, extend from the occupation to the personality. It is only when our appointed activities seem by a lucky accident to obey the particular earnestness of our temperament that we can taste the comfort of complete self-deception. The Assistant Commissioner did not like his work at home. The police work he had been engaged on in a distant part of the globe had the saving character of an irregular sort of warfare or at least the risk and excitement of open-air sport. His real abilities, which were mainly of an administrative order, were combined with an adventurous disposition. Chained to a desk in the thick of four millions of men, he considered himself the victim of an ironic fate—the same, no doubt, which had brought about his marriage with a woman exceptionally sensitive in the matter of colonial climate, besides other limitations testifying to the delicacy of her nature—and her tastes. Though he judged his alarm sardonically he did not dismiss the improper thought from his mind. The instinct of self-preservation was strong within him. On the contrary, he repeated it mentally with profane emphasis and a fuller precision: "Damn it! If that infernal Heat has his way the fellow'll die in prison smothered in his fat, and she'll never forgive me."

His black, narrow figure, with the white band of the collar under the silvery gleams on the close-cropped hair at the back of the head, remained motionless. The silence had lasted such a long time that Chief Inspector Heat ventured to clear his throat. This noise produced its effect. The zealous and intelligent officer was asked by his superior, whose back remained turned to him immovably:

"You connect Michaelis with this affair?"

Chief Inspector Heat was very positive, but cautious.

"Well, sir," he said, "we have enough to go upon. A man like that has no business to be at large, anyhow."

"You will want some conclusive evidence," came the observation in a murmur.

Chief Inspector Heat raised his eyebrows at the black, narrow back, which remained obstinately presented to his intelligence and his zeal.

"There will be no difficulty in getting up sufficient evidence against *him*," he said, with virtuous complacency. "You may trust me for that, sir," he added, quite unnecessarily, out of the fulness of his heart; for it seemed to him an excellent thing to have that man in hand to be thrown down to the public should it think fit to roar with any special indignation in this case. It was impossible to say yet whether it would roar or not. That in the last instance depended, of course, on the newspaper press. But in any case, Chief Inspector Heat, purveyor of prisons by trade, and a man of legal instincts, did logically believe that incarceration was the proper fate for every declared enemy of the law. In the strength of that conviction he committed a fault of tact. He allowed himself a little conceited laugh, and repeated:

"Trust me for that, sir."

This was too much for the forced calmness under which the Assistant Commissioner had for upwards of eighteen months concealed his irritation with the system and the subordinates of his office. A square peg forced into a round hole, he had felt like a daily outrage that long established smooth roundness into which a man of less sharply angular shape would have fitted himself, with voluptuous acquiescence, after a shrug or two. What he resented most was just the necessity of taking so much on trust. At the little laugh of Chief Inspector Heat's he spun swiftly on his heels, as if whirled away from the window-pane by an electric shock. He caught on the latter's face not only the complacency proper to the occasion lurking under the moustache, but the vestiges of experimental watchfulness in the round eyes, which had been, no doubt, fastened on his back, and now met his glance for a second before the intent character of their stare had the time to change to a merely startled appearance.

The Assistant Commissioner of Police had really some qualifications for his post. Suddenly his suspicion was awakened. It is but fair to say that his suspicions of the police methods (unless the police happened to be a semi-military body organised by himself) was not difficult to arouse. If it ever slumbered from sheer weariness, it was but lightly; and his appreciation of Chief Inspector Heat's zeal and ability, moderate in itself, excluded all notion of moral confidence. "He's up to something," he exclaimed mentally, and at once became angry. Crossing over to his desk with headlong strides, he sat down violently. "Here I am stuck in a litter of paper," he reflected, with unreasonable resentment, "supposed to hold all the threads in my hands, and yet I can but hold what is put in my hand, and nothing else. And they can fasten the other ends of the threads where they please."

He raised his head, and turned towards his subordinate a long, meagre face with the accentuated features of an energetic Don Quixote.

"Now what is it you've got up your sleeve?"

The other stared. He stared without winking in a perfect immobility of his round eyes, as he was used to stare at the various members of the criminal class when, after being duly cautioned, they made their statements in the tones of injured innocence, or false simplicity, or sullen resignation. But behind that professional and stony fixity there was some surprise too, for in such a tone, combining nicely the note of contempt and impatience, Chief Inspector Heat, the right-hand man of the department, was not used to be addressed. He began in a procrastinating manner, like a man taken unawares by a new and unexpected experience.

"What I've got against that man Michaelis you mean, sir?"

The Assistant Commissioner watched the bullet head; the points of that Norse rover's moustache, falling below the line of the heavy jaw; the whole full and pale physiognomy, whose determined character was marred by too much flesh; at the cunning wrinkles radiating from the outer corners of the eyes—and in that purposeful contemplation of the valuable and trusted officer he drew a conviction so sudden that it moved him like an inspiration.

"I have reason to think that when you came into this room," he said in measured tones, "it was not Michaelis who was in your mind; not principally—perhaps not at all."

"You have reason to think, sir?" muttered Chief Inspector Heat, with every appearance of astonishment, which up to a certain point was genuine enough. He had discovered in this affair a delicate and perplexing side, forcing upon the discoverer a certain amount of insincerity—that sort of insincerity which, under the names of skill, prudence, discretion, turns up at one point or another in most human affairs. He felt at the moment like a tight-rope artist might feel if suddenly, in the middle of the performance, the manager of the Music Hall were to rush out of the proper managerial seclusion and begin to shake the rope. Indignation, the sense of moral insecurity engendered by such a treacherous proceeding joined to the immediate apprehension of a broken neck, would, in the colloquial phrase, put him in a state. And there would be also some scandalised concern for his art too, since a man must identify himself with something more tangible than his own personality, and establish his pride somewhere, either in his social position, or in the quality of the work he is obliged to do, or simply in the superiority of the idleness he may be fortunate enough to enjoy.

"Yes," said the Assistant Commissioner; "I have. I do not mean to say that you have not thought of Michaelis at all. But you are giving the fact you've mentioned a prominence which strikes me as not quite candid, Inspector Heat. If that is really the track of discovery, why haven't you followed it up at once, either personally or by sending one of your men to that village?"

"Do you think, sir, I have failed in my duty there?" the Chief Inspector asked, in a tone which he sought to make simply reflective. Forced unexpectedly to concentrate his faculties upon the task of preserving his balance, he had seized upon that point, and exposed himself to a rebuke; for, the Assistant Commissioner frowning slightly, observed that this was a very improper remark to make.

"But since you've made it," he continued coldly, "I'll tell you that this is not my meaning."

He paused, with a straight glance of his sunken eyes which was a full equivalent of the unspoken termination "and you know it." The head of the so-called Special Crimes Department debarred by his position from going out of doors personally in quest of secrets locked up in guilty breasts, had a propensity to exercise his considerable gifts for the detection of incriminating truth upon his own subordinates. That peculiar instinct could hardly be called a weakness. It was natural. He was a born detective. It had unconsciously governed his choice of a career, and if it ever failed him in life it was perhaps in the one exceptional circumstance of his marriage—which was also natural. It fed, since it could not roam abroad, upon the human material which was brought to it in its official seclusion. We can never cease to be ourselves.

His elbow on the desk, his thin legs crossed, and nursing his cheek in the palm of his meagre hand, the Assistant Commissioner in charge of the Special Crimes branch was getting hold of the case with growing interest. His Chief Inspector, if not an absolutely worthy foeman of his penetration, was at any rate the most worthy of all within his reach. A mistrust of established reputations was strictly in character with the Assistant Commissioner's ability as detector. His memory evoked a certain old fat and wealthy native chief in the distant colony whom it was a tradition for the successive Colonial Governors to trust and make much of as a firm friend and supporter of the order and legality established by white men; whereas, when examined sceptically, he was found out to be principally his own good friend, and nobody else's. Not precisely a traitor, but still a man of many dangerous reservations in his fidelity, caused by a due regard for his own advantage, comfort, and safety. A fellow of some innocence in his naive duplicity, but none the less dangerous. He took some finding out. He was physically a big man, too, and (allowing for the difference of colour, of course) Chief Inspector Heat's appearance recalled him to the memory of his superior. It was not the eyes nor yet the lips exactly. It was bizarre. But does not Alfred Wallace relate in his famous book on the Malay Archipelago how, amongst the Aru Islanders, he discovered in an old and naked savage with a sooty skin a peculiar resemblance to a dear friend at home?

For the first time since he took up his appointment the Assistant Commissioner felt as if he were going to do some real work for his salary. And that was a pleasurable sensation. "I'll turn him inside out like an old glove," thought the Assistant Commissioner, with his eyes resting pensively upon Chief Inspector Heat.

"No, that was not my thought," he began again. "There is no doubt about you knowing your business—no doubt at all; and that's precisely why I—" He stopped short, and changing his tone: "What could you bring up against Michaelis of a definite nature? I mean apart from the fact that the two men under suspicion—you're certain there were two of them —came last from a railway station within three miles of the village where Michaelis is living now."

"This by itself is enough for us to go upon, sir, with that sort of man," said the Chief Inspector, with returning composure. The slight approving movement of the Assistant Commissioner's head went far to pacify the resentful astonishment of the renowned officer. For Chief Inspector Heat was a kind man, an excellent husband, a devoted father; and the public and departmental confidence he enjoyed acting favourably upon an amiable nature, disposed him to feel friendly towards the successive Assistant Commissioners he had seen pass through that very room. There had been three in his time. The first one, a soldierly, abrupt, red-faced person, with white eyebrows and an explosive temper, could be managed with a silken thread. He left on reaching the age limit. The second, a perfect gentleman, knowing his own and everybody else's place to a nicety, on resigning to take up a higher appointment out of England got decorated for (really) Inspector Heat's services. To work with him had been a pride and a pleasure. The third, a bit of a dark horse from the first, was at the end of eighteen months something of a dark horse still to the department. Upon the whole Chief Inspector Heat believed him to be in the main harmless—odd-looking, but harmless. He was speaking now, and the Chief Inspector listened with outward deference (which means nothing, being a matter of duty) and inwardly with benevolent toleration.

"Michaelis reported himself before leaving London for the country?"

"Yes, sir. He did."

"And what may he be doing there?" continued the Assistant Commissioner, who was perfectly informed on that point. Fitted with painful tightness into an old wooden arm-chair, before a worm-eaten oak table in an upstairs room of a four-roomed cottage with a roof of moss-grown tiles, Michaelis was writing night and day in a shaky, slanting hand that "Autobiography of a Prisoner" which was to be like a book of Revelation in the history of mankind. The conditions of confined space, seclusion, and solitude in a small four-roomed cottage were favourable to his inspiration. It was like being in prison, except that one was never disturbed for the odious purpose of taking exercise according to the tyrannical regulations of his old home in the penitentiary. He could not tell whether the sun still shone on the earth or not. The perspiration of the literary labour dropped from his brow. A delightful enthusiasm urged him on. It was the liberation of his inner life, the letting out of his soul into the wide world. And the zeal of his guileless vanity (first awakened by the offer of five hundred pounds from a publisher) seemed something predestined and holy.

"It would be, of course, most desirable to be informed exactly," insisted the Assistant Commissioner uncandidly.

Chief Inspector Heat, conscious of renewed irritation at this display of scrupulousness, said that the county police had been notified from the first of Michaelis' arrival, and that a full report could be obtained in a few hours. A wire to the superintendent—

Thus he spoke, rather slowly, while his mind seemed already to be weighing the consequences. A slight knitting of the brow was the outward sign of this. But he was interrupted by a question.

"You've sent that wire already?"

"No, sir," he answered, as if surprised.

The Assistant Commissioner uncrossed his legs suddenly. The briskness of that movement contrasted with the casual way in which he threw out a suggestion.

"Would you think that Michaelis had anything to do with the preparation of that bomb, for instance?"

The Chief Inspector assumed a reflective manner.

"I wouldn't say so. There's no necessity to say anything at present. He associates with men who are classed as dangerous. He was made a delegate of the Red Committee less than a year after his release on licence. A sort of compliment, I suppose."

And the Chief Inspector laughed a little angrily, a little scornfully. With a man of that sort scrupulousness was a misplaced and even an illegal sentiment. The celebrity bestowed upon Michaelis on his release two years ago by some emotional journalists in want of special copy had rankled ever since in his breast. It was perfectly legal to arrest that man on the barest suspicion. It was legal and expedient on the face of it. His two former chiefs would have seen the point at once; whereas this one, without saying either yes or no, sat there, as if lost in a dream. Moreover, besides being legal and expedient, the arrest of Michaelis solved a little personal difficulty which worried Chief Inspector Heat somewhat. This difficulty had its bearing upon his reputation, upon his comfort, and even upon the efficient performance of his duties. For, if Michaelis no doubt knew something about this outrage, the Chief Inspector was fairly certain that he did not know too much. This was just as well. He knew much less—the Chief Inspector was positive—than certain other individuals he had in his mind, but whose arrest seemed to him inexpedient, besides being a more complicated matter, on account of the rules of the game. The rules of the game did not protect so much Michaelis, who was an ex-convict. It would be stupid not to take advantage of legal facilities, and the journalists who had written him up with emotional gush would be ready to write him down with emotional indignation.

This prospect, viewed with confidence, had the attraction of a personal triumph for Chief Inspector Heat. And deep down in his blameless bosom of an average married citizen, almost unconscious but potent nevertheless, the dislike of being compelled by events to meddle with the desperate ferocity of the Professor had its say. This dislike had been strengthened by the chance meeting in the lane. The encounter did not leave behind with Chief Inspector Heat that satisfactory sense of superiority the members of the police force get from the unofficial but intimate side of their intercourse with the criminal classes, by which the vanity of power is soothed, and the vulgar love of domination over our fellow-creatures is flattered as worthily as it deserves.

The perfect anarchist was not recognised as a fellow-creature by Chief Inspector Heat. He was impossible—a mad dog to be left alone. Not that the Chief Inspector was afraid of him; on the contrary, he meant to have him some day. But not yet; he meant to get hold of him in his own time, properly and effectively according to the rules of the game. The present was not the right time for attempting that feat, not the right time for many reasons, personal and of public service. This being the strong feeling of Inspector Heat, it appeared to him just and proper that this affair should be shunted off its obscure and inconvenient track, leading goodness knows where, into a quiet (and lawful) siding called Michaelis. And he repeated, as if reconsidering the suggestion conscientiously:

"The bomb. No, I would not say that exactly. We may never find that out. But it's clear that he is connected with this in some way, which we can find out without much trouble."

His countenance had that look of grave, overbearing indifference once well known and much dreaded by the better sort of thieves. Chief Inspector Heat, though what is called a man, was not a smiling animal. But his inward state was that of satisfaction at the passively receptive attitude of the Assistant Commissioner, who murmured gently:

"And you really think that the investigation should be made in that direction?"

"I do, sir."

"Quite convinced?

"I am, sir. That's the true line for us to take."

The Assistant Commissioner withdrew the support of his hand from his reclining head with a suddenness that, considering his languid attitude, seemed to menace his whole person with collapse. But, on the contrary, he sat up, extremely alert, behind the great writing-table on which his hand had fallen with the sound of a sharp blow.

"What I want to know is what put it out of your head till now."

"Put it out of my head," repeated the Chief Inspector very slowly.

"Yes. Till you were called into this room—you know."

The Chief Inspector felt as if the air between his clothing and his skin had become unpleasantly hot. It was the sensation of an unprecedented and incredible experience.

"Of course," he said, exaggerating the deliberation of his utterance to the utmost limits of possibility, "if there is a reason, of which I know nothing, for not interfering with the convict Michaelis, perhaps it's just as well I didn't start the county police after him."

This took such a long time to say that the unflagging attention of the Assistant Commissioner seemed a wonderful feat of endurance. His retort came without delay.

"No reason whatever that I know of. Come, Chief Inspector, this finessing with me is highly improper on your part—highly improper. And it's also unfair, you know. You shouldn't leave me to puzzle things out for myself like this. Really, I am surprised."

He paused, then added smoothly: "I need scarcely tell you that this conversation is altogether unofficial."

These words were far from pacifying the Chief Inspector. The indignation of a betrayed tight-rope performer was strong within him. In his pride of a trusted servant he was affected by the assurance that the rope was not shaken for the purpose of breaking his neck, as by an exhibition of impudence. As if anybody were afraid! Assistant Commissioners come and go, but a valuable Chief Inspector is not an ephemeral office phenomenon. He was not afraid of getting a broken neck. To have his performance spoiled was more than enough to account for the glow of honest indignation. And as thought is no respecter of persons, the thought of Chief Inspector Heat took a threatening and prophetic shape. "You, my boy," he said to himself, keeping his round and habitually roving eyes fastened upon the Assistant Commissioner's face—"you, my boy, you don't know your place, and your place won't know you very long either, I bet."

As if in provoking answer to that thought, something like the ghost of an amiable smile passed on the lips of the Assistant Commissioner. His manner was easy and business-like while he persisted in administering another shake to the tight rope.

"Let us come now to what you have discovered on the spot, Chief Inspector," he said.

"A fool and his job are soon parted," went on the train of prophetic thought in Chief Inspector Heat's head. But it was immediately followed by the reflection that a higher official, even when "fired out" (this was the precise image), has still the time as he flies through the door to launch a nasty kick at the shin-bones of a subordinate. Without softening very much the basilisk nature of his stare, he said impassively:

"We are coming to that part of my investigation, sir."

"That's right. Well, what have you brought away from it?"

The Chief Inspector, who had made up his mind to jump off the rope, came to the ground with gloomy frankness.

"I've brought away an address," he said, pulling out of his pocket without haste a singed rag of dark blue cloth. "This belongs to the overcoat the fellow who got himself blown to pieces was wearing. Of course, the overcoat may not have been his, and may even have been stolen. But that's not at all probable if you look at this."

The Chief Inspector, stepping up to the table, smoothed out carefully the rag of blue cloth. He had picked it up from the repulsive heap in the mortuary, because a tailor's name is found sometimes under the collar. It is not often of much use, but still—He only half expected to find anything useful, but certainly he did not expect to find—not under the collar at all, but stitched carefully on the under side of the lapel—a square piece of calico with an address written on it in marking ink.

The Chief Inspector removed his smoothing hand.

"I carried it off with me without anybody taking notice," he said. "I thought it best. It can always be produced if required."

The Assistant Commissioner, rising a little in his chair, pulled the cloth over to his side of the table. He sat looking at it in silence. Only the number 32 and the name of Brett Street were written in marking ink on a piece of calico slightly larger than an ordinary cigarette paper. He was genuinely surprised.

"Can't understand why he should have gone about labelled like this," he said, looking up at Chief Inspector Heat. "It's a most extraordinary thing."

"I met once in the smoking-room of a hotel an old gentleman who went about with his name and address sewn on in all his coats in case of an accident or sudden illness," said the Chief Inspector. "He professed to be eighty-four years old, but he didn't look his age. He told me he was also afraid of losing his memory suddenly, like those people he has been reading of in the papers."

A question from the Assistant Commissioner, who wanted to know what was No. 32 Brett Street, interrupted that reminiscence abruptly. The Chief Inspector, driven down to the ground by unfair artifices, had elected to walk the path of unreserved openness. If he believed firmly that to know too much was not good for the department, the judicious holding back of knowledge was as far as his loyalty dared to go for the good of the service. If the Assistant Commissioner wanted to mismanage this affair nothing, of course, could prevent him. But, on his own part, he now saw no reason for a display of alacrity. So he answered concisely:

"It's a shop, sir."

The Assistant Commissioner, with his eyes lowered on the rag of blue cloth, waited for more information. As that did not come he proceeded to obtain it by a series of questions propounded with gentle patience. Thus he acquired an idea of the nature of Mr Verloc's commerce, of his personal appearance, and heard at last his name. In a pause the Assistant Commissioner raised his eyes, and discovered some animation on the Chief Inspector's face. They looked at each other in silence.

"Of course," said the latter, "the department has no record of that man."

"Did any of my predecessors have any knowledge of what you have told me now?" asked the Assistant Commissioner, putting his elbows on the table and raising his joined hands before his face, as if about to offer prayer, only that his eyes had not a pious expression.

"No, sir; certainly not. What would have been the object? That sort of man could never be produced publicly to any good purpose. It was sufficient for me to know who he was, and to make use of him in a way that could be used publicly."

"And do you think that sort of private knowledge consistent with the official position you occupy?"

"Perfectly, sir. I think it's quite proper. I will take the liberty to tell you, sir, that it makes me what I am—and I am looked upon as a man who knows his work. It's a private affair of my own. A personal friend of mine in the French police gave me the hint that the fellow was an Embassy spy. Private friendship, private information, private use of it—that's how I look upon it."

The Assistant Commissioner after remarking to himself that the mental state of the renowned Chief Inspector seemed to affect the outline of his lower jaw, as if the lively sense of his high professional distinction had been located in that part of his anatomy, dismissed the point for the moment with a calm "I see." Then leaning his cheek on his joined hands:

"Well then—speaking privately if you like—how long have you been in private touch with this Embassy spy?"

To this inquiry the private answer of the Chief Inspector, so private that it was never shaped into audible words, was:

"Long before you were even thought of for your place here."

The so-to-speak public utterance was much more precise.

"I saw him for the first time in my life a little more than seven years ago, when two Imperial Highnesses and the Imperial Chancellor were on a visit here. I was put in charge of all the arrangements for looking after them. Baron Stott-Wartenheim was Ambassador then. He was a very nervous old gentleman. One evening, three days before the Guildhall Banquet, he sent word that he wanted to see me for a moment. I was downstairs, and the carriages were at the door to take the Imperial Highnesses and the Chancellor to the opera. I went up at once. I found the Baron walking up and down his bedroom in a pitiable state of distress, squeezing his hands together. He assured me he had the fullest confidence in our police and in my abilities, but he had there a man just come over from Paris whose information could be trusted implicity. He wanted me to hear what that man had to say. He took me at once into a dressing-room next door, where I saw a big fellow in a heavy overcoat sitting all alone on a chair, and holding his hat and stick in one hand. The Baron said to him in French 'Speak, my friend.' The light in that room was not very good. I talked with him for some five minutes perhaps. He certainly gave me a piece of very startling news. Then the Baron took me aside nervously to praise him up to me, and when I turned round again I discovered that the fellow had vanished like a ghost. Got up and sneaked out down some back stairs, I suppose. There was no time to run after him, as I had to hurry off after the Ambassador down the great staircase, and see the party started safe for the opera. However, I acted upon the information that very night. Whether it was perfectly correct or not, it did look serious enough. Very likely it saved us from an ugly trouble on the day of the Imperial visit to the City.

"Some time later, a month or so after my promotion to Chief Inspector, my attention was attracted to a big burly man, I thought I had seen somewhere before, coming out in a hurry from a jeweller's shop in the Strand. I went after him, as it was on my way towards Charing Cross, and there seeing one of our detectives across the road, I beckoned him over, and pointed out the fellow to him, with instructions to watch his movements for a couple of days, and then report to me. No later than next afternoon my man turned up to tell me that the fellow had married his landlady's daughter at a registrar's office that very day at 11.30 a.m., and had gone off with her to Margate for a week. Our man had seen the luggage being put on the cab. There were some old Paris labels on one of the bags. Somehow I couldn't get the fellow out of my head, and the very next time I had to go to Paris on service I spoke about him to that friend of mine in the Paris police. My friend said: 'From what you tell me I think you must mean a rather well-known hanger-on and emissary of the Revolutionary Red Committee. He says he is an Englishman by birth. We have an idea that he has been for a good few years now a secret agent of one of the foreign Embassies in London.' This woke up my memory completely. He was the vanishing fellow I saw sitting on a chair in Baron Stott-Wartenheim's bathroom. I told my friend that he was quite right. The fellow was a secret agent to my certain knowledge. Afterwards my friend took the trouble to ferret out the complete record of that man for me. I thought I had better know all there was to know; but I don't suppose you want to hear his history now, sir?"

The Assistant Commissioner shook his supported head. "The history of your relations with that useful personage is the only thing that matters just now," he said, closing slowly his weary, deep-set eyes, and then opening them swiftly with a greatly refreshed glance.

"There's nothing official about them," said the Chief Inspector bitterly. "I went into his shop one evening, told him who I was, and reminded him of our first meeting. He didn't as much as twitch an eyebrow. He said that he was married and settled now, and that all he wanted was not to be interfered in his little business. I took it upon myself to promise him that, as long as he didn't go in for anything obviously outrageous, he would be left alone by the police. That was worth something to him, because a word from us to the Custom-House people would have been enough to get some of these packages he gets from Paris and Brussels opened in Dover, with confiscation to follow for certain, and perhaps a prosecution as well at the end of it."

"That's a very precarious trade," murmured the Assistant Commissioner. "Why did he go in for that?"

The Chief Inspector raised scornful eyebrows dispassionately.

"Most likely got a connection—friends on the Continent—amongst people who deal in such wares. They would be just the sort he would consort with. He's a lazy dog, too—like the rest of them."

"What do you get from him in exchange for your protection?"

The Chief Inspector was not inclined to enlarge on the value of Mr Verloc's services.

"He would not be much good to anybody but myself. One has got to know a good deal beforehand to make use of a man like that. I can understand the sort of hint he can give. And when I want a hint he can generally furnish it to me."

The Chief Inspector lost himself suddenly in a discreet reflective mood; and the Assistant Commissioner repressed a smile at the fleeting thought that the reputation of Chief Inspector Heat might possibly have been made in a great part by the Secret Agent Verloc.

"In a more general way of being of use, all our men of the Special Crimes section on duty at Charing Cross and Victoria have orders to take careful notice of anybody they may see with him. He meets the new arrivals frequently, and afterwards keeps track of them. He seems to have been told off for that sort of duty. When I want an address in a hurry, I can always get it from him. Of course, I know how to manage our relations. I haven't seen him to speak to three times in the last two years. I drop him a line, unsigned, and he answers me in the same way at my private address."

From time to time the Assistant Commissioner gave an almost imperceptible nod. The

Chief Inspector added that he did not suppose Mr Verloc to be deep in the confidence of the prominent members of the Revolutionary International Council, but that he was generally trusted of that there could be no doubt. "Whenever I've had reason to think there was something in the wind," he concluded, "I've always found he could tell me something worth knowing."

The Assistant Commissioner made a significant remark.

"He failed you this time."

"Neither had I wind of anything in any other way," retorted Chief Inspector Heat. "I asked him nothing, so he could tell me nothing. He isn't one of our men. It isn't as if he were in our pay."

"No," muttered the Assistant Commissioner. "He's a spy in the pay of a foreign government. We could never confess to him."

"I must do my work in my own way," declared the Chief Inspector. "When it comes to that I would deal with the devil himself, and take the consequences. There are things not fit for everybody to know."

"Your idea of secrecy seems to consist in keeping the chief of your department in the dark. That's stretching it perhaps a little too far, isn't it? He lives over his shop?"

"Who—Verloc? Oh yes. He lives over his shop. The wife's mother, I fancy, lives with them."

"Is the house watched?"

"Oh dear, no. It wouldn't do. Certain people who come there are watched. My opinion is that he knows nothing of this affair."

"How do you account for this?" The Assistant Commissioner nodded at the cloth rag lying before him on the table.

"I don't account for it at all, sir. It's simply unaccountable. It can't be explained by what I know." The Chief Inspector made those admissions with the frankness of a man whose reputation is established as if on a rock. "At any rate not at this present moment. I think that the man who had most to do with it will turn out to be Michaelis."

"You do?"

"Yes, sir; because I can answer for all the others."

"What about that other man supposed to have escaped from the park?"

"I should think he's far away by this time," opined the Chief Inspector.

The Assistant Commissioner looked hard at him, and rose suddenly, as though having made up his mind to some course of action. As a matter of fact, he had that very moment succumbed to a fascinating temptation. The Chief Inspector heard himself dismissed with instructions to meet his superior early next morning for further consultation upon the case. He listened with an impenetrable face, and walked out of the room with measured steps.

Whatever might have been the plans of the Assistant Commissioner they had nothing to do with that desk work, which was the bane of his existence because of its confined nature and apparent lack of reality. It could not have had, or else the general air of alacrity that came upon the Assistant Commissioner would have been inexplicable. As soon as he was left alone he looked for his hat impulsively, and put it on his head. Having done that, he sat down again to reconsider the whole matter. But as his mind was already made up, this did not take long. And before Chief Inspector Heat had gone very far on the way home, he also left the building.

7

THE ASSISTANT COMMISSIONER walked along a short and narrow street like a wet, muddy trench, then crossing a very broad thoroughfare entered a public edifice, and sought speech with a young private secretary (unpaid) of a great personage.

This fair, smooth-faced young man, whose symmetrically arranged hair gave him the air of a large and neat schoolboy, met the Assistant Commissioner's request with a doubtful look, and spoke with bated breath.

"Would he see you? I don't know about that. He has walked over from the House an hour ago to talk with the permanent Under-Secretary, and now he's ready to walk back again. He might have sent for him; but he does it for the sake of a little exercise, I suppose. It's all the exercise he can find time for while this session lasts. I don't complain; I rather enjoy these little strolls. He leans on my arm, and doesn't open his lips. But, I say, he's very tired, and—well—not in the sweetest of tempers just now."

"It's in connection with that Greenwich affair."

"Oh! I say! He's very bitter against you people. But I will go and see, if you insist."

"Do. That's a good fellow," said the Assistant Commissioner.

The unpaid secretary admired this pluck. Composing for himself an innocent face, he opened a door, and went in with the assurance of a nice and privileged child. And presently he reappeared, with a nod to the Assistant Commissioner, who passing through the same door left open for him, found himself with the great personage in a large room.

Vast in bulk and stature, with a long white face, which, broadened at the base by a big double chin, appeared egg-shaped in the fringe of thin greyish whisker, the great personage seemed an expanding man. Unfortunate from a tailoring point of view, the cross-folds in the middle of a buttoned black coat added to the impression, as if the fastenings of the garment were tried to the utmost. From the head, set upward on a thick neck, the eyes, with puffy lower lids, stared with a haughty droop on each side of a hooked aggressive nose, nobly salient in the vast pale circumference of the face. A shiny silk hat and a pair of worn gloves lying ready on the end of a long table looked expanded too, enormous.

He stood on the hearthrug in big, roomy boots, and uttered no word of greeting.

"I would like to know if this is the beginning of another dynamite campaign," he asked at once in a deep, very smooth voice. "Don't go into details. I have no time for that."

The Assistant Commissioner's figure before this big and rustic Presence had the frail slenderness of a reed addressing an oak. And indeed the unbroken record of that man's descent surpassed in the number of centuries the age of the oldest oak in the country.

"No. As far as one can be positive about anything I can assure you that it is not."

"Yes. But your idea of assurances over there," said the great man, with a contemptuous wave of his hand towards a window giving on the broad thoroughfare, "seems to consist mainly in making the Secretary of State look a fool. I have been told positively in this very room less than a month ago that nothing of the sort was even possible."

The Assistant Commissioner glanced in the direction of the window calmly.

"You will allow me to remark, Sir Ethelred, that so far I have had no opportunity to give you assurances of any kind."

The haughty droop of the eyes was focussed now upon the Assistant Commissioner.

"True," confessed the deep, smooth voice. "I sent for Heat. You are still rather a novice in your new berth. And how are you getting on over there?"

"I believe I am learning something every day."

"Of course, of course. I hope you will get on."

"Thank you, Sir Ethelred. I've learned something to-day, and even within the last hour or so. There is much in this affair of a kind that does not meet the eye in a usual anarchist outrage, even if one looked into it as deep as can be. That's why I am here."

The great man put his arms akimbo, the backs of his big hands resting on his hips.

"Very well. Go on. Only no details, pray. Spare me the details."

"You shall not be troubled with them, Sir Ethelred," the Assistant Commissioner began, with a calm and untroubled assurance. While he was speaking the hands on the face of the clock behind the great man's back—a heavy, glistening affair of massive scrolls in the same dark marble as the mantelpiece, and with a ghostly, evanescent tick—had moved through the space of seven minutes. He spoke with a studious fidelity to a parenthetical manner, into which every little fact—that is, every detail—fitted with delightful ease. Not a murmur nor even a movement hinted at interruption. The great Personage might have been the statue of one of his own princely ancestors stripped of a crusader's war harness, and put into an ill-fitting frock coat. The Assistant Commissioner felt as though he were at liberty to talk for an hour. But he kept his head, and at the end of the time mentioned above he broke off with a sudden conclusion, which, reproducing the opening statement, pleasantly surprised Sir Ethelred by its apparent swiftness and force.

"The kind of thing which meets us under the surface of this affair, otherwise without gravity, is unusual—in this precise form at least—and requires special treatment."

The tone of Sir Ethelred was deepened, full of conviction.

"I should think so—involving the Ambassador of a foreign power!"

"Oh! The Ambassador!" protested the other, erect and slender, allowing himself a mere half smile. "It would be stupid of me to advance anything of the kind. And it is absolutely unnecessary, because if I am right in my surmises, whether ambassador or hall porter it's a mere detail."

Sir Ethelred opened a wide mouth, like a cavern, into which the hooked nose seemed anxious to peer; there came from it a subdued rolling sound, as from a distant organ with the scornful indignation stop.

"No! These people are too impossible. What do they mean by importing their methods of Crim-Tartary here? A Turk would have more decency."

"You forget, Sir Ethelred, that strictly speaking we know nothing positively—as yet."

"No! But how would you define it? Shortly?"

"Barefaced audacity amounting to childishness of a peculiar sort."

"We can't put up with the innocence of nasty little children," said the great and expanded personage, expanding a little more, as it were. The haughty drooping glance struck crushingly the carpet at the Assistant Commissioner's feet. "They'll have to get a hard rap on the knuckles over this affair. We must be in a position to—What is your general idea, stated shortly? No need to go into details."

"No, Sir Ethelred. In principle, I should lay it down that the existence of secret agents should not be tolerated, as tending to augment the positive dangers of the evil against which they are used. That the spy will fabricate his information is a mere commonplace. But in the sphere of political and revolutionary action, relying partly on violence, the professional spy has every facility to fabricate the very facts themselves, and will spread the double evil of emulation in one direction, and of panic, hasty legislation, unreflecting hate, on the other. However, this is an imperfect world—"

The deep-voiced Presence on the hearthrug, motionless, with big elbows stuck out, said hastily:

"Be lucid, please."

"Yes, Sir Ethelred—An imperfect world. Therefore directly the character of this affair suggested itself to me, I thought it should be dealt with with special secrecy, and ventured to come over here."

"That's right," approved the great Personage, glancing down complacently over his double chin. "I am glad there's somebody over at your shop who thinks that the Secretary of State may be trusted now and then."

The Assistant Commissioner had an amused smile.

"I was really thinking that it might be better at this stage for Heat to be replaced by—"

"What! Heat? An ass—eh?" exclaimed the great man, with distinct animosity.

"Not at all. Pray, Sir Ethelred, don't put that unjust interpretation on my remarks."

"Then what? Too clever by half?"

"Neither—at least not as a rule. All the grounds of my surmises I have from him. The only thing I've discovered by myself is that he has been making use of that man privately. Who could blame him? He's an old police hand. He told me virtually that he must have tools to work with. It occurred to me that this tool should be surrendered to the Special Crimes division as a whole, instead of remaining the private property of Chief Inspector Heat. I extend my conception of our departmental duties to the suppression of the secret agent. But Chief Inspector Heat is an old departmental hand. He would accuse me of perverting its morality and attacking its efficiency. He would define it bitterly as protection extended to the criminal class of revolutionists. It would mean just that to him."

"Yes. But what do you mean?"

"I mean to say, first, that there's but poor comfort in being able to declare that any given act of violence—damaging property or destroying life—is not the work of anarchism at all, but of something else altogether—some species of authorised scoundrelism. This, I fancy, is much more frequent than we suppose. Next, it's obvious that the existence of these people in the pay of foreign governments destroys in a measure the efficiency of our supervision. A spy of that sort can afford to be more reckless than the most reckless of conspirators. His occupation is free from all restraint. He's without as much faith as is necessary for complete negation, and without that much law as is implied in lawlessness. Thirdly, the existence of these spies amongst the revolutionary groups, which we are reproached for harbouring here, does away with all certitude. You have received a reassuring statement from Chief Inspector Heat some time ago. It was by no means groundless—and yet this episode happens. I call it an episode, because this affair, I make bold to say, is episodic; it is no part of any general scheme, however wild. The very peculiarities which surprise and perplex Chief Inspector Heat establish its character in my eyes. I am keeping clear of details, Sir Ethelred."

The Personage on the hearthrug had been listening with profound attention.

"Just so. Be as concise as you can."

The Assistant Commissioner intimated by an earnest deferential gesture that he was anxious to be concise.

"There is a peculiar stupidity and feebleness in the conduct of this affair which gives me excellent hopes of getting behind it and finding there something else than an individual freak of fanaticism. For it is a planned thing, undoubtedly. The actual perpetrator seems to have been led by the hand to the spot, and then abandoned hurriedly to his own devices. The inference is that he was imported from abroad for the purpose of committing this outrage. At the same time one is forced to the conclusion that he did not know enough English to ask his way, unless one were to accept the fantastic theory that he was a deaf mute. I wonder now—But this is idle. He has destroyed himself by an accident, obviously. Not an extraordinary accident. But an extraordinary little fact remains: the address on his clothing discovered by the merest accident, too. It is an incredible little fact, so incredible that the explanation which will account for it is bound to touch the bottom of this affair. Instead of instructing Heat to go on with this case, my intention is to seek this explanation personally—by myself, I mean—where it may be picked up. That is in a certain shop in Brett Street, and on the lips of a certain secret agent once upon a time the confidential and trusted spy of the late Baron Stott-Wartenheim, Ambassador of a Great Power to the Court of St James."

The Assistant Commissioner paused, then added: "Those fellows are a perfect pest." In order to raise his drooping glance to the speaker's face, the Personage on the hearthrug had gradually tilted his head farther back, which gave him an aspect of extraordinary haughtiness.

"Why not leave it to Heat?"

"Because he is an old departmental hand. They have their own morality. My line of inquiry would appear to him an awful perversion of duty. For him the plain duty is to fasten the guilt upon as many prominent anarchists as he can on some slight indications he had picked up in the course of his investigation on the spot; whereas I, he would say, am bent upon vindicating their innocence. I am trying to be as lucid as I can in presenting this obscure matter to you without details."

"He would, would he?" muttered the proud head of Sir Ethelred from its lofty elevation.

"I am afraid so—with an indignation and disgust of which you or I can have no idea. He's an excellent servant. We must not put an undue strain on his loyalty. That's always a mistake. Besides, I want a free hand—a freer hand than it would be perhaps advisable to give Chief Inspector Heat. I haven't the slightest wish to spare this man Verloc. He will, I imagine, be extremely startled to find his connection with this affair, whatever it may be, brought home to him so quickly. Frightening him will not be very difficult. But our true objective lies behind him somewhere. I want your authority to give him such assurances of personal safety as I may think proper."

"Certainly," said the Personage on the hearthrug. "Find out as much as you can; find it out in your own way."

"I must set about it without loss of time, this very evening," said the Assistant Commissioner.

Sir Ethelred shifted one hand under his coat tails, and tilting back his head, looked at him steadily.

"We'll have a late sitting to-night," he said. "Come to the House with your discoveries if we are not gone home. I'll warn Toodles to look out for you. He'll take you into my room."

The numerous family and the wide connections of the youthful-looking Private Secretary cherished for him the hope of an austere and exalted destiny. Meantime the social sphere he adorned in his hours of idleness chose to pet him under the above nickname. And Sir Ethelred, hearing it on the lips of his wife and girls every day (mostly at breakfast-time), had conferred upon it the dignity of unsmiling adoption.

The Assistant Commissioner was surprised and gratified extremely.

"I shall certainly bring my discoveries to the House on the chance of you having the time to—"

"I won't have the time," interrupted the great Personage. "But I will see you. I haven't the time now—And you are going yourself?"

"Yes, Sir Ethelred. I think it the best way."

The Personage had tilted his head so far back that, in order to keep the Assistant Commissioner under his observation, he had to nearly close his eyes.

"H'm. Ha! And how do you propose—Will you assume a disguise?"

"Hardly a disguise! I'll change my clothes, of course."

"Of course," repeated the great man, with a sort of absent-minded loftiness. He turned his big head slowly, and over his shoulder gave a haughty oblique stare to the ponderous marble timepiece with the sly, feeble tick. The gilt hands had taken the opportunity to steal through no less than five and twenty minutes behind his back.

The Assistant Commissioner, who could not see them, grew a little nervous in the interval. But the great man presented to him a calm and undismayed face.

"Very well," he said, and paused, as if in deliberate contempt of the official clock. "But what first put you in motion in this direction?"

"I have been always of opinion," began the Assistant Commissioner.

"Ah. Yes! Opinion. That's of course. But the immediate motive?"

"What shall I say, Sir Ethelred? A new man's antagonism to old methods. A desire to know something at first hand. Some impatience. It's my old work, but the harness is different. It has been chafing me a little in one or two tender places."

"I hope you'll get on over there," said the great man kindly, extending his hand, soft to the touch, but broad and powerful like the hand of a glorified farmer. The Assistant Commissioner shook it, and withdrew.

In the outer room Toodles, who had been waiting perched on the edge of a table, advanced to meet him, subduing his natural buoyancy.

"Well? Satisfactory?" he asked, with airy importance.

"Perfectly. You've earned my undying gratitude," answered the Assistant Commissioner, whose long face looked wooden in contrast with the peculiar character of the other's gravity, which seemed perpetually ready to break into ripples and chuckles.

"That's all right. But seriously, you can't imagine how irritated he is by the attacks on his Bill for the Nationalisation of Fisheries. They call it the beginning of social revolution. Of course, it is a revolutionary measure. But these fellows have no decency. The personal attacks—"

"I read the papers," remarked the Assistant Commissioner.

"Odious? Eh? And you have no notion what a mass of work he has got to get through every day. He does it all himself. Seems unable to trust anyone with these Fisheries."

"And yet he's given a whole half hour to the consideration of my very small sprat," interjected the Assistant Commissioner.

"Small! Is it? I'm glad to hear that. But it's a pity you didn't keep away, then. This fight takes it out of him frightfully. The man's getting exhausted. I feel it by the way he leans on my arm as we walk over. And, I say, is he safe in the streets? Mullins has been marching his men up here this afternoon. There's a constable stuck by every lamp-post, and every second person we meet between this and Palace Yard is an obvious 'tec.' It will get on his nerves presently. I say, these foreign scoundrels aren't likely to throw something at him—are they? It would be a national calamity. The country can't spare him."

"Not to mention yourself. He leans on your arm," suggested the Assistant Commissioner soberly. "You would both go."

"It would be an easy way for a young man to go down into history? Not so many British Ministers have been assassinated as to make it a minor incident. But seriously now—"

"I am afraid that if you want to go down into history you'll have to do something for it. Seriously, there's no danger whatever for both of you but from overwork."

The sympathetic Toodles welcomed this opening for a chuckle.

"The Fisheries won't kill me. I am used to late hours," he declared, with ingenuous levity. But, feeling an instant compunction, he began to assume an air of statesman-like moodiness, as one draws on a glove. "His massive intellect will stand any amount of work. It's his nerves that I am afraid of. The reactionary gang, with that abusive brute Cheeseman at their head, insult him every night."

"If he will insist on beginning a revolution!" murmured the Assistant Commissioner.

"The time has come, and he is the only man great enough for the work," protested the revolutionary Toodles, flaring up under the calm, speculative gaze of the Assistant Commissioner. Somewhere in a corridor a distant bell tinkled urgently, and with devoted vigilance the young man pricked up his ears at the sound. "He's ready to go now," he exclaimed in a whisper, snatched up his hat, and vanished from the room.

The Assistant Commissioner went out by another door in a less elastic manner. Again he crossed the wide thoroughfare, walked along a narrow street, and re-entered hastily his own departmental buildings. He kept up this accelerated pace to the door of his private room. Before he had closed it fairly his eyes sought his desk. He stood still for a moment, then walked up, looked all round on the floor, sat down in his chair, rang a bell, and waited.

"Chief Inspector Heat gone yet?"

"Yes, sir. Went away half-an-hour ago."

He nodded. "That will do." And sitting still, with his hat pushed off his forehead, he thought that it was just like Heat's confounded cheek to carry off quietly the only piece of material evidence. But he thought this without animosity. Old and valued servants will take liberties. The piece of overcoat with the address sewn on was certainly not a thing to leave about. Dismissing from his mind this manifestation of Chief Inspector Heat's mistrust, he wrote and despatched a note to his wife, charging her to make his apologies to Michaelis' great lady, with whom they were engaged to dine that evening.

The short jacket and the low, round hat he assumed in a sort of curtained alcove containing a washstand, a row of wooden pegs and a shelf, brought out wonderfully the length of his grave, brown face. He stepped back into the full light of the room, looking like the vision of a cool, reflective Don Quixote, with the sunken eyes of a dark enthusiast and a very deliberate manner. He left the scene of his daily labours quickly like an unobtrusive shadow. His descent into the street was like the descent into a slimy aquarium from which the water had been run off. A murky, gloomy dampness enveloped him. The walls of the houses were wet, the mud of the roadway glistened with an effect of phosphorescence, and when he emerged into the Strand out of a narrow street by the side of Charing Cross Station the genius of the locality assimilated him. He might have been but one more of the queer foreign fish that can be seen of an evening about there flitting round the dark corners.

He came to a stand on the very edge of the pavement, and waited. His exercised eyes had made out in the confused movements of lights and shadows thronging the roadway the crawling approach of a hansom. He gave no sign; but when the low step gliding along the curbstone came to his feet he dodged in skilfully in front of the big turning wheel, and spoke up through the little trap door almost before the man gazing supinely ahead from his perch was aware of having been boarded by a fare.

It was not a long drive. It ended by signal abruptly, nowhere in particular, between two lamp-posts before a large drapery establishment—a long range of shops already lapped up in sheets of corrugated iron for the night. Tendering a coin through the trap door the fare slipped out and away, leaving an effect of uncanny, eccentric ghastliness upon the driver's mind. But the size of the coin was satisfactory to his touch, and his education not being literary, he remained untroubled by the fear of finding it presently turned to a dead leaf in his pocket. Raised above the world of fares by the nature of his calling, he contemplated their actions with a limited interest. The sharp pulling of his horse right round expressed his philosophy.

Meantime the Assistant Commissioner was already giving his order to a waiter in a little Italian restaurant round the corner—one of those traps for the hungry, long and narrow, baited with a perspective of mirrors and white napery; without air, but with an atmosphere of their own—an atmosphere of fraudulent cookery mocking an abject mankind in the most pressing of its miserable necessities. In this immoral atmosphere the Assistant Commissioner, reflecting upon his enterprise, seemed to lose some more of his identity. He had a sense of loneliness, of evil freedom. It was rather pleasant. When, after paying for his short meal, he stood up and waited for his change, he saw himself in the sheet of glass, and was struck by his foreign appearance. He contemplated his own image with a melancholy and inquisitive gaze, then by sudden inspiration raised the collar of his jacket. This arrangement appeared to him commendable, and he completed it by giving an upward twist to the ends of his black moustache. He was satisfied by the subtle modification of his personal aspect caused by these small changes. "That'll do very well," he thought. "I'll get a little wet, a little splashed—"

He became aware of the waiter at his elbow and of a small pile of silver coins on the edge of the table before him. The waiter kept one eye on it, while his other eye followed the long back of a tall, not very young girl, who passed up to a distant table looking perfectly sightless and altogether unapproachable. She seemed to be a habitual customer.

On going out the Assistant Commissioner made to himself the observation that the patrons of the place had lost in the frequentation of fraudulent cookery all their national and private characteristics. And this was strange, since the Italian restaurant is such a peculiarly British institution. But these people were as denationalised as the dishes set before them with every circumstance of unstamped respectability. Neither was their personality stamped in any way, professionally, socially or racially. They seemed created for the Italian restaurant, unless the Italian restaurant had been perchance created for them. But that last hypothesis was unthinkable, since one could not place them anywhere outside those special establishments. One never met these enigmatical persons elsewhere. It was impossible to form a precise idea what occupations they followed by day and where they went to bed at night. And he himself had become unplaced. It would have been impossible for anybody to guess his occupation. As to going to bed, there was a doubt even in his own mind. Not indeed in regard to his domicile itself, but very much so in respect of the time when he would be able to return there. A pleasurable feeling of independence possessed him when he heard the glass doors swing to behind his back with a sort of imperfect baffled thud. He advanced at once into an immensity of greasy slime and damp plaster interspersed with lamps, and enveloped, oppressed, penetrated, choked, and suffocated by the blackness of a wet London night, which is composed of soot and drops of water.

Brett Street was not very far away. It branched off, narrow, from the side of an open triangular space surrounded by dark and mysterious houses, temples of petty commerce emptied of traders for the night. Only a fruiterer's stall at the corner made a violent blaze of light and colour. Beyond all was black, and the few people passing in that direction vanished at one stride beyond the glowing heaps of oranges and lemons. No footsteps echoed. They would never be heard of again. The adventurous head of the Special Crimes Department watched these disappearances from a distance with an interested eye. He felt light-hearted, as though he had been ambushed all alone in a jungle many thousands of miles away from departmental desks and official inkstands. This joyousness and dispersion of thought before a task of some importance seems to prove that this world of ours is not such a very serious affair after all. For the Assistant Commissioner was not constitutionally inclined to levity.

The policeman on the beat projected his sombre and moving form against the luminous glory of oranges and lemons, and entered Brett Street without haste. The Assistant Commissioner, as though he were a member of the criminal classes, lingered out of sight, awaiting his return. But this constable seemed to be lost for ever to the force. He never returned: must have gone out at the other end of Brett Street.

The Assistant Commissioner, reaching this conclusion, entered the street in his turn, and came upon a large van arrested in front of the dimly lit window-panes of a carter's eating-house. The man was refreshing himself inside, and the horses, their big heads lowered to the ground, fed out of nose-bags steadily. Farther on, on the opposite side of the street, another suspect patch of dim light issued from Mr Verloc's shop front, hung with papers, heaving with vague piles of cardboard boxes and the shapes of books. The Assistant Commissioner stood observing it across the roadway. There could be no mistake. By the side of the front window, encumbered by the shadows of nondescript things, the door, standing ajar, let escape on the pavement a narrow, clear streak of gas-light within.

Behind the Assistant Commissioner the van and horses, merged into one mass, seemed something alive—a square-backed black monster blocking half the street, with sudden iron-shod stampings, fierce jingles, and heavy, blowing sighs. The harshly festive, ill-omened glare of a large and prosperous public-house faced the other end of Brett Street across a wide road. This barrier of blazing lights, opposing the shadows gathered about the humble abode of Mr Verloc's domestic happiness, seemed to drive the obscurity of the street back upon itself, make it more sullen, brooding, and sinister.

8

Having infused by persistent importunities some sort of heat into the chilly interest of several licensed victuallers (the acquaintances once upon a time of her late unlucky husband), Mrs Verloc's mother had at last secured her admission to certain almshouses founded by a wealthy innkeeper for the destitute widows of the trade.

This end, conceived in the astuteness of her uneasy heart, the old woman had pursued with secrecy and determination. That was the time when her daughter Winnie could not help passing a remark to Mr Verloc that "mother has been spending half-crowns and five shillings almost every day this last week in cab fares." But the remark was not made grudgingly. Winnie respected her mother's infirmities. She was only a little surprised at this sudden mania for locomotion. Mr Verloc, who was sufficiently magnificent in his way, had grunted the remark impatiently aside as interfering with his meditations. These were frequent, deep, and prolonged; they bore upon a matter more important than five shillings. Distinctly more important, and beyond all comparison more difficult to consider in all its aspects with philosophical serenity.

Her object attained in astute secrecy, the heroic old woman had made a clean breast of it to Mrs Verloc. Her soul was triumphant and her heart tremulous. Inwardly she quaked, because she dreaded and admired the calm, self-contained character of her daughter Winnie, whose displeasure was made redoubtable by a diversity of dreadful silences. But she did not allow her inward apprehensions to rob her of the advantage of venerable placidity conferred upon her outward person by her triple chin, the floating ampleness of her ancient form, and the impotent condition of her legs.

The shock of the information was so unexpected that Mrs Verloc, against her usual practice when addressed, interrupted the domestic occupation she was engaged upon. It was the dusting of the furniture in the parlour behind the shop. She turned her head towards her mother.

"Whatever did you want to do that for?" she exclaimed, in scandalised astonishment.

The shock must have been severe to make her depart from that distant and uninquiring acceptance of facts which was her force and her safeguard in life.

"Weren't you made comfortable enough here?"

She had lapsed into these inquiries, but next moment she saved the consistency of her conduct by resuming her dusting, while the old woman sat scared and dumb under her dingy white cap and lustreless dark wig.

Winnie finished the chair, and ran the duster along the mahogany at the back of the horse-hair sofa on which Mr Verloc loved to take his ease in hat and overcoat. She was intent on her work, but presently she permitted herself another question.

"How in the world did you manage it, mother?"

As not affecting the inwardness of things, which it was Mrs Verloc's principle to ignore, this curiosity was excusable. It bore merely on the methods. The old woman welcomed it eagerly as bringing forward something that could be talked about with much sincerity.

She favoured her daughter by an exhaustive answer, full of names and enriched by side comments upon the ravages of time as observed in the alteration of human countenances. The names were principally the names of licensed victuallers—"poor daddy's friends, my dear." She enlarged with special appreciation on the kindness and condescension of a large brewer, a Baronet and an M. P., the Chairman of the Governors of the Charity. She expressed herself thus warmly because she had been allowed to interview by appointment his Private Secretary—"a very polite gentleman, all in black, with a gentle, sad voice, but so very, very thin and quiet. He was like a shadow, my dear."

Winnie, prolonging her dusting operations till the tale was told to the end, walked out of the parlour into the kitchen (down two steps) in her usual manner, without the slightest comment.

Shedding a few tears in sign of rejoicing at her daughter's mansuetude in this terrible affair, Mrs Verloc's mother gave play to her astuteness in the direction of her furniture, because it was her own; and sometimes she wished it hadn't been. Heroism is all very well, but there are circumstances when the disposal of a few tables and chairs, brass bedsteads, and so on, may be big with remote and disastrous consequences. She required a few pieces herself, the Foundation which, after many importunities, had gathered her to its charitable breast, giving nothing but bare planks and cheaply papered bricks to the objects of its solicitude. The delicacy guiding her choice to the least valuable and most dilapidated articles passed unacknowledged, because Winnie's philosophy consisted in not taking notice of the inside of facts; she assumed that mother took what suited her best. As to Mr Verloc, his intense meditation, like a sort of Chinese wall, isolated him completely from the phenomena of this world of vain effort and illusory appearances.

Her selection made, the disposal of the rest became a perplexing question in a particular way. She was leaving it in Brett Street, of course. But she had two children. Winnie was provided for by her sensible union with that excellent husband, Mr Verloc. Stevie was destitute—and a little peculiar. His position had to be considered before the claims of legal justice and even the promptings of partiality. The possession of the furniture would not be in any sense a provision. He ought to have it—the poor boy. But to give it to him would be like tampering with his position of complete dependence. It was a sort of claim which she feared to weaken. Moreover, the susceptibilities of Mr Verloc would perhaps not brook being beholden to his brother-in-law for the chairs he sat on. In a long experience of gentlemen lodgers, Mrs Verloc's mother had acquired a dismal but resigned notion of the fantastic side of human nature. What if Mr Verloc suddenly took it into his head to tell Stevie to take his blessed sticks somewhere out of that? A division, on the other hand, however carefully made, might give some cause of offence to Winnie. No, Stevie must remain destitute and dependent. And at the moment of leaving Brett Street she had said to her daughter: "No use waiting till I am dead, is there? Everything I leave here is altogether your own now, my dear."

Winnie, with her hat on, silent behind her mother's back, went on arranging the collar of the old woman's cloak. She got her hand-bag, an umbrella, with an impassive face. The time had come for the expenditure of the sum of three-and-sixpence on what might well be supposed the last cab drive of Mrs Verloc's mother's life. They went out at the shop door.

The conveyance awaiting them would have illustrated the proverb that "truth can be more cruel than caricature," if such a proverb existed. Crawling behind an infirm horse, a metropolitan hackney carriage drew up on wobbly wheels and with a maimed driver on the box. This last peculiarity caused some embarrassment. Catching sight of a hooked iron contrivance protruding from the left sleeve of the man's coat, Mrs Verloc's mother lost suddenly the heroic courage of these days. She really couldn't trust herself. "What do you think, Winnie?" She hung back. The passionate expostulations of the big-faced cabman seemed to be squeezed out of a blocked throat. Leaning over from his box, he whispered with mysterious indignation. What was the matter now? Was it possible to treat a man so? His enormous and unwashed countenance flamed red in the muddy stretch of the street. Was it likely they would have given him a licence, he inquired desperately, if—

The police constable of the locality quieted him by a friendly glance; then addressing himself to the two women without marked consideration, said:

"He's been driving a cab for twenty years. I never knew him to have an accident."

"Accident!" shouted the driver in a scornful whisper.

The policeman's testimony settled it. The modest assemblage of seven people, mostly under age, dispersed. Winnie followed her mother into the cab. Stevie climbed on the box. His vacant mouth and distressed eyes depicted the state of his mind in regard to the transactions which were taking place. In the narrow streets the progress of the journey was made sensible to those within by the near fronts of the houses gliding past slowly and shakily, with a great rattle and jingling of glass, as if about to collapse behind the cab; and the infirm horse, with the harness hung over his sharp backbone flapping very loose about his thighs, appeared to be dancing mincingly on his toes with infinite patience. Later on, in the wider space of Whitehall, all visual evidences of motion became imperceptible. The rattle and jingle of glass went on indefinitely in front of the long Treasury building—and time itself seemed to stand still.

At last Winnie observed: "This isn't a very good horse."

Her eyes gleamed in the shadow of the cab straight ahead, immovable. On the box, Stevie shut his vacant mouth first, in order to ejaculate earnestly: "Don't."

The driver, holding high the reins twisted around the hook, took no notice. Perhaps he had not heard. Stevie's breast heaved.

"Don't whip."

The man turned slowly his bloated and sodden face of many colours bristling with white hairs. His little red eyes glistened with moisture. His big lips had a violet tint. They remained closed. With the dirty back of his whip-hand he rubbed the stubble sprouting on his enormous chin.

"You mustn't," stammered out Stevie violently. "It hurts."

"Mustn't whip," queried the other in a thoughtful whisper, and immediately whipped. He did this, not because his soul was cruel and his heart evil, but because he had to earn his fare. And for a time the walls of St Stephen's, with its towers and pinnacles, contemplated in immobility and silence a cab that jingled. It rolled too, however. But on the bridge there was a commotion. Stevie suddenly proceeded to get down from the box. There were shouts on the pavement, people ran forward, the driver pulled up, whispering curses of indignation and astonishment. Winnie lowered the window, and put her head out, white as a ghost. In the depths of the cab, her mother was exclaiming, in tones of anguish: "Is that boy hurt? Is that boy hurt?"

Stevie was not hurt, he had not even fallen, but excitement as usual had robbed him of the power of connected speech. He could do no more than stammer at the window. "Too heavy. Too heavy." Winnie put out her hand on to his shoulder.

"Stevie! Get up on the box directly, and don't try to get down again."

"No. No. Walk. Must walk."

In trying to state the nature of that necessity he stammered himself into utter incoherence. No physical impossibility stood in the way of his whim. Stevie could have managed easily to keep pace with the infirm, dancing horse without getting out of breath. But his sister withheld her consent decisively. "The idea! Whoever heard of such a thing! Run after a cab!" Her mother, frightened and helpless in the depths of the conveyance, entreated: "Oh, don't let him, Winnie. He'll get lost. Don't let him."

"Certainly not. What next! Mr Verloc will be sorry to hear of this nonsense, Stevie,—I can tell you. He won't be happy at all."

The idea of Mr Verloc's grief and unhappiness acting as usual powerfully upon Stevie's fundamentally docile disposition, he abandoned all resistance, and climbed up again on the box, with a face of despair.

The cabby turned at him his enormous and inflamed countenance truculently. "Don't you go for trying this silly game again, young fellow."

After delivering himself thus in a stern whisper, strained almost to extinction, he drove on, ruminating solemnly. To his mind the incident remained somewhat obscure. But his intellect, though it had lost its pristine vivacity in the benumbing years of sedentary exposure to the weather, lacked not independence or sanity. Gravely he dismissed the hypothesis of Stevie being a drunken young nipper.

Inside the cab the spell of silence, in which the two women had endured shoulder to shoulder the jolting, rattling, and jingling of the journey, had been broken by Stevie's outbreak. Winnie raised her voice.

"You've done what you wanted, mother. You'll have only yourself to thank for it if you aren't happy afterwards. And I don't think you'll be. That I don't. Weren't you comfortable enough in the house? Whatever people'll think of us—you throwing yourself like this on a Charity?"

"My dear," screamed the old woman earnestly above the noise, "you've been the best of daughters to me. As to Mr Verloc—there—"

Words failing her on the subject of Mr Verloc's excellence, she turned her old tearful eyes to the roof of the cab. Then she averted her head on the pretence of looking out of the window, as if to judge of their progress. It was insignificant, and went on close to the curbstone. Night, the early dirty night, the sinister, noisy, hopeless and rowdy night of South London, had overtaken her on her last cab drive. In the gas-light of the low-fronted shops her big cheeks glowed with an orange hue under a black and mauve bonnet.

Mrs Verloc's mother's complexion had become yellow by the effect of age and from a natural predisposition to biliousness, favoured by the trials of a difficult and worried existence, first as wife, then as widow. It was a complexion, that under the influence of a blush would take on an orange tint. And this woman, modest indeed but hardened in the fires of adversity, of an age, moreover, when blushes are not expected, had positively blushed before her daughter. In the privacy of a four-wheeler, on her way to a charity cottage (one of a row) which by the exiguity of its dimensions and the simplicity of its accommodation, might well have been devised in kindness as a place of training for the still more straitened circumstances of the grave, she was forced to hide from her own child a blush of remorse and shame.

Whatever people will think? She knew very well what they did think, the people Winnie had in her mind—the old friends of her husband, and others too, whose interest she had solicited with such flattering success. She had not known before what a good beggar she could be. But she guessed very well what inference was drawn from her application. On account of that shrinking delicacy, which exists side by side with aggressive brutality in masculine nature, the inquiries into her circumstances had not been pushed very far. She had checked them by a visible compression of the lips and some display of an emotion determined to be eloquently silent. And the men would become suddenly incurious, after the manner of their kind. She congratulated herself more than once on having nothing to do with women, who being naturally more callous and avid of details, would have been anxious to be exactly informed by what sort of unkind conduct her daughter and son-in-law had driven her to that sad extremity. It was only before the Secretary of the great brewer M. P. and Chairman of the Charity, who, acting for his principal, felt bound to be conscientiously inquisitive as to the real circumstances of the applicant, that she had burst into tears outright and aloud, as a cornered woman will weep. The thin and polite gentleman, after contemplating her with an air of being "struck all of a heap," abandoned his position under the cover of soothing remarks. She must not distress herself. The deed of the Charity did not absolutely specify "childless widows." In fact, it did not by any means disqualify her. But the discretion of the Committee must be an informed discretion. One could understand very well her unwillingness to be a burden, etc. etc. Thereupon, to his profound disappointment, Mrs Verloc's mother wept some more with an augmented vehemence.

The tears of that large female in a dark, dusty wig, and ancient silk dress festooned with dingy white cotton lace, were the tears of genuine distress. She had wept because she was heroic and unscrupulous and full of love for both her children. Girls frequently get sacrificed to the welfare of the boys. In this case she was sacrificing Winnie. By the suppression of truth she was slandering her. Of course, Winnie was independent, and need not care for the opinion of people that she would never see and who would never see her; whereas poor Stevie had nothing in the world he could call his own except his mother's heroism and unscrupulousness.

The first sense of security following on Winnie's marriage wore off in time (for nothing lasts), and Mrs Verloc's mother, in the seclusion of the back bedroom, had recalled the teaching of that experience which the world impresses upon a widowed woman. But she had recalled it without vain bitterness; her store of resignation amounted almost to dignity. She reflected stoically that everything decays, wears out, in this world; that the way of kindness should be made easy to the well disposed; that her daughter Winnie was a most devoted sister, and a very self-confident wife indeed. As regards Winnie's sisterly devotion, her stoicism flinched. She excepted that sentiment from the rule of decay affecting all things human and some things divine. She could not help it; not to do so would have frightened her too much. But in considering the conditions of her daughter's married state, she rejected firmly all flattering illusions. She took the cold and reasonable view that the less strain put on Mr Verloc's kindness the longer its effects were likely to last. That excellent man loved his wife, of course, but he would, no doubt, prefer to keep as few of her relations as was consistent with the proper display of that sentiment. It would be better if its whole effect were concentrated on poor Stevie. And the heroic old woman resolved on going away from her children as an act of devotion and as a move of deep policy.

The "virtue" of this policy consisted in this (Mrs Verloc's mother was subtle in her way), that Stevie's moral claim would be strengthened. The poor boy—a good, useful boy, if a little peculiar—had not a sufficient standing. He had been taken over with his mother, somewhat in the same way as the furniture of the Belgravian mansion had been taken over, as if on the ground of belonging to her exclusively. What will happen, she asked herself (for Mrs Verloc's mother was in a measure imaginative), when I die? And when she asked herself that question it was with dread. It was also terrible to think that she would not then have the means of knowing what happened to the poor boy. But by making him over to his sister, by going thus away, she gave him the advantage of a directly dependent position. This was the more subtle sanction of Mrs Verloc's mother's heroism and unscrupulousness. Her act of abandonment was really an arrangement for settling her son permanently in life. Other people made material sacrifices for such an object, she in that way. It was the only way. Moreover, she would be able to see how it worked. Ill or well she would avoid the horrible incertitude on the death-bed. But it was hard, hard, cruelly hard.

The cab rattled, jingled, jolted; in fact, the last was quite extraordinary. By its disproportionate violence and magnitude it obliterated every sensation of onward movement; and the effect was of being shaken in a stationary apparatus like a mediæval device for the punishment of crime, or some very newfangled invention for the cure of a sluggish liver. It was extremely distressing; and the raising of Mrs Verloc's mother's voice sounded like a wail of pain.

"I know, my dear, you'll come to see me as often as you can spare the time. Won't you?"

"Of course," answered Winnie shortly, staring straight before her.

And the cab jolted in front of a steamy, greasy shop in a blaze of gas and in the smell of fried fish.

The old woman raised a wail again.

"And, my dear, I must see that poor boy every Sunday. He won't mind spending the day with his old mother—"

Winnie screamed out stolidly:

"Mind! I should think not. That poor boy will miss you something cruel. I wish you had thought a little of that, mother."

Not think of it! The heroic woman swallowed a playful and inconvenient object like a billiard ball, which had tried to jump out of her throat. Winnie sat mute for a while, pouting at the front of the cab, then snapped out, which was an unusual tone with her:

"I expect I'll have a job with him at first, he'll be that restless—"

"Whatever you do, don't let him worry your husband, my dear."

Thus they discussed on familiar lines the bearings of a new situation. And the cab jolted. Mrs Verloc's mother expressed some misgivings. Could Stevie be trusted to come all that way alone? Winnie maintained that he was much less "absent-minded" now. They agreed as to that. It could not be denied. Much less—hardly at all. They shouted at each other in the jingle with comparative cheerfulness. But suddenly the maternal anxiety broke out afresh. There were two omnibuses to take, and a short walk between. It was too difficult! The old woman gave way to grief and consternation.

Winnie stared forward.

"Don't you upset yourself like this, mother. You must see him, of course."

"No, my dear. I'll try not to."

She mopped her streaming eyes.

"But you can't spare the time to come with him, and if he should forget himself and lose his way and somebody spoke to him sharply, his name and address may slip his memory, and he'll remain lost for days and days—"

The vision of a workhouse infirmary for poor Stevie—if only during inquiries—wrung her heart. For she was a proud woman. Winnie's stare had grown hard, intent, inventive.

"I can't bring him to you myself every week," she cried. "But don't you worry, mother. I'll see to it that he don't get lost for long."

They felt a peculiar bump; a vision of brick pillars lingered before the rattling windows of the cab; a sudden cessation of atrocious jolting and uproarious jingling dazed the two women. What had happened? They sat motionless and scared in the profound stillness, till the door came open, and a rough, strained whispering was heard:

"Here you are!"

A range of gabled little houses, each with one dim yellow window, on the ground floor, surrounded the dark open space of a grass plot planted with shrubs and railed off from the patchwork of lights and shadows in the wide road, resounding with the dull rumble of traffic. Before the door of one of these tiny houses—one without a light in the little downstairs window—the cab had come to a standstill. Mrs Verloc's mother got out first, backwards, with a key in her hand. Winnie lingered on the flagstone path to pay the cabman. Stevie, after helping to carry inside a lot of small parcels, came out and stood under the light of a gas-lamp belonging to the Charity. The cabman looked at the pieces of silver, which, appearing very minute in his big, grimy palm, symbolised the insignificant results which reward the ambitious courage and toil of a mankind whose day is short on this earth of evil.

He had been paid decently—four one-shilling pieces—and he contemplated them in perfect stillness, as if they had been the surprising terms of a melancholy problem. The slow transfer of that treasure to an inner pocket demanded much laborious groping in the depths of decayed clothing. His form was squat and without flexibility. Stevie, slender, his shoulders a little up, and his hands thrust deep in the side pockets of his warm overcoat, stood at the edge of the path, pouting.

The cabman, pausing in his deliberate movements, seemed struck by some misty recollection.

"Oh! 'Ere you are, young fellow," he whispered. "You'll know him again—won't you?"

Stevie was staring at the horse, whose hind quarters appeared unduly elevated by the effect of emaciation. The little stiff tail seemed to have been fitted in for a heartless joke; and at the other end the thin, flat neck, like a plank covered with old horse-hide, drooped to the ground under the weight of an enormous bony head. The ears hung at different angles, negligently; and the macabre figure of that mute dweller on the earth steamed straight up from ribs and backbone in the muggy stillness of the air.

The cabman struck lightly Stevie's breast with the iron hook protruding from a ragged, greasy sleeve.

"Look 'ere, young feller. 'Ow'd *you* like to sit behind this 'oss up to two o'clock in the morning p'raps?"

Stevie looked vacantly into the fierce little eyes with red-edged lids.

"He ain't lame," pursued the other, whispering with energy. "He ain't got no sore places on 'im. 'Ere he is. 'Ow would *you* like—"

His strained, extinct voice invested his utterance with a character of vehement secrecy. Stevie's vacant gaze was changing slowly into dread.

"You may well look! Till three and four o'clock in the morning. Cold and 'ungry. Looking for fares. Drunks."

His jovial purple cheeks bristled with white hairs; and like Virgil's Silenus, who, his face smeared with the juice of berries, discoursed of Olympian Gods to the innocent shepherds of Sicily, he talked to Stevie of domestic matters and the affairs of men whose sufferings are great and immortality by no means assured.

"I am a night cabby, I am," he whispered, with a sort of boastful exasperation. "I've got to take out what they will blooming well give me at the yard. I've got my missus and four kids at 'ome."

The monstrous nature of that declaration of paternity seemed to strike the world dumb. A silence reigned during which the flanks of the old horse, the steed of apocalyptic misery, smoked upwards in the light of the charitable gas-lamp.

The cabman grunted, then added in his mysterious whisper:

"This ain't an easy world." Stevie's face had been twitching for some time, and at last his feelings burst out in their usual concise form.

"Bad! Bad!"

His gaze remained fixed on the ribs of the horse, self-conscious and sombre, as though he were afraid to look about him at the badness of the world. And his slenderness, his rosy lips and pale, clear complexion, gave him the aspect of a delicate boy, notwithstanding the fluffy growth of golden hair on his cheeks. He pouted in a scared way like a child. The cabman, short and broad, eyed him with his fierce little eyes that seemed to smart in a clear and corroding liquid.

"'Ard on 'osses, but dam' sight 'arder on poor chaps like me," he wheezed just audibly.

"Poor! Poor!" stammered out Stevie, pushing his hands deeper into his pockets with convulsive sympathy. He could say nothing; for the tenderness to all pain and all misery, the desire to make the horse happy and the cabman happy, had reached the point of a bizarre longing to take them to bed with him. And that, he knew, was impossible. For Stevie was not mad. It was, as it were, a symbolic longing; and at the same time it was very distinct, because springing from experience, the mother of wisdom. Thus when as a child he cowered in a dark corner scared, wretched, sore, and miserable with the black, black misery of the soul, his sister Winnie used to come along, and carry him off to bed with her, as into a heaven of consoling peace. Stevie, though apt to forget mere facts, such as his name and address for instance, had a faithful memory of sensations. To be taken into a bed of compassion was the supreme remedy, with the only one disadvantage of being difficult of application on a large scale. And looking at the cabman, Stevie perceived this clearly, because he was reasonable.

The cabman went on with his leisurely preparations as if Stevie had not existed. He made as if to hoist himself on the box, but at the last moment from some obscure motive, perhaps merely from disgust with carriage exercise, desisted. He approached instead the motionless partner of his labours, and stooping to seize the bridle, lifted up the big, weary head to the height of his shoulder with one effort of his right arm, like a feat of strength.

"Come on," he whispered secretly.

Limping, he led the cab away. There was an air of austerity in this departure, the scrunched gravel of the drive crying out under the slowly turning wheels, the horse's lean thighs moving with ascetic deliberation away from the light into the obscurity of the open space bordered dimly by the pointed roofs and the feebly shining windows of the little alms-houses. The plaint of the gravel travelled slowly all round the drive. Between the lamps of the charitable gateway the slow cortege reappeared, lighted up for a moment, the short, thick man limping busily, with the horse's head held aloft in his fist, the lank animal walking in stiff and forlorn dignity, the dark, low box on wheels rolling behind comically with an air of waddling. They turned to the left. There was a pub down the street, within fifty yards of the gate.

Stevie left alone beside the private lamp-post of the Charity, his hands thrust deep into his pockets, glared with vacant sulkiness. At the bottom of his pockets his incapable weak hands were clinched hard into a pair of angry fists. In the face of anything which affected directly or indirectly his morbid dread of pain, Stevie ended by turning vicious. A magnanimous indignation swelled his frail chest to bursting, and caused his candid eyes to squint. Supremely wise in knowing his own powerlessness, Stevie was not wise enough to restrain his passions. The tenderness of his universal charity had two phases as indissolubly joined and connected as the reverse and obverse sides of a medal. The anguish of immoderate compassion was succeeded by the pain of an innocent but pitiless rage. Those two states expressing themselves outwardly by the same signs of futile bodily agitation, his sister Winnie soothed his excitement without ever fathoming its twofold character. Mrs Verloc wasted no portion of this transient life in seeking for fundamental information. This is a sort of economy having all the appearances and some of the advantages of prudence. Obviously it may be good for one not to know too much. And such a view accords very well with constitutional indolence.

On that evening on which it may be said that Mrs Verloc's mother having parted for good from her children had also departed this life, Winnie Verloc did not investigate her brother's psychology. The poor boy was excited, of course. After once more assuring the old woman on the threshold that she would know how to guard against the risk of Stevie losing himself for very long on his pilgrimages of filial piety, she took her brother's arm to walk away. Stevie did not even mutter to himself, but with the special sense of sisterly devotion developed in her earliest infancy, she felt that the boy was very much excited indeed. Holding tight to his arm, under the appearance of leaning on it, she thought of some words suitable to the occasion.

"Now, Stevie, you must look well after me at the crossings, and get first into the 'bus, like a good brother."

This appeal to manly protection was received by Stevie with his usual docility. It flattered him. He raised his head and threw out his chest.

"Don't be nervous, Winnie. Mustn't be nervous! 'Bus all right," he answered in a brusque, slurring stammer partaking of the timorousness of a child and the resolution of a man. He advanced fearlessly with the woman on his arm, but his lower lip dropped. Nevertheless, on the pavement of the squalid and wide thoroughfare, whose poverty in all the amenities of life stood foolishly exposed by a mad profusion of gas-lights, their resemblance to each other was so pronounced as to strike the casual passers-by.

Before the doors of the public-house at the corner, where the profusion of gas-light reached the height of positive wickedness, a four-wheeled cab standing by the curbstone with no one on the box, seemed cast out into the gutter on account of irremediable decay. Mrs Verloc recognised the conveyance. Its aspect was so profoundly lamentable, with such a perfection of grotesque misery and weirdness of macabre detail, as if it were the Cab of Death itself, that Mrs Verloc, with that ready compassion of a woman for a horse (when she is not sitting behind him), exclaimed vaguely:

"Poor brute!"

Hanging back suddenly, Stevie inflicted an arresting jerk upon his sister.

"Poor! Poor!" he ejaculated appreciatively. "Cabman poor too. He told me himself."

The contemplation of the infirm and lonely steed overcame him. Jostled, but obstinate, he would remain there, trying to express the view newly opened to his sympathies of the human and equine misery in close association. But it was very difficult. "Poor brute, poor people!" was all he could repeat. It did not seem forcible enough, and he came to a stop with an angry splutter: "Shame!" Stevie was no master of phrases, and perhaps for that very reason his thoughts lacked clearness and precision. But he felt with greater completeness and some profundity. That little word contained all his sense of indignation and horror at one sort of wretchedness having to feed upon the anguish of the other—at the poor cabman beating the poor horse in the name, as it were, of his poor kids at home. And Stevie knew what it was to be beaten. He knew it from experience. It was a bad world. Bad! Bad!

Mrs Verloc, his only sister, guardian, and protector, could not pretend to such depths of insight. Moreover, she had not experienced the magic of the cabman's eloquence. She was in the dark as to the inwardness of the word "Shame." And she said placidly:

"Come along, Stevie. You can't help that."

The docile Stevie went along; but now he went along without pride, shamblingly, and muttering half words, and even words that would have been whole if they had not been made up of halves that did not belong to each other. It was as though he had been trying to fit all the words he could remember to his sentiments in order to get some sort of corresponding idea. And, as a matter of fact, he got it at last. He hung back to utter it at once.

"Bad world for poor people."

Directly he had expressed that thought he became aware that it was familiar to him already in all its consequences. This circumstance strengthened his conviction immensely, but also augmented his indignation. Somebody, he felt, ought to be punished for it—punished with great severity. Being no sceptic, but a moral creature, he was in a manner at the mercy of his righteous passions.

"Beastly!" he added concisely.

It was clear to Mrs Verloc that he was greatly excited.

"Nobody can help that," she said. "Do come along. Is that the way you're taking care of me?"

Stevie mended his pace obediently. He prided himself on being a good brother. His morality, which was very complete, demanded that from him. Yet he was pained at the information imparted by his sister Winnie who was good. Nobody could help that! He came along gloomily, but presently he brightened up. Like the rest of mankind, perplexed by the mystery of the universe, he had his moments of consoling trust in the organised powers of the earth.

"Police," he suggested confidently.

"The police aren't for that," observed Mrs Verloc cursorily, hurrying on her way.

Stevie's face lengthened considerably. He was thinking. The more intense his thinking, the slacker was the droop of his lower jaw.

And it was with an aspect of hopeless vacancy that he gave up his intellectual enterprise.

"Not for that?" he mumbled, resigned but surprised. "Not for that?" He had formed for himself an ideal conception of the metropolitan police as a sort of benevolent institution for the suppression of evil. The notion of benevolence especially was very closely associated with his sense of the power of the men in blue. He had liked all police constables tenderly, with a guileless trustfulness. And he was pained. He was irritated, too, by a suspicion of duplicity in the members of the force. For Stevie was frank and as open as the day himself. What did they mean by pretending then? Unlike his sister, who put her trust in face values, he wished to go to the bottom of the matter. He carried on his inquiry by means of an angry challenge.

"What for are they then, Winn? What are they for? Tell me."

Winnie disliked controversy. But fearing most a fit of black depression consequent on Stevie missing his mother very much at first, she did not altogether decline the discussion. Guiltless of all irony, she answered yet in a form which was not perhaps unnatural in the wife of Mr Verloc, Delegate of the Central Red Committee, personal friend of certain anarchists, and a votary of social revolution.

"Don't you know what the police are for, Stevie? They are there so that them as have nothing shouldn't take anything away from them who have."

She avoided using the verb "to steal," because it always made her brother uncomfortable. For Stevie was delicately honest. Certain simple principles had been instilled into him so anxiously (on account of his "queerness") that the mere names of certain transgressions filled him with horror. He had been always easily impressed by speeches. He was impressed and startled now, and his intelligence was very alert.

"What?" he asked at once anxiously. "Not even if they were hungry? Mustn't they?"

The two had paused in their walk.

"Not if they were ever so," said Mrs Verloc, with the equanimity of a person untroubled by the problem of the distribution of wealth, and exploring the perspective of the roadway for an omnibus of the right colour. "Certainly not. But what's the use of talking about all that? You aren't ever hungry."

She cast a swift glance at the boy, like a young man, by her side. She saw him amiable, attractive, affectionate, and only a little, a very little, peculiar. And she could not see him otherwise, for he was connected with what there was of the salt of passion in her tasteless life —the passion of indignation, of courage, of pity, and even of self-sacrifice. She did not add: "And you aren't likely ever to be as long as I live." But she might very well have done so, since she had taken effectual steps to that end. Mr Verloc was a very good husband. It was her honest impression that nobody could help liking the boy. She cried out suddenly:

"Quick, Stevie. Stop that green 'bus."

And Stevie, tremulous and important with his sister Winnie on his arm, flung up the other high above his head at the approaching 'bus, with complete success.

An hour afterwards Mr Verloc raised his eyes from a newspaper he was reading, or at any rate looking at, behind the counter, and in the expiring clatter of the door-bell beheld Winnie, his wife, enter and cross the shop on her way upstairs, followed by Stevie, his brother-in-law. The sight of his wife was agreeable to Mr Verloc. It was his idiosyncrasy. The figure of his brother-in-law remained imperceptible to him because of the morose thoughtfulness that lately had fallen like a veil between Mr Verloc and the appearances of the world of senses. He looked after his wife fixedly, without a word, as though she had been a phantom. His voice for home use was husky and placid, but now it was heard not at all. It was not heard at supper, to which he was called by his wife in the usual brief manner: "Adolf." He sat down to consume it without conviction, wearing his hat pushed far back on his head. It was not devotion to an outdoor life, but the frequentation of foreign cafés which was responsible for that habit, investing with a character of unceremonious impermanency Mr Verloc's steady fidelity to his own fireside. Twice at the clatter of the cracked bell he arose without a word, disappeared into the shop, and came back silently. During these absences Mrs Verloc, becoming acutely aware of the vacant place at her right hand, missed her mother very much, and stared stonily; while Stevie, from the same reason, kept on shuffling his feet, as though the floor under the table were uncomfortably hot. When Mr Verloc returned to sit in his place, like the very embodiment of silence, the character of Mrs Verloc's stare underwent a subtle change, and Stevie ceased to fidget with his feet, because of his great and awed regard for his sister's husband. He directed at him glances of respectful compassion. Mr Verloc was sorry. His sister Winnie had impressed upon him (in the omnibus) that Mr Verloc would be found at home in a state of sorrow, and must not be worried. His father's anger, the irritability of gentlemen lodgers, and Mr Verloc's predisposition to immoderate grief, had been the main sanctions of Stevie's self-restraint. Of these sentiments, all easily provoked, but not always easy to understand, the last had the greatest moral efficiency—because Mr Verloc was *good*. His mother and his sister had established that ethical fact on an unshakable foundation. They had established, erected, consecrated it behind Mr Verloc's back, for reasons that had nothing to do with abstract morality. And Mr Verloc was not aware of it. It is but bare justice to him to say that he had no notion of appearing good to Stevie. Yet so it was. He was even the only man so qualified in Stevie's knowledge, because the gentlemen lodgers had been too transient and too remote to have anything very distinct about them but perhaps their boots; and as regards the disciplinary measures of his father, the desolation of his mother and sister shrank from setting up a theory of goodness before the victim. It would have been too cruel. And it was even possible that Stevie would not have believed them. As far as Mr Verloc was concerned, nothing could stand in the way of Stevie's belief. Mr Verloc was obviously yet mysteriously *good*. And the grief of a good man is august.

Stevie gave glances of reverential compassion to his brother-in-law. Mr Verloc was sorry. The brother of Winnie had never before felt himself in such close communion with the mystery of that man's goodness. It was an understandable sorrow. And Stevie himself was sorry. He was very sorry. The same sort of sorrow. And his attention being drawn to this unpleasant state, Stevie shuffled his feet. His feelings were habitually manifested by the agitation of his limbs.

"Keep your feet quiet, dear," said Mrs Verloc, with authority and tenderness; then turning towards her husband in an indifferent voice, the masterly achievement of instinctive tact: "Are you going out to-night?" she asked.

The mere suggestion seemed repugnant to Mr Verloc. He shook his head moodily, and then sat still with downcast eyes, looking at the piece of cheese on his plate for a whole minute. At the end of that time he got up, and went out—went right out in the clatter of the shop-door bell. He acted thus inconsistently, not from any desire to make himself unpleasant, but because of an unconquerable restlessness. It was no earthly good going out. He could not find anywhere in London what he wanted. But he went out. He led a cortege of dismal thoughts along dark streets, through lighted streets, in and out of two flash bars, as if in a half-hearted attempt to make a night of it, and finally back again to his menaced home, where he sat down fatigued behind the counter, and they crowded urgently round him, like a pack of hungry black hounds. After locking up the house and putting out the gas he took them upstairs with him—a dreadful escort for a man going to bed. His wife had preceded him some time before, and with her ample form defined vaguely under the counterpane, her head on the pillow, and a hand under the cheek offered to his distraction the view of early drowsiness arguing the possession of an equable soul. Her big eyes stared wide open, inert and dark against the snowy whiteness of the linen. She did not move.

She had an equable soul. She felt profoundly that things do not stand much looking into. She made her force and her wisdom of that instinct. But the taciturnity of Mr Verloc had been lying heavily upon her for a good many days. It was, as a matter of fact, affecting her nerves. Recumbent and motionless, she said placidly:

"You'll catch cold walking about in your socks like this."

This speech, becoming the solicitude of the wife and the prudence of the woman, took Mr Verloc unawares. He had left his boots downstairs, but he had forgotten to put on his slippers, and he had been turning about the bedroom on noiseless pads like a bear in a cage. At the sound of his wife's voice he stopped and stared at her with a somnambulistic, expressionless gaze so long that Mrs Verloc moved her limbs slightly under the bed-clothes. But she did not move her black head sunk in the white pillow one hand under her cheek and the big, dark, unwinking eyes.

Under her husband's expressionless stare, and remembering her mother's empty room across the landing, she felt an acute pang of loneliness. She had never been parted from her mother before. They had stood by each other. She felt that they had, and she said to herself that now mother was gone—gone for good. Mrs Verloc had no illusions. Stevie remained, however. And she said:

"Mother's done what she wanted to do. There's no sense in it that I can see. I'm sure she couldn't have thought you had enough of her. It's perfectly wicked, leaving us like that."

Mr Verloc was not a well-read person; his range of allusive phrases was limited, but there was a peculiar aptness in circumstances which made him think of rats leaving a doomed ship. He very nearly said so. He had grown suspicious and embittered. Could it be that the old woman had such an excellent nose? But the unreasonableness of such a suspicion was patent, and Mr Verloc held his tongue. Not altogether, however. He muttered heavily:

"Perhaps it's just as well."

He began to undress. Mrs Verloc kept very still, perfectly still, with her eyes fixed in a dreamy, quiet stare. And her heart for the fraction of a second seemed to stand still too. That night she was "not quite herself," as the saying is, and it was borne upon her with some force that a simple sentence may hold several diverse meanings—mostly disagreeable. How was it just as well? And why? But she did not allow herself to fall into the idleness of barren speculation. She was rather confirmed in her belief that things did not stand being looked into. Practical and subtle in her way, she brought Stevie to the front without loss of time, because in her the singleness of purpose had the unerring nature and the force of an instinct.

"What I am going to do to cheer up that boy for the first few days I'm sure I don't know. He'll be worrying himself from morning till night before he gets used to mother being away. And he's such a good boy. I couldn't do without him."

Mr Verloc went on divesting himself of his clothing with the unnoticing inward concentration of a man undressing in the solitude of a vast and hopeless desert. For thus inhospitably did this fair earth, our common inheritance, present itself to the mental vision of Mr Verloc. All was so still without and within that the lonely ticking of the clock on the landing stole into the room as if for the sake of company.

Mr Verloc, getting into bed on his own side, remained prone and mute behind Mrs Verloc's back. His thick arms rested abandoned on the outside of the counterpane like dropped weapons, like discarded tools. At that moment he was within a hair's breadth of making a clean breast of it all to his wife. The moment seemed propitious. Looking out of the corners of his eyes, he saw her ample shoulders draped in white, the back of her head, with the hair done for the night in three plaits tied up with black tapes at the ends. And he forbore. Mr Verloc loved his wife as a wife should be loved—that is, maritally, with the regard one has for one's chief possession. This head arranged for the night, those ample shoulders, had an aspect of familiar sacredness—the sacredness of domestic peace. She moved not, massive and shapeless like a recumbent statue in the rough; he remembered her wide-open eyes looking into the empty room. She was mysterious, with the mysteriousness of living beings. The far-famed secret agent [delta] of the late Baron Stott-Wartenheim's alarmist despatches was not the man to break into such mysteries. He was easily intimidated. And he was also indolent, with the indolence which is so often the secret of good nature. He forbore touching that mystery out of love, timidity, and indolence. There would be always time enough. For several minutes he bore his sufferings silently in the drowsy silence of the room. And then he disturbed it by a resolute declaration.

"I am going on the Continent to-morrow."

His wife might have fallen asleep already. He could not tell. As a matter of fact, Mrs Verloc had heard him. Her eyes remained very wide open, and she lay very still, confirmed in her instinctive conviction that things don't bear looking into very much. And yet it was nothing very unusual for Mr Verloc to take such a trip. He renewed his stock from Paris and Brussels. Often he went over to make his purchases personally. A little select connection of amateurs was forming around the shop in Brett Street, a secret connection eminently proper for any business undertaken by Mr Verloc, who, by a mystic accord of temperament and necessity, had been set apart to be a secret agent all his life.

He waited for a while, then added: "I'll be away a week or perhaps a fortnight. Get Mrs Neale to come for the day."

Mrs Neale was the charwoman of Brett Street. Victim of her marriage with a debauched joiner, she was oppressed by the needs of many infant children. Red-armed, and aproned in coarse sacking up to the arm-pits, she exhaled the anguish of the poor in a breath of soapsuds and rum, in the uproar of scrubbing, in the clatter of tin pails.

Mrs Verloc, full of deep purpose, spoke in the tone of the shallowest indifference.

"There is no need to have the woman here all day. I shall do very well with Stevie."

She let the lonely clock on the landing count off fifteen ticks into the abyss of eternity, and asked:

"Shall I put the light out?"

Mr Verloc snapped at his wife huskily.

"Put it out."

9

Mr Verloc returning from the Continent at the end of ten days, brought back a mind evidently unrefreshed by the wonders of foreign travel and a countenance unlighted by the joys of home-coming. He entered in the clatter of the shop bell with an air of sombre and vexed exhaustion. His bag in hand, his head lowered, he strode straight behind the counter, and let himself fall into the chair, as though he had tramped all the way from Dover. It was early morning. Stevie, dusting various objects displayed in the front windows, turned to gape at him with reverence and awe.

"Here!" said Mr Verloc, giving a slight kick to the gladstone bag on the floor; and Stevie flung himself upon it, seized it, bore it off with triumphant devotion. He was so prompt that Mr Verloc was distinctly surprised.

Already at the clatter of the shop bell Mrs Neale, blackleading the parlour grate, had looked through the door, and rising from her knees had gone, aproned, and grimy with everlasting toil, to tell Mrs Verloc in the kitchen that "there was the master come back."

Winnie came no farther than the inner shop door.

"You'll want some breakfast," she said from a distance.

Mr Verloc moved his hands slightly, as if overcome by an impossible suggestion. But once enticed into the parlour he did not reject the food set before him. He ate as if in a public place, his hat pushed off his forehead, the skirts of his heavy overcoat hanging in a triangle on each side of the chair. And across the length of the table covered with brown oil-cloth Winnie, his wife, talked evenly at him the wifely talk, as artfully adapted, no doubt, to the circumstances of this return as the talk of Penelope to the return of the wandering Odysseus. Mrs Verloc, however, had done no weaving during her husband's absence. But she had had all the upstairs room cleaned thoroughly, had sold some wares, had seen Mr Michaelis several times. He had told her the last time that he was going away to live in a cottage in the country, somewhere on the London, Chatham, and Dover line. Karl Yundt had come too, once, led under the arm by that "wicked old housekeeper of his." He was "a disgusting old man." Of Comrade Ossipon, whom she had received curtly, entrenched behind the counter with a stony face and a faraway gaze, she said nothing, her mental reference to the robust anarchist being marked by a short pause, with the faintest possible blush. And bringing in her brother Stevie as soon as she could into the current of domestic events, she mentioned that the boy had moped a good deal.

"It's all along of mother leaving us like this."

Mr Verloc neither said, "Damn!" nor yet "Stevie be hanged!" And Mrs Verloc, not let into the secret of his thoughts, failed to appreciate the generosity of this restraint.

"It isn't that he doesn't work as well as ever," she continued. "He's been making himself very useful. You'd think he couldn't do enough for us."

Mr Verloc directed a casual and somnolent glance at Stevie, who sat on his right, delicate, pale-faced, his rosy mouth open vacantly. It was not a critical glance. It had no intention. And if Mr Verloc thought for a moment that his wife's brother looked uncommonly useless, it was only a dull and fleeting thought, devoid of that force and durability which enables sometimes a thought to move the world. Leaning back, Mr Verloc uncovered his head. Before his extended arm could put down the hat Stevie pounced upon it, and bore it off reverently into the kitchen. And again Mr Verloc was surprised.

"You could do anything with that boy, Adolf," Mrs Verloc said, with her best air of inflexible calmness. "He would go through fire for you. He—"

She paused attentive, her ear turned towards the door of the kitchen.

There Mrs Neale was scrubbing the floor. At Stevie's appearance she groaned lamentably, having observed that he could be induced easily to bestow for the benefit of her infant children the shilling his sister Winnie presented him with from time to time. On all fours amongst the puddles, wet and begrimed, like a sort of amphibious and domestic animal living in ash-bins and dirty water, she uttered the usual exordium: "It's all very well for you, kept doing nothing like a gentleman." And she followed it with the everlasting plaint of the poor, pathetically mendacious, miserably authenticated by the horrible breath of cheap rum and soap-suds. She scrubbed hard, snuffling all the time, and talking volubly. And she was sincere. And on each side of her thin red nose her bleared, misty eyes swam in tears, because she felt really the want of some sort of stimulant in the morning.

In the parlour Mrs Verloc observed, with knowledge:

"There's Mrs Neale at it again with her harrowing tales about her little children. They can't be all so little as she makes them out. Some of them must be big enough by now to try to do something for themselves. It only makes Stevie angry."

These words were confirmed by a thud as of a fist striking the kitchen table. In the normal evolution of his sympathy Stevie had become angry on discovering that he had no shilling in his pocket. In his inability to relieve at once Mrs Neale's "little 'uns'" privations, he felt that somebody should be made to suffer for it. Mrs Verloc rose, and went into the kitchen to "stop that nonsense." And she did it firmly but gently. She was well aware that directly Mrs Neale received her money she went round the corner to drink ardent spirits in a mean and musty public-house—the unavoidable station on the *via dolorosa* of her life. Mrs Verloc's comment upon this practice had an unexpected profundity, as coming from a person disinclined to look under the surface of things. "Of course, what is she to do to keep up? If I were like Mrs Neale I expect I wouldn't act any different."

In the afternoon of the same day, as Mr Verloc, coming with a start out of the last of a long series of dozes before the parlour fire, declared his intention of going out for a walk, Winnie said from the shop:

"I wish you would take that boy out with you, Adolf."

For the third time that day Mr Verloc was surprised. He stared stupidly at his wife. She continued in her steady manner. The boy, whenever he was not doing anything, moped in the house. It made her uneasy; it made her nervous, she confessed. And that from the calm Winnie sounded like exaggeration. But, in truth, Stevie moped in the striking fashion of an unhappy domestic animal. He would go up on the dark landing, to sit on the floor at the foot of the tall clock, with his knees drawn up and his head in his hands. To come upon his pallid face, with its big eyes gleaming in the dusk, was discomposing; to think of him up there was uncomfortable.

Mr Verloc got used to the startling novelty of the idea. He was fond of his wife as a man should be—that is, generously. But a weighty objection presented itself to his mind, and he formulated it.

"He'll lose sight of me perhaps, and get lost in the street," he said.

Mrs Verloc shook her head competently.

"He won't. You don't know him. That boy just worships you. But if you should miss him—"

Mrs Verloc paused for a moment, but only for a moment.

"You just go on, and have your walk out. Don't worry. He'll be all right. He's sure to turn up safe here before very long."

This optimism procured for Mr Verloc his fourth surprise of the day.

"Is he?" he grunted doubtfully. But perhaps his brother-in-law was not such an idiot as he looked. His wife would know best. He turned away his heavy eyes, saying huskily: "Well, let him come along, then," and relapsed into the clutches of black care, that perhaps prefers to sit behind a horseman, but knows also how to tread close on the heels of people not sufficiently well off to keep horses—like Mr Verloc, for instance.

Winnie, at the shop door, did not see this fatal attendant upon Mr Verloc's walks. She watched the two figures down the squalid street, one tall and burly, the other slight and short, with a thin neck, and the peaked shoulders raised slightly under the large semi-transparent ears. The material of their overcoats was the same, their hats were black and round in shape. Inspired by the similarity of wearing apparel, Mrs Verloc gave rein to her fancy.

"Might be father and son," she said to herself. She thought also that Mr Verloc was as much of a father as poor Stevie ever had in his life. She was aware also that it was her work. And with peaceful pride she congratulated herself on a certain resolution she had taken a few years before. It had cost her some effort, and even a few tears.

She congratulated herself still more on observing in the course of days that Mr Verloc seemed to be taking kindly to Stevie's companionship. Now, when ready to go out for his walk, Mr Verloc called aloud to the boy, in the spirit, no doubt, in which a man invites the attendance of the household dog, though, of course, in a different manner. In the house Mr Verloc could be detected staring curiously at Stevie a good deal. His own demeanour had changed. Taciturn still, he was not so listless. Mrs Verloc thought that he was rather jumpy at times. It might have been regarded as an improvement. As to Stevie, he moped no longer at the foot of the clock, but muttered to himself in corners instead in a threatening tone. When asked "What is it you're saying, Stevie?" he merely opened his mouth, and squinted at his sister. At odd times he clenched his fists without apparent cause, and when discovered in solitude would be scowling at the wall, with the sheet of paper and the pencil given him for drawing circles lying blank and idle on the kitchen table. This was a change, but it was no improvement. Mrs Verloc including all these vagaries under the general definition of excitement, began to fear that Stevie was hearing more than was good for him of her husband's conversations with his friends. During his "walks" Mr Verloc, of course, met and conversed with various persons. It could hardly be otherwise. His walks were an integral part of his outdoor activities, which his wife had never looked deeply into. Mrs Verloc felt that the position was delicate, but she faced it with the same impenetrable calmness which impressed and even astonished the customers of the shop and made the other visitors keep their distance a little wonderingly. No! She feared that there were things not good for Stevie to hear of, she told her husband. It only excited the poor boy, because he could not help them being so. Nobody could.

It was in the shop. Mr Verloc made no comment. He made no retort, and yet the retort was obvious. But he refrained from pointing out to his wife that the idea of making Stevie the companion of his walks was her own, and nobody else's. At that moment, to an impartial observer, Mr Verloc would have appeared more than human in his magnanimity. He took down a small cardboard box from a shelf, peeped in to see that the contents were all right, and put it down gently on the counter. Not till that was done did he break the silence, to the effect that most likely Stevie would profit greatly by being sent out of town for a while; only he supposed his wife could not get on without him.

"Could not get on without him!" repeated Mrs Verloc slowly. "I couldn't get on without him if it were for his good! The idea! Of course, I can get on without him. But there's nowhere for him to go."

Mr Verloc got out some brown paper and a ball of string; and meanwhile he muttered that Michaelis was living in a little cottage in the country. Michaelis wouldn't mind giving Stevie a room to sleep in. There were no visitors and no talk there. Michaelis was writing a book.

Mrs Verloc declared her affection for Michaelis; mentioned her abhorrence of Karl Yundt, "nasty old man"; and of Ossipon she said nothing. As to Stevie, he could be no other than very pleased. Mr Michaelis was always so nice and kind to him. He seemed to like the boy. Well, the boy was a good boy.

"You too seem to have grown quite fond of him of late," she added, after a pause, with her inflexible assurance.

Mr Verloc tying up the cardboard box into a parcel for the post, broke the string by an injudicious jerk, and muttered several swear words confidentially to himself. Then raising his tone to the usual husky mutter, he announced his willingness to take Stevie into the country himself, and leave him all safe with Michaelis.

He carried out this scheme on the very next day. Stevie offered no objection. He seemed rather eager, in a bewildered sort of way. He turned his candid gaze inquisitively to Mr Verloc's heavy countenance at frequent intervals, especially when his sister was not looking at him. His expression was proud, apprehensive, and concentrated, like that of a small child entrusted for the first time with a box of matches and the permission to strike a light. But Mrs Verloc, gratified by her brother's docility, recommended him not to dirty his clothes unduly in the country. At this Stevie gave his sister, guardian and protector a look, which for the first time in his life seemed to lack the quality of perfect childlike trustfulness. It was haughtily gloomy. Mrs Verloc smiled.

"Goodness me! You needn't be offended. You know you do get yourself very untidy when you get a chance, Stevie."

Mr Verloc was already gone some way down the street.

Thus in consequence of her mother's heroic proceedings, and of her brother's absence on this villegiature, Mrs Verloc found herself oftener than usual all alone not only in the shop, but in the house. For Mr Verloc had to take his walks. She was alone longer than usual on the day of the attempted bomb outrage in Greenwich Park, because Mr Verloc went out very early that morning and did not come back till nearly dusk. She did not mind being alone.

She had no desire to go out. The weather was too bad, and the shop was cosier than the streets. Sitting behind the counter with some sewing, she did not raise her eyes from her work when Mr Verloc entered in the aggressive clatter of the bell. She had recognised his step on the pavement outside.

She did not raise her eyes, but as Mr Verloc, silent, and with his hat rammed down upon his forehead, made straight for the parlour door, she said serenely:

"What a wretched day. You've been perhaps to see Stevie?"

"No! I haven't," said Mr Verloc softly, and slammed the glazed parlour door behind him with unexpected energy.

For some time Mrs Verloc remained quiescent, with her work dropped in her lap, before she put it away under the counter and got up to light the gas. This done, she went into the parlour on her way to the kitchen. Mr Verloc would want his tea presently. Confident of the power of her charms, Winnie did not expect from her husband in the daily intercourse of their married life a ceremonious amenity of address and courtliness of manner; vain and antiquated forms at best, probably never very exactly observed, discarded nowadays even in the highest spheres, and always foreign to the standards of her class. She did not look for courtesies from him. But he was a good husband, and she had a loyal respect for his rights.

Mrs Verloc would have gone through the parlour and on to her domestic duties in the kitchen with the perfect serenity of a woman sure of the power of her charms. But a slight, very slight, and rapid rattling sound grew upon her hearing. Bizarre and incomprehensible, it arrested Mrs Verloc's attention. Then as its character became plain to the ear she stopped short, amazed and concerned. Striking a match on the box she held in her hand, she turned on and lighted, above the parlour table, one of the two gas-burners, which, being defective, first whistled as if astonished, and then went on purring comfortably like a cat.

Mr Verloc, against his usual practice, had thrown off his overcoat. It was lying on the sofa. His hat, which he must also have thrown off, rested overturned under the edge of the sofa. He had dragged a chair in front of the fireplace, and his feet planted inside the fender, his head held between his hands, he was hanging low over the glowing grate. His teeth rattled with an ungovernable violence, causing his whole enormous back to tremble at the same rate. Mrs Verloc was startled.

"You've been getting wet," she said.

"Not very," Mr Verloc managed to falter out, in a profound shudder. By a great effort he suppressed the rattling of his teeth.

"I'll have you laid up on my hands," she said, with genuine uneasiness.

"I don't think so," remarked Mr Verloc, snuffling huskily.

He had certainly contrived somehow to catch an abominable cold between seven in the morning and five in the afternoon. Mrs Verloc looked at his bowed back.

"Where have you been to-day?" she asked.

"Nowhere," answered Mr Verloc in a low, choked nasal tone. His attitude suggested aggrieved sulks or a severe headache. The unsufficiency and uncandidness of his answer became painfully apparent in the dead silence of the room. He snuffled apologetically, and added: "I've been to the bank."

Mrs Verloc became attentive.

"You have!" she said dispassionately. "What for?"

Mr Verloc mumbled, with his nose over the grate, and with marked unwillingness.

"Draw the money out!"

"What do you mean? All of it?"

"Yes. All of it."

Mrs Verloc spread out with care the scanty table-cloth, got two knives and two forks out of the table drawer, and suddenly stopped in her methodical proceedings.

"What did you do that for?"

"May want it soon," snuffled vaguely Mr Verloc, who was coming to the end of his calculated indiscretions.

"I don't know what you mean," remarked his wife in a tone perfectly casual, but standing stock still between the table and the cupboard.

"You know you can trust me," Mr Verloc remarked to the grate, with hoarse feeling.

Mrs Verloc turned slowly towards the cupboard, saying with deliberation:

"Oh yes. I can trust you."

And she went on with her methodical proceedings. She laid two plates, got the bread, the butter, going to and fro quietly between the table and the cupboard in the peace and silence of her home. On the point of taking out the jam, she reflected practically: "He will be feeling hungry, having been away all day," and she returned to the cupboard once more to get the cold beef. She set it under the purring gas-jet, and with a passing glance at her motionless husband hugging the fire, she went (down two steps) into the kitchen. It was only when coming back, carving knife and fork in hand, that she spoke again.

"If I hadn't trusted you I wouldn't have married you."

Bowed under the overmantel, Mr Verloc, holding his head in both hands, seemed to have gone to sleep. Winnie made the tea, and called out in an undertone:

"Adolf."

Mr Verloc got up at once, and staggered a little before he sat down at the table. His wife examining the sharp edge of the carving knife, placed it on the dish, and called his attention to the cold beef. He remained insensible to the suggestion, with his chin on his breast.

"You should feed your cold," Mrs Verloc said dogmatically.

He looked up, and shook his head. His eyes were bloodshot and his face red. His fingers had ruffled his hair into a dissipated untidiness. Altogether he had a disreputable aspect, expressive of the discomfort, the irritation and the gloom following a heavy debauch. But Mr Verloc was not a debauched man. In his conduct he was respectable. His appearance might have been the effect of a feverish cold. He drank three cups of tea, but abstained from food entirely. He recoiled from it with sombre aversion when urged by Mrs Verloc, who said at last:

"Aren't your feet wet? You had better put on your slippers. You aren't going out any more this evening."

Mr Verloc intimated by morose grunts and signs that his feet were not wet, and that anyhow he did not care. The proposal as to slippers was disregarded as beneath his notice. But the question of going out in the evening received an unexpected development. It was not of going out in the evening that Mr Verloc was thinking. His thoughts embraced a vaster scheme. From moody and incomplete phrases it became apparent that Mr Verloc had been considering the expediency of emigrating. It was not very clear whether he had in his mind France or California.

The utter unexpectedness, improbability, and inconceivableness of such an event robbed this vague declaration of all its effect. Mrs Verloc, as placidly as if her husband had been threatening her with the end of the world, said:

"The idea!"

Mr Verloc declared himself sick and tired of everything, and besides—She interrupted him.

"You've a bad cold."

It was indeed obvious that Mr Verloc was not in his usual state, physically and even mentally. A sombre irresolution held him silent for a while. Then he murmured a few ominous generalities on the theme of necessity.

"Will have to," repeated Winnie, sitting calmly back, with folded arms, opposite her husband. "I should like to know who's to make you. You ain't a slave. No one need be a slave in this country—and don't you make yourself one." She paused, and with invincible and steady candour. "The business isn't so bad," she went on. "You've a comfortable home."

She glanced all round the parlour, from the corner cupboard to the good fire in the grate. Ensconced cosily behind the shop of doubtful wares, with the mysteriously dim window, and its door suspiciously ajar in the obscure and narrow street, it was in all essentials of domestic propriety and domestic comfort a respectable home. Her devoted affection missed out of it her brother Stevie, now enjoying a damp villegiature in the Kentish lanes under the care of Mr Michaelis. She missed him poignantly, with all the force of her protecting passion. This was the boy's home too—the roof, the cupboard, the stoked grate. On this thought Mrs Verloc rose, and walking to the other end of the table, said in the fulness of her heart:

"And you are not tired of me."

Mr Verloc made no sound. Winnie leaned on his shoulder from behind, and pressed her lips to his forehead. Thus she lingered. Not a whisper reached them from the outside world.

The sound of footsteps on the pavement died out in the discreet dimness of the shop. Only the gas-jet above the table went on purring equably in the brooding silence of the parlour.

During the contact of that unexpected and lingering kiss Mr Verloc, gripping with both hands the edges of his chair, preserved a hieratic immobility. When the pressure was removed he let go the chair, rose, and went to stand before the fireplace. He turned no longer his back to the room. With his features swollen and an air of being drugged, he followed his wife's movements with his eyes.

Mrs Verloc went about serenely, clearing up the table. Her tranquil voice commented the idea thrown out in a reasonable and domestic tone. It wouldn't stand examination. She condemned it from every point of view. But her only real concern was Stevie's welfare. He appeared to her thought in that connection as sufficiently "peculiar" not to be taken rashly abroad. And that was all. But talking round that vital point, she approached absolute vehemence in her delivery. Meanwhile, with brusque movements, she arrayed herself in an apron for the washing up of cups. And as if excited by the sound of her uncontradicted voice, she went so far as to say in a tone almost tart:

"If you go abroad you'll have to go without me."

"You know I wouldn't," said Mr Verloc huskily, and the unresonant voice of his private life trembled with an enigmatical emotion.

Already Mrs Verloc was regretting her words. They had sounded more unkind than she meant them to be. They had also the unwisdom of unnecessary things. In fact, she had not meant them at all. It was a sort of phrase that is suggested by the demon of perverse inspiration. But she knew a way to make it as if it had not been.

She turned her head over her shoulder and gave that man planted heavily in front of the fireplace a glance, half arch, half cruel, out of her large eyes—a glance of which the Winnie of the Belgravian mansion days would have been incapable, because of her respectability and her ignorance. But the man was her husband now, and she was no longer ignorant. She kept it on him for a whole second, with her grave face motionless like a mask, while she said playfully:

"You couldn't. You would miss me too much."

Mr Verloc started forward.

"Exactly," he said in a louder tone, throwing his arms out and making a step towards her. Something wild and doubtful in his expression made it appear uncertain whether he meant to strangle or to embrace his wife. But Mrs Verloc's attention was called away from that manifestation by the clatter of the shop bell.

"Shop, Adolf. You go."

He stopped, his arms came down slowly.

"You go," repeated Mrs Verloc. "I've got my apron on."

Mr Verloc obeyed woodenly, stony-eyed, and like an automaton whose face had been painted red. And this resemblance to a mechanical figure went so far that he had an automaton's absurd air of being aware of the machinery inside of him.

He closed the parlour door, and Mrs Verloc moving briskly, carried the tray into the kitchen. She washed the cups and some other things before she stopped in her work to listen. No sound reached her. The customer was a long time in the shop. It was a customer, because if he had not been Mr Verloc would have taken him inside. Undoing the strings of her apron with a jerk, she threw it on a chair, and walked back to the parlour slowly.

At that precise moment Mr Verloc entered from the shop.

He had gone in red. He came out a strange papery white. His face, losing its drugged, feverish stupor, had in that short time acquired a bewildered and harassed expression. He walked straight to the sofa, and stood looking down at his overcoat lying there, as though he were afraid to touch it.

"What's the matter?" asked Mrs Verloc in a subdued voice. Through the door left ajar she could see that the customer was not gone yet.

"I find I'll have to go out this evening," said Mr Verloc. He did not attempt to pick up his outer garment.

Without a word Winnie made for the shop, and shutting the door after her, walked in behind the counter. She did not look overtly at the customer till she had established herself comfortably on the chair. But by that time she had noted that he was tall and thin, and wore his moustaches twisted up. In fact, he gave the sharp points a twist just then. His long, bony face rose out of a turned-up collar. He was a little splashed, a little wet. A dark man, with the ridge of the cheek-bone well defined under the slightly hollow temple. A complete stranger. Not a customer either.

Mrs Verloc looked at him placidly.

"You came over from the Continent?" she said after a time.

The long, thin stranger, without exactly looking at Mrs Verloc, answered only by a faint and peculiar smile.

Mrs Verloc's steady, incurious gaze rested on him.

"You understand English, don't you?"

"Oh yes. I understand English."

There was nothing foreign in his accent, except that he seemed in his slow enunciation to be taking pains with it. And Mrs Verloc, in her varied experience, had come to the conclusion that some foreigners could speak better English than the natives. She said, looking at the door of the parlour fixedly:

"You don't think perhaps of staying in England for good?"

The stranger gave her again a silent smile. He had a kindly mouth and probing eyes. And he shook his head a little sadly, it seemed.

"My husband will see you through all right. Meantime for a few days you couldn't do better than take lodgings with Mr Giugliani. Continental Hotel it's called. Private. It's quiet. My husband will take you there."

"A good idea," said the thin, dark man, whose glance had hardened suddenly.

"You knew Mr Verloc before—didn't you? Perhaps in France?"

"I have heard of him," admitted the visitor in his slow, painstaking tone, which yet had a certain curtness of intention.

There was a pause. Then he spoke again, in a far less elaborate manner.

"Your husband has not gone out to wait for me in the street by chance?"

"In the street!" repeated Mrs Verloc, surprised. "He couldn't. There's no other door to the house."

For a moment she sat impassive, then left her seat to go and peep through the glazed door. Suddenly she opened it, and disappeared into the parlour.

Mr Verloc had done no more than put on his overcoat. But why he should remain afterwards leaning over the table propped up on his two arms as though he were feeling giddy or sick, she could not understand. "Adolf," she called out half aloud; and when he had raised himself:

"Do you know that man?" she asked rapidly.

"I've heard of him," whispered uneasily Mr Verloc, darting a wild glance at the door.

Mrs Verloc's fine, incurious eyes lighted up with a flash of abhorrence.

"One of Karl Yundt's friends—beastly old man."

"No! No!" protested Mr Verloc, busy fishing for his hat. But when he got it from under the sofa he held it as if he did not know the use of a hat.

"Well—he's waiting for you," said Mrs Verloc at last. "I say, Adolf, he ain't one of them Embassy people you have been bothered with of late?"

"Bothered with Embassy people," repeated Mr Verloc, with a heavy start of surprise and fear. "Who's been talking to you of the Embassy people?"

"Yourself."

"I! I! Talked of the Embassy to you!"

Mr Verloc seemed scared and bewildered beyond measure. His wife explained:

"You've been talking a little in your sleep of late, Adolf."

"What—what did I say? What do you know?"

"Nothing much. It seemed mostly nonsense. Enough to let me guess that something worried you."

Mr Verloc rammed his hat on his head. A crimson flood of anger ran over his face.

"Nonsense—eh? The Embassy people! I would cut their hearts out one after another. But let them look out. I've got a tongue in my head."

He fumed, pacing up and down between the table and the sofa, his open overcoat catching against the angles. The red flood of anger ebbed out, and left his face all white, with quivering nostrils. Mrs Verloc, for the purposes of practical existence, put down these appearances to the cold.

"Well," she said, "get rid of the man, whoever he is, as soon as you can, and come back home to me. You want looking after for a day or two."

Mr Verloc calmed down, and, with resolution imprinted on his pale face, had already opened the door, when his wife called him back in a whisper:

"Adolf! Adolf!" He came back startled. "What about that money you drew out?" she asked. "You've got it in your pocket? Hadn't you better—"

Mr Verloc gazed stupidly into the palm of his wife's extended hand for some time before he slapped his brow.

"Money! Yes! Yes! I didn't know what you meant."

He drew out of his breast pocket a new pigskin pocket-book. Mrs Verloc received it without another word, and stood still till the bell, clattering after Mr Verloc and Mr Verloc's visitor, had quieted down. Only then she peeped in at the amount, drawing the notes out for the purpose. After this inspection she looked round thoughtfully, with an air of mistrust in the silence and solitude of the house. This abode of her married life appeared to her as lonely and unsafe as though it had been situated in the midst of a forest. No receptacle she could think of amongst the solid, heavy furniture seemed other but flimsy and particularly tempting to her conception of a house-breaker. It was an ideal conception, endowed with sublime faculties and a miraculous insight. The till was not to be thought of. It was the first spot a thief would make for. Mrs Verloc unfastening hastily a couple of hooks, slipped the pocket-book under the bodice of her dress. Having thus disposed of her husband's capital, she was rather glad to hear the clatter of the door bell, announcing an arrival. Assuming the fixed, unabashed stare and the stony expression reserved for the casual customer, she walked in behind the counter.

A man standing in the middle of the shop was inspecting it with a swift, cool, all-round glance. His eyes ran over the walls, took in the ceiling, noted the floor—all in a moment. The points of a long fair moustache fell below the line of the jaw. He smiled the smile of an old if distant acquaintance, and Mrs Verloc remembered having seen him before. Not a customer. She softened her "customer stare" to mere indifference, and faced him across the counter.

He approached, on his side, confidentially, but not too markedly so.

"Husband at home, Mrs Verloc?" he asked in an easy, full tone.

"No. He's gone out."

"I am sorry for that. I've called to get from him a little private information."

This was the exact truth. Chief Inspector Heat had been all the way home, and had even gone so far as to think of getting into his slippers, since practically he was, he told himself, chucked out of that case. He indulged in some scornful and in a few angry thoughts, and found the occupation so unsatisfactory that he resolved to seek relief out of doors. Nothing prevented him paying a friendly call to Mr Verloc, casually as it were. It was in the character of a private citizen that walking out privately he made use of his customary conveyances. Their general direction was towards Mr Verloc's home. Chief Inspector Heat respected his own private character so consistently that he took especial pains to avoid all the police constables on point and patrol duty in the vicinity of Brett Street. This precaution was much more necessary for a man of his standing than for an obscure Assistant Commissioner. Private Citizen Heat entered the street, manoeuvring in a way which in a member of the criminal classes would have been stigmatised as slinking. The piece of cloth picked up in Greenwich was in his pocket. Not that he had the slightest intention of producing it in his private capacity. On the contrary, he wanted to know just what Mr Verloc would be disposed to say voluntarily. He hoped Mr Verloc's talk would be of a nature to incriminate Michaelis. It was a conscientiously professional hope in the main, but not without its moral value. For Chief Inspector Heat was a servant of justice. Finding Mr Verloc from home, he felt disappointed.

"I would wait for him a little if I were sure he wouldn't be long," he said.

Mrs Verloc volunteered no assurance of any kind.

"The information I need is quite private," he repeated. "You understand what I mean? I wonder if you could give me a notion where he's gone to?"

Mrs Verloc shook her head.

"Can't say."

She turned away to range some boxes on the shelves behind the counter. Chief Inspector Heat looked at her thoughtfully for a time.

"I suppose you know who I am?" he said.

Mrs Verloc glanced over her shoulder. Chief Inspector Heat was amazed at her coolness.

"Come! You know I am in the police," he said sharply.

"I don't trouble my head much about it," Mrs Verloc remarked, returning to the ranging of her boxes.

"My name is Heat. Chief Inspector Heat of the Special Crimes section."

Mrs Verloc adjusted nicely in its place a small cardboard box, and turning round, faced him again, heavy-eyed, with idle hands hanging down. A silence reigned for a time.

"So your husband went out a quarter of an hour ago! And he didn't say when he would be back?"

"He didn't go out alone," Mrs Verloc let fall negligently.

"A friend?"

Mrs Verloc touched the back of her hair. It was in perfect order.

"A stranger who called."

"I see. What sort of man was that stranger? Would you mind telling me?"

Mrs Verloc did not mind. And when Chief Inspector Heat heard of a man dark, thin, with a long face and turned up moustaches, he gave signs of perturbation, and exclaimed:

"Dash me if I didn't think so! He hasn't lost any time."

He was intensely disgusted in the secrecy of his heart at the unofficial conduct of his immediate chief. But he was not quixotic. He lost all desire to await Mr Verloc's return. What they had gone out for he did not know, but he imagined it possible that they would return together. The case is not followed properly, it's being tampered with, he thought bitterly.

"I am afraid I haven't time to wait for your husband," he said.

Mrs Verloc received this declaration listlessly. Her detachment had impressed Chief Inspector Heat all along. At this precise moment it whetted his curiosity. Chief Inspector Heat hung in the wind, swayed by his passions like the most private of citizens.

"I think," he said, looking at her steadily, "that you could give me a pretty good notion of what's going on if you liked."

Forcing her fine, inert eyes to return his gaze, Mrs Verloc murmured:

"Going on! What *is* going on?"

"Why, the affair I came to talk about a little with your husband."

That day Mrs Verloc had glanced at a morning paper as usual. But she had not stirred out of doors. The newsboys never invaded Brett Street. It was not a street for their business. And the echo of their cries drifting along the populous thoroughfares, expired between the dirty brick walls without reaching the threshold of the shop. Her husband had not brought an evening paper home. At any rate she had not seen it. Mrs Verloc knew nothing whatever of any affair. And she said so, with a genuine note of wonder in her quiet voice.

Chief Inspector Heat did not believe for a moment in so much ignorance. Curtly, without amiability, he stated the bare fact.

Mrs Verloc turned away her eyes.

"I call it silly," she pronounced slowly. She paused. "We ain't downtrodden slaves here."

The Chief Inspector waited watchfully. Nothing more came.

"And your husband didn't mention anything to you when he came home?"

Mrs Verloc simply turned her face from right to left in sign of negation. A languid, baffling silence reigned in the shop. Chief Inspector Heat felt provoked beyond endurance.

"There was another small matter," he began in a detached tone, "which I wanted to speak to your husband about. There came into our hands a—a—what we believe is—a stolen overcoat."

Mrs Verloc, with her mind specially aware of thieves that evening, touched lightly the bosom of her dress.

"We have lost no overcoat," she said calmly.

"That's funny," continued Private Citizen Heat. "I see you keep a lot of marking ink here—"

He took up a small bottle, and looked at it against the gas-jet in the middle of the shop.

"Purple—isn't it?" he remarked, setting it down again. "As I said, it's strange. Because the overcoat has got a label sewn on the inside with your address written in marking ink."

Mrs Verloc leaned over the counter with a low exclamation.

"That's my brother's, then."

"Where's your brother? Can I see him?" asked the Chief Inspector briskly. Mrs Verloc leaned a little more over the counter.

"No. He isn't here. I wrote that label myself."

"Where's your brother now?"

"He's been away living with—a friend—in the country."

"The overcoat comes from the country. And what's the name of the friend?"

"Michaelis," confessed Mrs Verloc in an awed whisper.

The Chief Inspector let out a whistle. His eyes snapped.

"Just so. Capital. And your brother now, what's he like—a sturdy, darkish chap—eh?"

"Oh no," exclaimed Mrs Verloc fervently. "That must be the thief. Stevie's slight and fair."

"Good," said the Chief Inspector in an approving tone. And while Mrs Verloc, wavering between alarm and wonder, stared at him, he sought for information. Why have the address sewn like this inside the coat? And he heard that the mangled remains he had inspected that morning with extreme repugnance were those of a youth, nervous, absent-minded, peculiar, and also that the woman who was speaking to him had had the charge of that boy since he was a baby.

"Easily excitable?" he suggested.

"Oh yes. He is. But how did he come to lose his coat—"

Chief Inspector Heat suddenly pulled out a pink newspaper he had bought less than half-an-hour ago. He was interested in horses. Forced by his calling into an attitude of doubt and suspicion towards his fellow-citizens, Chief Inspector Heat relieved the instinct of credulity implanted in the human breast by putting unbounded faith in the sporting prophets of that particular evening publication. Dropping the extra special on to the counter, he plunged his hand again into his pocket, and pulling out the piece of cloth fate had presented him with out of a heap of things that seemed to have been collected in shambles and rag shops, he offered it to Mrs Verloc for inspection.

"I suppose you recognise this?"

She took it mechanically in both her hands. Her eyes seemed to grow bigger as she looked.

"Yes," she whispered, then raised her head, and staggered backward a little.

"Whatever for is it torn out like this?"

The Chief Inspector snatched across the counter the cloth out of her hands, and she sat heavily on the chair. He thought: identification's perfect. And in that moment he had a glimpse into the whole amazing truth. Verloc was the "other man."

"Mrs Verloc," he said, "it strikes me that you know more of this bomb affair than even you yourself are aware of."

Mrs Verloc sat still, amazed, lost in boundless astonishment. What was the connection? And she became so rigid all over that she was not able to turn her head at the clatter of the bell, which caused the private investigator Heat to spin round on his heel. Mr Verloc had shut the door, and for a moment the two men looked at each other.

Mr Verloc, without looking at his wife, walked up to the Chief Inspector, who was relieved to see him return alone.

"You here!" muttered Mr Verloc heavily. "Who are you after?"

"No one," said Chief Inspector Heat in a low tone. "Look here, I would like a word or two with you."

Mr Verloc, still pale, had brought an air of resolution with him. Still he didn't look at his wife. He said:

"Come in here, then." And he led the way into the parlour.

The door was hardly shut when Mrs Verloc, jumping up from the chair, ran to it as if to fling it open, but instead of doing so fell on her knees, with her ear to the keyhole. The two men must have stopped directly they were through, because she heard plainly the Chief Inspector's voice, though she could not see his finger pressed against her husband's breast emphatically.

"You are the other man, Verloc. Two men were seen entering the park."

And the voice of Mr Verloc said:

"Well, take me now. What's to prevent you? You have the right."

"Oh no! I know too well who you have been giving yourself away to. He'll have to manage this little affair all by himself. But don't you make a mistake, it's I who found you out."

Then she heard only muttering. Inspector Heat must have been showing to Mr Verloc the piece of Stevie's overcoat, because Stevie's sister, guardian, and protector heard her husband a little louder.

"I never noticed that she had hit upon that dodge."

Again for a time Mrs Verloc heard nothing but murmurs, whose mysteriousness was less nightmarish to her brain than the horrible suggestions of shaped words. Then Chief Inspector Heat, on the other side of the door, raised his voice.

"You must have been mad."

And Mr Verloc's voice answered, with a sort of gloomy fury:

"I have been mad for a month or more, but I am not mad now. It's all over. It shall all come out of my head, and hang the consequences."

There was a silence, and then Private Citizen Heat murmured:

"What's coming out?"

"Everything," exclaimed the voice of Mr Verloc, and then sank very low.

After a while it rose again.

"You have known me for several years now, and you've found me useful, too. You know I was a straight man. Yes, straight."

This appeal to old acquaintance must have been extremely distasteful to the Chief Inspector.

His voice took on a warning note.

"Don't you trust so much to what you have been promised. If I were you I would clear out. I don't think we will run after you."

Mr Verloc was heard to laugh a little.

"Oh yes; you hope the others will get rid of me for you—don't you? No, no; you don't shake me off now. I have been a straight man to those people too long, and now everything must come out."

"Let it come out, then," the indifferent voice of Chief Inspector Heat assented. "But tell me now how did you get away."

"I was making for Chesterfield Walk," Mrs Verloc heard her husband's voice, "when I heard the bang. I started running then. Fog. I saw no one till I was past the end of George Street. Don't think I met anyone till then."

"So easy as that!" marvelled the voice of Chief Inspector Heat. "The bang startled you, eh?"

"Yes; it came too soon," confessed the gloomy, husky voice of Mr Verloc.

Mrs Verloc pressed her ear to the keyhole; her lips were blue, her hands cold as ice, and her pale face, in which the two eyes seemed like two black holes, felt to her as if it were enveloped in flames.

On the other side of the door the voices sank very low. She caught words now and then, sometimes in her husband's voice, sometimes in the smooth tones of the Chief Inspector. She heard this last say:

"We believe he stumbled against the root of a tree?"

There was a husky, voluble murmur, which lasted for some time, and then the Chief Inspector, as if answering some inquiry, spoke emphatically.

"Of course. Blown to small bits: limbs, gravel, clothing, bones, splinters—all mixed up together. I tell you they had to fetch a shovel to gather him up with."

Mrs Verloc sprang up suddenly from her crouching position, and stopping her ears, reeled to and fro between the counter and the shelves on the wall towards the chair. Her crazed eyes noted the sporting sheet left by the Chief Inspector, and as she knocked herself against the counter she snatched it up, fell into the chair, tore the optimistic, rosy sheet right across in trying to open it, then flung it on the floor. On the other side of the door, Chief Inspector Heat was saying to Mr Verloc, the secret agent:

"So your defence will be practically a full confession?"

"It will. I am going to tell the whole story."

"You won't be believed as much as you fancy you will."

And the Chief Inspector remained thoughtful. The turn this affair was taking meant the disclosure of many things—the laying waste of fields of knowledge, which, cultivated by a capable man, had a distinct value for the individual and for the society. It was sorry, sorry meddling. It would leave Michaelis unscathed; it would drag to light the Professor's home industry; disorganise the whole system of supervision; make no end of a row in the papers, which, from that point of view, appeared to him by a sudden illumination as invariably written by fools for the reading of imbeciles. Mentally he agreed with the words Mr Verloc let fall at last in answer to his last remark.

"Perhaps not. But it will upset many things. I have been a straight man, and I shall keep straight in this—"

"If they let you," said the Chief Inspector cynically. "You will be preached to, no doubt, before they put you into the dock. And in the end you may yet get let in for a sentence that will surprise you. I wouldn't trust too much the gentleman who's been talking to you."

Mr Verloc listened, frowning.

"My advice to you is to clear out while you may. I have no instructions. There are some of them," continued Chief Inspector Heat, laying a peculiar stress on the word "them," "who think you are already out of the world."

"Indeed!" Mr Verloc was moved to say. Though since his return from Greenwich he had spent most of his time sitting in the tap-room of an obscure little public-house, he could hardly have hoped for such favourable news.

"That's the impression about you." The Chief Inspector nodded at him. "Vanish. Clear out."

"Where to?" snarled Mr Verloc. He raised his head, and gazing at the closed door of the parlour, muttered feelingly: "I only wish you would take me away to-night. I would go quietly."

"I daresay," assented sardonically the Chief Inspector, following the direction of his glance.

The brow of Mr Verloc broke into slight moisture. He lowered his husky voice confidentially before the unmoved Chief Inspector.

"The lad was half-witted, irresponsible. Any court would have seen that at once. Only fit for the asylum. And that was the worst that would've happened to him if—"

The Chief Inspector, his hand on the door handle, whispered into Mr Verloc's face.

"He may've been half-witted, but you must have been crazy. What drove you off your head like this?"

Mr Verloc, thinking of Mr Vladimir, did not hesitate in the choice of words.

"A Hyperborean swine," he hissed forcibly. "A what you might call a—a gentleman."

The Chief Inspector, steady-eyed, nodded briefly his comprehension, and opened the door. Mrs Verloc, behind the counter, might have heard but did not see his departure, pursued by the aggressive clatter of the bell. She sat at her post of duty behind the counter. She sat rigidly erect in the chair with two dirty pink pieces of paper lying spread out at her feet. The palms of her hands were pressed convulsively to her face, with the tips of the fingers contracted against the forehead, as though the skin had been a mask which she was ready to tear off violently. The perfect immobility of her pose expressed the agitation of rage and despair, all the potential violence of tragic passions, better than any shallow display of shrieks, with the beating of a distracted head against the walls, could have done. Chief Inspector Heat, crossing the shop at his busy, swinging pace, gave her only a cursory glance. And when the cracked bell ceased to tremble on its curved ribbon of steel nothing stirred near Mrs Verloc, as if her attitude had the locking power of a spell. Even the butterfly-shaped gas flames posed on the ends of the suspended T-bracket burned without a quiver. In that shop of shady wares fitted with deal shelves painted a dull brown, which seemed to devour the sheen of the light, the gold circlet of the wedding ring on Mrs Verloc's left hand glittered exceedingly with the untarnished glory of a piece from some splendid treasure of jewels, dropped in a dust-bin.

10

The Assistant Commissioner, driven rapidly in a hansom from the neighbourhood of Soho in the direction of Westminster, got out at the very centre of the Empire on which the sun never sets. Some stalwart constables, who did not seem particularly impressed by the duty of watching the august spot, saluted him. Penetrating through a portal by no means lofty into the precincts of the House which is *the* House, *par excellence* in the minds of many millions of men, he was met at last by the volatile and revolutionary Toodles.

That neat and nice young man concealed his astonishment at the early appearance of the Assistant Commissioner, whom he had been told to look out for some time about midnight. His turning up so early he concluded to be the sign that things, whatever they were, had gone wrong. With an extremely ready sympathy, which in nice youngsters goes often with a joyous temperament, he felt sorry for the great Presence he called "The Chief," and also for the Assistant Commissioner, whose face appeared to him more ominously wooden than ever before, and quite wonderfully long. "What a queer, foreign-looking chap he is," he thought to himself, smiling from a distance with friendly buoyancy. And directly they came together he began to talk with the kind intention of burying the awkwardness of failure under a heap of words. It looked as if the great assault threatened for that night were going to fizzle out. An inferior henchman of "that brute Cheeseman" was up boring mercilessly a very thin House with some shamelessly cooked statistics. He, Toodles, hoped he would bore them into a count out every minute. But then he might be only marking time to let that guzzling Cheeseman dine at his leisure. Anyway, the Chief could not be persuaded to go home.

"He will see you at once, I think. He's sitting all alone in his room thinking of all the fishes of the sea," concluded Toodles airily. "Come along."

Notwithstanding the kindness of his disposition, the young private secretary (unpaid) was accessible to the common failings of humanity. He did not wish to harrow the feelings of the Assistant Commissioner, who looked to him uncommonly like a man who has made a mess of his job. But his curiosity was too strong to be restrained by mere compassion. He could not help, as they went along, to throw over his shoulder lightly:

"And your sprat?"

"Got him," answered the Assistant Commissioner with a concision which did not mean to be repellent in the least.

"Good. You've no idea how these great men dislike to be disappointed in small things."

After this profound observation the experienced Toodles seemed to reflect. At any rate he said nothing for quite two seconds. Then:

"I'm glad. But—I say—is it really such a very small thing as you make it out?"

"Do you know what may be done with a sprat?" the Assistant Commissioner asked in his turn.

"He's sometimes put into a sardine box," chuckled Toodles, whose erudition on the subject of the fishing industry was fresh and, in comparison with his ignorance of all other industrial matters, immense. "There are sardine canneries on the Spanish coast which—"

The Assistant Commissioner interrupted the apprentice statesman.

"Yes. Yes. But a sprat is also thrown away sometimes in order to catch a whale."

"A whale. Phew!" exclaimed Toodles, with bated breath. "You're after a whale, then?"

"Not exactly. What I am after is more like a dog-fish. You don't know perhaps what a dog-fish is like."

"Yes; I do. We're buried in special books up to our necks—whole shelves full of them—with plates. . . . It's a noxious, rascally-looking, altogether detestable beast, with a sort of smooth face and moustaches."

"Described to a T," commended the Assistant Commissioner. "Only mine is clean-shaven altogether. You've seen him. It's a witty fish."

"I have seen him!" said Toodles incredulously. "I can't conceive where I could have seen him."

"At the Explorers, I should say," dropped the Assistant Commissioner calmly. At the name of that extremely exclusive club Toodles looked scared, and stopped short.

"Nonsense," he protested, but in an awe-struck tone. "What do you mean? A member?"

"Honorary," muttered the Assistant Commissioner through his teeth.

"Heavens!"

Toodles looked so thunderstruck that the Assistant Commissioner smiled faintly.

"That's between ourselves strictly," he said.

"That's the beastliest thing I've ever heard in my life," declared Toodles feebly, as if astonishment had robbed him of all his buoyant strength in a second.

The Assistant Commissioner gave him an unsmiling glance. Till they came to the door of the great man's room, Toodles preserved a scandalised and solemn silence, as though he were offended with the Assistant Commissioner for exposing such an unsavoury and disturbing fact. It revolutionised his idea of the Explorers' Club's extreme selectness, of its social purity. Toodles was revolutionary only in politics; his social beliefs and personal feelings he wished to preserve unchanged through all the years allotted to him on this earth which, upon the whole, he believed to be a nice place to live on.

He stood aside.

"Go in without knocking," he said.

Shades of green silk fitted low over all the lights imparted to the room something of a forest's deep gloom. The haughty eyes were physically the great man's weak point. This point was wrapped up in secrecy. When an opportunity offered, he rested them conscientiously.

The Assistant Commissioner entering saw at first only a big pale hand supporting a big head, and concealing the upper part of a big pale face. An open despatch-box stood on the writing-table near a few oblong sheets of paper and a scattered handful of quill pens. There was absolutely nothing else on the large flat surface except a little bronze statuette draped in a toga, mysteriously watchful in its shadowy immobility. The Assistant Commissioner, invited to take a chair, sat down. In the dim light, the salient points of his personality, the long face, the black hair, his lankness, made him look more foreign than ever.

The great man manifested no surprise, no eagerness, no sentiment whatever. The attitude in which he rested his menaced eyes was profoundly meditative. He did not alter it the least bit. But his tone was not dreamy.

"Well! What is it that you've found out already? You came upon something unexpected on the first step."

"Not exactly unexpected, Sir Ethelred. What I mainly came upon was a psychological state."

The Great Presence made a slight movement. "You must be lucid, please."

"Yes, Sir Ethelred. You know no doubt that most criminals at some time or other feel an irresistible need of confessing—of making a clean breast of it to somebody—to anybody. And they do it often to the police. In that Verloc whom Heat wished so much to screen I've found a man in that particular psychological state. The man, figuratively speaking, flung himself on my breast. It was enough on my part to whisper to him who I was and to add 'I know that you are at the bottom of this affair.' It must have seemed miraculous to him that we should know already, but he took it all in the stride. The wonderfulness of it never checked him for a moment. There remained for me only to put to him the two questions: Who put you up to it? and Who was the man who did it? He answered the first with remarkable emphasis. As to the second question, I gather that the fellow with the bomb was his brother-in-law—quite a lad—a weak-minded creature. . . . It is rather a curious affair—too long perhaps to state fully just now."

"What then have you learned?" asked the great man.

"First, I've learned that the ex-convict Michaelis had nothing to do with it, though indeed the lad had been living with him temporarily in the country up to eight o'clock this morning. It is more than likely that Michaelis knows nothing of it to this moment."

"You are positive as to that?" asked the great man.

"Quite certain, Sir Ethelred. This fellow Verloc went there this morning, and took away the lad on the pretence of going out for a walk in the lanes. As it was not the first time that he did this, Michaelis could not have the slightest suspicion of anything unusual. For the rest, Sir Ethelred, the indignation of this man Verloc had left nothing in doubt—nothing whatever. He had been driven out of his mind almost by an extraordinary performance, which for you or me it would be difficult to take as seriously meant, but which produced a great impression obviously on him."

The Assistant Commissioner then imparted briefly to the great man, who sat still, resting his eyes under the screen of his hand, Mr Verloc's appreciation of Mr Vladimir's proceedings and character. The Assistant Commissioner did not seem to refuse it a certain amount of competency. But the great personage remarked:

"All this seems very fantastic."

"Doesn't it? One would think a ferocious joke. But our man took it seriously, it appears. He felt himself threatened. In the time, you know, he was in direct communication with old Stott-Wartenheim himself, and had come to regard his services as indispensable. It was an extremely rude awakening. I imagine that he lost his head. He became angry and frightened. Upon my word, my impression is that he thought these Embassy people quite capable not only to throw him out but, to give him away too in some manner or other—"

"How long were you with him," interrupted the Presence from behind his big hand.

"Some forty minutes, Sir Ethelred, in a house of bad repute called Continental Hotel, closeted in a room which by-the-by I took for the night. I found him under the influence of that reaction which follows the effort of crime. The man cannot be defined as a hardened criminal. It is obvious that he did not plan the death of that wretched lad—his brother-in-law. That was a shock to him—I could see that. Perhaps he is a man of strong sensibilities. Perhaps he was even fond of the lad—who knows? He might have hoped that the fellow would get clear away; in which case it would have been almost impossible to bring this thing home to anyone. At any rate he risked consciously nothing more but arrest for him."

The Assistant Commissioner paused in his speculations to reflect for a moment.

"Though how, in that last case, he could hope to have his own share in the business concealed is more than I can tell," he continued, in his ignorance of poor Stevie's devotion to Mr Verloc (who was *good*), and of his truly peculiar dumbness, which in the old affair of fireworks on the stairs had for many years resisted entreaties, coaxing, anger, and other means of investigation used by his beloved sister. For Stevie was loyal. . . . "No, I can't imagine. It's possible that he never thought of that at all. It sounds an extravagant way of putting it, Sir Ethelred, but his state of dismay suggested to me an impulsive man who, after committing suicide with the notion that it would end all his troubles, had discovered that it did nothing of the kind."

The Assistant Commissioner gave this definition in an apologetic voice. But in truth there is a sort of lucidity proper to extravagant language, and the great man was not offended. A slight jerky movement of the big body half lost in the gloom of the green silk shades, of the big head leaning on the big hand, accompanied an intermittent stifled but powerful sound. The great man had laughed.

"What have you done with him?"

The Assistant Commissioner answered very readily:

"As he seemed very anxious to get back to his wife in the shop I let him go, Sir Ethelred."

"You did? But the fellow will disappear."

"Pardon me. I don't think so. Where could he go to? Moreover, you must remember that he has got to think of the danger from his comrades too. He's there at his post. How could he explain leaving it? But even if there were no obstacles to his freedom of action he would do nothing. At present he hasn't enough moral energy to take a resolution of any sort. Permit me also to point out that if I had detained him we would have been committed to a course of action on which I wished to know your precise intentions first."

The great personage rose heavily, an imposing shadowy form in the greenish gloom of the room.

"I'll see the Attorney-General to-night, and will send for you to-morrow morning. Is there anything more you'd wish to tell me now?"

The Assistant Commissioner had stood up also, slender and flexible.

"I think not, Sir Ethelred, unless I were to enter into details which—"

"No. No details, please."

The great shadowy form seemed to shrink away as if in physical dread of details; then came forward, expanded, enormous, and weighty, offering a large hand. "And you say that this man has got a wife?"

"Yes, Sir Ethelred," said the Assistant Commissioner, pressing deferentially the extended hand. "A genuine wife and a genuinely, respectably, marital relation. He told me that after his interview at the Embassy he would have thrown everything up, would have tried to sell his shop, and leave the country, only he felt certain that his wife would not even hear of going abroad. Nothing could be more characteristic of the respectable bond than that," went on, with a touch of grimness, the Assistant Commissioner, whose own wife too had refused to hear of going abroad. "Yes, a genuine wife. And the victim was a genuine brother-in-law. From a certain point of view we are here in the presence of a domestic drama."

The Assistant Commissioner laughed a little; but the great man's thoughts seemed to have wandered far away, perhaps to the questions of his country's domestic policy, the battle-ground of his crusading valour against the paynim Cheeseman. The Assistant Commissioner withdrew quietly, unnoticed, as if already forgotten.

He had his own crusading instincts. This affair, which, in one way or another, disgusted Chief Inspector Heat, seemed to him a providentially given starting-point for a crusade. He had it much at heart to begin. He walked slowly home, meditating that enterprise on the way, and thinking over Mr Verloc's psychology in a composite mood of repugnance and satisfaction. He walked all the way home. Finding the drawing-room dark, he went upstairs, and spent some time between the bedroom and the dressing-room, changing his clothes, going to and fro with the air of a thoughtful somnambulist. But he shook it off before going out again to join his wife at the house of the great lady patroness of Michaelis.

He knew he would be welcomed there. On entering the smaller of the two drawing-rooms he saw his wife in a small group near the piano. A youngish composer in pass of becoming famous was discoursing from a music stool to two thick men whose backs looked old, and three slender women whose backs looked young. Behind the screen the great lady had only two persons with her: a man and a woman, who sat side by side on arm-chairs at the foot of her couch. She extended her hand to the Assistant Commissioner.

"I never hoped to see you here to-night. Annie told me—"

"Yes. I had no idea myself that my work would be over so soon."

The Assistant Commissioner added in a low tone: "I am glad to tell you that Michaelis is altogether clear of this—"

The patroness of the ex-convict received this assurance indignantly.

"Why? Were your people stupid enough to connect him with—"

"Not stupid," interrupted the Assistant Commissioner, contradicting deferentially. "Clever enough—quite clever enough for that."

A silence fell. The man at the foot of the couch had stopped speaking to the lady, and looked on with a faint smile.

"I don't know whether you ever met before," said the great lady.

Mr Vladimir and the Assistant Commissioner, introduced, acknowledged each other's existence with punctilious and guarded courtesy.

"He's been frightening me," declared suddenly the lady who sat by the side of Mr Vladimir, with an inclination of the head towards that gentleman. The Assistant Commissioner knew the lady.

"You do not look frightened," he pronounced, after surveying her conscientiously with his tired and equable gaze. He was thinking meantime to himself that in this house one met everybody sooner or later. Mr Vladimir's rosy countenance was wreathed in smiles, because he was witty, but his eyes remained serious, like the eyes of convinced man.

"Well, he tried to at least," amended the lady.

"Force of habit perhaps," said the Assistant Commissioner, moved by an irresistible inspiration.

"He has been threatening society with all sorts of horrors," continued the lady, whose enunciation was caressing and slow, "apropos of this explosion in Greenwich Park. It appears we all ought to quake in our shoes at what's coming if those people are not suppressed all over the world. I had no idea this was such a grave affair."

Mr Vladimir, affecting not to listen, leaned towards the couch, talking amiably in subdued tones, but he heard the Assistant Commissioner say:

"I've no doubt that Mr Vladimir has a very precise notion of the true importance of this affair."

Mr Vladimir asked himself what that confounded and intrusive policeman was driving at. Descended from generations victimised by the instruments of an arbitrary power, he was racially, nationally, and individually afraid of the police. It was an inherited weakness, altogether independent of his judgment, of his reason, of his experience. He was born to it. But that sentiment, which resembled the irrational horror some people have of cats, did not stand in the way of his immense contempt for the English police. He finished the sentence addressed to the great lady, and turned slightly in his chair.

"You mean that we have a great experience of these people. Yes; indeed, we suffer greatly from their activity, while you"—Mr Vladimir hesitated for a moment, in smiling perplexity—"while you suffer their presence gladly in your midst," he finished, displaying a dimple on each clean-shaven cheek. Then he added more gravely: "I may even say—because you do."

When Mr Vladimir ceased speaking the Assistant Commissioner lowered his glance, and the conversation dropped. Almost immediately afterwards Mr Vladimir took leave.

Directly his back was turned on the couch the Assistant Commissioner rose too.

"I thought you were going to stay and take Annie home," said the lady patroness of Michaelis.

"I find that I've yet a little work to do to-night."

"In connection—?"

"Well, yes—in a way."

"Tell me, what is it really—this horror?"

"It's difficult to say what it is, but it may yet be a *cause célèbre*," said the Assistant Commissioner.

He left the drawing-room hurriedly, and found Mr Vladimir still in the hall, wrapping up his throat carefully in a large silk handkerchief. Behind him a footman waited, holding his overcoat. Another stood ready to open the door. The Assistant Commissioner was duly helped into his coat, and let out at once. After descending the front steps he stopped, as if to consider the way he should take. On seeing this through the door held open, Mr Vladimir lingered in the hall to get out a cigar and asked for a light. It was furnished to him by an elderly man out of livery with an air of calm solicitude. But the match went out; the footman then closed the door, and Mr Vladimir lighted his large Havana with leisurely care.

When at last he got out of the house, he saw with disgust the "confounded policeman" still standing on the pavement.

"Can he be waiting for me," thought Mr Vladimir, looking up and down for some signs of a hansom. He saw none. A couple of carriages waited by the curbstone, their lamps blazing steadily, the horses standing perfectly still, as if carved in stone, the coachmen sitting motionless under the big fur capes, without as much as a quiver stirring the white thongs of their big whips. Mr Vladimir walked on, and the "confounded policeman" fell into step at his elbow. He said nothing. At the end of the fourth stride Mr Vladimir felt infuriated and uneasy. This could not last.

"Rotten weather," he growled savagely.

"Mild," said the Assistant Commissioner without passion. He remained silent for a little while. "We've got hold of a man called Verloc," he announced casually.

Mr Vladimir did not stumble, did not stagger back, did not change his stride. But he could not prevent himself from exclaiming: "What?" The Assistant Commissioner did not repeat his statement. "You know him," he went on in the same tone.

Mr Vladimir stopped, and became guttural. "What makes you say that?"

"I don't. It's Verloc who says that."

"A lying dog of some sort," said Mr Vladimir in somewhat Oriental phraseology. But in his heart he was almost awed by the miraculous cleverness of the English police. The change of his opinion on the subject was so violent that it made him for a moment feel slightly sick. He threw away his cigar, and moved on.

"What pleased me most in this affair," the Assistant went on, talking slowly, "is that it makes such an excellent starting-point for a piece of work which I've felt must be taken in hand—that is, the clearing out of this country of all the foreign political spies, police, and that sort of—of—dogs. In my opinion they are a ghastly nuisance; also an element of danger. But we can't very well seek them out individually. The only way is to make their employment unpleasant to their employers. The thing's becoming indecent. And dangerous too, for us, here."

Mr Vladimir stopped again for a moment.

"What do you mean?"

"The prosecution of this Verloc will demonstrate to the public both the danger and the indecency."

"Nobody will believe what a man of that sort says," said Mr Vladimir contemptuously.

"The wealth and precision of detail will carry conviction to the great mass of the public," advanced the Assistant Commissioner gently.

"So that is seriously what you mean to do."

"We've got the man; we have no choice."

"You will be only feeding up the lying spirit of these revolutionary scoundrels," Mr Vladimir protested. "What do you want to make a scandal for?—from morality—or what?"

Mr Vladimir's anxiety was obvious. The Assistant Commissioner having ascertained in this way that there must be some truth in the summary statements of Mr Verloc, said indifferently:

"There's a practical side too. We have really enough to do to look after the genuine article. You can't say we are not effective. But we don't intend to let ourselves be bothered by shams under any pretext whatever."

Mr Vladimir's tone became lofty.

"For my part, I can't share your view. It is selfish. My sentiments for my own country cannot be doubted; but I've always felt that we ought to be good Europeans besides—I mean governments and men."

"Yes," said the Assistant Commissioner simply. "Only you look at Europe from its other end. But," he went on in a good-natured tone, "the foreign governments cannot complain of the inefficiency of our police. Look at this outrage; a case specially difficult to trace inasmuch as it was a sham. In less than twelve hours we have established the identity of a man literally blown to shreds, have found the organiser of the attempt, and have had a glimpse of the inciter behind him. And we could have gone further; only we stopped at the limits of our territory."

"So this instructive crime was planned abroad," Mr Vladimir said quickly. "You admit it was planned abroad?"

"Theoretically. Theoretically only, on foreign territory; abroad only by a fiction," said the Assistant Commissioner, alluding to the character of Embassies, which are supposed to be part and parcel of the country to which they belong. "But that's a detail. I talked to you of this business because it's your government that grumbles most at our police. You see that we are not so bad. I wanted particularly to tell you of our success."

"I'm sure I'm very grateful," muttered Mr Vladimir through his teeth.

"We can put our finger on every anarchist here," went on the Assistant Commissioner, as though he were quoting Chief Inspector Heat. "All that's wanted now is to do away with the agent provocateur to make everything safe."

Mr Vladimir held up his hand to a passing hansom.

"You're not going in here," remarked the Assistant Commissioner, looking at a building of noble proportions and hospitable aspect, with the light of a great hall falling through its glass doors on a broad flight of steps.

But Mr Vladimir, sitting, stony-eyed, inside the hansom, drove off without a word.

The Assistant Commissioner himself did not turn into the noble building. It was the Explorers' Club. The thought passed through his mind that Mr Vladimir, honorary member, would not be seen very often there in the future. He looked at his watch. It was only half-past ten. He had had a very full evening.

II

After Chief Inspector Heat had left him Mr Verloc moved about the parlour.

From time to time he eyed his wife through the open door. "She knows all about it now," he thought to himself with commiseration for her sorrow and with some satisfaction as regarded himself. Mr Verloc's soul, if lacking greatness perhaps, was capable of tender sentiments. The prospect of having to break the news to her had put him into a fever. Chief Inspector Heat had relieved him of the task. That was good as far as it went. It remained for him now to face her grief.

Mr Verloc had never expected to have to face it on account of death, whose catastrophic character cannot be argued away by sophisticated reasoning or persuasive eloquence. Mr Verloc never meant Stevie to perish with such abrupt violence. He did not mean him to perish at all. Stevie dead was a much greater nuisance than ever he had been when alive. Mr Verloc had augured a favourable issue to his enterprise, basing himself not on Stevie's intelligence, which sometimes plays queer tricks with a man, but on the blind docility and on the blind devotion of the boy. Though not much of a psychologist, Mr Verloc had gauged the depth of Stevie's fanaticism. He dared cherish the hope of Stevie walking away from the walls of the Observatory as he had been instructed to do, taking the way shown to him several times previously, and rejoining his brother-in-law, the wise and good Mr Verloc, outside the precincts of the park. Fifteen minutes ought to have been enough for the veriest fool to deposit the engine and walk away. And the Professor had guaranteed more than fifteen minutes. But Stevie had stumbled within five minutes of being left to himself. And Mr Verloc was shaken morally to pieces. He had foreseen everything but that. He had foreseen Stevie distracted and lost—sought for—found in some police station or provincial workhouse in the end. He had foreseen Stevie arrested, and was not afraid, because Mr Verloc had a great opinion of Stevie's loyalty, which had been carefully indoctrinated with the necessity of silence in the course of many walks. Like a peripatetic philosopher, Mr Verloc, strolling along the streets of London, had modified Stevie's view of the police by conversations full of subtle reasonings. Never had a sage a more attentive and admiring disciple. The submission and worship were so apparent that Mr Verloc had come to feel something like a liking for the boy. In any case, he had not foreseen the swift bringing home of his connection. That his wife should hit upon the precaution of sewing the boy's address inside his overcoat was the last thing Mr Verloc would have thought of. One can't think of everything. That was what she meant when she said that he need not worry if he lost Stevie during their walks. She had assured him that the boy would turn up all right. Well, he had turned up with a vengeance!

"Well, well," muttered Mr Verloc in his wonder. What did she mean by it? Spare him the trouble of keeping an anxious eye on Stevie? Most likely she had meant well. Only she ought to have told him of the precaution she had taken.

Mr Verloc walked behind the counter of the shop. His intention was not to overwhelm his wife with bitter reproaches. Mr Verloc felt no bitterness. The unexpected march of events had converted him to the doctrine of fatalism. Nothing could be helped now. He said:

"I didn't mean any harm to come to the boy."

Mrs Verloc shuddered at the sound of her husband's voice. She did not uncover her face. The trusted secret agent of the late Baron Stott-Wartenheim looked at her for a time with a heavy, persistent, undiscerning glance. The torn evening paper was lying at her feet. It could not have told her much. Mr Verloc felt the need of talking to his wife.

"It's that damned Heat—eh?" he said. "He upset you. He's a brute, blurting it out like this to a woman. I made myself ill thinking how to break it to you. I sat for hours in the little parlour of Cheshire Cheese thinking over the best way. You understand I never meant any harm to come to that boy."

Mr Verloc, the Secret Agent, was speaking the truth. It was his marital affection that had received the greatest shock from the premature explosion. He added:

"I didn't feel particularly gay sitting there and thinking of you."

He observed another slight shudder of his wife, which affected his sensibility. As she persisted in hiding her face in her hands, he thought he had better leave her alone for a while. On this delicate impulse Mr Verloc withdrew into the parlour again, where the gas jet purred like a contented cat. Mrs Verloc's wifely forethought had left the cold beef on the table with carving knife and fork and half a loaf of bread for Mr Verloc's supper. He noticed all these things now for the first time, and cutting himself a piece of bread and meat, began to eat.

His appetite did not proceed from callousness. Mr Verloc had not eaten any breakfast that day. He had left his home fasting. Not being an energetic man, he found his resolution in nervous excitement, which seemed to hold him mainly by the throat. He could not have swallowed anything solid. Michaelis' cottage was as destitute of provisions as the cell of a prisoner. The ticket-of-leave apostle lived on a little milk and crusts of stale bread. Moreover, when Mr Verloc arrived he had already gone upstairs after his frugal meal. Absorbed in the toil and delight of literary composition, he had not even answered Mr Verloc's shout up the little staircase.

"I am taking this young fellow home for a day or two."

And, in truth, Mr Verloc did not wait for an answer, but had marched out of the cottage at once, followed by the obedient Stevie.

Now that all action was over and his fate taken out of his hands with unexpected swiftness, Mr Verloc felt terribly empty physically. He carved the meat, cut the bread, and devoured his supper standing by the table, and now and then casting a glance towards his wife. Her prolonged immobility disturbed the comfort of his refection. He walked again into the shop, and came up very close to her. This sorrow with a veiled face made Mr Verloc uneasy. He expected, of course, his wife to be very much upset, but he wanted her to pull herself together. He needed all her assistance and all her loyalty in these new conjunctures his fatalism had already accepted.

"Can't be helped," he said in a tone of gloomy sympathy. "Come, Winnie, we've got to think of to-morrow. You'll want all your wits about you after I am taken away."

He paused. Mrs Verloc's breast heaved convulsively. This was not reassuring to Mr Verloc, in whose view the newly created situation required from the two people most concerned in it calmness, decision, and other qualities incompatible with the mental disorder of passionate sorrow. Mr Verloc was a humane man; he had come home prepared to allow every latitude to his wife's affection for her brother.

Only he did not understand either the nature or the whole extent of that sentiment. And in this he was excusable, since it was impossible for him to understand it without ceasing to be himself. He was startled and disappointed, and his speech conveyed it by a certain roughness of tone.

"You might look at a fellow," he observed after waiting a while.

As if forced through the hands covering Mrs Verloc's face the answer came, deadened, almost pitiful.

"I don't want to look at you as long as I live."

"Eh? What!" Mr Verloc was merely startled by the superficial and literal meaning of this declaration. It was obviously unreasonable, the mere cry of exaggerated grief. He threw over it the mantle of his marital indulgence. The mind of Mr Verloc lacked profundity. Under the mistaken impression that the value of individuals consists in what they are in themselves, he could not possibly comprehend the value of Stevie in the eyes of Mrs Verloc. She was taking it confoundedly hard, he thought to himself. It was all the fault of that damned Heat. What did he want to upset the woman for? But she mustn't be allowed, for her own good, to carry on so till she got quite beside herself.

"Look here! You can't sit like this in the shop," he said with affected severity, in which there was some real annoyance; for urgent practical matters must be talked over if they had to sit up all night. "Somebody might come in at any minute," he added, and waited again. No effect was produced, and the idea of the finality of death occurred to Mr Verloc during the pause. He changed his tone. "Come. This won't bring him back," he said gently, feeling ready to take her in his arms and press her to his breast, where impatience and compassion dwelt side by side. But except for a short shudder Mrs Verloc remained apparently unaffected by the force of that terrible truism. It was Mr Verloc himself who was moved. He was moved in his simplicity to urge moderation by asserting the claims of his own personality.

"Do be reasonable, Winnie. What would it have been if you had lost me!"

He had vaguely expected to hear her cry out. But she did not budge. She leaned back a little, quieted down to a complete unreadable stillness. Mr Verloc's heart began to beat faster with exasperation and something resembling alarm. He laid his hand on her shoulder, saying:

"Don't be a fool, Winnie."

She gave no sign. It was impossible to talk to any purpose with a woman whose face one cannot see. Mr Verloc caught hold of his wife's wrists. But her hands seemed glued fast. She swayed forward bodily to his tug, and nearly went off the chair. Startled to feel her so helplessly limp, he was trying to put her back on the chair when she stiffened suddenly all over, tore herself out of his hands, ran out of the shop, across the parlour, and into the kitchen. This was very swift. He had just a glimpse of her face and that much of her eyes that he knew she had not looked at him.

It all had the appearance of a struggle for the possession of a chair, because Mr Verloc instantly took his wife's place in it. Mr Verloc did not cover his face with his hands, but a sombre thoughtfulness veiled his features. A term of imprisonment could not be avoided. He did not wish now to avoid it. A prison was a place as safe from certain unlawful vengeances as the grave, with this advantage, that in a prison there is room for hope. What he saw before him was a term of imprisonment, an early release and then life abroad somewhere, such as he had contemplated already, in case of failure. Well, it was a failure, if not exactly the sort of failure he had feared. It had been so near success that he could have positively terrified Mr Vladimir out of his ferocious scoffing with this proof of occult efficiency. So at least it seemed now to Mr Verloc. His prestige with the Embassy would have been immense if—if his wife had not had the unlucky notion of sewing on the address inside Stevie's overcoat. Mr Verloc, who was no fool, had soon perceived the extraordinary character of the influence he had over Stevie, though he did not understand exactly its origin—the doctrine of his supreme wisdom and goodness inculcated by two anxious women. In all the eventualities he had foreseen Mr Verloc had calculated with correct insight on Stevie's instinctive loyalty and blind discretion. The eventuality he had not foreseen had appalled him as a humane man and a fond husband. From every other point of view it was rather advantageous. Nothing can equal the everlasting discretion of death. Mr Verloc, sitting perplexed and frightened in the small parlour of the Cheshire Cheese, could not help acknowledging that to himself, because his sensibility did not stand in the way of his judgment. Stevie's violent disintegration, however disturbing to think about, only assured the success; for, of course, the knocking down of a wall was not the aim of Mr Vladimir's menaces, but the production of a moral effect. With much trouble and distress on Mr Verloc's part the effect might be said to have been produced. When, however, most unexpectedly, it came home to roost in Brett Street, Mr Verloc, who had been struggling like a man in a nightmare for the preservation of his position, accepted the blow in the spirit of a convinced fatalist. The position was gone through no one's fault really. A small, tiny fact had done it. It was like slipping on a bit of orange peel in the dark and breaking your leg.

Mr Verloc drew a weary breath. He nourished no resentment against his wife. He thought: She will have to look after the shop while they keep me locked up. And thinking also how cruelly she would miss Stevie at first, he felt greatly concerned about her health and spirits. How would she stand her solitude—absolutely alone in that house? It would not do for her to break down while he was locked up? What would become of the shop then? The shop was an asset. Though Mr Verloc's fatalism accepted his undoing as a secret agent, he had no mind to be utterly ruined, mostly, it must be owned, from regard for his wife.

Silent, and out of his line of sight in the kitchen, she frightened him. If only she had had her mother with her. But that silly old woman—An angry dismay possessed Mr Verloc. He must talk with his wife. He could tell her certainly that a man does get desperate under certain circumstances. But he did not go incontinently to impart to her that information. First of all, it was clear to him that this evening was no time for business. He got up to close the street door and put the gas out in the shop.

Having thus assured a solitude around his hearthstone Mr Verloc walked into the parlour, and glanced down into the kitchen. Mrs Verloc was sitting in the place where poor Stevie usually established himself of an evening with paper and pencil for the pastime of drawing these coruscations of innumerable circles suggesting chaos and eternity. Her arms were folded on the table, and her head was lying on her arms. Mr Verloc contemplated her back and the arrangement of her hair for a time, then walked away from the kitchen door. Mrs Verloc's philosophical, almost disdainful incuriosity, the foundation of their accord in domestic life made it extremely difficult to get into contact with her, now this tragic necessity had arisen. Mr Verloc felt this difficulty acutely. He turned around the table in the parlour with his usual air of a large animal in a cage.

Curiosity being one of the forms of self-revelation, a systematically incurious person remains always partly mysterious. Every time he passed near the door Mr Verloc glanced at his wife uneasily. It was not that he was afraid of her. Mr Verloc imagined himself loved by that woman. But she had not accustomed him to make confidences. And the confidence he had to make was of a profound psychological order. How with his want of practice could he tell her what he himself felt but vaguely: that there are conspiracies of fatal destiny, that a notion grows in a mind sometimes till it acquires an outward existence, an independent power of its own, and even a suggestive voice? He could not inform her that a man may be haunted by a fat, witty, clean-shaved face till the wildest expedient to get rid of it appears a child of wisdom.

On this mental reference to a First Secretary of a great Embassy, Mr Verloc stopped in the doorway, and looking down into the kitchen with an angry face and clenched fists, addressed his wife.

"You don't know what a brute I had to deal with."

He started off to make another perambulation of the table; then when he had come to the door again he stopped, glaring in from the height of two steps.

"A silly, jeering, dangerous brute, with no more sense than—After all these years! A man like me! And I have been playing my head at that game. You didn't know. Quite right, too. What was the good of telling you that I stood the risk of having a knife stuck into me any time these seven years we've been married? I am not a chap to worry a woman that's fond of me. You had no business to know." Mr Verloc took another turn round the parlour, fuming.

"A venomous beast," he began again from the doorway. "Drive me out into a ditch to starve for a joke. I could see he thought it was a damned good joke. A man like me! Look here! Some of the highest in the world got to thank me for walking on their two legs to this day. That's the man you've got married to, my girl!"

He perceived that his wife had sat up. Mrs Verloc's arms remained lying stretched on the table. Mr Verloc watched at her back as if he could read there the effect of his words.

"There isn't a murdering plot for the last eleven years that I hadn't my finger in at the risk of my life. There's scores of these revolutionists I've sent off, with their bombs in their blamed pockets, to get themselves caught on the frontier. The old Baron knew what I was worth to his country. And here suddenly a swine comes along—an ignorant, overbearing swine."

Mr Verloc, stepping slowly down two steps, entered the kitchen, took a tumbler off the dresser, and holding it in his hand, approached the sink, without looking at his wife. "It wasn't the old Baron who would have had the wicked folly of getting me to call on him at eleven in the morning. There are two or three in this town that, if they had seen me going in, would have made no bones about knocking me on the head sooner or later. It was a silly, murderous trick to expose for nothing a man—like me."

Mr Verloc, turning on the tap above the sink, poured three glasses of water, one after another, down his throat to quench the fires of his indignation. Mr Vladimir's conduct was like a hot brand which set his internal economy in a blaze. He could not get over the disloyalty of it. This man, who would not work at the usual hard tasks which society sets to its humbler members, had exercised his secret industry with an indefatigable devotion. There was in Mr Verloc a fund of loyalty. He had been loyal to his employers, to the cause of social stability,—and to his affections too—as became apparent when, after standing the tumbler in the sink, he turned about, saying:

"If I hadn't thought of you I would have taken the bullying brute by the throat and rammed his head into the fireplace. I'd have been more than a match for that pink-faced, smooth-shaved—"

Mr Verloc, neglected to finish the sentence, as if there could be no doubt of the terminal word. For the first time in his life he was taking that incurious woman into his confidence. The singularity of the event, the force and importance of the personal feelings aroused in the course of this confession, drove Stevie's fate clean out of Mr Verloc's mind. The boy's stuttering existence of fears and indignations, together with the violence of his end, had passed out of Mr Verloc's mental sight for a time. For that reason, when he looked up he was startled by the inappropriate character of his wife's stare. It was not a wild stare, and it was not inattentive, but its attention was peculiar and not satisfactory, inasmuch that it seemed concentrated upon some point beyond Mr Verloc's person. The impression was so strong that Mr Verloc glanced over his shoulder. There was nothing behind him: there was just the whitewashed wall. The excellent husband of Winnie Verloc saw no writing on the wall. He turned to his wife again, repeating, with some emphasis:

"I would have taken him by the throat. As true as I stand here, if I hadn't thought of you then I would have half choked the life out of the brute before I let him get up. And don't you think he would have been anxious to call the police either. He wouldn't have dared. You understand why—don't you?"

He blinked at his wife knowingly.

"No," said Mrs Verloc in an unresonant voice, and without looking at him at all. "What are you talking about?"

A great discouragement, the result of fatigue, came upon Mr Verloc. He had had a very full day, and his nerves had been tried to the utmost. After a month of maddening worry, ending in an unexpected catastrophe, the storm-tossed spirit of Mr Verloc longed for repose. His career as a secret agent had come to an end in a way no one could have foreseen; only, now, perhaps he could manage to get a night's sleep at last. But looking at his wife, he doubted it. She was taking it very hard—not at all like herself, he thought. He made an effort to speak.

"You'll have to pull yourself together, my girl," he said sympathetically. "What's done can't be undone."

Mrs Verloc gave a slight start, though not a muscle of her white face moved in the least. Mr Verloc, who was not looking at her, continued ponderously.

"You go to bed now. What you want is a good cry."

This opinion had nothing to recommend it but the general consent of mankind. It is universally understood that, as if it were nothing more substantial than vapour floating in the sky, every emotion of a woman is bound to end in a shower. And it is very probable that had Stevie died in his bed under her despairing gaze, in her protecting arms, Mrs Verloc's grief would have found relief in a flood of bitter and pure tears. Mrs Verloc, in common with other human beings, was provided with a fund of unconscious resignation sufficient to meet the normal manifestation of human destiny. Without "troubling her head about it," she was aware that it "did not stand looking into very much." But the lamentable circumstances of Stevie's end, which to Mr Verloc's mind had only an episodic character, as part of a greater disaster, dried her tears at their very source. It was the effect of a white-hot iron drawn across her eyes; at the same time her heart, hardened and chilled into a lump of ice, kept her body in an inward shudder, set her features into a frozen contemplative immobility addressed to a whitewashed wall with no writing on it. The exigencies of Mrs Verloc's temperament, which, when stripped of its philosophical reserve, was maternal and violent, forced her to roll a series of thoughts in her motionless head. These thoughts were rather imagined than expressed. Mrs Verloc was a woman of singularly few words, either for public or private use. With the rage and dismay of a betrayed woman, she reviewed the tenor of her life in visions concerned mostly with Stevie's difficult existence from its earliest days. It was a life of single purpose and of a noble unity of inspiration, like those rare lives that have left their mark on the thoughts and feelings of mankind. But the visions of Mrs Verloc lacked nobility and magnificence. She saw herself putting the boy to bed by the light of a single candle on the deserted top floor of a "business house," dark under the roof and scintillating exceedingly with lights and cut glass at the level of the street like a fairy palace. That meretricious splendour was the only one to be met in Mrs Verloc's visions. She remembered brushing the boy's hair and tying his pinafores—herself in a pinafore still; the consolations administered to a small and badly scared creature by another creature nearly as small but not quite so badly scared; she had the vision of the blows intercepted (often with her own head), of a door held desperately shut against a man's rage (not for very long); of a poker flung once (not very far), which stilled that particular storm into the dumb and awful silence which follows a thunder-clap. And all these scenes of violence came and went accompanied by the unrefined noise of deep vociferations proceeding from a man wounded in his paternal pride, declaring himself obviously accursed since one of his kids was a "slobbering idjut and the other a wicked she-devil." It was of her that this had been said many years ago.

Mrs Verloc heard the words again in a ghostly fashion, and then the dreary shadow of the Belgravian mansion descended upon her shoulders. It was a crushing memory, an exhausting vision of countless breakfast trays carried up and down innumerable stairs, of endless haggling over pence, of the endless drudgery of sweeping, dusting, cleaning, from basement to attics; while the impotent mother, staggering on swollen legs, cooked in a grimy kitchen, and poor Stevie, the unconscious presiding genius of all their toil, blacked the gentlemen's boots in the scullery. But this vision had a breath of a hot London summer in it, and for a central figure a young man wearing his Sunday best, with a straw hat on his dark head and a wooden pipe in his mouth. Affectionate and jolly, he was a fascinating companion for a voyage down the sparkling stream of life; only his boat was very small. There was room in it for a girl-partner at the oar, but no accommodation for passengers. He was allowed to drift away from the threshold of the Belgravian mansion while Winnie averted her tearful eyes. He was not a lodger. The lodger was Mr Verloc, indolent, and keeping late hours, sleepily jocular of a morning from under his bed-clothes, but with gleams of infatuation in his heavy lidded eyes, and always with some money in his pockets. There was no sparkle of any kind on the lazy stream of his life. It flowed through secret places. But his barque seemed a roomy craft, and his taciturn magnanimity accepted as a matter of course the presence of passengers.

Mrs Verloc pursued the visions of seven years' security for Stevie, loyally paid for on her part; of security growing into confidence, into a domestic feeling, stagnant and deep like a placid pool, whose guarded surface hardly shuddered on the occasional passage of Comrade Ossipon, the robust anarchist with shamelessly inviting eyes, whose glance had a corrupt clearness sufficient to enlighten any woman not absolutely imbecile.

A few seconds only had elapsed since the last word had been uttered aloud in the kitchen, and Mrs Verloc was staring already at the vision of an episode not more than a fortnight old. With eyes whose pupils were extremely dilated she stared at the vision of her husband and poor Stevie walking up Brett Street side by side away from the shop. It was the last scene of an existence created by Mrs Verloc's genius; an existence foreign to all grace and charm, without beauty and almost without decency, but admirable in the continuity of feeling and tenacity of purpose. And this last vision had such plastic relief, such nearness of form, such a fidelity of suggestive detail, that it wrung from Mrs Verloc an anguished and faint murmur, reproducing the supreme illusion of her life, an appalled murmur that died out on her blanched lips.

"Might have been father and son."

Mr Verloc stopped, and raised a care-worn face. "Eh? What did you say?" he asked. Receiving no reply, he resumed his sinister tramping. Then with a menacing flourish of a thick, fleshy fist, he burst out:

"Yes. The Embassy people. A pretty lot, ain't they! Before a week's out I'll make some of them wish themselves twenty feet underground. Eh? What?"

He glanced sideways, with his head down. Mrs Verloc gazed at the whitewashed wall. A blank wall—perfectly blank. A blankness to run at and dash your head against. Mrs Verloc remained immovably seated. She kept still as the population of half the globe would keep still in astonishment and despair, were the sun suddenly put out in the summer sky by the perfidy of a trusted providence.

"The Embassy," Mr Verloc began again, after a preliminary grimace which bared his teeth wolfishly. "I wish I could get loose in there with a cudgel for half-an-hour. I would keep on hitting till there wasn't a single unbroken bone left amongst the whole lot. But never mind, I'll teach them yet what it means trying to throw out a man like me to rot in the streets. I've a tongue in my head. All the world shall know what I've done for them. I am not afraid. I don't care. Everything'll come out. Every damned thing. Let them look out!"

In these terms did Mr Verloc declare his thirst for revenge. It was a very appropriate revenge. It was in harmony with the promptings of Mr Verloc's genius. It had also the advantage of being within the range of his powers and of adjusting itself easily to the practice of his life, which had consisted precisely in betraying the secret and unlawful proceedings of his fellow-men. Anarchists or diplomats were all one to him. Mr Verloc was temperamentally no respecter of persons. His scorn was equally distributed over the whole field of his operations. But as a member of a revolutionary proletariat—which he undoubtedly was—he nourished a rather inimical sentiment against social distinction.

"Nothing on earth can stop me now," he added, and paused, looking fixedly at his wife, who was looking fixedly at a blank wall.

The silence in the kitchen was prolonged, and Mr Verloc felt disappointed. He had expected his wife to say something. But Mrs Verloc's lips, composed in their usual form, preserved a statuesque immobility like the rest of her face. And Mr Verloc was disappointed. Yet the occasion did not, he recognised, demand speech from her. She was a woman of very few words. For reasons involved in the very foundation of his psychology, Mr Verloc was inclined to put his trust in any woman who had given herself to him. Therefore he trusted his wife. Their accord was perfect, but it was not precise. It was a tacit accord, congenial to Mrs Verloc's incuriosity and to Mr Verloc's habits of mind, which were indolent and secret. They refrained from going to the bottom of facts and motives.

This reserve, expressing, in a way, their profound confidence in each other, introduced at the same time a certain element of vagueness into their intimacy. No system of conjugal relations is perfect. Mr Verloc presumed that his wife had understood him, but he would have been glad to hear her say what she thought at the moment. It would have been a comfort.

There were several reasons why this comfort was denied him. There was a physical obstacle: Mrs Verloc had no sufficient command over her voice. She did not see any alternative between screaming and silence, and instinctively she chose the silence. Winnie Verloc was temperamentally a silent person. And there was the paralysing atrocity of the thought which occupied her. Her cheeks were blanched, her lips ashy, her immobility amazing. And she thought without looking at Mr Verloc: "This man took the boy away to murder him. He took the boy away from his home to murder him. He took the boy away from me to murder him!"

Mrs Verloc's whole being was racked by that inconclusive and maddening thought. It was in her veins, in her bones, in the roots of her hair. Mentally she assumed the biblical attitude of mourning—the covered face, the rent garments; the sound of wailing and lamentation filled her head. But her teeth were violently clenched, and her tearless eyes were hot with rage, because she was not a submissive creature. The protection she had extended over her brother had been in its origin of a fierce and indignant complexion. She had to love him with a militant love. She had battled for him—even against herself. His loss had the bitterness of defeat, with the anguish of a baffled passion. It was not an ordinary stroke of death. Moreover, it was not death that took Stevie from her. It was Mr Verloc who took him away. She had seen him. She had watched him, without raising a hand, take the boy away. And she had let him go, like—like a fool—a blind fool. Then after he had murdered the boy he came home to her. Just came home like any other man would come home to his wife. . . .

Through her set teeth Mrs Verloc muttered at the wall:

"And I thought he had caught a cold."

Mr Verloc heard these words and appropriated them.

"It was nothing," he said moodily. "I was upset. I was upset on your account."

Mrs Verloc, turning her head slowly, transferred her stare from the wall to her husband's person. Mr Verloc, with the tips of his fingers between his lips, was looking on the ground.

"Can't be helped," he mumbled, letting his hand fall. "You must pull yourself together. You'll want all your wits about you. It is you who brought the police about our ears. Never mind, I won't say anything more about it," continued Mr Verloc magnanimously. "You couldn't know."

"I couldn't," breathed out Mrs Verloc. It was as if a corpse had spoken. Mr Verloc took up the thread of his discourse.

"I don't blame you. I'll make them sit up. Once under lock and key it will be safe enough for me to talk—you understand. You must reckon on me being two years away from you," he continued, in a tone of sincere concern. "It will be easier for you than for me. You'll have something to do, while I—Look here, Winnie, what you must do is to keep this business going for two years. You know enough for that. You've a good head on you. I'll send you word when it's time to go about trying to sell. You'll have to be extra careful. The comrades will be keeping an eye on you all the time. You'll have to be as artful as you know how, and as close as the grave. No one must know what you are going to do. I have no mind to get a knock on the head or a stab in the back directly I am let out."

Thus spoke Mr Verloc, applying his mind with ingenuity and forethought to the problems of the future. His voice was sombre, because he had a correct sentiment of the situation. Everything which he did not wish to pass had come to pass. The future had become precarious. His judgment, perhaps, had been momentarily obscured by his dread of Mr Vladimir's truculent folly. A man somewhat over forty may be excusably thrown into considerable disorder by the prospect of losing his employment, especially if the man is a secret agent of political police, dwelling secure in the consciousness of his high value and in the esteem of high personages. He was excusable.

Now the thing had ended in a crash. Mr Verloc was cool; but he was not cheerful. A secret agent who throws his secrecy to the winds from desire of vengeance, and flaunts his achievements before the public eye, becomes the mark for desperate and bloodthirsty indignations. Without unduly exaggerating the danger, Mr Verloc tried to bring it clearly before his wife's mind. He repeated that he had no intention to let the revolutionists do away with him.

He looked straight into his wife's eyes. The enlarged pupils of the woman received his stare into their unfathomable depths.

"I am too fond of you for that," he said, with a little nervous laugh.

A faint flush coloured Mrs Verloc's ghastly and motionless face. Having done with the visions of the past, she had not only heard, but had also understood the words uttered by her husband. By their extreme disaccord with her mental condition these words produced on her a slightly suffocating effect. Mrs Verloc's mental condition had the merit of simplicity; but it was not sound. It was governed too much by a fixed idea. Every nook and cranny of her brain was filled with the thought that this man, with whom she had lived without distaste for seven years, had taken the "poor boy" away from her in order to kill him—the man to whom she had grown accustomed in body and mind; the man whom she had trusted, took the boy away to kill him! In its form, in its substance, in its effect, which was universal, altering even the aspect of inanimate things, it was a thought to sit still and marvel at for ever and ever. Mrs Verloc sat still. And across that thought (not across the kitchen) the form of Mr Verloc went to and fro, familiarly in hat and overcoat, stamping with his boots upon her brain. He was probably talking too; but Mrs Verloc's thought for the most part covered the voice.

Now and then, however, the voice would make itself heard. Several connected words emerged at times. Their purport was generally hopeful. On each of these occasions Mrs Verloc's dilated pupils, losing their far-off fixity, followed her husband's movements with the effect of black care and impenetrable attention. Well informed upon all matters relating to his secret calling, Mr Verloc augured well for the success of his plans and combinations. He really believed that it would be upon the whole easy for him to escape the knife of infuriated revolutionists. He had exaggerated the strength of their fury and the length of their arm (for professional purposes) too often to have many illusions one way or the other. For to exaggerate with judgment one must begin by measuring with nicety. He knew also how much virtue and how much infamy is forgotten in two years—two long years. His first really confidential discourse to his wife was optimistic from conviction. He also thought it good policy to display all the assurance he could muster. It would put heart into the poor woman. On his liberation, which, harmonising with the whole tenor of his life, would be secret, of course, they would vanish together without loss of time. As to covering up the tracks, he begged his wife to trust him for that. He knew how it was to be done so that the devil himself—

He waved his hand. He seemed to boast. He wished only to put heart into her. It was a benevolent intention, but Mr Verloc had the misfortune not to be in accord with his audience.

The self-confident tone grew upon Mrs Verloc's ear which let most of the words go by; for what were words to her now? What could words do to her, for good or evil in the face of her fixed idea? Her black glance followed that man who was asserting his impunity—the man who had taken poor Stevie from home to kill him somewhere. Mrs Verloc could not remember exactly where, but her heart began to beat very perceptibly.

Mr Verloc, in a soft and conjugal tone, was now expressing his firm belief that there were yet a good few years of quiet life before them both. He did not go into the question of means. A quiet life it must be and, as it were, nestling in the shade, concealed among men whose flesh is grass; modest, like the life of violets. The words used by Mr Verloc were: "Lie low for a bit." And far from England, of course. It was not clear whether Mr Verloc had in his mind Spain or South America; but at any rate somewhere abroad.

This last word, falling into Mrs Verloc's ear, produced a definite impression. This man was talking of going abroad. The impression was completely disconnected; and such is the force of mental habit that Mrs Verloc at once and automatically asked herself: "And what of Stevie?"

It was a sort of forgetfulness; but instantly she became aware that there was no longer any occasion for anxiety on that score. There would never be any occasion any more. The poor boy had been taken out and killed. The poor boy was dead.

This shaking piece of forgetfulness stimulated Mrs Verloc's intelligence. She began to perceive certain consequences which would have surprised Mr Verloc. There was no need for her now to stay there, in that kitchen, in that house, with that man—since the boy was gone for ever. No need whatever. And on that Mrs Verloc rose as if raised by a spring. But neither could she see what there was to keep her in the world at all. And this inability arrested her. Mr Verloc watched her with marital solicitude.

"You're looking more like yourself," he said uneasily. Something peculiar in the blackness of his wife's eyes disturbed his optimism. At that precise moment Mrs Verloc began to look upon herself as released from all earthly ties.

She had her freedom. Her contract with existence, as represented by that man standing over there, was at an end. She was a free woman. Had this view become in some way perceptible to Mr Verloc he would have been extremely shocked. In his affairs of the heart Mr Verloc had been always carelessly generous, yet always with no other idea than that of being loved for himself. Upon this matter, his ethical notions being in agreement with his vanity, he was completely incorrigible. That this should be so in the case of his virtuous and legal connection he was perfectly certain. He had grown older, fatter, heavier, in the belief that he lacked no fascination for being loved for his own sake. When he saw Mrs Verloc starting to walk out of the kitchen without a word he was disappointed.

"Where are you going to?" he called out rather sharply. "Upstairs?"

Mrs Verloc in the doorway turned at the voice. An instinct of prudence born of fear, the excessive fear of being approached and touched by that man, induced her to nod at him slightly (from the height of two steps), with a stir of the lips which the conjugal optimism of Mr Verloc took for a wan and uncertain smile.

"That's right," he encouraged her gruffly. "Rest and quiet's what you want. Go on. It won't be long before I am with you."

Mrs Verloc, the free woman who had had really no idea where she was going to, obeyed the suggestion with rigid steadiness.

Mr Verloc watched her. She disappeared up the stairs. He was disappointed. There was that within him which would have been more satisfied if she had been moved to throw herself upon his breast. But he was generous and indulgent. Winnie was always undemonstrative and silent. Neither was Mr Verloc himself prodigal of endearments and words as a rule. But this was not an ordinary evening. It was an occasion when a man wants to be fortified and strengthened by open proofs of sympathy and affection. Mr Verloc sighed, and put out the gas in the kitchen. Mr Verloc's sympathy with his wife was genuine and intense. It almost brought tears into his eyes as he stood in the parlour reflecting on the loneliness hanging over her head. In this mood Mr Verloc missed Stevie very much out of a difficult world. He thought mournfully of his end. If only that lad had not stupidly destroyed himself!

The sensation of unappeasable hunger, not unknown after the strain of a hazardous enterprise to adventurers of tougher fibre than Mr Verloc, overcame him again. The piece of roast beef, laid out in the likeness of funereal baked meats for Stevie's obsequies, offered itself largely to his notice. And Mr Verloc again partook. He partook ravenously, without restraint and decency, cutting thick slices with the sharp carving knife, and swallowing them without bread. In the course of that refection it occurred to Mr Verloc that he was not hearing his wife move about the bedroom as he should have done. The thought of finding her perhaps sitting on the bed in the dark not only cut Mr Verloc's appetite, but also took from him the inclination to follow her upstairs just yet. Laying down the carving knife, Mr Verloc listened with careworn attention.

He was comforted by hearing her move at last. She walked suddenly across the room, and threw the window up. After a period of stillness up there, during which he figured her to himself with her head out, he heard the sash being lowered slowly. Then she made a few steps, and sat down. Every resonance of his house was familiar to Mr Verloc, who was thoroughly domesticated. When next he heard his wife's footsteps overhead he knew, as well as if he had seen her doing it, that she had been putting on her walking shoes. Mr Verloc wriggled his shoulders slightly at this ominous symptom, and moving away from the table, stood with his back to the fireplace, his head on one side, and gnawing perplexedly at the tips of his fingers. He kept track of her movements by the sound. She walked here and there violently, with abrupt stoppages, now before the chest of drawers, then in front of the wardrobe. An immense load of weariness, the harvest of a day of shocks and surprises, weighed Mr Verloc's energies to the ground.

He did not raise his eyes till he heard his wife descending the stairs. It was as he had guessed. She was dressed for going out.

Mrs Verloc was a free woman. She had thrown open the window of the bedroom either with the intention of screaming Murder! Help! or of throwing herself out. For she did not exactly know what use to make of her freedom. Her personality seemed to have been torn into two pieces, whose mental operations did not adjust themselves very well to each other. The street, silent and deserted from end to end, repelled her by taking sides with that man who was so certain of his impunity. She was afraid to shout lest no one should come. Obviously no one would come. Her instinct of self-preservation recoiled from the depth of the fall into that sort of slimy, deep trench. Mrs Verloc closed the window, and dressed herself to go out into the street by another way. She was a free woman. She had dressed herself thoroughly, down to the tying of a black veil over her face. As she appeared before him in the light of the parlour, Mr Verloc observed that she had even her little handbag hanging from her left wrist. . . . Flying off to her mother, of course.

The thought that women were wearisome creatures after all presented itself to his fatigued brain. But he was too generous to harbour it for more than an instant. This man, hurt cruelly in his vanity, remained magnanimous in his conduct, allowing himself no satisfaction of a bitter smile or of a contemptuous gesture. With true greatness of soul, he only glanced at the wooden clock on the wall, and said in a perfectly calm but forcible manner:

"Five and twenty minutes past eight, Winnie. There's no sense in going over there so late. You will never manage to get back to-night."

Before his extended hand Mrs Verloc had stopped short. He added heavily: "Your mother will be gone to bed before you get there. This is the sort of news that can wait."

Nothing was further from Mrs Verloc's thoughts than going to her mother. She recoiled at the mere idea, and feeling a chair behind her, she obeyed the suggestion of the touch, and sat down. Her intention had been simply to get outside the door for ever. And if this feeling was correct, its mental form took an unrefined shape corresponding to her origin and station. "I would rather walk the streets all the days of my life," she thought. But this creature, whose moral nature had been subjected to a shock of which, in the physical order, the most violent earthquake of history could only be a faint and languid rendering, was at the mercy of mere trifles, of casual contacts. She sat down. With her hat and veil she had the air of a visitor, of having looked in on Mr Verloc for a moment. Her instant docility encouraged him, whilst her aspect of only temporary and silent acquiescence provoked him a little.

"Let me tell you, Winnie," he said with authority, "that your place is here this evening. Hang it all! you brought the damned police high and low about my ears. I don't blame you —but it's your doing all the same. You'd better take this confounded hat off. I can't let you go out, old girl," he added in a softened voice.

Mrs Verloc's mind got hold of that declaration with morbid tenacity. The man who had taken Stevie out from under her very eyes to murder him in a locality whose name was at the moment not present to her memory would not allow her go out. Of course he wouldn't.

Now he had murdered Stevie he would never let her go. He would want to keep her for nothing. And on this characteristic reasoning, having all the force of insane logic, Mrs Verloc's disconnected wits went to work practically. She could slip by him, open the door, run out. But he would dash out after her, seize her round the body, drag her back into the shop. She could scratch, kick, and bite—and stab too; but for stabbing she wanted a knife. Mrs Verloc sat still under her black veil, in her own house, like a masked and mysterious visitor of impenetrable intentions.

Mr Verloc's magnanimity was not more than human. She had exasperated him at last.

"Can't you say something? You have your own dodges for vexing a man. Oh yes! I know your deaf-and-dumb trick. I've seen you at it before to-day. But just now it won't do. And to begin with, take this damned thing off. One can't tell whether one is talking to a dummy or to a live woman."

He advanced, and stretching out his hand, dragged the veil off, unmasking a still, unreadable face, against which his nervous exasperation was shattered like a glass bubble flung against a rock. "That's better," he said, to cover his momentary uneasiness, and retreated back to his old station by the mantelpiece. It never entered his head that his wife could give him up. He felt a little ashamed of himself, for he was fond and generous. What could he do? Everything had been said already. He protested vehemently.

"By heavens! You know that I hunted high and low. I ran the risk of giving myself away to find somebody for that accursed job. And I tell you again I couldn't find anyone crazy enough or hungry enough. What do you take me for—a murderer, or what? The boy is gone. Do you think I wanted him to blow himself up? He's gone. His troubles are over. Ours are just going to begin, I tell you, precisely because he did blow himself. I don't blame you. But just try to understand that it was a pure accident; as much an accident as if he had been run over by a 'bus while crossing the street."

His generosity was not infinite, because he was a human being—and not a monster, as Mrs Verloc believed him to be. He paused, and a snarl lifting his moustaches above a gleam of white teeth gave him the expression of a reflective beast, not very dangerous—a slow beast with a sleek head, gloomier than a seal, and with a husky voice.

"And when it comes to that, it's as much your doing as mine. That's so. You may glare as much as you like. I know what you can do in that way. Strike me dead if I ever would have thought of the lad for that purpose. It was you who kept on shoving him in my way when I was half distracted with the worry of keeping the lot of us out of trouble. What the devil made you? One would think you were doing it on purpose. And I am damned if I know that you didn't. There's no saying how much of what's going on you have got hold of on the sly with your infernal don't-care-a-damn way of looking nowhere in particular, and saying nothing at all. . . . "

His husky domestic voice ceased for a while. Mrs Verloc made no reply. Before that silence he felt ashamed of what he had said. But as often happens to peaceful men in domestic tiffs, being ashamed he pushed another point.

"You have a devilish way of holding your tongue sometimes," he began again, without raising his voice. "Enough to make some men go mad. It's lucky for you that I am not so easily put out as some of them would be by your deaf-and-dumb sulks. I am fond of you. But don't you go too far. This isn't the time for it. We ought to be thinking of what we've got to do. And I can't let you go out to-night, galloping off to your mother with some crazy tale or other about me. I won't have it. Don't you make any mistake about it: if you will have it that I killed the boy, then you've killed him as much as I."

In sincerity of feeling and openness of statement, these words went far beyond anything that had ever been said in this home, kept up on the wages of a secret industry eked out by the sale of more or less secret wares: the poor expedients devised by a mediocre mankind for preserving an imperfect society from the dangers of moral and physical corruption, both secret too of their kind. They were spoken because Mr Verloc had felt himself really outraged; but the reticent decencies of this home life, nestling in a shady street behind a shop where the sun never shone, remained apparently undisturbed. Mrs Verloc heard him out with perfect propriety, and then rose from her chair in her hat and jacket like a visitor at the end of a call. She advanced towards her husband, one arm extended as if for a silent leave-taking. Her net veil dangling down by one end on the left side of her face gave an air of disorderly formality to her restrained movements. But when she arrived as far as the hearthrug, Mr Verloc was no longer standing there. He had moved off in the direction of the sofa, without raising his eyes to watch the effect of his tirade. He was tired, resigned in a truly marital spirit. But he felt hurt in the tender spot of his secret weakness. If she would go on sulking in that dreadful overcharged silence—why then she must. She was a master in that domestic art. Mr Verloc flung himself heavily upon the sofa, disregarding as usual the fate of his hat, which, as if accustomed to take care of itself, made for a safe shelter under the table.

He was tired. The last particle of his nervous force had been expended in the wonders and agonies of this day full of surprising failures coming at the end of a harassing month of scheming and insomnia. He was tired. A man isn't made of stone. Hang everything! Mr Verloc reposed characteristically, clad in his outdoor garments. One side of his open overcoat was lying partly on the ground. Mr Verloc wallowed on his back. But he longed for a more perfect rest—for sleep—for a few hours of delicious forgetfulness. That would come later. Provisionally he rested. And he thought: "I wish she would give over this damned nonsense. It's exasperating."

There must have been something imperfect in Mrs Verloc's sentiment of regained freedom. Instead of taking the way of the door she leaned back, with her shoulders against the tablet of the mantelpiece, as a wayfarer rests against a fence. A tinge of wildness in her aspect was derived from the black veil hanging like a rag against her cheek, and from the fixity of her black gaze where the light of the room was absorbed and lost without the trace of a single gleam. This woman, capable of a bargain the mere suspicion of which would have been infinitely shocking to Mr Verloc's idea of love, remained irresolute, as if scrupulously aware of something wanting on her part for the formal closing of the transaction.

On the sofa Mr Verloc wriggled his shoulders into perfect comfort, and from the fulness of his heart emitted a wish which was certainly as pious as anything likely to come from such a source.

"I wish to goodness," he growled huskily, "I had never seen Greenwich Park or anything belonging to it."

The veiled sound filled the small room with its moderate volume, well adapted to the modest nature of the wish. The waves of air of the proper length, propagated in accordance with correct mathematical formulas, flowed around all the inanimate things in the room, lapped against Mrs Verloc's head as if it had been a head of stone. And incredible as it may appear, the eyes of Mrs Verloc seemed to grow still larger. The audible wish of Mr Verloc's overflowing heart flowed into an empty place in his wife's memory. Greenwich Park. A park! That's where the boy was killed. A park—smashed branches, torn leaves, gravel, bits of brotherly flesh and bone, all spouting up together in the manner of a firework. She remembered now what she had heard, and she remembered it pictorially. They had to gather him up with the shovel. Trembling all over with irrepressible shudders, she saw before her the very implement with its ghastly load scraped up from the ground. Mrs Verloc closed her eyes desperately, throwing upon that vision the night of her eyelids, where after a rainlike fall of mangled limbs the decapitated head of Stevie lingered suspended alone, and fading out slowly like the last star of a pyrotechnic display. Mrs Verloc opened her eyes.

Her face was no longer stony. Anybody could have noted the subtle change on her features, in the stare of her eyes, giving her a new and startling expression; an expression seldom observed by competent persons under the conditions of leisure and security demanded for thorough analysis, but whose meaning could not be mistaken at a glance. Mrs Verloc's doubts as to the end of the bargain no longer existed; her wits, no longer disconnected, were working under the control of her will. But Mr Verloc observed nothing. He was reposing in that pathetic condition of optimism induced by excess of fatigue. He did not want any more trouble—with his wife too—of all people in the world. He had been unanswerable in his vindication. He was loved for himself. The present phase of her silence he interpreted favourably. This was the time to make it up with her. The silence had lasted long enough. He broke it by calling to her in an undertone.

"Winnie."

"Yes," answered obediently Mrs Verloc the free woman. She commanded her wits now, her vocal organs; she felt herself to be in an almost preternaturally perfect control of every fibre of her body. It was all her own, because the bargain was at an end. She was clear sighted. She had become cunning. She chose to answer him so readily for a purpose. She did not wish that man to change his position on the sofa which was very suitable to the circumstances. She succeeded. The man did not stir. But after answering him she remained leaning negligently against the mantelpiece in the attitude of a resting wayfarer. She was unhurried. Her brow was smooth. The head and shoulders of Mr Verloc were hidden from her by the high side of the sofa. She kept her eyes fixed on his feet.

She remained thus mysteriously still and suddenly collected till Mr Verloc was heard with an accent of marital authority, and moving slightly to make room for her to sit on the edge of the sofa.

"Come here," he said in a peculiar tone, which might have been the tone of brutality, but was intimately known to Mrs Verloc as the note of wooing.

She started forward at once, as if she were still a loyal woman bound to that man by an unbroken contract. Her right hand skimmed slightly the end of the table, and when she had passed on towards the sofa the carving knife had vanished without the slightest sound from the side of the dish. Mr Verloc heard the creaky plank in the floor, and was content. He waited. Mrs Verloc was coming. As if the homeless soul of Stevie had flown for shelter straight to the breast of his sister, guardian and protector, the resemblance of her face with that of her brother grew at every step, even to the droop of the lower lip, even to the slight divergence of the eyes. But Mr Verloc did not see that. He was lying on his back and staring upwards. He saw partly on the ceiling and partly on the wall the moving shadow of an arm with a clenched hand holding a carving knife. It flickered up and down. Its movements were leisurely. They were leisurely enough for Mr Verloc to recognise the limb and the weapon.

They were leisurely enough for him to take in the full meaning of the portent, and to taste the flavour of death rising in his gorge. His wife had gone raving mad—murdering mad. They were leisurely enough for the first paralysing effect of this discovery to pass away before a resolute determination to come out victorious from the ghastly struggle with that armed lunatic. They were leisurely enough for Mr Verloc to elaborate a plan of defence involving a dash behind the table, and the felling of the woman to the ground with a heavy wooden chair. But they were not leisurely enough to allow Mr Verloc the time to move either hand or foot. The knife was already planted in his breast. It met no resistance on its way. Hazard has such accuracies. Into that plunging blow, delivered over the side of the couch, Mrs Verloc had put all the inheritance of her immemorial and obscure descent, the simple ferocity of the age of caverns, and the unbalanced nervous fury of the age of bar-rooms. Mr Verloc, the Secret Agent, turning slightly on his side with the force of the blow, expired without stirring a limb, in the muttered sound of the word "Don't" by way of protest.

Mrs Verloc had let go the knife, and her extraordinary resemblance to her late brother had faded, had become very ordinary now. She drew a deep breath, the first easy breath since Chief Inspector Heat had exhibited to her the labelled piece of Stevie's overcoat. She leaned forward on her folded arms over the side of the sofa. She adopted that easy attitude not in order to watch or gloat over the body of Mr Verloc, but because of the undulatory and swinging movements of the parlour, which for some time behaved as though it were at sea in a tempest. She was giddy but calm. She had become a free woman with a perfection of freedom which left her nothing to desire and absolutely nothing to do, since Stevie's urgent claim on her devotion no longer existed. Mrs Verloc, who thought in images, was not troubled now by visions, because she did not think at all. And she did not move. She was a woman enjoying her complete irresponsibility and endless leisure, almost in the manner of a corpse. She did not move, she did not think. Neither did the mortal envelope of the late Mr Verloc reposing on the sofa. Except for the fact that Mrs Verloc breathed these two would have been perfect in accord: that accord of prudent reserve without superfluous words, and sparing of signs, which had been the foundation of their respectable home life. For it had been respectable, covering by a decent reticence the problems that may arise in the practice of a secret profession and the commerce of shady wares. To the last its decorum had remained undisturbed by unseemly shrieks and other misplaced sincerities of conduct. And after the striking of the blow, this respectability was continued in immobility and silence.

Nothing moved in the parlour till Mrs Verloc raised her head slowly and looked at the clock with inquiring mistrust. She had become aware of a ticking sound in the room. It grew upon her ear, while she remembered clearly that the clock on the wall was silent, had no audible tick. What did it mean by beginning to tick so loudly all of a sudden? Its face indicated ten minutes to nine. Mrs Verloc cared nothing for time, and the ticking went on. She concluded it could not be the clock, and her sullen gaze moved along the walls, wavered, and became vague, while she strained her hearing to locate the sound. Tic, tic, tic.

After listening for some time Mrs Verloc lowered her gaze deliberately on her husband's body. Its attitude of repose was so home-like and familiar that she could do so without feeling embarrassed by any pronounced novelty in the phenomena of her home life. Mr Verloc was taking his habitual ease. He looked comfortable.

By the position of the body the face of Mr Verloc was not visible to Mrs Verloc, his widow. Her fine, sleepy eyes, travelling downward on the track of the sound, became contemplative on meeting a flat object of bone which protruded a little beyond the edge of the sofa. It was the handle of the domestic carving knife with nothing strange about it but its position at right angles to Mr Verloc's waistcoat and the fact that something dripped from it. Dark drops fell on the floorcloth one after another, with a sound of ticking growing fast and furious like the pulse of an insane clock. At its highest speed this ticking changed into a continuous sound of trickling. Mrs Verloc watched that transformation with shadows of anxiety coming and going on her face. It was a trickle, dark, swift, thin. . . . Blood!

At this unforeseen circumstance Mrs Verloc abandoned her pose of idleness and irresponsibility.

With a sudden snatch at her skirts and a faint shriek she ran to the door, as if the trickle had been the first sign of a destroying flood. Finding the table in her way she gave it a push with both hands as though it had been alive, with such force that it went for some distance on its four legs, making a loud, scraping racket, whilst the big dish with the joint crashed heavily on the floor.

Then all became still. Mrs Verloc on reaching the door had stopped. A round hat disclosed in the middle of the floor by the moving of the table rocked slightly on its crown in the wind of her flight.

12

Winnie Verloc, the widow of Mr Verloc, the sister of the late faithful Stevie (blown to fragments in a state of innocence and in the conviction of being engaged in a humanitarian enterprise), did not run beyond the door of the parlour. She had indeed run away so far from a mere trickle of blood, but that was a movement of instinctive repulsion. And there she had paused, with staring eyes and lowered head. As though she had run through long years in her flight across the small parlour, Mrs Verloc by the door was quite a different person from the woman who had been leaning over the sofa, a little swimmy in her head, but otherwise free to enjoy the profound calm of idleness and irresponsibility. Mrs Verloc was no longer giddy. Her head was steady. On the other hand, she was no longer calm. She was afraid.

If she avoided looking in the direction of her reposing husband it was not because she was afraid of him. Mr Verloc was not frightful to behold. He looked comfortable. Moreover, he was dead. Mrs Verloc entertained no vain delusions on the subject of the dead. Nothing brings them back, neither love nor hate. They can do nothing to you. They are as nothing. Her mental state was tinged by a sort of austere contempt for that man who had let himself be killed so easily. He had been the master of a house, the husband of a woman, and the murderer of her Stevie. And now he was of no account in every respect. He was of less practical account than the clothing on his body, than his overcoat, than his boots—than that hat lying on the floor. He was nothing. He was not worth looking at. He was even no longer the murderer of poor Stevie. The only murderer that would be found in the room when people came to look for Mr Verloc would be—herself!

Her hands shook so that she failed twice in the task of refastening her veil. Mrs Verloc was no longer a person of leisure and responsibility. She was afraid. The stabbing of Mr Verloc had been only a blow. It had relieved the pent-up agony of shrieks strangled in her throat, of tears dried up in her hot eyes, of the maddening and indignant rage at the atrocious part played by that man, who was less than nothing now, in robbing her of the boy.

It had been an obscurely prompted blow. The blood trickling on the floor off the handle of the knife had turned it into an extremely plain case of murder. Mrs Verloc, who always refrained from looking deep into things, was compelled to look into the very bottom of this thing. She saw there no haunting face, no reproachful shade, no vision of remorse, no sort of ideal conception. She saw there an object. That object was the gallows. Mrs Verloc was afraid of the gallows.

She was terrified of them ideally. Having never set eyes on that last argument of men's justice except in illustrative woodcuts to a certain type of tales, she first saw them erect against a black and stormy background, festooned with chains and human bones, circled about by birds that peck at dead men's eyes. This was frightful enough, but Mrs Verloc, though not a well-informed woman, had a sufficient knowledge of the institutions of her country to know that gallows are no longer erected romantically on the banks of dismal rivers or on wind-swept headlands, but in the yards of jails. There within four high walls, as if into a pit, at dawn of day, the murderer was brought out to be executed, with a horrible quietness and, as the reports in the newspapers always said, "in the presence of the authorities." With her eyes staring on the floor, her nostrils quivering with anguish and shame, she imagined herself all alone amongst a lot of strange gentlemen in silk hats who were calmly proceeding about the business of hanging her by the neck. That—never! Never! And how was it done? The impossibility of imagining the details of such quiet execution added something maddening to her abstract terror. The newspapers never gave any details except one, but that one with some affectation was always there at the end of a meagre report. Mrs Verloc remembered its nature. It came with a cruel burning pain into her head, as if the words "The drop given was fourteen feet" had been scratched on her brain with a hot needle. "The drop given was fourteen feet."

These words affected her physically too. Her throat became convulsed in waves to resist strangulation; and the apprehension of the jerk was so vivid that she seized her head in both hands as if to save it from being torn off her shoulders. "The drop given was fourteen feet." No! that must never be. She could not stand *that*. The thought of it even was not bearable. She could not stand thinking of it. Therefore Mrs Verloc formed the resolution to go at once and throw herself into the river off one of the bridges.

This time she managed to refasten her veil. With her face as if masked, all black from head to foot except for some flowers in her hat, she looked up mechanically at the clock. She thought it must have stopped. She could not believe that only two minutes had passed since she had looked at it last. Of course not. It had been stopped all the time. As a matter of fact, only three minutes had elapsed from the moment she had drawn the first deep, easy breath after the blow, to this moment when Mrs Verloc formed the resolution to drown herself in the Thames. But Mrs Verloc could not believe that. She seemed to have heard or read that clocks and watches always stopped at the moment of murder for the undoing of the murderer. She did not care. "To the bridge—and over I go." . . . But her movements were slow.

She dragged herself painfully across the shop, and had to hold on to the handle of the door before she found the necessary fortitude to open it. The street frightened her, since it led either to the gallows or to the river. She floundered over the doorstep head forward, arms thrown out, like a person falling over the parapet of a bridge. This entrance into the open air had a foretaste of drowning; a slimy dampness enveloped her, entered her nostrils, clung to her hair. It was not actually raining, but each gas lamp had a rusty little halo of mist. The van and horses were gone, and in the black street the curtained window of the carters' eating-house made a square patch of soiled blood-red light glowing faintly very near the level of the pavement. Mrs Verloc, dragging herself slowly towards it, thought that she was a very friendless woman. It was true. It was so true that, in a sudden longing to see some friendly face, she could think of no one else but of Mrs Neale, the charwoman. She had no acquaintances of her own. Nobody would miss her in a social way. It must not be imagined that the Widow Verloc had forgotten her mother. This was not so. Winnie had been a good daughter because she had been a devoted sister. Her mother had always leaned on her for support. No consolation or advice could be expected there. Now that Stevie was dead the bond seemed to be broken. She could not face the old woman with the horrible tale. Moreover, it was too far. The river was her present destination. Mrs Verloc tried to forget her mother.

Each step cost her an effort of will which seemed the last possible. Mrs Verloc had dragged herself past the red glow of the eating-house window. "To the bridge—and over I go," she repeated to herself with fierce obstinacy. She put out her hand just in time to steady herself against a lamp-post. "I'll never get there before morning," she thought. The fear of death paralysed her efforts to escape the gallows. It seemed to her she had been staggering in that street for hours. "I'll never get there," she thought. "They'll find me knocking about the streets. It's too far." She held on, panting under her black veil.

"The drop given was fourteen feet."

She pushed the lamp-post away from her violently, and found herself walking. But another wave of faintness overtook her like a great sea, washing away her heart clean out of her breast. "I will never get there," she muttered, suddenly arrested, swaying lightly where she stood. "Never."

And perceiving the utter impossibility of walking as far as the nearest bridge, Mrs Verloc thought of a flight abroad.

It came to her suddenly. Murderers escaped. They escaped abroad. Spain or California. Mere names. The vast world created for the glory of man was only a vast blank to Mrs Verloc. She did not know which way to turn. Murderers had friends, relations, helpers—they had knowledge. She had nothing. She was the most lonely of murderers that ever struck a mortal blow. She was alone in London: and the whole town of marvels and mud, with its maze of streets and its mass of lights, was sunk in a hopeless night, rested at the bottom of a black abyss from which no unaided woman could hope to scramble out.

She swayed forward, and made a fresh start blindly, with an awful dread of falling down; but at the end of a few steps, unexpectedly, she found a sensation of support, of security. Raising her head, she saw a man's face peering closely at her veil. Comrade Ossipon was not afraid of strange women, and no feeling of false delicacy could prevent him from striking an acquaintance with a woman apparently very much intoxicated. Comrade Ossipon was interested in women. He held up this one between his two large palms, peering at her in a business-like way till he heard her say faintly "Mr Ossipon!" and then he very nearly let her drop to the ground.

"Mrs Verloc!" he exclaimed. "You here!"

It seemed impossible to him that she should have been drinking. But one never knows. He did not go into that question, but attentive not to discourage kind fate surrendering to him the widow of Comrade Verloc, he tried to draw her to his breast. To his astonishment she came quite easily, and even rested on his arm for a moment before she attempted to disengage herself. Comrade Ossipon would not be brusque with kind fate. He withdrew his arm in a natural way.

"You recognised me," she faltered out, standing before him, fairly steady on her legs.

"Of course I did," said Ossipon with perfect readiness. "I was afraid you were going to fall. I've thought of you too often lately not to recognise you anywhere, at any time. I've always thought of you—ever since I first set eyes on you."

Mrs Verloc seemed not to hear. "You were coming to the shop?" she said nervously.

"Yes; at once," answered Ossipon. "Directly I read the paper."

In fact, Comrade Ossipon had been skulking for a good two hours in the neighbourhood of Brett Street, unable to make up his mind for a bold move. The robust anarchist was not exactly a bold conqueror. He remembered that Mrs Verloc had never responded to his glances by the slightest sign of encouragement. Besides, he thought the shop might be watched by the police, and Comrade Ossipon did not wish the police to form an exaggerated notion of his revolutionary sympathies. Even now he did not know precisely what to do. In comparison with his usual amatory speculations this was a big and serious undertaking. He ignored how much there was in it and how far he would have to go in order to get hold of what there was to get—supposing there was a chance at all. These perplexities checking his elation imparted to his tone a soberness well in keeping with the circumstances.

"May I ask you where you were going?" he inquired in a subdued voice.

"Don't ask me!" cried Mrs Verloc with a shuddering, repressed violence. All her strong vitality recoiled from the idea of death. "Never mind where I was going. . . ."

Ossipon concluded that she was very much excited but perfectly sober. She remained silent by his side for moment, then all at once she did something which he did not expect. She slipped her hand under his arm. He was startled by the act itself certainly, and quite as much too by the palpably resolute character of this movement. But this being a delicate affair, Comrade Ossipon behaved with delicacy. He contented himself by pressing the hand slightly against his robust ribs. At the same time he felt himself being impelled forward, and yielded to the impulse. At the end of Brett Street he became aware of being directed to the left. He submitted.

The fruiterer at the corner had put out the blazing glory of his oranges and lemons, and Brett Place was all darkness, interspersed with the misty halos of the few lamps defining its triangular shape, with a cluster of three lights on one stand in the middle. The dark forms of the man and woman glided slowly arm in arm along the walls with a loverlike and homeless aspect in the miserable night.

"What would you say if I were to tell you that I was going to find you?" Mrs Verloc asked, gripping his arm with force.

"I would say that you couldn't find anyone more ready to help you in your trouble," answered Ossipon, with a notion of making tremendous headway. In fact, the progress of this delicate affair was almost taking his breath away.

"In my trouble!" Mrs Verloc repeated slowly.

"Yes."

"And do you know what my trouble is?" she whispered with strange intensity.

"Ten minutes after seeing the evening paper," explained Ossipon with ardour, "I met a fellow whom you may have seen once or twice at the shop perhaps, and I had a talk with him which left no doubt whatever in my mind. Then I started for here, wondering whether you—I've been fond of you beyond words ever since I set eyes on your face," he cried, as if unable to command his feelings.

Comrade Ossipon assumed correctly that no woman was capable of wholly disbelieving such a statement. But he did not know that Mrs Verloc accepted it with all the fierceness the instinct of self-preservation puts into the grip of a drowning person. To the widow of Mr Verloc the robust anarchist was like a radiant messenger of life.

They walked slowly, in step. "I thought so," Mrs Verloc murmured faintly.

"You've read it in my eyes," suggested Ossipon with great assurance.

"Yes," she breathed out into his inclined ear.

"A love like mine could not be concealed from a woman like you," he went on, trying to detach his mind from material considerations such as the business value of the shop, and the amount of money Mr Verloc might have left in the bank. He applied himself to the sentimental side of the affair. In his heart of hearts he was a little shocked at his success. Verloc had been a good fellow, and certainly a very decent husband as far as one could see. However, Comrade Ossipon was not going to quarrel with his luck for the sake of a dead man. Resolutely he suppressed his sympathy for the ghost of Comrade Verloc, and went on.

"I could not conceal it. I was too full of you. I daresay you could not help seeing it in my eyes. But I could not guess it. You were always so distant. . . ."

"What else did you expect?" burst out Mrs Verloc. "I was a respectable woman—"

She paused, then added, as if speaking to herself, in sinister resentment: "Till he made me what I am."

Ossipon let that pass, and took up his running. "He never did seem to me to be quite worthy of you," he began, throwing loyalty to the winds. "You were worthy of a better fate."

Mrs Verloc interrupted bitterly:

"Better fate! He cheated me out of seven years of life."

"You seemed to live so happily with him." Ossipon tried to exculpate the lukewarmness of his past conduct. "It's that what's made me timid. You seemed to love him. I was surprised—and jealous," he added.

"Love him!" Mrs Verloc cried out in a whisper, full of scorn and rage. "Love him! I was a good wife to him. I am a respectable woman. You thought I loved him! You did! Look here, Tom—"

The sound of this name thrilled Comrade Ossipon with pride. For his name was Alexander, and he was called Tom by arrangement with the most familiar of his intimates. It was a name of friendship—of moments of expansion. He had no idea that she had ever heard it used by anybody. It was apparent that she had not only caught it, but had treasured it in her memory—perhaps in her heart.

"Look here, Tom! I was a young girl. I was done up. I was tired. I had two people depending on what I could do, and it did seem as if I couldn't do any more. Two people—mother and the boy. He was much more mine than mother's. I sat up nights and nights with him on my lap, all alone upstairs, when I wasn't more than eight years old myself. And then —He was mine, I tell you. . . . You can't understand that. No man can understand it. What was I to do? There was a young fellow—"

The memory of the early romance with the young butcher survived, tenacious, like the image of a glimpsed ideal in that heart quailing before the fear of the gallows and full of revolt against death.

"That was the man I loved then," went on the widow of Mr Verloc. "I suppose he could see it in my eyes too. Five and twenty shillings a week, and his father threatened to kick him out of the business if he made such a fool of himself as to marry a girl with a crippled mother and a crazy idiot of a boy on her hands. But he would hang about me, till one evening I found the courage to slam the door in his face. I had to do it. I loved him dearly. Five and twenty shillings a week! There was that other man—a good lodger. What is a girl to do? Could I've gone on the streets? He seemed kind. He wanted me, anyhow. What was I to do with mother and that poor boy? Eh? I said yes. He seemed good-natured, he was freehanded, he had money, he never said anything. Seven years—seven years a good wife to him, the kind, the good, the generous, the—And he loved me. Oh yes. He loved me till I sometimes wished myself—Seven years. Seven years a wife to him. And do you know what he was, that dear friend of yours? Do you know what he was? He was a devil!"

The superhuman vehemence of that whispered statement completely stunned Comrade Ossipon. Winnie Verloc turning about held him by both arms, facing him under the falling mist in the darkness and solitude of Brett Place, in which all sounds of life seemed lost as if in a triangular well of asphalt and bricks, of blind houses and unfeeling stones.

"No; I didn't know," he declared, with a sort of flabby stupidity, whose comical aspect was lost upon a woman haunted by the fear of the gallows, "but I do now. I—I understand," he floundered on, his mind speculating as to what sort of atrocities Verloc could have practised under the sleepy, placid appearances of his married estate. It was positively awful. "I understand," he repeated, and then by a sudden inspiration uttered an—"Unhappy woman!" of lofty commiseration instead of the more familiar "Poor darling!" of his usual practice. This was no usual case. He felt conscious of something abnormal going on, while he never lost sight of the greatness of the stake. "Unhappy, brave woman!"

He was glad to have discovered that variation; but he could discover nothing else.

"Ah, but he is dead now," was the best he could do. And he put a remarkable amount of animosity into his guarded exclamation. Mrs Verloc caught at his arm with a sort of frenzy.

"You guessed then he was dead," she murmured, as if beside herself. "You! You guessed what I had to do. Had to!"

There were suggestions of triumph, relief, gratitude in the indefinable tone of these words. It engrossed the whole attention of Ossipon to the detriment of mere literal sense. He wondered what was up with her, why she had worked herself into this state of wild excitement. He even began to wonder whether the hidden causes of that Greenwich Park affair did not lie deep in the unhappy circumstances of the Verlocs' married life. He went so far as to suspect Mr Verloc of having selected that extraordinary manner of committing suicide. By Jove! that would account for the utter inanity and wrong-headedness of the thing. No anarchist manifestation was required by the circumstances. Quite the contrary; and Verloc was as well aware of that as any other revolutionist of his standing. What an immense joke if Verloc had simply made fools of the whole of Europe, of the revolutionary world, of the police, of the press, and of the cocksure Professor as well. Indeed, thought Ossipon, in astonishment, it seemed almost certain that he did! Poor beggar! It struck him as very possible that of that household of two it wasn't precisely the man who was the devil.

Alexander Ossipon, nicknamed the Doctor, was naturally inclined to think indulgently of his men friends. He eyed Mrs Verloc hanging on his arm. Of his women friends he thought in a specially practical way. Why Mrs Verloc should exclaim at his knowledge of Mr Verloc's death, which was no guess at all, did not disturb him beyond measure. They often talked like lunatics. But he was curious to know how she had been informed. The papers could tell her nothing beyond the mere fact: the man blown to pieces in Greenwich Park not having been identified. It was inconceivable on any theory that Verloc should have given her an inkling of his intention—whatever it was. This problem interested Comrade Ossipon immensely. He stopped short. They had gone then along the three sides of Brett Place, and were near the end of Brett Street again.

"How did you first come to hear of it?" he asked in a tone he tried to render appropriate to the character of the revelations which had been made to him by the woman at his side.

She shook violently for a while before she answered in a listless voice.

"From the police. A chief inspector came, Chief Inspector Heat he said he was. He showed me—"

Mrs Verloc choked. "Oh, Tom, they had to gather him up with a shovel."

Her breast heaved with dry sobs. In a moment Ossipon found his tongue.

"The police! Do you mean to say the police came already? That Chief Inspector Heat himself actually came to tell you."

"Yes," she confirmed in the same listless tone. "He came just like this. He came. I didn't know. He showed me a piece of overcoat, and—just like that. Do you know this? he says."

"Heat! Heat! And what did he do?"

Mrs Verloc's head dropped. "Nothing. He did nothing. He went away. The police were on that man's side," she murmured tragically. "Another one came too."

"Another—another inspector, do you mean?" asked Ossipon, in great excitement, and very much in the tone of a scared child.

"I don't know. He came. He looked like a foreigner. He may have been one of them Embassy people."

Comrade Ossipon nearly collapsed under this new shock.

"Embassy! Are you aware what you are saying? What Embassy? What on earth do you mean by Embassy?"

"It's that place in Chesham Square. The people he cursed so. I don't know. What does it matter!"

"And that fellow, what did he do or say to you?"

"I don't remember. . . . Nothing . . . . I don't care. Don't ask me," she pleaded in a weary voice.

"All right. I won't," assented Ossipon tenderly. And he meant it too, not because he was touched by the pathos of the pleading voice, but because he felt himself losing his footing in the depths of this tenebrous affair. Police! Embassy! Phew! For fear of adventuring his intelligence into ways where its natural lights might fail to guide it safely he dismissed resolutely all suppositions, surmises, and theories out of his mind. He had the woman there, absolutely flinging herself at him, and that was the principal consideration. But after what he had heard nothing could astonish him any more. And when Mrs Verloc, as if startled suddenly out of a dream of safety, began to urge upon him wildly the necessity of an immediate flight on the Continent, he did not exclaim in the least. He simply said with unaffected regret that there was no train till the morning, and stood looking thoughtfully at her face, veiled in black net, in the light of a gas lamp veiled in a gauze of mist.

Near him, her black form merged in the night, like a figure half chiselled out of a block of black stone. It was impossible to say what she knew, how deep she was involved with policemen and Embassies. But if she wanted to get away, it was not for him to object. He was anxious to be off himself. He felt that the business, the shop so strangely familiar to chief inspectors and members of foreign Embassies, was not the place for him. That must be dropped. But there was the rest. These savings. The money!

"You must hide me till the morning somewhere," she said in a dismayed voice.

"Fact is, my dear, I can't take you where I live. I share the room with a friend."

He was somewhat dismayed himself. In the morning the blessed 'tecs will be out in all the stations, no doubt. And if they once got hold of her, for one reason or another she would be lost to him indeed.

"But you must. Don't you care for me at all—at all? What are you thinking of?"

She said this violently, but she let her clasped hands fall in discouragement. There was a silence, while the mist fell, and darkness reigned undisturbed over Brett Place. Not a soul, not even the vagabond, lawless, and amorous soul of a cat, came near the man and the woman facing each other.

"It would be possible perhaps to find a safe lodging somewhere," Ossipon spoke at last. "But the truth is, my dear, I have not enough money to go and try with—only a few pence. We revolutionists are not rich."

He had fifteen shillings in his pocket. He added:

"And there's the journey before us, too—first thing in the morning at that."

She did not move, made no sound, and Comrade Ossipon's heart sank a little. Apparently she had no suggestion to offer. Suddenly she clutched at her breast, as if she had felt a sharp pain there.

"But I have," she gasped. "I have the money. I have enough money. Tom! Let us go from here."

"How much have you got?" he inquired, without stirring to her tug; for he was a cautious man.

"I have the money, I tell you. All the money."

"What do you mean by it? All the money there was in the bank, or what?" he asked incredulously, but ready not to be surprised at anything in the way of luck.

"Yes, yes!" she said nervously. "All there was. I've it all."

"How on earth did you manage to get hold of it already?" he marvelled.

"He gave it to me," she murmured, suddenly subdued and trembling. Comrade Ossipon put down his rising surprise with a firm hand.

"Why, then—we are saved," he uttered slowly.

She leaned forward, and sank against his breast. He welcomed her there. She had all the money. Her hat was in the way of very marked effusion; her veil too. He was adequate in his manifestations, but no more. She received them without resistance and without abandonment, passively, as if only half-sensible. She freed herself from his lax embraces without difficulty.

"You will save me, Tom," she broke out, recoiling, but still keeping her hold on him by the two lapels of his damp coat. "Save me. Hide me. Don't let them have me. You must kill me first. I couldn't do it myself—I couldn't, I couldn't—not even for what I am afraid of."

She was confoundedly bizarre, he thought. She was beginning to inspire him with an indefinite uneasiness. He said surlily, for he was busy with important thoughts:

"What the devil *are* you afraid of?"

"Haven't you guessed what I was driven to do!" cried the woman. Distracted by the vividness of her dreadful apprehensions, her head ringing with forceful words, that kept the horror of her position before her mind, she had imagined her incoherence to be clearness itself. She had no conscience of how little she had audibly said in the disjointed phrases completed only in her thought. She had felt the relief of a full confession, and she gave a special meaning to every sentence spoken by Comrade Ossipon, whose knowledge did not in the least resemble her own. "Haven't you guessed what I was driven to do!" Her voice fell. "You needn't be long in guessing then what I am afraid of," she continued, in a bitter and sombre murmur. "I won't have it. I won't. I won't. I won't. You must promise to kill me first!" She shook the lapels of his coat. "It must never be!"

He assured her curtly that no promises on his part were necessary, but he took good care not to contradict her in set terms, because he had had much to do with excited women, and he was inclined in general to let his experience guide his conduct in preference to applying his sagacity to each special case. His sagacity in this case was busy in other directions. Women's words fell into water, but the shortcomings of time-tables remained. The insular nature of Great Britain obtruded itself upon his notice in an odious form. "Might just as well be put under lock and key every night," he thought irritably, as nonplussed as though he had a wall to scale with the woman on his back. Suddenly he slapped his forehead. He had by dint of cudgelling his brains just thought of the Southampton—St Malo service. The boat left about midnight. There was a train at 10.30. He became cheery and ready to act.

"From Waterloo. Plenty of time. We are all right after all. . . . What's the matter now? This isn't the way," he protested.

Mrs Verloc, having hooked her arm into his, was trying to drag him into Brett Street again.

"I've forgotten to shut the shop door as I went out," she whispered, terribly agitated.

The shop and all that was in it had ceased to interest Comrade Ossipon. He knew how to limit his desires. He was on the point of saying "What of that? Let it be," but he refrained. He disliked argument about trifles. He even mended his pace considerably on the thought that she might have left the money in the drawer. But his willingness lagged behind her feverish impatience.

The shop seemed to be quite dark at first. The door stood ajar. Mrs Verloc, leaning against the front, gasped out:

"Nobody has been in. Look! The light—the light in the parlour."

Ossipon, stretching his head forward, saw a faint gleam in the darkness of the shop.

"There is," he said.

"I forgot it." Mrs Verloc's voice came from behind her veil faintly. And as he stood waiting for her to enter first, she said louder: "Go in and put it out—or I'll go mad."

He made no immediate objection to this proposal, so strangely motived. "Where's all that money?" he asked.

"On me! Go, Tom. Quick! Put it out. . . . Go in!" she cried, seizing him by both shoulders from behind.

Not prepared for a display of physical force, Comrade Ossipon stumbled far into the shop before her push. He was astonished at the strength of the woman and scandalised by her proceedings. But he did not retrace his steps in order to remonstrate with her severely in the street. He was beginning to be disagreeably impressed by her fantastic behaviour. Moreover, this or never was the time to humour the woman. Comrade Ossipon avoided easily the end of the counter, and approached calmly the glazed door of the parlour. The curtain over the panes being drawn back a little he, by a very natural impulse, looked in, just as he made ready to turn the handle. He looked in without a thought, without intention, without curiosity of any sort. He looked in because he could not help looking in. He looked in, and discovered Mr Verloc reposing quietly on the sofa.

A yell coming from the innermost depths of his chest died out unheard and transformed into a sort of greasy, sickly taste on his lips. At the same time the mental personality of Comrade Ossipon executed a frantic leap backward. But his body, left thus without intellectual guidance, held on to the door handle with the unthinking force of an instinct. The robust anarchist did not even totter. And he stared, his face close to the glass, his eyes protruding out of his head. He would have given anything to get away, but his returning reason informed him that it would not do to let go the door handle. What was it—madness, a nightmare, or a trap into which he had been decoyed with fiendish artfulness? Why—what for? He did not know. Without any sense of guilt in his breast, in the full peace of his conscience as far as these people were concerned, the idea that he would be murdered for mysterious reasons by the couple Verloc passed not so much across his mind as across the pit of his stomach, and went out, leaving behind a trail of sickly faintness—an indisposition. Comrade Ossipon did not feel very well in a very special way for a moment—a long moment. And he stared. Mr Verloc lay very still meanwhile, simulating sleep for reasons of his own, while that savage woman of his was guarding the door—invisible and silent in the dark and deserted street. Was all this a some sort of terrifying arrangement invented by the police for his especial benefit? His modesty shrank from that explanation.

But the true sense of the scene he was beholding came to Ossipon through the contemplation of the hat. It seemed an extraordinary thing, an ominous object, a sign. Black, and rim upward, it lay on the floor before the couch as if prepared to receive the contributions of pence from people who would come presently to behold Mr Verloc in the fullness of his domestic ease reposing on a sofa. From the hat the eyes of the robust anarchist wandered to the displaced table, gazed at the broken dish for a time, received a kind of optical shock from observing a white gleam under the imperfectly closed eyelids of the man on the couch. Mr Verloc did not seem so much asleep now as lying down with a bent head and looking insistently at his left breast. And when Comrade Ossipon had made out the handle of the knife he turned away from the glazed door, and retched violently.

The crash of the street door flung to made his very soul leap in a panic. This house with its harmless tenant could still be made a trap of—a trap of a terrible kind. Comrade Ossipon had no settled conception now of what was happening to him. Catching his thigh against the end of the counter, he spun round, staggered with a cry of pain, felt in the distracting clatter of the bell his arms pinned to his side by a convulsive hug, while the cold lips of a woman moved creepily on his very ear to form the words:

"Policeman! He has seen me!"

He ceased to struggle; she never let him go. Her hands had locked themselves with an inseparable twist of fingers on his robust back. While the footsteps approached, they breathed quickly, breast to breast, with hard, laboured breaths, as if theirs had been the attitude of a deadly struggle, while, in fact, it was the attitude of deadly fear. And the time was long.

The constable on the beat had in truth seen something of Mrs Verloc; only coming from the lighted thoroughfare at the other end of Brett Street, she had been no more to him than a flutter in the darkness. And he was not even quite sure that there had been a flutter. He had no reason to hurry up. On coming abreast of the shop he observed that it had been closed early. There was nothing very unusual in that. The men on duty had special instructions about that shop: what went on about there was not to be meddled with unless absolutely disorderly, but any observations made were to be reported. There were no observations to make; but from a sense of duty and for the peace of his conscience, owing also to that doubtful flutter of the darkness, the constable crossed the road, and tried the door. The spring latch, whose key was reposing for ever off duty in the late Mr Verloc's waistcoat pocket, held as well as usual. While the conscientious officer was shaking the handle, Ossipon felt the cold lips of the woman stirring again creepily against his very ear:

"If he comes in kill me—kill me, Tom."

The constable moved away, flashing as he passed the light of his dark lantern, merely for form's sake, at the shop window. For a moment longer the man and the woman inside stood motionless, panting, breast to breast; then her fingers came unlocked, her arms fell by her side slowly. Ossipon leaned against the counter. The robust anarchist wanted support badly. This was awful. He was almost too disgusted for speech. Yet he managed to utter a plaintive thought, showing at least that he realised his position.

"Only a couple of minutes later and you'd have made me blunder against the fellow poking about here with his damned dark lantern."

The widow of Mr Verloc, motionless in the middle of the shop, said insistently:

"Go in and put that light out, Tom. It will drive me crazy."

She saw vaguely his vehement gesture of refusal. Nothing in the world would have induced Ossipon to go into the parlour. He was not superstitious, but there was too much blood on the floor; a beastly pool of it all round the hat. He judged he had been already far too near that corpse for his peace of mind—for the safety of his neck, perhaps!

"At the meter then! There. Look. In that corner."

The robust form of Comrade Ossipon, striding brusque and shadowy across the shop, squatted in a corner obediently; but this obedience was without grace. He fumbled nervously—and suddenly in the sound of a muttered curse the light behind the glazed door flicked out to a gasping, hysterical sigh of a woman. Night, the inevitable reward of men's faithful labours on this earth, night had fallen on Mr Verloc, the tried revolutionist—"one of the old lot"—the humble guardian of society; the invaluable Secret Agent [delta] of Baron Stott-Wartenheim's despatches; a servant of law and order, faithful, trusted, accurate, admirable, with perhaps one single amiable weakness: the idealistic belief in being loved for himself.

Ossipon groped his way back through the stuffy atmosphere, as black as ink now, to the counter. The voice of Mrs Verloc, standing in the middle of the shop, vibrated after him in that blackness with a desperate protest.

"I will not be hanged, Tom. I will not—"

She broke off. Ossipon from the counter issued a warning: "Don't shout like this," then seemed to reflect profoundly. "You did this thing quite by yourself?" he inquired in a hollow voice, but with an appearance of masterful calmness which filled Mrs Verloc's heart with grateful confidence in his protecting strength.

"Yes," she whispered, invisible.

"I wouldn't have believed it possible," he muttered. "Nobody would." She heard him move about and the snapping of a lock in the parlour door. Comrade Ossipon had turned the key on Mr Verloc's repose; and this he did not from reverence for its eternal nature or any other obscurely sentimental consideration, but for the precise reason that he was not at all sure that there was not someone else hiding somewhere in the house. He did not believe the woman, or rather he was incapable by now of judging what could be true, possible, or even probable in this astounding universe. He was terrified out of all capacity for belief or disbelief in regard of this extraordinary affair, which began with police inspectors and Embassies and would end goodness knows where—on the scaffold for someone. He was terrified at the thought that he could not prove the use he made of his time ever since seven o'clock, for he had been skulking about Brett Street. He was terrified at this savage woman who had brought him in there, and would probably saddle him with complicity, at least if he were not careful. He was terrified at the rapidity with which he had been involved in such dangers—decoyed into it. It was some twenty minutes since he had met her—not more.

The voice of Mrs Verloc rose subdued, pleading piteously: "Don't let them hang me, Tom! Take me out of the country. I'll work for you. I'll slave for you. I'll love you. I've no one in the world. . . . Who would look at me if you don't!" She ceased for a moment; then in the depths of the loneliness made round her by an insignificant thread of blood trickling off the handle of a knife, she found a dreadful inspiration to her—who had been the respectable girl of the Belgravian mansion, the loyal, respectable wife of Mr Verloc. "I won't ask you to marry me," she breathed out in shame-faced accents.

She moved a step forward in the darkness. He was terrified at her. He would not have been surprised if she had suddenly produced another knife destined for his breast. He certainly would have made no resistance. He had really not enough fortitude in him just then to tell her to keep back. But he inquired in a cavernous, strange tone: "Was he asleep?"

"No," she cried, and went on rapidly. "He wasn't. Not he. He had been telling me that nothing could touch him. After taking the boy away from under my very eyes to kill him—

the loving, innocent, harmless lad. My own, I tell you. He was lying on the couch quite easy—after killing the boy—my boy. I would have gone on the streets to get out of his sight. And he says to me like this: 'Come here,' after telling me I had helped to kill the boy. You hear, Tom? He says like this: 'Come here,' after taking my very heart out of me along with the boy to smash in the dirt."

She ceased, then dreamily repeated twice: "Blood and dirt. Blood and dirt." A great light broke upon Comrade Ossipon. It was that half-witted lad then who had perished in the park. And the fooling of everybody all round appeared more complete than ever—colossal. He exclaimed scientifically, in the extremity of his astonishment: "The degenerate—by heavens!"

"Come here." The voice of Mrs Verloc rose again. "What did he think I was made of? Tell me, Tom. Come here! Me! Like this! I had been looking at the knife, and I thought I would come then if he wanted me so much. Oh yes! I came—for the last time. . . . With the knife."

He was excessively terrified at her—the sister of the degenerate—a degenerate herself of a murdering type . . . or else of the lying type. Comrade Ossipon might have been said to be terrified scientifically in addition to all other kinds of fear. It was an immeasurable and composite funk, which from its very excess gave him in the dark a false appearance of calm and thoughtful deliberation. For he moved and spoke with difficulty, being as if half frozen in his will and mind—and no one could see his ghastly face. He felt half dead.

He leaped a foot high. Unexpectedly Mrs Verloc had desecrated the unbroken reserved decency of her home by a shrill and terrible shriek.

"Help, Tom! Save me. I won't be hanged!"

He rushed forward, groping for her mouth with a silencing hand, and the shriek died out. But in his rush he had knocked her over. He felt her now clinging round his legs, and his terror reached its culminating point, became a sort of intoxication, entertained delusions, acquired the characteristics of delirium tremens. He positively saw snakes now. He saw the woman twined round him like a snake, not to be shaken off. She was not deadly. She was death itself—the companion of life.

Mrs Verloc, as if relieved by the outburst, was very far from behaving noisily now. She was pitiful.

"Tom, you can't throw me off now," she murmured from the floor. "Not unless you crush my head under your heel. I won't leave you."

"Get up," said Ossipon.

His face was so pale as to be quite visible in the profound black darkness of the shop; while Mrs Verloc, veiled, had no face, almost no discernible form. The trembling of something small and white, a flower in her hat, marked her place, her movements.

It rose in the blackness. She had got up from the floor, and Ossipon regretted not having run out at once into the street. But he perceived easily that it would not do. It would not do. She would run after him. She would pursue him shrieking till she sent every policeman within hearing in chase. And then goodness only knew what she would say of him. He was so frightened that for a moment the insane notion of strangling her in the dark passed through his mind. And he became more frightened than ever! She had him! He saw himself living in abject terror in some obscure hamlet in Spain or Italy; till some fine morning they found him dead too, with a knife in his breast—like Mr Verloc. He sighed deeply. He dared not move. And Mrs Verloc waited in silence the good pleasure of her saviour, deriving comfort from his reflective silence.

Suddenly he spoke up in an almost natural voice. His reflections had come to an end.

"Let's get out, or we will lose the train."

"Where are we going to, Tom?" she asked timidly. Mrs Verloc was no longer a free woman.

"Let's get to Paris first, the best way we can. . . . Go out first, and see if the way's clear."

She obeyed. Her voice came subdued through the cautiously opened door.

"It's all right."

Ossipon came out. Notwithstanding his endeavours to be gentle, the cracked bell clattered behind the closed door in the empty shop, as if trying in vain to warn the reposing Mr Verloc of the final departure of his wife—accompanied by his friend.

In the hansom they presently picked up, the robust anarchist became explanatory. He was still awfully pale, with eyes that seemed to have sunk a whole half-inch into his tense face. But he seemed to have thought of everything with extraordinary method.

"When we arrive," he discoursed in a queer, monotonous tone, "you must go into the station ahead of me, as if we did not know each other. I will take the tickets, and slip in yours into your hand as I pass you. Then you will go into the first-class ladies' waiting-room, and sit there till ten minutes before the train starts. Then you come out. I will be outside. You go in first on the platform, as if you did not know me. There may be eyes watching there that know what's what. Alone you are only a woman going off by train. I am known. With me, you may be guessed at as Mrs Verloc running away. Do you understand, my dear?" he added, with an effort.

"Yes," said Mrs Verloc, sitting there against him in the hansom all rigid with the dread of the gallows and the fear of death. "Yes, Tom." And she added to herself, like an awful refrain: "The drop given was fourteen feet."

Ossipon, not looking at her, and with a face like a fresh plaster cast of himself after a wasting illness, said: "By-the-by, I ought to have the money for the tickets now."

Mrs Verloc, undoing some hooks of her bodice, while she went on staring ahead beyond the splashboard, handed over to him the new pigskin pocket-book. He received it without a word, and seemed to plunge it deep somewhere into his very breast. Then he slapped his coat on the outside.

All this was done without the exchange of a single glance; they were like two people looking out for the first sight of a desired goal. It was not till the hansom swung round a corner and towards the bridge that Ossipon opened his lips again.

"Do you know how much money there is in that thing?" he asked, as if addressing slowly some hobgoblin sitting between the ears of the horse.

"No," said Mrs Verloc. "He gave it to me. I didn't count. I thought nothing of it at the time. Afterwards—"

She moved her right hand a little. It was so expressive that little movement of that right hand which had struck the deadly blow into a man's heart less than an hour before that Ossipon could not repress a shudder. He exaggerated it then purposely, and muttered:

"I am cold. I got chilled through."

Mrs Verloc looked straight ahead at the perspective of her escape. Now and then, like a sable streamer blown across a road, the words "The drop given was fourteen feet" got in the way of her tense stare. Through her black veil the whites of her big eyes gleamed lustrously like the eyes of a masked woman.

Ossipon's rigidity had something business-like, a queer official expression. He was heard again all of a sudden, as though he had released a catch in order to speak.

"Look here! Do you know whether your—whether he kept his account at the bank in his own name or in some other name."

Mrs Verloc turned upon him her masked face and the big white gleam of her eyes.

"Other name?" she said thoughtfully.

"Be exact in what you say," Ossipon lectured in the swift motion of the hansom. "It's extremely important. I will explain to you. The bank has the numbers of these notes. If they were paid to him in his own name, then when his—his death becomes known, the notes may serve to track us since we have no other money. You have no other money on you?"

She shook her head negatively.

"None whatever?" he insisted.

"A few coppers."

"It would be dangerous in that case. The money would have then to be dealt specially with. Very specially. We'd have perhaps to lose more than half the amount in order to get these notes changed in a certain safe place I know of in Paris. In the other case I mean if he had his account and got paid out under some other name—say Smith, for instance—the money is perfectly safe to use. You understand? The bank has no means of knowing that Mr Verloc and, say, Smith are one and the same person. Do you see how important it is that you should make no mistake in answering me? Can you answer that query at all? Perhaps not. Eh?"

She said composedly:

"I remember now! He didn't bank in his own name. He told me once that it was on deposit in the name of Prozor."

"You are sure?"

"Certain."

"You don't think the bank had any knowledge of his real name? Or anybody in the bank or—"

She shrugged her shoulders.

"How can I know? Is it likely, Tom?

"No. I suppose it's not likely. It would have been more comfortable to know. . . . Here we are. Get out first, and walk straight in. Move smartly."

He remained behind, and paid the cabman out of his own loose silver. The programme traced by his minute foresight was carried out. When Mrs Verloc, with her ticket for St Malo in her hand, entered the ladies' waiting-room, Comrade Ossipon walked into the bar, and in seven minutes absorbed three goes of hot brandy and water.

"Trying to drive out a cold," he explained to the barmaid, with a friendly nod and a grimacing smile. Then he came out, bringing out from that festive interlude the face of a man who had drunk at the very Fountain of Sorrow. He raised his eyes to the clock. It was time. He waited.

Punctual, Mrs Verloc came out, with her veil down, and all black—black as commonplace death itself, crowned with a few cheap and pale flowers. She passed close to a little group of men who were laughing, but whose laughter could have been struck dead by a single word. Her walk was indolent, but her back was straight, and Comrade Ossipon looked after it in terror before making a start himself.

The train was drawn up, with hardly anybody about its row of open doors. Owing to the time of the year and to the abominable weather there were hardly any passengers. Mrs Verloc walked slowly along the line of empty compartments till Ossipon touched her elbow from behind.

"In here."

She got in, and he remained on the platform looking about. She bent forward, and in a whisper:

"What is it, Tom? Is there any danger? Wait a moment. There's the guard."

She saw him accost the man in uniform. They talked for a while. She heard the guard say "Very well, sir," and saw him touch his cap. Then Ossipon came back, saying: "I told him not to let anybody get into our compartment."

She was leaning forward on her seat. "You think of everything. . . . You'll get me off, Tom?" she asked in a gust of anguish, lifting her veil brusquely to look at her saviour.

She had uncovered a face like adamant. And out of this face the eyes looked on, big, dry, enlarged, lightless, burnt out like two black holes in the white, shining globes.

"There is no danger," he said, gazing into them with an earnestness almost rapt, which to Mrs Verloc, flying from the gallows, seemed to be full of force and tenderness. This devotion deeply moved her—and the adamantine face lost the stern rigidity of its terror. Comrade Ossipon gazed at it as no lover ever gazed at his mistress's face. Alexander Ossipon, anarchist, nicknamed the Doctor, author of a medical (and improper) pamphlet, late lecturer on the social aspects of hygiene to working men's clubs, was free from the trammels of conventional morality—but he submitted to the rule of science. He was scientific, and he gazed scientifically at that woman, the sister of a degenerate, a degenerate herself—of a murdering type. He gazed at her, and invoked Lombroso, as an Italian peasant recommends himself to his favourite saint. He gazed scientifically. He gazed at her cheeks, at her nose, at her eyes, at her ears. . . . Bad! . . . Fatal! Mrs Verloc's pale lips parting, slightly relaxed under his passionately attentive gaze, he gazed also at her teeth. . . . Not a doubt remained . . . a murdering type. . . . If Comrade Ossipon did not recommend his terrified soul to Lombroso, it was only because on scientific grounds he could not believe that he carried about him such a thing as a soul. But he had in him the scientific spirit, which moved him to testify on the platform of a railway station in nervous jerky phrases.

"He was an extraordinary lad, that brother of yours. Most interesting to study. A perfect type in a way. Perfect!"

He spoke scientifically in his secret fear. And Mrs Verloc, hearing these words of commendation vouchsafed to her beloved dead, swayed forward with a flicker of light in her sombre eyes, like a ray of sunshine heralding a tempest of rain.

"He was that indeed," she whispered softly, with quivering lips. "You took a lot of notice of him, Tom. I loved you for it."

"It's almost incredible the resemblance there was between you two," pursued Ossipon, giving a voice to his abiding dread, and trying to conceal his nervous, sickening impatience for the train to start. "Yes; he resembled you."

These words were not especially touching or sympathetic. But the fact of that resemblance insisted upon was enough in itself to act upon her emotions powerfully. With a little faint cry, and throwing her arms out, Mrs Verloc burst into tears at last.

Ossipon entered the carriage, hastily closed the door and looked out to see the time by the station clock. Eight minutes more. For the first three of these Mrs Verloc wept violently and helplessly without pause or interruption. Then she recovered somewhat, and sobbed gently in an abundant fall of tears. She tried to talk to her saviour, to the man who was the messenger of life.

"Oh, Tom! How could I fear to die after he was taken away from me so cruelly! How could I! How could I be such a coward!"

She lamented aloud her love of life, that life without grace or charm, and almost without decency, but of an exalted faithfulness of purpose, even unto murder. And, as often happens in the lament of poor humanity, rich in suffering but indigent in words, the truth—the very cry of truth—was found in a worn and artificial shape picked up somewhere among the phrases of sham sentiment.

"How could I be so afraid of death! Tom, I tried. But I am afraid. I tried to do away with myself. And I couldn't. Am I hard? I suppose the cup of horrors was not full enough for such as me. Then when you came. . . . "

She paused. Then in a gust of confidence and gratitude, "I will live all my days for you, Tom!" she sobbed out.

"Go over into the other corner of the carriage, away from the platform," said Ossipon solicitously. She let her saviour settle her comfortably, and he watched the coming on of another crisis of weeping, still more violent than the first. He watched the symptoms with a sort of medical air, as if counting seconds. He heard the guard's whistle at last. An involuntary contraction of the upper lip bared his teeth with all the aspect of savage resolution as he felt the train beginning to move. Mrs Verloc heard and felt nothing, and Ossipon, her saviour, stood still. He felt the train roll quicker, rumbling heavily to the sound of the woman's loud sobs, and then crossing the carriage in two long strides he opened the door deliberately, and leaped out.

He had leaped out at the very end of the platform; and such was his determination in sticking to his desperate plan that he managed by a sort of miracle, performed almost in the air, to slam to the door of the carriage. Only then did he find himself rolling head over heels like a shot rabbit. He was bruised, shaken, pale as death, and out of breath when he got up. But he was calm, and perfectly able to meet the excited crowd of railway men who had gathered round him in a moment. He explained, in gentle and convincing tones, that his wife had started at a moment's notice for Brittany to her dying mother; that, of course, she was greatly up-set, and he considerably concerned at her state; that he was trying to cheer her up, and had absolutely failed to notice at first that the train was moving out. To the general exclamation, "Why didn't you go on to Southampton, then, sir?" he objected the inexperience of a young sister-in-law left alone in the house with three small children, and her alarm at his absence, the telegraph offices being closed. He had acted on impulse. "But I don't think I'll ever try that again," he concluded; smiled all round; distributed some small change, and marched without a limp out of the station.

Outside, Comrade Ossipon, flush of safe banknotes as never before in his life, refused the offer of a cab.

"I can walk," he said, with a little friendly laugh to the civil driver.

He could walk. He walked. He crossed the bridge. Later on the towers of the Abbey saw in their massive immobility the yellow bush of his hair passing under the lamps. The lights of Victoria saw him too, and Sloane Square, and the railings of the park. And Comrade Ossipon once more found himself on a bridge. The river, a sinister marvel of still shadows and flowing gleams mingling below in a black silence, arrested his attention. He stood looking over the parapet for a long time. The clock tower boomed a brazen blast above his drooping head. He looked up at the dial. . . . Half-past twelve of a wild night in the Channel.

And again Comrade Ossipon walked. His robust form was seen that night in distant parts of the enormous town slumbering monstrously on a carpet of mud under a veil of raw mist. It was seen crossing the streets without life and sound, or diminishing in the interminable straight perspectives of shadowy houses bordering empty roadways lined by strings of gas lamps. He walked through Squares, Places, Ovals, Commons, through monotonous streets with unknown names where the dust of humanity settles inert and hopeless out of the stream of life. He walked. And suddenly turning into a strip of a front garden with a mangy grass plot, he let himself into a small grimy house with a latch-key he took out of his pocket.

He threw himself down on his bed all dressed, and lay still for a whole quarter of an hour. Then he sat up suddenly, drawing up his knees, and clasping his legs. The first dawn found him open-eyed, in that same posture. This man who could walk so long, so far, so aimlessly, without showing a sign of fatigue, could also remain sitting still for hours without stirring a limb or an eyelid. But when the late sun sent its rays into the room he unclasped his hands, and fell back on the pillow. His eyes stared at the ceiling. And suddenly they closed. Comrade Ossipon slept in the sunlight.

13

THE ENORMOUS IRON padlock on the doors of the wall cupboard was the only object in the room on which the eye could rest without becoming afflicted by the miserable unloveliness of forms and the poverty of material. Unsaleable in the ordinary course of business on account of its noble proportions, it had been ceded to the Professor for a few pence by a marine dealer in the east of London. The room was large, clean, respectable, and poor with that poverty suggesting the starvation of every human need except mere bread. There was nothing on the walls but the paper, an expanse of arsenical green, soiled with indelible smudges here and there, and with stains resembling faded maps of uninhabited continents.

At a deal table near a window sat Comrade Ossipon, holding his head between his fists. The Professor, dressed in his only suit of shoddy tweeds, but flapping to and fro on the bare boards a pair of incredibly dilapidated slippers, had thrust his hands deep into the overstrained pockets of his jacket. He was relating to his robust guest a visit he had lately been paying to the Apostle Michaelis. The Perfect Anarchist had even been unbending a little.

"The fellow didn't know anything of Verloc's death. Of course! He never looks at the newspapers. They make him too sad, he says. But never mind. I walked into his cottage. Not a soul anywhere. I had to shout half-a-dozen times before he answered me. I thought he was fast asleep yet, in bed. But not at all. He had been writing his book for four hours already. He sat in that tiny cage in a litter of manuscript. There was a half-eaten raw carrot on the table near him. His breakfast. He lives on a diet of raw carrots and a little milk now."

"How does he look on it?" asked Comrade Ossipon listlessly.

"Angelic. . . . I picked up a handful of his pages from the floor. The poverty of reasoning is astonishing. He has no logic. He can't think consecutively. But that's nothing. He has divided his biography into three parts, entitled—'Faith, Hope, Charity.' He is elaborating now the idea of a world planned out like an immense and nice hospital, with gardens and flowers, in which the strong are to devote themselves to the nursing of the weak."

The Professor paused.

"Conceive you this folly, Ossipon? The weak! The source of all evil on this earth!" he continued with his grim assurance. "I told him that I dreamt of a world like shambles, where the weak would be taken in hand for utter extermination."

"Do you understand, Ossipon? The source of all evil! They are our sinister masters—the weak, the flabby, the silly, the cowardly, the faint of heart, and the slavish of mind. They have power. They are the multitude. Theirs is the kingdom of the earth. Exterminate, exterminate! That is the only way of progress. It is! Follow me, Ossipon. First the great multitude of the weak must go, then the only relatively strong. You see? First the blind, then the deaf and the dumb, then the halt and the lame—and so on. Every taint, every vice, every prejudice, every convention must meet its doom."

"And what remains?" asked Ossipon in a stifled voice.

"I remain—if I am strong enough," asserted the sallow little Professor, whose large ears, thin like membranes, and standing far out from the sides of his frail skull, took on suddenly a deep red tint.

"Haven't I suffered enough from this oppression of the weak?" he continued forcibly. Then tapping the breast-pocket of his jacket: "And yet *I am* the force," he went on. "But the time! The time! Give me time! Ah! that multitude, too stupid to feel either pity or fear. Sometimes I think they have everything on their side. Everything—even death—my own weapon."

"Come and drink some beer with me at the Silenus," said the robust Ossipon after an interval of silence pervaded by the rapid flap, flap of the slippers on the feet of the Perfect Anarchist. This last accepted. He was jovial that day in his own peculiar way. He slapped Ossipon's shoulder.

"Beer! So be it! Let us drink and he merry, for we are strong, and to-morrow we die."

He busied himself with putting on his boots, and talked meanwhile in his curt, resolute tones.

"What's the matter with you, Ossipon? You look glum and seek even my company. I hear that you are seen constantly in places where men utter foolish things over glasses of liquor. Why? Have you abandoned your collection of women? They are the weak who feed the strong—eh?"

He stamped one foot, and picked up his other laced boot, heavy, thick-soled, unblacked, mended many times. He smiled to himself grimly.

"Tell me, Ossipon, terrible man, has ever one of your victims killed herself for you—or are your triumphs so far incomplete—for blood alone puts a seal on greatness? Blood. Death. Look at history."

"You be damned," said Ossipon, without turning his head.

"Why? Let that be the hope of the weak, whose theology has invented hell for the strong. Ossipon, my feeling for you is amicable contempt. You couldn't kill a fly."

But rolling to the feast on the top of the omnibus the Professor lost his high spirits. The contemplation of the multitudes thronging the pavements extinguished his assurance under a load of doubt and uneasiness which he could only shake off after a period of seclusion in the room with the large cupboard closed by an enormous padlock.

"And so," said over his shoulder Comrade Ossipon, who sat on the seat behind. "And so Michaelis dreams of a world like a beautiful and cheery hospital."

"Just so. An immense charity for the healing of the weak," assented the Professor sardonically.

"That's silly," admitted Ossipon. "You can't heal weakness. But after all Michaelis may not be so far wrong. In two hundred years doctors will rule the world. Science reigns already. It reigns in the shade maybe—but it reigns. And all science must culminate at last in the science of healing—not the weak, but the strong. Mankind wants to live—to live."

"Mankind," asserted the Professor with a self-confident glitter of his iron-rimmed spectacles, "does not know what it wants."

"But you do," growled Ossipon. "Just now you've been crying for time—time. Well. The doctors will serve you out your time—if you are good. You profess yourself to be one of the strong—because you carry in your pocket enough stuff to send yourself and, say, twenty other people into eternity. But eternity is a damned hole. It's time that you need. You—if you met a man who could give you for certain ten years of time, you would call him your master."

"My device is: No God! No Master," said the Professor sententiously as he rose to get off the 'bus.

Ossipon followed. "Wait till you are lying flat on your back at the end of your time," he retorted, jumping off the footboard after the other. "Your scurvy, shabby, mangy little bit of time," he continued across the street, and hopping on to the curbstone.

"Ossipon, I think that you are a humbug," the Professor said, opening masterfully the doors of the renowned Silenus. And when they had established themselves at a little table he developed further this gracious thought. "You are not even a doctor. But you are funny. Your notion of a humanity universally putting out the tongue and taking the pill from pole to pole at the bidding of a few solemn jokers is worthy of the prophet. Prophecy! What's the good of thinking of what will be!" He raised his glass. "To the destruction of what is," he said calmly.

He drank and relapsed into his peculiarly close manner of silence. The thought of a mankind as numerous as the sands of the sea-shore, as indestructible, as difficult to handle, oppressed him. The sound of exploding bombs was lost in their immensity of passive grains without an echo. For instance, this Verloc affair. Who thought of it now?

Ossipon, as if suddenly compelled by some mysterious force, pulled a much-folded newspaper out of his pocket. The Professor raised his head at the rustle.

"What's that paper? Anything in it?" he asked.

Ossipon started like a scared somnambulist.

"Nothing. Nothing whatever. The thing's ten days old. I forgot it in my pocket, I suppose."

But he did not throw the old thing away. Before returning it to his pocket he stole a glance at the last lines of a paragraph. They ran thus: "*An impenetrable mystery seems destined to hang for ever over this act of madness or despair.*"

Such were the end words of an item of news headed: "Suicide of Lady Passenger from a cross-Channel Boat." Comrade Ossipon was familiar with the beauties of its journalistic style. "*An impenetrable mystery seems destined to hang for ever. . . .*" He knew every word by heart. "*An impenetrable mystery. . . .*"

And the robust anarchist, hanging his head on his breast, fell into a long reverie.

He was menaced by this thing in the very sources of his existence. He could not issue forth to meet his various conquests, those that he courted on benches in Kensington Gardens, and those he met near area railings, without the dread of beginning to talk to them of an impenetrable mystery destined. . . . He was becoming scientifically afraid of insanity lying in wait for him amongst these lines. "*To hang for ever over.*" It was an obsession, a torture. He had lately failed to keep several of these appointments, whose note used to be an unbounded trustfulness in the language of sentiment and manly tenderness. The confiding disposition of various classes of women satisfied the needs of his self-love, and put some material means into his hand. He needed it to live. It was there. But if he could no longer make use of it, he ran the risk of starving his ideals and his body . . . "*This act of madness or despair.*"

"An impenetrable mystery" was sure "to hang for ever" as far as all mankind was concerned. But what of that if he alone of all men could never get rid of the cursed knowledge? And Comrade Ossipon's knowledge was as precise as the newspaper man could make it—up to the very threshold of the "*mystery destined to hang for ever. . . .*"

Comrade Ossipon was well informed. He knew what the gangway man of the steamer had seen: "A lady in a black dress and a black veil, wandering at midnight alongside, on the quay. 'Are you going by the boat, ma'am,' he had asked her encouragingly. 'This way.' She seemed not to know what to do. He helped her on board. She seemed weak."

And he knew also what the stewardess had seen: A lady in black with a white face standing in the middle of the empty ladies' cabin. The stewardess induced her to lie down there. The lady seemed quite unwilling to speak, and as if she were in some awful trouble. The next the stewardess knew she was gone from the ladies' cabin. The stewardess then went on deck to look for her, and Comrade Ossipon was informed that the good woman found the unhappy lady lying down in one of the hooded seats. Her eyes were open, but she would not answer anything that was said to her. She seemed very ill. The stewardess fetched the chief steward, and those two people stood by the side of the hooded seat consulting over their extraordinary and tragic passenger. They talked in audible whispers (for she seemed past hearing) of St Malo and the Consul there, of communicating with her people in England. Then they went away to arrange for her removal down below, for indeed by what they could see of her face she seemed to them to be dying. But Comrade Ossipon knew that behind that white mask of despair there was struggling against terror and despair a vigour of vitality, a love of life that could resist the furious anguish which drives to murder and the fear, the blind, mad fear of the gallows. He knew. But the stewardess and the chief steward knew nothing, except that when they came back for her in less than five minutes the lady in black was no longer in the hooded seat. She was nowhere. She was gone. It was then five o'clock in the morning, and it was no accident either. An hour afterwards one of the steamer's hands found a wedding ring left lying on the seat. It had stuck to the wood in a bit of wet, and its glitter caught the man's eye. There was a date, 24th June 1879, engraved inside. "*An impenetrable mystery is destined to hang for ever. . . .*"

And Comrade Ossipon raised his bowed head, beloved of various humble women of these isles, Apollo-like in the sunniness of its bush of hair.

The Professor had grown restless meantime. He rose.

"Stay," said Ossipon hurriedly. "Here, what do you know of madness and despair?"

The Professor passed the tip of his tongue on his dry, thin lips, and said doctorally:

"There are no such things. All passion is lost now. The world is mediocre, limp, without force. And madness and despair are a force. And force is a crime in the eyes of the fools, the weak and the silly who rule the roost. You are mediocre. Verloc, whose affair the police has managed to smother so nicely, was mediocre. And the police murdered him. He was mediocre. Everybody is mediocre. Madness and despair! Give me that for a lever, and I'll move the world. Ossipon, you have my cordial scorn. You are incapable of conceiving even what the fat-fed citizen would call a crime. You have no force." He paused, smiling sardonically under the fierce glitter of his thick glasses.

"And let me tell you that this little legacy they say you've come into has not improved your intelligence. You sit at your beer like a dummy. Good-bye."

"Will you have it?" said Ossipon, looking up with an idiotic grin.

"Have what?"

"The legacy. All of it."

The incorruptible Professor only smiled. His clothes were all but falling off him, his boots, shapeless with repairs, heavy like lead, let water in at every step. He said:

"I will send you by-and-by a small bill for certain chemicals which I shall order to-morrow. I need them badly. Understood—eh?"

Ossipon lowered his head slowly. He was alone. *"An impenetrable mystery. . . . "* It seemed to him that suspended in the air before him he saw his own brain pulsating to the rhythm of an impenetrable mystery. It was diseased clearly. . . . *"This act of madness or despair."*

The mechanical piano near the door played through a valse cheekily, then fell silent all at once, as if gone grumpy.

Comrade Ossipon, nicknamed the Doctor, went out of the Silenus beer-hall. At the door he hesitated, blinking at a not too splendid sunlight—and the paper with the report of the suicide of a lady was in his pocket. His heart was beating against it. The suicide of a lady —*this act of madness or despair.*

He walked along the street without looking where he put his feet; and he walked in a direction which would not bring him to the place of appointment with another lady (an elderly nursery governess putting her trust in an Apollo-like ambrosial head). He was walking away from it. He could face no woman. It was ruin. He could neither think, work, sleep, nor eat. But he was beginning to drink with pleasure, with anticipation, with hope. It was ruin. His revolutionary career, sustained by the sentiment and trustfulness of many women, was menaced by an impenetrable mystery—the mystery of a human brain pulsating wrongfully to the rhythm of journalistic phrases. " . . . *Will hang for ever over this act.* . . . It was inclining towards the gutter . . . *of madness or despair."*

"I am seriously ill," he muttered to himself with scientific insight. Already his robust form, with an Embassy's secret-service money (inherited from Mr Verloc) in his pockets, was marching in the gutter as if in training for the task of an inevitable future. Already he bowed his broad shoulders, his head of ambrosial locks, as if ready to receive the leather yoke of the sandwich board. As on that night, more than a week ago, Comrade Ossipon walked without looking where he put his feet, feeling no fatigue, feeling nothing, seeing nothing, hearing not a sound. *"An impenetrable mystery. . . ."* He walked disregarded. . . . *"This act of madness or despair."*

And the incorruptible Professor walked too, averting his eyes from the odious multitude of mankind. He had no future. He disdained it. He was a force. His thoughts caressed the images of ruin and destruction. He walked frail, insignificant, shabby, miserable—and terrible in the simplicity of his idea calling madness and despair to the regeneration of the world. Nobody looked at him. He passed on unsuspected and deadly, like a pest in the street full of men.

AN OUTCAST OF THE ISLANDS

I

I

WHEN HE STEPPED off the straight and narrow path of his peculiar honesty, it was with an inward assertion of unflinching resolve to fall back again into the monotonous but safe stride of virtue as soon as his little excursion into the wayside quagmires had produced the desired effect. It was going to be a short episode—a sentence in brackets, so to speak—in the flowing tale of his life: a thing of no moment, to be done unwillingly, yet neatly, and to be quickly forgotten. He imagined that he could go on afterwards looking at the sunshine, enjoying the shade, breathing in the perfume of flowers in the small garden before his house. He fancied that nothing would be changed, that he would be able as heretofore to tyrannize good-humouredly over his half-caste wife, to notice with tender contempt his pale yellow child, to patronize loftily his dark-skinned brother-in-law, who loved pink neckties and wore patent-leather boots on his little feet, and was so humble before the white husband of the lucky sister. Those were the delights of his life, and he was unable to conceive that the moral significance of any act of his could interfere with the very nature of things, could dim the light of the sun, could destroy the perfume of the flowers, the submission of his wife, the smile of his child, the awe-struck respect of Leonard da Souza and of all the Da Souza family. That family's admiration was the great luxury of his life. It rounded and completed his existence in a perpetual assurance of unquestionable superiority. He loved to breathe the coarse incense they offered before the shrine of the successful white man; the man that had done them the honour to marry their daughter, sister, cousin; the rising man sure to climb very high; the confidential clerk of Hudig & Co. They were a numerous and an unclean crowd, living in ruined bamboo houses, surrounded by neglected compounds, on the outskirts of Macassar. He kept them at arm's length and even further off, perhaps, having no illusions as to their worth. They were a half-caste, lazy lot, and he saw them as they were—ragged, lean, unwashed, undersized men of various ages, shuffling about aimlessly in slippers; motionless old women who looked like monstrous bags of pink calico stuffed with shapeless lumps of fat, and deposited askew upon decaying rattan chairs in shady corners of dusty verandahs; young women, slim and yellow, big-eyed, long-haired, moving languidly amongst the dirt and rubbish of their dwellings as if every step they took was going to be their very last. He heard their shrill quarrellings, the squalling of their children, the grunting of their pigs; he smelt the odours of the heaps of garbage in their courtyards: and he was greatly disgusted. But he fed and clothed that shabby multitude; those degenerate descendants of Portuguese conquerors; he was their providence; he kept them singing his praises in the midst of their laziness, of their dirt, of their immense and hopeless squalor: and he was greatly delighted. They wanted much, but he could give them all they wanted without ruining himself. In exchange he had their silent fear, their loquacious love, their noisy veneration. It is a fine thing to be a providence, and to be told so on every day of one's life. It gives one a feeling of enormously remote superiority, and Willems revelled in it. He did not analyze the state of his mind, but probably his greatest delight lay in the unexpressed but intimate conviction that, should he close his hand, all those admiring human beings would starve. His munificence had demoralized them. An easy task. Since he descended amongst them and married Joanna they had lost the little aptitude and strength for work they might have had to put forth under the stress of extreme necessity. They lived now by the grace of his will. This was power. Willems loved it. In another, and perhaps a lower plane, his days did not want for their less complex but more obvious pleasures. He liked the simple games of skill—billiards; also games not so simple, and calling for quite another kind of skill—poker. He had been the aptest pupil of a steady-eyed, sententious American, who had drifted mysteriously into Macassar from the wastes of the Pacific, and, after knocking about for a time in the eddies of town life, had drifted out enigmatically into the sunny solitudes of the Indian Ocean. The memory of the Californian stranger was perpetuated in the game of poker—which became popular in the capital of Celebes from that time—and in a powerful cocktail, the recipe for which is transmitted—in the Kwang-tung dialect—from head boy to head boy of the Chinese servants in the Sunda Hotel even to this day. Willems was a connoisseur in the drink and an adept at the game. Of those accomplishments he was moderately proud. Of the confidence reposed in him by Hudig—the master—he was boastfully and obtrusively proud. This arose from his great benevolence, and from an exalted sense of his duty to himself and the world at large. He experienced that irresistible impulse to impart information which is inseparable from gross ignorance. There is always some one thing which the ignorant man knows, and that thing is the only thing worth knowing; it fills the ignorant man's universe. Willems knew all about himself. On the day when, with many misgivings, he ran away from a Dutch East-Indiaman in Samarang roads, he had commenced that study of himself, of his own ways, of his own abilities, of those fate-compelling qualities of his which led him toward that lucrative position which he now filled. Being of a modest and diffident nature, his successes amazed, almost frightened him, and ended—as he got over the succeeding shocks of surprise—by making him ferociously conceited. He believed in his genius and in his knowledge of the world. Others should know of it also; for their own good and for his greater glory. All those friendly men who slapped him on the back and greeted him noisily should have the benefit of his example. For that he must talk. He talked to them conscientiously. In the afternoon he expounded his theory of success over the little tables, dipping now and then his moustache in the crushed ice of the cocktails; in the evening he would often hold forth, cue in hand, to a young listener across the billiard table. The billiard balls stood still as if listening also, under the vivid brilliance of the shaded oil lamps hung low over the cloth; while away in the shadows of the big room the Chinaman marker would lean wearily against the wall, the blank mask of his face looking pale under the mahogany marking-board; his eyelids dropped in the drowsy fatigue of late hours and in the buzzing monotony of the unintelligible stream of words poured out by the white man. In a sudden pause of the talk the game would recommence with a sharp click and go on for a time in the flowing soft whirr and the subdued thuds as the balls rolled zig-zagging towards the inevitably successful cannon. Through the big windows and the open doors the salt dampness of the sea, the vague smell of mould and flowers from the garden of the hotel drifted in and mingled with the odour of lamp oil, growing heavier as the night advanced. The players' heads dived into the light as they bent down for the stroke, springing back again smartly into the greenish gloom of broad lamp-shades; the clock ticked methodically; the unmoved Chinaman continuously repeated the score in a lifeless voice, like a big talking doll —and Willems would win the game. With a remark that it was getting late, and that he was a married man, he would say a patronizing good-night and step out into the long, empty street. At that hour its white dust was like a dazzling streak of moonlight where the eye sought repose in the dimmer gleam of rare oil lamps. Willems walked homewards, following the line of walls overtopped by the luxuriant vegetation of the front gardens. The houses right and left were hidden behind the black masses of flowering shrubs. Willems had the street to himself. He would walk in the middle, his shadow gliding obsequiously before him. He looked down on it complacently. The shadow of a successful man! He would be slightly dizzy with the cocktails and with the intoxication of his own glory. As he often told people, he came east fourteen years ago—a cabin boy. A small boy. His shadow must have been very small at that time; he thought with a smile that he was not aware then he had anything—even a shadow—which he dared call his own. And now he was looking at the shadow of the confidential clerk of Hudig & Co. going home. How glorious! How good was life for those that were on the winning side! He had won the game of life; also the game of billiards. He walked faster, jingling his winnings, and thinking of the white stone days that had marked the path of his existence. He thought of the trip to Lombok for ponies—that first important transaction confided to him by Hudig; then he reviewed the more important affairs: the quiet deal in opium; the illegal traffic in gunpowder; the great affair of smuggled firearms, the difficult business of the Rajah of Goak. He carried that last through by sheer pluck; he had bearded the savage old ruler in his council room; he had bribed him with a gilt glass coach, which, rumour said, was used as a hen-coop now; he had over-persuaded him; he had bested him in every way. That was the way to get on. He disapproved of the elementary dishonesty that dips the hand in the cash-box, but one could evade the laws and push the principles of trade to their furthest consequences. Some call that cheating. Those are the fools, the weak, the contemptible. The wise, the strong, the respected, have no scruples. Where there are scruples there can be no power. On that text he preached often to the young men. It was his doctrine, and he, himself, was a shining example of its truth.

Night after night he went home thus, after a day of toil and pleasure, drunk with the sound of his own voice celebrating his own prosperity. On his thirtieth birthday he went home thus. He had spent in good company a nice, noisy evening, and, as he walked along the empty street, the feeling of his own greatness grew upon him, lifted him above the white dust of the road, and filled him with exultation and regrets. He had not done himself justice over there in the hotel, he had not talked enough about himself, he had not impressed his hearers enough. Never mind. Some other time. Now he would go home and make his wife get up and listen to him. Why should she not get up?—and mix a cocktail for him—and listen patiently. Just so. She shall. If he wanted he could make all the Da Souza family get up. He had only to say a word and they would all come and sit silently in their night vestments on the hard, cold ground of his compound and listen, as long as he wished to go on explaining to them from the top of the stairs, how great and good he was. They would. However, his wife would do—for to-night.

His wife! He winced inwardly. A dismal woman with startled eyes and dolorously drooping mouth, that would listen to him in pained wonder and mute stillness. She was used to those night-discourses now. She had rebelled once—at the beginning. Only once. Now, while he sprawled in the long chair and drank and talked, she would stand at the further end of the table, her hands resting on the edge, her frightened eyes watching his lips, without a sound, without a stir, hardly breathing, till he dismissed her with a contemptuous: "Go to bed, dummy." She would draw a long breath then and trail out of the room, relieved but unmoved. Nothing could startle her, make her scold or make her cry. She did not complain, she did not rebel. That first difference of theirs was decisive. Too decisive, thought Willems, discontentedly. It had frightened the soul out of her body apparently. A dismal woman! A damn'd business altogether! What the devil did he want to go and saddle himself. . . . Ah! Well! he wanted a home, and the match seemed to please Hudig, and Hudig gave him the bungalow, that flower-bowered house to which he was wending his way in the cool moonlight. And he had the worship of the Da Souza tribe. A man of his stamp could carry off anything, do anything, aspire to anything. In another five years those white people who attended the Sunday card-parties of the Governor would accept him—half-caste wife and all! Hooray! He saw his shadow dart forward and wave a hat, as big as a rum barrel, at the end of an arm several yards long. . . . Who shouted hooray? . . . He smiled shamefacedly to himself, and, pushing his hands deep into his pockets, walked faster with a suddenly grave face. Behind him—to the left—a cigar end glowed in the gateway of Mr. Vinck's front yard. Leaning against one of the brick pillars, Mr. Vinck, the cashier of Hudig & Co., smoked the last cheroot of the evening. Amongst the shadows of the trimmed bushes Mrs. Vinck crunched slowly, with measured steps, the gravel of the circular path before the house.

"There's Willems going home on foot—and drunk I fancy," said Mr. Vinck over his shoulder. "I saw him jump and wave his hat."

The crunching of the gravel stopped.

"Horrid man," said Mrs. Vinck, calmly. "I have heard he beats his wife."

"Oh no, my dear, no," muttered absently Mr. Vinck, with a vague gesture. The aspect of Willems as a wife-beater presented to him no interest. How women do misjudge! If Willems wanted to torture his wife he would have recourse to less primitive methods. Mr. Vinck knew Willems well, and believed him to be very able, very smart—objectionably so. As he took the last quick draws at the stump of his cheroot, Mr. Vinck reflected that the confidence accorded by Hudig to Willems was open, under the circumstances, to loyal criticism from Hudig's cashier.

"He is becoming dangerous; he knows too much. He will have to be got rid of," said Mr. Vinck aloud. But Mrs. Vinck had gone in already, and after shaking his head he threw away his cheroot and followed her slowly.

Willems walked on homeward weaving the splendid web of his future. The road to greatness lay plainly before his eyes, straight and shining, without any obstacle that he could see. He had stepped off the path of honesty, as he understood it, but he would soon regain it, never to leave it any more! It was a very small matter. He would soon put it right again. Meantime his duty was not to be found out, and he trusted in his skill, in his luck, in his well-established reputation that would disarm suspicion if anybody dared to suspect. But nobody would dare! True, he was conscious of a slight deterioration. He had appropriated temporarily some of Hudig's money. A deplorable necessity. But he judged himself with the indulgence that should be extended to the weaknesses of genius. He would make reparation and all would be as before; nobody would be the loser for it, and he would go on unchecked toward the brilliant goal of his ambition.

Hudig's partner!

Before going up the steps of his house he stood for awhile, his feet well apart, chin in hand, contemplating mentally Hudig's future partner. A glorious occupation. He saw him quite safe; solid as the hills; deep—deep as an abyss; discreet as the grave.

2

The sea, perhaps because of its saltness, roughens the outside but keeps sweet the kernel of its servants' soul. The old sea; the sea of many years ago, whose servants were devoted slaves and went from youth to age or to a sudden grave without needing to open the book of life, because they could look at eternity reflected on the element that gave the life and dealt the death. Like a beautiful and unscrupulous woman, the sea of the past was glorious in its smiles, irresistible in its anger, capricious, enticing, illogical, irresponsible; a thing to love, a thing to fear. It cast a spell, it gave joy, it lulled gently into boundless faith; then with quick and causeless anger it killed. But its cruelty was redeemed by the charm of its inscrutable mystery, by the immensity of its promise, by the supreme witchery of its possible favour. Strong men with childlike hearts were faithful to it, were content to live by its grace—to die by its will. That was the sea before the time when the French mind set the Egyptian muscle in motion and produced a dismal but profitable ditch. Then a great pall of smoke sent out by countless steam-boats was spread over the restless mirror of the Infinite. The hand of the engineer tore down the veil of the terrible beauty in order that greedy and faithless landlubbers might pocket dividends. The mystery was destroyed. Like all mysteries, it lived only in the hearts of its worshippers. The hearts changed; the men changed. The once loving and devoted servants went out armed with fire and iron, and conquering the fear of their own hearts became a calculating crowd of cold and exacting masters. The sea of the past was an incomparably beautiful mistress, with inscrutable face, with cruel and promising eyes. The sea of to-day is a used-up drudge, wrinkled and defaced by the churned-up wakes of brutal propellers, robbed of the enslaving charm of its vastness, stripped of its beauty, of its mystery and of its promise.

Tom Lingard was a master, a lover, a servant of the sea. The sea took him young, fashioned him body and soul; gave him his fierce aspect, his loud voice, his fearless eyes, his stupidly guileless heart. Generously it gave him his absurd faith in himself, his universal love of creation, his wide indulgence, his contemptuous severity, his straightforward simplicity of motive and honesty of aim. Having made him what he was, womanlike, the sea served him humbly and let him bask unharmed in the sunshine of its terribly uncertain favour. Tom

Lingard grew rich on the sea and by the sea. He loved it with the ardent affection of a lover, he made light of it with the assurance of perfect mastery, he feared it with the wise fear of a brave man, and he took liberties with it as a spoiled child might do with a paternal and good-natured ogre. He was grateful to it, with the gratitude of an honest heart. His greatest pride lay in his profound conviction of its faithfulness—in the deep sense of his unerring knowledge of its treachery.

The little brig Flash was the instrument of Lingard's fortune. They came north together—both young—out of an Australian port, and after a very few years there was not a white man in the islands, from Palembang to Ternate, from Ombawa to Palawan, that did not know Captain Tom and his lucky craft. He was liked for his reckless generosity, for his unswerving honesty, and at first was a little feared on account of his violent temper. Very soon, however, they found him out, and the word went round that Captain Tom's fury was less dangerous than many a man's smile. He prospered greatly. After his first—and successful—fight with the sea robbers, when he rescued, as rumour had it, the yacht of some big wig from home, somewhere down Carimata way, his great popularity began. As years went on it grew apace. Always visiting out-of-the-way places of that part of the world, always in search of new markets for his cargoes—not so much for profit as for the pleasure of finding them—he soon became known to the Malays, and by his successful recklessness in several encounters with pirates, established the terror of his name. Those white men with whom he had business, and who naturally were on the look-out for his weaknesses, could easily see that it was enough to give him his Malay title to flatter him greatly. So when there was anything to be gained by it, and sometimes out of pure and unprofitable good nature, they would drop the ceremonious "Captain Lingard" and address him half seriously as Rajah Laut—the King of the Sea.

He carried the name bravely on his broad shoulders. He had carried it many years already when the boy Willems ran barefooted on the deck of the ship Kosmopoliet IV. in Samarang roads, looking with innocent eyes on the strange shore and objurgating his immediate surroundings with blasphemous lips, while his childish brain worked upon the heroic idea of running away. From the poop of the Flash Lingard saw in the early morning the Dutch ship get lumberingly under weigh, bound for the eastern ports. Very late in the evening of the same day he stood on the quay of the landing canal, ready to go on board of his brig. The night was starry and clear; the little custom-house building was shut up, and as the gharry that brought him down disappeared up the long avenue of dusty trees leading to the town, Lingard thought himself alone on the quay. He roused up his sleeping boat-crew and stood waiting for them to get ready, when he felt a tug at his coat and a thin voice said, very distinctly—

"English captain."

Lingard turned round quickly, and what seemed to be a very lean boy jumped back with commendable activity.

"Who are you? Where do you spring from?" asked Lingard, in startled surprise.

From a safe distance the boy pointed toward a cargo lighter moored to the quay.

"Been hiding there, have you?" said Lingard. "Well, what do you want? Speak out, confound you. You did not come here to scare me to death, for fun, did you?"

The boy tried to explain in imperfect English, but very soon Lingard interrupted him.

"I see," he exclaimed, "you ran away from the big ship that sailed this morning. Well, why don't you go to your countrymen here?"

"Ship gone only a little way—to Sourabaya. Make me go back to the ship," explained the boy.

"Best thing for you," affirmed Lingard with conviction.

"No," retorted the boy; "me want stop here; not want go home. Get money here; home no good."

"This beats all my going a-fishing," commented the astonished Lingard. "It's money you want? Well! well! And you were not afraid to run away, you bag of bones, you!"

The boy intimated that he was frightened of nothing but of being sent back to the ship. Lingard looked at him in meditative silence.

"Come closer," he said at last. He took the boy by the chin, and turning up his face gave him a searching look. "How old are you?"

"Seventeen."

"There's not much of you for seventeen. Are you hungry?"

"A little."

"Will you come with me, in that brig there?"

The boy moved without a word towards the boat and scrambled into the bows.

"Knows his place," muttered Lingard to himself as he stepped heavily into the stern sheets and took up the yoke lines. "Give way there."

The Malay boat crew lay back together, and the gig sprang away from the quay heading towards the brig's riding light.

Such was the beginning of Willems' career.

Lingard learned in half an hour all that there was of Willems' commonplace story. Father outdoor clerk of some ship-broker in Rotterdam; mother dead. The boy quick in learning, but idle in school. The straitened circumstances in the house filled with small brothers and sisters, sufficiently clothed and fed but otherwise running wild, while the disconsolate widower tramped about all day in a shabby overcoat and imperfect boots on the muddy quays, and in the evening piloted wearily the half-intoxicated foreign skippers amongst the places of cheap delights, returning home late, sick with too much smoking and drinking—for company's sake—with these men, who expected such attentions in the way of business. Then the offer of the good-natured captain of Kosmopoliet IV., who was pleased to do something for the patient and obliging fellow; young Willems' great joy, his still greater disappointment with the sea that looked so charming from afar, but proved so hard and exacting on closer acquaintance—and then this running away by a sudden impulse. The boy was hopelessly at variance with the spirit of the sea. He had an instinctive contempt for the honest simplicity of that work which led to nothing he cared for. Lingard soon found this out. He offered to send him home in an English ship, but the boy begged hard to be permitted to remain. He wrote a beautiful hand, became soon perfect in English, was quick at figures; and Lingard made him useful in that way. As he grew older his trading instincts developed themselves astonishingly, and Lingard left him often to trade in one island or another while he, himself, made an intermediate trip to some out-of-the-way place. On Willems expressing a wish to that effect, Lingard let him enter Hudig's service. He felt a little sore at that abandonment because he had attached himself, in a way, to his protege. Still he was proud of him, and spoke up for him loyally. At first it was, "Smart boy that—never make a seaman though." Then when Willems was helping in the trading he referred to him as "that clever young fellow." Later when Willems became the confidential agent of Hudig, employed in many a delicate affair, the simple-hearted old seaman would point an admiring finger at his back and whisper to whoever stood near at the moment, "Long-headed chap that; deuced long-headed chap. Look at him. Confidential man of old Hudig. I picked him up in a ditch, you may say, like a starved cat. Skin and bone. 'Pon my word I did. And now he knows more than I do about island trading. Fact. I am not joking. More than I do," he would repeat, seriously, with innocent pride in his honest eyes.

From the safe elevation of his commercial successes Willems patronized Lingard. He had a liking for his benefactor, not unmixed with some disdain for the crude directness of the old fellow's methods of conduct. There were, however, certain sides of Lingard's character for which Willems felt a qualified respect. The talkative seaman knew how to be silent on certain matters that to Willems were very interesting. Besides, Lingard was rich, and that in itself was enough to compel Willems' unwilling admiration. In his confidential chats with Hudig, Willems generally alluded to the benevolent Englishman as the "lucky old fool" in a very distinct tone of vexation; Hudig would grunt an unqualified assent, and then the two would look at each other in a sudden immobility of pupils fixed by a stare of unexpressed thought.

"You can't find out where he gets all that india-rubber, hey Willems?" Hudig would ask at last, turning away and bending over the papers on his desk.

"No, Mr. Hudig. Not yet. But I am trying," was Willems' invariable reply, delivered with a ring of regretful deprecation.

"Try! Always try! You may try! You think yourself clever perhaps," rumbled on Hudig, without looking up. "I have been trading with him twenty—thirty years now. The old fox. And I have tried. Bah!"

He stretched out a short, podgy leg and contemplated the bare instep and the grass slipper hanging by the toes. "You can't make him drunk?" he would add, after a pause of stertorous breathing.

"No, Mr. Hudig, I can't really," protested Willems, earnestly.

"Well, don't try. I know him. Don't try," advised the master, and, bending again over his desk, his staring bloodshot eyes close to the paper, he would go on tracing laboriously with his thick fingers the slim unsteady letters of his correspondence, while Willems waited respectfully for his further good pleasure before asking, with great deference—

"Any orders, Mr. Hudig?"

"Hm! yes. Go to Bun-Hin yourself and see the dollars of that payment counted and packed, and have them put on board the mail-boat for Ternate. She's due here this afternoon."

"Yes, Mr. Hudig."

"And, look here. If the boat is late, leave the case in Bun-Hin's godown till to-morrow. Seal it up. Eight seals as usual. Don't take it away till the boat is here."

"No, Mr. Hudig."

"And don't forget about these opium cases. It's for to-night. Use my own boatmen. Transship them from the Caroline to the Arab barque," went on the master in his hoarse undertone. "And don't you come to me with another story of a case dropped overboard like last time," he added, with sudden ferocity, looking up at his confidential clerk.

"No, Mr. Hudig. I will take care."

"That's all. Tell that pig as you go out that if he doesn't make the punkah go a little better I will break every bone in his body," finished up Hudig, wiping his purple face with a red silk handkerchief nearly as big as a counterpane.

Noiselessly Willems went out, shutting carefully behind him the little green door through which he passed to the warehouse. Hudig, pen in hand, listened to him bullying the punkah boy with profane violence, born of unbounded zeal for the master's comfort, before he returned to his writing amid the rustling of papers fluttering in the wind sent down by the punkah that waved in wide sweeps above his head.

Willems would nod familiarly to Mr. Vinck, who had his desk close to the little door of the private office, and march down the warehouse with an important air. Mr. Vinck—extreme dislike lurking in every wrinkle of his gentlemanly countenance—would follow with his eyes the white figure flitting in the gloom amongst the piles of bales and cases till it passed out through the big archway into the glare of the street.

3

THE OPPORTUNITY and the temptation were too much for Willems, and under the pressure of sudden necessity he abused that trust which was his pride, the perpetual sign of his cleverness and a load too heavy for him to carry. A run of bad luck at cards, the failure of a small speculation undertaken on his own account, an unexpected demand for money from one or another member of the Da Souza family—and almost before he was well aware of it he was off the path of his peculiar honesty. It was such a faint and ill-defined track that it took him some time to find out how far he had strayed amongst the brambles of the dangerous wilderness he had been skirting for so many years, without any other guide than his own convenience and that doctrine of success which he had found for himself in the book of life—in those interesting chapters that the Devil has been permitted to write in it, to test the sharpness of men's eyesight and the steadfastness of their hearts. For one short, dark and solitary moment he was dismayed, but he had that courage that will not scale heights, yet will wade bravely through the mud—if there be no other road. He applied himself to the task of restitution, and devoted himself to the duty of not being found out. On his thirtieth birthday he had almost accomplished the task—and the duty had been faithfully and cleverly performed. He saw himself safe. Again he could look hopefully towards the goal of his legitimate ambition. Nobody would dare to suspect him, and in a few days there would be nothing to suspect. He was elated. He did not know that his prosperity had touched then its high-water mark, and that the tide was already on the turn.

Two days afterwards he knew. Mr. Vinck, hearing the rattle of the door-handle, jumped up from his desk—where he had been tremulously listening to the loud voices in the private office—and buried his face in the big safe with nervous haste. For the last time Willems passed through the little green door leading to Hudig's sanctum, which, during the past half-hour, might have been taken—from the fiendish noise within—for the cavern of some wild beast. Willems' troubled eyes took in the quick impression of men and things as he came out from the place of his humiliation. He saw the scared expression of the punkah boy; the Chinamen tellers sitting on their heels with unmovable faces turned up blankly towards him while their arrested hands hovered over the little piles of bright guilders ranged on the floor; Mr. Vinck's shoulder-blades with the fleshy rims of two red ears above. He saw the long avenue of gin cases stretching from where he stood to the arched doorway beyond which he would be able to breathe perhaps. A thin rope's end lay across his path and he saw it distinctly, yet stumbled heavily over it as if it had been a bar of iron. Then he found himself in the street at last, but could not find air enough to fill his lungs. He walked towards his home, gasping.

As the sound of Hudig's insults that lingered in his ears grew fainter by the lapse of time, the feeling of shame was replaced slowly by a passion of anger against himself and still more against the stupid concourse of circumstances that had driven him into his idiotic indiscretion. Idiotic indiscretion; that is how he defined his guilt to himself. Could there be anything worse from the point of view of his undeniable cleverness? What a fatal aberration of an acute mind! He did not recognize himself there. He must have been mad. That's it. A sudden gust of madness. And now the work of long years was destroyed utterly. What would become of him?

Before he could answer that question he found himself in the garden before his house, Hudig's wedding gift. He looked at it with a vague surprise to find it there. His past was so utterly gone from him that the dwelling which belonged to it appeared to him incongruous standing there intact, neat, and cheerful in the sunshine of the hot afternoon. The house was a pretty little structure all doors and windows, surrounded on all sides by the deep verandah supported on slender columns clothed in the green foliage of creepers, which also fringed the overhanging eaves of the high-pitched roof. Slowly, Willems mounted the dozen steps that led to the verandah. He paused at every step. He must tell his wife. He felt frightened at the prospect, and his alarm dismayed him. Frightened to face her! Nothing could give him a better measure of the greatness of the change around him, and in him. Another man—and another life with the faith in himself gone. He could not be worth much if he was afraid to face that woman.

He dared not enter the house through the open door of the dining-room, but stood irresolute by the little work-table where trailed a white piece of calico, with a needle stuck in it, as if the work had been left hurriedly. The pink-crested cockatoo started, on his appearance, into clumsy activity and began to climb laboriously up and down his perch, calling "Joanna" with indistinct loudness and a persistent screech that prolonged the last syllable of the name as if in a peal of insane laughter. The screen in the doorway moved gently once or twice in the breeze, and each time Willems started slightly, expecting his wife, but he never lifted his eyes, although straining his ears for the sound of her footsteps. Gradually he lost himself in his thoughts, in the endless speculation as to the manner in which she would receive his news—and his orders. In this preoccupation he almost forgot the fear of her presence. No doubt she will cry, she will lament, she will be helpless and frightened and passive as ever. And he would have to drag that limp weight on and on through the darkness of a spoiled life. Horrible! Of course he could not abandon her and the child to certain misery or possible starvation. The wife and the child of Willems. Willems the successful, the smart; Willems the conf . . . . Pah! And what was Willems now? Willems the. . . . He strangled the half-born thought, and cleared his throat to stifle a groan. Ah! Won't they talk to-night in the billiard-room—his world, where he had been first—all those men to whom he had been so superciliously condescending. Won't they talk with surprise, and affected regret, and grave faces, and wise nods. Some of them owed him money, but he never pressed anybody. Not he. Willems, the prince of good fellows, they called him. And now they will rejoice, no doubt, at his downfall. A crowd of imbeciles. In his abasement he was yet aware of his superiority over those fellows, who were merely honest or simply not found out yet. A crowd of imbeciles! He shook his fist at the evoked image of his friends, and the startled parrot fluttered its wings and shrieked in desperate fright.

In a short glance upwards Willems saw his wife come round the corner of the house. He lowered his eyelids quickly, and waited silently till she came near and stood on the other side of the little table. He would not look at her face, but he could see the red dressing-gown he knew so well. She trailed through life in that red dressing-gown, with its row of dirty blue bows down the front, stained, and hooked on awry; a torn flounce at the bottom following her like a snake as she moved languidly about, with her hair negligently caught up, and a tangled wisp straggling untidily down her back. His gaze travelled upwards from bow to bow, noticing those that hung only by a thread, but it did not go beyond her chin. He looked at her lean throat, at the obtrusive collarbone visible in the disarray of the upper part of her attire. He saw the thin arm and the bony hand clasping the child she carried, and he felt an immense distaste for those encumbrances of his life. He waited for her to say something, but as he felt her eyes rest on him in unbroken silence he sighed and began to speak.

It was a hard task. He spoke slowly, lingering amongst the memories of this early life in his reluctance to confess that this was the end of it and the beginning of a less splendid existence. In his conviction of having made her happiness in the full satisfaction of all material wants he never doubted for a moment that she was ready to keep him company on no matter how hard and stony a road. He was not elated by this certitude. He had married her to please Hudig, and the greatness of his sacrifice ought to have made her happy without any further exertion on his part. She had years of glory as Willems' wife, and years of comfort, of loyal care, and of such tenderness as she deserved. He had guarded her carefully from any bodily hurt; and of any other suffering he had no conception. The assertion of his superiority was only another benefit conferred on her. All this was a matter of course, but he told her all this so as to bring vividly before her the greatness of her loss. She was so dull of understanding that she would not grasp it else. And now it was at an end. They would have to go. Leave this house, leave this island, go far away where he was unknown. To the English Strait-Settlements perhaps. He would find an opening there for his abilities—and juster men to deal with than old Hudig. He laughed bitterly.

"You have the money I left at home this morning, Joanna?" he asked. "We will want it all now."

As he spoke those words he thought he was a fine fellow. Nothing new that. Still, he surpassed there his own expectations. Hang it all, there are sacred things in life, after all. The marriage tie was one of them, and he was not the man to break it. The solidity of his principles caused him great satisfaction, but he did not care to look at his wife, for all that. He waited for her to speak. Then he would have to console her; tell her not to be a crying fool; to get ready to go. Go where? How? When? He shook his head. They must leave at once; that was the principal thing. He felt a sudden need to hurry up his departure.

"Well, Joanna," he said, a little impatiently—"don't stand there in a trance. Do you hear? We must. . . ."

He looked up at his wife, and whatever he was going to add remained unspoken. She was staring at him with her big, slanting eyes, that seemed to him twice their natural size. The child, its dirty little face pressed to its mother's shoulder, was sleeping peacefully. The deep silence of the house was not broken, but rather accentuated, by the low mutter of the cockatoo, now very still on its perch. As Willems was looking at Joanna her upper lip was drawn up on one side, giving to her melancholy face a vicious expression altogether new to his experience. He stepped back in his surprise.

"Oh! You great man!" she said distinctly, but in a voice that was hardly above a whisper.

Those words, and still more her tone, stunned him as if somebody had fired a gun close to his ear. He stared back at her stupidly.

"Oh! you great man!" she repeated slowly, glancing right and left as if meditating a sudden escape. "And you think that I am going to starve with you. You are nobody now. You think my mamma and Leonard would let me go away? And with you! With you," she repeated scornfully, raising her voice, which woke up the child and caused it to whimper feebly.

"Joanna!" exclaimed Willems.

"Do not speak to me. I have heard what I have waited for all these years. You are less than dirt, you that have wiped your feet on me. I have waited for this. I am not afraid now. I do not want you; do not come near me. Ah-h!" she screamed shrilly, as he held out his hand in an entreating gesture—"Ah! Keep off me! Keep off me! Keep off!"

She backed away, looking at him with eyes both angry and frightened. Willems stared motionless, in dumb amazement at the mystery of anger and revolt in the head of his wife. Why? What had he ever done to her? This was the day of injustice indeed. First Hudig—and now his wife. He felt a terror at this hate that had lived stealthily so near him for years. He tried to speak, but she shrieked again, and it was like a needle through his heart. Again he raised his hand.

"Help!" called Mrs. Willems, in a piercing voice. "Help!"

"Be quiet! You fool!" shouted Willems, trying to drown the noise of his wife and child in his own angry accents and rattling violently the little zinc table in his exasperation.

From under the house, where there were bathrooms and a tool closet, appeared Leonard, a rusty iron bar in his hand. He called threateningly from the bottom of the stairs.

"Do not hurt her, Mr. Willems. You are a savage. Not at all like we, whites."

"You too!" said the bewildered Willems. "I haven't touched her. Is this a madhouse?" He moved towards the stairs, and Leonard dropped the bar with a clang and made for the gate of the compound. Willems turned back to his wife.

"So you expected this," he said. "It is a conspiracy. Who's that sobbing and groaning in the room? Some more of your precious family. Hey?"

She was more calm now, and putting hastily the crying child in the big chair walked towards him with sudden fearlessness.

"My mother," she said, "my mother who came to defend me from you—man from nowhere; a vagabond!"

"You did not call me a vagabond when you hung round my neck—before we were married," said Willems, contemptuously.

"You took good care that I should not hang round your neck after we were," she answered, clenching her hands, and putting her face close to his. "You boasted while I suffered and said nothing. What has become of your greatness; of our greatness—you were always speaking about? Now I am going to live on the charity of your master. Yes. That is true. He sent Leonard to tell me so. And you will go and boast somewhere else, and starve. So! Ah! I can breathe now! This house is mine."

"Enough!" said Willems, slowly, with an arresting gesture.

She leaped back, the fright again in her eyes, snatched up the child, pressed it to her breast, and, falling into a chair, drummed insanely with her heels on the resounding floor of the verandah.

"I shall go," said Willems, steadily. "I thank you. For the first time in your life you make me happy. You were a stone round my neck; you understand. I did not mean to tell you that as long as you lived, but you made me—now. Before I pass this gate you shall be gone from my mind. You made it very easy. I thank you."

He turned and went down the steps without giving her a glance, while she sat upright and quiet, with wide-open eyes, the child crying querulously in her arms. At the gate he came suddenly upon Leonard, who had been dodging about there and failed to get out of the way in time.

"Do not be brutal, Mr. Willems," said Leonard, hurriedly. "It is unbecoming between white men with all those natives looking on." Leonard's legs trembled very much, and his voice wavered between high and low tones without any attempt at control on his part. "Restrain your improper violence," he went on mumbling rapidly. "I am a respectable man of very good family, while you . . . it is regrettable . . . they all say so . . ."

"What?" thundered Willems. He felt a sudden impulse of mad anger, and before he knew what had happened he was looking at Leonard da Souza rolling in the dust at his feet. He stepped over his prostrate brother-in-law and tore blindly down the street, everybody making way for the frantic white man.

When he came to himself he was beyond the outskirts of the town, stumbling on the hard and cracked earth of reaped rice fields. How did he get there? It was dark. He must get back. As he walked towards the town slowly, his mind reviewed the events of the day and he felt a sense of bitter loneliness. His wife had turned him out of his own house. He had assaulted brutally his brother-in-law, a member of the Da Souza family—of that band of his worshippers. He did. Well, no! It was some other man. Another man was coming back. A man without a past, without a future, yet full of pain and shame and anger. He stopped and looked round. A dog or two glided across the empty street and rushed past him with a frightened snarl. He was now in the midst of the Malay quarter whose bamboo houses, hidden in the verdure of their little gardens, were dark and silent. Men, women and children slept in there. Human beings. Would he ever sleep, and where? He felt as if he was the outcast of all mankind, and as he looked hopelessly round, before resuming his weary march, it seemed to him that the world was bigger, the night more vast and more black; but he went on doggedly with his head down as if pushing his way through some thick brambles. Then suddenly he felt planks under his feet and, looking up, saw the red light at the end of the jetty. He walked quite to the end and stood leaning against the post, under the lamp, looking at the roadstead where two vessels at anchor swayed their slender rigging amongst the stars. The end of the jetty; and here in one step more the end of life; the end of everything. Better so. What else could he do? Nothing ever comes back. He saw it clearly. The respect and admiration of them all, the old habits and old affections finished abruptly in the clear perception of the cause of his disgrace. He saw all this; and for a time he came out of himself, out of his selfishness—out of the constant preoccupation of his interests and his desires—out of the temple of self and the concentration of personal thought.

His thoughts now wandered home. Standing in the tepid stillness of a starry tropical night he felt the breath of the bitter east wind, he saw the high and narrow fronts of tall houses under the gloom of a clouded sky; and on muddy quays he saw the shabby, high-shouldered figure—the patient, faded face of the weary man earning bread for the children that waited for him in a dingy home. It was miserable, miserable. But it would never come back. What was there in common between those things and Willems the clever, Willems the successful. He had cut himself adrift from that home many years ago. Better for him then.

Better for them now. All this was gone, never to come back again; and suddenly he shivered, seeing himself alone in the presence of unknown and terrible dangers.

For the first time in his life he felt afraid of the future, because he had lost his faith, the faith in his own success. And he had destroyed it foolishly with his own hands!

4

His meditation which resembled slow drifting into suicide was interrupted by Lingard, who, with a loud "I've got you at last!" dropped his hand heavily on Willems' shoulder. This time it was the old seaman himself going out of his way to pick up the uninteresting waif—all that there was left of that sudden and sordid shipwreck. To Willems, the rough, friendly voice was a quick and fleeting relief followed by a sharper pang of anger and unavailing regret. That voice carried him back to the beginning of his promising career, the end of which was very visible now from the jetty where they both stood. He shook himself free from the friendly grasp, saying with ready bitterness—

"It's all your fault. Give me a push now, do, and send me over. I have been standing here waiting for help. You are the man—of all men. You helped at the beginning; you ought to have a hand in the end."

"I have better use for you than to throw you to the fishes," said Lingard, seriously, taking Willems by the arm and forcing him gently to walk up the jetty. "I have been buzzing over this town like a bluebottle fly, looking for you high and low. I have heard a lot. I will tell you what, Willems; you are no saint, that's a fact. And you have not been over-wise either. I am not throwing stones," he added, hastily, as Willems made an effort to get away, "but I am not going to mince matters. Never could! You keep quiet while I talk. Can't you?"

With a gesture of resignation and a half-stifled groan Willems submitted to the stronger will, and the two men paced slowly up and down the resounding planks, while Lingard disclosed to Willems the exact manner of his undoing. After the first shock Willems lost the faculty of surprise in the over-powering feeling of indignation. So it was Vinck and Leonard who had served him so. They had watched him, tracked his misdeeds, reported them to Hudig. They had bribed obscure Chinamen, wormed out confidences from tipsy skippers, got at various boatmen, and had pieced out in that way the story of his irregularities. The blackness of this dark intrigue filled him with horror. He could understand Vinck. There was no love lost between them. But Leonard! Leonard!

"Why, Captain Lingard," he burst out, "the fellow licked my boots."

"Yes, yes, yes," said Lingard, testily, "we know that, and you did your best to cram your boot down his throat. No man likes that, my boy."

"I was always giving money to all that hungry lot," went on Willems, passionately. "Always my hand in my pocket. They never had to ask twice."

"Just so. Your generosity frightened them. They asked themselves where all that came from, and concluded that it was safer to throw you overboard. After all, Hudig is a much greater man than you, my friend, and they have a claim on him also."

"What do you mean, Captain Lingard?"

"What do I mean?" repeated Lingard, slowly. "Why, you are not going to make me believe you did not know your wife was Hudig's daughter. Come now!"

Willems stopped suddenly and swayed about.

"Ah! I understand," he gasped. "I never heard . . . Lately I thought there was . . . But no, I never guessed."

"Oh, you simpleton!" said Lingard, pityingly. "'Pon my word," he muttered to himself, "I don't believe the fellow knew. Well! well! Steady now. Pull yourself together. What's wrong there. She is a good wife to you."

"Excellent wife," said Willems, in a dreary voice, looking far over the black and scintillating water.

"Very well then," went on Lingard, with increasing friendliness. "Nothing wrong there. But did you really think that Hudig was marrying you off and giving you a house and I don't know what, out of love for you?"

"I had served him well," answered Willems. "How well, you know yourself—through thick and thin. No matter what work and what risk, I was always there; always ready."

How well he saw the greatness of his work and the immensity of that injustice which was his reward. She was that man's daughter!

In the light of this disclosure the facts of the last five years of his life stood clearly revealed in their full meaning. He had spoken first to Joanna at the gate of their dwelling as he went to his work in the brilliant flush of the early morning, when women and flowers are charming even to the dullest eyes. A most respectable family—two women and a young man—were his next-door neighbours. Nobody ever came to their little house but the priest, a native from the Spanish islands, now and then. The young man Leonard he had met in town, and was flattered by the little fellow's immense respect for the great Willems. He let him bring chairs, call the waiters, chalk his cues when playing billiards, express his admiration in choice words. He even condescended to listen patiently to Leonard's allusions to "our beloved father," a man of official position, a government agent in Koti, where he died of cholera, alas! a victim to duty, like a good Catholic, and a good man. It sounded very respectable, and Willems approved of those feeling references. Moreover, he prided himself upon having no colour-prejudices and no racial antipathies. He consented to drink curacoa one afternoon on the verandah of Mrs. da Souza's house. He remembered Joanna that day, swinging in a hammock. She was untidy even then, he remembered, and that was the only impression he carried away from that visit. He had no time for love in those glorious days, no time even for a passing fancy, but gradually he fell into the habit of calling almost every day at that little house where he was greeted by Mrs. da Souza's shrill voice screaming for Joanna to come and entertain the gentleman from Hudig & Co. And then the sudden and unexpected visit of the priest. He remembered the man's flat, yellow face, his thin legs, his propitiatory smile, his beaming black eyes, his conciliating manner, his veiled hints which he did not understand at the time. How he wondered what the man wanted, and how unceremoniously he got rid of him. And then came vividly into his recollection the morning when he met again that fellow coming out of Hudig's office, and how he was amused at the incongruous visit. And that morning with Hudig! Would he ever forget it? Would he ever forget his surprise as the master, instead of plunging at once into business, looked at him thoughtfully before turning, with a furtive smile, to the papers on the desk? He could hear him now, his nose in the paper before him, dropping astonishing words in the intervals of wheezy breathing.

"Heard said . . . called there often . . . most respectable ladies . . . knew the father very well . . . estimable . . . best thing for a young man . . . settle down. . . . Personally, very glad to hear . . . thing arranged. . . . Suitable recognition of valuable services. . . . Best thing—best thing to do."

And he believed! What credulity! What an ass! Hudig knew the father! Rather. And so did everybody else probably; all except himself. How proud he had been of Hudig's benevolent interest in his fate! How proud he was when invited by Hudig to stay with him at his little house in the country—where he could meet men, men of official position—as a friend. Vinck had been green with envy. Oh, yes! He had believed in the best thing, and took the girl like a gift of fortune. How he boasted to Hudig of being free from prejudices. The old scoundrel must have been laughing in his sleeve at his fool of a confidential clerk. He took the girl, guessing nothing. How could he? There had been a father of some kind to the common knowledge. Men knew him; spoke about him. A lank man of hopelessly mixed descent, but otherwise—apparently—unobjectionable. The shady relations came out afterward, but—with his freedom from prejudices—he did not mind them, because, with their humble dependence, they completed his triumphant life. Taken in! taken in! Hudig had found an easy way to provide for the begging crowd. He had shifted the burden of his youthful vagaries on to the shoulders of his confidential clerk; and while he worked for the master, the master had cheated him; had stolen his very self from him. He was married. He belonged to that woman, no matter what she might do! . . . Had sworn . . . for all life! . . . Thrown himself away. . . . And that man dared this very morning call him a thief! Damnation!

"Let go, Lingard!" he shouted, trying to get away by a sudden jerk from the watchful old seaman. "Let me go and kill that . . ."

"No you don't!" panted Lingard, hanging on manfully. "You want to kill, do you? You lunatic. Ah!—I've got you now! Be quiet, I say!"

They struggled violently, Lingard forcing Willems slowly towards the guard-rail. Under their feet the jetty sounded like a drum in the quiet night. On the shore end the native caretaker of the wharf watched the combat, squatting behind the safe shelter of some big cases. The next day he informed his friends, with calm satisfaction, that two drunken white men had fought on the jetty.

It had been a great fight. They fought without arms, like wild beasts, after the manner of white men. No! nobody was killed, or there would have been trouble and a report to make. How could he know why they fought? White men have no reason when they are like that.

Just as Lingard was beginning to fear that he would be unable to restrain much longer the violence of the younger man, he felt Willems' muscles relaxing, and took advantage of this opportunity to pin him, by a last effort, to the rail. They both panted heavily, speechless, their faces very close.

"All right," muttered Willems at last. "Don't break my back over this infernal rail. I will be quiet."

"Now you are reasonable," said Lingard, much relieved. "What made you fly into that passion?" he asked, leading him back to the end of the jetty, and, still holding him prudently with one hand, he fumbled with the other for his whistle and blew a shrill and prolonged blast. Over the smooth water of the roadstead came in answer a faint cry from one of the ships at anchor.

"My boat will be here directly," said Lingard. "Think of what you are going to do. I sail to-night."

"What is there for me to do, except one thing?" said Willems, gloomily.

"Look here," said Lingard; "I picked you up as a boy, and consider myself responsible for you in a way. You took your life into your own hands many years ago—but still . . ."

He paused, listening, till he heard the regular grind of the oars in the rowlocks of the approaching boat then went on again.

"I have made it all right with Hudig. You owe him nothing now. Go back to your wife. She is a good woman. Go back to her."

"Why, Captain Lingard," exclaimed Willems, "she . . ."

"It was most affecting," went on Lingard, without heeding him. "I went to your house to look for you and there I saw her despair. It was heart-breaking. She called for you; she entreated me to find you. She spoke wildly, poor woman, as if all this was her fault."

Willems listened amazed. The blind old idiot! How queerly he misunderstood! But if it was true, if it was even true, the very idea of seeing her filled his soul with intense loathing. He did not break his oath, but he would not go back to her. Let hers be the sin of that separation; of the sacred bond broken. He revelled in the extreme purity of his heart, and he would not go back to her. Let her come back to him. He had the comfortable conviction that he would never see her again, and that through her own fault only. In this conviction he told himself solemnly that if she would come to him he would receive her with generous forgiveness, because such was the praiseworthy solidity of his principles. But he hesitated whether he would or would not disclose to Lingard the revolting completeness of his humiliation. Turned out of his house—and by his wife; that woman who hardly dared to breathe in his presence, yesterday. He remained perplexed and silent. No. He lacked the courage to tell the ignoble story.

As the boat of the brig appeared suddenly on the black water close to the jetty, Lingard broke the painful silence.

"I always thought," he said, sadly, "I always thought you were somewhat heartless, Willems, and apt to cast adrift those that thought most of you. I appeal to what is best in you; do not abandon that woman."

"I have not abandoned her," answered Willems, quickly, with conscious truthfulness. "Why should I? As you so justly observed, she has been a good wife to me. A very good, quiet, obedient, loving wife, and I love her as much as she loves me. Every bit. But as to going back now, to that place where I . . . To walk again amongst those men who yesterday were ready to crawl before me, and then feel on my back the sting of their pitying or satisfied smiles—no! I can't. I would rather hide from them at the bottom of the sea," he went on, with resolute energy. "I don't think, Captain Lingard," he added, more quietly, "I don't think that you realize what my position was there."

In a wide sweep of his hand he took in the sleeping shore from north to south, as if wishing it a proud and threatening good-bye. For a short moment he forgot his downfall in the recollection of his brilliant triumphs. Amongst the men of his class and occupation who slept in those dark houses he had been indeed the first.

"It is hard," muttered Lingard, pensively. "But whose the fault? Whose the fault?"

"Captain Lingard!" cried Willems, under the sudden impulse of a felicitous inspiration, "if you leave me here on this jetty—it's murder. I shall never return to that place alive, wife or no wife. You may just as well cut my throat at once."

The old seaman started.

"Don't try to frighten me, Willems," he said, with great severity, and paused.

Above the accents of Willems' brazen despair he heard, with considerable uneasiness, the whisper of his own absurd conscience. He meditated for awhile with an irresolute air.

"I could tell you to go and drown yourself, and be damned to you," he said, with an unsuccessful assumption of brutality in his manner, "but I won't. We are responsible for one another—worse luck. I am almost ashamed of myself, but I can understand your dirty pride. I can! By . . ."

He broke off with a loud sigh and walked briskly to the steps, at the bottom of which lay his boat, rising and falling gently on the slight and invisible swell.

"Below there! Got a lamp in the boat? Well, light it and bring it up, one of you. Hurry now!"

He tore out a page of his pocketbook, moistened his pencil with great energy and waited, stamping his feet impatiently.

"I will see this thing through," he muttered to himself. "And I will have it all square and ship-shape; see if I don't! Are you going to bring that lamp, you son of a crippled mud-turtle? I am waiting."

The gleam of the light on the paper placated his professional anger, and he wrote rapidly, the final dash of his signature curling the paper up in a triangular tear.

"Take that to this white Tuan's house. I will send the boat back for you in half an hour."

The coxswain raised his lamp deliberately to Willem's face.

"This Tuan? Tau! I know."

"Quick then!" said Lingard, taking the lamp from him—and the man went off at a run.

"Kassi mem! To the lady herself," called Lingard after him.

Then, when the man disappeared, he turned to Willems.

"I have written to your wife," he said. "If you do not return for good, you do not go back to that house only for another parting. You must come as you stand. I won't have that poor woman tormented. I will see to it that you are not separated for long. Trust me!"

Willems shivered, then smiled in the darkness.

"No fear of that," he muttered, enigmatically. "I trust you implicitly, Captain Lingard," he added, in a louder tone.

Lingard led the way down the steps, swinging the lamp and speaking over his shoulder.

"It is the second time, Willems, I take you in hand. Mind it is the last. The second time; and the only difference between then and now is that you were bare-footed then and have boots now. In fourteen years. With all your smartness! A poor result that. A very poor result."

He stood for awhile on the lowest platform of the steps, the light of the lamp falling on the upturned face of the stroke oar, who held the gunwale of the boat close alongside, ready for the captain to step in.

"You see," he went on, argumentatively, fumbling about the top of the lamp, "you got yourself so crooked amongst those 'longshore quill-drivers that you could not run clear in any way. That's what comes of such talk as yours, and of such a life. A man sees so much falsehood that he begins to lie to himself. Pah!" he said, in disgust, "there's only one place for an honest man. The sea, my boy, the sea! But you never would; didn't think there was enough money in it; and now—look!"

He blew the light out, and, stepping into the boat, stretched quickly his hand towards Willems, with friendly care. Willems sat by him in silence, and the boat shoved off, sweeping in a wide circle towards the brig.

"Your compassion is all for my wife, Captain Lingard," said Willems, moodily. "Do you think I am so very happy?"

"No! no!" said Lingard, heartily. "Not a word more shall pass my lips. I had to speak my mind once, seeing that I knew you from a child, so to speak. And now I shall forget; but you are young yet. Life is very long," he went on, with unconscious sadness; "let this be a lesson to you."

He laid his hand affectionately on Willems' shoulder, and they both sat silent till the boat came alongside the ship's ladder.

When on board Lingard gave orders to his mate, and leading Willems on the poop, sat on the breech of one of the brass six-pounders with which his vessel was armed. The boat went off again to bring back the messenger. As soon as it was seen returning dark forms appeared on the brig's spars; then the sails fell in festoons with a swish of their heavy folds, and hung motionless under the yards in the dead calm of the clear and dewy night. From the forward end came the clink of the windlass, and soon afterwards the hail of the chief mate informing Lingard that the cable was hove short.

"Hold on everything," hailed back Lingard; "we must wait for the land-breeze before we let go our hold of the ground."

He approached Willems, who sat on the skylight, his body bent down, his head low, and his hands hanging listlessly between his knees.

"I am going to take you to Sambir," he said. "You've never heard of the place, have you? Well, it's up that river of mine about which people talk so much and know so little. I've found out the entrance for a ship of Flash's size. It isn't easy. You'll see. I will show you. You have been at sea long enough to take an interest. . . . Pity you didn't stick to it. Well, I am going there. I have my own trading post in the place. Almayer is my partner. You knew him when he was at Hudig's. Oh, he lives there as happy as a king. D'ye see, I have them all in my pocket. The rajah is an old friend of mine. My word is law—and I am the only trader. No other white man but Almayer had ever been in that settlement. You will live quietly there till I come back from my next cruise to the westward. We shall see then what can be done for you. Never fear. I have no doubt my secret will be safe with you. Keep mum about my river when you get amongst the traders again. There's many would give their ears for the knowledge of it. I'll tell you something: that's where I get all my guttah and rattans. Simply inexhaustible, my boy."

While Lingard spoke Willems looked up quickly, but soon his head fell on his breast in the discouraging certitude that the knowledge he and Hudig had wished for so much had come to him too late. He sat in a listless attitude.

"You will help Almayer in his trading if you have a heart for it," continued Lingard, "just to kill time till I come back for you. Only six weeks or so."

Over their heads the damp sails fluttered noisily in the first faint puff of the breeze; then, as the airs freshened, the brig tended to the wind, and the silenced canvas lay quietly aback. The mate spoke with low distinctness from the shadows of the quarter-deck.

"There's the breeze. Which way do you want to cast her, Captain Lingard?"

Lingard's eyes, that had been fixed aloft, glanced down at the dejected figure of the man sitting on the skylight. He seemed to hesitate for a minute.

"To the northward, to the northward," he answered, testily, as if annoyed at his own fleeting thought, "and bear a hand there. Every puff of wind is worth money in these seas."

He remained motionless, listening to the rattle of blocks and the creaking of trusses as the head-yards were hauled round. Sail was made on the ship and the windlass manned again while he stood still, lost in thought. He only roused himself when a barefooted seacannie glided past him silently on his way to the wheel.

"Put the helm aport! Hard over!" he said, in his harsh sea-voice, to the man whose face appeared suddenly out of the darkness in the circle of light thrown upwards from the binnacle lamps.

The anchor was secured, the yards trimmed, and the brig began to move out of the roadstead. The sea woke up under the push of the sharp cutwater, and whispered softly to the gliding craft in that tender and rippling murmur in which it speaks sometimes to those it nurses and loves. Lingard stood by the taff-rail listening, with a pleased smile till the Flash began to draw close to the only other vessel in the anchorage.

"Here, Willems," he said, calling him to his side, "d'ye see that barque here? That's an Arab vessel. White men have mostly given up the game, but this fellow drops in my wake often, and lives in hopes of cutting me out in that settlement. Not while I live, I trust. You see, Willems, I brought prosperity to that place. I composed their quarrels, and saw them grow under my eyes. There's peace and happiness there. I am more master there than his Dutch Excellency down in Batavia ever will be when some day a lazy man-of-war blunders at last against the river. I mean to keep the Arabs out of it, with their lies and their intrigues. I shall keep the venomous breed out, if it costs me my fortune."

The Flash drew quietly abreast of the barque, and was beginning to drop it astern when a white figure started up on the poop of the Arab vessel, and a voice called out—

"Greeting to the Rajah Laut!"

"To you greeting!" answered Lingard, after a moment of hesitating surprise. Then he turned to Willems with a grim smile. "That's Abdulla's voice," he said. "Mighty civil all of a sudden, isn't he? I wonder what it means. Just like his impudence! No matter! His civility or his impudence are all one to me. I know that this fellow will be under way and after me like a shot. I don't care! I have the heels of anything that floats in these seas," he added, while his proud and loving glance ran over and rested fondly amongst the brig's lofty and graceful spars.

5

"It was the writing on his forehead," said Babalatchi, adding a couple of small sticks to the little fire by which he was squatting, and without looking at Lakamba who lay down supported on his elbow on the other side of the embers. "It was written when he was born that he should end his life in darkness, and now he is like a man walking in a black night—with his eyes open, yet seeing not. I knew him well when he had slaves, and many wives, and much merchandise, and trading praus, and praus for fighting. Hai—ya! He was a great fighter in the days before the breath of the Merciful put out the light in his eyes. He was a pilgrim, and had many virtues: he was brave, his hand was open, and he was a great robber. For many years he led the men that drank blood on the sea: first in prayer and first in fight! Have I not stood behind him when his face was turned to the West? Have I not watched by his side ships with high masts burning in a straight flame on the calm water? Have I not followed him on dark nights amongst sleeping men that woke up only to die? His sword was swifter than the fire from Heaven, and struck before it flashed. Hai! Tuan! Those were the days and that was a leader, and I myself was younger; and in those days there were not so many fireships with guns that deal fiery death from afar. Over the hill and over the forest—O! Tuan Lakamba! they dropped whistling fireballs into the creek where our praus took refuge, and where they dared not follow men who had arms in their hands."

He shook his head with mournful regret and threw another handful of fuel on the fire. The burst of clear flame lit up his broad, dark, and pock-marked face, where the big lips, stained with betel-juice, looked like a deep and bleeding gash of a fresh wound. The reflection of the firelight gleamed brightly in his solitary eye, lending it for a moment a fierce animation that died out together with the short-lived flame. With quick touches of his bare hands he raked the embers into a heap, then, wiping the warm ash on his waistcloth—his only garment—he clasped his thin legs with his entwined fingers, and rested his chin on his drawn-up knees. Lakamba stirred slightly without changing his position or taking his eyes off the glowing coals, on which they had been fixed in dreamy immobility.

"Yes," went on Babalatchi, in a low monotone, as if pursuing aloud a train of thought that had its beginning in the silent contemplation of the unstable nature of earthly greatness

—"yes. He has been rich and strong, and now he lives on alms: old, feeble, blind, and without companions, but for his daughter. The Rajah Patalolo gives him rice, and the pale woman—his daughter—cooks it for him, for he has no slave."

"I saw her from afar," muttered Lakamba, disparagingly. "A she-dog with white teeth, like a woman of the Orang-Putih."

"Right, right," assented Babalatchi; "but you have not seen her near. Her mother was a woman from the west; a Baghdadi woman with veiled face. Now she goes uncovered, like our women do, for she is poor and he is blind, and nobody ever comes near them unless to ask for a charm or a blessing and depart quickly for fear of his anger and of the Rajah's hand. You have not been on that side of the river?"

"Not for a long time. If I go . . ."

"True! true!" interrupted Babalatchi, soothingly, "but I go often alone—for your good—and look—and listen. When the time comes; when we both go together towards the Rajah's campong, it will be to enter—and to remain."

Lakamba sat up and looked at Babalatchi gloomily.

"This is good talk, once, twice; when it is heard too often it becomes foolish, like the prattle of children."

"Many, many times have I seen the cloudy sky and have heard the wind of the rainy seasons," said Babalatchi, impressively.

"And where is your wisdom? It must be with the wind and the clouds of seasons past, for I do not hear it in your talk."

"Those are the words of the ungrateful!" shouted Babalatchi, with sudden exasperation. "Verily, our only refuge is with the One, the Mighty, the Redresser of . . ."

"Peace! Peace!" growled the startled Lakamba. "It is but a friend's talk."

Babalatchi subsided into his former attitude, muttering to himself. After awhile he went on again in a louder voice—

"Since the Rajah Laut left another white man here in Sambir, the daughter of the blind Omar el Badavi has spoken to other ears than mine."

"Would a white man listen to a beggar's daughter?" said Lakamba, doubtingly.

"Hai! I have seen . . ."

"And what did you see? O one-eyed one!" exclaimed Lakamba, contemptuously.

"I have seen the strange white man walking on the narrow path before the sun could dry the drops of dew on the bushes, and I have heard the whisper of his voice when he spoke through the smoke of the morning fire to that woman with big eyes and a pale skin. Woman in body, but in heart a man! She knows no fear and no shame. I have heard her voice too."

He nodded twice at Lakamba sagaciously and gave himself up to silent musing, his solitary eye fixed immovably upon the straight wall of forest on the opposite bank. Lakamba lay silent, staring vacantly. Under them Lingard's own river rippled softly amongst the piles supporting the bamboo platform of the little watch-house before which they were lying. Behind the house the ground rose in a gentle swell of a low hill cleared of the big timber, but thickly overgrown with the grass and bushes, now withered and burnt up in the long drought of the dry season. This old rice clearing, which had been several years lying fallow, was framed on three sides by the impenetrable and tangled growth of the untouched forest, and on the fourth came down to the muddy river bank. There was not a breath of wind on the land or river, but high above, in the transparent sky, little clouds rushed past the moon, now appearing in her diffused rays with the brilliance of silver, now obscuring her face with the blackness of ebony. Far away, in the middle of the river, a fish would leap now and then with a short splash, the very loudness of which measured the profundity of the overpowering silence that swallowed up the sharp sound suddenly.

Lakamba dozed uneasily off, but the wakeful Babalatchi sat thinking deeply, sighing from time to time, and slapping himself over his naked torso incessantly in a vain endeavour to keep off an occasional and wandering mosquito that, rising as high as the platform above the swarms of the riverside, would settle with a ping of triumph on the unexpected victim. The moon, pursuing her silent and toilsome path, attained her highest elevation, and chasing the shadow of the roof-eaves from Lakamba's face, seemed to hang arrested over their heads. Babalatchi revived the fire and woke up his companion, who sat up yawning and shivering discontentedly.

Babalatchi spoke again in a voice which was like the murmur of a brook that runs over the stones: low, monotonous, persistent; irresistible in its power to wear out and to destroy the hardest obstacles. Lakamba listened, silent but interested. They were Malay adventurers; ambitious men of that place and time; the Bohemians of their race. In the early days of the settlement, before the ruler Patalolo had shaken off his allegiance to the Sultan of Koti, Lakamba appeared in the river with two small trading vessels. He was disappointed to find already some semblance of organization amongst the settlers of various races who recognized the unobtrusive sway of old Patalolo, and he was not politic enough to conceal his disappointment. He declared himself to be a man from the east, from those parts where no white man ruled, and to be of an oppressed race, but of a princely family. And truly enough he had all the gifts of an exiled prince. He was discontented, ungrateful, turbulent; a man full of envy and ready for intrigue, with brave words and empty promises for ever on his lips. He was obstinate, but his will was made up of short impulses that never lasted long enough to carry him to the goal of his ambition. Received coldly by the suspicious Patalolo, he persisted—permission or no permission—in clearing the ground on a good spot some fourteen miles down the river from Sambir, and built himself a house there, which he fortified by a high palisade. As he had many followers and seemed very reckless, the old Rajah did not think it prudent at the time to interfere with him by force. Once settled, he began to intrigue. The quarrel of Patalolo with the Sultan of Koti was of his fomenting, but failed to produce the result he expected because the Sultan could not back him up effectively at such a great distance. Disappointed in that scheme, he promptly organized an outbreak of the Bugis settlers, and besieged the old Rajah in his stockade with much noisy valour and a fair chance of success; but Lingard then appeared on the scene with the armed brig, and the old seaman's hairy forefinger, shaken menacingly in his face, quelled his martial ardour. No man cared to encounter the Rajah Laut, and Lakamba, with momentary resignation, subsided into a half-cultivator, half-trader, and nursed in his fortified house his wrath and his ambition, keeping it for use on a more propitious occasion. Still faithful to his character of a prince-pretender, he would not recognize the constituted authorities, answering sulkily the Rajah's messenger, who claimed the tribute for the cultivated fields, that the Rajah had better come and take it himself. By Lingard's advice he was left alone, notwithstanding his rebellious mood; and for many days he lived undisturbed amongst his wives and retainers, cherishing that persistent and causeless hope of better times, the possession of which seems to be the universal privilege of exiled greatness.

But the passing days brought no change. The hope grew faint and the hot ambition burnt itself out, leaving only a feeble and expiring spark amongst a heap of dull and tepid ashes of indolent acquiescence with the decrees of Fate, till Babalatchi fanned it again into a bright flame. Babalatchi had blundered upon the river while in search of a safe refuge for his disreputable head.

He was a vagabond of the seas, a true Orang-Laut, living by rapine and plunder of coasts and ships in his prosperous days; earning his living by honest and irksome toil when the days of adversity were upon him. So, although at times leading the Sulu rovers, he had also served as Serang of country ships, and in that wise had visited the distant seas, beheld the glories of Bombay, the might of the Mascati Sultan; had even struggled in a pious throng for the privilege of touching with his lips the Sacred Stone of the Holy City. He gathered experience and wisdom in many lands, and after attaching himself to Omar el Badavi, he affected great piety (as became a pilgrim), although unable to read the inspired words of the Prophet. He was brave and bloodthirsty without any affection, and he hated the white men who interfered with the manly pursuits of throat-cutting, kidnapping, slave-dealing, and fire-raising, that were the only possible occupation for a true man of the sea. He found favour in the eyes of his chief, the fearless Omar el Badavi, the leader of Brunei rovers, whom he followed with unquestioning loyalty through the long years of successful depredation. And when that long career of murder, robbery and violence received its first serious check at the hands of white men, he stood faithfully by his chief, looked steadily at the bursting shells, was undismayed by the flames of the burning stronghold, by the death of his companions, by the shrieks of their women, the wailing of their children; by the sudden ruin and destruction of all that he deemed indispensable to a happy and glorious existence. The beaten ground between the houses was slippery with blood, and the dark mangroves of the muddy creeks were full of sighs of the dying men who were stricken down before they could see their enemy. They died helplessly, for into the tangled forest there was no escape, and their swift praus, in which they had so often scoured the coast and the seas, now wedged together in the narrow creek, were burning fiercely. Babalatchi, with the clear perception of the coming end, devoted all his energies to saving if it was but only one of them. He succeeded in time. When the end came in the explosion of the stored powder-barrels, he was ready to look for his chief. He found him half dead and totally blinded, with nobody near him but his daughter Aissa:—the sons had fallen earlier in the day, as became men of their courage. Helped by the girl with the steadfast heart, Babalatchi carried Omar on board the light prau and succeeded in escaping, but with very few companions only. As they hauled their craft into the network of dark and silent creeks, they could hear the cheering of the crews of the man-of-war's boats dashing to the attack of the rover's village. Aissa, sitting on the high after-deck, her father's blackened and bleeding head in her lap, looked up with fearless eyes at Babalatchi. "They shall find only smoke, blood and dead men, and women mad with fear there, but nothing else living," she said, mournfully. Babalatchi, pressing with his right hand the deep gash on his shoulder, answered sadly: "They are very strong. When we fight with them we can only die. Yet," he added, menacingly—"some of us still live! Some of us still live!"

For a short time he dreamed of vengeance, but his dream was dispelled by the cold reception of the Sultan of Sulu, with whom they sought refuge at first and who gave them only a contemptuous and grudging hospitality. While Omar, nursed by Aissa, was recovering from his wounds, Babalatchi attended industriously before the exalted Presence that had extended to them the hand of Protection. For all that, when Babalatchi spoke into the Sultan's ear certain proposals of a great and profitable raid, that was to sweep the islands from Ternate to Acheen, the Sultan was very angry. "I know you, you men from the west," he exclaimed, angrily. "Your words are poison in a Ruler's ears. Your talk is of fire and murder and booty—but on our heads falls the vengeance of the blood you drink. Begone!"

There was nothing to be done. Times were changed. So changed that, when a Spanish frigate appeared before the island and a demand was sent to the Sultan to deliver Omar and his companions, Babalatchi was not surprised to hear that they were going to be made the victims of political expediency. But from that sane appreciation of danger to tame submission was a very long step. And then began Omar's second flight. It began arms in hand, for the little band had to fight in the night on the beach for the possession of the small canoes in which those that survived got away at last. The story of that escape lives in the hearts of brave men even to this day. They talk of Babalatchi and of the strong woman who carried her blind father through the surf under the fire of the warship from the north. The companions of that piratical and son-less Aeneas are dead now, but their ghosts wander over the waters and the islands at night—after the manner of ghosts—and haunt the fires by which sit armed men, as is meet for the spirits of fearless warriors who died in battle. There they may hear the story of their own deeds, of their own courage, suffering and death, on the lips of living men. That story is told in many places. On the cool mats in breezy verandahs of Rajahs' houses it is alluded to disdainfully by impassive statesmen, but amongst armed men that throng the courtyards it is a tale which stills the murmur of voices and the tinkle of anklets; arrests the passage of the siri-vessel, and fixes the eyes in absorbed gaze. They talk of the fight, of the fearless woman, of the wise man; of long suffering on the thirsty sea in leaky canoes; of those who died. . . . Many died. A few survived. The chief, the woman, and another one who became great.

There was no hint of incipient greatness in Babalatchi's unostentatious arrival in Sambir. He came with Omar and Aissa in a small prau loaded with green cocoanuts, and claimed the ownership of both vessel and cargo. How it came to pass that Babalatchi, fleeing for his life in a small canoe, managed to end his hazardous journey in a vessel full of a valuable commodity, is one of those secrets of the sea that baffle the most searching inquiry. In truth nobody inquired much. There were rumours of a missing trading prau belonging to Menado, but they were vague and remained mysterious. Babalatchi told a story which—it must be said in justice to Patalolo's knowledge of the world—was not believed. When the Rajah ventured to state his doubts, Babalatchi asked him in tones of calm remonstrance whether he could reasonably suppose that two oldish men—who had only one eye amongst them—and a young woman were likely to gain possession of anything whatever by violence? Charity was a virtue recommended by the Prophet. There were charitable people, and their hand was open to the deserving. Patalolo wagged his aged head doubtingly, and Babalatchi withdrew with a shocked mien and put himself forthwith under Lakamba's protection. The two men who completed the prau's crew followed him into that magnate's campong. The blind Omar, with Aissa, remained under the care of the Rajah, and the Rajah confiscated the cargo. The prau hauled up on the mud-bank, at the junction of the two branches of the Pantai, rotted in the rain, warped in the sun, fell to pieces and gradually vanished into the smoke of household fires of the settlement. Only a forgotten plank and a rib or two, sticking neglected in the shiny ooze for a long time, served to remind Babalatchi during many months that he was a stranger in the land.

Otherwise, he felt perfectly at home in Lakamba's establishment, where his peculiar position and influence were quickly recognized and soon submitted to even by the women. He had all a true vagabond's pliability to circumstances and adaptiveness to momentary surroundings. In his readiness to learn from experience that contempt for early principles so necessary to a true statesman, he equalled the most successful politicians of any age; and he had enough persuasiveness and firmness of purpose to acquire a complete mastery over Lakamba's vacillating mind—where there was nothing stable but an all-pervading discontent. He kept the discontent alive, he rekindled the expiring ambition, he moderated the poor exile's not unnatural impatience to attain a high and lucrative position. He—the man of violence—deprecated the use of force, for he had a clear comprehension of the difficult situation. From the same cause, he—the hater of white men—would to some extent admit the eventual expediency of Dutch protection. But nothing should be done in a hurry. Whatever his master Lakamba might think, there was no use in poisoning old Patalolo, he maintained. It could be done, of course; but what then? As long as Lingard's influence was paramount—as long as Almayer, Lingard's representative, was the only great trader of the settlement, it was not worth Lakamba's while—even if it had been possible—to grasp the rule of the young state. Killing Almayer and Lingard was so difficult and so risky that it might be dismissed as impracticable. What was wanted was an alliance; somebody to set up against the white men's influence—and somebody who, while favourable to Lakamba, would at the same time be a person of a good standing with the Dutch authorities. A rich and considered trader was wanted. Such a person once firmly established in Sambir would help them to oust the old Rajah, to remove him from power or from life if there was no other way. Then it would be time to apply to the Orang Blanda for a flag; for a recognition of their meritorious services; for that protection which would make them safe for ever! The word of a rich and loyal trader would mean something with the Ruler down in Batavia. The first thing to do was to find such an ally and to induce him to settle in Sambir. A white trader would not do. A white man would not fall in with their ideas—would not be trustworthy. The man they wanted should be rich, unscrupulous, have many followers, and be a well-known personality in the islands. Such a man might be found amongst the Arab traders. Lingard's jealousy, said Babalatchi, kept all the traders out of the river. Some were afraid, and some did not know how to get there; others ignored the very existence of Sambir; a good many did not think it worth their while to run the risk of Lingard's enmity for the doubtful advantage of trade with a comparatively unknown settlement. The great majority were undesirable or untrustworthy. And Babalatchi mentioned regretfully the men he had known in his young days: wealthy, resolute, courageous, reckless, ready for any enterprise! But why lament the past and speak about the dead? There is one man—living—great—not far off . . .

Such was Babalatchi's line of policy laid before his ambitious protector. Lakamba assented, his only objection being that it was very slow work. In his extreme desire to grasp dollars and power, the unintellectual exile was ready to throw himself into the arms of any wandering cut-throat whose help could be secured, and Babalatchi experienced great difficulty in restraining him from unconsidered violence. It would not do to let it be seen that they had any hand in introducing a new element into the social and political life of Sambir. There was always a possibility of failure, and in that case Lingard's vengeance would be swift and certain. No risk should be run. They must wait.

Meantime he pervaded the settlement, squatting in the course of each day by many household fires, testing the public temper and public opinion—and always talking about his impending departure.

At night he would often take Lakamba's smallest canoe and depart silently to pay mysterious visits to his old chief on the other side of the river. Omar lived in odour of sanctity under the wing of Patalolo. Between the bamboo fence, enclosing the houses of the Rajah, and the wild forest, there was a banana plantation, and on its further edge stood two little houses built on low piles under a few precious fruit trees that grew on the banks of a clear brook, which, bubbling up behind the house, ran in its short and rapid course down to the big river. Along the brook a narrow path led through the dense second growth of a neglected clearing to the banana plantation and to the houses in it which the Rajah had given for residence to Omar. The Rajah was greatly impressed by Omar's ostentatious piety, by his oracular wisdom, by his many misfortunes, by the solemn fortitude with which he bore his affliction. Often the old ruler of Sambir would visit informally the blind Arab and listen gravely to his talk during the hot hours of an afternoon. In the night, Babalatchi would call and interrupt Omar's repose, unrebuked. Aissa, standing silently at the door of one of the huts, could see the two old friends as they sat very still by the fire in the middle of the beaten ground between the two houses, talking in an indistinct murmur far into the night. She could not hear their words, but she watched the two formless shadows curiously. Finally Babalatchi would rise and, taking her father by the wrist, would lead him back to the house, arrange his mats for him, and go out quietly. Instead of going away, Babalatchi, unconscious of Aissa's eyes, often sat again by the fire, in a long and deep meditation. Aissa looked with respect on that wise and brave man—she was accustomed to see at her father's side as long as she could remember—sitting alone and thoughtful in the silent night by the dying fire, his body motionless and his mind wandering in the land of memories, or—who knows?—perhaps groping for a road in the waste spaces of the uncertain future.

Babalatchi noted the arrival of Willems with alarm at this new accession to the white men's strength. Afterwards he changed his opinion. He met Willems one night on the path leading to Omar's house, and noticed later on, with only a moderate surprise, that the blind Arab did not seem to be aware of the new white man's visits to the neighbourhood of his dwelling. Once, coming unexpectedly in the daytime, Babalatchi fancied he could see the gleam of a white jacket in the bushes on the other side of the brook. That day he watched Aissa pensively as she moved about preparing the evening rice; but after awhile he went hurriedly away before sunset, refusing Omar's hospitable invitation, in the name of Allah, to share their meal. That same evening he startled Lakamba by announcing that the time had come at last to make the first move in their long-deferred game. Lakamba asked excitedly for explanation. Babalatchi shook his head and pointed to the flitting shadows of moving women and to the vague forms of men sitting by the evening fires in the courtyard. Not a word would he speak here, he declared. But when the whole household was reposing, Babalatchi and Lakamba passed silent amongst sleeping groups to the riverside, and, taking a canoe, paddled off stealthily on their way to the dilapidated guard-hut in the old rice-clearing. There they were safe from all eyes and ears, and could account, if need be, for their excursion by the wish to kill a deer, the spot being well known as the drinking-place of all kinds of game. In the seclusion of its quiet solitude Babalatchi explained his plan to the attentive Lakamba. His idea was to make use of Willems for the destruction of Lingard's influence.

"I know the white men, Tuan," he said, in conclusion. "In many lands have I seen them; always the slaves of their desires, always ready to give up their strength and their reason into the hands of some woman. The fate of the Believers is written by the hand of the Mighty One, but they who worship many gods are thrown into the world with smooth foreheads, for any woman's hand to mark their destruction there. Let one white man destroy another. The will of the Most High is that they should be fools. They know how to keep faith with their enemies, but towards each other they know only deception. Hai! I have seen! I have seen!"

He stretched himself full length before the fire, and closed his eye in real or simulated sleep. Lakamba, not quite convinced, sat for a long time with his gaze riveted on the dull embers. As the night advanced, a slight white mist rose from the river, and the declining moon, bowed over the tops of the forest, seemed to seek the repose of the earth, like a wayward and wandering lover who returns at last to lay his tired and silent head on his beloved's breast.

6

"LEND ME YOUR GUN, ALMAYER," said Willems, across the table on which a smoky lamp shone redly above the disorder of a finished meal. "I have a mind to go and look for a deer when the moon rises to-night."

Almayer, sitting sidewise to the table, his elbow pushed amongst the dirty plates, his chin on his breast and his legs stretched stiffly out, kept his eyes steadily on the toes of his grass slippers and laughed abruptly.

"You might say yes or no instead of making that unpleasant noise," remarked Willems, with calm irritation.

"If I believed one word of what you say, I would," answered Almayer without changing his attitude and speaking slowly, with pauses, as if dropping his words on the floor. "As it is —what's the use? You know where the gun is; you may take it or leave it. Gun. Deer. Bosh! Hunt deer! Pah! It's a . . . gazelle you are after, my honoured guest. You want gold anklets and silk sarongs for that game—my mighty hunter. And you won't get those for the asking, I promise you. All day amongst the natives. A fine help you are to me."

"You shouldn't drink so much, Almayer," said Willems, disguising his fury under an affected drawl. "You have no head. Never had, as far as I can remember, in the old days in Macassar. You drink too much."

"I drink my own," retorted Almayer, lifting his head quickly and darting an angry glance at Willems.

Those two specimens of the superior race glared at each other savagely for a minute, then turned away their heads at the same moment as if by previous arrangement, and both got up. Almayer kicked off his slippers and scrambled into his hammock, which hung between two wooden columns of the verandah so as to catch every rare breeze of the dry season, and Willems, after standing irresolutely by the table for a short time, walked without a word down the steps of the house and over the courtyard towards the little wooden jetty, where several small canoes and a couple of big white whale-boats were made fast, tugging at their short painters and bumping together in the swift current of the river. He jumped into the smallest canoe, balancing himself clumsily, slipped the rattan painter, and gave an unnecessary and violent shove, which nearly sent him headlong overboard. By the time he regained his balance the canoe had drifted some fifty yards down the river. He knelt in the bottom of his little craft and fought the current with long sweeps of the paddle. Almayer sat up in his hammock, grasping his feet and peering over the river with parted lips till he made out the shadowy form of man and canoe as they struggled past the jetty again.

"I thought you would go," he shouted. "Won't you take the gun? Hey?" he yelled, straining his voice. Then he fell back in his hammock and laughed to himself feebly till he fell asleep. On the river, Willems, his eyes fixed intently ahead, swept his paddle right and left, unheeding the words that reached him faintly.

It was now three months since Lingard had landed Willems in Sambir and had departed hurriedly, leaving him in Almayer's care.

The two white men did not get on well together. Almayer, remembering the time when they both served Hudig, and when the superior Willems treated him with offensive condescension, felt a great dislike towards his guest. He was also jealous of Lingard's favour. Almayer had married a Malay girl whom the old seaman had adopted in one of his accesses of unreasoning benevolence, and as the marriage was not a happy one from a domestic point of view, he looked to Lingard's fortune for compensation in his matrimonial unhappiness. The appearance of that man, who seemed to have a claim of some sort upon Lingard, filled him with considerable uneasiness, the more so because the old seaman did not choose to acquaint the husband of his adopted daughter with Willems' history, or to confide to him his intentions as to that individual's future fate. Suspicious from the first, Almayer discouraged Willems' attempts to help him in his trading, and then when Willems drew back, he made, with characteristic perverseness, a grievance of his unconcern. From cold civility in their relations, the two men drifted into silent hostility, then into outspoken enmity, and both wished ardently for Lingard's return and the end of a situation that grew more intolerable from day to day. The time dragged slowly. Willems watched the succeeding sunrises wondering dismally whether before the evening some change would occur in the deadly dullness of his life. He missed the commercial activity of that existence which seemed to him far off, irreparably lost, buried out of sight under the ruins of his past success—now gone from him beyond the possibility of redemption. He mooned disconsolately about Almayer's courtyard, watching from afar, with uninterested eyes, the up-country canoes discharging guttah or rattans, and loading rice or European goods on the little wharf of Lingard & Co. Big as was the extent of ground owned by Almayer, Willems yet felt that there was not enough room for him inside those neat fences. The man who, during long years, became accustomed to think of himself as indispensable to others, felt a bitter and savage rage at the cruel consciousness of his superfluity, of his uselessness; at the cold hostility visible in every look of the only white man in this barbarous corner of the world. He gnashed his teeth when he thought of the wasted days, of the life thrown away in the unwilling company of that peevish and suspicious fool. He heard the reproach of his idleness in the murmurs of the river, in the unceasing whisper of the great forests. Round him everything stirred, moved, swept by in a rush; the earth under his feet and the heavens above his head. The very savages around him strove, struggled, fought, worked—if only to prolong a miserable existence; but they lived, they lived! And it was only himself that seemed to be left outside the scheme of creation in a hopeless immobility filled with tormenting anger and with ever-stinging regret.

He took to wandering about the settlement. The afterwards flourishing Sambir was born in a swamp and passed its youth in malodorous mud. The houses crowded the bank, and, as if to get away from the unhealthy shore, stepped boldly into the river, shooting over it in a close row of bamboo platforms elevated on high piles, amongst which the current below spoke in a soft and unceasing plaint of murmuring eddies. There was only one path in the whole town and it ran at the back of the houses along the succession of blackened circular patches that marked the place of the household fires. On the other side the virgin forest bordered the path, coming close to it, as if to provoke impudently any passer-by to the solution of the gloomy problem of its depths. Nobody would accept the deceptive challenge. There were only a few feeble attempts at a clearing here and there, but the ground was low and the river, retiring after its yearly floods, left on each a gradually diminishing mudhole, where the imported buffaloes of the Bugis settlers wallowed happily during the heat of the day. When Willems walked on the path, the indolent men stretched on the shady side of the houses looked at him with calm curiosity, the women busy round the cooking fires would send after him wondering and timid glances, while the children would only look once, and then run away yelling with fright at the horrible appearance of the man with a red and white face. These manifestations of childish disgust and fear stung Willems with a sense of absurd humiliation; he sought in his walks the comparative solitude of the rudimentary clearings, but the very buffaloes snorted with alarm at his sight, scrambled lumberingly out of the cool mud and stared wildly in a compact herd at him as he tried to slink unperceived along the edge of the forest. One day, at some unguarded and sudden movement of his, the whole herd stampeded down the path, scattered the fires, sent the women flying with shrill cries, and left behind a track of smashed pots, trampled rice, overturned children, and a crowd of angry men brandishing sticks in loud-voiced pursuit. The innocent cause of that disturbance ran shamefacedly the gauntlet of black looks and unfriendly remarks, and hastily sought refuge in Almayer's campong. After that he left the settlement alone.

Later, when the enforced confinement grew irksome, Willems took one of Almayer's many canoes and crossed the main branch of the Pantai in search of some solitary spot where he could hide his discouragement and his weariness. He skirted in his little craft the wall of tangled verdure, keeping in the dead water close to the bank where the spreading nipa palms nodded their broad leaves over his head as if in contemptuous pity of the wandering outcast. Here and there he could see the beginnings of chopped-out pathways, and, with the fixed idea of getting out of sight of the busy river, he would land and follow the narrow and winding path, only to find that it led nowhere, ending abruptly in the discouragement of thorny thickets. He would go back slowly, with a bitter sense of unreasonable disappointment and sadness; oppressed by the hot smell of earth, dampness, and decay in that forest which seemed to push him mercilessly back into the glittering sunshine of the river. And he would recommence paddling with tired arms to seek another opening, to find another deception.

As he paddled up to the point where the Rajah's stockade came down to the river, the nipas were left behind rattling their leaves over the brown water, and the big trees would appear on the bank, tall, strong, indifferent in the immense solidity of their life, which endures for ages, to that short and fleeting life in the heart of the man who crept painfully amongst their shadows in search of a refuge from the unceasing reproach of his thoughts. Amongst their smooth trunks a clear brook meandered for a time in twining lacets before it made up its mind to take a leap into the hurrying river, over the edge of the steep bank. There was also a pathway there and it seemed frequented. Willems landed, and following the capricious promise of the track soon found himself in a comparatively clear space, where the confused tracery of sunlight fell through the branches and the foliage overhead, and lay on the stream that shone in an easy curve like a bright sword-blade dropped amongst the long and feathery grass.

Further on, the path continued, narrowed again in the thick undergrowth. At the end of the first turning Willems saw a flash of white and colour, a gleam of gold like a sun-ray lost in shadow, and a vision of blackness darker than the deepest shade of the forest. He stopped, surprised, and fancied he had heard light footsteps—growing lighter—ceasing. He looked around. The grass on the bank of the stream trembled and a tremulous path of its shivering, silver-grey tops ran from the water to the beginning of the thicket. And yet there was not a breath of wind. Somebody kind passed there. He looked pensive while the tremor died out in a quick tremble under his eyes; and the grass stood high, unstirring, with drooping heads in the warm and motionless air.

He hurried on, driven by a suddenly awakened curiosity, and entered the narrow way between the bushes. At the next turn of the path he caught again the glimpse of coloured stuff and of a woman's black hair before him. He hastened his pace and came in full view of the object of his pursuit. The woman, who was carrying two bamboo vessels full of water, heard his footsteps, stopped, and putting the bamboos down half turned to look back. Willems also stood still for a minute, then walked steadily on with a firm tread, while the woman moved aside to let him pass. He kept his eyes fixed straight before him, yet almost unconsciously he took in every detail of the tall and graceful figure. As he approached her the woman tossed her head slightly back, and with a free gesture of her strong, round arm, caught up the mass of loose black hair and brought it over her shoulder and across the lower part of her face. The next moment he was passing her close, walking rigidly, like a man in a trance. He heard her rapid breathing and he felt the touch of a look darted at him from half-open eyes. It touched his brain and his heart together. It seemed to him to be something loud and stirring like a shout, silent and penetrating like an inspiration. The momentum of his motion carried him past her, but an invisible force made up of surprise and curiosity and desire spun him round as soon as he had passed.

She had taken up her burden already, with the intention of pursuing her path. His sudden movement arrested her at the first step, and again she stood straight, slim, expectant, with a readiness to dart away suggested in the light immobility of her pose. High above, the branches of the trees met in a transparent shimmer of waving green mist, through which the rain of yellow rays descended upon her head, streamed in glints down her black tresses, shone with the changing glow of liquid metal on her face, and lost itself in vanishing sparks in the sombre depths of her eyes that, wide open now, with enlarged pupils, looked steadily at the man in her path. And Willems stared at her, charmed with a charm that carries with it a sense of irreparable loss, tingling with that feeling which begins like a caress and ends in a blow, in that sudden hurt of a new emotion making its way into a human heart, with the brusque stirring of sleeping sensations awakening suddenly to the rush of new hopes, new fears, new desires—and to the flight of one's old self.

She moved a step forward and again halted. A breath of wind that came through the trees, but in Willems' fancy seemed to be driven by her moving figure, rippled in a hot wave round his body and scorched his face in a burning touch. He drew it in with a long breath, the last long breath of a soldier before the rush of battle, of a lover before he takes in his arms the adored woman; the breath that gives courage to confront the menace of death or the storm of passion.

Who was she? Where did she come from? Wonderingly he took his eyes off her face to look round at the serried trees of the forest that stood big and still and straight, as if watching him and her breathlessly. He had been baffled, repelled, almost frightened by the intensity of that tropical life which wants the sunshine but works in gloom; which seems to be all grace of colour and form, all brilliance, all smiles, but is only the blossoming of the dead; whose mystery holds the promise of joy and beauty, yet contains nothing but poison and decay. He had been frightened by the vague perception of danger before, but now, as he looked at that life again, his eyes seemed able to pierce the fantastic veil of creepers and leaves, to look past the solid trunks, to see through the forbidding gloom—and the mystery was disclosed—enchanting, subduing, beautiful. He looked at the woman. Through the checkered light between them she appeared to him with the impalpable distinctness of a dream. The very spirit of that land of mysterious forests, standing before him like an apparition behind a transparent veil—a veil woven of sunbeams and shadows.

She had approached him still nearer. He felt a strange impatience within him at her advance. Confused thoughts rushed through his head, disordered, shapeless, stunning. Then he heard his own voice asking—

"Who are you?"

"I am the daughter of the blind Omar," she answered, in a low but steady tone. "And you," she went on, a little louder, "you are the white trader—the great man of this place."

"Yes," said Willems, holding her eyes with his in a sense of extreme effort, "Yes, I am white." Then he added, feeling as if he spoke about some other man, "But I am the outcast of my people."

She listened to him gravely. Through the mesh of scattered hair her face looked like the face of a golden statue with living eyes. The heavy eyelids dropped slightly, and from between the long eyelashes she sent out a sidelong look: hard, keen, and narrow, like the gleam of sharp steel. Her lips were firm and composed in a graceful curve, but the distended nostrils, the upward poise of the half-averted head, gave to her whole person the expression of a wild and resentful defiance.

A shadow passed over Willems' face. He put his hand over his lips as if to keep back the words that wanted to come out in a surge of impulsive necessity, the outcome of dominant thought that rushes from the heart to the brain and must be spoken in the face of doubt, of danger, of fear, of destruction itself.

"You are beautiful," he whispered.

She looked at him again with a glance that running in one quick flash of her eyes over his sunburnt features, his broad shoulders, his straight, tall, motionless figure, rested at last on the ground at his feet. Then she smiled. In the sombre beauty of her face that smile was like the first ray of light on a stormy daybreak that darts evanescent and pale through the gloomy clouds: the forerunner of sunrise and of thunder.

7

THERE ARE in our lives short periods which hold no place in memory but only as the recollection of a feeling. There is no remembrance of gesture, of action, of any outward manifestation of life; those are lost in the unearthly brilliance or in the unearthly gloom of such moments. We are absorbed in the contemplation of that something, within our bodies, which rejoices or suffers while the body goes on breathing, instinctively runs away or, not less instinctively, fights—perhaps dies. But death in such a moment is the privilege of the fortunate, it is a high and rare favour, a supreme grace.

Willems never remembered how and when he parted from Aissa. He caught himself drinking the muddy water out of the hollow of his hand, while his canoe was drifting in mid-stream past the last houses of Sambir. With his returning wits came the fear of something unknown that had taken possession of his heart, of something inarticulate and masterful which could not speak and would be obeyed. His first impulse was that of revolt. He would never go back there. Never! He looked round slowly at the brilliance of things in the deadly sunshine and took up his paddle! How changed everything seemed! The river was broader, the sky was higher. How fast the canoe flew under the strokes of his paddle! Since when had he acquired the strength of two men or more? He looked up and down the reach at the forests of the bank with a confused notion that with one sweep of his hand he could tumble all these trees into the stream. His face felt burning. He drank again, and shuddered with a depraved sense of pleasure at the after-taste of slime in the water.

It was late when he reached Almayer's house, but he crossed the dark and uneven courtyard, walking lightly in the radiance of some light of his own, invisible to other eyes. His host's sulky greeting jarred him like a sudden fall down a great height. He took his place at the table opposite Almayer and tried to speak cheerfully to his gloomy companion, but when the meal was ended and they sat smoking in silence he felt an abrupt discouragement, a lassitude in all his limbs, a sense of immense sadness as after some great and irreparable loss. The darkness of the night entered his heart, bringing with it doubt and hesitation and dull anger with himself and all the world. He had an impulse to shout horrible curses, to quarrel with Almayer, to do something violent. Quite without any immediate provocation he thought he would like to assault the wretched, sulky beast. He glanced at him ferociously from under his eyebrows. The unconscious Almayer smoked thoughtfully, planning to-morrow's work probably. The man's composure seemed to Willems an unpardonable insult. Why didn't that idiot talk to-night when he wanted him to? . . . on other nights he was ready enough to chatter. And such dull nonsense too! And Willems, trying hard to repress his own senseless rage, looked fixedly through the thick tobacco-smoke at the stained tablecloth.

They retired early, as usual, but in the middle of the night Willems leaped out of his hammock with a stifled execration and ran down the steps into the courtyard. The two night watchmen, who sat by a little fire talking together in a monotonous undertone, lifted their heads to look wonderingly at the discomposed features of the white man as he crossed the circle of light thrown out by their fire. He disappeared in the darkness and then came back again, passing them close, but with no sign of consciousness of their presence on his face. Backwards and forwards he paced, muttering to himself, and the two Malays, after a short consultation in whispers left the fire quietly, not thinking it safe to remain in the vicinity of a white man who behaved in such a strange manner. They retired round the corner of the godown and watched Willems curiously through the night, till the short daybreak was followed by the sudden blaze of the rising sun, and Almayer's establishment woke up to life and work.

As soon as he could get away unnoticed in the bustle of the busy riverside, Willems crossed the river on his way to the place where he had met Aissa. He threw himself down in the grass by the side of the brook and listened for the sound of her footsteps. The brilliant light of day fell through the irregular opening in the high branches of the trees and streamed down, softened, amongst the shadows of big trunks. Here and there a narrow sunbeam touched the rugged bark of a tree with a golden splash, sparkled on the leaping water of the brook, or rested on a leaf that stood out, shimmering and distinct, on the monotonous background of sombre green tints. The clear gap of blue above his head was crossed by the quick flight of white rice-birds whose wings flashed in the sunlight, while through it the heat poured down from the sky, clung about the steaming earth, rolled among the trees, and wrapped up Willems in the soft and odorous folds of air heavy with the faint scent of blossoms and with the acrid smell of decaying life. And in that atmosphere of Nature's workshop Willems felt soothed and lulled into forgetfulness of his past, into indifference as to his future. The recollections of his triumphs, of his wrongs and of his ambition vanished in that warmth, which seemed to melt all regrets, all hope, all anger, all strength out of his heart. And he lay there, dreamily contented, in the tepid and perfumed shelter, thinking of Aissa's eyes; recalling the sound of her voice, the quiver of her lips—her frowns and her smile.

She came, of course. To her he was something new, unknown and strange. He was bigger, stronger than any man she had seen before, and altogether different from all those she knew. He was of the victorious race. With a vivid remembrance of the great catastrophe of her life he appeared to her with all the fascination of a great and dangerous thing; of a terror vanquished, surmounted, made a plaything of. They spoke with just such a deep voice—those victorious men; they looked with just such hard blue eyes at their enemies. And she made that voice speak softly to her, those eyes look tenderly at her face! He was indeed a man. She could not understand all he told her of his life, but the fragments she understood she made up for herself into a story of a man great amongst his own people, valorous and unfortunate; an undaunted fugitive dreaming of vengeance against his enemies. He had all the attractiveness of the vague and the unknown—of the unforeseen and of the sudden; of a being strong, dangerous, alive, and human, ready to be enslaved.

She felt that he was ready. She felt it with the unerring intuition of a primitive woman confronted by a simple impulse. Day after day, when they met and she stood a little way off, listening to his words, holding him with her look, the undefined terror of the new conquest became faint and blurred like the memory of a dream, and the certitude grew distinct, and convincing, and visible to the eyes like some material thing in full sunlight. It was a deep joy, a great pride, a tangible sweetness that seemed to leave the taste of honey on her lips. He lay stretched at her feet without moving, for he knew from experience how a slight movement of his could frighten her away in those first days of their intercourse. He lay very quiet, with all the ardour of his desire ringing in his voice and shining in his eyes, whilst his body was still, like death itself. And he looked at her, standing above him, her head lost in the shadow of broad and graceful leaves that touched her cheek; while the slender spikes of pale green orchids streamed down from amongst the boughs and mingled with the black hair that framed her face, as if all those plants claimed her for their own—the animated and brilliant flower of all that exuberant life which, born in gloom, struggles for ever towards the sunshine.

Every day she came a little nearer. He watched her slow progress—the gradual taming of that woman by the words of his love. It was the monotonous song of praise and desire that, commencing at creation, wraps up the world like an atmosphere and shall end only in the end of all things—when there are no lips to sing and no ears to hear. He told her that she was beautiful and desirable, and he repeated it again and again; for when he told her that, he had said all there was within him—he had expressed his only thought, his only feeling. And he watched the startled look of wonder and mistrust vanish from her face with the passing days, her eyes soften, the smile dwell longer and longer on her lips; a smile as of one charmed by a delightful dream; with the slight exaltation of intoxicating triumph lurking in its dawning tenderness.

And while she was near there was nothing in the whole world—for that idle man—but her look and her smile. Nothing in the past, nothing in the future; and in the present only the luminous fact of her existence. But in the sudden darkness of her going he would be left weak and helpless, as though despoiled violently of all that was himself. He who had lived all his life with no preoccupation but that of his own career, contemptuously indifferent to all feminine influence, full of scorn for men that would submit to it, if ever so little; he, so strong, so superior even in his errors, realized at last that his very individuality was snatched from within himself by the hand of a woman. Where was the assurance and pride of his cleverness; the belief in success, the anger of failure, the wish to retrieve his fortune, the certitude of his ability to accomplish it yet? Gone. All gone. All that had been a man within him was gone, and there remained only the trouble of his heart—that heart which had become a contemptible thing; which could be fluttered by a look or a smile, tormented by a word, soothed by a promise.

When the longed-for day came at last, when she sank on the grass by his side and with a quick gesture took his hand in hers, he sat up suddenly with the movement and look of a man awakened by the crash of his own falling house. All his blood, all his sensation, all his life seemed to rush into that hand leaving him without strength, in a cold shiver, in the sudden clamminess and collapse as of a deadly gun-shot wound. He flung her hand away brutally, like something burning, and sat motionless, his head fallen forward, staring on the ground and catching his breath in painful gasps. His impulse of fear and apparent horror did not dismay her in the least. Her face was grave and her eyes looked seriously at him. Her fingers touched the hair of his temple, ran in a light caress down his cheek, twisted gently the end of his long moustache: and while he sat in the tremor of that contact she ran off with startling fleetness and disappeared in a peal of clear laughter, in the stir of grass, in the nod of young twigs growing over the path; leaving behind only a vanishing trail of motion and sound.

He scrambled to his feet slowly and painfully, like a man with a burden on his shoulders, and walked towards the riverside. He hugged to his breast the recollection of his fear and of his delight, but told himself seriously over and over again that this must be the end of that adventure. After shoving off his canoe into the stream he lifted his eyes to the bank and gazed at it long and steadily, as if taking his last look at a place of charming memories. He marched up to Almayer's house with the concentrated expression and the determined step of a man who had just taken a momentous resolution. His face was set and rigid, his gestures and movements were guarded and slow. He was keeping a tight hand on himself. A very tight hand. He had a vivid illusion—as vivid as reality almost—of being in charge of a slippery prisoner. He sat opposite Almayer during that dinner—which was their last meal together—with a perfectly calm face and within him a growing terror of escape from his own self.

Now and then he would grasp the edge of the table and set his teeth hard in a sudden wave of acute despair, like one who, falling down a smooth and rapid declivity that ends in a precipice, digs his finger nails into the yielding surface and feels himself slipping helplessly to inevitable destruction.

Then, abruptly, came a relaxation of his muscles, the giving way of his will. Something seemed to snap in his head, and that wish, that idea kept back during all those hours, darted into his brain with the heat and noise of a conflagration. He must see her! See her at once! Go now! To-night! He had the raging regret of the lost hour, of every passing moment. There was no thought of resistance now. Yet with the instinctive fear of the irrevocable, with the innate falseness of the human heart, he wanted to keep open the way of retreat. He had never absented himself during the night. What did Almayer know? What would Almayer think? Better ask him for the gun. A moonlight night. . . . Look for deer. . . . A colourable pretext. He would lie to Almayer. What did it matter! He lied to himself every minute of his life. And for what? For a woman. And such. . . .

Almayer's answer showed him that deception was useless. Everything gets to be known, even in this place. Well, he did not care. Cared for nothing but for the lost seconds. What if he should suddenly die. Die before he saw her. Before he could . . .

As, with the sound of Almayer's laughter in his ears, he urged his canoe in a slanting course across the rapid current, he tried to tell himself that he could return at any moment. He would just go and look at the place where they used to meet, at the tree under which he lay when she took his hand, at the spot where she sat by his side. Just go there and then return—nothing more; but when his little skiff touched the bank he leaped out, forgetting the painter, and the canoe hung for a moment amongst the bushes and then swung out of sight before he had time to dash into the water and secure it. He was thunderstruck at first. Now he could not go back unless he called up the Rajah's people to get a boat and rowers—and the way to Patalolo's campong led past Aissa's house!

He went up the path with the eager eyes and reluctant steps of a man pursuing a phantom, and when he found himself at a place where a narrow track branched off to the left towards Omar's clearing he stood still, with a look of strained attention on his face as if listening to a far-off voice—the voice of his fate. It was a sound inarticulate but full of meaning; and following it there came a rending and tearing within his breast. He twisted his fingers together, and the joints of his hands and arms cracked. On his forehead the perspiration stood out in small pearly drops. He looked round wildly. Above the shapeless darkness of the forest undergrowth rose the treetops with their high boughs and leaves standing out black on the pale sky—like fragments of night floating on moonbeams. Under his feet warm steam rose from the heated earth. Round him there was a great silence.

He was looking round for help. This silence, this immobility of his surroundings seemed to him a cold rebuke, a stern refusal, a cruel unconcern. There was no safety outside of himself—and in himself there was no refuge; there was only the image of that woman. He had a sudden moment of lucidity—of that cruel lucidity that comes once in life to the most benighted. He seemed to see what went on within him, and was horrified at the strange sight. He, a white man whose worst fault till then had been a little want of judgment and too much confidence in the rectitude of his kind! That woman was a complete savage, and . . . He tried to tell himself that the thing was of no consequence. It was a vain effort. The novelty of the sensations he had never experienced before in the slightest degree, yet had despised on hearsay from his safe position of a civilized man, destroyed his courage. He was disappointed with himself. He seemed to be surrendering to a wild creature the unstained purity of his life, of his race, of his civilization. He had a notion of being lost amongst shapeless things that were dangerous and ghastly. He struggled with the sense of certain defeat—lost his footing—fell back into the darkness. With a faint cry and an upward throw of his arms he gave up as a tired swimmer gives up: because the swamped craft is gone from under his feet; because the night is dark and the shore is far—because death is better than strife.

II

I

THE LIGHT and heat fell upon the settlement, the clearings, and the river as if flung down by an angry hand. The land lay silent, still, and brilliant under the avalanche of burning rays that had destroyed all sound and all motion, had buried all shadows, had choked every breath. No living thing dared to affront the serenity of this cloudless sky, dared to revolt against the oppression of this glorious and cruel sunshine. Strength and resolution, body and mind alike were helpless, and tried to hide before the rush of the fire from heaven. Only the frail butterflies, the fearless children of the sun, the capricious tyrants of the flowers, fluttered audaciously in the open, and their minute shadows hovered in swarms over the drooping blossoms, ran lightly on the withering grass, or glided on the dry and cracked earth. No voice was heard in this hot noontide but the faint murmur of the river that hurried on in swirls and eddies, its sparkling wavelets chasing each other in their joyous course to the sheltering depths, to the cool refuge of the sea.

Almayer had dismissed his workmen for the midday rest, and, his little daughter on his shoulder, ran quickly across the courtyard, making for the shade of the verandah of his house. He laid the sleepy child on the seat of the big rocking-chair, on a pillow which he took out of his own hammock, and stood for a while looking down at her with tender and pensive eyes. The child, tired and hot, moved uneasily, sighed, and looked up at him with the veiled look of sleepy fatigue. He picked up from the floor a broken palm-leaf fan, and began fanning gently the flushed little face. Her eyelids fluttered and Almayer smiled. A responsive smile brightened for a second her heavy eyes, broke with a dimple the soft outline of her cheek; then the eyelids dropped suddenly, she drew a long breath through the parted lips—and was in a deep sleep before the fleeting smile could vanish from her face.

Almayer moved lightly off, took one of the wooden armchairs, and placing it close to the balustrade of the verandah sat down with a sigh of relief. He spread his elbows on the top rail and resting his chin on his clasped hands looked absently at the river, at the dance of sunlight on the flowing water. Gradually the forest of the further bank became smaller, as if sinking below the level of the river. The outlines wavered, grew thin, dissolved in the air. Before his eyes there was now only a space of undulating blue—one big, empty sky growing dark at times. . . . Where was the sunshine? . . . He felt soothed and happy, as if some gentle and invisible hand had removed from his soul the burden of his body. In another second he seemed to float out into a cool brightness where there was no such thing as memory or pain. Delicious. His eyes closed—opened—closed again.

"Almayer!"

With a sudden jerk of his whole body he sat up, grasping the front rail with both his hands, and blinked stupidly.

"What? What's that?" he muttered, looking round vaguely.

"Here! Down here, Almayer."

Half rising in his chair, Almayer looked over the rail at the foot of the verandah, and fell back with a low whistle of astonishment.

"A ghost, by heavens!" he exclaimed softly to himself.

"Will you listen to me?" went on the husky voice from the courtyard. "May I come up, Almayer?"

Almayer stood up and leaned over the rail. "Don't you dare," he said, in a voice subdued but distinct. "Don't you dare! The child sleeps here. And I don't want to hear you—or speak to you either."

"You must listen to me! It's something important."

"Not to me, surely."

"Yes! To you. Very important."

"You were always a humbug," said Almayer, after a short silence, in an indulgent tone. "Always! I remember the old days. Some fellows used to say there was no one like you for smartness—but you never took me in. Not quite. I never quite believed in you, Mr. Willems."

"I admit your superior intelligence," retorted Willems, with scornful impatience, from below. "Listening to me would be a further proof of it. You will be sorry if you don't."

"Oh, you funny fellow!" said Almayer, banteringly. "Well, come up. Don't make a noise, but come up. You'll catch a sunstroke down there and die on my doorstep perhaps. I don't want any tragedy here. Come on!"

Before he finished speaking Willems' head appeared above the level of the floor, then his shoulders rose gradually and he stood at last before Almayer—a masquerading spectre of the once so very confidential clerk of the richest merchant in the islands. His jacket was soiled and torn; below the waist he was clothed in a worn-out and faded sarong. He flung off his hat, uncovering his long, tangled hair that stuck in wisps on his perspiring forehead and straggled over his eyes, which glittered deep down in the sockets like the last sparks amongst the black embers of a burnt-out fire. An unclean beard grew out of the caverns of his sunburnt cheeks. The hand he put out towards Almayer was very unsteady. The once firm mouth had the tell-tale droop of mental suffering and physical exhaustion. He was barefooted. Almayer surveyed him with leisurely composure.

"Well!" he said at last, without taking the extended hand which dropped slowly along Willems' body.

"I am come," began Willems.

"So I see," interrupted Almayer. "You might have spared me this treat without making me unhappy. You have been away five weeks, if I am not mistaken. I got on very well without you—and now you are here you are not pretty to look at."

"Let me speak, will you!" exclaimed Willems.

"Don't shout like this. Do you think yourself in the forest with your . . . your friends? This is a civilized man's house. A white man's. Understand?"

"I am come," began Willems again; "I am come for your good and mine."

"You look as if you had come for a good feed," chimed in the irrepressible Almayer, while Willems waved his hand in a discouraged gesture. "Don't they give you enough to eat," went on Almayer, in a tone of easy banter, "those—what am I to call them—those new relations of yours? That old blind scoundrel must be delighted with your company. You know, he was the greatest thief and murderer of those seas. Say! do you exchange confidences? Tell me, Willems, did you kill somebody in Macassar or did you only steal something?"

"It is not true!" exclaimed Willems, hotly. "I only borrowed. . . . They all lied! I . . ."

"Sh-sh!" hissed Almayer, warningly, with a look at the sleeping child. "So you did steal," he went on, with repressed exultation. "I thought there was something of the kind. And now, here, you steal again."

For the first time Willems raised his eyes to Almayer's face.

"Oh, I don't mean from me. I haven't missed anything," said Almayer, with mocking haste. "But that girl. Hey! You stole her. You did not pay the old fellow. She is no good to him now, is she?"

"Stop that. Almayer!"

Something in Willems' tone caused Almayer to pause. He looked narrowly at the man before him, and could not help being shocked at his appearance.

"Almayer," went on Willems, "listen to me. If you are a human being you will. I suffer horribly—and for your sake."

Almayer lifted his eyebrows. "Indeed! How? But you are raving," he added, negligently.

"Ah! You don't know," whispered Willems. "She is gone. Gone," he repeated, with tears in his voice, "gone two days ago."

"No!" exclaimed the surprised Almayer. "Gone! I haven't heard that news yet." He burst into a subdued laugh. "How funny! Had enough of you already? You know it's not flattering for you, my superior countryman."

Willems—as if not hearing him—leaned against one of the columns of the roof and looked over the river. "At first," he whispered, dreamily, "my life was like a vision of heaven—or hell; I didn't know which. Since she went I know what perdition means; what darkness is. I know what it is to be torn to pieces alive. That's how I feel."

"You may come and live with me again," said Almayer, coldly. "After all, Lingard—whom I call my father and respect as such—left you under my care. You pleased yourself by going away. Very good. Now you want to come back. Be it so. I am no friend of yours. I act for Captain Lingard."

"Come back?" repeated Willems, passionately. "Come back to you and abandon her? Do you think I am mad? Without her! Man! what are you made of? To think that she moves, lives, breathes out of my sight. I am jealous of the wind that fans her, of the air she breathes, of the earth that receives the caress of her foot, of the sun that looks at her now while I . . . I haven't seen her for two days—two days."

The intensity of Willems' feeling moved Almayer somewhat, but he affected to yawn elaborately, "You do bore me," he muttered. "Why don't you go after her instead of coming here?"

"Why indeed?"

"Don't you know where she is? She can't be very far. No native craft has left this river for the last fortnight."

"No! not very far—and I will tell you where she is. She is in Lakamba's campong." And Willems fixed his eyes steadily on Almayer's face.

"Phew! Patalolo never sent to let me know. Strange," said Almayer, thoughtfully. "Are you afraid of that lot?" he added, after a short pause.

"I—afraid!"

"Then is it the care of your dignity which prevents you from following her there, my high-minded friend?" asked Almayer, with mock solicitude. "How noble of you!"

There was a short silence; then Willems said, quietly, "You are a fool. I should like to kick you."

"No fear," answered Almayer, carelessly; "you are too weak for that. You look starved."

"I don't think I have eaten anything for the last two days; perhaps more—I don't remember. It does not matter. I am full of live embers," said Willems, gloomily. "Look!" and he bared an arm covered with fresh scars. "I have been biting myself to forget in that pain the fire that hurts me there!" He struck his breast violently with his fist, reeled under his own blow, fell into a chair that stood near and closed his eyes slowly.

"Disgusting exhibition," said Almayer, loftily. "What could father ever see in you? You are as estimable as a heap of garbage."

"You talk like that! You, who sold your soul for a few guilders," muttered Willems, wearily, without opening his eyes.

"Not so few," said Almayer, with instinctive readiness, and stopped confused for a moment. He recovered himself quickly, however, and went on: "But you—you have thrown yours away for nothing; flung it under the feet of a damned savage woman who has made you already the thing you are, and will kill you very soon, one way or another, with her love or with her hate. You spoke just now about guilders. You meant Lingard's money, I suppose. Well, whatever I have sold, and for whatever price, I never meant you—you of all people—to spoil my bargain. I feel pretty safe though. Even father, even Captain Lingard, would not touch you now with a pair of tongs; not with a ten-foot pole. . . ."

He spoke excitedly, all in one breath, and, ceasing suddenly, glared at Willems and breathed hard through his nose in sulky resentment. Willems looked at him steadily for a moment, then got up.

"Almayer," he said resolutely, "I want to become a trader in this place."

Almayer shrugged his shoulders.

"Yes. And you shall set me up. I want a house and trade goods—perhaps a little money. I ask you for it."

"Anything else you want? Perhaps this coat?" and here Almayer unbuttoned his jacket —"or my house—or my boots?"

"After all it's natural," went on Willems, without paying any attention to Almayer—"it's natural that she should expect the advantages which . . . and then I could shut up that old wretch and then . . ."

He paused, his face brightened with the soft light of dreamy enthusiasm, and he turned his eyes upwards. With his gaunt figure and dilapidated appearance he looked like some ascetic dweller in a wilderness, finding the reward of a self-denying life in a vision of dazzling glory. He went on in an impassioned murmur—

"And then I would have her all to myself away from her people—all to myself—under my own influence—to fashion—to mould—to adore—to soften—to . . . Oh! Delight! And then—then go away to some distant place where, far from all she knew, I would be all the world to her! All the world to her!"

His face changed suddenly. His eyes wandered for awhile and then became steady all at once.

"I would repay every cent, of course," he said, in a business-like tone, with something of his old assurance, of his old belief in himself, in it. "Every cent. I need not interfere with your business. I shall cut out the small native traders. I have ideas—but never mind that now. And

Captain Lingard would approve, I feel sure. After all it's a loan, and I shall be at hand. Safe thing for you."

"Ah! Captain Lingard would approve! He would app . . ." Almayer choked. The notion of Lingard doing something for Willems enraged him. His face was purple. He spluttered insulting words. Willems looked at him coolly.

"I assure you, Almayer," he said, gently, "that I have good grounds for my demand."

"Your cursed impudence!"

"Believe me, Almayer, your position here is not so safe as you may think. An unscrupulous rival here would destroy your trade in a year. It would be ruin. Now Lingard's long absence gives courage to certain individuals. You know?—I have heard much lately. They made proposals to me . . . You are very much alone here. Even Patalolo . . ."

"Damn Patalolo! I am master in this place."

"But, Almayer, don't you see . . ."

"Yes, I see. I see a mysterious ass," interrupted Almayer, violently. "What is the meaning of your veiled threats? Don't you think I know something also? They have been intriguing for years—and nothing has happened. The Arabs have been hanging about outside this river for years—and I am still the only trader here; the master here. Do you bring me a declaration of war? Then it's from yourself only. I know all my other enemies. I ought to knock you on the head. You are not worth powder and shot though. You ought to be destroyed with a stick—like a snake."

Almayer's voice woke up the little girl, who sat up on the pillow with a sharp cry. He rushed over to the chair, caught up the child in his arms, walked back blindly, stumbled against Willems' hat which lay on the floor, and kicked it furiously down the steps.

"Clear out of this! Clear out!" he shouted.

Willems made an attempt to speak, but Almayer howled him down.

"Take yourself off! Don't you see you frighten the child—you scarecrow! No, no! dear," he went on to his little daughter, soothingly, while Willems walked down the steps slowly. "No. Don't cry. See! Bad man going away. Look! He is afraid of your papa. Nasty, bad man. Never come back again. He shall live in the woods and never come near my little girl. If he comes papa will kill him—so!" He struck his fist on the rail of the balustrade to show how he would kill Willems, and, perching the consoled child on his shoulder held her with one hand, while he pointed toward the retreating figure of his visitor.

"Look how he runs away, dearest," he said, coaxingly. "Isn't he funny. Call 'pig' after him, dearest. Call after him."

The seriousness of her face vanished into dimples. Under the long eyelashes, glistening with recent tears, her big eyes sparkled and danced with fun. She took firm hold of Almayer's hair with one hand, while she waved the other joyously and called out with all her might, in a clear note, soft and distinct like the pipe of a bird:—

"Pig! Pig! Pig!"

2

A SIGH under the flaming blue, a shiver of the sleeping sea, a cool breath as if a door had been swung upon the frozen spaces of the universe, and with a stir of leaves, with the nod of boughs, with the tremble of slender branches the sea breeze struck the coast, rushed up the river, swept round the broad reaches, and travelled on in a soft ripple of darkening water, in the whisper of branches, in the rustle of leaves of the awakened forests. It fanned in Lakamba's campong the dull red of expiring embers into a pale brilliance; and, under its touch, the slender, upright spirals of smoke that rose from every glowing heap swayed, wavered, and eddying down filled the twilight of clustered shade trees with the aromatic scent of the burning wood. The men who had been dozing in the shade during the hot hours of the afternoon woke up, and the silence of the big courtyard was broken by the hesitating murmur of yet sleepy voices, by coughs and yawns, with now and then a burst of laughter, a loud hail, a name or a joke sent out in a soft drawl. Small groups squatted round the little fires, and the monotonous undertone of talk filled the enclosure; the talk of barbarians, persistent, steady, repeating itself in the soft syllables, in musical tones of the never-ending discourses of those men of the forests and the sea, who can talk most of the day and all the night; who never exhaust a subject, never seem able to thresh a matter out; to whom that talk is poetry and painting and music, all art, all history; their only accomplishment, their only superiority, their only amusement. The talk of camp fires, which speaks of bravery and cunning, of strange events and of far countries, of the news of yesterday and the news of to-morrow. The talk about the dead and the living—about those who fought and those who loved.

Lakamba came out on the platform before his own house and sat down—perspiring, half asleep, and sulky—in a wooden armchair under the shade of the overhanging eaves. Through the darkness of the doorway he could hear the soft warbling of his womenkind, busy round the looms where they were weaving the checkered pattern of his gala sarongs. Right and left of him on the flexible bamboo floor those of his followers to whom their distinguished birth, long devotion, or faithful service had given the privilege of using the chief's house, were sleeping on mats or just sat up rubbing their eyes: while the more wakeful had mustered enough energy to draw a chessboard with red clay on a fine mat and were now meditating silently over their moves. Above the prostrate forms of the players, who lay face downward supported on elbow, the soles of their feet waving irresolutely about, in the absorbed meditation of the game, there towered here and there the straight figure of an attentive spectator looking down with dispassionate but profound interest. On the edge of the platform a row of high-heeled leather sandals stood ranged carefully in a level line, and against the rough wooden rail leaned the slender shafts of the spears belonging to these gentlemen, the broad blades of dulled steel looking very black in the reddening light of approaching sunset.

A boy of about twelve—the personal attendant of Lakamba—squatted at his master's feet and held up towards him a silver siri box. Slowly Lakamba took the box, opened it, and tearing off a piece of green leaf deposited in it a pinch of lime, a morsel of gambier, a small bit of areca nut, and wrapped up the whole with a dexterous twist. He paused, morsel in hand, seemed to miss something, turned his head from side to side, slowly, like a man with a stiff neck, and ejaculated in an ill-humoured bass—

"Babalatchi!"

The players glanced up quickly, and looked down again directly. Those men who were standing stirred uneasily as if prodded by the sound of the chief's voice. The one nearest to Lakamba repeated the call, after a while, over the rail into the courtyard. There was a movement of upturned faces below by the fires, and the cry trailed over the enclosure in sing-song tones. The thumping of wooden pestles husking the evening rice stopped for a moment and Babalatchi's name rang afresh shrilly on women's lips in various keys. A voice far off shouted something—another, nearer, repeated it; there was a short hubbub which died out with extreme suddenness. The first crier turned to Lakamba, saying indolently—

"He is with the blind Omar."

Lakamba's lips moved inaudibly. The man who had just spoken was again deeply absorbed in the game going on at his feet; and the chief—as if he had forgotten all about it already—sat with a stolid face amongst his silent followers, leaning back squarely in his chair, his hands on the arms of his seat, his knees apart, his big blood-shot eyes blinking solemnly, as if dazzled by the noble vacuity of his thoughts.

Babalatchi had gone to see old Omar late in the afternoon. The delicate manipulation of the ancient pirate's susceptibilities, the skilful management of Aissa's violent impulses engrossed him to the exclusion of every other business—interfered with his regular attendance upon his chief and protector—even disturbed his sleep for the last three nights. That day when he left his own bamboo hut—which stood amongst others in Lakamba's campong—his heart was heavy with anxiety and with doubt as to the success of his intrigue. He walked slowly, with his usual air of detachment from his surroundings, as if unaware that many sleepy eyes watched from all parts of the courtyard his progress towards a small gate at its upper end. That gate gave access to a separate enclosure in which a rather large house, built of planks, had been prepared by Lakamba's orders for the reception of Omar and Aissa. It was a superior kind of habitation which Lakamba intended for the dwelling of his chief adviser—whose abilities were worth that honour, he thought. But after the consultation in the deserted clearing—when Babalatchi had disclosed his plan—they both had agreed that the new house should be used at first to shelter Omar and Aissa after they had been persuaded to leave the Rajah's place, or had been kidnapped from there—as the case might be. Babalatchi did not mind in the least the putting off of his own occupation of the house of honour, because it had many advantages for the quiet working out of his plans. It had a certain seclusion, having an enclosure of its own, and that enclosure communicated also with

Lakamba's private courtyard at the back of his residence—a place set apart for the female household of the chief. The only communication with the river was through the great front courtyard always full of armed men and watchful eyes. Behind the whole group of buildings there stretched the level ground of rice-clearings, which in their turn were closed in by the wall of untouched forests with undergrowth so thick and tangled that nothing but a bullet—and that fired at pretty close range—could penetrate any distance there.

Babalatchi slipped quietly through the little gate and, closing it, tied up carefully the rattan fastenings. Before the house there was a square space of ground, beaten hard into the level smoothness of asphalte. A big buttressed tree, a giant left there on purpose during the process of clearing the land, roofed in the clear space with a high canopy of gnarled boughs and thick, sombre leaves. To the right—and some small distance away from the large house—a little hut of reeds, covered with mats, had been put up for the special convenience of Omar, who, being blind and infirm, had some difficulty in ascending the steep plankway that led to the more substantial dwelling, which was built on low posts and had an uncovered verandah. Close by the trunk of the tree, and facing the doorway of the hut, the household fire glowed in a small handful of embers in the midst of a large circle of white ashes. An old woman—some humble relation of one of Lakamba's wives, who had been ordered to attend on Aissa—was squatting over the fire and lifted up her bleared eyes to gaze at Babalatchi in an uninterested manner, as he advanced rapidly across the courtyard.

Babalatchi took in the courtyard with a keen glance of his solitary eye, and without looking down at the old woman muttered a question. Silently, the woman stretched a tremulous and emaciated arm towards the hut. Babalatchi made a few steps towards the doorway, but stopped outside in the sunlight.

"O! Tuan Omar, Omar besar! It is I—Babalatchi!"

Within the hut there was a feeble groan, a fit of coughing and an indistinct murmur in the broken tones of a vague plaint. Encouraged evidently by those signs of dismal life within, Babalatchi entered the hut, and after some time came out leading with rigid carefulness the blind Omar, who followed with both his hands on his guide's shoulders. There was a rude seat under the tree, and there Babalatchi led his old chief, who sat down with a sigh of relief and leaned wearily against the rugged trunk. The rays of the setting sun, darting under the spreading branches, rested on the white-robed figure sitting with head thrown back in stiff dignity, on the thin hands moving uneasily, and on the stolid face with its eyelids dropped over the destroyed eyeballs; a face set into the immobility of a plaster cast yellowed by age.

"Is the sun near its setting?" asked Omar, in a dull voice.

"Very near," answered Babalatchi.

"Where am I? Why have I been taken away from the place which I knew—where I, blind, could move without fear? It is like black night to those who see. And the sun is near its setting—and I have not heard the sound of her footsteps since the morning! Twice a strange hand has given me my food to-day. Why? Why? Where is she?"

"She is near," said Babalatchi.

"And he?" went on Omar, with sudden eagerness, and a drop in his voice. "Where is he? Not here. Not here!" he repeated, turning his head from side to side as if in deliberate attempt to see.

"No! He is not here now," said Babalatchi, soothingly. Then, after a pause, he added very low, "But he shall soon return."

"Return! O crafty one! Will he return? I have cursed him three times," exclaimed Omar, with weak violence.

"He is—no doubt—accursed," assented Babalatchi, in a conciliating manner—"and yet he will be here before very long—I know!"

"You are crafty and faithless. I have made you great. You were dirt under my feet—less than dirt," said Omar, with tremulous energy.

"I have fought by your side many times," said Babalatchi, calmly.

"Why did he come?" went on Omar. "Did you send him? Why did he come to defile the air I breathe—to mock at my fate—to poison her mind and steal her body? She has grown hard of heart to me. Hard and merciless and stealthy like rocks that tear a ship's life out under the smooth sea." He drew a long breath, struggled with his anger, then broke down suddenly. "I have been hungry," he continued, in a whimpering tone—"often I have been very hungry—and cold—and neglected—and nobody near me. She has often forgotten me—and my sons are dead, and that man is an infidel and a dog. Why did he come? Did you show him the way?"

"He found the way himself, O Leader of the brave," said Babalatchi, sadly. "I only saw a way for their destruction and our own greatness. And if I saw aright, then you shall never suffer from hunger any more. There shall be peace for us, and glory and riches."

"And I shall die to-morrow," murmured Omar, bitterly.

"Who knows? Those things have been written since the beginning of the world," whispered Babalatchi, thoughtfully.

"Do not let him come back," exclaimed Omar.

"Neither can he escape his fate," went on Babalatchi. "He shall come back, and the power of men we always hated, you and I, shall crumble into dust in our hand." Then he added with enthusiasm, "They shall fight amongst themselves and perish both."

"And you shall see all this, while, I . . ."

"True!" murmured Babalatchi, regretfully. "To you life is darkness."

"No! Flame!" exclaimed the old Arab, half rising, then falling back in his seat. "The flame of that last day! I see it yet—the last thing I saw! And I hear the noise of the rent earth—when they all died. And I live to be the plaything of a crafty one," he added, with inconsequential peevishness.

"You are my master still," said Babalatchi, humbly. "You are very wise—and in your wisdom you shall speak to Syed Abdulla when he comes here—you shall speak to him as I advised, I, your servant, the man who fought at your right hand for many years. I have heard by a messenger that the Syed Abdulla is coming to-night, perhaps late; for those things must be done secretly, lest the white man, the trader up the river, should know of them. But he will be here. There has been a surat delivered to Lakamba. In it, Syed Abdulla says he will leave his ship, which is anchored outside the river, at the hour of noon to-day. He will be here before daylight if Allah wills."

He spoke with his eye fixed on the ground, and did not become aware of Aissa's presence till he lifted his head when he ceased speaking. She had approached so quietly that even Omar did not hear her footsteps, and she stood now looking at them with troubled eyes and parted lips, as if she was going to speak; but at Babalatchi's entreating gesture she remained silent. Omar sat absorbed in thought.

"Ay wa! Even so!" he said at last, in a weak voice. "I am to speak your wisdom, O Babalatchi! Tell him to trust the white man! I do not understand. I am old and blind and weak. I do not understand. I am very cold," he continued, in a lower tone, moving his shoulders uneasily. He ceased, then went on rambling in a faint whisper. "They are the sons of witches, and their father is Satan the stoned. Sons of witches. Sons of witches." After a short silence he asked suddenly, in a firmer voice—"How many white men are there here, O crafty one?"

"There are two here. Two white men to fight one another," answered Babalatchi, with alacrity.

"And how many will be left then? How many? Tell me, you who are wise."

"The downfall of an enemy is the consolation of the unfortunate," said Babalatchi, sententiously. "They are on every sea; only the wisdom of the Most High knows their number—but you shall know that some of them suffer."

"Tell me, Babalatchi, will they die? Will they both die?" asked Omar, in sudden agitation.

Aissa made a movement. Babalatchi held up a warning hand.

"They shall, surely, die," he said steadily, looking at the girl with unflinching eye.

"Ay wa! But die soon! So that I can pass my hand over their faces when Allah has made them stiff."

"If such is their fate and yours," answered Babalatchi, without hesitation. "God is great!"

A violent fit of coughing doubled Omar up, and he rocked himself to and fro, wheezing and moaning in turns, while Babalatchi and the girl looked at him in silence. Then he leaned back against the tree, exhausted.

"I am alone, I am alone," he wailed feebly, groping vaguely about with his trembling hands. "Is there anybody near me? Is there anybody? I am afraid of this strange place."

"I am by your side, O Leader of the brave," said Babalatchi, touching his shoulder lightly. "Always by your side as in the days when we both were young: as in the time when we both went with arms in our hands."

"Has there been such a time, Babalatchi?" said Omar, wildly; "I have forgotten. And now when I die there will be no man, no fearless man to speak of his father's bravery. There was a woman! A woman! And she has forsaken me for an infidel dog. The hand of the Compassionate is heavy on my head! Oh, my calamity! Oh, my shame!"

He calmed down after a while, and asked quietly—

"Is the sun set, Babalatchi?"

"It is now as low as the highest tree I can see from here," answered Babalatchi.

"It is the time of prayer," said Omar, attempting to get up.

Dutifully Babalatchi helped his old chief to rise, and they walked slowly towards the hut. Omar waited outside, while Babalatchi went in and came out directly, dragging after him the old Arab's praying carpet. Out of a brass vessel he poured the water of ablution on Omar's outstretched hands, and eased him carefully down into a kneeling posture, for the venerable robber was far too infirm to be able to stand. Then as Omar droned out the first words and made his first bow towards the Holy City, Babalatchi stepped noiselessly towards Aissa, who did not move all the time.

Aissa looked steadily at the one-eyed sage, who was approaching her slowly and with a great show of deference. For a moment they stood facing each other in silence. Babalatchi appeared embarrassed. With a sudden and quick gesture she caught hold of his arm, and with the other hand pointed towards the sinking red disc that glowed, rayless, through the floating mists of the evening.

"The third sunset! The last! And he is not here," she whispered; "what have you done, man without faith? What have you done?"

"Indeed I have kept my word," murmured Babalatchi, earnestly. "This morning Bulangi went with a canoe to look for him. He is a strange man, but our friend, and shall keep close to him and watch him without ostentation. And at the third hour of the day I have sent another canoe with four rowers. Indeed, the man you long for, O daughter of Omar! may come when he likes."

"But he is not here! I waited for him yesterday. To-day! To-morrow I shall go."

"Not alive!" muttered Babalatchi to himself. "And do you doubt your power," he went on in a louder tone—"you that to him are more beautiful than an houri of the seventh Heaven? He is your slave."

"A slave does run away sometimes," she said, gloomily, "and then the master must go and seek him out."

"And do you want to live and die a beggar?" asked Babalatchi, impatiently.

"I care not," she exclaimed, wringing her hands; and the black pupils of her wide-open eyes darted wildly here and there like petrels before the storm.

"Sh! Sh!" hissed Babalatchi, with a glance towards Omar. "Do you think, O girl! that he himself would live like a beggar, even with you?"

"He is great," she said, ardently. "He despises you all! He despises you all! He is indeed a man!"

"You know that best," muttered Babalatchi, with a fugitive smile—"but remember, woman with the strong heart, that to hold him now you must be to him like the great sea to thirsty men—a never-ceasing torment, and a madness."

He ceased and they stood in silence, both looking on the ground, and for a time nothing was heard above the crackling of the fire but the intoning of Omar glorifying the God—his God, and the Faith—his faith. Then Babalatchi cocked his head on one side and appeared to listen intently to the hum of voices in the big courtyard. The dull noise swelled into distinct shouts, then into a great tumult of voices, dying away, recommencing, growing louder, to cease again abruptly; and in those short pauses the shrill vociferations of women rushed up, as if released, towards the quiet heaven. Aissa and Babalatchi started, but the latter gripped in his turn the girl's arm and restrained her with a strong grasp.

"Wait," he whispered.

The little door in the heavy stockade which separated Lakamba's private ground from Omar's enclosure swung back quickly, and the noble exile appeared with disturbed mien and a naked short sword in his hand. His turban was half unrolled, and the end trailed on the ground behind him. His jacket was open. He breathed thickly for a moment before he spoke.

"He came in Bulangi's boat," he said, "and walked quietly till he was in my presence, when the senseless fury of white men caused him to rush upon me. I have been in great danger," went on the ambitious nobleman in an aggrieved tone. "Do you hear that, Babalatchi? That eater of swine aimed a blow at my face with his unclean fist. He tried to rush amongst my household. Six men are holding him now."

A fresh outburst of yells stopped Lakamba's discourse. Angry voices shouted: "Hold him. Beat him down. Strike at his head."

Then the clamour ceased with sudden completeness, as if strangled by a mighty hand, and after a second of surprising silence the voice of Willems was heard alone, howling maledictions in Malay, in Dutch, and in English.

"Listen," said Lakamba, speaking with unsteady lips, "he blasphemes his God. His speech is like the raving of a mad dog. Can we hold him for ever? He must be killed!"

"Fool!" muttered Babalatchi, looking up at Aissa, who stood with set teeth, with gleaming eyes and distended nostrils, yet obedient to the touch of his restraining hand. "It is the third day, and I have kept my promise," he said to her, speaking very low. "Remember," he added warningly—"like the sea to the thirsty! And now," he said aloud, releasing her and stepping back, "go, fearless daughter, go!"

Like an arrow, rapid and silent she flew down the enclosure, and disappeared through the gate of the courtyard. Lakamba and Babalatchi looked after her. They heard the renewed tumult, the girl's clear voice calling out, "Let him go!" Then after a pause in the din no longer than half the human breath the name of Aissa rang in a shout loud, discordant, and piercing, which sent through them an involuntary shudder. Old Omar collapsed on his carpet and moaned feebly; Lakamba stared with gloomy contempt in the direction of the inhuman sound; but Babalatchi, forcing a smile, pushed his distinguished protector through the narrow gate in the stockade, followed him, and closed it quickly.

The old woman, who had been most of the time kneeling by the fire, now rose, glanced round fearfully and crouched hiding behind the tree. The gate of the great courtyard flew open with a great clatter before a frantic kick, and Willems darted in carrying Aissa in his arms. He rushed up the enclosure like a tornado, pressing the girl to his breast, her arms round his neck, her head hanging back over his arm, her eyes closed and her long hair nearly touching the ground. They appeared for a second in the glare of the fire, then, with immense strides, he dashed up the planks and disappeared with his burden in the doorway of the big house.

Inside and outside the enclosure there was silence. Omar lay supporting himself on his elbow, his terrified face with its closed eyes giving him the appearance of a man tormented by a nightmare.

"What is it? Help! Help me to rise!" he called out faintly.

The old hag, still crouching in the shadow, stared with bleared eyes at the doorway of the big house, and took no notice of his call. He listened for a while, then his arm gave way, and, with a deep sigh of discouragement, he let himself fall on the carpet.

The boughs of the tree nodded and trembled in the unsteady currents of the light wind. A leaf fluttered down slowly from some high branch and rested on the ground, immobile, as if resting for ever, in the glow of the fire; but soon it stirred, then soared suddenly, and flew, spinning and turning before the breath of the perfumed breeze, driven helplessly into the dark night that had closed over the land.

3

FOR UPWARDS OF forty years Abdulla had walked in the way of his Lord. Son of the rich Syed Selim bin Sali, the great Mohammedan trader of the Straits, he went forth at the age of seventeen on his first commercial expedition, as his father's representative on board a pilgrim ship chartered by the wealthy Arab to convey a crowd of pious Malays to the Holy Shrine. That was in the days when steam was not in those seas—or, at least, not so much as now. The voyage was long, and the young man's eyes were opened to the wonders of many lands. Allah had made it his fate to become a pilgrim very early in life. This was a great favour of Heaven, and it could not have been bestowed upon a man who prized it more, or who made himself more worthy of it by the unswerving piety of his heart and by the religious solemnity of his demeanour. Later on it became clear that the book of his destiny contained the programme of a wandering life. He visited Bombay and Calcutta, looked in at the Persian Gulf, beheld in due course the high and barren coasts of the Gulf of Suez, and this was the limit of his wanderings westward. He was then twenty-seven, and the writing on his forehead decreed that the time had come for him to return to the Straits and take from his dying father's hands the many threads of a business that was spread over all the Archipelago: from Sumatra to New Guinea, from Batavia to Palawan.

Very soon his ability, his will—strong to obstinacy—his wisdom beyond his years, caused him to be recognized as the head of a family whose members and connections were found in every part of those seas. An uncle here—a brother there; a father-in-law in Batavia, another in Palembang; husbands of numerous sisters; cousins innumerable scattered north, south, east, and west—in every place where there was trade: the great family lay like a network over the islands. They lent money to princes, influenced the council-rooms, faced—if need be—with peaceful intrepidity the white rulers who held the land and the sea under the edge of sharp swords; and they all paid great deference to Abdulla, listened to his advice, entered into his plans—because he was wise, pious, and fortunate.

He bore himself with the humility becoming a Believer, who never forgets, even for one moment of his waking life, that he is the servant of the Most High. He was largely charitable because the charitable man is the friend of Allah, and when he walked out of his house—

built of stone, just outside the town of Penang—on his way to his godowns in the port, he had often to snatch his hand away sharply from under the lips of men of his race and creed; and often he had to murmur deprecating words, or even to rebuke with severity those who attempted to touch his knees with their finger-tips in gratitude or supplication. He was very handsome, and carried his small head high with meek gravity. His lofty brow, straight nose, narrow, dark face with its chiselled delicacy of feature, gave him an aristocratic appearance which proclaimed his pure descent. His beard was trimmed close and to a rounded point. His large brown eyes looked out steadily with a sweetness that was belied by the expression of his thin-lipped mouth. His aspect was serene. He had a belief in his own prosperity which nothing could shake.

Restless, like all his people, he very seldom dwelt for many days together in his splendid house in Penang. Owner of ships, he was often on board one or another of them, traversing in all directions the field of his operations. In every port he had a household—his own or that of a relation—to hail his advent with demonstrative joy. In every port there were rich and influential men eager to see him, there was business to talk over, there were important letters to read: an immense correspondence, enclosed in silk envelopes—a correspondence which had nothing to do with the infidels of colonial post-offices, but came into his hands by devious, yet safe, ways. It was left for him by taciturn nakhodas of native trading craft, or was delivered with profound salaams by travel-stained and weary men who would withdraw from his presence calling upon Allah to bless the generous giver of splendid rewards. And the news was always good, and all his attempts always succeeded, and in his ears there rang always a chorus of admiration, of gratitude, of humble entreaties.

A fortunate man. And his felicity was so complete that the good genii, who ordered the stars at his birth, had not neglected—by a refinement of benevolence strange in such primitive beings—to provide him with a desire difficult to attain, and with an enemy hard to overcome. The envy of Lingard's political and commercial successes, and the wish to get the best of him in every way, became Abdulla's mania, the paramount interest of his life, the salt of his existence.

For the last few months he had been receiving mysterious messages from Sambir urging him to decisive action. He had found the river a couple of years ago, and had been anchored more than once off that estuary where the, till then, rapid Pantai, spreading slowly over the lowlands, seems to hesitate, before it flows gently through twenty outlets; over a maze of mudflats, sandbanks and reefs, into the expectant sea. He had never attempted the entrance, however, because men of his race, although brave and adventurous travellers, lack the true seamanlike instincts, and he was afraid of getting wrecked. He could not bear the idea of the Rajah Laut being able to boast that Abdulla bin Selim, like other and lesser men, had also come to grief when trying to wrest his secret from him. Meantime he returned encouraging answers to his unknown friends in Sambir, and waited for his opportunity in the calm certitude of ultimate triumph.

Such was the man whom Lakamba and Babalatchi expected to see for the first time on the night of Willems' return to Aissa. Babalatchi, who had been tormented for three days by the fear of having over-reached himself in his little plot, now, feeling sure of his white man, felt lighthearted and happy as he superintended the preparations in the courtyard for Abdulla's reception. Half-way between Lakamba's house and the river a pile of dry wood was made ready for the torch that would set fire to it at the moment of Abdulla's landing. Between this and the house again there was, ranged in a semicircle, a set of low bamboo frames, and on those were piled all the carpets and cushions of Lakamba's household. It had been decided that the reception was to take place in the open air, and that it should be made impressive by the great number of Lakamba's retainers, who, clad in clean white, with their red sarongs gathered round their waists, chopper at side and lance in hand, were moving about the compound or, gathering into small knots, discussed eagerly the coming ceremony.

Two little fires burned brightly on the water's edge on each side of the landing place. A small heap of damar-gum torches lay by each, and between them Babalatchi strolled backwards and forwards, stopping often with his face to the river and his head on one side, listening to the sounds that came from the darkness over the water. There was no moon and the night was very clear overhead, but, after the afternoon breeze had expired in fitful puffs, the vapours hung thickening over the glancing surface of the Pantai and clung to the shore, hiding from view the middle of the stream.

A cry in the mist—then another—and, before Babalatchi could answer, two little canoes dashed up to the landing-place, and two of the principal citizens of Sambir, Daoud Sahamin and Hamet Bahassoen, who had been confidentially invited to meet Abdulla, landed quickly and after greeting Babalatchi walked up the dark courtyard towards the house. The little stir caused by their arrival soon subsided, and another silent hour dragged its slow length while Babalatchi tramped up and down between the fires, his face growing more anxious with every passing moment.

At last there was heard a loud hail from down the river. At a call from Babalatchi men ran down to the riverside and, snatching the torches, thrust them into the fires, then waved them above their heads till they burst into a flame. The smoke ascended in thick, wispy streams, and hung in a ruddy cloud above the glare that lit up the courtyard and flashed over the water, showing three long canoes manned by many paddlers lying a little off; the men in them lifting their paddles on high and dipping them down together, in an easy stroke that kept the small flotilla motionless in the strong current, exactly abreast of the landing-place. A man stood up in the largest craft and called out—

"Syed Abdulla bin Selim is here!"

Babalatchi answered aloud in a formal tone—

"Allah gladdens our hearts! Come to the land!"

Abdulla landed first, steadying himself by the help of Babalatchi's extended hand. In the short moment of his passing from the boat to the shore they exchanged sharp glances and a few rapid words.

"Who are you?"

"Babalatchi. The friend of Omar. The protected of Lakamba."

"You wrote?"

"My words were written, O Giver of alms!"

And then Abdulla walked with composed face between the two lines of men holding torches, and met Lakamba in front of the big fire that was crackling itself up into a great blaze. For a moment they stood with clasped hands invoking peace upon each other's head, then Lakamba, still holding his honoured guest by the hand, led him round the fire to the prepared seats. Babalatchi followed close behind his protector. Abdulla was accompanied by two Arabs. He, like his companions, was dressed in a white robe of starched muslin, which fell in stiff folds straight from the neck. It was buttoned from the throat halfway down with a close row of very small gold buttons; round the tight sleeves there was a narrow braid of gold lace. On his shaven head he wore a small skull-cap of plaited grass. He was shod in patent leather slippers over his naked feet. A rosary of heavy wooden beads hung by a round turn from his right wrist. He sat down slowly in the place of honour, and, dropping his slippers, tucked up his legs under him decorously.

The improvised divan was arranged in a wide semi-circle, of which the point most distant from the fire—some ten yards—was also the nearest to Lakamba's dwelling. As soon as the principal personages were seated, the verandah of the house was filled silently by the muffled-up forms of Lakamba's female belongings. They crowded close to the rail and looked down, whispering faintly. Below, the formal exchange of compliments went on for some time between Lakamba and Abdulla, who sat side by side. Babalatchi squatted humbly at his protector's feet, with nothing but a thin mat between himself and the hard ground.

Then there was a pause. Abdulla glanced round in an expectant manner, and after a while Babalatchi, who had been sitting very still in a pensive attitude, seemed to rouse himself with an effort, and began to speak in gentle and persuasive tones. He described in flowing sentences the first beginnings of Sambir, the dispute of the present ruler, Patalolo, with the Sultan of Koti, the consequent troubles ending with the rising of Bugis settlers under the leadership of Lakamba. At different points of the narrative he would turn for confirmation to Sahamin and Bahassoen, who sat listening eagerly and assented together with a "Betul! Betul! Right! Right!" ejaculated in a fervent undertone.

Warming up with his subject as the narrative proceeded, Babalatchi went on to relate the facts connected with Lingard's action at the critical period of those internal dissensions. He spoke in a restrained voice still, but with a growing energy of indignation. What was he, that man of fierce aspect, to keep all the world away from them? Was he a government? Who made him ruler? He took possession of Patalolo's mind and made his heart hard; he put severe words into his mouth and caused his hand to strike right and left. That unbeliever kept the Faithful panting under the weight of his senseless oppression. They had to trade with him—accept such goods as he would give—such credit as he would accord. And he exacted payment every year . . .

"Very true!" exclaimed Sahamin and Bahassoen together.

Babalatchi glanced at them approvingly and turned to Abdulla.

"Listen to those men, O Protector of the oppressed!" he exclaimed. "What could we do? A man must trade. There was nobody else."

Sahamin got up, staff in hand, and spoke to Abdulla with ponderous courtesy, emphasizing his words by the solemn flourishes of his right arm.

"It is so. We are weary of paying our debts to that white man here, who is the son of the Rajah Laut. That white man—may the grave of his mother be defiled!—is not content to hold us all in his hand with a cruel grasp. He seeks to cause our very death. He trades with the Dyaks of the forest, who are no better than monkeys. He buys from them guttah and rattans—while we starve. Only two days ago I went to him and said, 'Tuan Almayer'—even so; we must speak politely to that friend of Satan—'Tuan Almayer, I have such and such goods to sell. Will you buy?' And he spoke thus—because those white men have no understanding of any courtesy—he spoke to me as if I was a slave: 'Daoud, you are a lucky man'—remark, O First amongst the Believers! that by those words he could have brought misfortune on my head—'you are a lucky man to have anything in these hard times. Bring your goods quickly, and I shall receive them in payment of what you owe me from last year.' And he laughed, and struck me on the shoulder with his open hand. May Jehannum be his lot!"

"We will fight him," said young Bahassoen, crisply. "We shall fight if there is help and a leader. Tuan Abdulla, will you come among us?"

Abdulla did not answer at once. His lips moved in an inaudible whisper and the beads passed through his fingers with a dry click. All waited in respectful silence. "I shall come if my ship can enter this river," said Abdulla at last, in a solemn tone.

"It can, Tuan," exclaimed Babalatchi. "There is a white man here who . . ."

"I want to see Omar el Badavi and that white man you wrote about," interrupted Abdulla.

Babalatchi got on his feet quickly, and there was a general move.

The women on the verandah hurried indoors, and from the crowd that had kept discreetly in distant parts of the courtyard a couple of men ran with armfuls of dry fuel, which they cast upon the fire. One of them, at a sign from Babalatchi, approached and, after getting his orders, went towards the little gate and entered Omar's enclosure. While waiting for his return, Lakamba, Abdulla, and Babalatchi talked together in low tones. Sahamin sat by himself chewing betel-nut sleepily with a slight and indolent motion of his heavy jaw. Bahassoen, his hand on the hilt of his short sword, strutted backwards and forwards in the full light of the fire, looking very warlike and reckless; the envy and admiration of Lakamba's retainers, who stood in groups or flitted about noiselessly in the shadows of the courtyard.

The messenger who had been sent to Omar came back and stood at a distance, waiting till somebody noticed him. Babalatchi beckoned him close.

"What are his words?" asked Babalatchi.

"He says that Syed Abdulla is welcome now," answered the man.

Lakamba was speaking low to Abdulla, who listened to him with deep interest.

". . . We could have eighty men if there was need," he was saying—"eighty men in fourteen canoes. The only thing we want is gunpowder . . ."

"Hai! there will be no fighting," broke in Babalatchi. "The fear of your name will be enough and the terror of your coming."

"There may be powder too," muttered Abdulla with great nonchalance, "if only the ship enters the river safely."

"If the heart is stout the ship will be safe," said Babalatchi. "We will go now and see Omar el Badavi and the white man I have here."

Lakamba's dull eyes became animated suddenly.

"Take care, Tuan Abdulla," he said, "take care. The behaviour of that unclean white madman is furious in the extreme. He offered to strike . . ."

"On my head, you are safe, O Giver of alms!" interrupted Babalatchi.

Abdulla looked from one to the other, and the faintest flicker of a passing smile disturbed for a moment his grave composure. He turned to Babalatchi, and said with decision—

"Let us go."

"This way, O Uplifter of our hearts!" rattled on Babalatchi, with fussy deference. "Only a very few paces and you shall behold Omar the brave, and a white man of great strength and cunning. This way."

He made a sign for Lakamba to remain behind, and with respectful touches on the elbow steered Abdulla towards the gate at the upper end of the court-yard. As they walked on slowly, followed by the two Arabs, he kept on talking in a rapid undertone to the great man, who never looked at him once, although appearing to listen with flattering attention. When near the gate Babalatchi moved forward and stopped, facing Abdulla, with his hand on the fastenings.

"You shall see them both," he said. "All my words about them are true. When I saw him enslaved by the one of whom I spoke, I knew he would be soft in my hand like the mud of the river. At first he answered my talk with bad words of his own language, after the manner of white men. Afterwards, when listening to the voice he loved, he hesitated. He hesitated for many days—too many. I, knowing him well, made Omar withdraw here with his . . . household. Then this red-faced man raged for three days like a black panther that is hungry. And this evening, this very evening, he came. I have him here. He is in the grasp of one with a merciless heart. I have him here," ended Babalatchi, exultingly tapping the upright of the gate with his hand.

"That is good," murmured Abdulla.

"And he shall guide your ship and lead in the fight—if fight there be," went on Babalatchi. "If there is any killing—let him be the slayer. You should give him arms—a short gun that fires many times."

"Yes, by Allah!" assented Abdulla, with slow thoughtfulness.

"And you will have to open your hand, O First amongst the generous!" continued Babalatchi. "You will have to satisfy the rapacity of a white man, and also of one who is not a man, and therefore greedy of ornaments."

"They shall be satisfied," said Abdulla; "but . . ." He hesitated, looking down on the ground and stroking his beard, while Babalatchi waited, anxious, with parted lips. After a short time he spoke again jerkily in an indistinct whisper, so that Babalatchi had to turn his head to catch the words. "Yes. But Omar is the son of my father's uncle . . . and all belonging to him are of the Faith . . . while that man is an unbeliever. It is most unseemly . . . very unseemly. He cannot live under my shadow. Not that dog. Penitence! I take refuge with my God," he mumbled rapidly. "How can he live under my eyes with that woman, who is of the Faith? Scandal! O abomination!"

He finished with a rush and drew a long breath, then added dubiously—

"And when that man has done all we want, what is to be done with him?"

They stood close together, meditative and silent, their eyes roaming idly over the courtyard. The big bonfire burned brightly, and a wavering splash of light lay on the dark earth at their feet, while the lazy smoke wreathed itself slowly in gleaming coils amongst the black boughs of the trees. They could see Lakamba, who had returned to his place, sitting hunched up spiritlessly on the cushions, and Sahamin, who had got on his feet again and appeared to be talking to him with dignified animation. Men in twos or threes came out of the shadows into the light, strolling slowly, and passed again into the shadows, their faces turned to each other, their arms moving in restrained gestures. Bahassoen, his head proudly thrown back, his ornaments, embroideries, and sword-hilt flashing in the light, circled steadily round the fire like a planet round the sun. A cool whiff of damp air came from the darkness of the riverside; it made Abdulla and Babalatchi shiver, and woke them up from their abstraction.

"Open the gate and go first," said Abdulla; "there is no danger?"

"On my life, no!" answered Babalatchi, lifting the rattan ring. "He is all peace and content, like a thirsty man who has drunk water after many days."

He swung the gate wide, made a few paces into the gloom of the enclosure, and retraced his steps suddenly.

"He may be made useful in many ways," he whispered to Abdulla, who had stopped short, seeing him come back.

"O Sin! O Temptation!" sighed out Abdulla, faintly. "Our refuge is with the Most High. Can I feed this infidel for ever and for ever?" he added, impatiently.

"No," breathed out Babalatchi. "No! Not for ever. Only while he serves your designs, O Dispenser of Allah's gifts! When the time comes—and your order . . ."

He sidled close to Abdulla, and brushed with a delicate touch the hand that hung down listlessly, holding the prayer-beads.

"I am your slave and your offering," he murmured, in a distinct and polite tone, into Abdulla's ear. "When your wisdom speaks, there may be found a little poison that will not lie. Who knows?"

4

BABALATCHI SAW Abdulla pass through the low and narrow entrance into the darkness of Omar's hut; heard them exchange the usual greetings and the distinguished visitor's grave voice asking: "There is no misfortune—please God—but the sight?" and then, becoming aware of the disapproving looks of the two Arabs who had accompanied Abdulla, he followed their example and fell back out of earshot. He did it unwillingly, although he did not ignore that what was going to happen in there was now absolutely beyond his control. He roamed irresolutely about for awhile, and at last wandered with careless steps towards the fire, which had been moved, from under the tree, close to the hut and a little to windward of its entrance. He squatted on his heels and began playing pensively with live embers, as was his habit when engrossed in thought, withdrawing his hand sharply and shaking it above his head when he burnt his fingers in a fit of deeper abstraction. Sitting there he could hear the murmur of the talk inside the hut, and he could distinguish the voices but not the words. Abdulla spoke in deep tones, and now and then this flowing monotone was interrupted by a querulous exclamation, a weak moan or a plaintive quaver of the old man. Yes. It was annoying not to be able to make out what they were saying, thought Babalatchi, as he sat gazing fixedly at the unsteady glow of the fire. But it will be right. All will be right. Abdulla inspired him with confidence. He came up fully to his expectation. From the very first moment when he set his eye on him he felt sure that this man—whom he had known by reputation only—was very resolute. Perhaps too resolute. Perhaps he would want to grasp too much later on. A shadow flitted over Babalatchi's face. On the eve of the accomplishment of his desires he felt the bitter taste of that drop of doubt which is mixed with the sweetness of every success.

When, hearing footsteps on the verandah of the big house, he lifted his head, the shadow had passed away and on his face there was an expression of watchful alertness. Willems was coming down the plankway, into the courtyard. The light within trickled through the cracks of the badly joined walls of the house, and in the illuminated doorway appeared the moving form of Aissa. She also passed into the night outside and disappeared from view. Babalatchi wondered where she had got to, and for the moment forgot the approach of Willems. The voice of the white man speaking roughly above his head made him jump to his feet as if impelled upwards by a powerful spring.

"Where's Abdulla?"

Babalatchi waved his hand towards the hut and stood listening intently. The voices within had ceased, then recommenced again. He shot an oblique glance at Willems, whose indistinct form towered above the glow of dying embers.

"Make up this fire," said Willems, abruptly. "I want to see your face."

With obliging alacrity Babalatchi put some dry brushwood on the coals from a handy pile, keeping all the time a watchful eye on Willems. When he straightened himself up his hand wandered almost involuntarily towards his left side to feel the handle of a kriss amongst the folds of his sarong, but he tried to look unconcerned under the angry stare.

"You are in good health, please God?" he murmured.

"Yes!" answered Willems, with an unexpected loudness that caused Babalatchi to start nervously. "Yes! . . . Health! . . . You . . ."

He made a long stride and dropped both his hands on the Malay's shoulders. In the powerful grip Babalatchi swayed to and fro limply, but his face was as peaceful as when he sat—a little while ago—dreaming by the fire. With a final vicious jerk Willems let go suddenly, and turning away on his heel stretched his hands over the fire. Babalatchi stumbled backwards, recovered himself, and wriggled his shoulders laboriously.

"Tse! Tse! Tse!" he clicked, deprecatingly. After a short silence he went on with accentuated admiration: "What a man it is! What a strong man! A man like that"—he concluded, in a tone of meditative wonder—"a man like that could upset mountains —mountains!"

He gazed hopefully for a while at Willems' broad shoulders, and continued, addressing the inimical back, in a low and persuasive voice—

"But why be angry with me? With me who think only of your good? Did I not give her refuge, in my own house? Yes, Tuan! This is my own house. I will let you have it without any recompense because she must have a shelter. Therefore you and she shall live here. Who can know a woman's mind? And such a woman! If she wanted to go away from that other place, who am I—to say no! I am Omar's servant. I said: 'Gladden my heart by taking my house.' Did I say right?"

"I'll tell you something," said Willems, without changing his position; "if she takes a fancy to go away from this place it is you who shall suffer. I will wring your neck."

"When the heart is full of love there is no room in it for justice," recommenced Babalatchi, with unmoved and persistent softness. "Why slay me? You know, Tuan, what she wants. A splendid destiny is her desire—as of all women. You have been wronged and cast out by your people. She knows that. But you are brave, you are strong—you are a man; and, Tuan—I am older than you—you are in her hand. Such is the fate of strong men. And she is of noble birth and cannot live like a slave. You know her—and you are in her hand. You are like a snared bird, because of your strength. And—remember I am a man that has seen much—submit, Tuan! Submit! . . . Or else . . ."

He drawled out the last words in a hesitating manner and broke off his sentence. Still stretching his hands in turns towards the blaze and without moving his head, Willems gave a short, lugubrious laugh, and asked—

"Or else what?"

"She may go away again. Who knows?" finished Babalatchi, in a gentle and insinuating tone.

This time Willems spun round sharply. Babalatchi stepped back.

"If she does it will be the worse for you," said Willems, in a menacing voice. "It will be your doing, and I . . ."

Babalatchi spoke, from beyond the circle of light, with calm disdain.

"Hai—ya! I have heard before. If she goes—then I die. Good! Will that bring her back do you think—Tuan? If it is my doing it shall be well done, O white man! and—who knows—you will have to live without her."

Willems gasped and started back like a confident wayfarer who, pursuing a path he thinks safe, should see just in time a bottomless chasm under his feet. Babalatchi came into the light and approached Willems sideways, with his head thrown back and a little on one side so as to bring his only eye to bear full on the countenance of the tall white man.

"You threaten me," said Willems, indistinctly.

"I, Tuan!" exclaimed Babalatchi, with a slight suspicion of irony in the affected surprise of his tone. "I, Tuan? Who spoke of death? Was it I? No! I spoke of life only. Only of life. Of a long life for a lonely man!"

They stood with the fire between them, both silent, both aware, each in his own way, of the importance of the passing minutes. Babalatchi's fatalism gave him only an insignificant relief in his suspense, because no fatalism can kill the thought of the future, the desire of success, the pain of waiting for the disclosure of the immutable decrees of Heaven. Fatalism is born of the fear of failure, for we all believe that we carry success in our own hands, and we suspect that our hands are weak. Babalatchi looked at Willems and congratulated himself upon his ability to manage that white man. There was a pilot for Abdulla—a victim to appease Lingard's anger in case of any mishap. He would take good care to put him forward in everything. In any case let the white men fight it out amongst themselves. They were fools. He hated them—the strong fools—and knew that for his righteous wisdom was reserved the safe triumph.

Willems measured dismally the depth of his degradation. He—a white man, the admired of white men, was held by those miserable savages whose tool he was about to become. He felt for them all the hate of his race, of his morality, of his intelligence. He looked upon himself with dismay and pity. She had him. He had heard of such things. He had heard of women who . . . He would never believe such stories. . . . Yet they were true. But his own captivity seemed more complete, terrible, and final—without the hope of any redemption. He wondered at the wickedness of Providence that had made him what he was; that, worse still, permitted such a creature as Almayer to live. He had done his duty by going to him. Why did he not understand? All men were fools. He gave him his chance. The fellow did not see it. It was hard, very hard on himself—Willems. He wanted to take her from amongst her own people. That's why he had condescended to go to Almayer. He examined himself. With a sinking heart he thought that really he could not—somehow—live without her. It was terrible and sweet. He remembered the first days. Her appearance, her face, her smile, her eyes, her words. A savage woman! Yet he perceived that he could think of nothing else but of the three days of their separation, of the few hours since their reunion. Very well. If he could not take her away, then he would go to her. . . . He had, for a moment, a wicked pleasure in the thought that what he had done could not be undone. He had given himself up. He felt proud of it. He was ready to face anything, do anything. He cared for nothing, for nobody. He thought himself very fearless, but as a matter of fact he was only drunk; drunk with the poison of passionate memories.

He stretched his hands over the fire, looked round and called out—

"Aissa!"

She must have been near, for she appeared at once within the light of the fire. The upper part of her body was wrapped up in the thick folds of a head covering which was pulled down over her brow, and one end of it thrown across from shoulder to shoulder hid the lower part of her face. Only her eyes were visible—sombre and gleaming like a starry night.

Willems, looking at this strange, muffled figure, felt exasperated, amazed and helpless. The ex-confidential clerk of the rich Hudig would hug to his breast settled conceptions of respectable conduct. He sought refuge within his ideas of propriety from the dismal mangroves, from the darkness of the forests and of the heathen souls of the savages that were his masters. She looked like an animated package of cheap cotton goods! It made him furious. She had disguised herself so because a man of her race was near! He told her not to do it, and she did not obey. Would his ideas ever change so as to agree with her own notions of what was becoming, proper and respectable? He was really afraid they would, in time. It seemed to him awful. She would never change! This manifestation of her sense of proprieties was another sign of their hopeless diversity; something like another step downwards for him. She was too different from him. He was so civilized! It struck him suddenly that they had nothing in common—not a thought, not a feeling; he could not make clear to her the simplest motive of any act of his . . . and he could not live without her.

The courageous man who stood facing Babalatchi gasped unexpectedly with a gasp that was half a groan. This little matter of her veiling herself against his wish acted upon him like a disclosure of some great disaster. It increased his contempt for himself as the slave of a passion he had always derided, as the man unable to assert his will. This will, all his sensations, his personality—all this seemed to be lost in the abominable desire, in the priceless promise of that woman. He was not, of course, able to discern clearly the causes of his misery; but there are none so ignorant as not to know suffering, none so simple as not to feel and suffer from the shock of warring impulses. The ignorant must feel and suffer from their complexity as well as the wisest; but to them the pain of struggle and defeat appears strange, mysterious, remediable and unjust. He stood watching her, watching himself. He tingled with rage from head to foot, as if he had been struck in the face. Suddenly he laughed; but his laugh was like a distorted echo of some insincere mirth very far away.

From the other side of the fire Babalatchi spoke hurriedly—

"Here is Tuan Abdulla."

5

Directly on stepping outside Omar's hut Abdulla caught sight of Willems. He expected, of course, to see a white man, but not that white man, whom he knew so well. Everybody who traded in the islands, and who had any dealings with Hudig, knew Willems. For the last two years of his stay in Macassar the confidential clerk had been managing all the local trade of the house under a very slight supervision only on the part of the master. So everybody knew Willems, Abdulla amongst others—but he was ignorant of Willems' disgrace. As a matter of fact the thing had been kept very quiet—so quiet that a good many people in Macassar were expecting Willems' return there, supposing him to be absent on some confidential mission. Abdulla, in his surprise, hesitated on the threshold. He had prepared himself to see some seaman—some old officer of Lingard's; a common man—perhaps difficult to deal with, but still no match for him. Instead, he saw himself confronted by an individual whose reputation for sagacity in business was well known to him. How did he get here, and why? Abdulla, recovering from his surprise, advanced in a dignified manner towards the fire, keeping his eyes fixed steadily on Willems. When within two paces from Willems he stopped and lifted his right hand in grave salutation. Willems nodded slightly and spoke after a while.

"We know each other, Tuan Abdulla," he said, with an assumption of easy indifference.

"We have traded together," answered Abdulla, solemnly, "but it was far from here."

"And we may trade here also," said Willems.

"The place does not matter. It is the open mind and the true heart that are required in business."

"Very true. My heart is as open as my mind. I will tell you why I am here."

"What need is there? In leaving home one learns life. You travel. Travelling is victory! You shall return with much wisdom."

"I shall never return," interrupted Willems. "I have done with my people. I am a man without brothers. Injustice destroys fidelity."

Abdulla expressed his surprise by elevating his eyebrows. At the same time he made a vague gesture with his arm that could be taken as an equivalent of an approving and conciliating "just so!"

Till then the Arab had not taken any notice of Aissa, who stood by the fire, but now she spoke in the interval of silence following Willems' declaration. In a voice that was much deadened by her wrappings she addressed Abdulla in a few words of greeting, calling him a kinsman. Abdulla glanced at her swiftly for a second, and then, with perfect good breeding, fixed his eyes on the ground. She put out towards him her hand, covered with a corner of her face-veil, and he took it, pressed it twice, and dropping it turned towards Willems. She looked at the two men searchingly, then backed away and seemed to melt suddenly into the night.

"I know what you came for, Tuan Abdulla," said Willems; "I have been told by that man there." He nodded towards Babalatchi, then went on slowly, "It will be a difficult thing."

"Allah makes everything easy," interjected Babalatchi, piously, from a distance.

The two men turned quickly and stood looking at him thoughtfully, as if in deep consideration of the truth of that proposition. Under their sustained gaze Babalatchi experienced an unwonted feeling of shyness, and dared not approach nearer. At last Willems moved slightly, Abdulla followed readily, and they both walked down the courtyard, their voices dying away in the darkness. Soon they were heard returning, and the voices grew distinct as their forms came out of the gloom. By the fire they wheeled again, and Babalatchi caught a few words. Willems was saying—

"I have been at sea with him many years when young. I have used my knowledge to observe the way into the river when coming in, this time."

Abdulla assented in general terms.

"In the variety of knowledge there is safety," he said; and then they passed out of earshot.

Babalatchi ran to the tree and took up his position in the solid blackness under its branches, leaning against the trunk. There he was about midway between the fire and the other limit of the two men's walk. They passed him close. Abdulla slim, very straight, his head high, and his hands hanging before him and twisting mechanically the string of beads; Willems tall, broad, looking bigger and stronger in contrast to the slight white figure by the side of which he strolled carelessly, taking one step to the other's two; his big arms in constant motion as he gesticulated vehemently, bending forward to look Abdulla in the face.

They passed and repassed close to Babalatchi some half a dozen times, and, whenever they were between him and the fire, he could see them plain enough. Sometimes they would stop short, Willems speaking emphatically, Abdulla listening with rigid attention, then, when the other had ceased, bending his head slightly as if consenting to some demand, or admitting some statement. Now and then Babalatchi caught a word here and there, a fragment of a sentence, a loud exclamation. Impelled by curiosity he crept to the very edge of the black shadow under the tree. They were nearing him, and he heard Willems say—

"You will pay that money as soon as I come on board. That I must have."

He could not catch Abdulla's reply. When they went past again, Willems was saying—

"My life is in your hand anyway. The boat that brings me on board your ship shall take the money to Omar. You must have it ready in a sealed bag."

Again they were out of hearing, but instead of coming back they stopped by the fire facing each other. Willems moved his arm, shook his hand on high talking all the time, then brought it down jerkily—stamped his foot. A short period of immobility ensued. Babalatchi, gazing intently, saw Abdulla's lips move almost imperceptibly. Suddenly Willems seized the Arab's passive hand and shook it. Babalatchi drew the long breath of relieved suspense. The conference was over. All well, apparently.

He ventured now to approach the two men, who saw him and waited in silence. Willems had retired within himself already, and wore a look of grim indifference. Abdulla moved away a step or two. Babalatchi looked at him inquisitively.

"I go now," said Abdulla, "and shall wait for you outside the river, Tuan Willems, till the second sunset. You have only one word, I know."

"Only one word," repeated Willems.

Abdulla and Babalatchi walked together down the enclosure, leaving the white man alone by the fire. The two Arabs who had come with Abdulla preceded them and passed at once through the little gate into the light and the murmur of voices of the principal courtyard, but Babalatchi and Abdulla stopped on this side of it. Abdulla said—

"It is well. We have spoken of many things. He consents."

"When?" asked Babalatchi, eagerly.

"On the second day from this. I have promised every thing. I mean to keep much."

"Your hand is always open, O Most Generous amongst Believers! You will not forget your servant who called you here. Have I not spoken the truth? She has made roast meat of his heart."

With a horizontal sweep of his arm Abdulla seemed to push away that last statement, and said slowly, with much meaning—

"He must be perfectly safe; do you understand? Perfectly safe—as if he was amongst his own people—till . . ."

"Till when?" whispered Babalatchi.

"Till I speak," said Abdulla. "As to Omar." He hesitated for a moment, then went on very low: "He is very old."

"Hai-ya! Old and sick," murmured Babalatchi, with sudden melancholy.

"He wanted me to kill that white man. He begged me to have him killed at once," said Abdulla, contemptuously, moving again towards the gate.

"He is impatient, like those who feel death near them," exclaimed Babalatchi, apologetically.

"Omar shall dwell with me," went on Abdulla, "when . . . But no matter. Remember! The white man must be safe."

"He lives in your shadow," answered Babalatchi, solemnly. "It is enough!" He touched his forehead and fell back to let Abdulla go first.

And now they are back in the courtyard wherefrom, at their appearance, listlessness vanishes, and all the faces become alert and interested once more. Lakamba approaches his guest, but looks at Babalatchi, who reassures him by a confident nod. Lakamba clumsily attempts a smile, and looking, with natural and ineradicable sulkiness, from under his eyebrows at the man whom he wants to honour, asks whether he would condescend to visit the place of sitting down and take food. Or perhaps he would prefer to give himself up to repose? The house is his, and what is in it, and those many men that stand afar watching the interview are his. Syed Abdulla presses his host's hand to his breast, and informs him in a confidential murmur that his habits are ascetic and his temperament inclines to melancholy. No rest; no food; no use whatever for those many men who are his. Syed Abdulla is impatient to be gone. Lakamba is sorrowful but polite, in his hesitating, gloomy way. Tuan Abdulla must have fresh boatmen, and many, to shorten the dark and fatiguing road. Hai-ya! There! Boats!

By the riverside indistinct forms leap into a noisy and disorderly activity. There are cries, orders, banter, abuse. Torches blaze sending out much more smoke than light, and in their red glare Babalatchi comes up to say that the boats are ready.

Through that lurid glare Syed Abdulla, in his long white gown, seems to glide fantastically, like a dignified apparition attended by two inferior shades, and stands for a moment at the landing-place to take leave of his host and ally—whom he loves. Syed Abdulla says so distinctly before embarking, and takes his seat in the middle of the canoe under a small canopy of blue calico stretched on four sticks. Before and behind Syed Abdulla, the men squatting by the gunwales hold high the blades of their paddles in readiness for a dip, all together. Ready? Not yet. Hold on all! Syed Abdulla speaks again, while Lakamba and Babalatchi stand close on the bank to hear his words. His words are encouraging. Before the sun rises for the second time they shall meet, and Syed Abdulla's ship shall float on the waters of this river—at last! Lakamba and Babalatchi have no doubt—if Allah wills. They are in the hands of the Compassionate. No doubt. And so is Syed Abdulla, the great trader who does not know what the word failure means; and so is the white man—the smartest business man in the islands—who is lying now by Omar's fire with his head on Aissa's lap, while Syed Abdulla flies down the muddy river with current and paddles between the sombre walls of the sleeping forest; on his way to the clear and open sea where the Lord of the Isles (formerly of Greenock, but condemned, sold, and registered now as of Penang) waits for its owner, and swings erratically at anchor in the currents of the capricious tide, under the crumbling red cliffs of Tanjong Mirrah.

For some time Lakamba, Sahamin, and Bahassoen looked silently into the humid darkness which had swallowed the big canoe that carried Abdulla and his unvarying good fortune. Then the two guests broke into a talk expressive of their joyful anticipations. The venerable Sahamin, as became his advanced age, found his delight in speculation as to the activities of a rather remote future. He would buy praus, he would send expeditions up the river, he would enlarge his trade, and, backed by Abdulla's capital, he would grow rich in a very few years. Very few. Meantime it would be a good thing to interview Almayer to-morrow and, profiting by the last day of the hated man's prosperity, obtain some goods from him on credit. Sahamin thought it could be done by skilful wheedling. After all, that son of Satan was a fool, and the thing was worth doing, because the coming revolution would wipe all debts out. Sahamin did not mind imparting that idea to his companions, with much senile chuckling, while they strolled together from the riverside towards the residence. The bull-necked Lakamba, listening with pouted lips without the sign of a smile, without a gleam in his dull, bloodshot eyes, shuffled slowly across the courtyard between his two guests. But suddenly Bahassoen broke in upon the old man's prattle with the generous enthusiasm of his youth. . . . Trading was very good. But was the change that would make them happy effected yet? The white man should be despoiled with a strong hand! . . . He grew excited, spoke very loud, and his further discourse, delivered with his hand on the hilt of his sword, dealt incoherently with the honourable topics of throat-cutting, fire-raising, and with the far-famed valour of his ancestors.

Babalatchi remained behind, alone with the greatness of his conceptions. The sagacious statesman of Sambir sent a scornful glance after his noble protector and his noble protector's friends, and then stood meditating about that future which to the others seemed so assured. Not so to Babalatchi, who paid the penalty of his wisdom by a vague sense of insecurity that kept sleep at arm's length from his tired body. When he thought at last of leaving the waterside, it was only to strike a path for himself and to creep along the fences, avoiding the middle of the courtyard where small fires glimmered and winked as though the sinister darkness there had reflected the stars of the serene heaven. He slunk past the wicket-gate of Omar's enclosure, and crept on patiently along the light bamboo palisade till he was stopped by the angle where it joined the heavy stockade of Lakamba's private ground. Standing there, he could look over the fence and see Omar's hut and the fire before its door. He could also see the shadow of two human beings sitting between him and the red glow. A man and a woman. The sight seemed to inspire the careworn sage with a frivolous desire to sing. It could hardly be called a song; it was more in the nature of a recitative without any rhythm, delivered rapidly but distinctly in a croaking and unsteady voice; and if Babalatchi considered it a song, then it was a song with a purpose and, perhaps for that reason, artistically defective. It had all the imperfections of unskilful improvisation and its subject was gruesome. It told a tale of shipwreck and of thirst, and of one brother killing another for the sake of a gourd of water. A repulsive story which might have had a purpose but possessed no moral whatever. Yet it must have pleased Babalatchi for he repeated it twice, the second time even in louder tones than at first, causing a disturbance amongst the white rice-birds and the wild fruit-pigeons which roosted on the boughs of the big tree growing in Omar's compound. There was in the thick foliage above the singer's head a confused beating of wings, sleepy remarks in bird-language, a sharp stir of leaves. The forms by the fire moved; the shadow of the woman altered its shape, and Babalatchi's song was cut short abruptly by a fit of soft and persistent coughing. He did not try to resume his efforts after that interruption, but went away stealthily to seek—if not sleep—then, at least, repose.

6

As soon as Abdulla and his companions had left the enclosure, Aissa approached Willems and stood by his side. He took no notice of her expectant attitude till she touched him gently, when he turned furiously upon her and, tearing off her face-veil, trampled upon it as though it had been a mortal enemy. She looked at him with the faint smile of patient curiosity, with the puzzled interest of ignorance watching the running of a complicated piece of machinery. After he had exhausted his rage, he stood again severe and unbending looking down at the fire, but the touch of her fingers at the nape of his neck effaced instantly the hard lines round his mouth; his eyes wavered uneasily; his lips trembled slightly. Starting with the unresisting rapidity of a particle of iron—which, quiescent one moment, leaps in the next to a powerful magnet—he moved forward, caught her in his arms and pressed her violently to his breast. He released her as suddenly, and she stumbled a little, stepped back, breathed quickly through her parted lips, and said in a tone of pleased reproof—

"O Fool-man! And if you had killed me in your strong arms what would you have done?"

"You want to live . . . and to run away from me again," he said gently. "Tell me—do you?"

She moved towards him with very short steps, her head a little on one side, hands on hips, with a slight balancing of her body: an approach more tantalizing than an escape. He looked on, eager—charmed. She spoke jestingly.

"What am I to say to a man who has been away three days from me? Three!" she repeated, holding up playfully three fingers before Willems' eyes. He snatched at the hand, but she was on her guard and whisked it behind her back.

"No!" she said. "I cannot be caught. But I will come. I am coming myself because I like. Do not move. Do not touch me with your mighty hands, O child!"

As she spoke she made a step nearer, then another. Willems did not stir. Pressing against him she stood on tiptoe to look into his eyes, and her own seemed to grow bigger, glistening and tender, appealing and promising. With that look she drew the man's soul away from him through his immobile pupils, and from Willems' features the spark of reason vanished under her gaze and was replaced by an appearance of physical well-being, an ecstasy of the senses which had taken possession of his rigid body; an ecstasy that drove out regrets, hesitation and doubt, and proclaimed its terrible work by an appalling aspect of idiotic beatitude. He never stirred a limb, hardly breathed, but stood in stiff immobility, absorbing the delight of her close contact by every pore.

"Closer! Closer!" he murmured.

Slowly she raised her arms, put them over his shoulders, and clasping her hands at the back of his neck, swung off the full length of her arms. Her head fell back, the eyelids dropped slightly, and her thick hair hung straight down: a mass of ebony touched by the red gleams of the fire. He stood unyielding under the strain, as solid and motionless as one of the big trees of the surrounding forests; and his eyes looked at the modelling of her chin, at the outline of her neck, at the swelling lines of her bosom, with the famished and concentrated expression of a starving man looking at food. She drew herself up to him and rubbed her head against his cheek slowly and gently. He sighed. She, with her hands still on his shoulders, glanced up at the placid stars and said—

"The night is half gone. We shall finish it by this fire. By this fire you shall tell me all: your words and Syed Abdulla's words; and listening to you I shall forget the three days—because I am good. Tell me—am I good?"

He said "Yes" dreamily, and she ran off towards the big house.

When she came back, balancing a roll of fine mats on her head, he had replenished the fire and was ready to help her in arranging a couch on the side of it nearest to the hut. She sank down with a quick but gracefully controlled movement, and he threw himself full length with impatient haste, as if he wished to forestall somebody. She took his head on her knees, and when he felt her hands touching his face, her fingers playing with his hair, he had an expression of being taken possession of; he experienced a sense of peace, of rest, of happiness, and of soothing delight. His hands strayed upwards about her neck, and he drew her down so as to have her face above his. Then he whispered—"I wish I could die like this—now!" She looked at him with her big sombre eyes, in which there was no responsive light. His thought was so remote from her understanding that she let the words pass by unnoticed, like the breath of the wind, like the flight of a cloud. Woman though she was, she could not comprehend, in her simplicity, the tremendous compliment of that speech, that whisper of deadly happiness, so sincere, so spontaneous, coming so straight from the heart—like every corruption. It was the voice of madness, of a delirious peace, of happiness that is infamous, cowardly, and so exquisite that the debased mind refuses to contemplate its termination: for to the victims of such happiness the moment of its ceasing is the beginning afresh of that torture which is its price.

With her brows slightly knitted in the determined preoccupation of her own desires, she said—

"Now tell me all. All the words spoken between you and Syed Abdulla."

Tell what? What words? Her voice recalled back the consciousness that had departed under her touch, and he became aware of the passing minutes every one of which was like a reproach; of those minutes that falling, slow, reluctant, irresistible into the past, marked his footsteps on the way to perdition. Not that he had any conviction about it, any notion of the possible ending on that painful road. It was an indistinct feeling, a threat of suffering like the confused warning of coming disease, an inarticulate monition of evil made up of fear and pleasure, of resignation and of revolt. He was ashamed of his state of mind. After all, what was he afraid of? Were those scruples? Why that hesitation to think, to speak of what he intended doing? Scruples were for imbeciles. His clear duty was to make himself happy. Did he ever take an oath of fidelity to Lingard? No. Well then—he would not let any interest of that old fool stand between Willems and Willems' happiness. Happiness? Was he not, perchance, on a false track? Happiness meant money. Much money. At least he had always thought so till he had experienced those new sensations which . . .

Aissa's question, repeated impatiently, interrupted his musings, and looking up at her face shining above him in the dim light of the fire he stretched his limbs luxuriously and obedient to her desire, he spoke slowly and hardly above his breath. She, with her head close to his lips, listened absorbed, interested, in attentive immobility. The many noises of the great courtyard were hushed up gradually by the sleep that stilled all voices and closed all eyes. Then somebody droned out a song with a nasal drawl at the end of every verse. He stirred. She put her hand suddenly on his lips and sat upright. There was a feeble coughing, a rustle of leaves, and then a complete silence took possession of the land; a silence cold, mournful, profound; more like death than peace; more hard to bear than the fiercest tumult. As soon as she removed her hand he hastened to speak, so insupportable to him was that stillness perfect and absolute in which his thoughts seemed to ring with the loudness of shouts.

"Who was there making that noise?" he asked.

"I do not know. He is gone now," she answered, hastily. "Tell me, you will not return to your people; not without me. Not with me. Do you promise?"

"I have promised already. I have no people of my own. Have I not told you, that you are everybody to me?"

"Ah, yes," she said, slowly, "but I like to hear you say that again—every day, and every night, whenever I ask; and never to be angry because I ask. I am afraid of white women who are shameless and have fierce eyes." She scanned his features close for a moment and added:

"Are they very beautiful? They must be."

"I do not know," he whispered, thoughtfully. "And if I ever did know, looking at you I have forgotten."

"Forgotten! And for three days and two nights you have forgotten me also! Why? Why were you angry with me when I spoke at first of Tuan Abdulla, in the days when we lived beside the brook? You remembered somebody then. Somebody in the land whence you come. Your tongue is false. You are white indeed, and your heart is full of deception. I know it. And yet I cannot help believing you when you talk of your love for me. But I am afraid!"

He felt flattered and annoyed by her vehemence, and said—

"Well, I am with you now. I did come back. And it was you that went away."

"When you have helped Abdulla against the Rajah Laut, who is the first of white men, I shall not be afraid any more," she whispered.

"You must believe what I say when I tell you that there never was another woman; that there is nothing for me to regret, and nothing but my enemies to remember."

"Where do you come from?" she said, impulsive and inconsequent, in a passionate whisper. "What is that land beyond the great sea from which you come? A land of lies and of evil from which nothing but misfortune ever comes to us—who are not white. Did you not at first ask me to go there with you? That is why I went away."

"I shall never ask you again."

"And there is no woman waiting for you there?"

"No!" said Willems, firmly.

She bent over him. Her lips hovered above his face and her long hair brushed his cheeks.

"You taught me the love of your people which is of the Devil," she murmured, and bending still lower, she said faintly, "Like this?"

"Yes, like this!" he answered very low, in a voice that trembled slightly with eagerness; and she pressed suddenly her lips to his while he closed his eyes in an ecstasy of delight.

There was a long interval of silence. She stroked his head with gentle touches, and he lay dreamily, perfectly happy but for the annoyance of an indistinct vision of a well-known figure; a man going away from him and diminishing in a long perspective of fantastic trees, whose every leaf was an eye looking after that man, who walked away growing smaller, but never getting out of sight for all his steady progress. He felt a desire to see him vanish, a hurried impatience of his disappearance, and he watched for it with a careful and irksome effort. There was something familiar about that figure. Why! Himself! He gave a sudden start and opened his eyes, quivering with the emotion of that quick return from so far, of finding himself back by the fire with the rapidity of a flash of lightning. It had been half a dream; he had slumbered in her arms for a few seconds. Only the beginning of a dream—nothing more. But it was some time before he recovered from the shock of seeing himself go away so deliberately, so definitely, so unguardedly; and going away—where? Now, if he had not woke up in time he would never have come back again from there; from whatever place he was going to. He felt indignant. It was like an evasion, like a prisoner breaking his parole—that thing slinking off stealthily while he slept. He was very indignant, and was also astonished at the absurdity of his own emotions.

She felt him tremble, and murmuring tender words, pressed his head to her breast. Again he felt very peaceful with a peace that was as complete as the silence round them. He muttered—

"You are tired, Aissa."

She answered so low that it was like a sigh shaped into faint words.

"I shall watch your sleep, O child!"

He lay very quiet, and listened to the beating of her heart. That sound, light, rapid, persistent, and steady; her very life beating against his cheek, gave him a clear perception of secure ownership, strengthened his belief in his possession of that human being, was like an assurance of the vague felicity of the future. There were no regrets, no doubts, no hesitation now. Had there ever been? All that seemed far away, ages ago—as unreal and pale as the fading memory of some delirium. All the anguish, suffering, strife of the past days; the humiliation and anger of his downfall; all that was an infamous nightmare, a thing born in sleep to be forgotten and leave no trace—and true life was this: this dreamy immobility with his head against her heart that beat so steadily.

He was broad awake now, with that tingling wakefulness of the tired body which succeeds to the few refreshing seconds of irresistible sleep, and his wide-open eyes looked absently at the doorway of Omar's hut. The reed walls glistened in the light of the fire, the smoke of which, thin and blue, drifted slanting in a succession of rings and spirals across the doorway, whose empty blackness seemed to him impenetrable and enigmatical like a curtain hiding vast spaces full of unexpected surprises. This was only his fancy, but it was absorbing enough to make him accept the sudden appearance of a head, coming out of the gloom, as part of his idle fantasy or as the beginning of another short dream, of another vagary of his overtired brain. A face with drooping eyelids, old, thin, and yellow, above the scattered white of a long beard that touched the earth. A head without a body, only a foot above the ground, turning slightly from side to side on the edge of the circle of light as if to catch the radiating heat of the fire on either cheek in succession. He watched it in passive amazement, growing distinct, as if coming nearer to him, and the confused outlines of a body crawling on all fours came out, creeping inch by inch towards the fire, with a silent and all but imperceptible movement. He was astounded at the appearance of that blind head dragging that crippled body behind, without a sound, without a change in the composure of the sightless face, which was plain one second, blurred the next in the play of the light that drew it to itself steadily. A mute face with a kriss between its lips. This was no dream. Omar's face. But why? What was he after?

He was too indolent in the happy languor of the moment to answer the question. It darted through his brain and passed out, leaving him free to listen again to the beating of her heart; to that precious and delicate sound which filled the quiet immensity of the night. Glancing upwards he saw the motionless head of the woman looking down at him in a tender gleam of liquid white between the long eyelashes, whose shadow rested on the soft curve of her cheek; and under the caress of that look, the uneasy wonder and the obscure fear of that apparition, crouching and creeping in turns towards the fire that was its guide, were lost—were drowned in the quietude of all his senses, as pain is drowned in the flood of drowsy serenity that follows upon a dose of opium.

He altered the position of his head by ever so little, and now could see easily that apparition which he had seen a minute before and had nearly forgotten already. It had moved closer, gliding and noiseless like the shadow of some nightmare, and now it was there, very near, motionless and still as if listening; one hand and one knee advanced; the neck stretched out and the head turned full towards the fire. He could see the emaciated face, the skin shiny over the prominent bones, the black shadows of the hollow temples and sunken cheeks, and the two patches of blackness over the eyes, over those eyes that were dead and could not see. What was the impulse which drove out this blind cripple into the night to creep and crawl towards that fire? He looked at him, fascinated, but the face, with its shifting lights and shadows, let out nothing, closed and impenetrable like a walled door.

Omar raised himself to a kneeling posture and sank on his heels, with his hands hanging down before him. Willems, looking out of his dreamy numbness, could see plainly the kriss between the thin lips, a bar across the face; the handle on one side where the polished wood caught a red gleam from the fire and the thin line of the blade running to a dull black point on the other. He felt an inward shock, which left his body passive in Aissa's embrace, but filled his breast with a tumult of powerless fear; and he perceived suddenly that it was his own death that was groping towards him; that it was the hate of himself and the hate of her love for him which drove this helpless wreck of a once brilliant and resolute pirate, to attempt a desperate deed that would be the glorious and supreme consolation of an unhappy old age. And while he looked, paralyzed with dread, at the father who had resumed his cautious advance—blind like fate, persistent like destiny—he listened with greedy eagerness to the heart of the daughter beating light, rapid, and steady against his head.

He was in the grip of horrible fear; of a fear whose cold hand robs its victim of all will and of all power; of all wish to escape, to resist, or to move; which destroys hope and despair alike, and holds the empty and useless carcass as if in a vise under the coming stroke. It was not the fear of death—he had faced danger before—it was not even the fear of that particular form of death. It was not the fear of the end, for he knew that the end would not come then. A movement, a leap, a shout would save him from the feeble hand of the blind old man, from that hand that even now was, with cautious sweeps along the ground, feeling for his body in the darkness. It was the unreasoning fear of this glimpse into the unknown things, into those motives, impulses, desires he had ignored, but that had lived in the breasts of despised men, close by his side, and were revealed to him for a second, to be hidden again behind the black mists of doubt and deception. It was not death that frightened him: it was the horror of bewildered life where he could understand nothing and nobody round him; where he could guide, control, comprehend nothing and no one—not even himself.

He felt a touch on his side. That contact, lighter than the caress of a mother's hand on the cheek of a sleeping child, had for him the force of a crushing blow. Omar had crept close, and now, kneeling above him, held the kriss in one hand while the other skimmed over his jacket up towards his breast in gentle touches; but the blind face, still turned to the heat of the fire, was set and immovable in its aspect of stony indifference to things it could not hope to see. With an effort Willems took his eyes off the deathlike mask and turned them up to Aissa's head. She sat motionless as if she had been part of the sleeping earth, then suddenly he saw her big sombre eyes open out wide in a piercing stare and felt the convulsive pressure of her hands pinning his arms along his body. A second dragged itself out, slow and bitter, like a day of mourning; a second full of regret and grief for that faith in her which took its flight from the shattered ruins of his trust. She was holding him! She too! He felt her heart give a great leap, his head slipped down on her knees, he closed his eyes and there was nothing. Nothing! It was as if she had died; as though her heart had leaped out into the night, abandoning him, defenceless and alone, in an empty world.

His head struck the ground heavily as she flung him aside in her sudden rush. He lay as if stunned, face up and, daring not move, did not see the struggle, but heard the piercing shriek of mad fear, her low angry words; another shriek dying out in a moan. When he got up at last he looked at Aissa kneeling over her father, he saw her bent back in the effort of holding him down, Omar's contorted limbs, a hand thrown up above her head and her quick movement grasping the wrist. He made an impulsive step forward, but she turned a wild face to him and called out over her shoulder—

"Keep back! Do not come near! Do not. . . ."

And he stopped short, his arms hanging lifelessly by his side, as if those words had changed him into stone. She was afraid of his possible violence, but in the unsettling of all his convictions he was struck with the frightful thought that she preferred to kill her father all by herself; and the last stage of their struggle, at which he looked as though a red fog had filled his eyes, loomed up with an unnatural ferocity, with a sinister meaning; like something monstrous and depraved, forcing its complicity upon him under the cover of that awful night. He was horrified and grateful; drawn irresistibly to her—and ready to run away. He could not move at first—then he did not want to stir. He wanted to see what would happen. He saw her lift, with a tremendous effort, the apparently lifeless body into the hut, and remained standing, after they disappeared, with the vivid image in his eyes of that head swaying on her shoulder, the lower jaw hanging down, collapsed, passive, meaningless, like the head of a corpse.

Then after a while he heard her voice speaking inside, harshly, with an agitated abruptness of tone; and in answer there were groans and broken murmurs of exhaustion. She spoke louder. He heard her saying violently—"No! No! Never!"

And again a plaintive murmur of entreaty as of some one begging for a supreme favour, with a last breath. Then she said—

"Never! I would sooner strike it into my own heart."

She came out, stood panting for a short moment in the doorway, and then stepped into the firelight. Behind her, through the darkness came the sound of words calling the vengeance of heaven on her head, rising higher, shrill, strained, repeating the curse over and over again—till the voice cracked in a passionate shriek that died out into hoarse muttering ending with a deep and prolonged sigh. She stood facing Willems, one hand behind her back, the other raised in a gesture compelling attention, and she listened in that attitude till all was still inside the hut. Then she made another step forward and her hand dropped slowly.

"Nothing but misfortune," she whispered, absently, to herself. "Nothing but misfortune to us who are not white." The anger and excitement died out of her face, and she looked straight at Willems with an intense and mournful gaze.

He recovered his senses and his power of speech with a sudden start.

"Aissa," he exclaimed, and the words broke out through his lips with hurried nervousness. "Aissa! How can I live here? Trust me. Believe in me. Let us go away from here. Go very far away! Very far; you and I!"

He did not stop to ask himself whether he could escape, and how, and where. He was carried away by the flood of hate, disgust, and contempt of a white man for that blood which is not his blood, for that race which is not his race; for the brown skins; for the hearts false like the sea, blacker than night. This feeling of repulsion overmastered his reason in a clear conviction of the impossibility for him to live with her people. He urged her passionately to fly with him because out of all that abhorred crowd he wanted this one woman, but wanted her away from them, away from that race of slaves and cut-throats from which she sprang. He wanted her for himself—far from everybody, in some safe and dumb solitude. And as he spoke his anger and contempt rose, his hate became almost fear; and his desire of her grew immense, burning, illogical and merciless; crying to him through all his senses; louder than his hate, stronger than his fear, deeper than his contempt—irresistible and certain like death itself.

Standing at a little distance, just within the light—but on the threshold of that darkness from which she had come—she listened, one hand still behind her back, the other arm stretched out with the hand half open as if to catch the fleeting words that rang around her, passionate, menacing, imploring, but all tinged with the anguish of his suffering, all hurried by the impatience that gnawed his breast. And while she listened she felt a slowing down of her heart-beats as the meaning of his appeal grew clearer before her indignant eyes, as she saw with rage and pain the edifice of her love, her own work, crumble slowly to pieces, destroyed by that man's fears, by that man's falseness. Her memory recalled the days by the brook when she had listened to other words—to other thoughts—to promises and to pleadings for other things, which came from that man's lips at the bidding of her look or her smile, at the nod of her head, at the whisper of her lips. Was there then in his heart something else than her image, other desires than the desires of her love, other fears than the fear of losing her? How could that be? Had she grown ugly or old in a moment? She was appalled, surprised and angry with the anger of unexpected humiliation; and her eyes looked fixedly, sombre and steady, at that man born in the land of violence and of evil wherefrom nothing but misfortune comes to those who are not white. Instead of thinking of her caresses, instead of forgetting all the world in her embrace, he was thinking yet of his people; of that people that steals every land, masters every sea, that knows no mercy and no truth—knows nothing but its own strength. O man of strong arm and of false heart! Go with him to a far country, be lost in the throng of cold eyes and false hearts—lose him there! Never! He was mad—mad with fear; but he should not escape her! She would keep him here a slave and a master; here where he was alone with her; where he must live for her—or die. She had a right to his love which was of her making, to the love that was in him now, while he spoke those words without sense. She must put between him and other white men a barrier of hate. He must not only stay, but he must also keep his promise to Abdulla, the fulfilment of which would make her safe.

"Aissa, let us go! With you by my side I would attack them with my naked hands. Or no! Tomorrow we shall be outside, on board Abdulla's ship. You shall come with me and then I could . . . If the ship went ashore by some chance, then we could steal a canoe and escape in the confusion. . . . You are not afraid of the sea . . . of the sea that would give me freedom . . ."

He was approaching her gradually with extended arms, while he pleaded ardently in incoherent words that ran over and tripped each other in the extreme eagerness of his speech. She stepped back, keeping her distance, her eyes on his face, watching on it the play of his doubts and of his hopes with a piercing gaze, that seemed to search out the innermost recesses of his thought; and it was as if she had drawn slowly the darkness round her, wrapping herself in its undulating folds that made her indistinct and vague. He followed her step by step till at last they both stopped, facing each other under the big tree of the enclosure. The solitary exile of the forests, great, motionless and solemn in his abandonment, left alone by the life of ages that had been pushed away from him by those pigmies that crept at his foot, towered high and straight above their heads. He seemed to look on, dispassionate and imposing, in his lonely greatness, spreading his branches wide in a gesture of lofty protection, as if to hide them in the sombre shelter of innumerable leaves; as if moved by the disdainful compassion of the strong, by the scornful pity of an aged giant, to screen this struggle of two human hearts from the cold scrutiny of glittering stars.

The last cry of his appeal to her mercy rose loud, vibrated under the sombre canopy, darted among the boughs startling the white birds that slept wing to wing—and died without an echo, strangled in the dense mass of unstirring leaves. He could not see her face, but he heard her sighs and the distracted murmur of indistinct words. Then, as he listened holding his breath, she exclaimed suddenly—

"Have you heard him? He has cursed me because I love you. You brought me suffering and strife—and his curse. And now you want to take me far away where I would lose you, lose my life; because your love is my life now. What else is there? Do not move," she cried violently, as he stirred a little—"do not speak! Take this! Sleep in peace!"

He saw a shadowy movement of her arm. Something whizzed past and struck the ground behind him, close to the fire. Instinctively he turned round to look at it. A kriss without its sheath lay by the embers; a sinuous dark object, looking like something that had been alive and was now crushed, dead and very inoffensive; a black wavy outline very distinct and still in the dull red glow. Without thinking he moved to pick it up, stooping with the sad and humble movement of a beggar gathering the alms flung into the dust of the roadside. Was this the answer to his pleading, to the hot and living words that came from his heart? Was this the answer thrown at him like an insult, that thing made of wood and iron, insignificant and venomous, fragile and deadly? He held it by the blade and looked at the handle stupidly for a moment before he let it fall again at his feet; and when he turned round he faced only the night:—the night immense, profound and quiet; a sea of darkness in which she had disappeared without leaving a trace.

He moved forward with uncertain steps, putting out both his hands before him with the anguish of a man blinded suddenly.

"Aissa!" he cried—"come to me at once."

He peered and listened, but saw nothing, heard nothing. After a while the solid blackness seemed to wave before his eyes like a curtain disclosing movements but hiding forms, and he heard light and hurried footsteps, then the short clatter of the gate leading to Lakamba's private enclosure. He sprang forward and brought up against the rough timber in time to hear the words, "Quick! Quick!" and the sound of the wooden bar dropped on the other side, securing the gate. With his arms thrown up, the palms against the paling, he slid down in a heap on the ground.

"Aissa," he said, pleadingly, pressing his lips to a chink between the stakes. "Aissa, do you hear me? Come back! I will do what you want, give you all you desire—if I have to set the whole Sambir on fire and put that fire out with blood. Only come back. Now! At once! Are you there? Do you hear me? Aissa!"

On the other side there were startled whispers of feminine voices; a frightened little laugh suddenly interrupted; some woman's admiring murmur—"This is brave talk!" Then after a short silence Aissa cried—

"Sleep in peace—for the time of your going is near. Now I am afraid of you. Afraid of your fear. When you return with Tuan Abdulla you shall be great. You will find me here. And there will be nothing but love. Nothing else!—Always!—Till we die!"

He listened to the shuffle of footsteps going away, and staggered to his feet, mute with the excess of his passionate anger against that being so savage and so charming; loathing her, himself, everybody he had ever known; the earth, the sky, the very air he drew into his oppressed chest; loathing it because it made him live, loathing her because she made him suffer. But he could not leave that gate through which she had passed. He wandered a little way off, then swerved round, came back and fell down again by the stockade only to rise suddenly in another attempt to break away from the spell that held him, that brought him back there, dumb, obedient and furious. And under the immobilized gesture of lofty protection in the branches outspread wide above his head, under the high branches where white birds slept wing to wing in the shelter of countless leaves, he tossed like a grain of dust in a whirlwind—sinking and rising—round and round—always near that gate. All through the languid stillness of that night he fought with the impalpable; he fought with the shadows, with the darkness, with the silence. He fought without a sound, striking futile blows, dashing from side to side; obstinate, hopeless, and always beaten back; like a man bewitched within the invisible sweep of a magic circle.

III

I

"Yes! Cat, dog, anything that can scratch or bite; as long as it is harmful enough and mangy enough. A sick tiger would make you happy—of all things. A half-dead tiger that you could weep over and palm upon some poor devil in your power, to tend and nurse for you. Never mind the consequences—to the poor devil. Let him be mangled or eaten up, of course! You haven't any pity to spare for the victims of your infernal charity. Not you! Your tender heart bleeds only for what is poisonous and deadly. I curse the day when you set your benevolent eyes on him. I curse it . . ."

"Now then! Now then!" growled Lingard in his moustache. Almayer, who had talked himself up to the choking point, drew a long breath and went on—

"Yes! It has been always so. Always. As far back as I can remember. Don't you recollect? What about that half-starved dog you brought on board in Bankok in your arms. In your arms by . . . ! It went mad next day and bit the serang. You don't mean to say you have forgotten? The best serang you ever had! You said so yourself while you were helping us to lash him down to the chain-cable, just before he died in his fits. Now, didn't you? Two wives and ever so many children the man left. That was your doing. . . . And when you went out of your way and risked your ship to rescue some Chinamen from a water-logged junk in Formosa Straits, that was also a clever piece of business. Wasn't it? Those damned Chinamen rose on you before forty-eight hours. They were cut-throats, those poor fishermen. You knew they were cut-throats before you made up your mind to run down on a lee shore in a gale of wind to save them. A mad trick! If they hadn't been scoundrels—hopeless scoundrels—you would not have put your ship in jeopardy for them, I know. You would not have risked the lives of your crew—that crew you loved so—and your own life. Wasn't that foolish! And, besides, you were not honest. Suppose you had been drowned? I would have been in a pretty mess then, left alone here with that adopted daughter of yours. Your duty was to myself first. I married that girl because you promised to make my fortune. You know you did! And then three months afterwards you go and do that mad trick—for a lot of Chinamen too. Chinamen! You have no morality. I might have been ruined for the sake of those murderous scoundrels that, after all, had to be driven overboard after killing ever so many of your crew —of your beloved crew! Do you call that honest?"

"Well, well!" muttered Lingard, chewing nervously the stump of his cheroot that had gone out and looking at Almayer—who stamped wildly about the verandah—much as a shepherd might look at a pet sheep in his obedient flock turning unexpectedly upon him in enraged revolt. He seemed disconcerted, contemptuously angry yet somewhat amused; and also a little hurt as if at some bitter jest at his own expense. Almayer stopped suddenly, and crossing his arms on his breast, bent his body forward and went on speaking.

"I might have been left then in an awkward hole—all on account of your absurd disregard for your safety—yet I bore no grudge. I knew your weaknesses. But now—when I think of it! Now we are ruined. Ruined! Ruined! My poor little Nina. Ruined!"

He slapped his thighs smartly, walked with small steps this way and that, seized a chair, planted it with a bang before Lingard, and sat down staring at the old seaman with haggard eyes. Lingard, returning his stare steadily, dived slowly into various pockets, fished out at last a box of matches and proceeded to light his cheroot carefully, rolling it round and round between his lips, without taking his gaze for a moment off the distressed Almayer. Then from behind a cloud of tobacco smoke he said calmly—

"If you had been in trouble as often as I have, my boy, you wouldn't carry on so. I have been ruined more than once. Well, here I am."

"Yes, here you are," interrupted Almayer. "Much good it is to me. Had you been here a month ago it would have been of some use. But now! . . You might as well be a thousand miles off."

"You scold like a drunken fish-wife," said Lingard, serenely. He got up and moved slowly to the front rail of the verandah. The floor shook and the whole house vibrated under his heavy step. For a moment he stood with his back to Almayer, looking out on the river and forest of the east bank, then turned round and gazed mildly down upon him.

"It's very lonely this morning here. Hey?" he said.

Almayer lifted up his head.

"Ah! you notice it—don't you? I should think it is lonely! Yes, Captain Lingard, your day is over in Sambir. Only a month ago this verandah would have been full of people coming to greet you. Fellows would be coming up those steps grinning and salaaming—to you and to me. But our day is over. And not by my fault either. You can't say that. It's all the doing of that pet rascal of yours. Ah! He is a beauty! You should have seen him leading that hellish crowd. You would have been proud of your old favourite."

"Smart fellow that," muttered Lingard, thoughtfully. Almayer jumped up with a shriek.

"And that's all you have to say! Smart fellow! O Lord!"

"Don't make a show of yourself. Sit down. Let's talk quietly. I want to know all about it. So he led?"

"He was the soul of the whole thing. He piloted Abdulla's ship in. He ordered everything and everybody," said Almayer, who sat down again, with a resigned air.

"When did it happen—exactly?"

"On the sixteenth I heard the first rumours of Abdulla's ship being in the river; a thing I refused to believe at first. Next day I could not doubt any more. There was a great council held openly in Lakamba's place where almost everybody in Sambir attended. On the eighteenth the Lord of the Isles was anchored in Sambir reach, abreast of my house. Let's see. Six weeks to-day, exactly."

"And all that happened like this? All of a sudden. You never heard anything—no warning. Nothing. Never had an idea that something was up? Come, Almayer!"

"Heard! Yes, I used to hear something every day. Mostly lies. Is there anything else in Sambir?"

"You might not have believed them," observed Lingard. "In fact you ought not to have believed everything that was told to you, as if you had been a green hand on his first voyage."

Almayer moved in his chair uneasily.

"That scoundrel came here one day," he said. "He had been away from the house for a couple of months living with that woman. I only heard about him now and then from Patalolo's people when they came over. Well one day, about noon, he appeared in this courtyard, as if he had been jerked up from hell-where he belongs."

Lingard took his cheroot out, and, with his mouth full of white smoke that oozed out through his parted lips, listened, attentive. After a short pause Almayer went on, looking at the floor moodily—

"I must say he looked awful. Had a bad bout of the ague probably. The left shore is very unhealthy. Strange that only the breadth of the river . . ."

He dropped off into deep thoughtfulness as if he had forgotten his grievances in a bitter meditation upon the unsanitary condition of the virgin forests on the left bank. Lingard took this opportunity to expel the smoke in a mighty expiration and threw the stump of his cheroot over his shoulder.

"Go on," he said, after a while. "He came to see you . . ."

"But it wasn't unhealthy enough to finish him, worse luck!" went on Almayer, rousing himself, "and, as I said, he turned up here with his brazen impudence. He bullied me, he threatened vaguely. He wanted to scare me, to blackmail me. Me! And, by heaven—he said you would approve. You! Can you conceive such impudence? I couldn't exactly make out what he was driving at. Had I known, I would have approved him. Yes! With a bang on the head. But how could I guess that he knew enough to pilot a ship through the entrance you always said was so difficult. And, after all, that was the only danger. I could deal with anybody here—but when Abdulla came. . . . That barque of his is armed. He carries twelve brass six-pounders, and about thirty men. Desperate beggars. Sumatra men, from Deli and Acheen. Fight all day and ask for more in the evening. That kind."

"I know, I know," said Lingard, impatiently.

"Of course, then, they were cheeky as much as you please after he anchored abreast of our jetty. Willems brought her up himself in the best berth. I could see him from this verandah standing forward, together with the half-caste master. And that woman was there too. Close to him. I heard they took her on board off Lakamba's place. Willems said he would not go higher without her. Stormed and raged. Frightened them, I believe. Abdulla had to interfere. She came off alone in a canoe, and no sooner on deck than she fell at his feet before all hands, embraced his knees, wept, raved, begged his pardon. Why? I wonder. Everybody in Sambir is talking of it. They never heard tell or saw anything like it. I have all this from Ali, who goes about in the settlement and brings me the news. I had better know what is going on—hadn't I? From what I can make out, they—he and that woman—are looked upon as something mysterious—beyond comprehension. Some think them mad. They live alone with an old woman in a house outside Lakamba's campong and are greatly respected—or feared, I should say rather. At least, he is. He is very violent. She knows nobody, sees nobody, will speak to nobody but him. Never leaves him for a moment. It's the talk of the place. There are other rumours. From what I hear I suspect that Lakamba and Abdulla are tired of him. There's also talk of him going away in the Lord of the Isles—when she leaves here for the southward—as a kind of Abdulla's agent. At any rate, he must take the ship out. The half-caste is not equal to it as yet."

Lingard, who had listened absorbed till then, began now to walk with measured steps. Almayer ceased talking and followed him with his eyes as he paced up and down with a quarter-deck swing, tormenting and twisting his long white beard, his face perplexed and thoughtful.

"So he came to you first of all, did he?" asked Lingard, without stopping.

"Yes. I told you so. He did come. Came to extort money, goods—I don't know what else. Wanted to set up as a trader—the swine! I kicked his hat into the courtyard, and he went after it, and that was the last of him till he showed up with Abdulla. How could I know that he could do harm in that way? Or in any way at that! Any local rising I could put down easy with my own men and with Patalolo's help."

"Oh! yes. Patalolo. No good. Eh? Did you try him at all?"

"Didn't I!" exclaimed Almayer. "I went to see him myself on the twelfth. That was four days before Abdulla entered the river. In fact, same day Willems tried to get at me. I did feel a little uneasy then. Patalolo assured me that there was no human being that did not love me in Sambir. Looked as wise as an owl. Told me not to listen to the lies of wicked people from down the river. He was alluding to that man Bulangi, who lives up the sea reach, and who had sent me word that a strange ship was anchored outside—which, of course, I repeated to Patalolo. He would not believe. Kept on mumbling 'No! No! No!' like an old parrot, his head all of a tremble, all beslobbered with betel-nut juice. I thought there was something queer about him. Seemed so restless, and as if in a hurry to get rid of me. Well. Next day that one-eyed malefactor who lives with Lakamba—what's his name—Babalatchi, put in an appearance here! Came about mid-day, casually like, and stood there on this verandah chatting about one thing and another. Asking when I expected you, and so on. Then, incidentally, he mentioned that they—his master and himself—were very much bothered by a ferocious white man—my friend—who was hanging about that woman—Omar's daughter. Asked my advice. Very deferential and proper. I told him the white man was not my friend, and that they had better kick him out. Whereupon he went away salaaming, and protesting his friendship and his master's goodwill. Of course I know now the infernal nigger came to spy and to talk over some of my men. Anyway, eight were missing at the evening muster. Then I took alarm. Did not dare to leave my house unguarded. You know what my wife is, don't you? And I did not care to take the child with me—it being late—so I sent a message to Patalolo to say that we ought to consult; that there were rumours and uneasiness in the settlement. Do you know what answer I got?"

Lingard stopped short in his walk before Almayer, who went on, after an impressive pause, with growing animation.

"All brought it: 'The Rajah sends a friend's greeting, and does not understand the message.' That was all. Not a word more could Ali get out of him. I could see that Ali was pretty well scared. He hung about, arranging my hammock—one thing and another. Then just before going away he mentioned that the water-gate of the Rajah's place was heavily barred, but that he could see only very few men about the courtyard. Finally he said, 'There is darkness in our Rajah's house, but no sleep. Only darkness and fear and the wailing of women.' Cheerful, wasn't it? It made me feel cold down my back somehow. After Ali slipped away I stood here—by this table, and listened to the shouting and drumming in the settlement. Racket enough for twenty weddings. It was a little past midnight then."

Again Almayer stopped in his narrative with an abrupt shutting of lips, as if he had said all that there was to tell, and Lingard stood staring at him, pensive and silent. A big bluebottle fly flew in recklessly into the cool verandah, and darted with loud buzzing between the two men. Lingard struck at it with his hat. The fly swerved, and Almayer dodged his head out of the way. Then Lingard aimed another ineffectual blow; Almayer jumped up and waved his arms about. The fly buzzed desperately, and the vibration of minute wings sounded in the peace of the early morning like a far-off string orchestra accompanying the hollow, determined stamping of the two men, who, with heads thrown back and arms gyrating on high, or again bending low with infuriated lunges, were intent upon killing the intruder. But suddenly the buzz died out in a thin thrill away in the open space of the courtyard, leaving Lingard and Almayer standing face to face in the fresh silence of the young day, looking very puzzled and idle, their arms hanging uselessly by their sides —like men disheartened by some portentous failure.

"Look at that!" muttered Lingard. "Got away after all."

"Nuisance," said Almayer in the same tone. "Riverside is overrun with them. This house is badly placed . . . mosquitos . . . and these big flies . . . . last week stung Nina . . . been ill four days . . . poor child. . . . I wonder what such damned things are made for!"

2

After a long silence, during which Almayer had moved towards the table and sat down, his head between his hands, staring straight before him, Lingard, who had recommenced walking, cleared his throat and said—

"What was it you were saying?"

"Ah! Yes! You should have seen this settlement that night. I don't think anybody went to bed. I walked down to the point, and could see them. They had a big bonfire in the palm grove, and the talk went on there till the morning. When I came back here and sat in the dark verandah in this quiet house I felt so frightfully lonely that I stole in and took the child out of her cot and brought her here into my hammock. If it hadn't been for her I am sure I would have gone mad; I felt so utterly alone and helpless. Remember, I hadn't heard from you for four months. Didn't know whether you were alive or dead. Patalolo would have nothing to do with me. My own men were deserting me like rats do a sinking hulk. That was a black night for me, Captain Lingard. A black night as I sat here not knowing what would happen next. They were so excited and rowdy that I really feared they would come and burn the house over my head. I went and brought my revolver. Laid it loaded on the table. There were such awful yells now and then. Luckily the child slept through it, and seeing her so pretty and peaceful steadied me somehow. Couldn't believe there was any violence in this world, looking at her lying so quiet and so unconscious of what went on. But it was very hard. Everything was at an end. You must understand that on that night there was no government in Sambir. Nothing to restrain those fellows. Patalolo had collapsed. I was abandoned by my own people, and all that lot could vent their spite on me if they wanted. They know no gratitude. How many times haven't I saved this settlement from starvation? Absolute starvation. Only three months ago I distributed again a lot of rice on credit. There was nothing to eat in this infernal place. They came begging on their knees. There isn't a man in Sambir, big or little, who is not in debt to Lingard & Co. Not one. You ought to be satisfied. You always said that was the right policy for us. Well, I carried it out. Ah! Captain Lingard, a policy like that should be backed by loaded rifles . . ."

"You had them!" exclaimed Lingard in the midst of his promenade, that went on more rapid as Almayer talked: the headlong tramp of a man hurrying on to do something violent. The verandah was full of dust, oppressive and choking, which rose under the old seaman's feet, and made Almayer cough again and again.

"Yes, I had! Twenty. And not a finger to pull a trigger. It's easy to talk," he spluttered, his face very red.

Lingard dropped into a chair, and leaned back with one hand stretched out at length upon the table, the other thrown over the back of his seat. The dust settled, and the sun surging above the forest flooded the verandah with a clear light. Almayer got up and busied himself in lowering the split rattan screens that hung between the columns of the verandah.

"Phew!" said Lingard, "it will be a hot day. That's right, my boy. Keep the sun out. We don't want to be roasted alive here."

Almayer came back, sat down, and spoke very calmly—

"In the morning I went across to see Patalolo. I took the child with me, of course. I found the water-gate barred, and had to walk round through the bushes. Patalolo received me lying on the floor, in the dark, all the shutters closed. I could get nothing out of him but lamentations and groans. He said you must be dead. That Lakamba was coming now with Abdulla's guns to kill everybody. Said he did not mind being killed, as he was an old man, but that the wish of his heart was to make a pilgrimage. He was tired of men's ingratitude—he had no heirs—he wanted to go to Mecca and die there. He would ask Abdulla to let him go. Then he abused Lakamba—between sobs—and you, a little. You prevented him from asking for a flag that would have been respected—he was right there—and now when his enemies were strong he was weak, and you were not there to help him. When I tried to put some heart into him, telling him he had four big guns—you know the brass six-pounders you left here last year—and that I would get powder, and that, perhaps, together we could make head against Lakamba, he simply howled at me. No matter which way he turned—he shrieked—the white men would be the death of him, while he wanted only to be a pilgrim and be at peace. My belief is," added Almayer, after a short pause, and fixing a dull stare upon Lingard, "that the old fool saw this thing coming for a long time, and was not only too frightened to do anything himself, but actually too scared to let you or me know of his suspicions. Another of your particular pets! Well! You have a lucky hand, I must say!"

Lingard struck a sudden blow on the table with his clenched hand. There was a sharp crack of splitting wood. Almayer started up violently, then fell back in his chair and looked at the table.

"There!" he said, moodily, "you don't know your own strength. This table is completely ruined. The only table I had been able to save from my wife. By and by I will have to eat squatting on the floor like a native."

Lingard laughed heartily. "Well then, don't nag at me like a woman at a drunken husband!" He became very serious after awhile, and added, "If it hadn't been for the loss of the Flash I would have been here three months ago, and all would have been well. No use crying over that. Don't you be uneasy, Kaspar. We will have everything ship-shape here in a very short time."

"What? You don't mean to expel Abdulla out of here by force! I tell you, you can't."

"Not I!" exclaimed Lingard. "That's all over, I am afraid. Great pity. They will suffer for it. He will squeeze them. Great pity. Damn it! I feel so sorry for them if I had the Flash here I would try force. Eh! Why not? However, the poor Flash is gone, and there is an end of it. Poor old hooker. Hey, Almayer? You made a voyage or two with me. Wasn't she a sweet craft? Could make her do anything but talk. She was better than a wife to me. Never scolded. Hey? . . . And to think that it should come to this. That I should leave her poor old bones sticking on a reef as though I had been a damned fool of a southern-going man who must have half a mile of water under his keel to be safe! Well! well! It's only those who do nothing that make no mistakes, I suppose. But it's hard. Hard."

He nodded sadly, with his eyes on the ground. Almayer looked at him with growing indignation.

"Upon my word, you are heartless," he burst out; "perfectly heartless—and selfish. It does not seem to strike you—in all that—that in losing your ship—by your recklessness, I am sure—you ruin me—us, and my little Nina. What's going to become of me and of her? That's what I want to know. You brought me here, made me your partner, and now, when everything is gone to the devil—through your fault, mind you—you talk about your ship . . . ship! You can get another. But here. This trade. That's gone now, thanks to Willems. . . . Your dear Willems!"

"Never you mind about Willems. I will look after him," said Lingard, severely. "And as to the trade . . . I will make your fortune yet, my boy. Never fear. Have you got any cargo for the schooner that brought me here?"

"The shed is full of rattans," answered Almayer, "and I have about eighty tons of guttah in the well. The last lot I ever will have, no doubt," he added, bitterly.

"So, after all, there was no robbery. You've lost nothing actually. Well, then, you must . . . Hallo! What's the matter! . . . Here! . . ."

"Robbery! No!" screamed Almayer, throwing up his hands.

He fell back in the chair and his face became purple. A little white foam appeared on his lips and trickled down his chin, while he lay back, showing the whites of his upturned eyes. When he came to himself he saw Lingard standing over him, with an empty water-chatty in his hand.

"You had a fit of some kind," said the old seaman with much concern. "What is it? You did give me a fright. So very sudden."

Almayer, his hair all wet and stuck to his head, as if he had been diving, sat up and gasped.

"Outrage! A fiendish outrage. I . . ."

Lingard put the chatty on the table and looked at him in attentive silence. Almayer passed his hand over his forehead and went on in an unsteady tone:

"When I remember that, I lose all control," he said. "I told you he anchored Abdulla's ship abreast our jetty, but over to the other shore, near the Rajah's place. The ship was surrounded with boats. From here it looked as if she had been landed on a raft. Every dugout in Sambir was there. Through my glass I could distinguish the faces of people on the poop—Abdulla, Willems, Lakamba—everybody. That old cringing scoundrel Sahamin was there. I could see quite plain. There seemed to be much talk and discussion. Finally I saw a ship's boat lowered. Some Arab got into her, and the boat went towards Patalolo's landing-place. It seems they had been refused admittance—so they say. I think myself that the water-gate was not unbarred quick enough to please the exalted messenger. At any rate I saw the boat come back almost directly. I was looking on, rather interested, when I saw Willems and some more go forward—very busy about something there. That woman was also amongst them. Ah, that woman . . ."

Almayer choked, and seemed on the point of having a relapse, but by a violent effort regained a comparative composure.

"All of a sudden," he continued—"bang! They fired a shot into Patalolo's gate, and before I had time to catch my breath—I was startled, you may believe—they sent another and burst the gate open. Whereupon, I suppose, they thought they had done enough for a while, and probably felt hungry, for a feast began aft. Abdulla sat amongst them like an idol, cross-legged, his hands on his lap. He's too great altogether to eat when others do, but he presided, you see. Willems kept on dodging about forward, aloof from the crowd, and looking at my house through the ship's long glass. I could not resist it. I shook my fist at him."

"Just so," said Lingard, gravely. "That was the thing to do, of course. If you can't fight a man the best thing is to exasperate him."

Almayer waved his hand in a superior manner, and continued, unmoved: "You may say what you like. You can't realize my feelings. He saw me, and, with his eye still at the small end of the glass, lifted his arm as if answering a hail. I thought my turn to be shot at would come next after Patalolo, so I ran up the Union Jack to the flagstaff in the yard. I had no other protection. There were only three men besides Ali that stuck to me—three cripples, for that matter, too sick to get away. I would have fought singlehanded, I think, I was that angry, but there was the child. What to do with her? Couldn't send her up the river with the mother. You know I can't trust my wife. I decided to keep very quiet, but to let nobody land on our shore. Private property, that; under a deed from Patalolo. I was within my right—wasn't I? The morning was very quiet. After they had a feed on board the barque with Abdulla most of them went home; only the big people remained. Towards three o'clock Sahamin crossed alone in a small canoe. I went down on our wharf with my gun to speak to him, but didn't let him land. The old hypocrite said Abdulla sent greetings and wished to talk with me on business; would I come on board? I said no; I would not. Told him that Abdulla may write and I would answer, but no interview, neither on board his ship nor on shore. I also said that if anybody attempted to land within my fences I would shoot—no matter whom. On that he lifted his hands to heaven, scandalized, and then paddled away pretty smartly—to report, I suppose. An hour or so afterwards I saw Willems land a boat party at the Rajah's. It was very quiet. Not a shot was fired, and there was hardly any shouting. They tumbled those brass guns you presented to Patalolo last year down the bank into the river. It's deep there close to. The channel runs that way, you know. About five, Willems went back on board, and I saw him join Abdulla by the wheel aft. He talked a lot, swinging his arms about—seemed to explain things—pointed at my house, then down the reach. Finally, just before sunset, they hove upon the cable and dredged the ship down nearly half a mile to the junction of the two branches of the river—where she is now, as you might have seen."

Lingard nodded.

"That evening, after dark—I was informed—Abdulla landed for the first time in Sambir. He was entertained in Sahamin's house. I sent Ali to the settlement for news. He returned about nine, and reported that Patalolo was sitting on Abdulla's left hand before Sahamin's fire. There was a great council. Ali seemed to think that Patalolo was a prisoner, but he was wrong there. They did the trick very neatly. Before midnight everything was arranged as I can make out. Patalolo went back to his demolished stockade, escorted by a dozen boats with torches. It appears he begged Abdulla to let him have a passage in the Lord of the Isles to Penang. From there he would go to Mecca. The firing business was alluded to as a mistake. No doubt it was in a sense. Patalolo never meant resisting. So he is going as soon as the ship is ready for sea. He went on board next day with three women and half a dozen fellows as old as himself. By Abdulla's orders he was received with a salute of seven guns, and he has been living on board ever since—five weeks. I doubt whether he will leave the river alive. At any rate he won't live to reach Penang. Lakamba took over all his goods, and gave him a draft on Abdulla's house payable in Penang. He is bound to die before he gets there. Don't you see?"

He sat silent for a while in dejected meditation, then went on:

"Of course there were several rows during the night. Various fellows took the opportunity of the unsettled state of affairs to pay off old scores and settle old grudges. I passed the night in that chair there, dozing uneasily. Now and then there would be a great tumult and yelling which would make me sit up, revolver in hand. However, nobody was killed. A few broken heads—that's all. Early in the morning Willems caused them to make a fresh move which I must say surprised me not a little. As soon as there was daylight they busied themselves in setting up a flag-pole on the space at the other end of the settlement, where Abdulla is having his houses built now. Shortly after sunrise there was a great gathering at the flag-pole. All went there. Willems was standing leaning against the mast, one arm over that woman's shoulders. They had brought an armchair for Patalolo, and Lakamba stood on the right hand of the old man, who made a speech. Everybody in Sambir was there: women, slaves, children—everybody! Then Patalolo spoke. He said that by the mercy of the Most High he was going on a pilgrimage. The dearest wish of his heart was to be accomplished. Then, turning to Lakamba, he begged him to rule justly during his—Patalolo's—absence There was a bit of play-acting there. Lakamba said he was unworthy of the honourable burden, and Patalolo insisted. Poor old fool! It must have been bitter to him. They made him actually entreat that scoundrel. Fancy a man compelled to beg of a robber to despoil him! But the old Rajah was so frightened. Anyway, he did it, and Lakamba accepted at last. Then Willems made a speech to the crowd. Said that on his way to the west the Rajah—he meant Patalolo—would see the Great White Ruler in Batavia and obtain his protection for Sambir. Meantime, he went on, I, an Orang Blanda and your friend, hoist the flag under the shadow of which there is safety. With that he ran up a Dutch flag to the mast-head. It was made hurriedly, during the night, of cotton stuffs, and, being heavy, hung down the mast, while the crowd stared. Ali told me there was a great sigh of surprise, but not a word was spoken till Lakamba advanced and proclaimed in a loud voice that during all that day every one passing by the flagstaff must uncover his head and salaam before the emblem."

"But, hang it all!" exclaimed Lingard—"Abdulla is British!"

"Abdulla wasn't there at all—did not go on shore that day. Yet Ali, who has his wits about him, noticed that the space where the crowd stood was under the guns of the Lord of the Isles. They had put a coir warp ashore, and gave the barque a cant in the current, so as to bring the broadside to bear on the flagstaff. Clever! Eh? But nobody dreamt of resistance. When they recovered from the surprise there was a little quiet jeering; and Bahassoen abused Lakamba violently till one of Lakamba's men hit him on the head with a staff. Frightful crack, I am told. Then they left off jeering. Meantime Patalolo went away, and Lakamba sat in the chair at the foot of the flagstaff, while the crowd surged around, as if they could not make up their minds to go. Suddenly there was a great noise behind Lakamba's chair. It was that woman, who went for Willems. Ali says she was like a wild beast, but he twisted her wrist and made her grovel in the dust. Nobody knows exactly what it was about. Some say it was about that flag. He carried her off, flung her into a canoe, and went on board Abdulla's ship. After that Sahamin was the first to salaam to the flag. Others followed suit. Before noon everything was quiet in the settlement, and Ali came back and told me all this."

Almayer drew a long breath. Lingard stretched out his legs.

"Go on!" he said.

Almayer seemed to struggle with himself. At last he spluttered out:

"The hardest is to tell yet. The most unheard-of thing! An outrage! A fiendish outrage!"

3

"WELL! Let's know all about it. I can't imagine . . ." began Lingard, after waiting for some time in silence.

"Can't imagine! I should think you couldn't," interrupted Almayer. "Why! . . . You just listen. When Ali came back I felt a little easier in my mind. There was then some semblance of order in Sambir. I had the Jack up since the morning and began to feel safer. Some of my men turned up in the afternoon. I did not ask any questions; set them to work as if nothing had happened. Towards the evening—it might have been five or half-past—I was on our jetty with the child when I heard shouts at the far-off end of the settlement. At first I didn't take much notice. By and by Ali came to me and says, 'Master, give me the child, there is much trouble in the settlement.' So I gave him Nina and went in, took my revolver, and passed through the house into the back courtyard. As I came down the steps I saw all the serving girls clear out from the cooking shed, and I heard a big crowd howling on the other side of the dry ditch which is the limit of our ground. Could not see them on account of the fringe of bushes along the ditch, but I knew that crowd was angry and after somebody. As I stood wondering, that Jim-Eng—you know the Chinaman who settled here a couple of years ago?"

"He was my passenger; I brought him here," exclaimed Lingard. "A first-class Chinaman that."

"Did you? I had forgotten. Well, that Jim-Eng, he burst through the bush and fell into my arms, so to speak. He told me, panting, that they were after him because he wouldn't take off his hat to the flag. He was not so much scared, but he was very angry and indignant. Of course he had to run for it; there were some fifty men after him—Lakamba's friends—but he was full of fight. Said he was an Englishman, and would not take off his hat to any flag but English. I tried to soothe him while the crowd was shouting on the other side of the ditch. I told him he must take one of my canoes and cross the river. Stop on the other side for a couple of days. He wouldn't. Not he. He was English, and he would fight the whole lot. Says he: 'They are only black fellows. We white men,' meaning me and himself, 'can fight everybody in Sambir.' He was mad with passion. The crowd quieted a little, and I thought I could shelter Jim-Eng without much risk, when all of a sudden I heard Willems' voice. He shouted to me in English: 'Let four men enter your compound to get that Chinaman!' I said nothing. Told Jim-Eng to keep quiet too. Then after a while Willems shouts again: 'Don't resist, Almayer. I give you good advice. I am keeping this crowd back. Don't resist them!' That beggar's voice enraged me; I could not help it. I cried to him: 'You are a liar!' and just then Jim-Eng, who had flung off his jacket and had tucked up his trousers ready for a fight; just then that fellow he snatches the revolver out of my hand and lets fly at them through the bush. There was a sharp cry—he must have hit somebody—and a great yell, and before I could wink twice they were over the ditch and through the bush and on top of us! Simply rolled over us! There wasn't the slightest chance to resist. I was trampled under foot, Jim-Eng got a dozen gashes about his body, and we were carried halfway up the yard in the first rush. My eyes and mouth were full of dust; I was on my back with three or four fellows sitting on me. I could hear Jim-Eng trying to shout not very far from me. Now and then they would throttle him and he would gurgle. I could hardly breathe myself with two heavy fellows on my chest. Willems came up running and ordered them to raise me up, but to keep good hold. They led me into the verandah. I looked round, but did not see either Ali or the child. Felt easier. Struggled a little. . . . Oh, my God!"

Almayer's face was distorted with a passing spasm of rage. Lingard moved in his chair slightly. Almayer went on after a short pause:

"They held me, shouting threats in my face. Willems took down my hammock and threw it to them. He pulled out the drawer of this table, and found there a palm and needle and some sail-twine. We were making awnings for your brig, as you had asked me last voyage before you left. He knew, of course, where to look for what he wanted. By his orders they laid me out on the floor, wrapped me in my hammock, and he started to stitch me in, as if I had been a corpse, beginning at the feet. While he worked he laughed wickedly. I called him all the names I could think of. He told them to put their dirty paws over my mouth and nose. I was nearly choked. Whenever I moved they punched me in the ribs. He went on taking fresh needlefuls as he wanted them, and working steadily. Sewed me up to my throat. Then he rose, saying, 'That will do; let go.' That woman had been standing by; they must have been reconciled. She clapped her hands. I lay on the floor like a bale of goods while he stared at me, and the woman shrieked with delight. Like a bale of goods! There was a grin on every face, and the verandah was full of them. I wished myself dead—'pon my word, Captain Lingard, I did! I do now whenever I think of it!"

Lingard's face expressed sympathetic indignation. Almayer dropped his head upon his arms on the table, and spoke in that position in an indistinct and muffled voice, without looking up.

"Finally, by his directions, they flung me into the big rocking-chair. I was sewed in so tight that I was stiff like a piece of wood. He was giving orders in a very loud voice, and that man Babalatchi saw that they were executed. They obeyed him implicitly. Meantime I lay there in the chair like a log, and that woman capered before me and made faces; snapped her fingers before my nose. Women are bad!—ain't they? I never saw her before, as far as I know. Never done anything to her. Yet she was perfectly fiendish. Can you understand it? Now and then she would leave me alone to hang round his neck for awhile, and then she would return before my chair and begin her exercises again. He looked on, indulgent. The perspiration ran down my face, got into my eyes—my arms were sewn in. I was blinded half the time; at times I could see better. She drags him before my chair. 'I am like white women,' she says, her arms round his neck. You should have seen the faces of the fellows in the verandah! They were scandalized and ashamed of themselves to see her behaviour. Suddenly she asks him, alluding to me: 'When are you going to kill him?' Imagine how I felt. I must have swooned; I don't remember exactly. I fancy there was a row; he was angry. When I got my wits again he was sitting close to me, and she was gone. I understood he sent her to my wife, who was hiding in the back room and never came out during this affair. Willems says to me—I fancy I can hear his voice, hoarse and dull—he says to me: 'Not a hair of your head shall be touched.' I made no sound. Then he goes on: 'Please remark that the flag you have hoisted—which, by the by, is not yours—has been respected. Tell Captain Lingard so when you do see him. But,' he says, 'you first fired at the crowd.' 'You are a liar, you blackguard!' I shouted. He winced, I am sure. It hurt him to see I was not frightened. 'Anyways,' he says, 'a shot had been fired out of your compound and a man was hit. Still, all your property shall be respected on account of the Union Jack. Moreover, I have no quarrel with Captain Lingard, who is the senior partner in this business. As to you,' he continued, 'you will not forget this day—not if you live to be a hundred years old—or I don't know your nature. You will keep the bitter taste of this humiliation to the last day of your life, and so your kindness to me shall be repaid. I shall remove all the powder you have. This coast is under the protection of the Netherlands, and you have no right to have any powder. There are the Governor's Orders in Council to that effect, and you know it. Tell me where the key of the small storehouse is?' I said not a word, and he waited a little, then rose, saying: 'It's your own fault if there is any damage done.' He ordered Babalatchi to have the lock of the office-room forced, and went in—rummaged amongst my drawers—could not find the key. Then that woman Aissa asked my wife, and she gave them the key. After awhile they tumbled every barrel into the river. Eighty-three hundredweight! He superintended himself, and saw every barrel roll into the water. There were mutterings. Babalatchi was angry and tried to expostulate, but he gave him a good shaking. I must say he was perfectly fearless with those fellows. Then he came back to the verandah, sat down by me again, and says: 'We found your man Ali with your little daughter hiding in the bushes up the river. We brought them in. They are perfectly safe, of course. Let me congratulate you, Almayer, upon the cleverness of your child. She recognized me at once, and cried "pig" as naturally as you would yourself. Circumstances alter feelings. You should have seen how frightened your man Ali was. Clapped his hands over her mouth. I think you spoil her, Almayer. But I am not angry. Really, you look so ridiculous in this chair that I can't feel angry.' I made a frantic effort to burst out of my hammock to get at that scoundrel's throat, but I only fell off and upset the chair over myself. He laughed and said only: 'I leave you half of your revolver cartridges and take half myself; they will fit mine. We are both white men, and should back each other up. I may want them.' I shouted at him from under the chair: 'You are a thief,' but he never looked, and went away, one hand round that woman's waist, the other on Babalatchi's shoulder, to whom he was talking—laying down the law about something or other. In less than five minutes there was nobody inside our fences. After awhile Ali came to look for me and cut me free. I haven't seen Willems since—nor anybody else for that matter. I have been left alone. I offered sixty dollars to the man who had been wounded, which were accepted. They released Jim-Eng the next day, when the flag had been hauled down. He sent six cases of opium to me for safe keeping but has not left his house. I think he is safe enough now. Everything is very quiet."

Towards the end of his narrative Almayer lifted his head off the table, and now sat back in his chair and stared at the bamboo rafters of the roof above him. Lingard lolled in his seat with his legs stretched out. In the peaceful gloom of the verandah, with its lowered screens, they heard faint noises from the world outside in the blazing sunshine: a hail on the river, the answer from the shore, the creak of a pulley; sounds short, interrupted, as if lost suddenly in the brilliance of noonday. Lingard got up slowly, walked to the front rail, and holding one of the screens aside, looked out in silence. Over the water and the empty courtyard came a distinct voice from a small schooner anchored abreast of the Lingard jetty.

"Serang! Take a pull at the main peak halyards. This gaff is down on the boom."

There was a shrill pipe dying in long-drawn cadence, the song of the men swinging on the rope. The voice said sharply: "That will do!" Another voice—the serang's probably—shouted: "Ikat!" and as Lingard dropped the blind and turned away all was silent again, as if there had been nothing on the other side of the swaying screen; nothing but the light, brilliant, crude, heavy, lying on a dead land like a pall of fire. Lingard sat down again, facing Almayer, his elbow on the table, in a thoughtful attitude.

"Nice little schooner," muttered Almayer, wearily. "Did you buy her?"

"No," answered Lingard. "After I lost the Flash we got to Palembang in our boats. I chartered her there, for six months. From young Ford, you know. Belongs to him. He wanted a spell ashore, so I took charge myself. Of course all Ford's people on board. Strangers to me. I had to go to Singapore about the insurance; then I went to Macassar, of course. Had long passages. No wind. It was like a curse on me. I had lots of trouble with old Hudig. That delayed me much."

"Ah! Hudig! Why with Hudig?" asked Almayer, in a perfunctory manner.

"Oh! about a . . . a woman," mumbled Lingard.

Almayer looked at him with languid surprise. The old seaman had twisted his white beard into a point, and now was busy giving his moustaches a fierce curl. His little red eyes —those eyes that had smarted under the salt sprays of every sea, that had looked unwinking to windward in the gales of all latitudes—now glared at Almayer from behind the lowered eyebrows like a pair of frightened wild beasts crouching in a bush.

"Extraordinary! So like you! What can you have to do with Hudig's women? The old sinner!" said Almayer, negligently.

"What are you talking about! Wife of a friend of . . . I mean of a man I know . . ."

"Still, I don't see . . ." interjected Almayer carelessly.

"Of a man you know too. Well. Very well."

"I knew so many men before you made me bury myself in this hole!" growled Almayer, unamiably. "If she had anything to do with Hudig—that wife—then she can't be up to much. I would be sorry for the man," added Almayer, brightening up with the recollection of the scandalous tittle-tattle of the past, when he was a young man in the second capital of the Islands—and so well informed, so well informed. He laughed. Lingard's frown deepened.

"Don't talk foolish! It's Willems' wife."

Almayer grasped the sides of his seat, his eyes and mouth opened wide.

"What? Why!" he exclaimed, bewildered.

"Willems'—wife," repeated Lingard distinctly. "You ain't deaf, are you? The wife of Willems. Just so. As to why! There was a promise. And I did not know what had happened here."

"What is it. You've been giving her money, I bet," cried Almayer.

"Well, no!" said Lingard, deliberately. "Although I suppose I shall have to . . ."

Almayer groaned.

"The fact is," went on Lingard, speaking slowly and steadily, "the fact is that I have . . . I have brought her here. Here. To Sambir."

"In heaven's name! why?" shouted Almayer, jumping up. The chair tilted and fell slowly over. He raised his clasped hands above his head and brought them down jerkily, separating his fingers with an effort, as if tearing them apart. Lingard nodded, quickly, several times.

"I have. Awkward. Hey?" he said, with a puzzled look upwards.

"Upon my word," said Almayer, tearfully. "I can't understand you at all. What will you do next! Willems' wife!"

"Wife and child. Small boy, you know. They are on board the schooner."

Almayer looked at Lingard with sudden suspicion, then turning away busied himself in picking up the chair, sat down in it turning his back upon the old seaman, and tried to whistle, but gave it up directly. Lingard went on—

"Fact is, the fellow got into trouble with Hudig. Worked upon my feelings. I promised to arrange matters. I did. With much trouble. Hudig was angry with her for wishing to join her husband. Unprincipled old fellow. You know she is his daughter. Well, I said I would see her through it all right; help Willems to a fresh start and so on. I spoke to Craig in Palembang. He is getting on in years, and wanted a manager or partner. I promised to guarantee Willems' good behaviour. We settled all that. Craig is an old crony of mine. Been shipmates in the forties. He's waiting for him now. A pretty mess! What do you think?"

Almayer shrugged his shoulders.

"That woman broke with Hudig on my assurance that all would be well," went on Lingard, with growing dismay. "She did. Proper thing, of course. Wife, husband . . . together . . . as it should be . . . Smart fellow . . . Impossible scoundrel . . . Jolly old go! Oh! damn!"

Almayer laughed spitefully.

"How delighted he will be," he said, softly. "You will make two people happy. Two at least!" He laughed again, while Lingard looked at his shaking shoulders in consternation.

"I am jammed on a lee shore this time, if ever I was," muttered Lingard.

"Send her back quick," suggested Almayer, stifling another laugh.

"What are you sniggering at?" growled Lingard, angrily. "I'll work it out all clear yet. Meantime you must receive her into this house."

"My house!" cried Almayer, turning round.

"It's mine too—a little isn't it?" said Lingard. "Don't argue," he shouted, as Almayer opened his mouth. "Obey orders and hold your tongue!"

"Oh! If you take it in that tone!" mumbled Almayer, sulkily, with a gesture of assent.

"You are so aggravating too, my boy," said the old seaman, with unexpected placidity. "You must give me time to turn round. I can't keep her on board all the time. I must tell her something. Say, for instance, that he is gone up the river. Expected back every day. That's it. D'ye hear? You must put her on that tack and dodge her along easy, while I take the kinks out of the situation. By God!" he exclaimed, mournfully, after a short pause, "life is foul! Foul like a lee forebrace on a dirty night. And yet. And yet. One must see it clear for running before going below—for good. Now you attend to what I said," he added, sharply, "if you don't want to quarrel with me, my boy."

"I don't want to quarrel with you," murmured Almayer with unwilling deference. "Only I wish I could understand you. I know you are my best friend, Captain Lingard; only, upon my word, I can't make you out sometimes! I wish I could . . ."

Lingard burst into a loud laugh which ended shortly in a deep sigh. He closed his eyes, tilting his head over the back of his armchair; and on his face, baked by the unclouded suns of many hard years, there appeared for a moment a weariness and a look of age which startled Almayer, like an unexpected disclosure of evil.

"I am done up," said Lingard, gently. "Perfectly done up. All night on deck getting that schooner up the river. Then talking with you. Seems to me I could go to sleep on a clothes-line. I should like to eat something though. Just see about that, Kaspar."

Almayer clapped his hands, and receiving no response was going to call, when in the central passage of the house, behind the red curtain of the doorway opening upon the verandah, they heard a child's imperious voice speaking shrilly.

"Take me up at once. I want to be carried into the verandah. I shall be very angry. Take me up."

A man's voice answered, subdued, in humble remonstrance. The faces of Almayer and Lingard brightened at once. The old seaman called out—

"Bring the child. Lekas!"

"You will see how she has grown," exclaimed Almayer, in a jubilant tone.

Through the curtained doorway Ali appeared with little Nina Almayer in his arms. The child had one arm round his neck, and with the other she hugged a ripe pumelo nearly as big as her own head. Her little pink, sleeveless robe had half slipped off her shoulders, but the long black hair, that framed her olive face, in which the big black eyes looked out in childish solemnity, fell in luxuriant profusion over her shoulders, all round her and over Ali's arms, like a close-meshed and delicate net of silken threads. Lingard got up to meet Ali, and as soon as she caught sight of the old seaman she dropped the fruit and put out both her hands with a cry of delight. He took her from the Malay, and she laid hold of his moustaches with an affectionate goodwill that brought unaccustomed tears into his little red eyes.

"Not so hard, little one, not so hard," he murmured, pressing with an enormous hand, that covered it entirely, the child's head to his face.

"Pick up my pumelo, O Rajah of the sea!" she said, speaking in a high-pitched, clear voice with great volubility. "There, under the table. I want it quick! Quick! You have been away fighting with many men. Ali says so. You are a mighty fighter. Ali says so. On the great sea far away, away, away."

She waved her hand, staring with dreamy vacancy, while Lingard looked at her, and squatting down groped under the table after the pumelo.

"Where does she get those notions?" said Lingard, getting up cautiously, to Almayer, who had been giving orders to Ali.

"She is always with the men. Many a time I've found her with her fingers in their rice dish, of an evening. She does not care for her mother though—I am glad to say. How pretty she is—and so sharp. My very image!"

Lingard had put the child on the table, and both men stood looking at her with radiant faces.

"A perfect little woman," whispered Lingard. "Yes, my dear boy, we shall make her somebody. You'll see!"

"Very little chance of that now," remarked Almayer, sadly.

"You do not know!" exclaimed Lingard, taking up the child again, and beginning to walk up and down the verandah. "I have my plans. I have—listen."

And he began to explain to the interested Almayer his plans for the future. He would interview Abdulla and Lakamba. There must be some understanding with those fellows now they had the upper hand. Here he interrupted himself to swear freely, while the child, who had been diligently fumbling about his neck, had found his whistle and blew a loud blast now and then close to his ear—which made him wince and laugh as he put her hands down, scolding her lovingly. Yes—that would be easily settled. He was a man to be reckoned with yet. Nobody knew that better than Almayer. Very well. Then he must patiently try and keep some little trade together. It would be all right. But the great thing—and here Lingard spoke lower, bringing himself to a sudden standstill before the entranced Almayer—the great thing would be the gold hunt up the river. He—Lingard—would devote himself to it. He had been in the interior before. There were immense deposits of alluvial gold there. Fabulous. He felt sure. Had seen places. Dangerous work? Of course! But what a reward! He would explore—and find. Not a shadow of doubt. Hang the danger! They would first get as much as they could for themselves. Keep the thing quiet. Then after a time form a Company. In Batavia or in England. Yes, in England. Much better. Splendid! Why, of course. And that baby would be the richest woman in the world. He—Lingard—would not, perhaps, see it—although he felt good for many years yet—but Almayer would. Here was something to live for yet! Hey?

But the richest woman in the world had been for the last five minutes shouting shrilly—"Rajah Laut! Rajah Laut! Hai! Give ear!" while the old seaman had been speaking louder, unconsciously, to make his deep bass heard above the impatient clamour. He stopped now and said tenderly—

"What is it, little woman?"

"I am not a little woman. I am a white child. Anak Putih. A white child; and the white men are my brothers. Father says so. And Ali says so too. Ali knows as much as father. Everything."

Almayer almost danced with paternal delight.

"I taught her. I taught her," he repeated, laughing with tears in his eyes. "Isn't she sharp?"

"I am the slave of the white child," said Lingard, with playful solemnity. "What is the order?"

"I want a house," she warbled, with great eagerness. "I want a house, and another house on the roof, and another on the roof—high. High! Like the places where they dwell—my brothers—in the land where the sun sleeps."

"To the westward," explained Almayer, under his breath. "She remembers everything. She wants you to build a house of cards. You did, last time you were here."

Lingard sat down with the child on his knees, and Almayer pulled out violently one drawer after another, looking for the cards, as if the fate of the world depended upon his haste. He produced a dirty double pack which was only used during Lingard's visit to Sambir, when he would sometimes play—of an evening—with Almayer, a game which he called Chinese bezique. It bored Almayer, but the old seaman delighted in it, considering it a remarkable product of Chinese genius—a race for which he had an unaccountable liking and admiration.

"Now we will get on, my little pearl," he said, putting together with extreme precaution two cards that looked absurdly flimsy between his big fingers. Little Nina watched him with intense seriousness as he went on erecting the ground floor, while he continued to speak to Almayer with his head over his shoulder so as not to endanger the structure with his breath.

"I know what I am talking about. . . . Been in California in forty-nine. . . . Not that I made much . . . then in Victoria in the early days . . . . I know all about it. Trust me. Moreover a blind man could . . . Be quiet, little sister, or you will knock this affair down. . . . My hand pretty steady yet! Hey, Kaspar? . . . Now, delight of my heart, we shall put a third house on the top of these two . . . keep very quiet. . . . As I was saying, you got only to stoop and gather handfuls of gold . . . dust . . . there. Now here we are. Three houses on top of one another. Grand!"

He leaned back in his chair, one hand on the child's head, which he smoothed mechanically, and gesticulated with the other, speaking to Almayer.

"Once on the spot, there would be only the trouble to pick up the stuff. Then we shall all go to Europe. The child must be educated. We shall be rich. Rich is no name for it. Down in Devonshire where I belong, there was a fellow who built a house near Teignmouth which had as many windows as a three-decker has ports. Made all his money somewhere out here in the good old days. People around said he had been a pirate. We boys—I was a boy in a

Brixham trawler then—certainly believed that. He went about in a bath-chair in his grounds. Had a glass eye . . ."

"Higher, Higher!" called out Nina, pulling the old seaman's beard.

"You do worry me—don't you?" said Lingard, gently, giving her a tender kiss. "What? One more house on top of all these? Well! I will try."

The child watched him breathlessly. When the difficult feat was accomplished she clapped her hands, looked on steadily, and after a while gave a great sigh of content.

"Oh! Look out!" shouted Almayer.

The structure collapsed suddenly before the child's light breath. Lingard looked discomposed for a moment. Almayer laughed, but the little girl began to cry.

"Take her," said the old seaman, abruptly. Then, after Almayer went away with the crying child, he remained sitting by the table, looking gloomily at the heap of cards.

"Damn this Willems," he muttered to himself. "But I will do it yet!"

He got up, and with an angry push of his hand swept the cards off the table. Then he fell back in his chair.

"Tired as a dog," he sighed out, closing his eyes.

4

Consciously or unconsciously, men are proud of their firmness, steadfastness of purpose, directness of aim. They go straight towards their desire, to the accomplishment of virtue—sometimes of crime—in an uplifting persuasion of their firmness. They walk the road of life, the road fenced in by their tastes, prejudices, disdains or enthusiasms, generally honest, invariably stupid, and are proud of never losing their way. If they do stop, it is to look for a moment over the hedges that make them safe, to look at the misty valleys, at the distant peaks, at cliffs and morasses, at the dark forests and the hazy plains where other human beings grope their days painfully away, stumbling over the bones of the wise, over the unburied remains of their predecessors who died alone, in gloom or in sunshine, halfway from anywhere. The man of purpose does not understand, and goes on, full of contempt. He never loses his way. He knows where he is going and what he wants. Travelling on, he achieves great length without any breadth, and battered, besmirched, and weary, he touches the goal at last; he grasps the reward of his perseverance, of his virtue, of his healthy optimism: an untruthful tombstone over a dark and soon forgotten grave.

Lingard had never hesitated in his life. Why should he? He had been a most successful trader, and a man lucky in his fights, skilful in navigation, undeniably first in seamanship in those seas. He knew it. Had he not heard the voice of common consent?

The voice of the world that respected him so much; the whole world to him—for to us the limits of the universe are strictly defined by those we know. There is nothing for us outside the babble of praise and blame on familiar lips, and beyond our last acquaintance there lies only a vast chaos; a chaos of laughter and tears which concerns us not; laughter and tears unpleasant, wicked, morbid, contemptible—because heard imperfectly by ears rebellious to strange sounds. To Lingard—simple himself—all things were simple. He seldom read. Books were not much in his way, and he had to work hard navigating, trading, and also, in obedience to his benevolent instincts, shaping stray lives he found here and there under his busy hand. He remembered the Sunday-school teachings of his native village and the discourses of the black-coated gentleman connected with the Mission to Fishermen and Seamen, whose yawl-rigged boat darting through rain-squalls amongst the coasters wind-bound in Falmouth Bay, was part of those precious pictures of his youthful days that lingered in his memory. "As clever a sky-pilot as you could wish to see," he would say with conviction, "and the best man to handle a boat in any weather I ever did meet!" Such were the agencies that had roughly shaped his young soul before he went away to see the world in a southern-going ship—before he went, ignorant and happy, heavy of hand, pure in heart, profane in speech, to give himself up to the great sea that took his life and gave him his fortune. When thinking of his rise in the world—commander of ships, then shipowner, then a man of much capital, respected wherever he went, Lingard in a word, the Rajah Laut—he was amazed and awed by his fate, that seemed to his ill-informed mind the most wondrous known in the annals of men. His experience appeared to him immense and conclusive, teaching him the lesson of the simplicity of life. In life—as in seamanship—there were only two ways of doing a thing: the right way and the wrong way. Common sense and experience taught a man the way that was right. The other was for lubbers and fools, and led, in seamanship, to loss of spars and sails or shipwreck; in life, to loss of money and consideration, or to an unlucky knock on the head. He did not consider it his duty to be angry with rascals. He was only angry with things he could not understand, but for the weaknesses of humanity he could find a contemptuous tolerance. It being manifest that he was wise and lucky—otherwise how could he have been as successful in life as he had been? —he had an inclination to set right the lives of other people, just as he could hardly refrain—in defiance of nautical etiquette—from interfering with his chief officer when the crew was sending up a new topmast, or generally when busy about, what he called, "a heavy job." He was meddlesome with perfect modesty; if he knew a thing or two there was no merit in it. "Hard knocks taught me wisdom, my boy," he used to say, "and you had better take the advice of a man who has been a fool in his time. Have another." And "my boy" as a rule took the cool drink, the advice, and the consequent help which Lingard felt himself bound in honour to give, so as to back up his opinion like an honest man. Captain Tom went sailing from island to island, appearing unexpectedly in various localities, beaming, noisy, anecdotal, commendatory or comminatory, but always welcome.

It was only since his return to Sambir that the old seaman had for the first time known doubt and unhappiness, The loss of the Flash—planted firmly and for ever on a ledge of rock at the north end of Gaspar Straits in the uncertain light of a cloudy morning—shook him considerably; and the amazing news which he heard on his arrival in Sambir were not made to soothe his feelings. A good many years ago—prompted by his love of adventure—he, with infinite trouble, had found out and surveyed—for his own benefit only—the entrances to that river, where, he had heard through native report, a new settlement of Malays was forming. No doubt he thought at the time mostly of personal gain; but, received with hearty friendliness by Patalolo, he soon came to like the ruler and the people, offered his counsel and his help, and—knowing nothing of Arcadia—he dreamed of Arcadian happiness for that little corner of the world which he loved to think all his own. His deep-seated and immovable conviction that only he—he, Lingard—knew what was good for them was characteristic of him and, after all, not so very far wrong. He would make them happy whether or no, he said, and he meant it. His trade brought prosperity to the young state, and the fear of his heavy hand secured its internal peace for many years.

He looked proudly upon his work. With every passing year he loved more the land, the people, the muddy river that, if he could help it, would carry no other craft but the Flash on its unclean and friendly surface. As he slowly warped his vessel up-stream he would scan with knowing looks the riverside clearings, and pronounce solemn judgment upon the prospects of the season's rice-crop. He knew every settler on the banks between the sea and

Sambir; he knew their wives, their children; he knew every individual of the multi-coloured groups that, standing on the flimsy platforms of tiny reed dwellings built over the water, waved their hands and shouted shrilly: "O! Kapal layer! Hai!" while the Flash swept slowly through the populated reach, to enter the lonely stretches of sparkling brown water bordered by the dense and silent forest, whose big trees nodded their outspread boughs gently in the faint, warm breeze—as if in sign of tender but melancholy welcome. He loved it all: the landscape of brown golds and brilliant emeralds under the dome of hot sapphire; the whispering big trees; the loquacious nipa-palms that rattled their leaves volubly in the night breeze, as if in haste to tell him all the secrets of the great forest behind them. He loved the heavy scents of blossoms and black earth, that breath of life and of death which lingered over his brig in the damp air of tepid and peaceful nights. He loved the narrow and sombre creeks, strangers to sunshine: black, smooth, tortuous—like byways of despair. He liked even the troops of sorrowful-faced monkeys that profaned the quiet spots with capricious gambols and insane gestures of inhuman madness. He loved everything there, animated or inanimated; the very mud of the riverside; the very alligators, enormous and stolid, basking on it with impertinent unconcern. Their size was a source of pride to him. "Immense fellows! Make two of them Palembang reptiles! I tell you, old man!" he would shout, poking some crony of his playfully in the ribs: "I tell you, big as you are, they could swallow you in one gulp, hat, boots and all! Magnificent beggars! Wouldn't you like to see them? Wouldn't you! Ha! ha! ha!" His thunderous laughter filled the verandah, rolled over the hotel garden, overflowed into the street, paralyzing for a short moment the noiseless traffic of bare brown feet; and its loud reverberations would even startle the landlord's tame bird—a shameless mynah—into a momentary propriety of behaviour under the nearest chair. In the big billiard-room perspiring men in thin cotton singlets would stop the game, listen, cue in hand, for a while through the open windows, then nod their moist faces at each other sagaciously and whisper: "The old fellow is talking about his river."

His river! The whispers of curious men, the mystery of the thing, were to Lingard a source of never-ending delight. The common talk of ignorance exaggerated the profits of his queer monopoly, and, although strictly truthful in general, he liked, on that matter, to mislead speculation still further by boasts full of cold raillery. His river! By it he was not only rich—he was interesting. This secret of his which made him different to the other traders of those seas gave intimate satisfaction to that desire for singularity which he shared with the rest of mankind, without being aware of its presence within his breast. It was the greater part of his happiness, but he only knew it after its loss, so unforeseen, so sudden and so cruel.

After his conversation with Almayer he went on board the schooner, sent Joanna on shore, and shut himself up in his cabin, feeling very unwell. He made the most of his indisposition to Almayer, who came to visit him twice a day. It was an excuse for doing nothing just yet. He wanted to think. He was very angry. Angry with himself, with Willems. Angry at what Willems had done—and also angry at what he had left undone. The scoundrel was not complete. The conception was perfect, but the execution, unaccountably, fell short. Why? He ought to have cut Almayer's throat and burnt the place to ashes—then cleared out. Got out of his way; of him, Lingard! Yet he didn't. Was it impudence, contempt—or what? He felt hurt at the implied disrespect of his power, and the incomplete rascality of the proceeding disturbed him exceedingly. There was something short, something wanting, something that would have given him a free hand in the work of retribution. The obvious, the right thing to do, was to shoot Willems. Yet how could he? Had the fellow resisted, showed fight, or ran away; had he shown any consciousness of harm done, it would have been more possible, more natural. But no! The fellow actually had sent him a message.

Wanted to see him. What for? The thing could not be explained. An unexampled, cold-blooded treachery, awful, incomprehensible. Why did he do it? Why? Why? The old seaman in the stuffy solitude of his little cabin on board the schooner groaned out many times that question, striking with an open palm his perplexed forehead.

During his four days of seclusion he had received two messages from the outer world; from that world of Sambir which had, so suddenly and so finally, slipped from his grasp. One, a few words from Willems written on a torn-out page of a small notebook; the other, a communication from Abdulla caligraphed carefully on a large sheet of flimsy paper and delivered to him in a green silk wrapper. The first he could not understand. It said: "Come and see me. I am not afraid. Are you? W." He tore it up angrily, but before the small bits of dirty paper had the time to flutter down and settle on the floor, the anger was gone and was replaced by a sentiment that induced him to go on his knees, pick up the fragments of the torn message, piece it together on the top of his chronometer box, and contemplate it long and thoughtfully, as if he had hoped to read the answer of the horrible riddle in the very form of the letters that went to make up that fresh insult. Abdulla's letter he read carefully and rammed it into his pocket, also with anger, but with anger that ended in a half-resigned, half-amused smile. He would never give in as long as there was a chance. "It's generally the safest way to stick to the ship as long as she will swim," was one of his favourite sayings: "The safest and the right way. To abandon a craft because it leaks is easy—but poor work. Poor work!" Yet he was intelligent enough to know when he was beaten, and to accept the situation like a man, without repining. When Almayer came on board that afternoon he handed him the letter without comment.

Almayer read it, returned it in silence, and leaning over the taffrail (the two men were on deck) looked down for some time at the play of the eddies round the schooner's rudder. At last he said without looking up—

"That's a decent enough letter. Abdulla gives him up to you. I told you they were getting sick of him. What are you going to do?"

Lingard cleared his throat, shuffled his feet, opened his mouth with great determination, but said nothing for a while. At last he murmured—

"I'll be hanged if I know—just yet."

"I wish you would do something soon . . ."

"What's the hurry?" interrupted Lingard. "He can't get away. As it stands he is at my mercy, as far as I can see."

"Yes," said Almayer, reflectively—"and very little mercy he deserves too. Abdulla's meaning—as I can make it out amongst all those compliments—is: 'Get rid for me of that white man—and we shall live in peace and share the trade.'"

"You believe that?" asked Lingard, contemptuously.

"Not altogether," answered Almayer. "No doubt we will share the trade for a time—till he can grab the lot. Well, what are you going to do?"

He looked up as he spoke and was surprised to see Lingard's discomposed face.

"You ain't well. Pain anywhere?" he asked, with real solicitude.

"I have been queer—you know—these last few days, but no pain." He struck his broad chest several times, cleared his throat with a powerful "Hem!" and repeated: "No. No pain. Good for a few years yet. But I am bothered with all this, I can tell you!"

"You must take care of yourself," said Almayer. Then after a pause he added: "You will see Abdulla. Won't you?"

"I don't know. Not yet. There's plenty of time," said Lingard, impatiently.

"I wish you would do something," urged Almayer, moodily. "You know, that woman is a perfect nuisance to me. She and her brat! Yelps all day. And the children don't get on together. Yesterday the little devil wanted to fight with my Nina. Scratched her face, too. A perfect savage! Like his honourable papa. Yes, really. She worries about her husband, and whimpers from morning to night. When she isn't weeping she is furious with me. Yesterday she tormented me to tell her when he would be back and cried because he was engaged in such dangerous work. I said something about it being all right—no necessity to make a fool of herself, when she turned upon me like a wild cat. Called me a brute, selfish, heartless; raved about her beloved Peter risking his life for my benefit, while I did not care. Said I took advantage of his generous good-nature to get him to do dangerous work—my work. That he was worth twenty of the likes of me. That she would tell you—open your eyes as to the kind of man I was, and so on. That's what I've got to put up with for your sake. You really might consider me a little. I haven't robbed anybody," went on Almayer, with an attempt at bitter irony—"or sold my best friend, but still you ought to have some pity on me. It's like living in a hot fever. She is out of her wits. You make my house a refuge for scoundrels and lunatics. It isn't fair. 'Pon my word it isn't! When she is in her tantrums she is ridiculously ugly and screeches so—it sets my teeth on edge. Thank God! my wife got a fit of the sulks and cleared out of the house. Lives in a riverside hut since that affair—you know. But this Willems' wife by herself is almost more than I can bear. And I ask myself why should I? You are exacting and no mistake. This morning I thought she was going to claw me. Only think! She wanted to go prancing about the settlement. She might have heard something there, so I told her she mustn't. It wasn't safe outside our fences, I said. Thereupon she rushes at me with her ten nails up to my eyes. 'You miserable man,' she yells, 'even this place is not safe, and you've sent him up this awful river where he may lose his head. If he dies before forgiving me, Heaven will punish you for your crime . . .' My crime! I ask myself sometimes whether I am dreaming! It will make me ill, all this. I've lost my appetite already."

He flung his hat on deck and laid hold of his hair despairingly. Lingard looked at him with concern.

"What did she mean by it?" he muttered, thoughtfully.

"Mean! She is crazy, I tell you—and I will be, very soon, if this lasts!"

"Just a little patience, Kaspar," pleaded Lingard. "A day or so more."

Relieved or tired by his violent outburst, Almayer calmed down, picked up his hat and, leaning against the bulwark, commenced to fan himself with it.

"Days do pass," he said, resignedly—"but that kind of thing makes a man old before his time. What is there to think about?—I can't imagine! Abdulla says plainly that if you undertake to pilot his ship out and instruct the half-caste, he will drop Willems like a hot potato and be your friend ever after. I believe him perfectly, as to Willems. It's so natural. As to being your friend it's a lie of course, but we need not bother about that just yet. You just say yes to Abdulla, and then whatever happens to Willems will be nobody's business."

He interrupted himself and remained silent for a while, glaring about with set teeth and dilated nostrils.

"You leave it to me. I'll see to it that something happens to him," he said at last, with calm ferocity. Lingard smiled faintly.

"The fellow isn't worth a shot. Not the trouble of it," he whispered, as if to himself. Almayer fired up suddenly.

"That's what you think," he cried. "You haven't been sewn up in your hammock to be made a laughing-stock of before a parcel of savages. Why! I daren't look anybody here in the face while that scoundrel is alive. I will . . . I will settle him."

"I don't think you will," growled Lingard.

"Do you think I am afraid of him?"

"Bless you! no!" said Lingard with alacrity. "Afraid! Not you. I know you. I don't doubt your courage. It's your head, my boy, your head that I . . ."

"That's it," said the aggrieved Almayer. "Go on. Why don't you call me a fool at once?"

"Because I don't want to," burst out Lingard, with nervous irritability. "If I wanted to call you a fool, I would do so without asking your leave." He began to walk athwart the narrow quarter-deck, kicking ropes' ends out of his way and growling to himself: "Delicate gentleman . . . what next? . . . I've done man's work before you could toddle. Understand . . . say what I like."

"Well! well!" said Almayer, with affected resignation. "There's no talking to you these last few days." He put on his hat, strolled to the gangway and stopped, one foot on the little inside ladder, as if hesitating, came back and planted himself in Lingard's way, compelling him to stand still and listen.

"Of course you will do what you like. You never take advice—I know that; but let me tell you that it wouldn't be honest to let that fellow get away from here. If you do nothing, that scoundrel will leave in Abdulla's ship for sure. Abdulla will make use of him to hurt you and others elsewhere. Willems knows too much about your affairs. He will cause you lots of trouble. You mark my words. Lots of trouble. To you—and to others perhaps. Think of that, Captain Lingard. That's all I've got to say. Now I must go back on shore. There's lots of work. We will begin loading this schooner to-morrow morning, first thing. All the bundles are ready. If you should want me for anything, hoist some kind of flag on the mainmast. At night two shots will fetch me." Then he added, in a friendly tone, "Won't you come and dine in the house to-night? It can't be good for you to stew on board like that, day after day."

Lingard did not answer. The image evoked by Almayer; the picture of Willems ranging over the islands and disturbing the harmony of the universe by robbery, treachery, and violence, held him silent, entranced—painfully spellbound. Almayer, after waiting for a little while, moved reluctantly towards the gangway, lingered there, then sighed and got over the side, going down step by step. His head disappeared slowly below the rail. Lingard, who had been staring at him absently, started suddenly, ran to the side, and looking over, called out—

"Hey! Kaspar! Hold on a bit!"

Almayer signed to his boatmen to cease paddling, and turned his head towards the schooner. The boat drifted back slowly abreast of Lingard, nearly alongside.

"Look here," said Lingard, looking down—"I want a good canoe with four men to-day."

"Do you want it now?" asked Almayer.

"No! Catch this rope. Oh, you clumsy devil! . . . No, Kaspar," went on Lingard, after the bow-man had got hold of the end of the brace he had thrown down into the canoe—"No, Kaspar. The sun is too much for me. And it would be better to keep my affairs quiet, too. Send the canoe—four good paddlers, mind, and your canvas chair for me to sit in. Send it about sunset. D'ye hear?"

"All right, father," said Almayer, cheerfully—"I will send Ali for a steersman, and the best men I've got. Anything else?"

"No, my lad. Only don't let them be late."

"I suppose it's no use asking you where you are going," said Almayer, tentatively. "Because if it is to see Abdulla, I . . ."

"I am not going to see Abdulla. Not to-day. Now be off with you."

He watched the canoe dart away shorewards, waved his hand in response to Almayer's nod, and walked to the taffrail smoothing out Abdulla's letter, which he had pulled out of his pocket. He read it over carefully, crumpled it up slowly, smiling the while and closing his fingers firmly over the crackling paper as though he had hold there of Abdulla's throat. Halfway to his pocket he changed his mind, and flinging the ball overboard looked at it thoughtfully as it spun round in the eddies for a moment, before the current bore it away down-stream, towards the sea.

IV

I

THE NIGHT WAS VERY DARK. For the first time in many months the East Coast slept unseen by the stars under a veil of motionless cloud that, driven before the first breath of the rainy monsoon, had drifted slowly from the eastward all the afternoon; pursuing the declining sun with its masses of black and grey that seemed to chase the light with wicked intent, and with an ominous and gloomy steadiness, as though conscious of the message of violence and turmoil they carried. At the sun's disappearance below the western horizon, the immense cloud, in quickened motion, grappled with the glow of retreating light, and rolling down to the clear and jagged outline of the distant mountains, hung arrested above the steaming forests; hanging low, silent and menacing over the unstirring tree-tops; withholding the blessing of rain, nursing the wrath of its thunder; undecided—as if brooding over its own power for good or for evil.

Babalatchi, coming out of the red and smoky light of his little bamboo house, glanced upwards, drew in a long breath of the warm and stagnant air, and stood for a moment with his good eye closed tightly, as if intimidated by the unwonted and deep silence of Lakamba's courtyard. When he opened his eye he had recovered his sight so far, that he could distinguish the various degrees of formless blackness which marked the places of trees, of abandoned houses, of riverside bushes, on the dark background of the night.

The careworn sage walked cautiously down the deserted courtyard to the waterside, and stood on the bank listening to the voice of the invisible river that flowed at his feet; listening to the soft whispers, to the deep murmurs, to the sudden gurgles and the short hisses of the swift current racing along the bank through the hot darkness.

He stood with his face turned to the river, and it seemed to him that he could breathe easier with the knowledge of the clear vast space before him; then, after a while he leaned heavily forward on his staff, his chin fell on his breast, and a deep sigh was his answer to the selfish discourse of the river that hurried on unceasing and fast, regardless of joy or sorrow, of suffering and of strife, of failures and triumphs that lived on its banks. The brown water was there, ready to carry friends or enemies, to nurse love or hate on its submissive and heartless bosom, to help or to hinder, to save life or give death; the great and rapid river: a deliverance, a prison, a refuge or a grave.

Perchance such thoughts as these caused Babalatchi to send another mournful sigh into the trailing mists of the unconcerned Pantai. The barbarous politician had forgotten the recent success of his plottings in the melancholy contemplation of a sorrow that made the night blacker, the clammy heat more oppressive, the still air more heavy, the dumb solitude more significant of torment than of peace. He had spent the night before by the side of the dying Omar, and now, after twenty-four hours, his memory persisted in returning to that low and sombre reed hut from which the fierce spirit of the incomparably accomplished pirate took its flight, to learn too late, in a worse world, the error of its earthly ways. The mind of the savage statesman, chastened by bereavement, felt for a moment the weight of his loneliness with keen perception worthy even of a sensibility exasperated by all the refinements of tender sentiment that a glorious civilization brings in its train, among other blessings and virtues, into this excellent world. For the space of about thirty seconds, a half-naked, betel-chewing pessimist stood upon the bank of the tropical river, on the edge of the still and immense forests; a man angry, powerless, empty-handed, with a cry of bitter discontent ready on his lips; a cry that, had it come out, would have rung through the virgin solitudes of the woods, as true, as great, as profound, as any philosophical shriek that ever came from the depths of an easy-chair to disturb the impure wilderness of chimneys and roofs.

For half a minute and no more did Babalatchi face the gods in the sublime privilege of his revolt, and then the one-eyed puller of wires became himself again, full of care and wisdom and far-reaching plans, and a victim to the tormenting superstitions of his race. The night, no matter how quiet, is never perfectly silent to attentive ears, and now Babalatchi fancied he could detect in it other noises than those caused by the ripples and eddies of the river. He turned his head sharply to the right and to the left in succession, and then spun round quickly in a startled and watchful manner, as if he had expected to see the blind ghost of his departed leader wandering in the obscurity of the empty courtyard behind his back. Nothing there. Yet he had heard a noise; a strange noise! No doubt a ghostly voice of a complaining and angry spirit. He listened. Not a sound. Reassured, Babalatchi made a few paces towards his house, when a very human noise, that of hoarse coughing, reached him from the river. He stopped, listened attentively, but now without any sign of emotion, and moving briskly back to the waterside stood expectant with parted lips, trying to pierce with his eye the wavering curtain of mist that hung low over the water. He could see nothing, yet some people in a canoe must have been very near, for he heard words spoken in an ordinary tone.

"Do you think this is the place, Ali? I can see nothing."

"It must be near here, Tuan," answered another voice. "Shall we try the bank?"

"No! . . . Let drift a little. If you go poking into the bank in the dark you might stove the canoe on some log. We must be careful. . . . Let drift! Let drift! . . . This does seem to be a clearing of some sort. We may see a light by and by from some house or other. In Lakamba's campong there are many houses? Hey?"

"A great number, Tuan . . . I do not see any light."

"Nor I," grumbled the first voice again, this time nearly abreast of the silent Babalatchi who looked uneasily towards his own house, the doorway of which glowed with the dim light of a torch burning within. The house stood end on to the river, and its doorway faced down-stream, so Babalatchi reasoned rapidly that the strangers on the river could not see the light from the position their boat was in at the moment. He could not make up his mind to call out to them, and while he hesitated he heard the voices again, but now some way below the landing-place where he stood.

"Nothing. This cannot be it. Let them give way, Ali! Dayong there!"

That order was followed by the splash of paddles, then a sudden cry—

"I see a light. I see it! Now I know where to land, Tuan."

There was more splashing as the canoe was paddled sharply round and came back up-stream close to the bank.

"Call out," said very near a deep voice, which Babalatchi felt sure must belong to a white man. "Call out—and somebody may come with a torch. I can't see anything."

The loud hail that succeeded these words was emitted nearly under the silent listener's nose. Babalatchi, to preserve appearances, ran with long but noiseless strides halfway up the courtyard, and only then shouted in answer and kept on shouting as he walked slowly back again towards the river bank. He saw there an indistinct shape of a boat, not quite alongside the landing-place.

"Who speaks on the river?" asked Babalatchi, throwing a tone of surprise into his question.

"A white man," answered Lingard from the canoe. "Is there not one torch in rich Lakamba's campong to light a guest on his landing?"

"There are no torches and no men. I am alone here," said Babalatchi, with some hesitation.

"Alone!" exclaimed Lingard. "Who are you?"

"Only a servant of Lakamba. But land, Tuan Putih, and see my face. Here is my hand. No! Here! . . . By your mercy. . . . Ada! . . . Now you are safe."

"And you are alone here?" said Lingard, moving with precaution a few steps into the courtyard. "How dark it is," he muttered to himself—"one would think the world had been painted black."

"Yes. Alone. What more did you say, Tuan? I did not understand your talk."

"It is nothing. I expected to find here . . . But where are they all?"

"What matters where they are?" said Babalatchi, gloomily. "Have you come to see my people? The last departed on a long journey—and I am alone. Tomorrow I go too."

"I came to see a white man," said Lingard, walking on slowly. "He is not gone, is he?"

"No!" answered Babalatchi, at his elbow. "A man with a red skin and hard eyes," he went on, musingly, "whose hand is strong, and whose heart is foolish and weak. A white man indeed . . . But still a man."

They were now at the foot of the short ladder which led to the split-bamboo platform surrounding Babalatchi's habitation. The faint light from the doorway fell down upon the two men's faces as they stood looking at each other curiously.

"Is he there?" asked Lingard, in a low voice, with a wave of his hand upwards.

Babalatchi, staring hard at his long-expected visitor, did not answer at once. "No, not there," he said at last, placing his foot on the lowest rung and looking back. "Not there, Tuan—yet not very far. Will you sit down in my dwelling? There may be rice and fish and clear water—not from the river, but from a spring . . ."

"I am not hungry," interrupted Lingard, curtly, "and I did not come here to sit in your dwelling. Lead me to the white man who expects me. I have no time to lose."

"The night is long, Tuan," went on Babalatchi, softly, "and there are other nights and other days. Long. Very long . . . How much time it takes for a man to die! O Rajah Laut!"

Lingard started.

"You know me!" he exclaimed.

"Ay—wa! I have seen your face and felt your hand before—many years ago," said Babalatchi, holding on halfway up the ladder, and bending down from above to peer into Lingard's upturned face. "You do not remember—but I have not forgotten. There are many men like me: there is only one Rajah Laut."

He climbed with sudden agility the last few steps, and stood on the platform waving his hand invitingly to Lingard, who followed after a short moment of indecision.

The elastic bamboo floor of the hut bent under the heavy weight of the old seaman, who, standing within the threshold, tried to look into the smoky gloom of the low dwelling. Under the torch, thrust into the cleft of a stick, fastened at a right angle to the middle stay of the ridge pole, lay a red patch of light, showing a few shabby mats and a corner of a big wooden chest the rest of which was lost in shadow. In the obscurity of the more remote parts of the house a lance-head, a brass tray hung on the wall, the long barrel of a gun leaning against the chest, caught the stray rays of the smoky illumination in trembling gleams that wavered, disappeared, reappeared, went out, came back—as if engaged in a doubtful struggle with the darkness that, lying in wait in distant corners, seemed to dart out viciously towards its feeble enemy. The vast space under the high pitch of the roof was filled with a thick cloud of smoke, whose under-side—level like a ceiling—reflected the light of the swaying dull flame, while at the top it oozed out through the imperfect thatch of dried palm leaves. An indescribable and complicated smell, made up of the exhalation of damp earth below, of the taint of dried fish and of the effluvia of rotting vegetable matter, pervaded the place and caused Lingard to sniff strongly as he strode over, sat on the chest, and, leaning his elbows on his knees, took his head between his hands and stared at the doorway thoughtfully.

Babalatchi moved about in the shadows, whispering to an indistinct form or two that flitted about at the far end of the hut. Without stirring Lingard glanced sideways, and caught sight of muffled-up human shapes that hovered for a moment near the edge of light and retreated suddenly back into the darkness. Babalatchi approached, and sat at Lingard's feet on a rolled-up bundle of mats.

"Will you eat rice and drink sagueir?" he said. "I have waked up my household."

"My friend," said Lingard, without looking at him, "when I come to see Lakamba, or any of Lakamba's servants, I am never hungry and never thirsty. Tau! Savee! Never! Do you think I am devoid of reason? That there is nothing there?"

He sat up, and, fixing abruptly his eyes on Babalatchi, tapped his own forehead significantly.

"Tse! Tse! Tse! How can you talk like that, Tuan!" exclaimed Babalatchi, in a horrified tone.

"I talk as I think. I have lived many years," said Lingard, stretching his arm negligently to take up the gun, which he began to examine knowingly, cocking it, and easing down the hammer several times. "This is good. Mataram make. Old, too," he went on.

"Hai!" broke in Babalatchi, eagerly. "I got it when I was young. He was an Aru trader, a man with a big stomach and a loud voice, and brave—very brave. When we came up with his prau in the grey morning, he stood aft shouting to his men and fired this gun at us once. Only once!" . . . He paused, laughed softly, and went on in a low, dreamy voice. "In the grey morning we came up: forty silent men in a swift Sulu prau; and when the sun was so high"—here he held up his hands about three feet apart—"when the sun was only so high, Tuan, our work was done—and there was a feast ready for the fishes of the sea."

"Aye! aye!" muttered Lingard, nodding his head slowly. "I see. You should not let it get rusty like this," he added.

He let the gun fall between his knees, and moving back on his seat, leaned his head against the wall of the hut, crossing his arms on his breast.

"A good gun," went on Babalatchi. "Carry far and true. Better than this—there."

With the tips of his fingers he touched gently the butt of a revolver peeping out of the right pocket of Lingard's white jacket.

"Take your hand off that," said Lingard sharply, but in a good-humoured tone and without making the slightest movement.

Babalatchi smiled and hitched his seat a little further off.

For some time they sat in silence. Lingard, with his head tilted back, looked downwards with lowered eyelids at Babalatchi, who was tracing invisible lines with his finger on the mat between his feet. Outside, they could hear Ali and the other boatmen chattering and laughing round the fire they had lighted in the big and deserted courtyard.

"Well, what about that white man?" said Lingard, quietly.

It seemed as if Babalatchi had not heard the question. He went on tracing elaborate patterns on the floor for a good while. Lingard waited motionless. At last the Malay lifted his head.

"Hai! The white man. I know!" he murmured absently. "This white man or another. . . . Tuan," he said aloud with unexpected animation, "you are a man of the sea?"

"You know me. Why ask?" said Lingard, in a low tone.

"Yes. A man of the sea—even as we are. A true Orang Laut," went on Babalatchi, thoughtfully, "not like the rest of the white men."

"I am like other whites, and do not wish to speak many words when the truth is short. I came here to see the white man that helped Lakamba against Patalolo, who is my friend. Show me where that white man lives; I want him to hear my talk."

"Talk only? Tuan! Why hurry? The night is long and death is swift—as you ought to know; you who have dealt it to so many of my people. Many years ago I have faced you, arms in hand. Do you not remember? It was in Carimata—far from here."

"I cannot remember every vagabond that came in my way," protested Lingard, seriously.

"Hai! Hai!" continued Babalatchi, unmoved and dreamy. "Many years ago. Then all this"—and looking up suddenly at Lingard's beard, he flourished his fingers below his own beardless chin—"then all this was like gold in sunlight, now it is like the foam of an angry sea."

"Maybe, maybe," said Lingard, patiently, paying the involuntary tribute of a faint sigh to the memories of the past evoked by Babalatchi's words.

He had been living with Malays so long and so close that the extreme deliberation and deviousness of their mental proceedings had ceased to irritate him much. To-night, perhaps, he was less prone to impatience than ever. He was disposed, if not to listen to Babalatchi, then to let him talk. It was evident to him that the man had something to say, and he hoped that from the talk a ray of light would shoot through the thick blackness of inexplicable treachery, to show him clearly—if only for a second—the man upon whom he would have to execute the verdict of justice. Justice only! Nothing was further from his thoughts than such an useless thing as revenge. Justice only. It was his duty that justice should be done—and by his own hand. He did not like to think how. To him, as to Babalatchi, it seemed that the night would be long enough for the work he had to do. But he did not define to himself the nature of the work, and he sat very still, and willingly dilatory, under the fearsome oppression of his call. What was the good to think about it? It was inevitable, and its time was near. Yet he could not command his memories that came crowding round him in that evil-smelling hut, while Babalatchi talked on in a flowing monotone, nothing of him moving but the lips, in the artificially inanimated face. Lingard, like an anchored ship that had broken her sheer, darted about here and there on the rapid tide of his recollections. The subdued sound of soft words rang around him, but his thoughts were lost, now in the contemplation of the past sweetness and strife of Carimata days, now in the uneasy wonder at the failure of his judgment; at the fatal blindness of accident that had caused him, many years ago, to rescue a half-starved runaway from a Dutch ship in Samarang roads. How he had liked the man: his assurance, his push, his desire to get on, his conceited good-humour and his selfish eloquence. He had liked his very faults—those faults that had so many, to him, sympathetic sides.

And he had always dealt fairly by him from the very beginning; and he would deal fairly by him now—to the very end. This last thought darkened Lingard's features with a responsive and menacing frown. The doer of justice sat with compressed lips and a heavy heart, while in the calm darkness outside the silent world seemed to be waiting breathlessly for that justice he held in his hand—in his strong hand:—ready to strike—reluctant to move.

2

BABALATCHI CEASED SPEAKING. Lingard shifted his feet a little, uncrossed his arms, and shook his head slowly. The narrative of the events in Sambir, related from the point of view of the astute statesman, the sense of which had been caught here and there by his inattentive ears, had been yet like a thread to guide him out of the sombre labyrinth of his thoughts; and now he had come to the end of it, out of the tangled past into the pressing necessities of the present. With the palms of his hands on his knees, his elbows squared out, he looked down on Babalatchi who sat in a stiff attitude, inexpressive and mute as a talking doll the mechanism of which had at length run down.

"You people did all this," said Lingard at last, "and you will be sorry for it before the dry wind begins to blow again. Abdulla's voice will bring the Dutch rule here."

Babalatchi waved his hand towards the dark doorway.

"There are forests there. Lakamba rules the land now. Tell me, Tuan, do you think the big trees know the name of the ruler? No. They are born, they grow, they live and they die—yet know not, feel not. It is their land."

"Even a big tree may be killed by a small axe," said Lingard, drily. "And, remember, my one-eyed friend, that axes are made by white hands. You will soon find that out, since you have hoisted the flag of the Dutch."

"Ay—wa!" said Babalatchi, slowly. "It is written that the earth belongs to those who have fair skins and hard but foolish hearts. The farther away is the master, the easier it is for the slave, Tuan! You were too near. Your voice rang in our ears always. Now it is not going to be so. The great Rajah in Batavia is strong, but he may be deceived. He must speak very loud to be heard here. But if we have need to shout, then he must hear the many voices that call for protection. He is but a white man."

"If I ever spoke to Patalolo, like an elder brother, it was for your good—for the good of all," said Lingard with great earnestness.

"This is a white man's talk," exclaimed Babalatchi, with bitter exultation. "I know you. That is how you all talk while you load your guns and sharpen your swords; and when you are ready, then to those who are weak you say: 'Obey me and be happy, or die! You are strange, you white men. You think it is only your wisdom and your virtue and your happiness that are true. You are stronger than the wild beasts, but not so wise. A black tiger knows when he is not hungry—you do not. He knows the difference between himself and those that can speak; you do not understand the difference between yourselves and us—who are men. You are wise and great—and you shall always be fools."

He threw up both his hands, stirring the sleeping cloud of smoke that hung above his head, and brought the open palms on the flimsy floor on each side of his outstretched legs. The whole hut shook. Lingard looked at the excited statesman curiously.

"Apa! Apa! What's the matter?" he murmured, soothingly. "Whom did I kill here? Where are my guns? What have I done? What have I eaten up?"

Babalatchi calmed down, and spoke with studied courtesy.

"You, Tuan, are of the sea, and more like what we are. Therefore I speak to you all the words that are in my heart. . . . Only once has the sea been stronger than the Rajah of the sea."

"You know it; do you?" said Lingard, with pained sharpness.

"Hai! We have heard about your ship—and some rejoiced. Not I. Amongst the whites, who are devils, you are a man."

"Trima kassi! I give you thanks," said Lingard, gravely.

Babalatchi looked down with a bashful smile, but his face became saddened directly, and when he spoke again it was in a mournful tone.

"Had you come a day sooner, Tuan, you would have seen an enemy die. You would have seen him die poor, blind, unhappy—with no son to dig his grave and speak of his wisdom and courage. Yes; you would have seen the man that fought you in Carimata many years ago, die alone—but for one friend. A great sight to you."

"Not to me," answered Lingard. "I did not even remember him till you spoke his name just now. You do not understand us. We fight, we vanquish—and we forget."

"True, true," said Babalatchi, with polite irony; "you whites are so great that you disdain to remember your enemies. No! No!" he went on, in the same tone, "you have so much mercy for us, that there is no room for any remembrance. Oh, you are great and good! But it is in my mind that amongst yourselves you know how to remember. Is it not so, Tuan?"

Lingard said nothing. His shoulders moved imperceptibly. He laid his gun across his knees and stared at the flint lock absently.

"Yes," went on Babalatchi, falling again into a mournful mood, "yes, he died in darkness. I sat by his side and held his hand, but he could not see the face of him who watched the faint breath on his lips. She, whom he had cursed because of the white man, was there too, and wept with covered face. The white man walked about the courtyard making many noises. Now and then he would come to the doorway and glare at us who mourned. He stared with wicked eyes, and then I was glad that he who was dying was blind. This is true talk. I was glad; for a white man's eyes are not good to see when the devil that lives within is looking out through them."

"Devil! Hey?" said Lingard, half aloud to himself, as if struck with the obviousness of some novel idea. Babalatchi went on:

"At the first hour of the morning he sat up—he so weak—and said plainly some words that were not meant for human ears. I held his hand tightly, but it was time for the leader of brave men to go amongst the Faithful who are happy. They of my household brought a white sheet, and I began to dig a grave in the hut in which he died. She mourned aloud. The white man came to the doorway and shouted. He was angry. Angry with her because she beat her breast, and tore her hair, and mourned with shrill cries as a woman should. Do you understand what I say, Tuan? That white man came inside the hut with great fury, and took her by the shoulder, and dragged her out. Yes, Tuan. I saw Omar dead, and I saw her at the feet of that white dog who has deceived me. I saw his face grey, like the cold mist of the morning; I saw his pale eyes looking down at Omar's daughter beating her head on the ground at his feet. At the feet of him who is Abdulla's slave. Yes, he lives by Abdulla's will. That is why I held my hand while I saw all this. I held my hand because we are now under the flag of the Orang Blanda, and Abdulla can speak into the ears of the great. We must not have any trouble with white men. Abdulla has spoken—and I must obey."

"That's it, is it?" growled Lingard in his moustache. Then in Malay, "It seems that you are angry, O Babalatchi!"

"No; I am not angry, Tuan," answered Babalatchi, descending from the insecure heights of his indignation into the insincere depths of safe humility. "I am not angry. What am I to be angry? I am only an Orang Laut, and I have fled before your people many times. Servant of this one—protected of another; I have given my counsel here and there for a handful of rice. What am I, to be angry with a white man? What is anger without the power to strike? But you whites have taken all: the land, the sea, and the power to strike! And there is nothing left for us in the islands but your white men's justice; your great justice that knows not anger."

He got up and stood for a moment in the doorway, sniffing the hot air of the courtyard, then turned back and leaned against the stay of the ridge pole, facing Lingard who kept his seat on the chest. The torch, consumed nearly to the end, burned noisily. Small explosions took place in the heart of the flame, driving through its smoky blaze strings of hard, round puffs of white smoke, no bigger than peas, which rolled out of doors in the faint draught that came from invisible cracks of the bamboo walls. The pungent taint of unclean things below and about the hut grew heavier, weighing down Lingard's resolution and his thoughts in an irresistible numbness of the brain. He thought drowsily of himself and of that man who wanted to see him—who waited to see him. Who waited! Night and day. Waited. . . . A spiteful but vaporous idea floated through his brain that such waiting could not be very pleasant to the fellow. Well, let him wait. He would see him soon enough. And for how long? Five seconds—five minutes—say nothing—say something. What? No! Just give him time to take one good look, and then . . .

Suddenly Babalatchi began to speak in a soft voice. Lingard blinked, cleared his throat—sat up straight.

"You know all now, Tuan. Lakamba dwells in the stockaded house of Patalolo; Abdulla has begun to build godowns of plank and stone; and now that Omar is dead, I myself shall depart from this place and live with Lakamba and speak in his ear. I have served many. The best of them all sleeps in the ground in a white sheet, with nothing to mark his grave but the ashes of the hut in which he died. Yes, Tuan! the white man destroyed it himself. With a blazing brand in his hand he strode around, shouting to me to come out—shouting to me, who was throwing earth on the body of a great leader. Yes; swearing to me by the name of your God and ours that he would burn me and her in there if we did not make haste. . . . Hai! The white men are very masterful and wise. I dragged her out quickly!"

"Oh, damn it!" exclaimed Lingard—then went on in Malay, speaking earnestly. "Listen. That man is not like other white men. You know he is not. He is not a man at all. He is . . . I don't know."

Babalatchi lifted his hand deprecatingly. His eye twinkled, and his red-stained big lips, parted by an expressionless grin, uncovered a stumpy row of black teeth filed evenly to the gums.

"Hai! Hai! Not like you. Not like you," he said, increasing the softness of his tones as he neared the object uppermost in his mind during that much-desired interview. "Not like you, Tuan, who are like ourselves, only wiser and stronger. Yet he, also, is full of great cunning, and speaks of you without any respect, after the manner of white men when they talk of one another."

Lingard leaped in his seat as if he had been prodded.

"He speaks! What does he say?" he shouted.

"Nay, Tuan," protested the composed Babalatchi; "what matters his talk if he is not a man? I am nothing before you—why should I repeat words of one white man about another? He did boast to Abdulla of having learned much from your wisdom in years past. Other words I have forgotten. Indeed, Tuan, I have . . ."

Lingard cut short Babalatchi's protestations by a contemptuous wave of the hand and reseated himself with dignity.

"I shall go," said Babalatchi, "and the white man will remain here, alone with the spirit of the dead and with her who has been the delight of his heart. He, being white, cannot hear the voice of those that died. . . . Tell me, Tuan," he went on, looking at Lingard with curiosity —"tell me, Tuan, do you white people ever hear the voices of the invisible ones?"

"We do not," answered Lingard, "because those that we cannot see do not speak."

"Never speak! And never complain with sounds that are not words?" exclaimed Babalatchi, doubtingly. "It may be so—or your ears are dull. We Malays hear many sounds near the places where men are buried. To-night I heard . . . Yes, even I have heard. . . . I do not want to hear any more," he added, nervously. "Perhaps I was wrong when I . . . There are things I regret. The trouble was heavy in his heart when he died. Sometimes I think I was wrong . . . but I do not want to hear the complaint of invisible lips. Therefore I go, Tuan. Let the unquiet spirit speak to his enemy the white man who knows not fear, or love, or mercy—knows nothing but contempt and violence. I have been wrong! I have! Hai! Hai!"

He stood for awhile with his elbow in the palm of his left hand, the fingers of the other over his lips as if to stifle the expression of inconvenient remorse; then, after glancing at the torch, burnt out nearly to its end, he moved towards the wall by the chest, fumbled about there and suddenly flung open a large shutter of attaps woven in a light framework of sticks. Lingard swung his legs quickly round the corner of his seat.

"Hallo!" he said, surprised.

The cloud of smoke stirred, and a slow wisp curled out through the new opening. The torch flickered, hissed, and went out, the glowing end falling on the mat, whence Babalatchi snatched it up and tossed it outside through the open square. It described a vanishing curve of red light, and lay below, shining feebly in the vast darkness. Babalatchi remained with his arm stretched out into the empty night.

"There," he said, "you can see the white man's courtyard, Tuan, and his house."

"I can see nothing," answered Lingard, putting his head through the shutter-hole. "It's too dark."

"Wait, Tuan," urged Babalatchi. "You have been looking long at the burning torch. You will soon see. Mind the gun, Tuan. It is loaded."

"There is no flint in it. You could not find a fire-stone for a hundred miles round this spot," said Lingard, testily. "Foolish thing to load that gun."

"I have a stone. I had it from a man wise and pious that lives in Menang Kabau. A very pious man—very good fire. He spoke words over that stone that make its sparks good. And the gun is good—carries straight and far. Would carry from here to the door of the white man's house, I believe, Tuan."

"Tida apa. Never mind your gun," muttered Lingard, peering into the formless darkness. "Is that the house—that black thing over there?" he asked.

"Yes," answered Babalatchi; "that is his house. He lives there by the will of Abdulla, and shall live there till . . . From where you stand, Tuan, you can look over the fence and across the courtyard straight at the door—at the door from which he comes out every morning, looking like a man that had seen Jehannum in his sleep."

Lingard drew his head in. Babalatchi touched his shoulder with a groping hand.

"Wait a little, Tuan. Sit still. The morning is not far off now—a morning without sun after a night without stars. But there will be light enough to see the man who said not many days ago that he alone has made you less than a child in Sambir."

He felt a slight tremor under his hand, but took it off directly and began feeling all over the lid of the chest, behind Lingard's back, for the gun.

"What are you at?" said Lingard, impatiently. "You do worry about that rotten gun. You had better get a light."

"A light! I tell you, Tuan, that the light of heaven is very near," said Babalatchi, who had now obtained possession of the object of his solicitude, and grasping it strongly by its long barrel, grounded the stock at his feet.

"Perhaps it is near," said Lingard, leaning both his elbows on the lower cross-piece of the primitive window and looking out. "It is very black outside yet," he remarked carelessly.

Babalatchi fidgeted about.

"It is not good for you to sit where you may be seen," he muttered.

"Why not?" asked Lingard.

"The white man sleeps, it is true," explained Babalatchi, softly; "yet he may come out early, and he has arms."

"Ah! he has arms?" said Lingard.

"Yes; a short gun that fires many times—like yours here. Abdulla had to give it to him."

Lingard heard Babalatchi's words, but made no movement. To the old adventurer the idea that fire arms could be dangerous in other hands than his own did not occur readily, and certainly not in connection with Willems. He was so busy with the thoughts about what he considered his own sacred duty, that he could not give any consideration to the probable actions of the man of whom he thought—as one may think of an executed criminal—with wondering indignation tempered by scornful pity. While he sat staring into the darkness, that every minute grew thinner before his pensive eyes, like a dispersing mist, Willems appeared to him as a figure belonging already wholly to the past—a figure that could come in no way into his life again. He had made up his mind, and the thing was as well as done. In his weary thoughts he had closed this fatal, inexplicable, and horrible episode in his life. The worst had happened. The coming days would see the retribution.

He had removed an enemy once or twice before, out of his path; he had paid off some very heavy scores a good many times. Captain Tom had been a good friend to many: but it was generally understood, from Honolulu round about to Diego Suarez, that Captain Tom's enmity was rather more than any man single-handed could easily manage. He would not, as he said often, hurt a fly as long as the fly left him alone; yet a man does not live for years beyond the pale of civilized laws without evolving for himself some queer notions of justice. Nobody of those he knew had ever cared to point out to him the errors of his conceptions.

It was not worth anybody's while to run counter to Lingard's ideas of the fitness of things—that fact was acquired to the floating wisdom of the South Seas, of the Eastern Archipelago, and was nowhere better understood than in out-of-the-way nooks of the world; in those nooks which he filled, unresisted and masterful, with the echoes of his noisy presence. There is not much use in arguing with a man who boasts of never having regretted a single action of his life, whose answer to a mild criticism is a good-natured shout—"You know nothing about it. I would do it again. Yes, sir!" His associates and his acquaintances accepted him, his opinions, his actions like things preordained and unchangeable; looked upon his many-sided manifestations with passive wonder not unmixed with that admiration which is only the rightful due of a successful man. But nobody had ever seen him in the mood he was in now. Nobody had seen Lingard doubtful and giving way to doubt, unable to make up his mind and unwilling to act; Lingard timid and hesitating one minute, angry yet inactive the next; Lingard puzzled in a word, because confronted with a situation that discomposed him by its unprovoked malevolence, by its ghastly injustice, that to his rough but unsophisticated palate tasted distinctly of sulphurous fumes from the deepest hell.

The smooth darkness filling the shutter-hole grew paler and became blotchy with ill-defined shapes, as if a new universe was being evolved out of sombre chaos. Then outlines came out, defining forms without any details, indicating here a tree, there a bush; a black belt of forest far off; the straight lines of a house, the ridge of a high roof near by. Inside the hut, Babalatchi, who lately had been only a persuasive voice, became a human shape leaning its chin imprudently on the muzzle of a gun and rolling an uneasy eye over the reappearing world. The day came rapidly, dismal and oppressed by the fog of the river and by the heavy vapours of the sky—a day without colour and without sunshine: incomplete, disappointing, and sad.

Babalatchi twitched gently Lingard's sleeve, and when the old seaman had lifted up his head interrogatively, he stretched out an arm and a pointing forefinger towards Willems' house, now plainly visible to the right and beyond the big tree of the courtyard.

"Look, Tuan!" he said. "He lives there. That is the door—his door. Through it he will appear soon, with his hair in disorder and his mouth full of curses. That is so. He is a white man, and never satisfied. It is in my mind he is angry even in his sleep. A dangerous man. As Tuan may observe," he went on, obsequiously, "his door faces this opening, where you condescend to sit, which is concealed from all eyes. Faces it—straight—and not far. Observe, Tuan, not at all far."

"Yes, yes; I can see. I shall see him when he wakes."

"No doubt, Tuan. When he wakes. . . . If you remain here he can not see you. I shall withdraw quickly and prepare my canoe myself. I am only a poor man, and must go to Sambir to greet Lakamba when he opens his eyes. I must bow before Abdulla who has strength—even more strength than you. Now if you remain here, you shall easily behold the man who boasted to Abdulla that he had been your friend, even while he prepared to fight those who called you protector. Yes, he plotted with Abdulla for that cursed flag. Lakamba was blind then, and I was deceived. But you, Tuan! Remember, he deceived you more. Of that he boasted before all men."

He leaned the gun quietly against the wall close to the window, and said softly: "Shall I go now, Tuan? Be careful of the gun. I have put the fire-stone in. The fire-stone of the wise man, which never fails."

Lingard's eyes were fastened on the distant doorway. Across his line of sight, in the grey emptiness of the courtyard, a big fruit-pigeon flapped languidly towards the forests with a loud booming cry, like the note of a deep gong: a brilliant bird looking in the gloom of threatening day as black as a crow. A serried flock of white rice birds rose above the trees with a faint scream, and hovered, swaying in a disordered mass that suddenly scattered in all directions, as if burst asunder by a silent explosion. Behind his back Lingard heard a shuffle of feet—women leaving the hut. In the other courtyard a voice was heard complaining of cold, and coming very feeble, but exceedingly distinct, out of the vast silence of the abandoned houses and clearings. Babalatchi coughed discreetly. From under the house the thumping of wooden pestles husking the rice started with unexpected abruptness. The weak but clear voice in the yard again urged, "Blow up the embers, O brother!" Another voice answered, drawling in modulated, thin sing-song, "Do it yourself, O shivering pig!" and the drawl of the last words stopped short, as if the man had fallen into a deep hole. Babalatchi coughed again a little impatiently, and said in a confidential tone—

"Do you think it is time for me to go, Tuan? Will you take care of my gun, Tuan? I am a man that knows how to obey; even obey Abdulla, who has deceived me. Nevertheless this gun carries far and true—if you would want to know, Tuan. And I have put in a double measure of powder, and three slugs. Yes, Tuan. Now—perhaps—I go."

When Babalatchi commenced speaking, Lingard turned slowly round and gazed upon him with the dull and unwilling look of a sick man waking to another day of suffering. As the astute statesman proceeded, Lingard's eyebrows came close, his eyes became animated, and a big vein stood out on his forehead, accentuating a lowering frown. When speaking his last words Babalatchi faltered, then stopped, confused, before the steady gaze of the old seaman.

Lingard rose. His face cleared, and he looked down at the anxious Babalatchi with sudden benevolence.

"So! That's what you were after," he said, laying a heavy hand on Babalatchi's yielding shoulder. "You thought I came here to murder him. Hey? Speak! You faithful dog of an Arab trader!"

"And what else, Tuan?" shrieked Babalatchi, exasperated into sincerity. "What else, Tuan! Remember what he has done; he poisoned our ears with his talk about you. You are a man. If you did not come to kill, Tuan, then either I am a fool or . . ."

He paused, struck his naked breast with his open palm, and finished in a discouraged whisper—"or, Tuan, you are."

Lingard looked down at him with scornful serenity. After his long and painful gropings amongst the obscure abominations of Willems' conduct, the logical if tortuous evolutions of Babalatchi's diplomatic mind were to him welcome as daylight. There was something at last he could understand—the clear effect of a simple cause. He felt indulgent towards the disappointed sage.

"So you are angry with your friend, O one-eyed one!" he said slowly, nodding his fierce countenance close to Babalatchi's discomfited face. "It seems to me that you must have had much to do with what happened in Sambir lately. Hey? You son of a burnt father."

"May I perish under your hand, O Rajah of the sea, if my words are not true!" said Babalatchi, with reckless excitement. "You are here in the midst of your enemies. He the greatest. Abdulla would do nothing without him, and I could do nothing without Abdulla. Strike me—so that you strike all!"

"Who are you," exclaimed Lingard contemptuously—"who are you to dare call yourself my enemy! Dirt! Nothing! Go out first," he went on severely. "Lakas! quick. March out!"

He pushed Babalatchi through the doorway and followed him down the short ladder into the courtyard. The boatmen squatting over the fire turned their slow eyes with apparent difficulty towards the two men; then, unconcerned, huddled close together again, stretching forlornly their hands over the embers. The women stopped in their work and with uplifted pestles flashed quick and curious glances from the gloom under the house.

"Is that the way?" asked Lingard with a nod towards the little wicket-gate of Willems' enclosure.

"If you seek death, that is surely the way," answered Babalatchi in a dispassionate voice, as if he had exhausted all the emotions. "He lives there: he who destroyed your friends; who hastened Omar's death; who plotted with Abdulla first against you, then against me. I have been like a child. O shame! . . . But go, Tuan. Go there."

"I go where I like," said Lingard, emphatically, "and you may go to the devil; I do not want you any more. The islands of these seas shall sink before I, Rajah Laut, serve the will of any of your people. Tau? But I tell you this: I do not care what you do with him after to-day. And I say that because I am merciful."

"Tida! I do nothing," said Babalatchi, shaking his head with bitter apathy. "I am in Abdulla's hand and care not, even as you do. No! no!" he added, turning away, "I have learned much wisdom this morning. There are no men anywhere. You whites are cruel to your friends and merciful to your enemies—which is the work of fools."

He went away towards the riverside, and, without once looking back, disappeared in the low bank of mist that lay over the water and the shore. Lingard followed him with his eyes thoughtfully. After awhile he roused himself and called out to his boatmen—

"Hai—ya there! After you have eaten rice, wait for me with your paddles in your hands. You hear?"

"Ada, Tuan!" answered Ali through the smoke of the morning fire that was spreading itself, low and gentle, over the courtyard—"we hear!"

Lingard opened slowly the little wicket-gate, made a few steps into the empty enclosure, and stopped. He had felt about his head the short breath of a puff of wind that passed him, made every leaf of the big tree shiver—and died out in a hardly perceptible tremor of branches and twigs. Instinctively he glanced upwards with a seaman's impulse. Above him, under the grey motionless waste of a stormy sky, drifted low black vapours, in stretching bars, in shapeless patches, in sinuous wisps and tormented spirals. Over the courtyard and the house floated a round, sombre, and lingering cloud, dragging behind a tail of tangled and filmy streamers—like the dishevelled hair of a mourning woman.

3

"Beware!"

The tremulous effort and the broken, inadequate tone of the faint cry, surprised Lingard more than the unexpected suddenness of the warning conveyed, he did not know by whom and to whom. Besides himself there was no one in the courtyard as far as he could see.

The cry was not renewed, and his watchful eyes, scanning warily the misty solitude of Willems' enclosure, were met everywhere only by the stolid impassiveness of inanimate things: the big sombre-looking tree, the shut-up, sightless house, the glistening bamboo fences, the damp and drooping bushes further off—all these things, that condemned to look for ever at the incomprehensible afflictions or joys of mankind, assert in their aspect of cold unconcern the high dignity of lifeless matter that surrounds, incurious and unmoved, the restless mysteries of the ever-changing, of the never-ending life.

Lingard, stepping aside, put the trunk of the tree between himself and the house, then, moving cautiously round one of the projecting buttresses, had to tread short in order to avoid scattering a small heap of black embers upon which he came unexpectedly on the other side. A thin, wizened, little old woman, who, standing behind the tree, had been looking at the house, turned towards him with a start, gazed with faded, expressionless eyes at the intruder, then made a limping attempt to get away. She seemed, however, to realize directly the hopelessness or the difficulty of the undertaking, stopped, hesitated, tottered back slowly; then, after blinking dully, fell suddenly on her knees amongst the white ashes, and, bending over the heap of smouldering coals, distended her sunken cheeks in a steady effort to blow up the hidden sparks into a useful blaze. Lingard looked down on her, but she seemed to have made up her mind that there was not enough life left in her lean body for anything else than the discharge of the simple domestic duty, and, apparently, she begrudged him the least moment of attention.

After waiting for awhile, Lingard asked—

"Why did you call, O daughter?"

"I saw you enter," she croaked feebly, still grovelling with her face near the ashes and without looking up, "and I called—the cry of warning. It was her order. Her order," she repeated, with a moaning sigh.

"And did she hear?" pursued Lingard, with gentle composure.

Her projecting shoulder-blades moved uneasily under the thin stuff of the tight body jacket. She scrambled up with difficulty to her feet, and hobbled away, muttering peevishly to herself, towards a pile of dry brushwood heaped up against the fence.

Lingard, looking idly after her, heard the rattle of loose planks that led from the ground to the door of the house. He moved his head beyond the shelter of the tree and saw Aissa coming down the inclined way into the courtyard. After making a few hurried paces towards the tree, she stopped with one foot advanced in an appearance of sudden terror, and her eyes glanced wildly right and left. Her head was uncovered. A blue cloth wrapped her from her head to foot in close slanting folds, with one end thrown over her shoulder. A tress of her black hair strayed across her bosom. Her bare arms pressed down close to her body, with hands open and outstretched fingers; her slightly elevated shoulders and the backward inclination of her torso gave her the aspect of one defiant yet shrinking from a coming blow. She had closed the door of the house behind her; and as she stood solitary in the unnatural and threatening twilight of the murky day, with everything unchanged around her, she appeared to Lingard as if she had been made there, on the spot, out of the black vapours of the sky and of the sinister gleams of feeble sunshine that struggled, through the thickening clouds, into the colourless desolation of the world.

After a short but attentive glance towards the shut-up house, Lingard stepped out from behind the tree and advanced slowly towards her. The sudden fixity of her—till then—restless eyes and a slight twitch of her hands were the only signs she gave at first of having seen him. She made a long stride forward, and putting herself right in his path, stretched her arms across; her black eyes opened wide, her lips parted as if in an uncertain attempt to speak—but no sound came out to break the significant silence of their meeting. Lingard stopped and looked at her with stern curiosity. After a while he said composedly—

"Let me pass. I came here to talk to a man. Does he hide? Has he sent you?"

She made a step nearer, her arms fell by her side, then she put them straight out nearly touching Lingard's breast.

"He knows not fear," she said, speaking low, with a forward throw of her head, in a voice trembling but distinct. "It is my own fear that has sent me here. He sleeps."

"He has slept long enough," said Lingard, in measured tones. "I am come—and now is the time of his waking. Go and tell him this—or else my own voice will call him up. A voice he knows well."

He put her hands down firmly and again made as if to pass by her.

"Do not!" she exclaimed, and fell at his feet as if she had been cut down by a scythe. The unexpected suddenness of her movement startled Lingard, who stepped back.

"What's this?" he exclaimed in a wondering whisper—then added in a tone of sharp command: "Stand up!"

She rose at once and stood looking at him, timorous and fearless; yet with a fire of recklessness burning in her eyes that made clear her resolve to pursue her purpose even to the death. Lingard went on in a severe voice—

"Go out of my path. You are Omar's daughter, and you ought to know that when men meet in daylight women must be silent and abide their fate."

"Women!" she retorted, with subdued vehemence. "Yes, I am a woman! Your eyes see that, O Rajah Laut, but can you see my life? I also have heard—O man of many fights—I also have heard the voice of fire-arms; I also have felt the rain of young twigs and of leaves cut up by bullets fall down about my head; I also know how to look in silence at angry faces and at strong hands raised high grasping sharp steel. I also saw men fall dead around me without a cry of fear and of mourning; and I have watched the sleep of weary fugitives, and looked at night shadows full of menace and death with eyes that knew nothing but watchfulness. And," she went on, with a mournful drop in her voice, "I have faced the heartless sea, held on my lap the heads of those who died raving from thirst, and from their cold hands took the paddle and worked so that those with me did not know that one man more was dead. I did all this. What more have you done? That was my life. What has been yours?"

The matter and the manner of her speech held Lingard motionless, attentive and approving against his will. She ceased speaking, and from her staring black eyes with a narrow border of white above and below, a double ray of her very soul streamed out in a fierce desire to light up the most obscure designs of his heart. After a long silence, which served to emphasize the meaning of her words, she added in the whisper of bitter regret—

"And I have knelt at your feet! And I am afraid!"

"You," said Lingard deliberately, and returning her look with an interested gaze, "you are a woman whose heart, I believe, is great enough to fill a man's breast: but still you are a woman, and to you, I, Rajah Laut, have nothing to say."

She listened bending her head in a movement of forced attention; and his voice sounded to her unexpected, far off, with the distant and unearthly ring of voices that we hear in dreams, saying faintly things startling, cruel or absurd, to which there is no possible reply. To her he had nothing to say! She wrung her hands, glanced over the courtyard with that eager and distracted look that sees nothing, then looked up at the hopeless sky of livid grey and drifting black; at the unquiet mourning of the hot and brilliant heaven that had seen the beginning of her love, that had heard his entreaties and her answers, that had seen his desire and her fear; that had seen her joy, her surrender—and his defeat. Lingard moved a little, and this slight stir near her precipitated her disordered and shapeless thoughts into hurried words.

"Wait!" she exclaimed in a stifled voice, and went on disconnectedly and rapidly—"Stay. I have heard. Men often spoke by the fires . . . men of my people. And they said of you—the first on the sea—they said that to men's cries you were deaf in battle, but after . . . No! even while you fought, your ears were open to the voice of children and women. They said . . . that. Now I, a woman, I . . ."

She broke off suddenly and stood before him with dropped eyelids and parted lips, so still now that she seemed to have been changed into a breathless, an unhearing, an unseeing figure, without knowledge of fear or hope, of anger or despair. In the astounding repose that came on her face, nothing moved but the delicate nostrils that expanded and collapsed quickly, flutteringly, in interrupted beats, like the wings of a snared bird.

"I am white," said Lingard, proudly, looking at her with a steady gaze where simple curiosity was giving way to a pitying annoyance, "and men you have heard, spoke only what is true over the evening fires. My ears are open to your prayer. But listen to me before you speak. For yourself you need not be afraid. You can come even now with me and you shall find refuge in the household of Syed Abdulla—who is of your own faith. And this also you must know: nothing that you may say will change my purpose towards the man who is sleeping—or hiding—in that house."

Again she gave him the look that was like a stab, not of anger but of desire; of the intense, over-powering desire to see in, to see through, to understand everything: every thought, emotion, purpose; every impulse, every hesitation inside that man; inside that white-clad foreign being who looked at her, who spoke to her, who breathed before her like any other man, but bigger, red-faced, white-haired and mysterious. It was the future clothed in flesh; the to-morrow; the day after; all the days, all the years of her life standing there before her alive and secret, with all their good or evil shut up within the breast of that man; of that man who could be persuaded, cajoled, entreated, perhaps touched, worried; frightened—who knows?—if only first he could be understood! She had seen a long time ago whither events were tending. She had noted the contemptuous yet menacing coldness of Abdulla; she had heard—alarmed yet unbelieving—Babalatchi's gloomy hints, covert allusions and veiled suggestions to abandon the useless white man whose fate would be the price of the peace secured by the wise and good who had no need of him any more. And he—himself! She clung to him. There was nobody else. Nothing else. She would try to cling to him always—all the life! And yet he was far from her. Further every day. Every day he seemed more distant, and she followed him patiently, hopefully, blindly, but steadily, through all the devious wanderings of his mind. She followed as well as she could. Yet at times—very often lately—she had felt lost like one strayed in the thickets of tangled undergrowth of a great forest. To her the ex-clerk of old Hudig appeared as remote, as brilliant, as terrible, as necessary, as the sun that gives life to these lands: the sun of unclouded skies that dazzles and withers; the sun beneficent and wicked—the giver of light, perfume, and pestilence. She had watched him—watched him close; fascinated by love, fascinated by danger. He was alone now—but for her; and she saw—she thought she saw—that he was like a man afraid of something. Was it possible? He afraid? Of what? Was it of that old white man who was coming—who had come? Possibly. She had heard of that man ever since she could remember. The bravest were afraid of him! And now what was in the mind of this old, old man who looked so strong? What was he going to do with the light of her life? Put it out? Take it away? Take it away for ever!—for ever!—and leave her in darkness:—not in the stirring, whispering, expectant night in which the hushed world awaits the return of sunshine; but in the night without end, the night of the grave, where nothing breathes, nothing moves, nothing thinks—the last darkness of cold and silence without hope of another sunrise.

She cried—"Your purpose! You know nothing. I must . . ."

He interrupted—unreasonably excited, as if she had, by her look, inoculated him with some of her own distress.

"I know enough."

She approached, and stood facing him at arm's length, with both her hands on his shoulders; and he, surprised by that audacity, closed and opened his eyes two or three times, aware of some emotion arising within him, from her words, her tone, her contact; an emotion unknown, singular, penetrating and sad—at the close sight of that strange woman, of that being savage and tender, strong and delicate, fearful and resolute, that had got entangled so fatally between their two lives—his own and that other white man's, the abominable scoundrel.

"How can you know?" she went on, in a persuasive tone that seemed to flow out of her very heart—"how can you know? I live with him all the days. All the nights. I look at him; I see his every breath, every glance of his eye, every movement of his lips. I see nothing else! What else is there? And even I do not understand. I do not understand him!—Him!—My life! Him who to me is so great that his presence hides the earth and the water from my sight!"

Lingard stood straight, with his hands deep in the pockets of his jacket. His eyes winked quickly, because she spoke very close to his face. She disturbed him and he had a sense of the efforts he was making to get hold of her meaning, while all the time he could not help telling himself that all this was of no use.

She added after a pause—"There has been a time when I could understand him. When I knew what was in his mind better than he knew it himself. When I felt him. When I held him. . . . And now he has escaped."

"Escaped? What? Gone away!" shouted Lingard.

"Escaped from me," she said; "left me alone. Alone. And I am ever near him. Yet alone."

Her hands slipped slowly off Lingard's shoulders and her arms fell by her side, listless, discouraged, as if to her—to her, the savage, violent, and ignorant creature—had been revealed clearly in that moment the tremendous fact of our isolation, of the loneliness impenetrable and transparent, elusive and everlasting; of the indestructible loneliness that surrounds, envelopes, clothes every human soul from the cradle to the grave, and, perhaps, beyond.

"Aye! Very well! I understand. His face is turned away from you," said Lingard. "Now, what do you want?"

"I want . . . I have looked—for help . . . everywhere . . . against men. . . . All men . . . I do not know. First they came, the invisible whites, and dealt death from afar . . . then he came. He came to me who was alone and sad. He came; angry with his brothers; great amongst his own people; angry with those I have not seen: with the people where men have no mercy and women have no shame. He was of them, and great amongst them. For he was great?"

Lingard shook his head slightly. She frowned at him, and went on in disordered haste—

"Listen. I saw him. I have lived by the side of brave men . . . of chiefs. When he came I was the daughter of a beggar—of a blind man without strength and hope. He spoke to me as if I had been brighter than the sunshine—more delightful than the cool water of the brook by which we met—more . . ." Her anxious eyes saw some shade of expression pass on her listener's face that made her hold her breath for a second, and then explode into pained fury so violent that it drove Lingard back a pace, like an unexpected blast of wind. He lifted both his hands, incongruously paternal in his venerable aspect, bewildered and soothing, while she stretched her neck forward and shouted at him.

"I tell you I was all that to him. I know it! I saw it! . . . There are times when even you white men speak the truth. I saw his eyes. I felt his eyes, I tell you! I saw him tremble when I came near—when I spoke—when I touched him. Look at me! You have been young. Look at me. Look, Rajah Laut!"

She stared at Lingard with provoking fixity, then, turning her head quickly, she sent over her shoulder a glance, full of humble fear, at the house that stood high behind her back—dark, closed, rickety and silent on its crooked posts.

Lingard's eyes followed her look, and remained gazing expectantly at the house. After a minute or so he muttered, glancing at her suspiciously—

"If he has not heard your voice now, then he must be far away—or dead."

"He is there," she whispered, a little calmed but still anxious—"he is there. For three days he waited. Waited for you night and day. And I waited with him. I waited, watching his face, his eyes, his lips; listening to his words.—To the words I could not understand.—To the words he spoke in daylight; to the words he spoke at night in his short sleep. I listened. He spoke to himself walking up and down here—by the river; by the bushes. And I followed. I wanted to know—and I could not! He was tormented by things that made him speak in the words of his own people. Speak to himself—not to me. Not to me! What was he saying? What was he going to do? Was he afraid of you?—Of death? What was in his heart? . . . Fear? . . . Or anger? . . . what desire? . . . what sadness? He spoke; spoke; many words. All the time! And I could not know! I wanted to speak to him. He was deaf to me. I followed him everywhere, watching for some word I could understand; but his mind was in the land of his people—away from me. When I touched him he was angry—so!"

She imitated the movement of some one shaking off roughly an importunate hand, and looked at Lingard with tearful and unsteady eyes.

After a short interval of laboured panting, as if she had been out of breath with running or fighting, she looked down and went on—

"Day after day, night after night, I lived watching him—seeing nothing. And my heart was heavy—heavy with the presence of death that dwelt amongst us. I could not believe. I thought he was afraid. Afraid of you! Then I, myself, knew fear. . . . Tell me, Rajah Laut, do you know the fear without voice—the fear of silence—the fear that comes when there is no one near—when there is no battle, no cries, no angry faces or armed hands anywhere? . . . The fear from which there is no escape!"

She paused, fastened her eyes again on the puzzled Lingard, and hurried on in a tone of despair—

"And I knew then he would not fight you! Before—many days ago—I went away twice to make him obey my desire; to make him strike at his own people so that he could be mine—mine! O calamity! His hand was false as your white hearts. It struck forward, pushed by my desire—by his desire of me. . . . It struck that strong hand, and—O shame!—it killed nobody! Its fierce and lying blow woke up hate without any fear. Round me all was lies. His strength was a lie. My own people lied to me and to him. And to meet you—you, the great!—he had no one but me? But me with my rage, my pain, my weakness. Only me! And to me he would not even speak. The fool!"

She came up close to Lingard, with the wild and stealthy aspect of a lunatic longing to whisper out an insane secret—one of those misshapen, heart-rending, and ludicrous secrets; one of those thoughts that, like monsters—cruel, fantastic, and mournful, wander about terrible and unceasing in the night of madness. Lingard looked at her, astounded but unflinching. She spoke in his face, very low.

"He is all! Everything. He is my breath, my light, my heart. . . . Go away. . . . Forget him. . . . He has no courage and no wisdom any more . . . and I have lost my power. . . . Go away and forget. There are other enemies. . . . Leave him to me. He had been a man once. . . . You are too great. Nobody can withstand you. . . . I tried. . . . I know now . . . . I cry for mercy. Leave him to me and go away."

The fragments of her supplicating sentences were as if tossed on the crest of her sobs. Lingard, outwardly impassive, with his eyes fixed on the house, experienced that feeling of condemnation, deep-seated, persuasive, and masterful; that illogical impulse of disapproval which is half disgust, half vague fear, and that wakes up in our hearts in the presence of anything new or unusual, of anything that is not run into the mould of our own conscience; the accursed feeling made up of disdain, of anger, and of the sense of superior virtue that leaves us deaf, blind, contemptuous and stupid before anything which is not like ourselves.

He answered, not looking at her at first, but speaking towards the house that fascinated him—

"*I* go away! He wanted me to come—he himself did! . . . *You* must go away. You do not know what you are asking for. Listen. Go to your own people. Leave him. He is . . ."

He paused, looked down at her with his steady eyes; hesitated, as if seeking an adequate expression; then snapped his fingers, and said—

"Finish."

She stepped back, her eyes on the ground, and pressed her temples with both her hands, which she raised to her head in a slow and ample movement full of unconscious tragedy. The tone of her words was gentle and vibrating, like a loud meditation. She said—

"Tell the brook not to run to the river; tell the river not to run to the sea. Speak loud.

Speak angrily. Maybe they will obey you. But it is in my mind that the brook will not care. The brook that springs out of the hillside and runs to the great river. He would not care for your words: he that cares not for the very mountain that gave him life; he that tears the earth from which he springs. Tears it, eats it, destroys it—to hurry faster to the river—to the river in which he is lost for ever. . . . O Rajah Laut! I do not care."

She drew close again to Lingard, approaching slowly, reluctantly, as if pushed by an invisible hand, and added in words that seemed to be torn out of her—

"I cared not for my own father. For him that died. I would have rather . . . You do not know what I have done . . . I . . ."

"You shall have his life," said Lingard, hastily.

They stood together, crossing their glances; she suddenly appeased, and Lingard thoughtful and uneasy under a vague sense of defeat. And yet there was no defeat. He never intended to kill the fellow—not after the first moment of anger, a long time ago. The days of bitter wonder had killed anger; had left only a bitter indignation and a bitter wish for complete justice. He felt discontented and surprised. Unexpectedly he had come upon a human being—a woman at that—who had made him disclose his will before its time. She should have his life. But she must be told, she must know, that for such men as Willems there was no favour and no grace.

"Understand," he said slowly, "that I leave him his life not in mercy but in punishment."

She started, watched every word on his lips, and after he finished speaking she remained still and mute in astonished immobility. A single big drop of rain, a drop enormous, pellucid and heavy—like a super-human tear coming straight and rapid from above, tearing its way through the sombre sky—struck loudly the dry ground between them in a starred splash. She wrung her hands in the bewilderment of the new and incomprehensible fear. The anguish of her whisper was more piercing than the shrillest cry.

"What punishment! Will you take him away then? Away from me? Listen to what I have done. . . . It is I who . . ."

"Ah!" exclaimed Lingard, who had been looking at the house.

"Don't you believe her, Captain Lingard," shouted Willems from the doorway, where he appeared with swollen eyelids and bared breast. He stood for a while, his hands grasping the lintels on each side of the door, and writhed about, glaring wildly, as if he had been crucified there. Then he made a sudden rush head foremost down the plankway that responded with hollow, short noises to every footstep.

She heard him. A slight thrill passed on her face and the words that were on her lips fell back unspoken into her benighted heart; fell back amongst the mud, the stones—and the flowers, that are at the bottom of every heart.

4

When he felt the solid ground of the courtyard under his feet, Willems pulled himself up in his headlong rush and moved forward with a moderate gait. He paced stiffly, looking with extreme exactitude at Lingard's face; looking neither to the right nor to the left but at the face only, as if there was nothing in the world but those features familiar and dreaded; that white-haired, rough and severe head upon which he gazed in a fixed effort of his eyes, like a man trying to read small print at the full range of human vision. As soon as Willems' feet had left the planks, the silence which had been lifted up by the jerky rattle of his footsteps fell down again upon the courtyard; the silence of the cloudy sky and of the windless air, the sullen silence of the earth oppressed by the aspect of coming turmoil, the silence of the world collecting its faculties to withstand the storm. Through this silence Willems pushed his way, and stopped about six feet from Lingard. He stopped simply because he could go no further. He had started from the door with the reckless purpose of clapping the old fellow on the shoulder. He had no idea that the man would turn out to be so tall, so big and so unapproachable. It seemed to him that he had never, never in his life, seen Lingard.

He tried to say—

"Do not believe . . ."

A fit of coughing checked his sentence in a faint splutter. Directly afterwards he swallowed—as it were—a couple of pebbles, throwing his chin up in the act; and Lingard, who looked at him narrowly, saw a bone, sharp and triangular like the head of a snake, dart up and down twice under the skin of his throat. Then that, too, did not move. Nothing moved.

"Well," said Lingard, and with that word he came unexpectedly to the end of his speech. His hand in his pocket closed firmly round the butt of his revolver bulging his jacket on the hip, and he thought how soon and how quickly he could terminate his quarrel with that man who had been so anxious to deliver himself into his hands—and how inadequate would be that ending! He could not bear the idea of that man escaping from him by going out of life; escaping from fear, from doubt, from remorse into the peaceful certitude of death. He held him now. And he was not going to let him go—to let him disappear for ever in the faint blue smoke of a pistol shot. His anger grew within him. He felt a touch as of a burning hand on his heart. Not on the flesh of his breast, but a touch on his heart itself, on the palpitating and untiring particle of matter that responds to every emotion of the soul; that leaps with joy, with terror, or with anger.

He drew a long breath. He could see before him the bare chest of the man expanding and collapsing under the wide-open jacket. He glanced aside, and saw the bosom of the woman near him rise and fall in quick respirations that moved slightly up and down her hand, which was pressed to her breast with all the fingers spread out and a little curved, as if grasping something too big for its span. And nearly a minute passed. One of those minutes when the voice is silenced, while the thoughts flutter in the head, like captive birds inside a cage, in rushes desperate, exhausting and vain.

During that minute of silence Lingard's anger kept rising, immense and towering, such as a crested wave running over the troubled shallows of the sands. Its roar filled his cars; a roar so powerful and distracting that, it seemed to him, his head must burst directly with the expanding volume of that sound. He looked at that man. That infamous figure upright on its feet, still, rigid, with stony eyes, as if its rotten soul had departed that moment and the carcass hadn't had the time yet to topple over. For the fraction of a second he had the illusion and the fear of the scoundrel having died there before the enraged glance of his eyes. Willems' eyelids fluttered, and the unconscious and passing tremor in that stiffly erect body exasperated Lingard like a fresh outrage. The fellow dared to stir! Dared to wink, to breathe, to exist; here, right before his eyes! His grip on the revolver relaxed gradually. As the transport of his rage increased, so also his contempt for the instruments that pierce or stab, that interpose themselves between the hand and the object of hate. He wanted another kind of satisfaction. Naked hands, by heaven! No firearms. Hands that could take him by the throat, beat down his defence, batter his face into shapeless flesh; hands that could feel all the desperation of his resistance and overpower it in the violent delight of a contact lingering and furious, intimate and brutal.

He let go the revolver altogether, stood hesitating, then throwing his hands out, strode forward—and everything passed from his sight. He could not see the man, the woman, the earth, the sky—saw nothing, as if in that one stride he had left the visible world behind to step into a black and deserted space. He heard screams round him in that obscurity, screams like the melancholy and pitiful cries of sea-birds that dwell on the lonely reefs of great oceans. Then suddenly a face appeared within a few inches of his own. His face. He felt something in his left hand. His throat . . . Ah! the thing like a snake's head that darts up and down . . . He squeezed hard. He was back in the world. He could see the quick beating of eyelids over a pair of eyes that were all whites, the grin of a drawn-up lip, a row of teeth gleaming through the drooping hair of a moustache . . . Strong white teeth. Knock them down his lying throat . . . He drew back his right hand, the fist up to the shoulder, knuckles out. From under his feet rose the screams of sea-birds. Thousands of them. Something held his legs . . . What the devil . . . He delivered his blow straight from the shoulder, felt the jar right up his arm, and realized suddenly that he was striking something passive and unresisting. His heart sank within him with disappointment, with rage, with mortification. He pushed with his left arm, opening the hand with haste, as if he had just perceived that he got hold by accident of something repulsive—and he watched with stupefied eyes Willems tottering backwards in groping strides, the white sleeve of his jacket across his face. He watched his distance from that man increase, while he remained motionless, without being able to account to himself for the fact that so much empty space had come in between them. It should have been the other way. They ought to have been very close, and . . . Ah! He wouldn't fight, he wouldn't resist, he wouldn't defend himself! A cur! Evidently a cur! . . . He was amazed and aggrieved—profoundly, bitterly—with the immense and blank desolation of a small child robbed of a toy. He shouted—unbelieving:

"Will you be a cheat to the end?"

He waited for some answer. He waited anxiously with an impatience that seemed to lift him off his feet. He waited for some word, some sign; for some threatening stir. Nothing! Only two unwinking eyes glittered intently at him above the white sleeve. He saw the raised arm detach itself from the face and sink along the body. A white clad arm, with a big stain on the white sleeve. A red stain. There was a cut on the cheek. It bled. The nose bled too. The blood ran down, made one moustache look like a dark rag stuck over the lip, and went on in a wet streak down the clipped beard on one side of the chin. A drop of blood hung on the end of some hairs that were glued together; it hung for a while and took a leap down on the ground. Many more followed, leaping one after another in close file. One alighted on the breast and glided down instantly with devious vivacity, like a small insect running away; it left a narrow dark track on the white skin. He looked at it, looked at the tiny and active drops, looked at what he had done, with obscure satisfaction, with anger, with regret. This wasn't much like an act of justice. He had a desire to go up nearer to the man, to hear him speak, to hear him say something atrocious and wicked that would justify the violence of the blow. He made an attempt to move, and became aware of a close embrace round both his legs, just above the ankles. Instinctively, he kicked out with his foot, broke through the close bond and felt at once the clasp transferred to his other leg; the clasp warm, desperate and soft, of human arms. He looked down bewildered. He saw the body of the woman stretched at length, flattened on the ground like a dark blue rag. She trailed face downwards, clinging to his leg with both arms in a tenacious hug. He saw the top of her head, the long black hair streaming over his foot, all over the beaten earth, around his boot. He couldn't see his foot for it. He heard the short and repeated moaning of her breath. He imagined the invisible face close to his heel. With one kick into that face he could free himself. He dared not stir, and shouted down—

"Let go! Let go! Let go!"

The only result of his shouting was a tightening of the pressure of her arms. With a tremendous effort he tried to bring his right foot up to his left, and succeeded partly. He heard distinctly the rub of her body on the ground as he jerked her along. He tried to disengage himself by drawing up his foot. He stamped. He heard a voice saying sharply—

"Steady, Captain Lingard, steady!"

His eyes flew back to Willems at the sound of that voice, and, in the quick awakening of sleeping memories, Lingard stood suddenly still, appeased by the clear ring of familiar words. Appeased as in days of old, when they were trading together, when Willems was his trusted and helpful companion in out-of-the-way and dangerous places; when that fellow, who could keep his temper so much better than he could himself, had spared him many a difficulty, had saved him from many an act of hasty violence by the timely and good-humoured warning, whispered or shouted, "Steady, Captain Lingard, steady." A smart fellow. He had brought him up. The smartest fellow in the islands. If he had only stayed with him, then all this . . . He called out to Willems—

"Tell her to let me go or . . ."

He heard Willems shouting something, waited for awhile, then glanced vaguely down and saw the woman still stretched out perfectly mute and unstirring, with her head at his feet. He felt a nervous impatience that, somehow, resembled fear.

"Tell her to let go, to go away, Willems, I tell you. I've had enough of this," he cried.

"All right, Captain Lingard," answered the calm voice of Willems, "she has let go. Take your foot off her hair; she can't get up."

Lingard leaped aside, clean away, and spun round quickly. He saw her sit up and cover her face with both hands, then he turned slowly on his heel and looked at the man. Willems held himself very straight, but was unsteady on his feet, and moved about nearly on the same spot, like a tipsy man attempting to preserve his balance. After gazing at him for a while, Lingard called, rancorous and irritable—

"What have you got to say for yourself?"

Willems began to walk towards him. He walked slowly, reeling a little before he took each step, and Lingard saw him put his hand to his face, then look at it holding it up to his eyes, as if he had there, concealed in the hollow of the palm, some small object which he wanted to examine secretly. Suddenly he drew it, with a brusque movement, down the front of his jacket and left a long smudge.

"That's a fine thing to do," said Willems.

He stood in front of Lingard, one of his eyes sunk deep in the increasing swelling of his cheek, still repeating mechanically the movement of feeling his damaged face; and every time he did this he pressed the palm to some clean spot on his jacket, covering the white cotton with bloody imprints as of some deformed and monstrous hand. Lingard said nothing, looking on. At last Willems left off staunching the blood and stood, his arms hanging by his side, with his face stiff and distorted under the patches of coagulated blood; and he seemed as though he had been set up there for a warning: an incomprehensible figure marked all over with some awful and symbolic signs of deadly import. Speaking with difficulty, he repeated in a reproachful tone—

"That was a fine thing to do."

"After all," answered Lingard, bitterly, "I had too good an opinion of you."

"And I of you. Don't you see that I could have had that fool over there killed and the whole thing burnt to the ground, swept off the face of the earth. You wouldn't have found as much as a heap of ashes had I liked. I could have done all that. And I wouldn't."

"You—could—not. You dared not. You scoundrel!" cried Lingard.

"What's the use of calling me names?"

"True," retorted Lingard—"there's no name bad enough for you."

There was a short interval of silence. At the sound of their rapidly exchanged words, Aissa had got up from the ground where she had been sitting, in a sorrowful and dejected pose, and approached the two men. She stood on one side and looked on eagerly, in a desperate effort of her brain, with the quick and distracted eyes of a person trying for her life to penetrate the meaning of sentences uttered in a foreign tongue: the meaning portentous and fateful that lurks in the sounds of mysterious words; in the sounds surprising, unknown and strange.

Willems let the last speech of Lingard pass by; seemed by a slight movement of his hand to help it on its way to join the other shadows of the past. Then he said—

"You have struck me; you have insulted me . . ."

"Insulted you!" interrupted Lingard, passionately. "Who—what can insult you . . . you . . ."

He choked, advanced a step.

"Steady! steady!" said Willems calmly. "I tell you I sha'n't fight. Is it clear enough to you that I sha'n't? I—shall—not—lift—a—finger."

As he spoke, slowly punctuating each word with a slight jerk of his head, he stared at Lingard, his right eye open and big, the left small and nearly closed by the swelling of one half of his face, that appeared all drawn out on one side like faces seen in a concave glass. And they stood exactly opposite each other: one tall, slight and disfigured; the other tall, heavy and severe.

Willems went on—

"If I had wanted to hurt you—if I had wanted to destroy you, it was easy. I stood in the doorway long enough to pull a trigger—and you know I shoot straight."

"You would have missed," said Lingard, with assurance. "There is, under heaven, such a thing as justice."

The sound of that word on his own lips made him pause, confused, like an unexpected and unanswerable rebuke. The anger of his outraged pride, the anger of his outraged heart, had gone out in the blow; and there remained nothing but the sense of some immense infamy—of something vague, disgusting and terrible, which seemed to surround him on all sides, hover about him with shadowy and stealthy movements, like a band of assassins in the darkness of vast and unsafe places. Was there, under heaven, such a thing as justice? He looked at the man before him with such an intensity of prolonged glance that he seemed to see right through him, that at last he saw but a floating and unsteady mist in human shape. Would it blow away before the first breath of the breeze and leave nothing behind?

The sound of Willems' voice made him start violently. Willems was saying—

"I have always led a virtuous life; you know I have. You always praised me for my steadiness; you know you have. You know also I never stole—if that's what you're thinking of. I borrowed. You know how much I repaid. It was an error of judgment. But then consider my position there. I had been a little unlucky in my private affairs, and had debts. Could I let myself go under before the eyes of all those men who envied me? But that's all over. It was an error of judgment. I've paid for it. An error of judgment."

Lingard, astounded into perfect stillness, looked down. He looked down at Willems' bare feet. Then, as the other had paused, he repeated in a blank tone—

"An error of judgment . . ."

"Yes," drawled out Willems, thoughtfully, and went on with increasing animation: "As I said, I have always led a virtuous life. More so than Hudig—than you. Yes, than you. I drank a little, I played cards a little. Who doesn't? But I had principles from a boy. Yes, principles. Business is business, and I never was an ass. I never respected fools. They had to suffer for their folly when they dealt with me. The evil was in them, not in me. But as to principles, it's another matter. I kept clear of women. It's forbidden—I had no time—and I despised them. Now I hate them!"

He put his tongue out a little; a tongue whose pink and moist end ran here and there, like something independently alive, under his swollen and blackened lip; he touched with the tips of his fingers the cut on his cheek, felt all round it with precaution: and the unharmed side of his face appeared for a moment to be preoccupied and uneasy about the state of that other side which was so very sore and stiff.

He recommenced speaking, and his voice vibrated as though with repressed emotion of some kind.

"You ask my wife, when you see her in Macassar, whether I have no reason to hate her. She was nobody, and I made her Mrs. Willems. A half-caste girl! You ask her how she showed her gratitude to me. You ask . . . Never mind that. Well, you came and dumped me here like a load of rubbish; dumped me here and left me with nothing to do—nothing good to remember—and damn little to hope for. You left me here at the mercy of that fool, Almayer, who suspected me of something. Of what? Devil only knows. But he suspected and hated me from the first; I suppose because you befriended me. Oh! I could read him like a book. He isn't very deep, your Sambir partner, Captain Lingard, but he knows how to be disagreeable. Months passed. I thought I would die of sheer weariness, of my thoughts, of my regrets And then . . ."

He made a quick step nearer to Lingard, and as if moved by the same thought, by the same instinct, by the impulse of his will, Aissa also stepped nearer to them. They stood in a close group, and the two men could feel the calm air between their faces stirred by the light breath of the anxious woman who enveloped them both in the uncomprehending, in the despairing and wondering glances of her wild and mournful eyes.

5

Willems turned a little from her and spoke lower.

"Look at that," he said, with an almost imperceptible movement of his head towards the woman to whom he was presenting his shoulder. "Look at that! Don't believe her! What has she been saying to you? What? I have been asleep. Had to sleep at last. I've been waiting for you three days and nights. I had to sleep some time. Hadn't I? I told her to remain awake and watch for you, and call me at once. She did watch. You can't believe her. You can't believe any woman. Who can tell what's inside their heads? No one. You can know nothing. The only thing you can know is that it isn't anything like what comes through their lips. They live by the side of you. They seem to hate you, or they seem to love you; they caress or torment you; they throw you over or stick to you closer than your skin for some inscrutable and awful reason of their own—which you can never know! Look at her—and look at me. At me! —her infernal work. What has she been saying?"

His voice had sunk to a whisper. Lingard listened with great attention, holding his chin in his hand, which grasped a great handful of his white beard. His elbow was in the palm of his other hand, and his eyes were still fixed on the ground. He murmured, without looking up—

"She begged me for your life—if you want to know—as if the thing were worth giving or taking!"

"And for three days she begged me to take yours," said Willems quickly. "For three days she wouldn't give me any peace. She was never still. She planned ambushes. She has been looking for places all over here where I could hide and drop you with a safe shot as you walked up. It's true. I give you my word."

"Your word," muttered Lingard, contemptuously.

Willems took no notice.

"Ah! She is a ferocious creature," he went on. "You don't know . . . I wanted to pass the time—to do something—to have something to think about—to forget my troubles till you came back. And . . . look at her . . . she took me as if I did not belong to myself. She did. I did not know there was something in me she could get hold of. She, a savage. I, a civilized European, and clever! She that knew no more than a wild animal! Well, she found out something in me. She found it out, and I was lost. I knew it. She tormented me. I was ready to do anything. I resisted—but I was ready. I knew that too. That frightened me more than anything; more than my own sufferings; and that was frightful enough, I assure you."

Lingard listened, fascinated and amazed like a child listening to a fairy tale, and, when Willems stopped for breath, he shuffled his feet a little.

"What does he say?" cried out Aissa, suddenly.

The two men looked at her quickly, and then looked at one another.

Willems began again, speaking hurriedly—

"I tried to do something. Take her away from those people. I went to Almayer; the biggest blind fool that you ever . . . Then Abdulla came—and she went away. She took away with her something of me which I had to get back. I had to do it. As far as you are concerned, the change here had to happen sooner or later; you couldn't be master here for ever. It isn't what I have done that torments me. It is the why. It's the madness that drove me to it. It's that thing that came over me. That may come again, some day."

"It will do no harm to anybody then, I promise you," said Lingard, significantly.

Willems looked at him for a second with a blank stare, then went on—

"I fought against her. She goaded me to violence and to murder. Nobody knows why. She pushed me to it persistently, desperately, all the time. Fortunately Abdulla had sense. I don't know what I wouldn't have done. She held me then. Held me like a nightmare that is terrible and sweet. By and by it was another life. I woke up. I found myself beside an animal as full of harm as a wild cat. You don't know through what I have passed. Her father tried to kill me—and she very nearly killed him. I believe she would have stuck at nothing. I don't know which was more terrible! She would have stuck at nothing to defend her own. And when I think that it was me—me—Willems . . . I hate her. To-morrow she may want my life. How can I know what's in her? She may want to kill me next!"

He paused in great trepidation, then added in a scared tone—

"I don't want to die here."

"Don't you?" said Lingard, thoughtfully.

Willems turned towards Aissa and pointed at her with a bony forefinger.

"Look at her! Always there. Always near. Always watching, watching . . . for something. Look at her eyes. Ain't they big? Don't they stare? You wouldn't think she can shut them like human beings do. I don't believe she ever does. I go to sleep, if I can, under their stare, and when I wake up I see them fixed on me and moving no more than the eyes of a corpse. While I am still they are still. By God—she can't move them till I stir, and then they follow me like a pair of jailers. They watch me; when I stop they seem to wait patient and glistening till I am off my guard—for to do something. To do something horrible. Look at them! You can see nothing in them. They are big, menacing—and empty. The eyes of a savage; of a damned mongrel, half-Arab, half-Malay. They hurt me! I am white! I swear to you I can't stand this! Take me away. I am white! All white!"

He shouted towards the sombre heaven, proclaiming desperately under the frown of thickening clouds the fact of his pure and superior descent. He shouted, his head thrown up, his arms swinging about wildly; lean, ragged, disfigured; a tall madman making a great disturbance about something invisible; a being absurd, repulsive, pathetic, and droll. Lingard, who was looking down as if absorbed in deep thought, gave him a quick glance from under his eyebrows: Aissa stood with clasped hands. At the other end of the courtyard the old woman, like a vague and decrepit apparition, rose noiselessly to look, then sank down again with a stealthy movement and crouched low over the small glow of the fire. Willems' voice filled the enclosure, rising louder with every word, and then, suddenly, at its very loudest, stopped short—like water stops running from an over-turned vessel. As soon as it had ceased the thunder seemed to take up the burden in a low growl coming from the inland hills. The noise approached in confused mutterings which kept on increasing, swelling into a roar that came nearer, rushed down the river, passed close in a tearing crash—and instantly sounded faint, dying away in monotonous and dull repetitions amongst the endless sinuosities of the lower reaches. Over the great forests, over all the innumerable people of unstirring trees—over all that living people immense, motionless, and mute—the silence, that had rushed in on the track of the passing tumult, remained suspended as deep and complete as if it had never been disturbed from the beginning of remote ages. Then, through it, after a time, came to Lingard's ears the voice of the running river: a voice low, discreet, and sad, like the persistent and gentle voices that speak of the past in the silence of dreams.

He felt a great emptiness in his heart. It seemed to him that there was within his breast a great space without any light, where his thoughts wandered forlornly, unable to escape, unable to rest, unable to die, to vanish—and to relieve him from the fearful oppression of their existence. Speech, action, anger, forgiveness, all appeared to him alike useless and vain, appeared to him unsatisfactory, not worth the effort of hand or brain that was needed to give them effect. He could not see why he should not remain standing there, without ever doing anything, to the end of time. He felt something, something like a heavy chain, that held him there. This wouldn't do. He backed away a little from Willems and Aissa, leaving them close together, then stopped and looked at both. The man and the woman appeared to him much further than they really were. He had made only about three steps backward, but he believed for a moment that another step would take him out of earshot for ever. They appeared to him slightly under life size, and with a great cleanness of outlines, like figures carved with great precision of detail and highly finished by a skilful hand. He pulled himself together. The strong consciousness of his own personality came back to him. He had a notion of surveying them from a great and inaccessible height.

He said slowly: "You have been possessed of a devil."

"Yes," answered Willems gloomily, and looking at Aissa. "Isn't it pretty?"

"I've heard this kind of talk before," said Lingard, in a scornful tone; then paused, and went on steadily after a while: "I regret nothing. I picked you up by the waterside, like a starving cat—by God. I regret nothing; nothing that I have done. Abdulla—twenty others—no doubt Hudig himself, were after me. That's business—for them. But that you should . . . Money belongs to him who picks it up and is strong enough to keep it—but this thing was different. It was part of my life. . . . I am an old fool."

He was. The breath of his words, of the very words he spoke, fanned the spark of divine folly in his breast, the spark that made him—the hard-headed, heavy-handed adventurer—stand out from the crowd, from the sordid, from the joyous, unscrupulous, and noisy crowd of men that were so much like himself.

Willems said hurriedly: "It wasn't me. The evil was not in me, Captain Lingard."

"And where else confound you! Where else?" interrupted Lingard, raising his voice. "Did you ever see me cheat and lie and steal? Tell me that. Did you? Hey? I wonder where in perdition you came from when I found you under my feet. . . . No matter. You will do no more harm."

Willems moved nearer, gazing upon him anxiously. Lingard went on with distinct deliberation—

"What did you expect when you asked me to see you? What? You know me. I am

Lingard. You lived with me. You've heard men speak. You knew what you had done. Well! What did you expect?"

"How can I know?" groaned Willems, wringing his hands; "I was alone in that infernal savage crowd. I was delivered into their hands. After the thing was done, I felt so lost and weak that I would have called the devil himself to my aid if it had been any good—if he hadn't put in all his work already. In the whole world there was only one man that had ever cared for me. Only one white man. You! Hate is better than being alone! Death is better! I expected . . . anything. Something to expect. Something to take me out of this. Out of her sight!"

He laughed. His laugh seemed to be torn out from him against his will, seemed to be brought violently on the surface from under his bitterness, his self-contempt, from under his despairing wonder at his own nature.

"When I think that when I first knew her it seemed to me that my whole life wouldn't be enough to . . . And now when I look at her! She did it all. I must have been mad. I was mad. Every time I look at her I remember my madness. It frightens me. . . . And when I think that of all my life, of all my past, of all my future, of my intelligence, of my work, there is nothing left but she, the cause of my ruin, and you whom I have mortally offended . . ."

He hid his face for a moment in his hands, and when he took them away he had lost the appearance of comparative calm and gave way to a wild distress.

"Captain Lingard . . . anything . . . a deserted island . . . anywhere . . . I promise . . ."

"Shut up!" shouted Lingard, roughly.

He became dumb, suddenly, completely.

The wan light of the clouded morning retired slowly from the courtyard, from the clearings, from the river, as if it had gone unwillingly to hide in the enigmatical solitudes of the gloomy and silent forests. The clouds over their heads thickened into a low vault of uniform blackness. The air was still and inexpressibly oppressive. Lingard unbuttoned his jacket, flung it wide open and, inclining his body sideways a little, wiped his forehead with his hand, which he jerked sharply afterwards. Then he looked at Willems and said—

"No promise of yours is any good to me. I am going to take your conduct into my own hands. Pay attention to what I am going to say. You are my prisoner."

Willems' head moved imperceptibly; then he became rigid and still. He seemed not to breathe.

"You shall stay here," continued Lingard, with sombre deliberation. "You are not fit to go amongst people. Who could suspect, who could guess, who could imagine what's in you? I couldn't! You are my mistake. I shall hide you here. If I let you out you would go amongst unsuspecting men, and lie, and steal, and cheat for a little money or for some woman. I don't care about shooting you. It would be the safest way though. But I won't. Do not expect me to forgive you. To forgive one must have been angry and become contemptuous, and there is nothing in me now—no anger, no contempt, no disappointment. To me you are not Willems, the man I befriended and helped through thick and thin, and thought much of . . . You are not a human being that may be destroyed or forgiven. You are a bitter thought, a something without a body and that must be hidden . . . You are my shame."

He ceased and looked slowly round. How dark it was! It seemed to him that the light was dying prematurely out of the world and that the air was already dead.

"Of course," he went on, "I shall see to it that you don't starve."

"You don't mean to say that I must live here, Captain Lingard?" said Willems, in a kind of mechanical voice without any inflections.

"Did you ever hear me say something I did not mean?" asked Lingard. "You said you didn't want to die here—well, you must live . . . Unless you change your mind," he added, as if in involuntary afterthought.

He looked at Willems narrowly, then shook his head.

"You are alone," he went on. "Nothing can help you. Nobody will. You are neither white nor brown. You have no colour as you have no heart. Your accomplices have abandoned you to me because I am still somebody to be reckoned with. You are alone but for that woman there. You say you did this for her. Well, you have her."

Willems mumbled something, and then suddenly caught his hair with both his hands and remained standing so. Aissa, who had been looking at him, turned to Lingard.

"What did you say, Rajah Laut?" she cried.

There was a slight stir amongst the filmy threads of her disordered hair, the bushes by the river sides trembled, the big tree nodded precipitately over them with an abrupt rustle, as if waking with a start from a troubled sleep—and the breath of hot breeze passed, light, rapid, and scorching, under the clouds that whirled round, unbroken but undulating, like a restless phantom of a sombre sea.

Lingard looked at her pityingly before he said—

"I have told him that he must live here all his life . . . and with you."

The sun seemed to have gone out at last like a flickering light away up beyond the clouds, and in the stifling gloom of the courtyard the three figures stood colourless and shadowy, as if surrounded by a black and superheated mist. Aissa looked at Willems, who remained still, as though he had been changed into stone in the very act of tearing his hair. Then she turned her head towards Lingard and shouted—

"You lie! You lie! . . . White man. Like you all do. You . . . whom Abdulla made small. You lie!"

Her words rang out shrill and venomous with her secret scorn, with her overpowering desire to wound regardless of consequences; in her woman's reckless desire to cause suffering at any cost, to cause it by the sound of her own voice—by her own voice, that would carry the poison of her thought into the hated heart.

Willems let his hands fall, and began to mumble again. Lingard turned his ear towards him instinctively, caught something that sounded like "Very well"—then some more mumbling—then a sigh.

"As far as the rest of the world is concerned," said Lingard, after waiting for awhile in an attentive attitude, "your life is finished. Nobody will be able to throw any of your villainies in my teeth; nobody will be able to point at you and say, 'Here goes a scoundrel of Lingard's up-bringing.' You are buried here."

"And you think that I will stay . . . that I will submit?" exclaimed Willems, as if he had suddenly recovered the power of speech.

"You needn't stay here—on this spot," said Lingard, drily. "There are the forests—and here is the river. You may swim. Fifteen miles up, or forty down. At one end you will meet Almayer, at the other the sea. Take your choice."

He burst into a short, joyless laugh, then added with severe gravity—

"There is also another way."

"If you want to drive my soul into damnation by trying to drive me to suicide you will not succeed," said Willems in wild excitement. "I will live. I shall repent. I may escape. . . . Take that woman away—she is sin."

A hooked dart of fire tore in two the darkness of the distant horizon and lit up the gloom of the earth with a dazzling and ghastly flame. Then the thunder was heard far away, like an incredibly enormous voice muttering menaces.

Lingard said—

"I don't care what happens, but I may tell you that without that woman your life is not worth much—not twopence. There is a fellow here who . . . and Abdulla himself wouldn't stand on any ceremony. Think of that! And then she won't go."

He began, even while he spoke, to walk slowly down towards the little gate. He didn't look, but he felt as sure that Willems was following him as if he had been leading him by a string. Directly he had passed through the wicket-gate into the big courtyard he heard a voice, behind his back, saying—

"I think she was right. I ought to have shot you. I couldn't have been worse off."

"Time yet," answered Lingard, without stopping or looking back. "But, you see, you can't. There is not even that in you."

"Don't provoke me, Captain Lingard," cried Willems.

Lingard turned round sharply. Willems and Aissa stopped. Another forked flash of lightning split up the clouds overhead, and threw upon their faces a sudden burst of light—a blaze violent, sinister and fleeting; and in the same instant they were deafened by a near, single crash of thunder, which was followed by a rushing noise, like a frightened sigh of the startled earth.

"Provoke you!" said the old adventurer, as soon as he could make himself heard. "Provoke you! Hey! What's there in you to provoke? What do I care?"

"It is easy to speak like that when you know that in the whole world—in the whole world—I have no friend," said Willems.

"Whose fault?" said Lingard, sharply.

Their voices, after the deep and tremendous noise, sounded to them very unsatisfactory—thin and frail, like the voices of pigmies—and they became suddenly silent, as if on that account. From up the courtyard Lingard's boatmen came down and passed them, keeping step in a single file, their paddles on shoulder, and holding their heads straight with their eyes fixed on the river. Ali, who was walking last, stopped before Lingard, very stiff and upright. He said—

"That one-eyed Babalatchi is gone, with all his women. He took everything. All the pots and boxes. Big. Heavy. Three boxes."

He grinned as if the thing had been amusing, then added with an appearance of anxious concern, "Rain coming."

"We return," said Lingard. "Make ready."

"Aye, aye, sir!" ejaculated Ali with precision, and moved on. He had been quartermaster with Lingard before making up his mind to stay in Sambir as Almayer's head man. He strutted towards the landing-place thinking proudly that he was not like those other ignorant boatmen, and knew how to answer properly the very greatest of white captains.

"You have misunderstood me from the first, Captain Lingard," said Willems.

"Have I? It's all right, as long as there is no mistake about my meaning," answered Lingard, strolling slowly to the landing-place. Willems followed him, and Aissa followed Willems.

Two hands were extended to help Lingard in embarking. He stepped cautiously and heavily into the long and narrow canoe, and sat in the canvas folding-chair that had been placed in the middle. He leaned back and turned his head to the two figures that stood on the bank a little above him. Aissa's eyes were fastened on his face in a visible impatience to see him gone. Willems' look went straight above the canoe, straight at the forest on the other side of the river.

"All right, Ali," said Lingard, in a low voice.

A slight stir animated the faces, and a faint murmur ran along the line of paddlers. The foremost man pushed with the point of his paddle, canted the fore end out of the dead water into the current; and the canoe fell rapidly off before the rush of brown water, the stern rubbing gently against the low bank.

"We shall meet again, Captain Lingard!" cried Willems, in an unsteady voice.

"Never!" said Lingard, turning half round in his chair to look at Willems. His fierce red eyes glittered remorselessly over the high back of his seat.

"Must cross the river. Water less quick over there," said Ali.

He pushed in his turn now with all his strength, throwing his body recklessly right out over the stern. Then he recovered himself just in time into the squatting attitude of a monkey perched on a high shelf, and shouted: "Dayong!"

The paddles struck the water together. The canoe darted forward and went on steadily crossing the river with a sideways motion made up of its own speed and the downward drift of the current.

Lingard watched the shore astern. The woman shook her hand at him, and then squatted at the feet of the man who stood motionless. After a while she got up and stood beside him, reaching up to his head—and Lingard saw then that she had wetted some part of her covering and was trying to wash the dried blood off the man's immovable face, which did not seem to know anything about it. Lingard turned away and threw himself back in his chair, stretching his legs out with a sigh of fatigue. His head fell forward; and under his red face the white beard lay fan-like on his breast, the ends of fine long hairs all astir in the faint draught made by the rapid motion of the craft that carried him away from his prisoner—from the only thing in his life he wished to hide.

In its course across the river the canoe came into the line of Willems' sight and his eyes caught the image, followed it eagerly as it glided, small but distinct, on the dark background of the forest. He could see plainly the figure of the man sitting in the middle. All his life he had felt that man behind his back, a reassuring presence ready with help, with commendation, with advice; friendly in reproof, enthusiastic in approbation; a man inspiring confidence by his strength, by his fearlessness, by the very weakness of his simple heart. And now that man was going away. He must call him back.

He shouted, and his words, which he wanted to throw across the river, seemed to fall helplessly at his feet. Aissa put her hand on his arm in a restraining attempt, but he shook it off. He wanted to call back his very life that was going away from him. He shouted again—and this time he did not even hear himself. No use. He would never return. And he stood in sullen silence looking at the white figure over there, lying back in the chair in the middle of the boat; a figure that struck him suddenly as very terrible, heartless and astonishing, with its unnatural appearance of running over the water in an attitude of languid repose.

For a time nothing on earth stirred, seemingly, but the canoe, which glided up-stream with a motion so even and smooth that it did not convey any sense of movement. Overhead, the massed clouds appeared solid and steady as if held there in a powerful grip, but on their uneven surface there was a continuous and trembling glimmer, a faint reflection of the distant lightning from the thunderstorm that had broken already on the coast and was working its way up the river with low and angry growls. Willems looked on, as motionless as everything round him and above him. Only his eyes seemed to live, as they followed the canoe on its course that carried it away from him, steadily, unhesitatingly, finally, as if it were going, not up the great river into the momentous excitement of Sambir, but straight into the past, into the past crowded yet empty, like an old cemetery full of neglected graves, where lie dead hopes that never return.

From time to time he felt on his face the passing, warm touch of an immense breath coming from beyond the forest, like the short panting of an oppressed world. Then the heavy air round him was pierced by a sharp gust of wind, bringing with it the fresh, damp feel of the falling rain; and all the innumerable tree-tops of the forests swayed to the left and sprang back again in a tumultuous balancing of nodding branches and shuddering leaves. A light frown ran over the river, the clouds stirred slowly, changing their aspect but not their place, as if they had turned ponderously over; and when the sudden movement had died out in a quickened tremor of the slenderest twigs, there was a short period of formidable immobility above and below, during which the voice of the thunder was heard, speaking in a sustained, emphatic and vibrating roll, with violent louder bursts of crashing sound, like a wrathful and threatening discourse of an angry god. For a moment it died out, and then another gust of wind passed, driving before it a white mist which filled the space with a cloud of waterdust that hid suddenly from Willems the canoe, the forests, the river itself; that woke him up from his numbness in a forlorn shiver, that made him look round despairingly to see nothing but the whirling drift of rain spray before the freshening breeze, while through it the heavy big drops fell about him with sonorous and rapid beats upon the dry earth. He made a few hurried steps up the courtyard and was arrested by an immense sheet of water that fell all at once on him, fell sudden and overwhelming from the clouds, cutting his respiration, streaming over his head, clinging to him, running down his body, off his arms, off his legs. He stood gasping while the water beat him in a vertical downpour, drove on him slanting in squalls, and he felt the drops striking him from above, from everywhere; drops thick, pressed and dashing at him as if flung from all sides by a mob of infuriated hands. From under his feet a great vapour of broken water floated up, he felt the ground become soft—melt under him—and saw the water spring out from the dry earth to meet the water that fell from the sombre heaven. An insane dread took possession of him, the dread of all that water around him, of the water that ran down the courtyard towards him, of the water that pressed him on every side, of the slanting water that drove across his face in wavering sheets which gleamed pale red with the flicker of lightning streaming through them, as if fire and water were falling together, monstrously mixed, upon the stunned earth.

He wanted to run away, but when he moved it was to slide about painfully and slowly upon that earth which had become mud so suddenly under his feet. He fought his way up the courtyard like a man pushing through a crowd, his head down, one shoulder forward, stopping often, and sometimes carried back a pace or two in the rush of water which his heart was not stout enough to face. Aissa followed him step by step, stopping when he stopped, recoiling with him, moving forward with him in his toilsome way up the slippery declivity of the courtyard, of that courtyard, from which everything seemed to have been swept away by the first rush of the mighty downpour. They could see nothing. The tree, the bushes, the house, and the fences—all had disappeared in the thickness of the falling rain. Their hair stuck, streaming, to their heads; their clothing clung to them, beaten close to their bodies; water ran off them, off their heads over their shoulders. They moved, patient, upright, slow and dark, in the gleam clear or fiery of the falling drops, under the roll of unceasing thunder, like two wandering ghosts of the drowned that, condemned to haunt the water for ever, had come up from the river to look at the world under a deluge.

On the left the tree seemed to step out to meet them, appearing vaguely, high, motionless and patient; with a rustling plaint of its innumerable leaves through which every drop of water tore its separate way with cruel haste. And then, to the right, the house surged up in the mist, very black, and clamorous with the quick patter of rain on its high-pitched roof above the steady splash of the water running off the eaves. Down the plankway leading to the door flowed a thin and pellucid stream, and when Willems began his ascent it broke over his foot as if he were going up a steep ravine in the bed of a rapid and shallow torrent. Behind his heels two streaming smudges of mud stained for an instant the purity of the rushing water, and then he splashed his way up with a spurt and stood on the bamboo platform before the open door under the shelter of the overhanging eaves—under shelter at last!

A low moan ending in a broken and plaintive mutter arrested Willems on the threshold. He peered round in the half-light under the roof and saw the old woman crouching close to the wall in a shapeless heap, and while he looked he felt a touch of two arms on his shoulders. Aissa! He had forgotten her. He turned, and she clasped him round the neck instantly, pressing close to him as if afraid of violence or escape. He stiffened himself in repulsion, in horror, in the mysterious revolt of his heart; while she clung to him—clung to him as if he were a refuge from misery, from storm, from weariness, from fear, from despair; and it was on the part of that being an embrace terrible, enraged and mournful, in which all her strength went out to make him captive, to hold him for ever.

He said nothing. He looked into her eyes while he struggled with her fingers about the nape of his neck, and suddenly he tore her hands apart, holding her arms up in a strong grip of her wrists, and bending his swollen face close over hers, he said—

"It is all your doing. You . . ."

She did not understand him—not a word. He spoke in the language of his people—of his people that know no mercy and no shame. And he was angry. Alas! he was always angry now, and always speaking words that she could not understand. She stood in silence, looking at him through her patient eyes, while he shook her arms a little and then flung them down.

"Don't follow me!" he shouted. "I want to be alone—I mean to be left alone!"

He went in, leaving the door open.

She did not move. What need to understand the words when they are spoken in such a voice? In that voice which did not seem to be his voice—his voice when he spoke by the brook, when he was never angry and always smiling! Her eyes were fixed upon the dark doorway, but her hands strayed mechanically upwards; she took up all her hair, and, inclining her head slightly over her shoulder, wrung out the long black tresses, twisting them persistently, while she stood, sad and absorbed, like one listening to an inward voice—the voice of bitter, of unavailing regret. The thunder had ceased, the wind had died out, and the rain fell perpendicular and steady through a great pale clearness—the light of remote sun coming victorious from amongst the dissolving blackness of the clouds. She stood near the doorway. He was there—alone in the gloom of the dwelling. He was there. He spoke not. What was in his mind now? What fear? What desire? Not the desire of her as in the days when he used to smile . . . How could she know? . . .

A sigh coming from the bottom of her heart, flew out into the world through her parted lips. A sigh faint, profound, and broken; a sigh full of pain and fear, like the sigh of those who are about to face the unknown: to face it in loneliness, in doubt, and without hope. She let go her hair, that fell scattered over her shoulders like a funeral veil, and she sank down suddenly by the door. Her hands clasped her ankles; she rested her head on her drawn-up knees, and remained still, very still, under the streaming mourning of her hair. She was thinking of him; of the days by the brook; she was thinking of all that had been their love—and she sat in the abandoned posture of those who sit weeping by the dead, of those who watch and mourn over a corpse.

V

I

Almayer propped, alone on the verandah of his house, with both his elbows on the table, and holding his head between his hands, stared before him, away over the stretch of sprouting young grass in his courtyard, and over the short jetty with its cluster of small canoes, amongst which his big whale-boat floated high, like a white mother of all that dark and aquatic brood. He stared on the river, past the schooner anchored in mid-stream, past the forests of the left bank; he stared through and past the illusion of the material world.

The sun was sinking. Under the sky was stretched a network of white threads, a network fine and close-meshed, where here and there were caught thicker white vapours of globular shape; and to the eastward, above the ragged barrier of the forests, surged the summits of a chain of great clouds, growing bigger slowly, in imperceptible motion, as if careful not to disturb the glowing stillness of the earth and of the sky. Abreast of the house the river was empty but for the motionless schooner. Higher up, a solitary log came out from the bend above and went on drifting slowly down the straight reach: a dead and wandering tree going out to its grave in the sea, between two ranks of trees motionless and living.

And Almayer sat, his face in his hands, looking on and hating all this: the muddy river; the faded blue of the sky; the black log passing by on its first and last voyage; the green sea of leaves—the sea that glowed shimmered, and stirred above the uniform and impenetrable gloom of the forests—the joyous sea of living green powdered with the brilliant dust of oblique sunrays.

He hated all this; he begrudged every day—every minute—of his life spent amongst all these things; he begrudged it bitterly, angrily, with enraged and immense regret, like a miser compelled to give up some of his treasure to a near relation. And yet all this was very precious to him. It was the present sign of a splendid future.

He pushed the table away impatiently, got up, made a few steps aimlessly, then stood by the balustrade and again looked at the river—at that river which would have been the instrument for the making of his fortune if . . . if . . .

"What an abominable brute!" he said.

He was alone, but he spoke aloud, as one is apt to do under the impulse of a strong, of an overmastering thought.

"What a brute!" he muttered again.

The river was dark now, and the schooner lay on it, a black, a lonely, and a graceful form, with the slender masts darting upwards from it in two frail and raking lines. The shadows of the evening crept up the trees, crept up from bough to bough, till at last the long sunbeams coursing from the western horizon skimmed lightly over the topmost branches, then flew upwards amongst the piled-up clouds, giving them a sombre and fiery aspect in the last flush of light. And suddenly the light disappeared as if lost in the immensity of the great, blue, and empty hollow overhead. The sun had set: and the forests became a straight wall of formless blackness. Above them, on the edge of lingering clouds, a single star glimmered fitfully, obscured now and then by the rapid flight of high and invisible vapours.

Almayer fought with the uneasiness within his breast. He heard Ali, who moved behind him preparing his evening meal, and he listened with strange attention to the sounds the man made—to the short, dry bang of the plate put upon the table, to the clink of glass and the metallic rattle of knife and fork. The man went away. Now he was coming back. He would speak directly; and Almayer, notwithstanding the absorbing gravity of his thoughts, listened for the sound of expected words. He heard them, spoken in English with painstaking distinctness.

"Ready, sir!"

"All right," said Almayer, curtly. He did not move. He remained pensive, with his back to the table upon which stood the lighted lamp brought by Ali. He was thinking: "Where was Lingard now? Halfway down the river probably, in Abdulla's ship. He would be back in about three days—perhaps less. And then? Then the schooner would have to be got out of the river, and when that craft was gone they—he and Lingard—would remain here; alone with the constant thought of that other man, that other man living near them! What an extraordinary idea to keep him there for ever. For ever! What did that mean—for ever? Perhaps a year, perhaps ten years. Preposterous! Keep him there ten years—or may be twenty! The fellow was capable of living more than twenty years. And for all that time he would have to be watched, fed, looked after. There was nobody but Lingard to have such notions. Twenty years! Why, no! In less than ten years their fortune would be made and they would leave this place, first for Batavia—yes, Batavia—and then for Europe. England, no doubt. Lingard would want to go to England. And would they leave that man here? How would that fellow look in ten years? Very old probably. Well, devil take him. Nina would be fifteen. She would be rich and very pretty and he himself would not be so old then. . . ."

Almayer smiled into the night.

. . . Yes, rich! Why! Of course! Captain Lingard was a resourceful man, and he had plenty of money even now. They were rich already; but not enough. Decidedly not enough. Money brings money. That gold business was good. Famous! Captain Lingard was a remarkable man. He said the gold was there—and it was there. Lingard knew what he was talking about. But he had queer ideas. For instance, about Willems. Now what did he want to keep him alive for? Why?

"That scoundrel," muttered Almayer again.

"Makan Tuan!" ejaculated Ali suddenly, very loud in a pressing tone.

Almayer walked to the table, sat down, and his anxious visage dropped from above into the light thrown down by the lamp-shade. He helped himself absently, and began to eat in great mouthfuls.

. . . Undoubtedly, Lingard was the man to stick to! The man undismayed, masterful and ready. How quickly he had planned a new future when Willems' treachery destroyed their established position in Sambir! And the position even now was not so bad. What an immense prestige that Lingard had with all those people—Arabs, Malays and all. Ah, it was good to be able to call a man like that father. Fine! Wonder how much money really the old fellow had. People talked—they exaggerated surely, but if he had only half of what they said . . .

He drank, throwing his head up, and fell to again.

. . . Now, if that Willems had known how to play his cards well, had he stuck to the old fellow he would have been in his position, he would be now married to Lingard's adopted daughter with his future assured—splendid . . .

"The beast!" growled Almayer, between two mouthfuls.

Ali stood rigidly straight with an uninterested face, his gaze lost in the night which pressed round the small circle of light that shone on the table, on the glass, on the bottle, and on Almayer's head as he leaned over his plate moving his jaws.

. . . A famous man Lingard—yet you never knew what he would do next. It was notorious that he had shot a white man once for less than Willems had done. For less? . . . Why, for nothing, so to speak! It was not even his own quarrel. It was about some Malay returning from pilgrimage with wife and children. Kidnapped, or robbed, or something. A stupid story—an old story. And now he goes to see that Willems and—nothing. Comes back talking big about his prisoner; but after all he said very little. What did that Willems tell him? What passed between them? The old fellow must have had something in his mind when he let that scoundrel off. And Joanna! She would get round the old fellow. Sure. Then he would forgive perhaps. Impossible. But at any rate he would waste a lot of money on them. The old man was tenacious in his hates, but also in his affections. He had known that beast Willems from a boy. They would make it up in a year or so. Everything is possible: why did he not rush off at first and kill the brute? That would have been more like Lingard. . . .

Almayer laid down his spoon suddenly, and pushing his plate away, threw himself back in the chair.

. . . Unsafe. Decidedly unsafe. He had no mind to share Lingard's money with anybody. Lingard's money was Nina's money in a sense. And if Willems managed to become friendly with the old man it would be dangerous for him—Almayer. Such an unscrupulous scoundrel! He would oust him from his position. He would lie and slander. Everything would be lost. Lost. Poor Nina. What would become of her? Poor child. For her sake he must remove that Willems. Must. But how? Lingard wanted to be obeyed. Impossible to kill Willems. Lingard might be angry. Incredible, but so it was. He might . . .

A wave of heat passed through Almayer's body, flushed his face, and broke out of him in copious perspiration. He wriggled in his chair, and pressed his hands together under the table. What an awful prospect! He fancied he could see Lingard and Willems reconciled and going away arm-in-arm, leaving him alone in this God-forsaken hole—in Sambir—in this deadly swamp! And all his sacrifices, the sacrifice of his independence, of his best years, his surrender to Lingard's fancies and caprices, would go for nothing! Horrible! Then he thought of his little daughter—his daughter!—and the ghastliness of his supposition overpowered him. He had a deep emotion, a sudden emotion that made him feel quite faint at the idea of that young life spoiled before it had fairly begun. His dear child's life! Lying back in his chair he covered his face with both his hands.

Ali glanced down at him and said, unconcernedly—"Master finish?"

Almayer was lost in the immensity of his commiseration for himself, for his daughter, who was—perhaps—not going to be the richest woman in the world—notwithstanding

Lingard's promises. He did not understand the other's question, and muttered through his fingers in a doleful tone—

"What did you say? What? Finish what?"

"Clear up meza," explained Ali.

"Clear up!" burst out Almayer, with incomprehensible exasperation. "Devil take you and the table. Stupid! Chatterer! Chelakka! Get out!"

He leaned forward, glaring at his head man, then sank back in his seat with his arms hanging straight down on each side of the chair. And he sat motionless in a meditation so concentrated and so absorbing, with all his power of thought so deep within himself, that all expression disappeared from his face in an aspect of staring vacancy.

Ali was clearing the table. He dropped negligently the tumbler into the greasy dish, flung there the spoon and fork, then slipped in the plate with a push amongst the remnants of food. He took up the dish, tucked up the bottle under his armpit, and went off.

"My hammock!" shouted Almayer after him.

"Ada! I come soon," answered Ali from the doorway in an offended tone, looking back over his shoulder. . . . How could he clear the table and hang the hammock at the same time. Ya-wa! Those white men were all alike. Wanted everything done at once. Like children . . .

The indistinct murmur of his criticism went away, faded and died out together with the soft footfall of his bare feet in the dark passage.

For some time Almayer did not move. His thoughts were busy at work shaping a momentous resolution, and in the perfect silence of the house he believed that he could hear the noise of the operation as if the work had been done with a hammer. He certainly felt a thumping of strokes, faint, profound, and startling, somewhere low down in his breast; and he was aware of a sound of dull knocking, abrupt and rapid, in his ears. Now and then he held his breath, unconsciously, too long, and had to relieve himself by a deep expiration that whistled dully through his pursed lips. The lamp standing on the far side of the table threw a section of a lighted circle on the floor, where his out-stretched legs stuck out from under the table with feet rigid and turned up like the feet of a corpse; and his set face with fixed eyes would have been also like the face of the dead, but for its vacant yet conscious aspect; the hard, the stupid, the stony aspect of one not dead, but only buried under the dust, ashes, and corruption of personal thoughts, of base fears, of selfish desires.

"I will do it!"

Not till he heard his own voice did he know that he had spoken. It startled him. He stood up. The knuckles of his hand, somewhat behind him, were resting on the edge of the table as he remained still with one foot advanced, his lips a little open, and thought: It would not do to fool about with Lingard. But I must risk it. It's the only way I can see. I must tell her. She has some little sense. I wish they were a thousand miles off already. A hundred thousand miles. I do. And if it fails. And she blabs out then to Lingard? She seemed a fool. No; probably they will get away. And if they did, would Lingard believe me? Yes. I never lied to him. He would believe. I don't know . . . Perhaps he won't. . . . "I must do it. Must!" he argued aloud to himself.

For a long time he stood still, looking before him with an intense gaze, a gaze rapt and immobile, that seemed to watch the minute quivering of a delicate balance, coming to a rest.

To the left of him, in the whitewashed wall of the house that formed the back of the verandah, there was a closed door. Black letters were painted on it proclaiming the fact that behind that door there was the office of Lingard & Co. The interior had been furnished by Lingard when he had built the house for his adopted daughter and her husband, and it had been furnished with reckless prodigality. There was an office desk, a revolving chair, bookshelves, a safe: all to humour the weakness of Almayer, who thought all those paraphernalia necessary to successful trading. Lingard had laughed, but had taken immense trouble to get the things. It pleased him to make his protege, his adopted son-in-law, happy. It had been the sensation of Sambir some five years ago. While the things were being landed, the whole settlement literally lived on the river bank in front of the Rajah Laut's house, to look, to wonder, to admire. . . . What a big meza, with many boxes fitted all over it and under it! What did the white man do with such a table? And look, look, O Brothers! There is a green square box, with a gold plate on it, a box so heavy that those twenty men cannot drag it up the bank. Let us go, brothers, and help pull at the ropes, and perchance we may see what's inside. Treasure, no doubt. Gold is heavy and hard to hold, O Brothers! Let us go and earn a recompense from the fierce Rajah of the Sea who shouts over there, with a red face. See! There is a man carrying a pile of books from the boat! What a number of books. What were they for? . . . And an old invalided jurumudi, who had travelled over many seas and had heard holy men speak in far-off countries, explained to a small knot of unsophisticated citizens of Sambir that those books were books of magic—of magic that guides the white men's ships over the seas, that gives them their wicked wisdom and their strength; of magic that makes them great, powerful, and irresistible while they live, and—praise be to Allah!—the victims of Satan, the slaves of Jehannum when they die.

And when he saw the room furnished, Almayer had felt proud. In his exultation of an empty-headed quill-driver, he thought himself, by the virtue of that furniture, at the head of a serious business. He had sold himself to Lingard for these things—married the Malay girl of his adoption for the reward of these things and of the great wealth that must necessarily follow upon conscientious book-keeping. He found out very soon that trade in Sambir meant something entirely different. He could not guide Patalolo, control the irrepressible old Sahamin, or restrain the youthful vagaries of the fierce Bahassoen with pen, ink, and paper. He found no successful magic in the blank pages of his ledgers; and gradually he lost his old point of view in the saner appreciation of his situation. The room known as the office became neglected then like a temple of an exploded superstition. At first, when his wife reverted to her original savagery, Almayer, now and again, had sought refuge from her there; but after their child began to speak, to know him, he became braver, for he found courage and consolation in his unreasoning and fierce affection for his daughter—in the impenetrable mantle of selfishness he wrapped round both their lives: round himself, and that young life that was also his.

When Lingard ordered him to receive Joanna into his house, he had a truckle bed put into the office—the only room he could spare. The big office desk was pushed on one side, and Joanna came with her little shabby trunk and with her child and took possession in her dreamy, slack, half-asleep way; took possession of the dust, dirt, and squalor, where she appeared naturally at home, where she dragged a melancholy and dull existence; an existence made up of sad remorse and frightened hope, amongst the hopeless disorder—the senseless and vain decay of all these emblems of civilized commerce. Bits of white stuff; rags yellow, pink, blue: rags limp, brilliant and soiled, trailed on the floor, lay on the desk amongst the sombre covers of books soiled, grimy, but stiff-backed, in virtue, perhaps, of their European origin. The biggest set of bookshelves was partly hidden by a petticoat, the waistband of which was caught upon the back of a slender book pulled a little out of the row so as to make an improvised clothespeg. The folding canvas bedstead stood nearly in the middle of the room, stood anyhow, parallel to no wall, as if it had been, in the process of transportation to some remote place, dropped casually there by tired bearers. And on the tumbled blankets that lay in a disordered heap on its edge, Joanna sat almost all day with her stockingless feet upon one of the bed pillows that were somehow always kicking about the floor. She sat there, vaguely tormented at times by the thought of her absent husband, but most of the time thinking tearfully of nothing at all, looking with swimming eyes at her little son—at the big-headed, pasty-faced, and sickly Louis Willems—who rolled a glass inkstand, solid with dried ink, about the floor, and tottered after it with the portentous gravity of demeanour and absolute absorption by the business in hand that characterize the pursuits of early childhood. Through the half-open shutter a ray of sunlight, a ray merciless and crude, came into the room, beat in the early morning upon the safe in the far-off corner, then, travelling against the sun, cut at midday the big desk in two with its solid and clean-edged brilliance; with its hot brilliance in which a swarm of flies hovered in dancing flight over some dirty plate forgotten there amongst yellow papers for many a day. And towards the evening the cynical ray seemed to cling to the ragged petticoat, lingered on it with wicked enjoyment of that misery it had exposed all day; lingered on the corner of the dusty bookshelf, in a red glow intense and mocking, till it was suddenly snatched by the setting sun out of the way of the coming night. And the night entered the room. The night abrupt, impenetrable and all-filling with its flood of darkness; the night cool and merciful; the blind night that saw nothing, but could hear the fretful whimpering of the child, the creak of the bedstead, Joanna's deep sighs as she turned over, sleepless, in the confused conviction of her wickedness, thinking of that man masterful, fair-headed, and strong—a man hard perhaps, but her husband; her clever and handsome husband to whom she had acted so cruelly on the advice of bad people, if her own people; and of her poor, dear, deceived mother.

To Almayer, Joanna's presence was a constant worry, a worry unobtrusive yet intolerable; a constant, but mostly mute, warning of possible danger. In view of the absurd softness of Lingard's heart, every one in whom Lingard manifested the slightest interest was to Almayer a natural enemy. He was quite alive to that feeling, and in the intimacy of the secret intercourse with his inner self had often congratulated himself upon his own wide-awake comprehension of his position. In that way, and impelled by that motive, Almayer had hated many and various persons at various times. But he never had hated and feared anybody so much as he did hate and fear Willems. Even after Willems' treachery, which seemed to remove him beyond the pale of all human sympathy, Almayer mistrusted the situation and groaned in spirit every time he caught sight of Joanna.

He saw her very seldom in the daytime. But in the short and opal-tinted twilights, or in the azure dusk of starry evenings, he often saw, before he slept, the slender and tall figure trailing to and fro the ragged tail of its white gown over the dried mud of the riverside in front of the house. Once or twice when he sat late on the verandah, with his feet upon the deal table on a level with the lamp, reading the seven months' old copy of the North China Herald, brought by Lingard, he heard the stairs creak, and, looking round the paper, he saw her frail and meagre form rise step by step and toil across the verandah, carrying with difficulty the big, fat child, whose head, lying on the mother's bony shoulder, seemed of the same size as Joanna's own. Several times she had assailed him with tearful clamour or mad entreaties: asking about her husband, wanting to know where he was, when he would be back; and ending every such outburst with despairing and incoherent self-reproaches that were absolutely incomprehensible to Almayer. On one or two occasions she had overwhelmed her host with vituperative abuse, making him responsible for her husband's absence. Those scenes, begun without any warning, ended abruptly in a sobbing flight and a bang of the door; stirred the house with a sudden, a fierce, and an evanescent disturbance; like those inexplicable whirlwinds that rise, run, and vanish without apparent cause upon the sun-scorched dead level of arid and lamentable plains.

But to-night the house was quiet, deadly quiet, while Almayer stood still, watching that delicate balance where he was weighing all his chances: Joanna's intelligence, Lingard's credulity, Willems' reckless audacity, desire to escape, readiness to seize an unexpected opportunity. He weighed, anxious and attentive, his fears and his desires against the tremendous risk of a quarrel with Lingard. . . . Yes. Lingard would be angry. Lingard might suspect him of some connivance in his prisoner's escape—but surely he would not quarrel with him—Almayer—about those people once they were gone—gone to the devil in their own way. And then he had hold of Lingard through the little girl. Good. What an annoyance! A prisoner! As if one could keep him in there. He was bound to get away some time or other. Of course. A situation like that can't last. Anybody could see that. Lingard's eccentricity passed all bounds. You may kill a man, but you mustn't torture him. It was almost criminal. It caused worry, trouble, and unpleasantness. . . . Almayer for a moment felt very angry with Lingard. He made him responsible for the anguish he suffered from, for the anguish of doubt and fear; for compelling him—the practical and innocent Almayer—to such painful efforts of mind in order to find out some issue for absurd situations created by the unreasonable sentimentality of Lingard's unpractical impulses.

"Now if the fellow were dead it would be all right," said Almayer to the verandah.

He stirred a little, and scratching his nose thoughtfully, revelled in a short flight of fancy, showing him his own image crouching in a big boat, that floated arrested—say fifty yards off—abreast of Willems' landing-place. In the bottom of the boat there was a gun. A loaded gun. One of the boatmen would shout, and Willems would answer—from the bushes. The rascal would be suspicious. Of course. Then the man would wave a piece of paper urging Willems to come to the landing-place and receive an important message. "From the Rajah Laut" the man would yell as the boat edged in-shore, and that would fetch Willems out. Wouldn't it? Rather! And Almayer saw himself jumping up at the right moment, taking aim, pulling the trigger—and Willems tumbling over, his head in the water—the swine!

He seemed to hear the report of the shot. It made him thrill from head to foot where he stood. . . . How simple! . . . Unfortunate . . . Lingard . . . He sighed, shook his head. Pity. Couldn't be done. And couldn't leave him there either! Suppose the Arabs were to get hold of him again—for instance to lead an expedition up the river! Goodness only knows what harm would come of it. . . .

The balance was at rest now and inclining to the side of immediate action. Almayer walked to the door, walked up very close to it, knocked loudly, and turned his head away, looking frightened for a moment at what he had done. After waiting for a while he put his ear against the panel and listened. Nothing. He composed his features into an agreeable expression while he stood listening and thinking to himself: I hear her. Crying. Eh? I believe she has lost the little wits she had and is crying night and day since I began to prepare her for the news of her husband's death—as Lingard told me. I wonder what she thinks. It's just like father to make me invent all these stories for nothing at all. Out of kindness. Kindness! Damn! . . . She isn't deaf, surely.

He knocked again, then said in a friendly tone, grinning benevolently at the closed door—

"It's me, Mrs. Willems. I want to speak to you. I have . . . have . . . important news. . . ."

"What is it?"

"News," repeated Almayer, distinctly. "News about your husband. Your husband! . . . Damn him!" he added, under his breath.

He heard a stumbling rush inside. Things were overturned. Joanna's agitated voice cried—

"News! What? What? I am coming out."

"No," shouted Almayer. "Put on some clothes, Mrs. Willems, and let me in. It's . . . very confidential. You have a candle, haven't you?"

She was knocking herself about blindly amongst the furniture in that room. The candlestick was upset. Matches were struck ineffectually. The matchbox fell. He heard her drop on her knees and grope over the floor while she kept on moaning in maddened distraction.

"Oh, my God! News! Yes . . . yes. . . . Ah! where . . . where . . . candle. Oh, my God! . . . I can't find . . . Don't go away, for the love of Heaven . . ."

"I don't want to go away," said Almayer, impatiently, through the keyhole; "but look sharp. It's coni . . . it's pressing."

He stamped his foot lightly, waiting with his hand on the door-handle. He thought anxiously: The woman's a perfect idiot. Why should I go away? She will be off her head. She will never catch my meaning. She's too stupid.

She was moving now inside the room hurriedly and in silence. He waited. There was a moment of perfect stillness in there, and then she spoke in an exhausted voice, in words that were shaped out of an expiring sigh—out of a sigh light and profound, like words breathed out by a woman before going off into a dead faint—

"Come in."

He pushed the door. Ali, coming through the passage with an armful of pillows and blankets pressed to his breast high up under his chin, caught sight of his master before the door closed behind him. He was so astonished that he dropped his bundle and stood staring at the door for a long time. He heard the voice of his master talking. Talking to that Sirani woman! Who was she? He had never thought about that really. He speculated for a while hazily upon things in general. She was a Sirani woman—and ugly. He made a disdainful grimace, picked up the bedding, and went about his work, slinging the hammock between two uprights of the verandah. . . . Those things did not concern him. She was ugly, and brought here by the Rajah Laut, and his master spoke to her in the night. Very well. He, Ali, had his work to do. Sling the hammock—go round and see that the watchmen were awake—take a look at the moorings of the boats, at the padlock of the big storehouse—then go to sleep. To sleep! He shivered pleasantly. He leaned with both arms over his master's hammock and fell into a light doze.

A scream, unexpected, piercing—a scream beginning at once in the highest pitch of a woman's voice and then cut short, so short that it suggested the swift work of death—caused Ali to jump on one side away from the hammock, and the silence that succeeded seemed to him as startling as the awful shriek. He was thunderstruck with surprise. Almayer came out of the office, leaving the door ajar, passed close to his servant without taking any notice, and made straight for the water-chatty hung on a nail in a draughty place. He took it down and came back, missing the petrified Ali by an inch. He moved with long strides, yet, notwithstanding his haste, stopped short before the door, and, throwing his head back, poured a thin stream of water down his throat. While he came and went, while he stopped to drink, while he did all this, there came steadily from the dark room the sound of feeble and persistent crying, the crying of a sleepy and frightened child. After he had drunk, Almayer went in, closing the door carefully.

Ali did not budge. That Sirani woman shrieked! He felt an immense curiosity very unusual to his stolid disposition. He could not take his eyes off the door. Was she dead in there? How interesting and funny! He stood with open mouth till he heard again the rattle of the door-handle. Master coming out. He pivoted on his heels with great rapidity and made believe to be absorbed in the contemplation of the night outside. He heard Almayer moving about behind his back. Chairs were displaced. His master sat down.

"Ali," said Almayer.

His face was gloomy and thoughtful. He looked at his head man, who had approached the table, then he pulled out his watch. It was going. Whenever Lingard was in Sambir Almayer's watch was going. He would set it by the cabin clock, telling himself every time that he must really keep that watch going for the future. And every time, when Lingard went away, he would let it run down and would measure his weariness by sunrises and sunsets in an apathetic indifference to mere hours; to hours only; to hours that had no importance in Sambir life, in the tired stagnation of empty days; when nothing mattered to him but the quality of guttah and the size of rattans; where there were no small hopes to be watched for; where to him there was nothing interesting, nothing supportable, nothing desirable to expect; nothing bitter but the slowness of the passing days; nothing sweet but the hope, the distant and glorious hope—the hope wearying, aching and precious, of getting away.

He looked at the watch. Half-past eight. Ali waited stolidly.

"Go to the settlement," said Almayer, "and tell Mahmat Banjer to come and speak to me to-night."

Ali went off muttering. He did not like his errand. Banjer and his two brothers were Bajow vagabonds who had appeared lately in Sambir and had been allowed to take possession of a tumbledown abandoned hut, on three posts, belonging to Lingard & Co., and standing just outside their fence. Ali disapproved of the favour shown to those strangers. Any kind of dwelling was valuable in Sambir at that time, and if master did not want that old rotten house he might have given it to him, Ali, who was his servant, instead of bestowing it upon those bad men. Everybody knew they were bad. It was well known that they had stolen a boat from Hinopari, who was very aged and feeble and had no sons; and that afterwards, by the truculent recklessness of their demeanour, they had frightened the poor old man into holding his tongue about it. Yet everybody knew of it. It was one of the tolerated scandals of Sambir, disapproved and accepted, a manifestation of that base acquiescence in success, of that inexpressed and cowardly toleration of strength, that exists, infamous and irremediable, at the bottom of all hearts, in all societies; whenever men congregate; in bigger and more virtuous places than Sambir, and in Sambir also, where, as in other places, one man could steal a boat with impunity while another would have no right to look at a paddle.

Almayer, leaning back in his chair, meditated. The more he thought, the more he felt convinced that Banjer and his brothers were exactly the men he wanted. Those fellows were sea gipsies, and could disappear without attracting notice; and if they returned, nobody—and Lingard least of all—would dream of seeking information from them. Moreover, they had no personal interest of any kind in Sambir affairs—had taken no sides—would know nothing anyway.

He called in a strong voice: "Mrs. Willems!"

She came out quickly, almost startling him, so much did she appear as though she had surged up through the floor, on the other side of the table. The lamp was between them, and Almayer moved it aside, looking up at her from his chair. She was crying. She was crying gently, silently, in a ceaseless welling up of tears that did not fall in drops, but seemed to overflow in a clear sheet from under her eyelids—seemed to flow at once all over her face, her cheeks, and over her chin that glistened with moisture in the light. Her breast and her shoulders were shaken repeatedly by a convulsive and noiseless catching in her breath, and after every spasmodic sob her sorrowful little head, tied up in a red kerchief, trembled on her long neck, round which her bony hand gathered and clasped the disarranged dress.

"Compose yourself, Mrs. Willems," said Almayer.

She emitted an inarticulate sound that seemed to be a faint, a very far off, a hardly audible cry of mortal distress. Then the tears went on flowing in profound stillness.

"You must understand that I have told you all this because I am your friend—real friend," said Almayer, after looking at her for some time with visible dissatisfaction. "You, his wife, ought to know the danger he is in. Captain Lingard is a terrible man, you know."

She blubbered out, sniffing and sobbing together.

"Do you . . . you . . . speak . . . the . . . the truth now?"

"Upon my word of honour. On the head of my child," protested Almayer. "I had to deceive you till now because of Captain Lingard. But I couldn't bear it. Think only what a risk I run in telling you—if ever Lingard was to know! Why should I do it? Pure friendship. Dear Peter was my colleague in Macassar for years, you know."

"What shall I do . . . what shall I do!" she exclaimed, faintly, looking around on every side as if she could not make up her mind which way to rush off.

"You must help him to clear out, now Lingard is away. He offended Lingard, and that's no joke. Lingard said he would kill him. He will do it, too," said Almayer, earnestly.

She wrung her hands. "Oh! the wicked man. The wicked, wicked man!" she moaned, swaying her body from side to side.

"Yes. Yes! He is terrible," assented Almayer. "You must not lose any time. I say! Do you understand me, Mrs. Willems? Think of your husband. Of your poor husband. How happy he will be. You will bring him his life—actually his life. Think of him."

She ceased her swaying movement, and now, with her head sunk between her shoulders, she hugged herself with both her arms; and she stared at Almayer with wild eyes, while her teeth chattered, rattling violently and uninterruptedly, with a very loud sound, in the deep peace of the house.

"Oh! Mother of God!" she wailed. "I am a miserable woman. Will he forgive me? The poor, innocent man. Will he forgive me? Oh, Mr. Almayer, he is so severe. Oh! help me. . . . I dare not. . . . You don't know what I've done to him. . . . I daren't! . . . I can't! . . . God help me!"

The last words came in a despairing cry. Had she been flayed alive she could not have sent to heaven a more terrible, a more heartrending and anguished plaint.

"Sh! Sh!" hissed Almayer, jumping up. "You will wake up everybody with your shouting."

She kept on sobbing then without any noise, and Almayer stared at her in boundless astonishment. The idea that, maybe, he had done wrong by confiding in her, upset him so much that for a moment he could not find a connected thought in his head.

At last he said: "I swear to you that your husband is in such a position that he would welcome the devil . . . listen well to me . . . the devil himself if the devil came to him in a canoe. Unless I am much mistaken," he added, under his breath. Then again, loudly: "If you have any little difference to make up with him, I assure you—I swear to you—this is your time!"

The ardently persuasive tone of his words—he thought—would have carried irresistible conviction to a graven image. He noticed with satisfaction that Joanna seemed to have got some inkling of his meaning. He continued, speaking slowly—

"Look here, Mrs. Willems. I can't do anything. Daren't. But I will tell you what I will do. There will come here in about ten minutes a Bugis man—you know the language; you are from Macassar. He has a large canoe; he can take you there. To the new Rajah's clearing, tell him. They are three brothers, ready for anything if you pay them . . . you have some money. Haven't you?"

She stood—perhaps listening—but giving no sign of intelligence, and stared at the floor in sudden immobility, as if the horror of the situation, the overwhelming sense of her own wickedness and of her husband's great danger, had stunned her brain, her heart, her will—had left her no faculty but that of breathing and of keeping on her feet. Almayer swore to himself with much mental profanity that he had never seen a more useless, a more stupid being.

"D'ye hear me?" he said, raising his voice. "Do try to understand. Have you any money? Money. Dollars. Guilders. Money! What's the matter with you?"

Without raising her eyes she said, in a voice that sounded weak and undecided as if she had been making a desperate effort of memory—

"The house has been sold. Mr. Hudig was angry."

Almayer gripped the edge of the table with all his strength. He resisted manfully an almost uncontrollable impulse to fly at her and box her ears.

"It was sold for money, I suppose," he said with studied and incisive calmness. "Have you got it? Who has got it?"

She looked up at him, raising her swollen eyelids with a great effort, in a sorrowful expression of her drooping mouth, of her whole besmudged and tear-stained face. She whispered resignedly—

"Leonard had some. He wanted to get married. And uncle Antonio; he sat at the door and would not go away. And Aghostina—she is so poor . . . and so many, many children—little children. And Luiz the engineer. He never said a word against my husband. Also our cousin Maria. She came and shouted, and my head was so bad, and my heart was worse. Then cousin Salvator and old Daniel da Souza, who . . ."

Almayer had listened to her speechless with rage. He thought: I must give money now to that idiot. Must! Must get her out of the way now before Lingard is back. He made two attempts to speak before he managed to burst out—

"I don't want to know their blasted names! Tell me, did all those infernal people leave you anything? To you! That's what I want to know!"

"I have two hundred and fifteen dollars," said Joanna, in a frightened tone.

Almayer breathed freely. He spoke with great friendliness—

"That will do. It isn't much, but it will do. Now when the man comes I will be out of the way. You speak to him. Give him some money; only a little, mind! And promise more. Then when you get there you will be guided by your husband, of course. And don't forget to tell him that Captain Lingard is at the mouth of the river—the northern entrance. You will remember. Won't you? The northern branch. Lingard is—death."

Joanna shivered. Almayer went on rapidly—

"I would have given you money if you had wanted it. 'Pon my word! Tell your husband I've sent you to him. And tell him not to lose any time. And also say to him from me that we shall meet—some day. That I could not die happy unless I met him once more. Only once. I love him, you know. I prove it. Tremendous risk to me—this business is!"

Joanna snatched his hand and before he knew what she would be at, pressed it to her lips.

"Mrs. Willems! Don't. What are you . . ." cried the abashed Almayer, tearing his hand away.

"Oh, you are good!" she cried, with sudden exaltation, "You are noble . . . I shall pray every day . . . to all the saints . . . I shall . . ."

"Never mind . . . never mind!" stammered out Almayer, confusedly, without knowing very well what he was saying. "Only look out for Lingard. . . . I am happy to be able . . . in your sad situation . . . believe me. . . ."

They stood with the table between them, Joanna looking down, and her face, in the half-light above the lamp, appeared like a soiled carving of old ivory—a carving, with accentuated anxious hollows, of old, very old ivory. Almayer looked at her, mistrustful, hopeful. He was saying to himself: How frail she is! I could upset her by blowing at her. She seems to have got some idea of what must be done, but will she have the strength to carry it through? I must trust to luck now!

Somewhere far in the back courtyard Ali's voice rang suddenly in angry remonstrance—

"Why did you shut the gate, O father of all mischief? You a watchman! You are only a wild man. Did I not tell you I was coming back? You . . ."

"I am off, Mrs. Willems," exclaimed Almayer. "That man is here—with my servant. Be calm. Try to . . ."

He heard the footsteps of the two men in the passage, and without finishing his sentence ran rapidly down the steps towards the riverside.

2

For the next half-hour Almayer, who wanted to give Joanna plenty of time, stumbled amongst the lumber in distant parts of his enclosure, sneaked along the fences; or held his breath, flattened against grass walls behind various outhouses: all this to escape Ali's inconveniently zealous search for his master. He heard him talk with the head watchman—sometimes quite close to him in the darkness—then moving off, coming back, wondering, and, as the time passed, growing uneasy.

"He did not fall into the river?—say, thou blind watcher!" Ali was growling in a bullying tone, to the other man. "He told me to fetch Mahmat, and when I came back swiftly I found him not in the house. There is that Sirani woman there, so that Mahmat cannot steal anything, but it is in my mind, the night will be half gone before I rest."

He shouted—

"Master! O master! O mast . . ."

"What are you making that noise for?" said Almayer, with severity, stepping out close to them.

The two Malays leaped away from each other in their surprise.

"You may go. I don't want you any more tonight, Ali," went on Almayer. "Is Mahmat there?"

"Unless the ill-behaved savage got tired of waiting. Those men know not politeness. They should not be spoken to by white men," said Ali, resentfully.

Almayer went towards the house, leaving his servants to wonder where he had sprung from so unexpectedly. The watchman hinted obscurely at powers of invisibility possessed by the master, who often at night . . . Ali interrupted him with great scorn. Not every white man has the power. Now, the Rajah Laut could make himself invisible. Also, he could be in two places at once, as everybody knew; except he—the useless watchman—who knew no more about white men than a wild pig! Ya-wa!

And Ali strolled towards his hut, yawning loudly.

As Almayer ascended the steps he heard the noise of a door flung to, and when he entered the verandah he saw only Mahmat there, close to the doorway of the passage.

Mahmat seemed to be caught in the very act of slinking away, and Almayer noticed that with satisfaction. Seeing the white man, the Malay gave up his attempt and leaned against the wall. He was a short, thick, broad-shouldered man with very dark skin and a wide, stained, bright-red mouth that uncovered, when he spoke, a close row of black and glistening teeth. His eyes were big, prominent, dreamy and restless. He said sulkily, looking all over the place from under his eyebrows—

"White Tuan, you are great and strong—and I a poor man. Tell me what is your will, and let me go in the name of God. It is late."

Almayer examined the man thoughtfully. How could he find out whether . . . He had it! Lately he had employed that man and his two brothers as extra boatmen to carry stores, provisions, and new axes to a camp of rattan cutters some distance up the river. A three days' expedition. He would test him now in that way. He said negligently—

"I want you to start at once for the camp, with surat for the Kavitan. One dollar a day."

The man appeared plunged in dull hesitation, but Almayer, who knew his Malays, felt pretty sure from his aspect that nothing would induce the fellow to go. He urged—

"It is important—and if you are swift I shall give two dollars for the last day."

"No, Tuan. We do not go," said the man, in a hoarse whisper.

"Why?"

"We start on another journey."

"Where?"

"To a place we know of," said Mahmat, a little louder, in a stubborn manner, and looking at the floor.

Almayer experienced a feeling of immense joy. He said, with affected annoyance—

"You men live in my house and it is as if it were your own. I may want my house soon."

Mahmat looked up.

"We are men of the sea and care not for a roof when we have a canoe that will hold three, and a paddle apiece. The sea is our house. Peace be with you, Tuan."

He turned and went away rapidly, and Almayer heard him directly afterwards in the courtyard calling to the watchman to open the gate. Mahmat passed through the gate in silence, but before the bar had been put up behind him he had made up his mind that if the white man ever wanted to eject him from his hut, he would burn it and also as many of the white man's other buildings as he could safely get at. And he began to call his brothers before he was inside the dilapidated dwelling.

"All's well!" muttered Almayer to himself, taking some loose Java tobacco from a drawer in the table. "Now if anything comes out I am clear. I asked the man to go up the river. I urged him. He will say so himself. Good."

He began to charge the china bowl of his pipe, a pipe with a long cherry stem and a curved mouthpiece, pressing the tobacco down with his thumb and thinking: No. I sha'n't see her again. Don't want to. I will give her a good start, then go in chase—and send an express boat after father. Yes! that's it.

He approached the door of the office and said, holding his pipe away from his lips—

"Good luck to you, Mrs. Willems. Don't lose any time. You may get along by the bushes; the fence there is out of repair. Don't lose time. Don't forget that it is a matter of . . . life and death. And don't forget that I know nothing. I trust you."

He heard inside a noise as of a chest-lid falling down. She made a few steps. Then a sigh, profound and long, and some faint words which he did not catch. He moved away from the door on tiptoe, kicked off his slippers in a corner of the verandah, then entered the passage puffing at his pipe; entered cautiously in a gentle creaking of planks and turned into a curtained entrance to the left. There was a big room. On the floor a small binnacle lamp—that had found its way to the house years ago from the lumber-room of the Flash—did duty for a night-light. It glimmered very small and dull in the great darkness. Almayer walked to it, and picking it up revived the flame by pulling the wick with his fingers, which he shook directly after with a grimace of pain. Sleeping shapes, covered—head and all—with white sheets, lay about on the mats on the floor. In the middle of the room a small cot, under a square white mosquito net, stood—the only piece of furniture between the four walls—looking like an altar of transparent marble in a gloomy temple. A woman, half-lying on the floor with her head dropped on her arms, which were crossed on the foot of the cot, woke up as Almayer strode over her outstretched legs. She sat up without a word, leaning forward, and, clasping her knees, stared down with sad eyes, full of sleep.

Almayer, the smoky light in one hand, his pipe in the other, stood before the curtained cot looking at his daughter—at his little Nina—at that part of himself, at that small and unconscious particle of humanity that seemed to him to contain all his soul. And it was as if he had been bathed in a bright and warm wave of tenderness, in a tenderness greater than the world, more precious than life; the only thing real, living, sweet, tangible, beautiful and safe amongst the elusive, the distorted and menacing shadows of existence. On his face, lit up indistinctly by the short yellow flame of the lamp, came a look of rapt attention while he looked into her future. And he could see things there! Things charming and splendid passing before him in a magic unrolling of resplendent pictures; pictures of events brilliant, happy, inexpressibly glorious, that would make up her life. He would do it! He would do it. He would! He would—for that child! And as he stood in the still night, lost in his enchanting and gorgeous dreams, while the ascending, thin thread of tobacco smoke spread into a faint bluish cloud above his head, he appeared strangely impressive and ecstatic: like a devout and mystic worshipper, adoring, transported and mute; burning incense before a shrine, a diaphanous shrine of a child-idol with closed eyes; before a pure and vaporous shrine of a small god—fragile, powerless, unconscious and sleeping.

When Ali, roused by loud and repeated shouting of his name, stumbled outside the door of his hut, he saw a narrow streak of trembling gold above the forests and a pale sky with faded stars overhead: signs of the coming day. His master stood before the door waving a piece of paper in his hand and shouting excitedly—"Quick, Ali! Quick!" When he saw his servant he rushed forward, and pressing the paper on him objurgated him, in tones which induced Ali to think that something awful had happened, to hurry up and get the whale-boat ready to go immediately—at once, at once—after Captain Lingard. Ali remonstrated, agitated also, having caught the infection of distracted haste.

"If must go quick, better canoe. Whale-boat no can catch, same as small canoe."

"No, no! Whale-boat! whale-boat! You dolt! you wretch!" howled Almayer, with all the appearance of having gone mad. "Call the men! Get along with it. Fly!"

And Ali rushed about the courtyard kicking the doors of huts open to put his head in and yell frightfully inside; and as he dashed from hovel to hovel, men shivering and sleepy were coming out, looking after him stupidly, while they scratched their ribs with bewildered apathy. It was hard work to put them in motion. They wanted time to stretch themselves and to shiver a little. Some wanted food. One said he was sick. Nobody knew where the rudder was. Ali darted here and there, ordering, abusing, pushing one, then another, and stopping in his exertions at times to wring his hands hastily and groan, because the whale-boat was much slower than the worst canoe and his master would not listen to his protestations.

Almayer saw the boat go off at last, pulled anyhow by men that were cold, hungry, and sulky; and he remained on the jetty watching it down the reach. It was broad day then, and the sky was perfectly cloudless. Almayer went up to the house for a moment. His household was all astir and wondering at the strange disappearance of the Sirani woman, who had taken her child and had left her luggage. Almayer spoke to no one, got his revolver, and went down to the river again. He jumped into a small canoe and paddled himself towards the schooner. He worked very leisurely, but as soon as he was nearly alongside he began to hail the silent craft with the tone and appearance of a man in a tremendous hurry.

"Schooner ahoy! schooner ahoy!" he shouted.

A row of blank faces popped up above the bulwark. After a while a man with a woolly head of hair said—

"Sir!"

"The mate! the mate! Call him, steward!" said Almayer, excitedly, making a frantic grab at a rope thrown down to him by somebody.

In less than a minute the mate put his head over. He asked, surprised—

"What can I do for you, Mr. Almayer?"

"Let me have the gig at once, Mr. Swan—at once. I ask in Captain Lingard's name. I must have it. Matter of life and death."

The mate was impressed by Almayer's agitation

"You shall have it, sir. . . . Man the gig there! Bear a hand, serang! . . . It's hanging astern, Mr. Almayer," he said, looking down again. "Get into it, sir. The men are coming down by the painter."

By the time Almayer had clambered over into the stern sheets, four calashes were in the boat and the oars were being passed over the taffrail. The mate was looking on. Suddenly he said—

"Is it dangerous work? Do you want any help? I would come . . ."

"Yes, yes!" cried Almayer. "Come along. Don't lose a moment. Go and get your revolver. Hurry up! hurry up!"

Yet, notwithstanding his feverish anxiety to be off, he lolled back very quiet and unconcerned till the mate got in and, passing over the thwarts, sat down by his side. Then he seemed to wake up, and called out—

"Let go—let go the painter!"

"Let go the painter—the painter!" yelled the bowman, jerking at it.

People on board also shouted "Let go!" to one another, till it occurred at last to somebody to cast off the rope; and the boat drifted rapidly away from the schooner in the sudden silencing of all voices.

Almayer steered. The mate sat by his side, pushing the cartridges into the chambers of his revolver. When the weapon was loaded he asked—

"What is it? Are you after somebody?"

"Yes," said Almayer, curtly, with his eyes fixed ahead on the river. "We must catch a dangerous man."

"I like a bit of a chase myself," declared the mate, and then, discouraged by Almayer's aspect of severe thoughtfulness, said nothing more.

Nearly an hour passed. The calashes stretched forward head first and lay back with their faces to the sky, alternately, in a regular swing that sent the boat flying through the water; and the two sitters, very upright in the stern sheets, swayed rhythmically a little at every stroke of the long oars plied vigorously.

The mate observed: "The tide is with us."

"The current always runs down in this river," said Almayer.

"Yes—I know," retorted the other; "but it runs faster on the ebb. Look by the land at the way we get over the ground! A five-knot current here, I should say."

"H'm!" growled Almayer. Then suddenly: "There is a passage between two islands that will save us four miles. But at low water the two islands, in the dry season, are like one with only a mud ditch between them. Still, it's worth trying."

"Ticklish job that, on a falling tide," said the mate, coolly. "You know best whether there's time to get through."

"I will try," said Almayer, watching the shore intently. "Look out now!"

He tugged hard at the starboard yoke-line.

"Lay in your oars!" shouted the mate.

The boat swept round and shot through the narrow opening of a creek that broadened out before the craft had time to lose its way.

"Out oars! . . . Just room enough," muttered the mate.

It was a sombre creek of black water speckled with the gold of scattered sunlight falling through the boughs that met overhead in a soaring, restless arc full of gentle whispers passing, tremulous, aloft amongst the thick leaves. The creepers climbed up the trunks of serried trees that leaned over, looking insecure and undermined by floods which had eaten away the earth from under their roots. And the pungent, acrid smell of rotting leaves, of flowers, of blossoms and plants dying in that poisonous and cruel gloom, where they pined for sunshine in vain, seemed to lay heavy, to press upon the shiny and stagnant water in its tortuous windings amongst the everlasting and invincible shadows.

Almayer looked anxious. He steered badly. Several times the blades of the oars got foul of the bushes on one side or the other, checking the way of the gig. During one of those occurrences, while they were getting clear, one of the calashes said something to the others in a rapid whisper. They looked down at the water. So did the mate.

"Hallo!" he exclaimed. "Eh, Mr. Almayer! Look! The water is running out. See there! We will be caught."

"Back! back! We must go back!" cried Almayer.

"Perhaps better go on."

"No; back! back!"

He pulled at the steering line, and ran the nose of the boat into the bank. Time was lost again in getting clear.

"Give way, men! give way!" urged the mate, anxiously.

The men pulled with set lips and dilated nostrils, breathing hard.

"Too late," said the mate, suddenly. "The oars touch the bottom already. We are done."

The boat stuck. The men laid in the oars, and sat, panting, with crossed arms.

"Yes, we are caught," said Almayer, composedly. "That is unlucky!"

The water was falling round the boat. The mate watched the patches of mud coming to the surface. Then in a moment he laughed, and pointing his finger at the creek—

"Look!" he said; "the blamed river is running away from us. Here's the last drop of water clearing out round that bend."

Almayer lifted his head. The water was gone, and he looked only at a curved track of mud—of mud soft and black, hiding fever, rottenness, and evil under its level and glazed surface.

"We are in for it till the evening," he said, with cheerful resignation. "I did my best. Couldn't help it."

"We must sleep the day away," said the mate. "There's nothing to eat," he added, gloomily.

Almayer stretched himself in the stern sheets. The Malays curled down between thwarts.

"Well, I'm jiggered!" said the mate, starting up after a long pause. "I was in a devil of a hurry to go and pass the day stuck in the mud. Here's a holiday for you! Well! well!"

They slept or sat unmoving and patient. As the sun mounted higher the breeze died out, and perfect stillness reigned in the empty creek. A troop of long-nosed monkeys appeared, and crowding on the outer boughs, contemplated the boat and the motionless men in it with grave and sorrowful intensity, disturbed now and then by irrational outbreaks of mad gesticulation. A little bird with sapphire breast balanced a slender twig across a slanting beam of light, and flashed in it to and fro like a gem dropped from the sky. His minute round eye stared at the strange and tranquil creatures in the boat. After a while he sent out a thin twitter that sounded impertinent and funny in the solemn silence of the great wilderness; in the great silence full of struggle and death.

3

On Lingard's departure solitude and silence closed round Willems; the cruel solitude of one abandoned by men; the reproachful silence which surrounds an outcast ejected by his kind, the silence unbroken by the slightest whisper of hope; an immense and impenetrable silence that swallows up without echo the murmur of regret and the cry of revolt. The bitter peace of the abandoned clearings entered his heart, in which nothing could live now but the memory and hate of his past. Not remorse. In the breast of a man possessed by the masterful consciousness of his individuality with its desires and its rights; by the immovable conviction of his own importance, of an importance so indisputable and final that it clothes all his wishes, endeavours, and mistakes with the dignity of unavoidable fate, there could be no place for such a feeling as that of remorse.

The days passed. They passed unnoticed, unseen, in the rapid blaze of glaring sunrises, in the short glow of tender sunsets, in the crushing oppression of high noons without a cloud. How many days? Two—three—or more? He did not know. To him, since Lingard had gone, the time seemed to roll on in profound darkness. All was night within him. All was gone from his sight. He walked about blindly in the deserted courtyards, amongst the empty houses that, perched high on their posts, looked down inimically on him, a white stranger, a man from other lands; seemed to look hostile and mute out of all the memories of native life that lingered between their decaying walls. His wandering feet stumbled against the blackened brands of extinct fires, kicking up a light black dust of cold ashes that flew in drifting clouds and settled to leeward on the fresh grass sprouting from the hard ground, between the shade trees. He moved on, and on; ceaseless, unresting, in widening circles, in zigzagging paths that led to no issue; he struggled on wearily with a set, distressed face behind which, in his tired brain, seethed his thoughts: restless, sombre, tangled, chilling, horrible and venomous, like a nestful of snakes.

From afar, the bleared eyes of the old serving woman, the sombre gaze of Aissa followed the gaunt and tottering figure in its unceasing prowl along the fences, between the houses, amongst the wild luxuriance of riverside thickets. Those three human beings abandoned by all were like shipwrecked people left on an insecure and slippery ledge by the retiring tide of an angry sea—listening to its distant roar, living anguished between the menace of its return and the hopeless horror of their solitude—in the midst of a tempest of passion, of regret, of disgust, of despair. The breath of the storm had cast two of them there, robbed of everything—even of resignation. The third, the decrepit witness of their struggle and their torture, accepted her own dull conception of facts; of strength and youth gone; of her useless old age; of her last servitude; of being thrown away by her chief, by her nearest, to use up the last and worthless remnant of flickering life between those two incomprehensible and sombre outcasts: a shrivelled, an unmoved, a passive companion of their disaster.

To the river Willems turned his eyes like a captive that looks fixedly at the door of his cell. If there was any hope in the world it would come from the river, by the river. For hours together he would stand in sunlight while the sea breeze sweeping over the lonely reach fluttered his ragged garments; the keen salt breeze that made him shiver now and then under the flood of intense heat. He looked at the brown and sparkling solitude of the flowing water, of the water flowing ceaseless and free in a soft, cool murmur of ripples at his feet. The world seemed to end there. The forests of the other bank appeared unattainable, enigmatical, for ever beyond reach like the stars of heaven—and as indifferent. Above and below, the forests on his side of the river came down to the water in a serried multitude of tall, immense trees towering in a great spread of twisted boughs above the thick undergrowth; great, solid trees, looking sombre, severe, and malevolently stolid, like a giant crowd of pitiless enemies pressing round silently to witness his slow agony. He was alone, small, crushed. He thought of escape—of something to be done. What? A raft! He imagined himself working at it, feverishly, desperately; cutting down trees, fastening the logs together and then drifting down with the current, down to the sea into the straits. There were ships there—ships, help, white men. Men like himself. Good men who would rescue him, take him away, take him far away where there was trade, and houses, and other men that could understand him exactly, appreciate his capabilities; where there was proper food, and money; where there were beds, knives, forks, carriages, brass bands, cool drinks, churches with well-dressed people praying in them. He would pray also. The superior land of refined delights where he could sit on a chair, eat his tiffin off a white tablecloth, nod to fellows—good fellows; he would be popular; always was—where he could be virtuous, correct, do business, draw a salary, smoke cigars, buy things in shops—have boots . . . be happy, free, become rich. O God! What was wanted? Cut down a few trees. No! One would do. They used to make canoes by burning out a tree trunk, he had heard. Yes! One would do. One tree to cut down . . . He rushed forward, and suddenly stood still as if rooted in the ground. He had a pocket-knife.

And he would throw himself down on the ground by the riverside. He was tired, exhausted; as if that raft had been made, the voyage accomplished, the fortune attained. A glaze came over his staring eyes, over his eyes that gazed hopelessly at the rising river where big logs and uprooted trees drifted in the shine of mid-stream: a long procession of black and ragged specks. He could swim out and drift away on one of these trees. Anything to escape! Anything! Any risk! He could fasten himself up between the dead branches. He was torn by desire, by fear; his heart was wrung by the faltering of his courage. He turned over, face downwards, his head on his arms. He had a terrible vision of shadowless horizons where the blue sky and the blue sea met; or a circular and blazing emptiness where a dead tree and a dead man drifted together, endlessly, up and down, upon the brilliant undulations of the straits. No ships there. Only death. And the river led to it.

He sat up with a profound groan.

Yes, death. Why should he die? No! Better solitude, better hopeless waiting, alone. Alone. No! he was not alone, he saw death looking at him from everywhere; from the bushes, from the clouds—he heard her speaking to him in the murmur of the river, filling the space, touching his heart, his brain with a cold hand. He could see and think of nothing else. He saw it—the sure death—everywhere. He saw it so close that he was always on the point of throwing out his arms to keep it off. It poisoned all he saw, all he did; the miserable food he ate, the muddy water he drank; it gave a frightful aspect to sunrises and sunsets, to the brightness of hot noon, to the cooling shadows of the evenings. He saw the horrible form among the big trees, in the network of creepers in the fantastic outlines of leaves, of the great indented leaves that seemed to be so many enormous hands with big broad palms, with stiff fingers outspread to lay hold of him; hands gently stirring, or hands arrested in a frightful immobility, with a stillness attentive and watching for the opportunity to take him, to enlace him, to strangle him, to hold him till he died; hands that would hold him dead, that would never let go, that would cling to his body for ever till it perished—disappeared in their frantic and tenacious grasp.

And yet the world was full of life. All the things, all the men he knew, existed, moved, breathed; and he saw them in a long perspective, far off, diminished, distinct, desirable, unattainable, precious . . . lost for ever. Round him, ceaselessly, there went on without a sound the mad turmoil of tropical life. After he had died all this would remain! He wanted to clasp, to embrace solid things; he had an immense craving for sensations; for touching, pressing, seeing, handling, holding on, to all these things. All this would remain—remain for years, for ages, for ever. After he had miserably died there, all this would remain, would live, would exist in joyous sunlight, would breathe in the coolness of serene nights. What for, then? He would be dead. He would be stretched upon the warm moisture of the ground, feeling nothing, seeing nothing, knowing nothing; he would lie stiff, passive, rotting slowly; while over him, under him, through him—unopposed, busy, hurried—the endless and minute throngs of insects, little shining monsters of repulsive shapes, with horns, with claws, with pincers, would swarm in streams, in rushes, in eager struggle for his body; would swarm countless, persistent, ferocious and greedy—till there would remain nothing but the white gleam of bleaching bones in the long grass; in the long grass that would shoot its feathery heads between the bare and polished ribs. There would be that only left of him; nobody would miss him; no one would remember him.

Nonsense! It could not be. There were ways out of this. Somebody would turn up. Some human beings would come. He would speak, entreat—use force to extort help from them. He felt strong; he was very strong. He would . . . The discouragement, the conviction of the futility of his hopes would return in an acute sensation of pain in his heart. He would begin again his aimless wanderings. He tramped till he was ready to drop, without being able to calm by bodily fatigue the trouble of his soul. There was no rest, no peace within the cleared grounds of his prison. There was no relief but in the black release of sleep, of sleep without memory and without dreams; in the sleep coming brutal and heavy, like the lead that kills. To forget in annihilating sleep; to tumble headlong, as if stunned, out of daylight into the night of oblivion, was for him the only, the rare respite from this existence which he lacked the courage to endure—or to end.

He lived, he struggled with the inarticulate delirium of his thoughts under the eyes of the silent Aissa. She shared his torment in the poignant wonder, in the acute longing, in the despairing inability to understand the cause of his anger and of his repulsion; the hate of his looks; the mystery of his silence; the menace of his rare words—of those words in the speech of white people that were thrown at her with rage, with contempt, with the evident desire to hurt her; to hurt her who had given herself, her life—all she had to give—to that white man; to hurt her who had wanted to show him the way to true greatness, who had tried to help him, in her woman's dream of everlasting, enduring, unchangeable affection. From the short contact with the whites in the crashing collapse of her old life, there remained with her the imposing idea of irresistible power and of ruthless strength. She had found a man of their race—and with all their qualities. All whites are alike. But this man's heart was full of anger against his own people, full of anger existing there by the side of his desire of her. And to her it had been an intoxication of hope for great things born in the proud and tender consciousness of her influence. She had heard the passing whisper of wonder and fear in the presence of his hesitation, of his resistance, of his compromises; and yet with a woman's belief in the durable steadfastness of hearts, in the irresistible charm of her own personality, she had pushed him forward, trusting the future, blindly, hopefully; sure to attain by his side the ardent desire of her life, if she could only push him far beyond the possibility of retreat. She did not know, and could not conceive, anything of his—so exalted—ideals. She thought the man a warrior and a chief, ready for battle, violence, and treachery to his own people—for her. What more natural? Was he not a great, strong man? Those two, surrounded each by the impenetrable wall of their aspirations, were hopelessly alone, out of sight, out of earshot of each other; each the centre of dissimilar and distant horizons; standing each on a different earth, under a different sky. She remembered his words, his eyes, his trembling lips, his outstretched hands; she remembered the great, the immeasurable sweetness of her surrender, that beginning of her power which was to last until death. He remembered the quaysides and the warehouses; the excitement of a life in a whirl of silver coins; the glorious uncertainty of a money hunt; his numerous successes, the lost possibilities of wealth and consequent glory. She, a woman, was the victim of her heart, of her woman's belief that there is nothing in the world but love—the everlasting thing. He was the victim of his strange principles, of his continence, of his blind belief in himself, of his solemn veneration for the voice of his boundless ignorance.

In a moment of his idleness, of suspense, of discouragement, she had come—that creature—and by the touch of her hand had destroyed his future, his dignity of a clever and civilized man; had awakened in his breast the infamous thing which had driven him to what he had done, and to end miserably in the wilderness and be forgotten, or else remembered with hate or contempt. He dared not look at her, because now whenever he looked at her his thought seemed to touch crime, like an outstretched hand. She could only look at him—and at nothing else. What else was there? She followed him with a timorous gaze, with a gaze for ever expecting, patient, and entreating. And in her eyes there was the wonder and desolation of an animal that knows only suffering, of the incomplete soul that knows pain but knows not hope; that can find no refuge from the facts of life in the illusory conviction of its dignity, of an exalted destiny beyond; in the heavenly consolation of a belief in the momentous origin of its hate.

For the first three days after Lingard went away he would not even speak to her. She preferred his silence to the sound of hated and incomprehensible words he had been lately addressing to her with a wild violence of manner, passing at once into complete apathy. And during these three days he hardly ever left the river, as if on that muddy bank he had felt himself nearer to his freedom. He would stay late; he would stay till sunset; he would look at the glow of gold passing away amongst sombre clouds in a bright red flush, like a splash of warm blood. It seemed to him ominous and ghastly with a foreboding of violent death that beckoned him from everywhere—even from the sky.

One evening he remained by the riverside long after sunset, regardless of the night mist that had closed round him, had wrapped him up and clung to him like a wet winding-sheet. A slight shiver recalled him to his senses, and he walked up the courtyard towards his house.

Aissa rose from before the fire, that glimmered red through its own smoke, which hung thickening under the boughs of the big tree. She approached him from the side as he neared the plankway of the house. He saw her stop to let him begin his ascent. In the darkness her figure was like the shadow of a woman with clasped hands put out beseechingly. He stopped —could not help glancing at her. In all the sombre gracefulness of the straight figure, her limbs, features—all was indistinct and vague but the gleam of her eyes in the faint starlight. He turned his head away and moved on. He could feel her footsteps behind him on the bending planks, but he walked up without turning his head. He knew what she wanted. She wanted to come in there. He shuddered at the thought of what might happen in the impenetrable darkness of that house if they were to find themselves alone—even for a moment. He stopped in the doorway, and heard her say—

"Let me come in. Why this anger? Why this silence? . . . Let me watch . . . by your side. . . . Have I not watched faithfully? Did harm ever come to you when you closed your eyes while I was by? . . . I have waited . .. I have waited for your smile, for your words . . . I can wait no more.. . . Look at me . . . speak to me. Is there a bad spirit in you? A bad spirit that has eaten up your courage and your love? Let me touch you. Forget all . . . All. Forget the wicked hearts, the angry faces . . . and remember only the day I came to you . . . to you! O my heart! O my life!"

The pleading sadness of her appeal filled the space with the tremor of her low tones, that carried tenderness and tears into the great peace of the sleeping world. All around them the forests, the clearings, the river, covered by the silent veil of night, seemed to wake up and listen to her words in attentive stillness. After the sound of her voice had died out in a stifled sigh they appeared to listen yet; and nothing stirred among the shapeless shadows but the innumerable fireflies that twinkled in changing clusters, in gliding pairs, in wandering and solitary points—like the glimmering drift of scattered star-dust.

Willems turned round slowly, reluctantly, as if compelled by main force. Her face was hidden in her hands, and he looked above her bent head, into the sombre brilliance of the night. It was one of those nights that give the impression of extreme vastness, when the sky seems higher, when the passing puffs of tepid breeze seem to bring with them faint whispers from beyond the stars. The air was full of sweet scent, of the scent charming, penetrating and violent like the impulse of love. He looked into that great dark place odorous with the breath of life, with the mystery of existence, renewed, fecund, indestructible; and he felt afraid of his solitude, of the solitude of his body, of the loneliness of his soul in the presence of this unconscious and ardent struggle, of this lofty indifference, of this merciless and mysterious purpose, perpetuating strife and death through the march of ages. For the second time in his life he felt, in a sudden sense of his significance, the need to send a cry for help into the wilderness, and for the second time he realized the hopelessness of its unconcern. He could shout for help on every side—and nobody would answer. He could stretch out his hands, he could call for aid, for support, for sympathy, for relief—and nobody would come. Nobody. There was no one there—but that woman.

His heart was moved, softened with pity at his own abandonment. His anger against her, against her who was the cause of all his misfortunes, vanished before his extreme need for some kind of consolation. Perhaps—if he must resign himself to his fate—she might help him to forget. To forget! For a moment, in an access of despair so profound that it seemed like the beginning of peace, he planned the deliberate descent from his pedestal, the throwing away of his superiority, of all his hopes, of old ambitions, of the ungrateful civilization. For a moment, forgetfulness in her arms seemed possible; and lured by that possibility the semblance of renewed desire possessed his breast in a burst of reckless contempt for everything outside himself—in a savage disdain of Earth and of Heaven. He said to himself that he would not repent. The punishment for his only sin was too heavy. There was no mercy under Heaven. He did not want any. He thought, desperately, that if he could find with her again the madness of the past, the strange delirium that had changed him, that had worked his undoing, he would be ready to pay for it with an eternity of perdition. He was intoxicated by the subtle perfumes of the night; he was carried away by the suggestive stir of the warm breeze; he was possessed by the exaltation of the solitude, of the silence, of his memories, in the presence of that figure offering herself in a submissive and patient devotion; coming to him in the name of the past, in the name of those days when he could see nothing, think of nothing, desire nothing—but her embrace.

He took her suddenly in his arms, and she clasped her hands round his neck with a low cry of joy and surprise. He took her in his arms and waited for the transport, for the madness, for the sensations remembered and lost; and while she sobbed gently on his breast he held her and felt cold, sick, tired, exasperated with his failure—and ended by cursing himself. She clung to him trembling with the intensity of her happiness and her love. He heard her whispering—her face hidden on his shoulder—of past sorrow, of coming joy that would last for ever; of her unshaken belief in his love. She had always believed. Always! Even while his face was turned away from her in the dark days while his mind was wandering in his own land, amongst his own people. But it would never wander away from her any more, now it had come back. He would forget the cold faces and the hard hearts of the cruel people. What was there to remember? Nothing? Was it not so? . . .

He listened hopelessly to the faint murmur. He stood still and rigid, pressing her mechanically to his breast while he thought that there was nothing for him in the world. He was robbed of everything; robbed of his passion, of his liberty, of forgetfulness, of consolation. She, wild with delight, whispered on rapidly, of love, of light, of peace, of long years. . . . He looked drearily above her head down into the deeper gloom of the courtyard. And, all at once, it seemed to him that he was peering into a sombre hollow, into a deep black hole full of decay and of whitened bones; into an immense and inevitable grave full of corruption where sooner or later he must, unavoidably, fall.

In the morning he came out early, and stood for a time in the doorway, listening to the light breathing behind him—in the house. She slept. He had not closed his eyes through all that night. He stood swaying—then leaned against the lintel of the door. He was exhausted, done up; fancied himself hardly alive. He had a disgusted horror of himself that, as he looked at the level sea of mist at his feet, faded quickly into dull indifference. It was like a sudden and final decrepitude of his senses, of his body, of his thoughts. Standing on the high platform, he looked over the expanse of low night fog above which, here and there, stood out the feathery heads of tall bamboo clumps and the round tops of single trees, resembling small islets emerging black and solid from a ghostly and impalpable sea. Upon the faintly luminous background of the eastern sky, the sombre line of the great forests bounded that smooth sea of white vapours with an appearance of a fantastic and unattainable shore.

He looked without seeing anything—thinking of himself. Before his eyes the light of the rising sun burst above the forest with the suddenness of an explosion. He saw nothing. Then, after a time, he murmured with conviction—speaking half aloud to himself in the shock of the penetrating thought:

"I am a lost man."

He shook his hand above his head in a gesture careless and tragic, then walked down into the mist that closed above him in shining undulations under the first breath of the morning breeze.

4

Willems moved languidly towards the river, then retraced his steps to the tree and let himself fall on the seat under its shade. On the other side of the immense trunk he could hear the old woman moving about, sighing loudly, muttering to herself, snapping dry sticks, blowing up the fire. After a while a whiff of smoke drifted round to where he sat. It made him feel hungry, and that feeling was like a new indignity added to an intolerable load of humiliations. He felt inclined to cry. He felt very weak. He held up his arm before his eyes and watched for a little while the trembling of the lean limb. Skin and bone, by God! How thin he was! . . . He had suffered from fever a good deal, and now he thought with tearful dismay that Lingard, although he had sent him food—and what food, great Lord: a little rice and dried fish; quite unfit for a white man—had not sent him any medicine. Did the old savage think that he was like the wild beasts that are never ill? He wanted quinine.

He leaned the back of his head against the tree and closed his eyes. He thought feebly that if he could get hold of Lingard he would like to flay him alive; but it was only a blurred, a short and a passing thought. His imagination, exhausted by the repeated delineations of his own fate, had not enough strength left to grip the idea of revenge. He was not indignant and rebellious. He was cowed. He was cowed by the immense cataclysm of his disaster. Like most men, he had carried solemnly within his breast the whole universe, and the approaching end of all things in the destruction of his own personality filled him with paralyzing awe. Everything was toppling over. He blinked his eyes quickly, and it seemed to him that the very sunshine of the morning disclosed in its brightness a suggestion of some hidden and sinister meaning. In his unreasoning fear he tried to hide within himself. He drew his feet up, his head sank between his shoulders, his arms hugged his sides. Under the high and enormous tree soaring superbly out of the mist in a vigorous spread of lofty boughs, with a restless and eager flutter of its innumerable leaves in the clear sunshine, he remained motionless, huddled up on his seat: terrified and still.

Willems' gaze roamed over the ground, and then he watched with idiotic fixity half a dozen black ants entering courageously a tuft of long grass which, to them, must have appeared a dark and a dangerous jungle. Suddenly he thought: There must be something dead in there. Some dead insect. Death everywhere! He closed his eyes again in an access of trembling pain. Death everywhere—wherever one looks. He did not want to see the ants. He did not want to see anybody or anything. He sat in the darkness of his own making, reflecting bitterly that there was no peace for him. He heard voices now. . . . Illusion! Misery! Torment! Who would come? Who would speak to him? What business had he to hear voices? . . . yet he heard them faintly, from the river. Faintly, as if shouted far off over there, came the words "We come back soon." . . . Delirium and mockery! Who would come back? Nobody ever comes back! Fever comes back. He had it on him this morning. That was it. . . . He heard unexpectedly the old woman muttering something near by. She had come round to his side of the tree. He opened his eyes and saw her bent back before him. She stood, with her hand shading her eyes, looking towards the landing-place. Then she glided away. She had seen—and now she was going back to her cooking; a woman incurious; expecting nothing; without fear and without hope.

She had gone back behind the tree, and now Willems could see a human figure on the path to the landing-place. It appeared to him to be a woman, in a red gown, holding some heavy bundle in her arms; it was an apparition unexpected, familiar and odd. He cursed through his teeth . . . It had wanted only this! See things like that in broad daylight! He was very bad—very bad. . . . He was horribly scared at this awful symptom of the desperate state of his health.

This scare lasted for the space of a flash of lightning, and in the next moment it was revealed to him that the woman was real; that she was coming towards him; that she was his wife! He put his feet down to the ground quickly, but made no other movement. His eyes opened wide. He was so amazed that for a time he absolutely forgot his own existence. The only idea in his head was: Why on earth did she come here?

Joanna was coming up the courtyard with eager, hurried steps. She carried in her arms the child, wrapped up in one of Almayer's white blankets that she had snatched off the bed at the last moment, before leaving the house. She seemed to be dazed by the sun in her eyes; bewildered by her strange surroundings. She moved on, looking quickly right and left in impatient expectation of seeing her husband at any moment. Then, approaching the tree, she perceived suddenly a kind of a dried-up, yellow corpse, sitting very stiff on a bench in the shade and looking at her with big eyes that were alive. That was her husband.

She stopped dead short. They stared at one another in profound stillness, with astounded eyes, with eyes maddened by the memories of things far off that seemed lost in the lapse of time. Their looks crossed, passed each other, and appeared to dart at them through fantastic distances, to come straight from the incredible.

Looking at him steadily she came nearer, and deposited the blanket with the child in it on the bench. Little Louis, after howling with terror in the darkness of the river most of the night, now slept soundly and did not wake. Willems' eyes followed his wife, his head turning slowly after her. He accepted her presence there with a tired acquiescence in its fabulous improbability. Anything might happen. What did she come for? She was part of the general scheme of his misfortune. He half expected that she would rush at him, pull his hair, and scratch his face. Why not? Anything might happen! In an exaggerated sense of his great bodily weakness he felt somewhat apprehensive of possible assault. At any rate, she would scream at him. He knew her of old. She could screech. He had thought that he was rid of her for ever. She came now probably to see the end. . . .

Suddenly she turned, and embracing him slid gently to the ground.

This startled him. With her forehead on his knees she sobbed noiselessly. He looked down dismally at the top of her head. What was she up to? He had not the strength to move—to get away. He heard her whispering something, and bent over to listen. He caught the word "Forgive."

That was what she came for! All that way. Women are queer. Forgive. Not he! . . . All at once this thought darted through his brain: How did she come? In a boat. Boat! boat!

He shouted "Boat!" and jumped up, knocking her over. Before she had time to pick herself up he pounced upon her and was dragging her up by the shoulders. No sooner had she regained her feet than she clasped him tightly round the neck, covering his face, his eyes, his mouth, his nose with desperate kisses. He dodged his head about, shaking her arms, trying to keep her off, to speak, to ask her. . . . She came in a boat, boat, boat! . . . They struggled and swung round, tramping in a semicircle. He blurted out, "Leave off. Listen," while he tore at her hands. This meeting of lawful love and sincere joy resembled fight. Louis Willems slept peacefully under his blanket.

At last Willems managed to free himself, and held her off, pressing her arms down. He looked at her. He had half a suspicion that he was dreaming. Her lips trembled; her eyes wandered unsteadily, always coming back to his face. He saw her the same as ever, in his presence. She appeared startled, tremulous, ready to cry. She did not inspire him with confidence. He shouted—

"How did you come?"

She answered in hurried words, looking at him intently—

"In a big canoe with three men. I know everything. Lingard's away. I come to save you. I know. . . . Almayer told me."

"Canoe!—Almayer—Lies. Told you—You!" stammered Willems in a distracted manner. "Why you?—Told what?"

Words failed him. He stared at his wife, thinking with fear that she—stupid woman—had been made a tool in some plan of treachery . . . in some deadly plot.

She began to cry—

"Don't look at me like that, Peter. What have I done? I come to beg—to beg—forgiveness. . . . Save—Lingard—danger."

He trembled with impatience, with hope, with fear. She looked at him and sobbed out in a fresh outburst of grief—

"Oh! Peter. What's the matter?—Are you ill? . . . Oh! you look so ill . . ."

He shook her violently into a terrified and wondering silence.

"How dare you!—I am well—perfectly well. . . . Where's that boat? Will you tell me where that boat is—at last? The boat, I say . . . You! . . ."

"You hurt me," she moaned.

He let her go, and, mastering her terror, she stood quivering and looking at him with strange intensity. Then she made a movement forward, but he lifted his finger, and she restrained herself with a long sigh. He calmed down suddenly and surveyed her with cold criticism, with the same appearance as when, in the old days, he used to find fault with the household expenses. She found a kind of fearful delight in this abrupt return into the past, into her old subjection.

He stood outwardly collected now, and listened to her disconnected story. Her words seemed to fall round him with the distracting clatter of stunning hail. He caught the meaning here and there, and straightway would lose himself in a tremendous effort to shape out some intelligible theory of events. There was a boat. A boat. A big boat that could take him to sea if necessary. That much was clear. She brought it. Why did Almayer lie to her so? Was it a plan to decoy him into some ambush? Better that than hopeless solitude. She had money. The men were ready to go anywhere . . . she said.

He interrupted her—

"Where are they now?"

"They are coming directly," she answered, tearfully. "Directly. There are some fishing stakes near here—they said. They are coming directly."

Again she was talking and sobbing together. She wanted to be forgiven. Forgiven? What for? Ah! the scene in Macassar. As if he had time to think of that! What did he care what she had done months ago? He seemed to struggle in the toils of complicated dreams where everything was impossible, yet a matter of course, where the past took the aspects of the future and the present lay heavy on his heart—seemed to take him by the throat like the hand of an enemy. And while she begged, entreated, kissed his hands, wept on his shoulder, adjured him in the name of God, to forgive, to forget, to speak the word for which she longed, to look at his boy, to believe in her sorrow and in her devotion—his eyes, in the fascinated immobility of shining pupils, looked far away, far beyond her, beyond the river, beyond this land, through days, weeks, months; looked into liberty, into the future, into his triumph . . . into the great possibility of a startling revenge.

He felt a sudden desire to dance and shout. He shouted—

"After all, we shall meet again, Captain Lingard."

"Oh, no! No!" she cried, joining her hands.

He looked at her with surprise. He had forgotten she was there till the break of her cry in the monotonous tones of her prayer recalled him into that courtyard from the glorious turmoil of his dreams. It was very strange to see her there—near him. He felt almost affectionate towards her. After all, she came just in time. Then he thought: That other one. I must get away without a scene. Who knows; she may be dangerous! . . . And all at once he felt he hated Aissa with an immense hatred that seemed to choke him. He said to his wife—

"Wait a moment."

She, obedient, seemed to gulp down some words which wanted to come out. He muttered: "Stay here," and disappeared round the tree.

The water in the iron pan on the cooking fire boiled furiously, belching out volumes of white steam that mixed with the thin black thread of smoke. The old woman appeared to him through this as if in a fog, squatting on her heels, impassive and weird.

Willems came up near and asked, "Where is she?"

The woman did not even lift her head, but answered at once, readily, as though she had expected the question for a long time.

"While you were asleep under the tree, before the strange canoe came, she went out of the house. I saw her look at you and pass on with a great light in her eyes. A great light. And she went towards the place where our master Lakamba had his fruit trees. When we were many here. Many, many. Men with arms by their side. Many . . . men. And talk . . . and songs . . ."

She went on like that, raving gently to herself for a long time after Willems had left her.

Willems went back to his wife. He came up close to her and found he had nothing to say. Now all his faculties were concentrated upon his wish to avoid Aissa. She might stay all the morning in that grove. Why did those rascally boatmen go? He had a physical repugnance to set eyes on her. And somewhere, at the very bottom of his heart, there was a fear of her. Why? What could she do? Nothing on earth could stop him now. He felt strong, reckless, pitiless, and superior to everything. He wanted to preserve before his wife the lofty purity of his character. He thought: She does not know. Almayer held his tongue about Aissa. But if she finds out, I am lost. If it hadn't been for the boy I would . . . free of both of them. . . . The idea darted through his head. Not he! Married. . . . Swore solemnly. No . . . sacred tie. . . . Looking on his wife, he felt for the first time in his life something approaching remorse. Remorse, arising from his conception of the awful nature of an oath before the altar. . . . She mustn't find out. . . . Oh, for that boat! He must run in and get his revolver. Couldn't think of trusting himself unarmed with those Bajow fellows. Get it now while she is away. Oh, for that boat! . . . He dared not go to the river and hail. He thought: She might hear me. . . . I'll go and get . . . cartridges . . . then will be all ready . . . nothing else. No.

And while he stood meditating profoundly before he could make up his mind to run to the house, Joanna pleaded, holding to his arm—pleaded despairingly, broken-hearted, hopeless whenever she glanced up at his face, which to her seemed to wear the aspect of unforgiving rectitude, of virtuous severity, of merciless justice. And she pleaded humbly—abashed before him, before the unmoved appearance of the man she had wronged in defiance of human and divine laws. He heard not a word of what she said till she raised her voice in a final appeal—

". . . Don't you see I loved you always? They told me horrible things about you. . . . My own mother! They told me—you have been—you have been unfaithful to me, and I . . ."

"It's a damned lie!" shouted Willems, waking up for a moment into righteous indignation.

"I know! I know—Be generous.—Think of my misery since you went away—Oh! I could have torn my tongue out. . . . I will never believe anybody—Look at the boy—Be merciful—I could never rest till I found you. . . . Say—a word—one word. . ."

"What the devil do you want?" exclaimed Willems, looking towards the river. "Where's that damned boat? Why did you let them go away? You stupid!"

"Oh, Peter!—I know that in your heart you have forgiven me—You are so generous—I want to hear you say so. . . . Tell me—do you?"

"Yes! yes!" said Willems, impatiently. "I forgive you. Don't be a fool."

"Don't go away. Don't leave me alone here. Where is the danger? I am so frightened. . . . Are you alone here? Sure? . . . Let us go away!"

"That's sense," said Willems, still looking anxiously towards the river.

She sobbed gently, leaning on his arm.

"Let me go," he said.

He had seen above the steep bank the heads of three men glide along smoothly. Then, where the shore shelved down to the landing-place, appeared a big canoe which came slowly to land.

"Here they are," he went on, briskly. "I must get my revolver."

He made a few hurried paces towards the house, but seemed to catch sight of something, turned short round and came back to his wife. She stared at him, alarmed by the sudden change in his face. He appeared much discomposed. He stammered a little as he began to speak.

"Take the child. Walk down to the boat and tell them to drop it out of sight, quick, behind the bushes. Do you hear? Quick! I will come to you there directly. Hurry up!"

"Peter! What is it? I won't leave you. There is some danger in this horrible place."

"Will you do what I tell you?" said Willems, in an irritable whisper.

"No! no! no! I won't leave you. I will not lose you again. Tell me, what is it?"

From beyond the house came a faint voice singing. Willems shook his wife by the shoulder.

"Do what I tell you! Run at once!"

She gripped his arm and clung to him desperately. He looked up to heaven as if taking it to witness of that woman's infernal folly.

The song grew louder, then ceased suddenly, and Aissa appeared in sight, walking slowly, her hands full of flowers.

She had turned the corner of the house, coming out into the full sunshine, and the light seemed to leap upon her in a stream brilliant, tender, and caressing, as if attracted by the radiant happiness of her face. She had dressed herself for a festive day, for the memorable day of his return to her, of his return to an affection that would last for ever. The rays of the morning sun were caught by the oval clasp of the embroidered belt that held the silk sarong round her waist. The dazzling white stuff of her body jacket was crossed by a bar of yellow and silver of her scarf, and in the black hair twisted high on her small head shone the round balls of gold pins amongst crimson blossoms and white star-shaped flowers, with which she had crowned herself to charm his eyes; those eyes that were henceforth to see nothing in the world but her own resplendent image. And she moved slowly, bending her face over the mass of pure white champakas and jasmine pressed to her breast, in a dreamy intoxication of sweet scents and of sweeter hopes.

She did not seem to see anything, stopped for a moment at the foot of the plankway leading to the house, then, leaving her high-heeled wooden sandals there, ascended the planks in a light run; straight, graceful, flexible, and noiseless, as if she had soared up to the door on invisible wings. Willems pushed his wife roughly behind the tree, and made up his mind quickly for a rush to the house, to grab his revolver and . . . Thoughts, doubts, expedients seemed to boil in his brain. He had a flashing vision of delivering a stunning blow, of tying up that flower bedecked woman in the dark house—a vision of things done swiftly with enraged haste—to save his prestige, his superiority—something of immense importance. . . . He had not made two steps when Joanna bounded after him, caught the back of his ragged jacket, tore out a big piece, and instantly hooked herself with both hands to the collar, nearly dragging him down on his back. Although taken by surprise, he managed to keep his feet. From behind she panted into his ear—

"That woman! Who's that woman? Ah! that's what those boatmen were talking about. I heard them . . . heard them . . . heard . . . in the night. They spoke about some woman. I dared not understand. I would not ask . . . listen . . . believe! How could I? Then it's true. No. Say no. . . . Who's that woman?"

He swayed, tugging forward. She jerked at him till the button gave way, and then he slipped half out of his jacket and, turning round, remained strangely motionless. His heart seemed to beat in his throat. He choked—tried to speak—could not find any words. He thought with fury: I will kill both of them.

For a second nothing moved about the courtyard in the great vivid clearness of the day. Only down by the landing-place a waringan-tree, all in a blaze of clustering red berries, seemed alive with the stir of little birds that filled with the feverish flutter of their feathers the tangle of overloaded branches. Suddenly the variegated flock rose spinning in a soft whirr and dispersed, slashing the sunlit haze with the sharp outlines of stiffened wings. Mahmat and one of his brothers appeared coming up from the landing-place, their lances in their hands, to look for their passengers.

Aissa coming now empty-handed out of the house, caught sight of the two armed men. In her surprise she emitted a faint cry, vanished back and in a flash reappeared in the doorway with Willems' revolver in her hand. To her the presence of any man there could only have an ominous meaning. There was nothing in the outer world but enemies. She and the man she loved were alone, with nothing round them but menacing dangers. She did not mind that, for if death came, no matter from what hand, they would die together.

Her resolute eyes took in the courtyard in a circular glance. She noticed that the two strangers had ceased to advance and now were standing close together leaning on the polished shafts of their weapons. The next moment she saw Willems, with his back towards her, apparently struggling under the tree with some one. She saw nothing distinctly, and, unhesitating, flew down the plankway calling out: "I come!"

He heard her cry, and with an unexpected rush drove his wife backwards to the seat. She fell on it; he jerked himself altogether out of his jacket, and she covered her face with the soiled rags. He put his lips close to her, asking—

"For the last time, will you take the child and go?"

She groaned behind the unclean ruins of his upper garment. She mumbled something. He bent lower to hear. She was saying—

"I won't. Order that woman away. I can't look at her!"

"You fool!"

He seemed to spit the words at her, then, making up his mind, spun round to face Aissa. She was coming towards them slowly now, with a look of unbounded amazement on her face. Then she stopped and stared at him—who stood there, stripped to the waist, bareheaded and sombre.

Some way off, Mahmat and his brother exchanged rapid words in calm undertones. . . . This was the strong daughter of the holy man who had died. The white man is very tall. There would be three women and the child to take in the boat, besides that white man who had the money . . . . The brother went away back to the boat, and Mahmat remained looking on. He stood like a sentinel, the leaf-shaped blade of his lance glinting above his head.

Willems spoke suddenly.

"Give me this," he said, stretching his hand towards the revolver.

Aissa stepped back. Her lips trembled. She said very low: "Your people?"

He nodded slightly. She shook her head thoughtfully, and a few delicate petals of the flowers dying in her hair fell like big drops of crimson and white at her feet.

"Did you know?" she whispered.

"No!" said Willems. "They sent for me."

"Tell them to depart. They are accursed. What is there between them and you—and you who carry my life in your heart!"

Willems said nothing. He stood before her looking down on the ground and repeating to himself: I must get that revolver away from her, at once, at once. I can't think of trusting myself with those men without firearms. I must have it.

She asked, after gazing in silence at Joanna, who was sobbing gently—

"Who is she?"

"My wife," answered Willems, without looking up. "My wife according to our white law, which comes from God!"

"Your law! Your God!" murmured Aissa, contemptuously.

"Give me this revolver," said Willems, in a peremptory tone. He felt an unwillingness to close with her, to get it by force.

She took no notice and went on—

"Your law . . . or your lies? What am I to believe? I came—I ran to defend you when I saw the strange men. You lied to me with your lips, with your eyes. You crooked heart! . . . Ah!" she added, after an abrupt pause. "She is the first! Am I then to be a slave?"

"You may be what you like," said Willems, brutally. "I am going."

Her gaze was fastened on the blanket under which she had detected a slight movement. She made a long stride towards it. Willems turned half round. His legs seemed to him to be made of lead. He felt faint and so weak that, for a moment, the fear of dying there where he stood, before he could escape from sin and disaster, passed through his mind in a wave of despair.

She lifted up one corner of the blanket, and when she saw the sleeping child a sudden quick shudder shook her as though she had seen something inexpressibly horrible. She looked at Louis Willems with eyes fixed in an unbelieving and terrified stare. Then her fingers opened slowly, and a shadow seemed to settle on her face as if something obscure and fatal had come between her and the sunshine. She stood looking down, absorbed, as though she had watched at the bottom of a gloomy abyss the mournful procession of her thoughts.

Willems did not move. All his faculties were concentrated upon the idea of his release. And it was only then that the assurance of it came to him with such force that he seemed to hear a loud voice shouting in the heavens that all was over, that in another five, ten minutes, he would step into another existence; that all this, the woman, the madness, the sin, the regrets, all would go, rush into the past, disappear, become as dust, as smoke, as drifting clouds—as nothing! Yes! All would vanish in the unappeasable past which would swallow up all—even the very memory of his temptation and of his downfall. Nothing mattered. He cared for nothing. He had forgotten Aissa, his wife, Lingard, Hudig—everybody, in the rapid vision of his hopeful future.

After a while he heard Aissa saying—

"A child! A child! What have I done to be made to devour this sorrow and this grief? And while your man-child and the mother lived you told me there was nothing for you to remember in the land from which you came! And I thought you could be mine. I thought that I would . . ."

Her voice ceased in a broken murmur, and with it, in her heart, seemed to die the greater and most precious hope of her new life.

She had hoped that in the future the frail arms of a child would bind their two lives together in a bond which nothing on earth could break, a bond of affection, of gratitude, of tender respect. She the first—the only one! But in the instant she saw the son of that other woman she felt herself removed into the cold, the darkness, the silence of a solitude impenetrable and immense—very far from him, beyond the possibility of any hope, into an infinity of wrongs without any redress.

She strode nearer to Joanna. She felt towards that woman anger, envy, jealousy. Before her she felt humiliated and enraged. She seized the hanging sleeve of the jacket in which Joanna was hiding her face and tore it out of her hands, exclaiming loudly—

"Let me see the face of her before whom I am only a servant and a slave. Ya-wa! I see you!"

Her unexpected shout seemed to fill the sunlit space of cleared grounds, rise high and run on far into the land over the unstirring tree-tops of the forests. She stood in sudden stillness, looking at Joanna with surprised contempt.

"A Sirani woman!" she said, slowly, in a tone of wonder.

Joanna rushed at Willems—clung to him, shrieking: "Defend me, Peter! Defend me from that woman!"

"Be quiet. There is no danger," muttered Willems, thickly.

Aissa looked at them with scorn. "God is great! I sit in the dust at your feet," she exclaimed jeeringly, joining her hands above her head in a gesture of mock humility. "Before you I am as nothing." She turned to Willems fiercely, opening her arms wide. "What have you made of me?" she cried, "you lying child of an accursed mother! What have you made of me? The slave of a slave. Don't speak! Your words are worse than the poison of snakes. A Sirani woman. A woman of a people despised by all."

She pointed her finger at Joanna, stepped back, and began to laugh.

"Make her stop, Peter!" screamed Joanna. "That heathen woman. Heathen! Heathen! Beat her, Peter."

Willems caught sight of the revolver which Aissa had laid on the seat near the child. He spoke in Dutch to his wife, without moving his head.

"Snatch the boy—and my revolver there. See. Run to the boat. I will keep her back. Now's the time."

Aissa came nearer. She stared at Joanna, while between the short gusts of broken laughter she raved, fumbling distractedly at the buckle of her belt.

"To her! To her—the mother of him who will speak of your wisdom, of your courage. All to her. I have nothing. Nothing. Take, take."

She tore the belt off and threw it at Joanna's feet. She flung down with haste the armlets, the gold pins, the flowers; and the long hair, released, fell scattered over her shoulders, framing in its blackness the wild exaltation of her face.

"Drive her off, Peter. Drive off the heathen savage," persisted Joanna. She seemed to have lost her head altogether. She stamped, clinging to Willems' arm with both her hands.

"Look," cried Aissa. "Look at the mother of your son! She is afraid. Why does she not go from before my face? Look at her. She is ugly."

Joanna seemed to understand the scornful tone of the words. As Aissa stepped back again nearer to the tree she let go her husband's arm, rushed at her madly, slapped her face, then, swerving round, darted at the child who, unnoticed, had been wailing for some time, and, snatching him up, flew down to the waterside, sending shriek after shriek in an access of insane terror.

Willems made for the revolver. Aissa passed swiftly, giving him an unexpected push that sent him staggering away from the tree. She caught up the weapon, put it behind her back, and cried—

"You shall not have it. Go after her. Go to meet danger. . . . Go to meet death. . . . Go unarmed. . . . Go with empty hands and sweet words . . . as you came to me. . . . Go helpless and lie to the forests, to the sea . . . to the death that waits for you. . . ."

She ceased as if strangled. She saw in the horror of the passing seconds the half-naked, wild-looking man before her; she heard the faint shrillness of Joanna's insane shrieks for help somewhere down by the riverside. The sunlight streamed on her, on him, on the mute land, on the murmuring river—the gentle brilliance of a serene morning that, to her, seemed traversed by ghastly flashes of uncertain darkness. Hate filled the world, filled the space between them—the hate of race, the hate of hopeless diversity, the hate of blood; the hate against the man born in the land of lies and of evil from which nothing but misfortune comes to those who are not white. And as she stood, maddened, she heard a whisper near her, the whisper of the dead Omar's voice saying in her ear: "Kill! Kill!"

She cried, seeing him move—

"Do not come near me . . . or you die now! Go while I remember yet . . . remember. . . ."

Willems pulled himself together for a struggle. He dared not go unarmed. He made a long stride, and saw her raise the revolver. He noticed that she had not cocked it, and said to himself that, even if she did fire, she would surely miss. Go too high; it was a stiff trigger. He made a step nearer—saw the long barrel moving unsteadily at the end of her extended arm. He thought: This is my time . . . He bent his knees slightly, throwing his body forward, and took off with a long bound for a tearing rush.

He saw a burst of red flame before his eyes, and was deafened by a report that seemed to him louder than a clap of thunder. Something stopped him short, and he stood aspiring in his nostrils the acrid smell of the blue smoke that drifted from before his eyes like an immense cloud. . . . Missed, by Heaven! . . . Thought so! . . . And he saw her very far off, throwing her arms up, while the revolver, very small, lay on the ground between them. . . . Missed! . . . He would go and pick it up now. Never before did he understand, as in that second, the joy, the triumphant delight of sunshine and of life. His mouth was full of something salt and warm. He tried to cough; spat out. . . . Who shrieks: In the name of God, he dies!—he dies!—Who dies?—Must pick up—Night!—What? . . . Night already. . . .

Many years afterwards Almayer was telling the story of the great revolution in Sambir to a chance visitor from Europe. He was a Roumanian, half naturalist, half orchid-hunter for commercial purposes, who used to declare to everybody, in the first five minutes of acquaintance, his intention of writing a scientific book about tropical countries. On his way to the interior he had quartered himself upon Almayer. He was a man of some education, but he drank his gin neat, or only, at most, would squeeze the juice of half a small lime into the raw spirit. He said it was good for his health, and, with that medicine before him, he would describe to the surprised Almayer the wonders of European capitals; while Almayer, in exchange, bored him by expounding, with gusto, his unfavourable opinions of Sambir's social and political life. They talked far into the night, across the deal table on the verandah, while, between them, clear-winged, small, and flabby insects, dissatisfied with moonlight, streamed in and perished in thousands round the smoky light of the evil-smelling lamp.

Almayer, his face flushed, was saying—

"Of course, I did not see that. I told you I was stuck in the creek on account of father's—Captain Lingard's—susceptible temper. I am sure I did it all for the best in trying to facilitate the fellow's escape; but Captain Lingard was that kind of man—you know—one couldn't argue with. Just before sunset the water was high enough, and we got out of the creek. We got to Lakamba's clearing about dark. All very quiet; I thought they were gone, of course, and felt very glad. We walked up the courtyard—saw a big heap of something lying in the middle. Out of that she rose and rushed at us. By God. . . . You know those stories of faithful dogs watching their masters' corpses . . . don't let anybody approach . . . got to beat them off —and all that. . . . Well, 'pon my word we had to beat her off. Had to! She was like a fury. Wouldn't let us touch him. Dead—of course. Should think so. Shot through the lung, on the left side, rather high up, and at pretty close quarters too, for the two holes were small. Bullet came out through the shoulder-blade. After we had overpowered her—you can't imagine how strong that woman was; it took three of us—we got the body into the boat and shoved off. We thought she had fainted then, but she got up and rushed into the water after us. Well, I let her clamber in. What could I do? The river's full of alligators. I will never forget that pull up-stream in the night as long as I live. She sat in the bottom of the boat, holding his head in her lap, and now and again wiping his face with her hair. There was a lot of blood dried about his mouth and chin. And for all the six hours of that journey she kept on whispering tenderly to that corpse! . . . I had the mate of the schooner with me. The man said afterwards that he wouldn't go through it again—not for a handful of diamonds. And I believed him—I did. It makes me shiver. Do you think he heard? No! I mean somebody—something—heard? . . ."

"I am a materialist," declared the man of science, tilting the bottle shakily over the emptied glass.

Almayer shook his head and went on—

"Nobody saw how it really happened but that man Mahmat. He always said that he was no further off from them than two lengths of his lance. It appears the two women rowed each other while that Willems stood between them. Then Mahmat says that when Joanna struck her and ran off, the other two seemed to become suddenly mad together. They rushed here and there. Mahmat says—those were his very words: 'I saw her standing holding the pistol that fires many times and pointing it all over the campong. I was afraid—lest she might shoot me, and jumped on one side. Then I saw the white man coming at her swiftly. He came like our master the tiger when he rushes out of the jungle at the spears held by men. She did not take aim. The barrel of her weapon went like this—from side to side, but in her eyes I could see suddenly a great fear. There was only one shot. She shrieked while the white man stood blinking his eyes and very straight, till you could count slowly one, two, three; then he coughed and fell on his face. The daughter of Omar shrieked without drawing breath, till he fell. I went away then and left silence behind me. These things did not concern me, and in my boat there was that other woman who had promised me money. We left directly, paying no attention to her cries. We are only poor men—and had but a small reward for our trouble!' That's what Mahmat said. Never varied. You ask him yourself. He's the man you hired the boats from, for your journey up the river."

"The most rapacious thief I ever met!" exclaimed the traveller, thickly.

"Ah! He is a respectable man. His two brothers got themselves speared—served them right. They went in for robbing Dyak graves. Gold ornaments in them you know. Serve them right. But he kept respectable and got on. Aye! Everybody got on—but I. And all through that scoundrel who brought the Arabs here."

"De mortuis nil ni . . . num," muttered Almayer's guest.

"I wish you would speak English instead of jabbering in your own language, which no one can understand," said Almayer, sulkily.

"Don't be angry," hiccoughed the other. "It's Latin, and it's wisdom. It means: Don't waste your breath in abusing shadows. No offence there. I like you. You have a quarrel with Providence—so have I. I was meant to be a professor, while—look."

His head nodded. He sat grasping the glass. Almayer walked up and down, then stopped suddenly.

"Yes, they all got on but I. Why? I am better than any of them. Lakamba calls himself a Sultan, and when I go to see him on business sends that one-eyed fiend of his—Babalatchi—to tell me that the ruler is asleep; and shall sleep for a long time. And that Babalatchi! He is the Shahbandar of the State—if you please. Oh Lord! Shahbandar! The pig! A vagabond I wouldn't let come up these steps when he first came here. . . . Look at Abdulla now. He lives here because—he says—here he is away from white men. But he has hundreds of thousands. Has a house in Penang. Ships. What did he not have when he stole my trade from me! He knocked everything here into a cocked hat, drove father to gold-hunting—then to Europe, where he disappeared. Fancy a man like Captain Lingard disappearing as though he had been a common coolie. Friends of mine wrote to London asking about him. Nobody ever heard of him there! Fancy! Never heard of Captain Lingard!"

The learned gatherer of orchids lifted his head.

"He was a sen—sentimen—tal old buc—buccaneer," he stammered out, "I like him. I'm sent—tal myself."

He winked slowly at Almayer, who laughed.

"Yes! I told you about that gravestone. Yes! Another hundred and twenty dollars thrown away. Wish I had them now. He would do it. And the inscription. Ha! ha! ha! 'Peter Willems, Delivered by the Mercy of God from his Enemy.' What enemy—unless Captain Lingard himself? And then it has no sense. He was a great man—father was—but strange in many ways. . . . You haven't seen the grave? On the top of that hill, there, on the other side of the river. I must show you. We will go there."

"Not I!" said the other. "No interest—in the sun—too tiring. . . . Unless you carry me there."

As a matter of fact he was carried there a few months afterwards, and his was the second white man's grave in Sambir; but at present he was alive if rather drunk. He asked abruptly—

"And the woman?"

"Oh! Lingard, of course, kept her and her ugly brat in Macassar. Sinful waste of money—that! Devil only knows what became of them since father went home. I had my daughter to look after. I shall give you a word to Mrs. Vinck in Singapore when you go back. You shall see my Nina there. Lucky man. She is beautiful, and I hear so accomplished, so . . ."

"I have heard already twenty . . . a hundred times about your daughter. What ab—about —that—that other one, Ai—ssa?"

"She! Oh! we kept her here. She was mad for a long time in a quiet sort of way. Father thought a lot of her. He gave her a house to live in, in my campong. She wandered about, speaking to nobody unless she caught sight of Abdulla, when she would have a fit of fury, and shriek and curse like anything. Very often she would disappear—and then we all had to turn out and hunt for her, because father would worry till she was brought back. Found her in all kinds of places. Once in the abandoned campong of Lakamba. Sometimes simply wandering in the bush. She had one favourite spot we always made for at first. It was ten to one on finding her there—a kind of a grassy glade on the banks of a small brook. Why she preferred that place, I can't imagine! And such a job to get her away from there. Had to drag her away by main force. Then, as the time passed, she became quieter and more settled, like. Still, all my people feared her greatly. It was my Nina that tamed her. You see the child was naturally fearless and used to have her own way, so she would go to her and pull at her sarong, and order her about, as she did everybody. Finally she, I verily believe, came to love the child. Nothing could resist that little one—you know. She made a capital nurse. Once when the little devil ran away from me and fell into the river off the end of the jetty, she jumped in and pulled her out in no time. I very nearly died of fright. Now of course she lives with my serving girls, but does what she likes. As long as I have a handful of rice or a piece of cotton in the store she sha'n't want for anything. You have seen her. She brought in the dinner with Ali."

"What! That doubled-up crone?"

"Ah!" said Almayer. "They age quickly here. And long foggy nights spent in the bush will soon break the strongest backs—as you will find out yourself soon."

"Dis . . . disgusting," growled the traveller.

He dozed off. Almayer stood by the balustrade looking out at the bluish sheen of the moonlit night. The forests, unchanged and sombre, seemed to hang over the water, listening to the unceasing whisper of the great river; and above their dark wall the hill on which Lingard had buried the body of his late prisoner rose in a black, rounded mass, upon the silver paleness of the sky. Almayer looked for a long time at the clean-cut outline of the summit, as if trying to make out through darkness and distance the shape of that expensive tombstone. When he turned round at last he saw his guest sleeping, his arms on the table, his head on his arms.

"Now, look here!" he shouted, slapping the table with the palm of his hand.

The naturalist woke up, and sat all in a heap, staring owlishly.

"Here!" went on Almayer, speaking very loud and thumping the table, "I want to know. You, who say you have read all the books, just tell me . . . why such infernal things are ever allowed. Here I am! Done harm to nobody, lived an honest life . . . and a scoundrel like that is born in Rotterdam or some such place at the other end of the world somewhere, travels out here, robs his employer, runs away from his wife, and ruins me and my Nina—he ruined me, I tell you—and gets himself shot at last by a poor miserable savage, that knows nothing at all about him really. Where's the sense of all this? Where's your Providence? Where's the good for anybody in all this? The world's a swindle! A swindle! Why should I suffer? What have I done to be treated so?"

He howled out his string of questions, and suddenly became silent. The man who ought to have been a professor made a tremendous effort to articulate distinctly—

"My dear fellow, don't—don't you see that the ba-bare fac—the fact of your existence is off—offensive. . . . I—I like you—like . . ."

He fell forward on the table, and ended his remarks by an unexpected and prolonged snore.

Almayer shrugged his shoulders and walked back to the balustrade.

He drank his own trade gin very seldom, but when he did, a ridiculously small quantity of the stuff could induce him to assume a rebellious attitude towards the scheme of the universe. And now, throwing his body over the rail, he shouted impudently into the night, turning his face towards that far-off and invisible slab of imported granite upon which Lingard had thought fit to record God's mercy and Willems' escape.

"Father was wrong—wrong!" he yelled. "I want you to smart for it. You must smart for it! Where are you, Willems? Hey? . . . Hey? . . . Where there is no mercy for you—I hope!"

"Hope," repeated in a whispering echo the startled forests, the river and the hills; and Almayer, who stood waiting, with a smile of tipsy attention on his lips, heard no other answer.

A SMILE OF FORTUNE

A SMILE OF FORTUNE

HARBOUR STORY

Ever since the sun rose I had been looking ahead. The ship glided gently in smooth water. After a sixty days' passage I was anxious to make my landfall, a fertile and beautiful island of the tropics. The more enthusiastic of its inhabitants delight in describing it as the "Pearl of the Ocean." Well, let us call it the "Pearl." It's a good name. A pearl distilling much sweetness upon the world.

This is only a way of telling you that first-rate sugar-cane is grown there. All the population of the Pearl lives for it and by it. Sugar is their daily bread, as it were. And I was coming to them for a cargo of sugar in the hope of the crop having been good and of the freights being high.

Mr. Burns, my chief mate, made out the land first; and very soon I became entranced by this blue, pinnacled apparition, almost transparent against the light of the sky, a mere emanation, the astral body of an island risen to greet me from afar. It is a rare phenomenon, such a sight of the Pearl at sixty miles off. And I wondered half seriously whether it was a good omen, whether what would meet me in that island would be as luckily exceptional as this beautiful, dreamlike vision so very few seamen have been privileged to behold.

But horrid thoughts of business interfered with my enjoyment of an accomplished passage. I was anxious for success and I wished, too, to do justice to the flattering latitude of my owners' instructions contained in one noble phrase: "We leave it to you to do the best you can with the ship." . . . All the world being thus given me for a stage, my abilities appeared to me no bigger than a pinhead.

Meantime the wind dropped, and Mr. Burns began to make disagreeable remarks about my usual bad luck. I believe it was his devotion for me which made him critically outspoken on every occasion. All the same, I would not have put up with his humours if it had not been my lot at one time to nurse him through a desperate illness at sea. After snatching him out of the jaws of death, so to speak, it would have been absurd to throw away such an efficient officer. But sometimes I wished he would dismiss himself.

We were late in closing in with the land, and had to anchor outside the harbour till next day. An unpleasant and unrestful night followed. In this roadstead, strange to us both,

Burns and I remained on deck almost all the time. Clouds swirled down the porphyry crags under which we lay. The rising wind made a great bullying noise amongst the naked spars, with interludes of sad moaning. I remarked that we had been in luck to fetch the anchorage before dark. It would have been a nasty, anxious night to hang off a harbour under canvas. But my chief mate was uncompromising in his attitude.

"Luck, you call it, sir! Ay—our usual luck. The sort of luck to thank God it's no worse!"

And so he fretted through the dark hours, while I drew on my fund of philosophy. Ah, but it was an exasperating, weary, endless night, to be lying at anchor close under that black coast! The agitated water made snarling sounds all round the ship. At times a wild gust of wind out of a gully high up on the cliffs struck on our rigging a harsh and plaintive note like the wail of a forsaken soul.

I

BY HALF-PAST seven in the morning, the ship being then inside the harbour at last and moored within a long stone's-throw from the quay, my stock of philosophy was nearly exhausted. I was dressing hurriedly in my cabin when the steward came tripping in with a morning suit over his arm.

Hungry, tired, and depressed, with my head engaged inside a white shirt irritatingly stuck together by too much starch, I desired him peevishly to "heave round with that breakfast." I wanted to get ashore as soon as possible.

"Yes, sir. Ready at eight, sir. There's a gentleman from the shore waiting to speak to you, sir."

This statement was curiously slurred over. I dragged the shirt violently over my head and emerged staring.

"So early!" I cried. "Who's he? What does he want?"

On coming in from sea one has to pick up the conditions of an utterly unrelated existence. Every little event at first has the peculiar emphasis of novelty. I was greatly surprised by that early caller; but there was no reason for my steward to look so particularly foolish.

"Didn't you ask for the name?" I inquired in a stern tone.

"His name's Jacobus, I believe," he mumbled shamefacedly.

"Mr. Jacobus!" I exclaimed loudly, more surprised than ever, but with a total change of feeling. "Why couldn't you say so at once?"

But the fellow had scuttled out of my room. Through the momentarily opened door I had a glimpse of a tall, stout man standing in the cuddy by the table on which the cloth was already laid; a "harbour" table-cloth, stainless and dazzlingly white. So far good.

I shouted courteously through the closed door, that I was dressing and would be with him in a moment. In return the assurance that there was no hurry reached me in the visitor's deep, quiet undertone. His time was my own. He dared say I would give him a cup of coffee presently.

"I am afraid you will have a poor breakfast," I cried apologetically. "We have been sixty-one days at sea, you know."

A quiet little laugh, with a "That'll be all right, Captain," was his answer. All this, words, intonation, the glimpsed attitude of the man in the cuddy, had an unexpected character, a something friendly in it—propitiatory. And my surprise was not diminished thereby. What did this call mean? Was it the sign of some dark design against my commercial innocence?

Ah! These commercial interests—spoiling the finest life under the sun. Why must the sea be used for trade—and for war as well? Why kill and traffic on it, pursuing selfish aims of no great importance after all? It would have been so much nicer just to sail about with here and there a port and a bit of land to stretch one's legs on, buy a few books and get a change of cooking for a while. But, living in a world more or less homicidal and desperately mercantile, it was plainly my duty to make the best of its opportunities.

My owners' letter had left it to me, as I have said before, to do my best for the ship, according to my own judgment. But it contained also a postscript worded somewhat as follows:

"Without meaning to interfere with your liberty of action we are writing by the outgoing mail to some of our business friends there who may be of assistance to you. We desire you particularly to call on Mr. Jacobus, a prominent merchant and charterer. Should you hit it off with him he may be able to put you in the way of profitable employment for the ship."

Hit it off! Here was the prominent creature absolutely on board asking for the favour of a cup of coffee! And life not being a fairy-tale the improbability of the event almost shocked me. Had I discovered an enchanted nook of the earth where wealthy merchants rush fasting on board ships before they are fairly moored? Was this white magic or merely some black trick of trade? I came in the end (while making the bow of my tie) to suspect that perhaps I did not get the name right. I had been thinking of the prominent Mr. Jacobus pretty frequently during the passage and my hearing might have been deceived by some remote similarity of sound... The steward might have said Antrobus—or maybe Jackson.

But coming out of my stateroom with an interrogative "Mr. Jacobus?" I was met by a quiet "Yes," uttered with a gentle smile. The "yes" was rather perfunctory. He did not seem to make much of the fact that he was Mr. Jacobus. I took stock of a big, pale face, hair thin on the top, whiskers also thin, of a faded nondescript colour, heavy eyelids. The thick, smooth lips in repose looked as if glued together. The smile was faint. A heavy, tranquil man. I named my two officers, who just then came down to breakfast; but why Mr. Burns's silent demeanour should suggest suppressed indignation I could not understand.

While we were taking our seats round the table some disconnected words of an altercation going on in the companionway reached my ear. A stranger apparently wanted to come down to interview me, and the steward was opposing him.

"You can't see him."

"Why can't I?"

"The Captain is at breakfast, I tell you. He'll be going on shore presently, and you can speak to him on deck."

"That's not fair. You let—"

"I've had nothing to do with that."

"Oh, yes, you have. Everybody ought to have the same chance. You let that fellow—"

The rest I lost. The person having been repulsed successfully, the steward came down. I can't say he looked flushed—he was a mulatto—but he looked flustered. After putting the dishes on the table he remained by the sideboard with that lackadaisical air of indifference he used to assume when he had done something too clever by half and was afraid of getting into a scrape over it. The contemptuous expression of Mr. Burns's face as he looked from him to me was really extraordinary. I couldn't imagine what new bee had stung the mate now.

The Captain being silent, nobody else cared to speak, as is the way in ships. And I was saying nothing simply because I had been made dumb by the splendour of the entertainment. I had expected the usual sea-breakfast, whereas I beheld spread before us a veritable feast of shore provisions: eggs, sausages, butter which plainly did not come from a Danish tin, cutlets, and even a dish of potatoes. It was three weeks since I had seen a real, live potato. I contemplated them with interest, and Mr. Jacobus disclosed himself as a man of human, homely sympathies, and something of a thought-reader.

"Try them, Captain," he encouraged me in a friendly undertone. "They are excellent."

"They look that," I admitted. "Grown on the island, I suppose."

"Oh, no, imported. Those grown here would be more expensive."

I was grieved at the ineptitude of the conversation. Were these the topics for a prominent and wealthy merchant to discuss? I thought the simplicity with which he made himself at home rather attractive; but what is one to talk about to a man who comes on one suddenly, after sixty-one days at sea, out of a totally unknown little town in an island one has never seen before? What were (besides sugar) the interests of that crumb of the earth, its gossip, its topics of conversation? To draw him on business at once would have been almost indecent—or even worse: impolitic. All I could do at the moment was to keep on in the old groove.

"Are the provisions generally dear here?" I asked, fretting inwardly at my inanity.

"I wouldn't say that," he answered placidly, with that appearance of saving his breath his restrained manner of speaking suggested.

He would not be more explicit, yet he did not evade the subject. Eyeing the table in a spirit of complete abstemiousness (he wouldn't let me help him to any eatables) he went into details of supply. The beef was for the most part imported from Madagascar; mutton of course was rare and somewhat expensive, but good goat's flesh—

"Are these goat's cutlets?" I exclaimed hastily, pointing at one of the dishes.

Posed sentimentally by the sideboard, the steward gave a start.

"Lor', no, sir! It's real mutton!"

Mr. Burns got through his breakfast impatiently, as if exasperated by being made a party to some monstrous foolishness, muttered a curt excuse, and went on deck. Shortly afterwards the second mate took his smooth red countenance out of the cabin. With the appetite of a schoolboy, and after two months of sea-fare, he appreciated the generous spread. But I did not. It smacked of extravagance. All the same, it was a remarkable feat to have produced it so quickly, and I congratulated the steward on his smartness in a somewhat ominous tone. He gave me a deprecatory smile and, in a way I didn't know what to make of, blinked his fine dark eyes in the direction of the guest.

The latter asked under his breath for another cup of coffee, and nibbled ascetically at a piece of very hard ship's biscuit. I don't think he consumed a square inch in the end; but meantime he gave me, casually as it were, a complete account of the sugar crop, of the local business houses, of the state of the freight market. All that talk was interspersed with hints as to personalities, amounting to veiled warnings, but his pale, fleshy face remained equable, without a gleam, as if ignorant of his voice. As you may imagine I opened my ears very wide. Every word was precious. My ideas as to the value of business friendship were being favourably modified. He gave me the names of all the disponible ships together with their tonnage and the names of their commanders. From that, which was still commercial information, he condescended to mere harbour gossip. The *Hilda* had unaccountably lost her figurehead in the Bay of Bengal, and her captain was greatly affected by this. He and the ship had been getting on in years together and the old gentleman imagined this strange event to be the forerunner of his own early dissolution. The *Stella* had experienced awful weather off the Cape—had her decks swept, and the chief officer washed overboard. And only a few hours before reaching port the baby died.

Poor Captain H— and his wife were terribly cut up. If they had only been able to bring it into port alive it could have been probably saved; but the wind failed them for the last week or so, light breezes, and . . . the baby was going to be buried this afternoon. He supposed I would attend—

"Do you think I ought to?" I asked, shrinkingly.

He thought so, decidedly. It would be greatly appreciated. All the captains in the harbour were going to attend. Poor Mrs. H— was quite prostrated. Pretty hard on H— altogether.

"And you, Captain—you are not married I suppose?"

"No, I am not married," I said. "Neither married nor even engaged."

Mentally I thanked my stars; and while he smiled in a musing, dreamy fashion, I expressed my acknowledgments for his visit and for the interesting business information he had been good enough to impart to me. But I said nothing of my wonder thereat.

"Of course, I would have made a point of calling on you in a day or two," I concluded.

He raised his eyelids distinctly at me, and somehow managed to look rather more sleepy than before.

"In accordance with my owners' instructions," I explained. "You have had their letter, of course?"

By that time he had raised his eyebrows too but without any particular emotion. On the contrary he struck me then as absolutely imperturbable.

"Oh! You must be thinking of my brother."

It was for me, then, to say "Oh!" But I hope that no more than civil surprise appeared in my voice when I asked him to what, then, I owed the pleasure. . . . He was reaching for an inside pocket leisurely.

"My brother's a very different person. But I am well known in this part of the world. You've probably heard—"

I took a card he extended to me. A thick business card, as I lived! Alfred Jacobus—the other was Ernest—dealer in every description of ship's stores! Provisions salt and fresh, oils, paints, rope, canvas, etc., etc. Ships in harbour victualled by contract on moderate terms—

"I've never heard of you," I said brusquely.

His low-pitched assurance did not abandon him.

"You will be very well satisfied," he breathed out quietly.

I was not placated. I had the sense of having been circumvented somehow. Yet I had deceived myself—if there was any deception. But the confounded cheek of inviting himself to breakfast was enough to deceive any one. And the thought struck me: Why! The fellow had provided all these eatables himself in the way of business. I said:

"You must have got up mighty early this morning."

He admitted with simplicity that he was on the quay before six o'clock waiting for my ship to come in. He gave me the impression that it would be impossible to get rid of him now.

"If you think we are going to live on that scale," I said, looking at the table with an irritated eye, "you are jolly well mistaken."

"You'll find it all right, Captain. I quite understand."

Nothing could disturb his equanimity. I felt dissatisfied, but I could not very well fly out at him. He had told me many useful things—and besides he was the brother of that wealthy merchant. That seemed queer enough.

I rose and told him curtly that I must now go ashore. At once he offered the use of his boat for all the time of my stay in port.

"I only make a nominal charge," he continued equably. "My man remains all day at the landing-steps. You have only to blow a whistle when you want the boat."

And, standing aside at every doorway to let me go through first, he carried me off in his custody after all. As we crossed the quarter-deck two shabby individuals stepped forward and in mournful silence offered me business cards which I took from them without a word under his heavy eye. It was a useless and gloomy ceremony. They were the touts of the other ship-chandlers, and he placid at my back, ignored their existence.

We parted on the quay, after he had expressed quietly the hope of seeing me often "at the store." He had a smoking-room for captains there, with newspapers and a box of "rather decent cigars." I left him very unceremoniously.

My consignees received me with the usual business heartiness, but their account of the state of the freight-market was by no means so favourable as the talk of the wrong Jacobus had led me to expect. Naturally I became inclined now to put my trust in his version, rather. As I closed the door of the private office behind me I thought to myself: "H'm. A lot of lies. Commercial diplomacy. That's the sort of thing a man coming from sea has got to expect. They would try to charter the ship under the market rate."

In the big, outer room, full of desks, the chief clerk, a tall, lean, shaved person in immaculate white clothes and with a shiny, closely-cropped black head on which silvery gleams came and went, rose from his place and detained me affably. Anything they could do for me, they would be most happy. Was I likely to call again in the afternoon? What? Going to a funeral? Oh, yes, poor Captain H—.

He pulled a long, sympathetic face for a moment, then, dismissing from this workaday world the baby, which had got ill in a tempest and had died from too much calm at sea, he asked me with a dental, shark-like smile—if sharks had false teeth—whether I had yet made my little arrangements for the ship's stay in port.

"Yes, with Jacobus," I answered carelessly. "I understand he's the brother of Mr. Ernest Jacobus to whom I have an introduction from my owners."

I was not sorry to let him know I was not altogether helpless in the hands of his firm. He screwed his thin lips dubiously.

"Why," I cried, "isn't he the brother?"

"Oh, yes. . . . They haven't spoken to each other for eighteen years," he added impressively after a pause.

"Indeed! What's the quarrel about?"

"Oh, nothing! Nothing that one would care to mention," he protested primly. "He's got quite a large business. The best ship-chandler here, without a doubt. Business is all very well, but there is such a thing as personal character, too, isn't there? Good-morning, Captain."

He went away mincingly to his desk. He amused me. He resembled an old maid, a commercial old maid, shocked by some impropriety. Was it a commercial impropriety? Commercial impropriety is a serious matter, for it aims at one's pocket. Or was he only a purist in conduct who disapproved of Jacobus doing his own touting? It was certainly undignified. I wondered how the merchant brother liked it. But then different countries, different customs. In a community so isolated and so exclusively "trading" social standards have their own scale.

2

I WOULD HAVE gladly dispensed with the mournful opportunity of becoming acquainted by sight with all my fellow-captains at once. However I found my way to the cemetery. We made a considerable group of bareheaded men in sombre garments. I noticed that those of our company most approaching to the now obsolete sea-dog type were the most moved—perhaps because they had less "manner" than the new generation. The old sea-dog, away from his natural element, was a simple and sentimental animal. I noticed one—he was facing me across the grave—who was dropping tears. They trickled down his weather-beaten face like drops of rain on an old rugged wall. I learned afterwards that he was looked upon as the terror of sailors, a hard man; that he had never had wife or chick of his own, and that, engaged from his tenderest years in deep-sea voyages, he knew women and children merely by sight.

Perhaps he was dropping those tears over his lost opportunities, from sheer envy of paternity and in strange jealousy of a sorrow which he could never know. Man, and even the sea-man, is a capricious animal, the creature and the victim of lost opportunities. But he made me feel ashamed of my callousness. I had no tears.

I listened with horribly critical detachment to that service I had had to read myself, once or twice, over childlike men who had died at sea. The words of hope and defiance, the winged words so inspiring in the free immensity of water and sky, seemed to fall wearily into the little grave. What was the use of asking Death where her sting was, before that small, dark hole in the ground? And then my thoughts escaped me altogether—away into matters of life—and no very high matters at that—ships, freights, business. In the instability of his emotions man resembles deplorably a monkey. I was disgusted with my thoughts—and I thought: Shall I be able to get a charter soon? Time's money. . . . Will that Jacobus really put good business in my way? I must go and see him in a day or two.

Don't imagine that I pursued these thoughts with any precision. They pursued me rather: vague, shadowy, restless, shamefaced. Theirs was a callous, abominable, almost revolting, pertinacity. And it was the presence of that pertinacious ship-chandler which had started them. He stood mournfully amongst our little band of men from the sea, and I was angry at his presence, which, suggesting his brother the merchant, had caused me to become outrageous to myself. For indeed I had preserved some decency of feeling. It was only the mind which—

It was over at last. The poor father—a man of forty with black, bushy side-whiskers and a pathetic gash on his freshly-shaved chin—thanked us all, swallowing his tears. But for some reason, either because I lingered at the gate of the cemetery being somewhat hazy as to my way back, or because I was the youngest, or ascribing my moodiness caused by remorse to some more worthy and appropriate sentiment, or simply because I was even more of a stranger to him than the others—he singled me out. Keeping at my side, he renewed his thanks, which I listened to in a gloomy, conscience-stricken silence. Suddenly he slipped one hand under my arm and waved the other after a tall, stout figure walking away by itself down a street in a flutter of thin, grey garments:

"That's a good fellow—a real good fellow"—he swallowed down a belated sob—"this Jacobus."

And he told me in a low voice that Jacobus was the first man to board his ship on arrival, and, learning of their misfortune, had taken charge of everything, volunteered to attend to all routine business, carried off the ship's papers on shore, arranged for the funeral—

"A good fellow. I was knocked over. I had been looking at my wife for ten days. And helpless. Just you think of that! The dear little chap died the very day we made the land. How I managed to take the ship in God alone knows! I couldn't see anything; I couldn't speak; I couldn't. . . . You've heard, perhaps, that we lost our mate overboard on the passage? There was no one to do it for me. And the poor woman nearly crazy down below there all alone with the . . . By the Lord! It isn't fair."

We walked in silence together. I did not know how to part from him. On the quay he let go my arm and struck fiercely his fist into the palm of his other hand.

"By God, it isn't fair!" he cried again. "Don't you ever marry unless you can chuck the sea first. . . . It isn't fair."

I had no intention to "chuck the sea," and when he left me to go aboard his ship I felt convinced that I would never marry. While I was waiting at the steps for Jacobus's boatman, who had gone off somewhere, the captain of the *Hilda* joined me, a slender silk umbrella in his hand and the sharp points of his archaic, Gladstonian shirt-collar framing a small, clean-shaved, ruddy face. It was wonderfully fresh for his age, beautifully modelled and lit up by remarkably clear blue eyes. A lot of white hair, glossy like spun glass, curled upwards slightly under the brim of his valuable, ancient, panama hat with a broad black ribbon. In the aspect of that vivacious, neat, little old man there was something quaintly angelic and also boyish.

He accosted me, as though he had been in the habit of seeing me every day of his life from my earliest childhood, with a whimsical remark on the appearance of a stout negro woman who was sitting upon a stool near the edge of the quay. Presently he observed amiably that I had a very pretty little barque.

I returned this civil speech by saying readily:

"Not so pretty as the *Hilda*."

At once the corners of his clear-cut, sensitive mouth dropped dismally.

"Oh, dear! I can hardly bear to look at her now."

Did I know, he asked anxiously, that he had lost the figurehead of his ship; a woman in a blue tunic edged with gold, the face perhaps not so very, very pretty, but her bare white arms beautifully shaped and extended as if she were swimming? Did I? Who would have expected such a things . . . After twenty years too!

Nobody could have guessed from his tone that the woman was made of wood; his trembling voice, his agitated manner gave to his lamentations a ludicrously scandalous flavour. . . . Disappeared at night—a clear fine night with just a slight swell—in the gulf of Bengal. Went off without a splash; no one in the ship could tell why, how, at what hour—after twenty years last October. . . . Did I ever hear! . . .

I assured him sympathetically that I had never heard—and he became very doleful. This meant no good he was sure. There was something in it which looked like a warning. But when I remarked that surely another figure of a woman could be procured I found myself being soundly rated for my levity. The old boy flushed pink under his clear tan as if I had proposed something improper. One could replace masts, I was told, or a lost rudder—any working part of a ship; but where was the use of sticking up a new figurehead? What satisfaction? How could one care for it? It was easy to see that I had never been shipmates with a figurehead for over twenty years.

"A new figurehead!" he scolded in unquenchable indignation. "Why! I've been a widower now for eight-and-twenty years come next May and I would just as soon think of getting a new wife. You're as bad as that fellow Jacobus."

I was highly amused.

"What has Jacobus done? Did he want you to marry again, Captain?" I inquired in a deferential tone. But he was launched now and only grinned fiercely.

"Procure—indeed! He's the sort of chap to procure you anything you like for a price. I hadn't been moored here for an hour when he got on board and at once offered to sell me a figurehead he happens to have in his yard somewhere. He got Smith, my mate, to talk to me about it. 'Mr. Smith,' says I, 'don't you know me better than that? Am I the sort that would pick up with another man's cast-off figurehead?' And after all these years too! The way some of you young fellows talk—"

I affected great compunction, and as I stepped into the boat I said soberly:

"Then I see nothing for it but to fit in a neat fiddlehead—perhaps. You know, carved scrollwork, nicely gilt."

He became very dejected after his outburst.

"Yes. Scrollwork. Maybe. Jacobus hinted at that too. He's never at a loss when there's any money to be extracted from a sailorman. He would make me pay through the nose for that carving. A gilt fiddlehead did you say—eh? I dare say it would do for you. You young fellows don't seem to have any feeling for what's proper."

He made a convulsive gesture with his right arm.

"Never mind. Nothing can make much difference. I would just as soon let the old thing go about the world with a bare cutwater," he cried sadly. Then as the boat got away from the steps he raised his voice on the edge of the quay with comical animosity:

"I would! If only to spite that figurehead-procuring bloodsucker. I am an old bird here and don't you forget it. Come and see me on board some day!"

I spent my first evening in port quietly in my ship's cuddy; and glad enough was I to think that the shore life which strikes one as so pettily complex, discordant, and so full of new faces on first coming from sea, could be kept off for a few hours longer. I was however fated to hear the Jacobus note once more before I slept.

Mr. Burns had gone ashore after the evening meal to have, as he said, "a look round." As it was quite dark when he announced his intention I didn't ask him what it was he expected to see. Some time about midnight, while sitting with a book in the saloon, I heard cautious movements in the lobby and hailed him by name.

Burns came in, stick and hat in hand, incredibly vulgarised by his smart shore togs, with a jaunty air and an odious twinkle in his eye. Being asked to sit down he laid his hat and stick on the table and after we had talked of ship affairs for a little while:

"I've been hearing pretty tales on shore about that ship-chandler fellow who snatched the job from you so neatly, sir."

I remonstrated with my late patient for his manner of expressing himself. But he only tossed his head disdainfully. A pretty dodge indeed: boarding a strange ship with breakfast in two baskets for all hands and calmly inviting himself to the captain's table! Never heard of anything so crafty and so impudent in his life.

I found myself defending Jacobus's unusual methods.

"He's the brother of one of the wealthiest merchants in the port." The mate's eyes fairly snapped green sparks.

"His grand brother hasn't spoken to him for eighteen or twenty years," he declared triumphantly. "So there!"

"I know all about that," I interrupted loftily.

"Do you sir? H'm!" His mind was still running on the ethics of commercial competition. "I don't like to see your good nature taken advantage of. He's bribed that steward of ours with a five-rupee note to let him come down—or ten for that matter. He don't care. He will shove that and more into the bill presently."

"Is that one of the tales you have heard ashore?" I asked.

He assured me that his own sense could tell him that much. No; what he had heard on shore was that no respectable person in the whole town would come near Jacobus. He lived in a large old-fashioned house in one of the quiet streets with a big garden. After telling me this Burns put on a mysterious air. "He keeps a girl shut up there who, they say—"

"I suppose you've heard all this gossip in some eminently respectable place?" I snapped at him in a most sarcastic tone.

The shaft told, because Mr. Burns, like many other disagreeable people, was very sensitive himself. He remained as if thunderstruck, with his mouth open for some further communication, but I did not give him the chance. "And, anyhow, what the deuce do I care?" I added, retiring into my room.

And this was a natural thing to say. Yet somehow I was not indifferent. I admit it is absurd to be concerned with the morals of one's ship-chandler, if ever so well connected; but his personality had stamped itself upon my first day in harbour, in the way you know.

After this initial exploit Jacobus showed himself anything but intrusive. He was out in a boat early every morning going round the ships he served, and occasionally remaining on board one of them for breakfast with the captain.

As I discovered that this practice was generally accepted, I just nodded to him familiarly when one morning, on coming out of my room, I found him in the cabin. Glancing over the table I saw that his place was already laid. He stood awaiting my appearance, very bulky and placid, holding a beautiful bunch of flowers in his thick hand. He offered them to my notice with a faint, sleepy smile. From his own garden; had a very fine old garden; picked them himself that morning before going out to business; thought I would like. . . . He turned away. "Steward, can you oblige me with some water in a large jar, please."

I assured him jocularly, as I took my place at the table, that he made me feel as if I were a pretty girl, and that he mustn't be surprised if I blushed. But he was busy arranging his floral tribute at the sideboard. "Stand it before the Captain's plate, steward, please." He made this request in his usual undertone.

The offering was so pointed that I could do no less than to raise it to my nose, and as he sat down noiselessly he breathed out the opinion that a few flowers improved notably the appearance of a ship's saloon. He wondered why I did not have a shelf fitted all round the skylight for flowers in pots to take with me to sea. He had a skilled workman able to fit up shelves in a day, and he could procure me two or three dozen good plants—

The tips of his thick, round fingers rested composedly on the edge of the table on each side of his cup of coffee. His face remained immovable. Mr. Burns was smiling maliciously to himself. I declared that I hadn't the slightest intention of turning my skylight into a conservatory only to keep the cabin-table in a perpetual mess of mould and dead vegetable matter.

"Rear most beautiful flowers," he insisted with an upward glance. "It's no trouble really."

"Oh, yes, it is. Lots of trouble," I contradicted. "And in the end some fool leaves the skylight open in a fresh breeze, a flick of salt water gets at them and the whole lot is dead in a week."

Mr. Burns snorted a contemptuous approval. Jacobus gave up the subject passively. After a time he unglued his thick lips to ask me if I had seen his brother yet. I was very curt in my answer.

"No, not yet."

"A very different person," he remarked dreamily and got up. His movements were particularly noiseless. "Well—thank you, Captain. If anything is not to your liking please mention it to your steward. I suppose you will be giving a dinner to the office-clerks presently."

"What for?" I cried with some warmth. "If I were a steady trader to the port I could understand it. But a complete stranger! . . . I may not turn up again here for years. I don't see why! . . . Do you mean to say it is customary?"

"It will be expected from a man like you," he breathed out placidly. "Eight of the principal clerks, the manager, that's nine, you three gentlemen, that's twelve. It needn't be very expensive. If you tell your steward to give me a day's notice—"

"It will be expected of me! Why should it be expected of me? Is it because I look particularly soft—or what?"

His immobility struck me as dignified suddenly, his imperturbable quality as dangerous. "There's plenty of time to think about that," I concluded weakly with a gesture that tried to wave him away. But before he departed he took time to mention regretfully that he had not yet had the pleasure of seeing me at his "store" to sample those cigars. He had a parcel of six thousand to dispose of, very cheap.

"I think it would be worth your while to secure some," he added with a fat, melancholy smile and left the cabin.

Mr. Burns struck his fist on the table excitedly.

"Did you ever see such impudence! He's made up his mind to get something out of you one way or another, sir."

At once feeling inclined to defend Jacobus, I observed philosophically that all this was business, I supposed. But my absurd mate, muttering broken disjointed sentences, such as: "I cannot bear! . . . Mark my words! . . ." and so on, flung out of the cabin. If I hadn't nursed him through that deadly fever I wouldn't have suffered such manners for a single day.

3

Jacobus having put me in mind of his wealthy brother I concluded I would pay that business call at once. I had by that time heard a little more of him. He was a member of the Council, where he made himself objectionable to the authorities. He exercised a considerable influence on public opinion. Lots of people owed him money. He was an importer on a great scale of all sorts of goods. For instance, the whole supply of bags for sugar was practically in his hands. This last fact I did not learn till afterwards. The general impression conveyed to me was that of a local personage. He was a bachelor and gave weekly card-parties in his house out of town, which were attended by the best people in the colony.

The greater, then, was my surprise to discover his office in shabby surroundings, quite away from the business quarter, amongst a lot of hovels. Guided by a black board with white lettering, I climbed a narrow wooden staircase and entered a room with a bare floor of planks littered with bits of brown paper and wisps of packing straw. A great number of what looked like wine-cases were piled up against one of the walls. A lanky, inky, light-yellow, mulatto youth, miserably long-necked and generally recalling a sick chicken, got off a three-legged stool behind a cheap deal desk and faced me as if gone dumb with fright. I had some difficulty in persuading him to take in my name, though I could not get from him the nature of his objection. He did it at last with an almost agonised reluctance which ceased to be mysterious to me when I heard him being sworn at menacingly with savage, suppressed growls, then audibly cuffed and finally kicked out without any concealment whatever; because he came back flying head foremost through the door with a stifled shriek.

To say I was startled would not express it. I remained still, like a man lost in a dream. Clapping both his hands to that part of his frail anatomy which had received the shock, the poor wretch said to me simply:

"Will you go in, please." His lamentable self-possession was wonderful; but it did not do away with the incredibility of the experience. A preposterous notion that I had seen this boy somewhere before, a thing obviously impossible, was like a delicate finishing touch of weirdness added to a scene fit to raise doubts as to one's sanity. I stared anxiously about me like an awakened somnambulist.

"I say," I cried loudly, "there isn't a mistake, is there? This is Mr. Jacobus's office."

The boy gazed at me with a pained expression—and somehow so familiar! A voice within growled offensively:

"Come in, come in, since you are there. . . . I didn't know."

I crossed the outer room as one approaches the den of some unknown wild beast; with intrepidity but in some excitement. Only no wild beast that ever lived would rouse one's indignation; the power to do that belongs to the odiousness of the human brute. And I was very indignant, which did not prevent me from being at once struck by the extraordinary resemblance of the two brothers.

This one was dark instead of being fair like the other; but he was as big. He was without his coat and waistcoat; he had been doubtless snoozing in the rocking-chair which stood in a corner furthest from the window. Above the great bulk of his crumpled white shirt, buttoned with three diamond studs, his round face looked swarthy. It was moist; his brown moustache hung limp and ragged. He pushed a common, cane-bottomed chair towards me with his foot.

"Sit down."

I glanced at it casually, then, turning my indignant eyes full upon him, I declared in precise and incisive tones that I had called in obedience to my owners' instructions.

"Oh! Yes. H'm! I didn't understand what that fool was saying. . . . But never mind! It will teach the scoundrel to disturb me at this time of the day," he added, grinning at me with savage cynicism.

I looked at my watch. It was past three o'clock—quite the full swing of afternoon office work in the port. He snarled imperiously: "Sit down, Captain."

I acknowledged the gracious invitation by saying deliberately:

"I can listen to all you may have to say without sitting down."

Emitting a loud and vehement "Pshaw!" he glared for a moment, very round-eyed and fierce. It was like a gigantic tomcat spitting at one suddenly. "Look at him! . . . What do you fancy yourself to be? What did you come here for? If you won't sit down and talk business you had better go to the devil."

"I don't know him personally," I said. "But after this I wouldn't mind calling on him. It would be refreshing to meet a gentleman."

He followed me, growling behind my back:

"The impudence! I've a good mind to write to your owners what I think of you."

I turned on him for a moment:

"As it happens I don't care. For my part I assure you I won't even take the trouble to mention you to them."

He stopped at the door of his office while I traversed the littered anteroom. I think he was somewhat taken aback.

"I will break every bone in your body," he roared suddenly at the miserable mulatto lad, "if you ever dare to disturb me before half-past three for anybody. D'ye hear? For anybody! . . . Let alone any damned skipper," he added, in a lower growl.

The frail youngster, swaying like a reed, made a low moaning sound. I stopped short and addressed this sufferer with advice. It was prompted by the sight of a hammer (used for opening the wine-cases, I suppose) which was lying on the floor.

"If I were you, my boy, I would have that thing up my sleeve when I went in next and at the first occasion I would—"

What was there so familiar in that lad's yellow face? Entrenched and quaking behind the flimsy desk, he never looked up. His heavy, lowered eyelids gave me suddenly the clue of the puzzle. He resembled—yes, those thick glued lips—he resembled the brothers Jacobus. He resembled both, the wealthy merchant and the pushing shopkeeper (who resembled each other); he resembled them as much as a thin, light-yellow mulatto lad may resemble a big, stout, middle-aged white man. It was the exotic complexion and the slightness of his build which had put me off so completely. Now I saw in him unmistakably the Jacobus strain, weakened, attenuated, diluted as it were in a bucket of water—and I refrained from finishing my speech. I had intended to say: "Crack this brute's head for him." I still felt the conclusion to be sound. But it is no trifling responsibility to counsel parricide to any one, however deeply injured.

"Beggarly—cheeky—skippers."

I despised the emphatic growl at my back; only, being much vexed and upset, I regret to say that I slammed the door behind me in a most undignified manner.

It may not appear altogether absurd if I say that I brought out from that interview a kindlier view of the other Jacobus. It was with a feeling resembling partisanship that, a few days later, I called at his "store." That long, cavern-like place of business, very dim at the back and stuffed full of all sorts of goods, was entered from the street by a lofty archway. At the far end I saw my Jacobus exerting himself in his shirt-sleeves among his assistants. The captains' room was a small, vaulted apartment with a stone floor and heavy iron bars in its windows like a dungeon converted to hospitable purposes. A couple of cheerful bottles and several gleaming glasses made a brilliant cluster round a tall, cool red earthenware pitcher on the centre table which was littered with newspapers from all parts of the world. A well-groomed stranger in a smart grey check suit, sitting with one leg flung over his knee, put down one of these sheets briskly and nodded to me.

I guessed him to be a steamer-captain. It was impossible to get to know these men. They came and went too quickly and their ships lay moored far out, at the very entrance of the harbour. Theirs was another life altogether. He yawned slightly.

"Dull hole, isn't it?"

I understood this to allude to the town.

"Do you find it so?" I murmured.

"Don't you? But I'm off to-morrow, thank goodness."

He was a very gentlemanly person, good-natured and superior. I watched him draw the open box of cigars to his side of the table, take a big cigar-case out of his pocket and begin to fill it very methodically. Presently, on our eyes meeting, he winked like a common mortal and invited me to follow his example. "They are really decent smokes." I shook my head.

"I am not off to-morrow."

"What of that? Think I am abusing old Jacobus's hospitality? Heavens! It goes into the bill, of course. He spreads such little matters all over his account. He can take care of himself! Why, it's business—"

I noted a shadow fall over his well-satisfied expression, a momentary hesitation in closing his cigar-case. But he ended by putting it in his pocket jauntily. A placid voice uttered in the doorway: "That's quite correct, Captain."

The large noiseless Jacobus advanced into the room. His quietness, in the circumstances, amounted to cordiality. He had put on his jacket before joining us, and he sat down in the chair vacated by the steamer-man, who nodded again to me and went out with a short, jarring laugh. A profound silence reigned. With his drowsy stare Jacobus seemed to be slumbering open-eyed. Yet, somehow, I was aware of being profoundly scrutinised by those heavy eyes. In the enormous cavern of the store somebody began to nail down a case, expertly: tap-tap . . . tap-tap-tap.

Two other experts, one slow and nasal, the other shrill and snappy, started checking an invoice.

"A half-coil of three-inch manilla rope."

"Right!"

"Six assorted shackles."

"Right!"

"Six tins assorted soups, three of paté, two asparagus, fourteen pounds tobacco, cabin."

"Right!"

"It's for the captain who was here just now," breathed out the immovable Jacobus. "These steamer orders are very small. They pick up what they want as they go along. That man will be in Samarang in less than a fortnight. Very small orders indeed."

The calling over of the items went on in the shop; an extraordinary jumble of varied articles, paint-brushes, Yorkshire Relish, etc., etc. . . . "Three sacks of best potatoes," read out the nasal voice.

At this Jacobus blinked like a sleeping man roused by a shake, and displayed some animation. At his order, shouted into the shop, a smirking half-caste clerk with his ringlets much oiled and with a pen stuck behind his ear, brought in a sample of six potatoes which he paraded in a row on the table.

Being urged to look at their beauty I gave them a cold and hostile glance. Calmly, Jacobus proposed that I should order ten or fifteen tons—tons! I couldn't believe my ears. My crew could not have eaten such a lot in a year; and potatoes (excuse these practical remarks) are a highly perishable commodity. I thought he was joking—or else trying to find out whether I was an unutterable idiot. But his purpose was not so simple. I discovered that he meant me to buy them on my own account.

"I am proposing you a bit of business, Captain. I wouldn't charge you a great price."

I told him that I did not go in for trade. I even added grimly that I knew only too well how that sort of spec. generally ended.

He sighed and clasped his hands on his stomach with exemplary resignation. I admired the placidity of his impudence. Then waking up somewhat:

"Won't you try a cigar, Captain?"

"No, thanks. I don't smoke cigars."

"For once!" he exclaimed, in a patient whisper. A melancholy silence ensued. You know how sometimes a person discloses a certain unsuspected depth and acuteness of thought; that is, in other words, utters something unexpected. It was unexpected enough to hear Jacobus say:

"The man who just went out was right enough. You might take one, Captain. Here everything is bound to be in the way of business."

I felt a little ashamed of myself. The remembrance of his horrid brother made him appear quite a decent sort of fellow. It was with some compunction that I said a few words to the effect that I could have no possible objection to his hospitality.

Before I was a minute older I saw where this admission was leading me. As if changing the subject, Jacobus mentioned that his private house was about ten minutes' walk away. It had a beautiful old walled garden. Something really remarkable. I ought to come round some day and have a look at it.

He seemed to be a lover of gardens. I too take extreme delight in them; but I did not mean my compunction to carry me as far as Jacobus's flower-beds, however beautiful and old. He added, with a certain homeliness of tone:

"There's only my girl there."

It is difficult to set everything down in due order; so I must revert here to what happened a week or two before. The medical officer of the port had come on board my ship to have a look at one of my crew who was ailing, and naturally enough he was asked to step into the cabin. A fellow-shipmaster of mine was there too; and in the conversation, somehow or other, the name of Jacobus came to be mentioned. It was pronounced with no particular reverence by the other man, I believe. I don't remember now what I was going to say. The doctor—a pleasant, cultivated fellow, with an assured manner—prevented me by striking in, in a sour tone:

"Ah! You're talking about my respected papa-in-law."

Of course, that sally silenced us at the time. But I remembered the episode, and at this juncture, pushed for something noncommittal to say, I inquired with polite surprise:

"You have your married daughter living with you, Mr. Jacobus?"

He moved his big hand from right to left quietly. No! That was another of his girls, he stated, ponderously and under his breath as usual. She . . . He seemed in a pause to be ransacking his mind for some kind of descriptive phrase. But my hopes were disappointed. He merely produced his stereotyped definition.

"She's a very different sort of person."

"Indeed. . . . And by the by, Jacobus, I called on your brother the other day. It's no great compliment if I say that I found him a very different sort of person from you."

He had an air of profound reflection, then remarked quaintly:

"He's a man of regular habits."

He might have been alluding to the habit of late siesta; but I mumbled something about "beastly habits anyhow"—and left the store abruptly.

4

My little passage with Jacobus the merchant became known generally. One or two of my acquaintances made distant allusions to it. Perhaps the mulatto boy had talked. I must confess that people appeared rather scandalised, but not with Jacobus's brutality. A man I knew remonstrated with me for my hastiness.

I gave him the whole story of my visit, not forgetting the tell-tale resemblance of the wretched mulatto boy to his tormentor. He was not surprised. No doubt, no doubt. What of that? In a jovial tone he assured me that there must be many of that sort. The elder Jacobus had been a bachelor all his life. A highly respectable bachelor. But there had never been open scandal in that connection. His life had been quite regular. It could cause no offence to any one.

I said that I had been offended considerably. My interlocutor opened very wide eyes. Why? Because a mulatto lad got a few knocks? That was not a great affair, surely. I had no idea how insolent and untruthful these half-castes were. In fact he seemed to think Mr. Jacobus rather kind than otherwise to employ that youth at all; a sort of amiable weakness which could be forgiven.

This acquaintance of mine belonged to one of the old French families, descendants of the old colonists; all noble, all impoverished, and living a narrow domestic life in dull, dignified decay. The men, as a rule, occupy inferior posts in Government offices or in business houses. The girls are almost always pretty, ignorant of the world, kind and agreeable and generally bilingual; they prattle innocently both in French and English. The emptiness of their existence passes belief.

I obtained my entry into a couple of such households because some years before, in Bombay, I had occasion to be of use to a pleasant, ineffectual young man who was rather stranded there, not knowing what to do with himself or even how to get home to his island again. It was a matter of two hundred rupees or so, but, when I turned up, the family made a point of showing their gratitude by admitting me to their intimacy. My knowledge of the French language made me specially acceptable. They had meantime managed to marry the fellow to a woman nearly twice his age, comparatively well off: the only profession he was really fit for. But it was not all cakes and ale. The first time I called on the couple she spied a little spot of grease on the poor devil's pantaloons and made him a screaming scene of reproaches so full of sincere passion that I sat terrified as at a tragedy of Racine.

Of course there was never question of the money I had advanced him; but his sisters, Miss Angele and Miss Mary, and the aunts of both families, who spoke quaint archaic French of pre-Revolution period, and a host of distant relations adopted me for a friend outright in a manner which was almost embarrassing.

It was with the eldest brother (he was employed at a desk in my consignee's office) that I was having this talk about the merchant Jacobus. He regretted my attitude and nodded his head sagely. An influential man. One never knew when one would need him. I expressed my immense preference for the shopkeeper of the two. At that my friend looked grave.

"What on earth are you pulling that long face about?" I cried impatiently. "He asked me to see his garden and I have a good mind to go some day."

"Don't do that," he said, so earnestly that I burst into a fit of laughter; but he looked at me without a smile.

This was another matter altogether. At one time the public conscience of the island had been mightily troubled by my Jacobus. The two brothers had been partners for years in great harmony, when a wandering circus came to the island and my Jacobus became suddenly infatuated with one of the lady-riders. What made it worse was that he was married. He had not even the grace to conceal his passion. It must have been strong indeed to carry away such a large placid creature. His behaviour was perfectly scandalous. He followed that woman to the Cape, and apparently travelled at the tail of that beastly circus to other parts of the world, in a most degrading position. The woman soon ceased to care for him, and treated him worse than a dog. Most extraordinary stories of moral degradation were reaching the island at that time. He had not the strength of mind to shake himself free. . . .

The grotesque image of a fat, pushing ship-chandler, enslaved by an unholy love-spell, fascinated me; and I listened rather open-mouthed to the tale as old as the world, a tale which had been the subject of legend, of moral fables, of poems, but which so ludicrously failed to fit the personality. What a strange victim for the gods!

Meantime his deserted wife had died. His daughter was taken care of by his brother, who married her as advantageously as was possible in the circumstances.

"Oh! The Mrs. Doctor!" I exclaimed.

"You know that? Yes. A very able man. He wanted a lift in the world, and there was a good bit of money from her mother, besides the expectations. . . Of course, they don't know him," he added. "The doctor nods in the street, I believe, but he avoids speaking to him when they meet on board a ship, as must happen sometimes."

I remarked that this surely was an old story by now.

My friend assented. But it was Jacobus's own fault that it was neither forgiven nor forgotten. He came back ultimately. But how? Not in a spirit of contrition, in a way to propitiate his scandalised fellow-citizens. He must needs drag along with him a child—a girl. . . .

"He spoke to me of a daughter who lives with him," I observed, very much interested.

"She's certainly the daughter of the circus-woman," said my friend. "She may be his daughter too; I am willing to admit that she is. In fact I have no doubt—"

But he did not see why she should have been brought into a respectable community to perpetuate the memory of the scandal. And that was not the worst. Presently something much more distressing happened. That abandoned woman turned up. Landed from a mail-boat. . . .

"What! Here? To claim the child perhaps," I suggested.

"Not she!" My friendly informant was very scornful. "Imagine a painted, haggard, agitated, desperate hag. Been cast off in Mozambique by somebody who paid her passage here. She had been injured internally by a kick from a horse; she hadn't a cent on her when she got ashore; I don't think she even asked to see the child. At any rate, not till the last day of her life. Jacobus hired for her a bungalow to die in. He got a couple of Sisters from the hospital to nurse her through these few months. If he didn't marry her *in extremis* as the good Sisters tried to bring about, it's because she wouldn't even hear of it. As the nuns said: 'The woman died impenitent.' It was reported that she ordered Jacobus out of the room with her last breath. This may be the real reason why he didn't go into mourning himself; he only put the child into black. While she was little she was to be seen sometimes about the streets attended by a negro woman, but since she became of age to put her hair up I don't think she has set foot outside that garden once. She must be over eighteen now."

Thus my friend, with some added details; such as, that he didn't think the girl had spoken to three people of any position in the island; that an elderly female relative of the brothers Jacobus had been induced by extreme poverty to accept the position of gouvernante to the girl. As to Jacobus's business (which certainly annoyed his brother) it was a wise choice on his part. It brought him in contact only with strangers of passage; whereas any other would have given rise to all sorts of awkwardness with his social equals. The man was not wanting in a certain tact—only he was naturally shameless. For why did he want to keep that girl with him? It was most painful for everybody.

I thought suddenly (and with profound disgust) of the other Jacobus, and I could not refrain from saying slily:

"I suppose if he employed her, say, as a scullion in his household and occasionally pulled her hair or boxed her ears, the position would have been more regular—less shocking to the respectable class to which he belongs."

He was not so stupid as to miss my intention, and shrugged his shoulders impatiently.

"You don't understand. To begin with, she's not a mulatto. And a scandal is a scandal. People should be given a chance to forget. I dare say it would have been better for her if she had been turned into a scullion or something of that kind. Of course he's trying to make money in every sort of petty way, but in such a business there'll never be enough for anybody to come forward."

When my friend left me I had a conception of Jacobus and his daughter existing, a lonely pair of castaways, on a desert island; the girl sheltering in the house as if it were a cavern in a cliff, and Jacobus going out to pick up a living for both on the beach—exactly like two shipwrecked people who always hope for some rescuer to bring them back at last into touch with the rest of mankind.

But Jacobus's bodily reality did not fit in with this romantic view. When he turned up on board in the usual course, he sipped the cup of coffee placidly, asked me if I was satisfied—and I hardly listened to the harbour gossip he dropped slowly in his low, voice-saving enunciation. I had then troubles of my own. My ship chartered, my thoughts dwelling on the success of a quick round voyage, I had been suddenly confronted by a shortage of bags. A catastrophe! The stock of one especial kind, called pockets, seemed to be totally exhausted. A consignment was shortly expected—it was afloat, on its way, but, meantime, the loading of my ship dead stopped, I had enough to worry about. My consignees, who had received me with such heartiness on my arrival, now, in the character of my charterers, listened to my complaints with polite helplessness. Their manager, the old-maidish, thin man, who so prudishly didn't even like to speak about the impure Jacobus, gave me the correct commercial view of the position.

"My dear Captain"—he was retracting his leathery cheeks into a condescending, shark-like smile—"we were not morally obliged to tell you of a possible shortage before you signed the charter-party. It was for you to guard against the contingency of a delay—strictly speaking. But of course we shouldn't have taken any advantage. This is no one's fault really. We ourselves have been taken unawares," he concluded primly, with an obvious lie.

This lecture I confess had made me thirsty. Suppressed rage generally produces that effect; and as I strolled on aimlessly I bethought myself of the tall earthenware pitcher in the captains' room of the Jacobus "store."

With no more than a nod to the men I found assembled there, I poured down a deep, cool draught on my indignation, then another, and then, becoming dejected, I sat plunged in cheerless reflections. The others read, talked, smoked, bandied over my head some unsubtle chaff. But my abstraction was respected. And it was without a word to any one that I rose and went out, only to be quite unexpectedly accosted in the bustle of the store by Jacobus the outcast.

"Glad to see you, Captain. What? Going away? You haven't been looking so well these last few days, I notice. Run down, eh?"

He was in his shirt-sleeves, and his words were in the usual course of business, but they had a human note. It was commercial amenity, but I had been a stranger to amenity in that connection. I do verily believe (from the direction of his heavy glance towards a certain shelf) that he was going to suggest the purchase of Clarkson's Nerve Tonic, which he kept in stock, when I said impulsively:

"I am rather in trouble with my loading."

Wide awake under his sleepy, broad mask with glued lips, he understood at once, had a movement of the head so appreciative that I relieved my exasperation by exclaiming:

"Surely there must be eleven hundred quarter-bags to be found in the colony. It's only a matter of looking for them."

Again that slight movement of the big head, and in the noise and activity of the store that tranquil murmur:

"To be sure. But then people likely to have a reserve of quarter-bags wouldn't want to sell. They'd need that size themselves."

"That's exactly what my consignees are telling me. Impossible to buy. Bosh! They don't want to. It suits them to have the ship hung up. But if I were to discover the lot they would have to—Look here, Jacobus! You are the man to have such a thing up your sleeve."

He protested with a ponderous swing of his big head. I stood before him helplessly, being looked at by those heavy eyes with a veiled expression as of a man after some soul-shaking crisis. Then, suddenly:

"It's impossible to talk quietly here," he whispered. "I am very busy. But if you could go and wait for me in my house. It's less than ten minutes' walk. Oh, yes, you don't know the way."

He called for his coat and offered to take me there himself. He would have to return to the store at once for an hour or so to finish his business, and then he would be at liberty to talk over with me that matter of quarter-bags. This programme was breathed out at me through slightly parted, still lips; his heavy, motionless glance rested upon me, placid as ever, the glance of a tired man—but I felt that it was searching, too. I could not imagine what he was looking for in me and kept silent, wondering.

"I am asking you to wait for me in my house till I am at liberty to talk this matter over. You will?"

"Why, of course!" I cried.

"But I cannot promise—"

"I dare say not," I said. "I don't expect a promise."

"I mean I can't even promise to try the move I've in my mind. One must see first . . . h'm!"

"All right. I'll take the chance. I'll wait for you as long as you like. What else have I to do in this infernal hole of a port!"

Before I had uttered my last words we had set off at a swinging pace. We turned a couple of corners and entered a street completely empty of traffic, of semi-rural aspect, paved with cobblestones nestling in grass tufts. The house came to the line of the roadway; a single story on an elevated basement of rough-stones, so that our heads were below the level of the windows as we went along. All the jalousies were tightly shut, like eyes, and the house seemed fast asleep in the afternoon sunshine. The entrance was at the side, in an alley even more grass-grown than the street: a small door, simply on the latch.

With a word of apology as to showing me the way, Jacobus preceded me up a dark passage and led me across the naked parquet floor of what I supposed to be the dining-room. It was lighted by three glass doors which stood wide open on to a verandah or rather loggia running its brick arches along the garden side of the house. It was really a magnificent garden: smooth green lawns and a gorgeous maze of flower-beds in the foreground, displayed around a basin of dark water framed in a marble rim, and in the distance the massed foliage of varied trees concealing the roofs of other houses. The town might have been miles away. It was a brilliantly coloured solitude, drowsing in a warm, voluptuous silence. Where the long, still shadows fell across the beds, and in shady nooks, the massed colours of the flowers had an extraordinary magnificence of effect. I stood entranced. Jacobus grasped me delicately above the elbow, impelling me to a half-turn to the left.

I had not noticed the girl before. She occupied a low, deep, wickerwork arm-chair, and I saw her in exact profile like a figure in a tapestry, and as motionless. Jacobus released my arm.

"This is Alice," he announced tranquilly; and his subdued manner of speaking made it sound so much like a confidential communication that I fancied myself nodding understandingly and whispering: "I see, I see." . . . Of course, I did nothing of the kind. Neither of us did anything; we stood side by side looking down at the girl. For quite a time she did not stir, staring straight before her as if watching the vision of some pageant passing through the garden in the deep, rich glow of light and the splendour of flowers.

Then, coming to the end of her reverie, she looked round and up. If I had not at first noticed her, I am certain that she too had been unaware of my presence till she actually perceived me by her father's side. The quickened upward movement of the heavy eyelids, the widening of the languid glance, passing into a fixed stare, put that beyond doubt.

Under her amazement there was a hint of fear, and then came a flash as of anger. Jacobus, after uttering my name fairly loud, said: "Make yourself at home, Captain—I won't be gone long," and went away rapidly. Before I had time to make a bow I was left alone with the girl—who, I remembered suddenly, had not been seen by any man or woman of that town since she had found it necessary to put up her hair. It looked as though it had not been touched again since that distant time of first putting up; it was a mass of black, lustrous locks, twisted anyhow high on her head, with long, untidy wisps hanging down on each side of the clear sallow face; a mass so thick and strong and abundant that, nothing but to look at, it gave you a sensation of heavy pressure on the top of your head and an impression of magnificently cynical untidiness. She leaned forward, hugging herself with crossed legs; a dingy, amber-coloured, flounced wrapper of some thin stuff revealed the young supple body drawn together tensely in the deep low seat as if crouching for a spring. I detected a slight, quivering start or two, which looked uncommonly like bounding away. They were followed by the most absolute immobility.

The absurd impulse to run out after Jacobus (for I had been startled, too) once repressed, I took a chair, placed it not very far from her, sat down deliberately, and began to talk about the garden, caring not what I said, but using a gentle caressing intonation as one talks to soothe a startled wild animal. I could not even be certain that she understood me. She never raised her face nor attempted to look my way. I kept on talking only to prevent her from taking flight. She had another of those quivering, repressed starts which made me catch my breath with apprehension.

Ultimately I formed a notion that what prevented her perhaps from going off in one great, nervous leap, was the scantiness of her attire. The wicker armchair was the most substantial thing about her person. What she had on under that dingy, loose, amber wrapper must have been of the most flimsy and airy character. One could not help being aware of it. It was obvious. I felt it actually embarrassing at first; but that sort of embarrassment is got over easily by a mind not enslaved by narrow prejudices. I did not avert my gaze from Alice. I went on talking with ingratiating softness, the recollection that, most likely, she had never before been spoken to by a strange man adding to my assurance. I don't know why an emotional tenseness should have crept into the situation. But it did. And just as I was becoming aware of it a slight scream cut short my flow of urbane speech.

The scream did not proceed from the girl. It was emitted behind me, and caused me to turn my head sharply. I understood at once that the apparition in the doorway was the elderly relation of Jacobus, the companion, the gouvernante. While she remained thunderstruck, I got up and made her a low bow.

The ladies of Jacobus's household evidently spent their days in light attire. This stumpy old woman with a face like a large wrinkled lemon, beady eyes, and a shock of iron-grey hair, was dressed in a garment of some ash-coloured, silky, light stuff. It fell from her thick neck down to her toes with the simplicity of an unadorned nightgown. It made her appear truly cylindrical. She exclaimed: "How did you get here?"

Before I could say a word she vanished and presently I heard a confusion of shrill protestations in a distant part of the house. Obviously no one could tell her how I got there. In a moment, with great outcries from two negro women following her, she waddled back to the doorway, infuriated.

"What do you want here?"

I turned to the girl. She was sitting straight up now, her hands posed on the arms of the chair. I appealed to her.

"Surely, Miss Alice, you will not let them drive me out into the street?"

Her magnificent black eyes, narrowed, long in shape, swept over me with an indefinable expression, then in a harsh, contemptuous voice she let fall in French a sort of explanation:

"*C'est papa.*"

I made another low bow to the old woman.

She turned her back on me in order to drive away her black henchwomen, then surveying my person in a peculiar manner with one small eye nearly closed and her face all drawn up on that side as if with a twinge of toothache, she stepped out on the verandah, sat down in a rocking-chair some distance away, and took up her knitting from a little table. Before she started at it she plunged one of the needles into the mop of her grey hair and stirred it vigorously.

Her elementary nightgown-sort of frock clung to her ancient, stumpy, and floating form. She wore white cotton stockings and flat brown velvet slippers. Her feet and ankles were obtrusively visible on the foot-rest. She began to rock herself slightly, while she knitted. I had resumed my seat and kept quiet, for I mistrusted that old woman. What if she ordered me to depart? She seemed capable of any outrage. She had snorted once or twice; she was knitting violently. Suddenly she piped at the young girl in French a question which I translate colloquially:

"What's your father up to, now?"

The young creature shrugged her shoulders so comprehensively that her whole body swayed within the loose wrapper; and in that unexpectedly harsh voice which yet had a seductive quality to the senses, like certain kinds of natural rough wines one drinks with pleasure:

"It's some captain. Leave me alone—will you!"

The chair rocked quicker, the old, thin voice was like a whistle.

"You and your father make a pair. He would stick at nothing—that's well known. But I didn't expect this."

I thought it high time to air some of my own French. I remarked modestly, but firmly, that this was business. I had some matters to talk over with Mr. Jacobus.

At once she piped out a derisive "Poor innocent!" Then, with a change of tone: "The shop's for business. Why don't you go to the shop to talk with him?"

The furious speed of her fingers and knitting-needles made one dizzy; and with squeaky indignation:

"Sitting here staring at that girl—is that what you call business?"

"No," I said suavely. "I call this pleasure—an unexpected pleasure. And unless Miss Alice objects—"

I half turned to her. She flung at me an angry and contemptuous "Don't care!" and leaning her elbow on her knees took her chin in her hand—a Jacobus chin undoubtedly. And those heavy eyelids, this black irritated stare reminded me of Jacobus, too—the wealthy merchant, the respected one. The design of her eyebrows also was the same, rigid and ill-omened. Yes! I traced in her a resemblance to both of them. It came to me as a sort of surprising remote inference that both these Jacobuses were rather handsome men after all. I said:

"Oh! Then I shall stare at you till you smile."

She favoured me again with an even more viciously scornful "Don't care!"

The old woman broke in blunt and shrill:

"Hear his impudence! And you too! Don't care! Go at least and put some more clothes on. Sitting there like this before this sailor riff-raff."

The sun was about to leave the Pearl of the Ocean for other seas, for other lands. The walled garden full of shadows blazed with colour as if the flowers were giving up the light absorbed during the day. The amazing old woman became very explicit. She suggested to the girl a corset and a petticoat with a cynical unreserve which humiliated me. Was I of no more account than a wooden dummy? The girl snapped out: "Shan't!"

It was not the naughty retort of a vulgar child; it had a note of desperation. Clearly my intrusion had somehow upset the balance of their established relations. The old woman knitted with furious accuracy, her eyes fastened down on her work.

"Oh, you are the true child of your father! And *that* talks of entering a convent! Letting herself be stared at by a fellow."

"Leave off."

"Shameless thing!"

"Old sorceress," the girl uttered distinctly, preserving her meditative pose, chin in hand, and a far-away stare over the garden.

It was like the quarrel of the kettle and the pot. The old woman flew out of the chair, banged down her work, and with a great play of thick limb perfectly visible in that weird, clinging garment of hers, strode at the girl—who never stirred. I was experiencing a sort of trepidation when, as if awed by that unconscious attitude, the aged relative of Jacobus turned short upon me.

She was, I perceived, armed with a knitting-needle; and as she raised her hand her intention seemed to be to throw it at me like a dart. But she only used it to scratch her head with, examining me the while at close range, one eye nearly shut and her face distorted by a whimsical, one-sided grimace.

"My dear man," she asked abruptly, "do you expect any good to come of this?"

"I do hope so indeed, Miss Jacobus." I tried to speak in the easy tone of an afternoon caller. "You see, I am here after some bags."

"Bags! Look at that now! Didn't I hear you holding forth to that graceless wretch?"

"You would like to see me in my grave," uttered the motionless girl hoarsely.

"Grave! What about me? Buried alive before I am dead for the sake of a thing blessed with such a pretty father!" she cried; and turning to me: "You're one of these men he does business with. Well—why don't you leave us in peace, my good fellow?"

It was said in a tone—this "leave us in peace!" There was a sort of ruffianly familiarity, a superiority, a scorn in it. I was to hear it more than once, for you would show an imperfect knowledge of human nature if you thought that this was my last visit to that house—where no respectable person had put foot for ever so many years. No, you would be very much mistaken if you imagined that this reception had scared me away. First of all I was not going to run before a grotesque and ruffianly old woman.

And then you mustn't forget these necessary bags. That first evening Jacobus made me stay to dinner; after, however, telling me loyally that he didn't know whether he could do anything at all for me. He had been thinking it over. It was too difficult, he feared. . . . But he did not give it up in so many words.

We were only three at table; the girl by means of repeated "Won't!" "Shan't!" and "Don't care!" having conveyed and affirmed her intention not to come to the table, not to have any dinner, not to move from the verandah. The old relative hopped about in her flat slippers and piped indignantly, Jacobus towered over her and murmured placidly in his throat; I joined jocularly from a distance, throwing in a few words, for which under the cover of the night I received secretly a most vicious poke in the ribs from the old woman's elbow or perhaps her fist. I restrained a cry. And all the time the girl didn't even condescend to raise her head to look at any of us. All this may sound childish—and yet that stony, petulant sullenness had an obscurely tragic flavour.

And so we sat down to the food around the light of a good many candles while she remained crouching out there, staring in the dark as if feeding her bad temper on the heavily scented air of the admirable garden.

Before leaving I said to Jacobus that I would come next day to hear if the bag affair had made any progress. He shook his head slightly at that.

"I'll haunt your house daily till you pull it off. You'll be always finding me here."

His faint, melancholy smile did not part his thick lips.

"That will be all right, Captain."

Then seeing me to the door, very tranquil, he murmured earnestly the recommendation: "Make yourself at home," and also the hospitable hint about there being always "a plate of soup." It was only on my way to the quay, down the ill-lighted streets, that I remembered I had been engaged to dine that very evening with the S— family. Though vexed with my forgetfulness (it would be rather awkward to explain) I couldn't help thinking that it had procured me a more amusing evening. And besides—business. The sacred business—.

In a barefooted negro who overtook me at a run and bolted down the landing-steps I recognised Jacobus's boatman, who must have been feeding in the kitchen. His usual "Good-night, sah!" as I went up my ship's ladder had a more cordial sound than on previous occasions.

5

I KEPT my word to Jacobus. I haunted his home. He was perpetually finding me there of an afternoon when he popped in for a moment from the "store." The sound of my voice talking to his Alice greeted him on his doorstep; and when he returned for good in the evening, ten to one he would hear it still going on in the verandah. I just nodded to him; he would sit down heavily and gently, and watch with a sort of approving anxiety my efforts to make his daughter smile.

I called her often "Alice," right before him; sometimes I would address her as Miss "Don't Care," and I exhausted myself in nonsensical chatter without succeeding once in taking her out of her peevish and tragic self. There were moments when I felt I must break out and start swearing at her till all was blue. And I fancied that had I done so Jacobus would not have moved a muscle. A sort of shady, intimate understanding seemed to have been established between us.

I must say the girl treated her father exactly in the same way she treated me.

And how could it have been otherwise? She treated me as she treated her father. She had never seen a visitor. She did not know how men behaved. I belonged to the low lot with whom her father did business at the port. I was of no account. So was her father. The only decent people in the world were the people of the island, who would have nothing to do with him because of something wicked he had done. This was apparently the explanation Miss Jacobus had given her of the household's isolated position. For she had to be told something! And I feel convinced that this version had been assented to by Jacobus. I must say the old woman was putting it forward with considerable gusto. It was on her lips the universal explanation, the universal allusion, the universal taunt.

One day Jacobus came in early and, beckoning me into the dining-room, wiped his brow with a weary gesture and told me that he had managed to unearth a supply of quarter-bags.

"It's fourteen hundred your ship wanted, did you say, Captain?"

"Yes, yes!" I replied eagerly; but he remained calm. He looked more tired than I had ever seen him before.

"Well, Captain, you may go and tell your people that they can get that lot from my brother."

As I remained open-mouthed at this, he added his usual placid formula of assurance:

"You'll find it correct, Captain."

"You spoke to your brother about it?" I was distinctly awed. "And for me? Because he must have known that my ship's the only one hung up for bags. How on earth—"

He wiped his brow again. I noticed that he was dressed with unusual care, in clothes in which I had never seen him before. He avoided my eye.

"You've heard people talk, of course. . . . That's true enough. He . . . I . . . We certainly. . . for several years . . ." His voice declined to a mere sleepy murmur. "You see I had something to tell him of, something which—"

His murmur stopped. He was not going to tell me what this something was. And I didn't care. Anxious to carry the news to my charterers, I ran back on the verandah to get my hat.

At the bustle I made the girl turned her eyes slowly in my direction, and even the old woman was checked in her knitting. I stopped a moment to exclaim excitedly:

"Your father's a brick, Miss Don't Care. That's what he is."

She beheld my elation in scornful surprise. Jacobus with unwonted familiarity seized my arm as I flew through the dining-room, and breathed heavily at me a proposal about "A plate of soup" that evening. I answered distractedly: "Eh? What? Oh, thanks! Certainly. With pleasure," and tore myself away. Dine with him? Of course. The merest gratitude—

But some three hours afterwards, in the dusky, silent street, paved with cobble-stones, I became aware that it was not mere gratitude which was guiding my steps towards the house with the old garden, where for years no guest other than myself had ever dined. Mere gratitude does not gnaw at one's interior economy in that particular way. Hunger might; but I was not feeling particularly hungry for Jacobus's food.

On that occasion, too, the girl refused to come to the table.

My exasperation grew. The old woman cast malicious glances at me. I said suddenly to Jacobus: "Here! Put some chicken and salad on that plate." He obeyed without raising his eyes. I carried it with a knife and fork and a serviette out on the verandah. The garden was one mass of gloom, like a cemetery of flowers buried in the darkness, and she, in the chair, seemed to muse mournfully over the extinction of light and colour. Only whiffs of heavy scent passed like wandering, fragrant souls of that departed multitude of blossoms. I talked volubly, jocularly, persuasively, tenderly; I talked in a subdued tone. To a listener it would have sounded like the murmur of a pleading lover. Whenever I paused expectantly there was only a deep silence. It was like offering food to a seated statue.

"I haven't been able to swallow a single morsel thinking of you out here starving yourself in the dark. It's positively cruel to be so obstinate. Think of my sufferings."

"Don't care."

I felt as if I could have done her some violence—shaken her, beaten her maybe. I said:

"Your absurd behaviour will prevent me coming here any more."

"What's that to me?"

"You like it."

"It's false," she snarled.

My hand fell on her shoulder; and if she had flinched I verily believe I would have shaken her. But there was no movement and this immobility disarmed my anger.

"You do. Or you wouldn't be found on the verandah every day. Why are you here, then? There are plenty of rooms in the house. You have your own room to stay in—if you did not want to see me. But you do. You know you do."

I felt a slight shudder under my hand and released my grip as if frightened by that sign of animation in her body. The scented air of the garden came to us in a warm wave like a voluptuous and perfumed sigh.

"Go back to them," she whispered, almost pitifully.

As I re-entered the dining-room I saw Jacobus cast down his eyes. I banged the plate on the table. At this demonstration of ill-humour he murmured something in an apologetic tone, and I turned on him viciously as if he were accountable to me for these "abominable eccentricities," I believe I called them.

"But I dare say Miss Jacobus here is responsible for most of this offensive manner," I added loftily.

She piped out at once in her brazen, ruffianly manner:

"Eh? Why don't you leave us in peace, my good fellow?"

I was astonished that she should dare before Jacobus. Yet what could he have done to repress her? He needed her too much. He raised a heavy, drowsy glance for an instant, then looked down again. She insisted with shrill finality:

"Haven't you done your business, you two? Well, then—"

She had the true Jacobus impudence, that old woman. Her mop of iron-grey hair was parted, on the side like a man's, raffishly, and she made as if to plunge her fork into it, as she used to do with the knitting-needle, but refrained. Her little black eyes sparkled venomously. I turned to my host at the head of the table—menacingly as it were.

"Well, and what do you say to that, Jacobus? Am I to take it that we have done with each other?"

I had to wait a little. The answer when it came was rather unexpected, and in quite another spirit than the question.

"I certainly think we might do some business yet with those potatoes of mine, Captain. You will find that—"

I cut him short.

"I've told you before that I don't trade."

His broad chest heaved without a sound in a noiseless sigh.

"Think it over, Captain," he murmured, tenacious and tranquil; and I burst into a jarring laugh, remembering how he had stuck to the circus-rider woman—the depth of passion under that placid surface, which even cuts with a riding-whip (so the legend had it) could never raffle into the semblance of a storm; something like the passion of a fish would be if one could imagine such a thing as a passionate fish.

That evening I experienced more distinctly than ever the sense of moral discomfort which always attended me in that house lying under the ban of all "decent" people. I refused to stay on and smoke after dinner; and when I put my hand into the thickly-cushioned palm of Jacobus, I said to myself that it would be for the last time under his roof. I pressed his bulky paw heartily nevertheless. Hadn't he got me out of a serious difficulty? To the few words of acknowledgment I was bound, and indeed quite willing, to utter, he answered by stretching his closed lips in his melancholy, glued-together smile.

"That will be all right, I hope, Captain," he breathed out weightily.

"What do you mean?" I asked, alarmed. "That your brother might yet—"

"Oh, no," he reassured me. "He . . . he's a man of his word, Captain."

My self-communion as I walked away from his door, trying to believe that this was for the last time, was not satisfactory. I was aware myself that I was not sincere in my reflections as to Jacobus's motives, and, of course, the very next day I went back again.

How weak, irrational, and absurd we are! How easily carried away whenever our awakened imagination brings us the irritating hint of a desire! I cared for the girl in a particular way, seduced by the moody expression of her face, by her obstinate silences, her rare, scornful words; by the perpetual pout of her closed lips, the black depths of her fixed gaze turned slowly upon me as if in contemptuous provocation, only to be averted next moment with an exasperating indifference.

Of course the news of my assiduity had spread all over the little town. I noticed a change in the manner of my acquaintances and even something different in the nods of the other captains, when meeting them at the landing-steps or in the offices where business called me. The old-maidish head clerk treated me with distant punctiliousness and, as it were, gathered his skirts round him for fear of contamination. It seemed to me that the very niggers on the quays turned to look after me as I passed; and as to Jacobus's boatman his "Good-night, sah!" when he put me on board was no longer merely cordial—it had a familiar, confidential sound as though we had been partners in some villainy.

My friend S— the elder passed me on the other side of the street with a wave of the hand and an ironic smile. The younger brother, the one they had married to an elderly shrew, he, on the strength of an older friendship and as if paying a debt of gratitude, took the liberty to utter a word of warning.

"You're doing yourself no good by your choice of friends, my dear chap," he said with infantile gravity.

As I knew that the meeting of the brothers Jacobus was the subject of excited comment in the whole of the sugary Pearl of the Ocean I wanted to know why I was blamed.

"I have been the occasion of a move which may end in a reconciliation surely desirable from the point of view of the proprieties—don't you know?"

"Of course, if that girl were disposed of it would certainly facilitate—" he mused sagely, then, inconsequential creature, gave me a light tap on the lower part of my waistcoat. "You old sinner," he cried jovially, "much you care for proprieties. But you had better look out for yourself, you know, with a personage like Jacobus who has no sort of reputation to lose."

He had recovered his gravity of a respectable citizen by that time and added regretfully:

"All the women of our family are perfectly scandalised."

But by that time I had given up visiting the S— family and the D— family. The elder ladies pulled such faces when I showed myself, and the multitude of related young ladies received me with such a variety of looks: wondering, awed, mocking (except Miss Mary, who spoke to me and looked at me with hushed, pained compassion as though I had been ill), that I had no difficulty in giving them all up. I would have given up the society of the whole town, for the sake of sitting near that girl, snarling and superb and barely clad in that flimsy, dingy, amber wrapper, open low at the throat. She looked, with the wild wisps of hair hanging down her tense face, as though she had just jumped out of bed in the panic of a fire.

She sat leaning on her elbow, looking at nothing. Why did she stay listening to my absurd chatter? And not only that; but why did she powder her face in preparation for my arrival? It seemed to be her idea of making a toilette, and in her untidy negligence a sign of great effort towards personal adornment.

But I might have been mistaken. The powdering might have been her daily practice and her presence in the verandah a sign of an indifference so complete as to take no account of my existence. Well, it was all one to me.

I loved to watch her slow changes of pose, to look at her long immobilities composed in the graceful lines of her body, to observe the mysterious narrow stare of her splendid black eyes, somewhat long in shape, half closed, contemplating the void. She was like a spellbound creature with the forehead of a goddess crowned by the dishevelled magnificent hair of a gipsy tramp. Even her indifference was seductive. I felt myself growing attached to her by the bond of an irrealisable desire, for I kept my head—quite. And I put up with the moral discomfort of Jacobus's sleepy watchfulness, tranquil, and yet so expressive; as if there had been a tacit pact between us two. I put up with the insolence of the old woman's: "Aren't you ever going to leave us in peace, my good fellow?" with her taunts; with her brazen and sinister scolding. She was of the true Jacobus stock, and no mistake.

Directly I got away from the girl I called myself many hard names. What folly was this? I would ask myself. It was like being the slave of some depraved habit. And I returned to her with my head clear, my heart certainly free, not even moved by pity for that castaway (she was as much of a castaway as any one ever wrecked on a desert island), but as if beguiled by some extraordinary promise. Nothing more unworthy could be imagined. The recollection of that tremulous whisper when I gripped her shoulder with one hand and held a plate of chicken with the other was enough to make me break all my good resolutions.

Her insulting taciturnity was enough sometimes to make one gnash one's teeth with rage. When she opened her mouth it was only to be abominably rude in harsh tones to the associate of her reprobate father; and the full approval of her aged relative was conveyed to her by offensive chuckles. If not that, then her remarks, always uttered in the tone of scathing contempt, were of the most appalling inanity.

How could it have been otherwise? That plump, ruffianly Jacobus old maid in the tight grey frock had never taught her any manners. Manners I suppose are not necessary for born castaways. No educational establishment could ever be induced to accept her as a pupil—on account of the proprieties, I imagine. And Jacobus had not been able to send her away anywhere. How could he have done it? Who with? Where to? He himself was not enough of an adventurer to think of settling down anywhere else. His passion had tossed him at the tail of a circus up and down strange coasts, but, the storm over, he had drifted back shamelessly where, social outcast as he was, he remained still a Jacobus—one of the oldest families on the island, older than the French even. There must have been a Jacobus in at the death of the last Dodo. . . . The girl had learned nothing, she had never listened to a general conversation, she knew nothing, she had heard of nothing. She could read certainly; but all the reading matter that ever came in her way were the newspapers provided for the captains' room of the "store." Jacobus had the habit of taking these sheets home now and then in a very stained and ragged condition.

As her mind could not grasp the meaning of any matters treated there except police-court reports and accounts of crimes, she had formed for herself a notion of the civilised world as a scene of murders, abductions, burglaries, stabbing affrays, and every sort of desperate violence. England and France, Paris and London (the only two towns of which she seemed to have heard), appeared to her sinks of abomination, reeking with blood, in contrast to her little island where petty larceny was about the standard of current misdeeds, with, now and then, some more pronounced crime—and that only amongst the imported coolie labourers on sugar estates or the negroes of the town. But in Europe these things were being done daily by a wicked population of white men amongst whom, as that ruffianly, aristocratic old Miss Jacobus pointed out, the wandering sailors, the associates of her precious papa, were the lowest of the low.

It was impossible to give her a sense of proportion. I suppose she figured England to herself as about the size of the Pearl of the Ocean; in which case it would certainly have been reeking with gore and a mere wreck of burgled houses from end to end. One could not make her understand that these horrors on which she fed her imagination were lost in the mass of orderly life like a few drops of blood in the ocean. She directed upon me for a moment the uncomprehending glance of her narrowed eyes and then would turn her scornful powdered face away without a word. She would not even take the trouble to shrug her shoulders.

At that time the batches of papers brought by the last mail reported a series of crimes in the East End of London, there was a sensational case of abduction in France and a fine display of armed robbery in Australia. One afternoon crossing the dining-room I heard Miss Jacobus piping in the verandah with venomous animosity: "I don't know what your precious papa is plotting with that fellow. But he's just the sort of man who's capable of carrying you off far away somewhere and then cutting your throat some day for your money."

There was a good half of the length of the verandah between their chairs. I came out and sat down fiercely midway between them.

"Yes, that's what we do with girls in Europe," I began in a grimly matter-of-fact tone. I think Miss Jacobus was disconcerted by my sudden appearance. I turned upon her with cold ferocity:

"As to objectionable old women, they are first strangled quietly, then cut up into small pieces and thrown away, a bit here and a bit there. They vanish—"

I cannot go so far as to say I had terrified her. But she was troubled by my truculence, the more so because I had been always addressing her with a politeness she did not deserve. Her plump, knitting hands fell slowly on her knees. She said not a word while I fixed her with severe determination. Then as I turned away from her at last, she laid down her work gently and, with noiseless movements, retreated from the verandah. In fact, she vanished.

But I was not thinking of her. I was looking at the girl. It was what I was coming for daily; troubled, ashamed, eager; finding in my nearness to her a unique sensation which I indulged with dread, self-contempt, and deep pleasure, as if it were a secret vice bound to end in my undoing, like the habit of some drug or other which ruins and degrades its slave.

I looked her over, from the top of her dishevelled head, down the lovely line of the shoulder, following the curve of the hip, the draped form of the long limb, right down to her fine ankle below a torn, soiled flounce; and as far as the point of the shabby, high-heeled, blue slipper, dangling from her well-shaped foot, which she moved slightly, with quick, nervous jerks, as if impatient of my presence. And in the scent of the massed flowers I seemed to breathe her special and inexplicable charm, the heady perfume of the everlastingly irritated captive of the garden.

I looked at her rounded chin, the Jacobus chin; at the full, red lips pouting in the powdered, sallow face; at the firm modelling of the cheek, the grains of white in the hairs of the straight sombre eyebrows; at the long eyes, a narrowed gleam of liquid white and intense motionless black, with their gaze so empty of thought, and so absorbed in their fixity that she seemed to be staring at her own lonely image, in some far-off mirror hidden from my sight amongst the trees.

And suddenly, without looking at me, with the appearance of a person speaking to herself, she asked, in that voice slightly harsh yet mellow and always irritated:

"Why do you keep on coming here?"

"Why do I keep on coming here?" I repeated, taken by surprise. I could not have told her. I could not even tell myself with sincerity why I was coming there. "What's the good of you asking a question like that?"

"Nothing is any good," she observed scornfully to the empty air, her chin propped on her hand, that hand never extended to any man, that no one had ever grasped—for I had only grasped her shoulder once—that generous, fine, somewhat masculine hand. I knew well the peculiarly efficient shape—broad at the base, tapering at the fingers—of that hand, for which there was nothing in the world to lay hold of. I pretended to be playful.

"No! But do you really care to know?"

She shrugged indolently her magnificent shoulders, from which the dingy thin wrapper was slipping a little.

"Oh—never mind—never mind!"

There was something smouldering under those airs of lassitude. She exasperated me by the provocation of her nonchalance, by something elusive and defiant in her very form which I wanted to seize. I said roughly:

"Why? Don't you think I should tell you the truth?"

Her eyes glided my way for a sidelong look, and she murmured, moving only her full, pouting lips:

"I think you would not dare."

"Do you imagine I am afraid of you? What on earth. . . . Well, it's possible, after all, that I don't know exactly why I am coming here. Let us say, with Miss Jacobus, that it is for no good. You seem to believe the outrageous things she says, if you do have a row with her now and then."

She snapped out viciously:

"Who else am I to believe?

"I don't know," I had to own, seeing her suddenly very helpless and condemned to moral solitude by the verdict of a respectable community. "You might believe me, if you chose."

She made a slight movement and asked me at once, with an effort as if making an experiment:

"What is the business between you and papa?"

"Don't you know the nature of your father's business? Come! He sells provisions to ships."

She became rigid again in her crouching pose.

"Not that. What brings you here—to this house?"

"And suppose it's you? You would not call that business? Would you? And now let us drop the subject. It's no use. My ship will be ready for sea the day after to-morrow."

She murmured a distinctly scared "So soon," and getting up quickly, went to the little table and poured herself a glass of water. She walked with rapid steps and with an indolent swaying of her whole young figure above the hips; when she passed near me I felt with tenfold force the charm of the peculiar, promising sensation I had formed the habit to seek near her. I thought with sudden dismay that this was the end of it; that after one more day I would be no longer able to come into this verandah, sit on this chair, and taste perversely the flavour of contempt in her indolent poses, drink in the provocation of her scornful looks, and listen to the curt, insolent remarks uttered in that harsh and seductive voice. As if my innermost nature had been altered by the action of some moral poison, I felt an abject dread of going to sea.

I had to exercise a sudden self-control, as one puts on a brake, to prevent myself jumping up to stride about, shout, gesticulate, make her a scene. What for? What about? I had no idea. It was just the relief of violence that I wanted; and I lolled back in my chair, trying to keep my lips formed in a smile; that half-indulgent, half-mocking smile which was my shield against the shafts of her contempt and the insulting sallies flung at me by the old woman.

She drank the water at a draught, with the avidity of raging thirst, and let herself fall on the nearest chair, as if utterly overcome. Her attitude, like certain tones of her voice, had in it something masculine: the knees apart in the ample wrapper, the clasped hands hanging between them, her body leaning forward, with drooping head. I stared at the heavy black coil of twisted hair. It was enormous, crowning the bowed head with a crushing and disdained glory. The escaped wisps hung straight down. And suddenly I perceived that the girl was trembling from head to foot, as though that glass of iced water had chilled her to the bone.

"What's the matter now?" I said, startled, but in no very sympathetic mood.

She shook her bowed, overweighted head and cried in a stifled voice but with a rising inflection:

"Go away! Go away! Go away!"

I got up then and approached her, with a strange sort of anxiety. I looked down at her round, strong neck, then stooped low enough to peep at her face. And I began to tremble a little myself.

"What on earth are you gone wild about, Miss Don't Care?"

She flung herself backwards violently, her head going over the back of the chair. And now it was her smooth, full, palpitating throat that lay exposed to my bewildered stare. Her eyes were nearly closed, with only a horrible white gleam under the lids as if she were dead.

"What has come to you?" I asked in awe. "What are you terrifying yourself with?"

She pulled herself together, her eyes open frightfully wide now. The tropical afternoon was lengthening the shadows on the hot, weary earth, the abode of obscure desires, of extravagant hopes, of unimaginable terrors.

"Never mind! Don't care!" Then, after a gasp, she spoke with such frightful rapidity that I could hardly make out the amazing words: "For if you were to shut me up in an empty place as smooth all round as the palm of my hand, I could always strangle myself with my hair."

For a moment, doubting my ears, I let this inconceivable declaration sink into me. It is ever impossible to guess at the wild thoughts that pass through the heads of our fellow-creatures. What monstrous imaginings of violence could have dwelt under the low forehead of that girl who had been taught to regard her father as "capable of anything" more in the light of a misfortune than that of a disgrace; as, evidently, something to be resented and feared rather than to be ashamed of? She seemed, indeed, as unaware of shame as of anything else in the world; but in her ignorance, her resentment and fear took a childish and violent shape.

Of course she spoke without knowing the value of words. What could she know of death —she who knew nothing of life? It was merely as the proof of her being beside herself with some odious apprehension, that this extraordinary speech had moved me, not to pity, but to a fascinated, horrified wonder. I had no idea what notion she had of her danger. Some sort of abduction. It was quite possible with the talk of that atrocious old woman. Perhaps she thought she could be carried off, bound hand and foot and even gagged. At that surmise I felt as if the door of a furnace had been opened in front of me.

"Upon my honour!" I cried. "You shall end by going crazy if you listen to that abominable old aunt of yours—"

I studied her haggard expression, her trembling lips. Her cheeks even seemed sunk a little. But how I, the associate of her disreputable father, the "lowest of the low" from the criminal Europe, could manage to reassure her I had no conception. She was exasperating.

"Heavens and earth! What do you think I can do?"

"I don't know."

Her chin certainly trembled. And she was looking at me with extreme attention. I made a step nearer to her chair.

"I shall do nothing. I promise you that. Will that do? Do you understand? I shall do nothing whatever, of any kind; and the day after to-morrow I shall be gone."

What else could I have said? She seemed to drink in my words with the thirsty avidity with which she had emptied the glass of water. She whispered tremulously, in that touching tone I had heard once before on her lips, and which thrilled me again with the same emotion:

"I would believe you. But what about papa—"

"He be hanged!" My emotion betrayed itself by the brutality of my tone. "I've had enough of your papa. Are you so stupid as to imagine that I am frightened of him? He can't make me do anything."

All that sounded feeble to me in the face of her ignorance. But I must conclude that the "accent of sincerity" has, as some people say, a really irresistible power. The effect was far beyond my hopes,—and even beyond my conception. To watch the change in the girl was like watching a miracle—the gradual but swift relaxation of her tense glance, of her stiffened muscles, of every fibre of her body. That black, fixed stare into which I had read a tragic meaning more than once, in which I had found a sombre seduction, was perfectly empty now, void of all consciousness whatever, and not even aware any longer of my presence; it had become a little sleepy, in the Jacobus fashion.

But, man being a perverse animal, instead of rejoicing at my complete success, I beheld it with astounded and indignant eyes. There was something cynical in that unconcealed alteration, the true Jacobus shamelessness. I felt as though I had been cheated in some rather complicated deal into which I had entered against my better judgment. Yes, cheated without any regard for, at least, the forms of decency.

With an easy, indolent, and in its indolence supple, feline movement, she rose from the chair, so provokingly ignoring me now, that for very rage I held my ground within less than a foot of her. Leisurely and tranquil, behaving right before me with the ease of a person alone in a room, she extended her beautiful arms, with her hands clenched, her body swaying, her head thrown back a little, revelling contemptuously in a sense of relief, easing her limbs in freedom after all these days of crouching, motionless poses when she had been so furious and so afraid.

All this with supreme indifference, incredible, offensive, exasperating, like ingratitude doubled with treachery.

I ought to have been flattered, perhaps, but, on the contrary, my anger grew; her movement to pass by me as if I were a wooden post or a piece of furniture, that unconcerned movement brought it to a head.

I won't say I did not know what I was doing, but, certainly, cool reflection had nothing to do with the circumstance that next moment both my arms were round her waist. It was an impulsive action, as one snatches at something falling or escaping; and it had no hypocritical gentleness about it either. She had no time to make a sound, and the first kiss I planted on her closed lips was vicious enough to have been a bite.

She did not resist, and of course I did not stop at one. She let me go on, not as if she were inanimate—I felt her there, close against me, young, full of vigour, of life, a strong desirable creature, but as if she did not care in the least, in the absolute assurance of her safety, what I did or left undone. Our faces brought close together in this storm of haphazard caresses, her big, black, wide-open eyes looked into mine without the girl appearing either angry or pleased or moved in any way. In that steady gaze which seemed impersonally to watch my madness I could detect a slight surprise, perhaps—nothing more. I showered kisses upon her face and there did not seem to be any reason why this should not go on for ever.

That thought flashed through my head, and I was on the point of desisting, when, all at once, she began to struggle with a sudden violence which all but freed her instantly, which revived my exasperation with her, indeed a fierce desire never to let her go any more. I tightened my embrace in time, gasping out: "No—you don't!" as if she were my mortal enemy. On her part not a word was said. Putting her hands against my chest, she pushed with all her might without succeeding to break the circle of my arms. Except that she seemed thoroughly awake now, her eyes gave me no clue whatever. To meet her black stare was like looking into a deep well, and I was totally unprepared for her change of tactics. Instead of trying to tear my hands apart, she flung herself upon my breast and with a downward, undulating, serpentine motion, a quick sliding dive, she got away from me smoothly. It was all very swift; I saw her pick up the tail of her wrapper and run for the door at the end of the verandah not very gracefully. She appeared to be limping a little—and then she vanished; the door swung behind her so noiselessly that I could not believe it was completely closed. I had a distinct suspicion of her black eye being at the crack to watch what I would do. I could not make up my mind whether to shake my fist in that direction or blow a kiss.

6

Either would have been perfectly consistent with my feelings. I gazed at the door, hesitating, but in the end I did neither. The monition of some sixth sense—the sense of guilt, maybe, that sense which always acts too late, alas!—warned me to look round; and at once I became aware that the conclusion of this tumultuous episode was likely to be a matter of lively anxiety. Jacobus was standing in the doorway of the dining-room. How long he had been there it was impossible to guess; and remembering my struggle with the girl I thought he must have been its mute witness from beginning to end. But this supposition seemed almost incredible. Perhaps that impenetrable girl had heard him come in and had got away in time.

He stepped on to the verandah in his usual manner, heavy-eyed, with glued lips. I marvelled at the girl's resemblance to this man. Those long, Egyptian eyes, that low forehead of a stupid goddess, she had found in the sawdust of the circus; but all the rest of the face, the design and the modelling, the rounded chin, the very lips—all that was Jacobus, fined down, more finished, more expressive.

His thick hand fell on and grasped with force the back of a light chair (there were several standing about) and I perceived the chance of a broken head at the end of all this—most likely. My mortification was extreme. The scandal would be horrible; that was unavoidable. But how to act so as to satisfy myself I did not know. I stood on my guard and at any rate faced him. There was nothing else for it. Of one thing I was certain, that, however brazen my attitude, it could never equal the characteristic Jacobus impudence.

He gave me his melancholy, glued smile and sat down. I own I was relieved. The perspective of passing from kisses to blows had nothing particularly attractive in it. Perhaps—perhaps he had seen nothing? He behaved as usual, but he had never before found me alone on the verandah. If he had alluded to it, if he had asked: "Where's Alice?" or something of the sort, I would have been able to judge from the tone. He would give me no opportunity. The striking peculiarity was that he had never looked up at me yet. "He knows," I said to myself confidently. And my contempt for him relieved my disgust with myself.

"You are early home," I remarked.

"Things are very quiet; nothing doing at the store to-day," he explained with a cast-down air.

"Oh, well, you know, I am off," I said, feeling that this, perhaps, was the best thing to do.

"Yes," he breathed out. "Day after to-morrow."

This was not what I had meant; but as he gazed persistently on the floor, I followed the direction of his glance. In the absolute stillness of the house we stared at the high-heeled slipper the girl had lost in her flight. We stared. It lay overturned.

After what seemed a very long time to me, Jacobus hitched his chair forward, stooped with extended arm and picked it up. It looked a slender thing in his big, thick hands. It was not really a slipper, but a low shoe of blue, glazed kid, rubbed and shabby. It had straps to go over the instep, but the girl only thrust her feet in, after her slovenly manner. Jacobus raised his eyes from the shoe to look at me.

"Sit down, Captain," he said at last, in his subdued tone.

As if the sight of that shoe had renewed the spell, I gave up suddenly the idea of leaving the house there and then. It had become impossible. I sat down, keeping my eyes on the fascinating object. Jacobus turned his daughter's shoe over and over in his cushioned paws as if studying the way the thing was made. He contemplated the thin sole for a time; then glancing inside with an absorbed air:

"I am glad I found you here, Captain."

I answered this by some sort of grunt, watching him covertly. Then I added: "You won't have much more of me now."

He was still deep in the interior of that shoe on which my eyes too were resting.

"Have you thought any more of this deal in potatoes I spoke to you about the other day?"

"No, I haven't," I answered curtly. He checked my movement to rise by an austere, commanding gesture of the hand holding that fatal shoe. I remained seated and glared at him. "You know I don't trade."

"You ought to, Captain. You ought to."

I reflected. If I left that house now I would never see the girl again. And I felt I must see her once more, if only for an instant. It was a need, not to be reasoned with, not to be disregarded. No, I did not want to go away. I wanted to stay for one more experience of that strange provoking sensation and of indefinite desire, the habit of which had made me—me of all people!—dread the prospect of going to sea.

"Mr. Jacobus," I pronounced slowly. "Do you really think that upon the whole and taking various' matters into consideration—I mean everything, do you understand?—it would be a good thing for me to trade, let us say, with you?"

I waited for a while. He went on looking at the shoe which he held now crushed in the middle, the worn point of the toe and the high heel protruding on each side of his heavy fist.

"That will be all right," he said, facing me squarely at last.

"Are you sure?"

"You'll find it quite correct, Captain." He had uttered his habitual phrases in his usual placid, breath-saving voice and stood my hard, inquisitive stare sleepily without as much as a wink.

"Then let us trade," I said, turning my shoulder to him. "I see you are bent on it."

I did not want an open scandal, but I thought that outward decency may be bought too dearly at times. I included Jacobus, myself, the whole population of the island, in the same contemptuous disgust as though we had been partners in an ignoble transaction. And the remembered vision at sea, diaphanous and blue, of the Pearl of the Ocean at sixty miles off;

the unsubstantial, clear marvel of it as if evoked by the art of a beautiful and pure magic, turned into a thing of horrors too. Was this the fortune this vaporous and rare apparition had held for me in its hard heart, hidden within the shape as of fair dreams and mist? Was this my luck?

"I think"—Jacobus became suddenly audible after what seemed the silence of vile meditation—"that you might conveniently take some thirty tons. That would be about the lot, Captain."

"Would it? The lot! I dare say it would be convenient, but I haven't got enough money for that."

I had never seen him so animated.

"No!" he exclaimed with what I took for the accent of grim menace. "That's a pity." He paused, then, unrelenting: "How much money have you got, Captain?" he inquired with awful directness.

It was my turn to face him squarely. I did so and mentioned the amount I could dispose of. And I perceived that he was disappointed. He thought it over, his calculating gaze lost in mine, for quite a long time before he came out in a thoughtful tone with the rapacious suggestion:

"You could draw some more from your charterers. That would be quite easy, Captain."

"No, I couldn't," I retorted brusquely. "I've drawn my salary up to date, and besides, the ship's accounts are closed."

I was growing furious. I pursued: "And I'll tell you what: if I could do it I wouldn't." Then throwing off all restraint, I added: "You are a bit too much of a Jacobus, Mr. Jacobus."

The tone alone was insulting enough, but he remained tranquil, only a little puzzled, till something seemed to dawn upon him; but the unwonted light in his eyes died out instantly. As a Jacobus on his native heath, what a mere skipper chose to say could not touch him, outcast as he was. As a ship-chandler he could stand anything. All I caught of his mumble was a vague—"quite correct," than which nothing could have been more egregiously false at bottom—to my view, at least. But I remembered—I had never forgotten—that I must see the girl. I did not mean to go. I meant to stay in the house till I had seen her once more.

"Look here!" I said finally. "I'll tell you what I'll do. I'll take as many of your confounded potatoes as my money will buy, on condition that you go off at once down to the wharf to see them loaded in the lighter and sent alongside the ship straight away. Take the invoice and a signed receipt with you. Here's the key of my desk. Give it to Burns. He will pay you."

He got up from his chair before I had finished speaking, but he refused to take the key. Burns would never do it. He wouldn't like to ask him even.

"Well, then," I said, eyeing him slightingly, "there's nothing for it, Mr. Jacobus, but you must wait on board till I come off to settle with you."

"That will be all right, Captain. I will go at once."

He seemed at a loss what to do with the girl's shoe he was still holding in his fist. Finally, looking dully at me, he put it down on the chair from which he had risen.

"And you, Captain? Won't you come along, too, just to see—"

"Don't bother about me. I'll take care of myself."

He remained perplexed for a moment, as if trying to understand; and then his weighty: "Certainly, certainly, Captain," seemed to be the outcome of some sudden thought. His big chest heaved. Was it a sigh? As he went out to hurry off those potatoes he never looked back at me.

I waited till the noise of his footsteps had died out of the dining-room, and I waited a little longer. Then turning towards the distant door I raised my voice along the verandah:

"Alice!"

Nothing answered me, not even a stir behind the door. Jacobus's house might have been made empty for me to make myself at home in. I did not call again. I had become aware of a great discouragement. I was mentally jaded, morally dejected. I turned to the garden again, sitting down with my elbows spread on the low balustrade, and took my head in my hands.

The evening closed upon me. The shadows lengthened, deepened, mingled together into a pool of twilight in which the flower-beds glowed like coloured embers; whiffs of heavy scent came to me as if the dusk of this hemisphere were but the dimness of a temple and the garden an enormous censer swinging before the altar of the stars. The colours of the blossoms deepened, losing their glow one by one.

The girl, when I turned my head at a slight noise, appeared to me very tall and slender, advancing with a swaying limp, a floating and uneven motion which ended in the sinking of her shadowy form into the deep low chair. And I don't know why or whence I received the impression that she had come too late. She ought to have appeared at my call. She ought to have . . . It was as if a supreme opportunity had been missed.

I rose and took a seat close to her, nearly opposite her arm-chair. Her ever discontented voice addressed me at once, contemptuously:

"You are still here."

I pitched mine low.

"You have come out at last."

"I came to look for my shoe—before they bring in the lights."

It was her harsh, enticing whisper, subdued, not very steady, but its low tremulousness gave me no thrill now. I could only make out the oval of her face, her uncovered throat, the long, white gleam of her eyes. She was mysterious enough. Her hands were resting on the arms of the chair. But where was the mysterious and provoking sensation which was like the perfume of her flower-like youth? I said quietly:

"I have got your shoe here." She made no sound and I continued: "You had better give me your foot and I will put it on for you."

She made no movement. I bent low down and groped for her foot under the flounces of the wrapper. She did not withdraw it and I put on the shoe, buttoning the instep-strap. It was an inanimate foot. I lowered it gently to the floor.

"If you buttoned the strap you would not be losing your shoe, Miss Don't Care," I said, trying to be playful without conviction. I felt more like wailing over the lost illusion of vague desire, over the sudden conviction that I would never find again near her the strange, half-evil, half-tender sensation which had given its acrid flavour to so many days, which had made her appear tragic and promising, pitiful and provoking. That was all over.

"Your father picked it up," I said, thinking she may just as well be told of the fact.

"I am not afraid of papa—by himself," she declared scornfully.

"Oh! It's only in conjunction with his disreputable associates, strangers, the 'riff-raff of Europe' as your charming aunt or great-aunt says—men like me, for instance—that you—"

"I am not afraid of you," she snapped out.

"That's because you don't know that I am now doing business with your father. Yes, I am in fact doing exactly what he wants me to do. I've broken my promise to you. That's the sort of man I am. And now—aren't you afraid? If you believe what that dear, kind, truthful old lady says you ought to be."

It was with unexpected modulated softness that the affirmed:

"No. I am not afraid." She hesitated. . . . "Not now."

"Quite right. You needn't be. I shall not see you again before I go to sea." I rose and stood near her chair. "But I shall often think of you in this old garden, passing under the trees over there, walking between these gorgeous flower-beds. You must love this garden—"

"I love nothing."

I heard in her sullen tone the faint echo of that resentfully tragic note which I had found once so provoking. But it left me unmoved except for a sudden and weary conviction of the emptiness of all things under Heaven.

"Good-bye, Alice," I said.

She did not answer, she did not move. To merely take her hand, shake it, and go away seemed impossible, almost improper. I stooped without haste and pressed my lips to her smooth forehead. This was the moment when I realised clearly with a sort of terror my complete detachment from that unfortunate creature. And as I lingered in that cruel self-knowledge I felt the light touch of her arms falling languidly on my neck and received a hasty, awkward, haphazard kiss which missed my lips. No! She was not afraid; but I was no longer moved. Her arms slipped off my neck slowly, she made no sound, the deep wicker arm-chair creaked slightly; only a sense of my dignity prevented me fleeing headlong from that catastrophic revelation.

I traversed the dining-room slowly. I thought: She's listening to my footsteps; she can't help it; she'll hear me open and shut that door. And I closed it as gently behind me as if I had been a thief retreating with his ill-gotten booty. During that stealthy act I experienced the last touch of emotion in that house, at the thought of the girl I had left sitting there in the obscurity, with her heavy hair and empty eyes as black as the night itself, staring into the walled garden, silent, warm, odorous with the perfume of imprisoned flowers, which, like herself, were lost to sight in a world buried in darkness.

The narrow, ill-lighted, rustic streets I knew so well on my way to the harbour were extremely quiet. I felt in my heart that the further one ventures the better one understands how everything in our life is common, short, and empty; that it is in seeking the unknown in our sensations that we discover how mediocre are our attempts and how soon defeated! Jacobus's boatman was waiting at the steps with an unusual air of readiness. He put me alongside the ship, but did not give me his confidential "Good-evening, sah," and, instead of shoving off at once, remained holding by the ladder.

I was a thousand miles from commercial affairs, when on the dark quarter-deck Mr. Burns positively rushed at me, stammering with excitement. He had been pacing the deck distractedly for hours awaiting my arrival. Just before sunset a lighter loaded with potatoes had come alongside with that fat ship-chandler himself sitting on the pile of sacks. He was now stuck immovable in the cabin. What was the meaning of it all? Surely I did not—

"Yes, Mr. Burns, I did," I cut him short. He was beginning to make gestures of despair when I stopped that, too, by giving him the key of my desk and desiring him, in a tone which admitted of no argument, to go below at once, pay Mr. Jacobus's bill, and send him out of the ship.

"I don't want to see him," I confessed frankly, climbing the poop-ladder. I felt extremely tired. Dropping on the seat of the skylight, I gave myself up to idle gazing at the lights about the quay and at the black mass of the mountain on the south side of the harbour. I never heard Jacobus leave the ship with every single sovereign of my ready cash in his pocket. I never heard anything till, a long time afterwards, Mr. Burns, unable to contain himself any longer, intruded upon me with his ridiculously angry lamentations at my weakness and good nature.

"Of course, there's plenty of room in the after-hatch. But they are sure to go rotten down there. Well! I never heard . . . seventeen tons! I suppose I must hoist in that lot first thing to-morrow morning."

"I suppose you must. Unless you drop them overboard. But I'm afraid you can't do that. I wouldn't mind myself, but it's forbidden to throw rubbish into the harbour, you know."

"That is the truest word you have said for many a day, sir—rubbish. That's just what I expect they are. Nearly eighty good gold sovereigns gone; a perfectly clean sweep of your drawer, sir. Bless me if I understand!"

As it was impossible to throw the right light on this commercial transaction I left him to his lamentations and under the impression that I was a hopeless fool. Next day I did not go ashore. For one thing, I had no money to go ashore with—no, not enough to buy a cigarette. Jacobus had made a clean sweep. But that was not the only reason. The Pearl of the Ocean had in a few short hours grown odious to me. And I did not want to meet any one. My reputation had suffered. I knew I was the object of unkind and sarcastic comments.

The following morning at sunrise, just as our stern-fasts had been let go and the tug plucked us out from between the buoys, I saw Jacobus standing up in his boat. The nigger was pulling hard; several baskets of provisions for ships were stowed between the thwarts. The father of Alice was going his morning round. His countenance was tranquil and friendly. He raised his arm and shouted something with great heartiness. But his voice was of the sort that doesn't carry any distance; all I could catch faintly, or rather guess at, were the words "next time" and "quite correct." And it was only of these last that I was certain. Raising my arm perfunctorily for all response, I turned away. I rather resented the familiarity of the thing. Hadn't I settled accounts finally with him by means of that potato bargain?

This being a harbour story it is not my purpose to speak of our passage. I was glad enough to be at sea, but not with the gladness of old days. Formerly I had no memories to take away with me. I shared in the blessed forgetfulness of sailors, that forgetfulness natural and invincible, which resembles innocence in so far that it prevents self-examination. Now however I remembered the girl. During the first few days I was for ever questioning myself as to the nature of facts and sensations connected with her person and with my conduct.

And I must say also that Mr. Burns' intolerable fussing with those potatoes was not calculated to make me forget the part which I had played. He looked upon it as a purely commercial transaction of a particularly foolish kind, and his devotion—if it was devotion and not mere cussedness as I came to regard it before long—inspired him with a zeal to minimise my loss as much as possible. Oh, yes! He took care of those infamous potatoes with a vengeance, as the saying goes.

Everlastingly, there was a tackle over the after-hatch and everlastingly the watch on deck were pulling up, spreading out, picking over, rebagging, and lowering down again, some part of that lot of potatoes. My bargain with all its remotest associations, mental and visual —the garden of flowers and scents, the girl with her provoking contempt and her tragic loneliness of a hopeless castaway—was everlastingly dangled before my eyes, for thousands of miles along the open sea. And as if by a satanic refinement of irony it was accompanied by a most awful smell. Whiffs from decaying potatoes pursued me on the poop, they mingled with my thoughts, with my food, poisoned my very dreams. They made an atmosphere of corruption for the ship.

I remonstrated with Mr. Burns about this excessive care. I would have been well content to batten the hatch down and let them perish under the deck.

That perhaps would have been unsafe. The horrid emanations might have flavoured the cargo of sugar. They seemed strong enough to taint the very ironwork. In addition Mr.

Burns made it a personal matter. He assured me he knew how to treat a cargo of potatoes at sea—had been in the trade as a boy, he said. He meant to make my loss as small as possible. What between his devotion—it must have been devotion—and his vanity, I positively dared not give him the order to throw my commercial-venture overboard. I believe he would have refused point blank to obey my lawful command. An unprecedented and comical situation would have been created with which I did not feel equal to deal.

I welcomed the coming of bad weather as no sailor had ever done. When at last I hove the ship to, to pick up the pilot outside Port Philip Heads, the after-hatch had not been opened for more than a week and I might have believed that no such thing as a potato had ever been on board.

It was an abominable day, raw, blustering, with great squalls of wind and rain; the pilot, a cheery person, looked after the ship and chatted to me, streaming from head to foot; and the heavier the lash of the downpour the more pleased with himself and everything around him he seemed to be. He rubbed his wet hands with a satisfaction, which to me, who had stood that kind of thing for several days and nights, seemed inconceivable in any non-aquatic creature.

"You seem to enjoy getting wet, Pilot," I remarked.

He had a bit of land round his house in the suburbs and it was of his garden he was thinking. At the sound of the word garden, unheard, unspoken for so many days, I had a vision of gorgeous colour, of sweet scents, of a girlish figure crouching in a chair. Yes. That was a distinct emotion breaking into the peace I had found in the sleepless anxieties of my responsibility during a week of dangerous bad weather. The Colony, the pilot explained, had suffered from unparalleled drought. This was the first decent drop of water they had had for seven months. The root crops were lost. And, trying to be casual, but with visible interest, he asked me if I had perchance any potatoes to spare.

Potatoes! I had managed to forget them. In a moment I felt plunged into corruption up to my neck. Mr. Burns was making eyes at me behind the pilot's back.

Finally, he obtained a ton, and paid ten pounds for it. This was twice the price of my bargain with Jacobus. The spirit of covetousness woke up in me. That night, in harbour, before I slept, the Custom House galley came alongside. While his underlings were putting seals on the storerooms, the officer in charge took me aside confidentially. "I say, Captain, you don't happen to have any potatoes to sell."

Clearly there was a potato famine in the land. I let him have a ton for twelve pounds and he went away joyfully. That night I dreamt of a pile of gold in the form of a grave in which a girl was buried, and woke up callous with greed. On calling at my ship-broker's office, that man, after the usual business had been transacted, pushed his spectacles up on his forehead.

"I was thinking, Captain, that coming from the Pearl of the Ocean you may have some potatoes to sell."

I said negligently: "Oh, yes, I could spare you a ton. Fifteen pounds."

He exclaimed: "I say!" But after studying my face for a while accepted my terms with a faint grimace. It seems that these people could not exist without potatoes. I could. I didn't want to see a potato as long as I lived; but the demon of lucre had taken possession of me. How the news got about I don't know, but, returning on board rather late, I found a small group of men of the coster type hanging about the waist, while Mr. Burns walked to and fro the quarterdeck loftily, keeping a triumphant eye on them. They had come to buy potatoes.

"These chaps have been waiting here in the sun for hours," Burns whispered to me excitedly. "They have drank the water-cask dry. Don't you throw away your chances, sir. You are too good-natured."

I selected a man with thick legs and a man with a cast in his eye to negotiate with; simply because they were easily distinguishable from the rest. "You have the money on you?" I inquired, before taking them down into the cabin.

"Yes, sir," they answered in one voice, slapping their pockets. I liked their air of quiet determination. Long before the end of the day all the potatoes were sold at about three times the price I had paid for them. Mr. Burns, feverish and exulting, congratulated himself on his skilful care of my commercial venture, but hinted plainly that I ought to have made more of it.

That night I did not sleep very well. I thought of Jacobus by fits and starts, between snatches of dreams concerned with castaways starving on a desert island covered with flowers. It was extremely unpleasant. In the morning, tired and unrefreshed, I sat down and wrote a long letter to my owners, giving them a carefully-thought-out scheme for the ship's employment in the East and about the China Seas for the next two years. I spent the day at that task and felt somewhat more at peace when it was done.

Their reply came in due course. They were greatly struck with my project; but considering that, notwithstanding the unfortunate difficulty with the bags (which they trusted I would know how to guard against in the future), the voyage showed a very fair profit, they thought it would be better to keep the ship in the sugar trade—at least for the present.

I turned over the page and read on:

"We have had a letter from our good friend Mr. Jacobus. We are pleased to see how well you have hit it off with him; for, not to speak of his assistance in the unfortunate matter of the bags, he writes us that should you, by using all possible dispatch, manage to bring the ship back early in the season he would be able to give us a good rate of freight. We have no doubt that your best endeavours . . . etc. . . . etc."

I dropped the letter and sat motionless for a long time. Then I wrote my answer (it was a short one) and went ashore myself to post it. But I passed one letter-box, then another, and in the end found myself going up Collins Street with the letter still in my pocket—against my heart. Collins Street at four o'clock in the afternoon is not exactly a desert solitude; but I had never felt more isolated from the rest of mankind as when I walked that day its crowded pavement, battling desperately with my thoughts and feeling already vanquished.

There came a moment when the awful tenacity of Jacobus, the man of one passion and of one idea, appeared to me almost heroic. He had not given me up. He had gone again to his odious brother. And then he appeared to me odious himself. Was it for his own sake or for the sake of the poor girl? And on that last supposition the memory of the kiss which missed my lips appalled me; for whatever he had seen, or guessed at, or risked, he knew nothing of that. Unless the girl had told him. How could I go back to fan that fatal spark with my cold breath? No, no, that unexpected kiss had to be paid for at its full price.

At the first letter-box I came to I stopped and reaching into my breast-pocket I took out the letter—it was as if I were plucking out my very heart—and dropped it through the slit. Then I went straight on board.

I wondered what dreams I would have that night; but as it turned out I did not sleep at all. At breakfast I informed Mr. Burns that I had resigned my command.

He dropped his knife and fork and looked at me with indignation.

"You have, sir! I thought you loved the ship."

"So I do, Burns," I said. "But the fact is that the Indian Ocean and everything that is in it has lost its charm for me. I am going home as passenger by the Suez Canal."

"Everything that is in it," he repeated angrily. "I've never heard anybody talk like this.

And to tell you the truth, sir, all the time we have been together I've never quite made you out. What's one ocean more than another? Charm, indeed!"

He was really devoted to me, I believe. But he cheered up when I told him that I had recommended him for my successor.

"Anyhow," he remarked, "let people say what they like, this Jacobus has served your turn. I must admit that this potato business has paid extremely well. Of course, if only you had—"

"Yes, Mr. Burns," I interrupted. "Quite a smile of fortune."

But I could not tell him that it was driving me out of the ship I had learned to love. And as I sat heavy-hearted at that parting, seeing all my plans destroyed, my modest future endangered—for this command was like a foot in the stirrup for a young man—he gave up completely for the first time his critical attitude.

"A wonderful piece of luck!" he said.

GASPAR RUIZ

I

A REVOLUTIONARY WAR raises many strange characters out of the obscurity which is the common lot of humble lives in an undisturbed state of society.

Certain individualities grow into fame through their vices and their virtues, or simply by their actions, which may have a temporary importance; and then they become forgotten. The names of a few leaders alone survive the end of armed strife and are further preserved in history; so that, vanishing from men's active memories, they still exist in books.

The name of General Santierra attained that cold paper-and-ink immortality. He was a South American of good family, and the books published in his lifetime numbered him amongst the liberators of that continent from the oppressive rule of Spain.

That long contest, waged for independence on one side and for dominion on the other, developed in the course of years and the vicissitudes of changing fortune the fierceness and inhumanity of a struggle for life. All feelings of pity and compassion disappeared in the growth of political hatred. And, as is usual in war, the mass of the people, who had the least to gain by the issue, suffered most in their obscure persons and their humble fortunes.

General Santierra began his service as lieutenant in the patriot army raised and commanded by the famous San Martin, afterwards conqueror of Lima and liberator of Peru. A great battle had just been fought on the banks of the river Bio-Bio. Amongst the prisoners made upon the routed Royalist troops there was a soldier called Gaspar Ruiz. His powerful build and his big head rendered him remarkable amongst his fellow-captives. The personality of the man was unmistakable. Some months before he had been missed from the ranks of Republican troops after one of the many skirmishes which preceded the great battle. And now, having been captured arms in hand amongst Royalists, he could expect no other fate but to be shot as a deserter.

Gaspar Ruiz, however, was not a deserter; his mind was hardly active enough to take a discriminating view of the advantages or perils of treachery. Why should he change sides? He had really been made a prisoner, had suffered ill-usage and many privations. Neither side showed tenderness to its adversaries. There came a day when he was ordered, together with some other captured rebels, to march in the front rank of the Royal troops. A musket had been thrust into his hands. He had taken it. He had marched. He did not want to be killed with circumstances of peculiar atrocity for refusing to march. He did not understand heroism but it was his intention to throw his musket away at the first opportunity. Meantime he had gone on loading and firing, from fear of having his brains blown out at the first sign of unwillingness, by some non-commissioned officer of the King of Spain. He tried to set forth these elementary considerations before the sergeant of the guard set over him and some twenty other such deserters, who had been condemned summarily to be shot.

It was in the quadrangle of the fort at the back of the batteries which command the roadstead of Valparaiso. The officer who had identified him had gone on without listening to his protestations. His doom was sealed; his hands were tied very tightly together behind his back; his body was sore all over from the many blows with sticks and butts of muskets which had hurried him along on the painful road from the place of his capture to the gate of the fort. This was the only kind of systematic attention the prisoners had received from their escort during a four days' journey across a scantily watered tract of country. At the crossings of rare streams they were permitted to quench their thirst by lapping hurriedly like dogs. In the evening a few scraps of meat were thrown amongst them as they dropped down dead-beat upon the stony ground of the halting-place.

As he stood in the courtyard of the castle in the early morning, after having been driven hard all night, Gaspar Ruiz's throat was parched, and his tongue felt very large and dry in his mouth.

And Gaspar Ruiz, besides being very thirsty, was stirred by a feeling of sluggish anger, which he could not very well express, as though the vigour of his spirit were by no means equal to the strength of his body.

The other prisoners in the batch of the condemned hung their heads, looking obstinately on the ground. But Gaspar Ruiz kept on repeating: "What should I desert for to the Royalists? Why should I desert? Tell me, Estaban!"

He addressed himself to the sergeant, who happened to belong to the same part of the country as himself. But the sergeant, after shrugging his meagre shoulders once, paid no further attention to the deep murmuring voice at his back. It was indeed strange that Gaspar Ruiz should desert. His people were in too humble a station to feel much the disadvantages of any form of government. There was no reason why Gaspar Ruiz should wish to uphold in his own person the rule of the King of Spain. Neither had he been anxious to exert himself for its subversion. He had joined the side of Independence in an extremely reasonable and natural manner. A band of patriots appeared one morning early, surrounding his father's ranche, spearing the watch-dogs and ham-stringing a fat cow all in the twinkling of an eye, to the cries of "Viva la Libertad!" Their officer discoursed of Liberty with enthusiasm and eloquence after a long and refreshing sleep. When they left in the evening, taking with them some of Ruiz, the father's, best horses to replace their own lamed animals, Gaspar Ruiz went away with them, having been invited pressingly to do so by the eloquent officer.

Shortly afterwards a detachment of Royalist troops coming to pacify the district, burnt the ranche, carried off the remaining horses and cattle, and having thus deprived the old people of all their worldly possessions, left them sitting under a bush in the enjoyment of the inestimable boon of life.

2

Gaspar Ruiz, condemned to death as a deserter, was not thinking either of his native place or of his parents, to whom he had been a good son on account of the mildness of his character and the great strength of his limbs. The practical advantage of this last was made still more valuable to his father by his obedient disposition. Gaspar Ruiz had an acquiescent soul.

But it was stirred now to a sort of dim revolt by his dislike to die the death of a traitor. He was not a traitor. He said again to the sergeant: "You know I did not desert, Estaban. You know I remained behind amongst the trees with three others to keep the enemy back while the detachment was running away!"

Lieutenant Santierra, little more than a boy at the time, and unused as yet to the sanguinary imbecilities of a state of war, had lingered near by, as if fascinated by the sight of these men who were to be shot presently—"for an example"—as the Commandante had said.

The sergeant, without deigning to look at the prisoner, addressed himself to the young officer with a superior smile.

"Ten men would not have been enough to make him a prisoner, mi teniente. Moreover, the other three rejoined the detachment after dark. Why should he, unwounded and the strongest of them all, have failed to do so?"

"My strength is as nothing against a mounted man with a lasso," Gaspar Ruiz protested, eagerly. "He dragged me behind his horse for half a mile."

At this excellent reason the sergeant only laughed contemptuously. The young officer hurried away after the Commandante.

Presently the adjutant of the castle came by. He was a truculent, raw-boned man in a ragged uniform. His spluttering voice issued out of a flat yellow face. The sergeant learned from him that the condemned men would not be shot till sunset. He begged then to know what he was to do with them meantime.

The adjutant looked savagely round the courtyard and, pointing to the door of a small dungeon-like guardroom, receiving light and air through one heavily barred window, said: "Drive the scoundrels in there."

The sergeant, tightening his grip upon the stick he carried in virtue of his rank, executed this order with alacrity and zeal. He hit Gaspar Ruiz, whose movements were slow, over his head and shoulders. Gaspar Ruiz stood still for a moment under the shower of blows, biting his lip thoughtfully as if absorbed by a perplexing mental process—then followed the others without haste. The door was locked, and the adjutant carried off the key.

By noon the heat of that vaulted place crammed to suffocation had become unbearable. The prisoners crowded towards the window, begging their guards for a drop of water; but the soldiers remained lying in indolent attitudes wherever there was a little shade under a wall, while the sentry sat with his back against the door smoking a cigarette, and raising his eyebrows philosophically from time to time. Gaspar Ruiz had pushed his way to the window with irresistible force. His capacious chest needed more air than the others; his big face, resting with its chin on the ledge, pressed close to the bars, seemed to support the other faces crowding up for breath. From moaned entreaties they had passed to desperate cries, and the tumultuous howling of those thirsty men obliged a young officer who was just then crossing the courtyard to shout in order to make himself heard.

"Why don't you give some water to these prisoners?"

The sergeant, with an air of surprised innocence, excused himself by the remark that all those men were condemned to die in a very few hours.

Lieutenant Santierra stamped his foot. "They are condemned to death, not to torture," he shouted. "Give them some water at once."

Impressed by this appearance of anger, the soldiers bestirred themselves, and the sentry, snatching up his musket, stood to attention.

But when a couple of buckets were found and filled from the well, it was discovered that they could not be passed through the bars, which were set too close. At the prospect of quenching their thirst, the shrieks of those trampled down in the struggle to get near the opening became very heartrending. But when the soldiers who had lifted the buckets towards the window put them to the ground again helplessly, the yell of disappointment was still more terrible.

The soldiers of the army of Independence were not equipped with canteens. A small tin cup was found, but its approach to the opening caused such a commotion, such yells of rage and pain in the vague mass of limbs behind the straining faces at the window, that Lieutenant Santierra cried out hurriedly, "No, no—you must open the door, sergeant."

The sergeant, shrugging his shoulders, explained that he had no right to open the door even if he had had the key. But he had not the key. The adjutant of the garrison kept the key. Those men were giving much unnecessary trouble, since they had to die at sunset in any case. Why they had not been shot at once early in the morning he could not understand.

Lieutenant Santierra kept his back studiously to the window. It was at his earnest solicitations that the Commandante had delayed the execution. This favour had been granted to him in consideration of his distinguished family and of his father's high position amongst the chiefs of the Republican party. Lieutenant Santierra believed that the General commanding would visit the fort some time in the afternoon, and he ingenuously hoped that his naive intercession would induce that severe man to pardon some, at least, of those criminals. In the revulsion of his feeling his interference stood revealed now as guilty and futile meddling. It appeared to him obvious that the general would never even consent to listen to his petition. He could never save those men, and he had only made himself responsible for the sufferings added to the cruelty of their fate.

"Then go at once and get the key from the adjutant," said Lieutenant Santierra.

The sergeant shook his head with a sort of bashful smile, while his eyes glanced sideways at Gaspar Ruiz's face, motionless and silent, staring through the bars at the bottom of a heap of other haggard, distorted, yelling faces.

His worship the adjutant de Plaza, the sergeant murmured, was having his siesta; and supposing that he, the sergeant, would be allowed access to him, the only result he expected would be to have his soul flogged out of his body for presuming to disturb his worship's repose. He made a deprecatory movement with his hands, and stood stock-still, looking down modestly upon his brown toes.

Lieutenant Santierra glared with indignation, but hesitated. His handsome oval face, as smooth as a girl's, flushed with the shame of his perplexity. Its nature humiliated his spirit. His hairless upper lip trembled; he seemed on the point of either bursting into a fit of rage or into tears of dismay.

Fifty years later, General Santierra, the venerable relic of revolutionary times, was well able to remember the feelings of the young lieutenant. Since he had given up riding altogether, and found it difficult to walk beyond the limits of his garden, the general's greatest delight was to entertain in his house the officers of the foreign men-of-war visiting the harbour. For Englishmen he had a preference, as for old companions in arms. English naval men of all ranks accepted his hospitality with curiosity, because he had known Lord Cochrane and had taken part, on board the patriot squadron commanded by that marvellous seaman, in the cutting out and blockading operations before Callao—an episode of unalloyed glory in the wars of Independence and of endless honour in the fighting tradition of Englishmen. He was a fair linguist, this ancient survivor of the Liberating armies. A trick of smoothing his long white beard whenever he was short of a word in French or English imparted an air of leisurely dignity to the tone of his reminiscences.

3

"YES, MY FRIENDS," he used to say to his guests, "what would you have? A youth of seventeen summers, without worldly experience, and owing my rank only to the glorious patriotism of my father, may God rest his soul. I suffered immense humiliation, not so much from the disobedience of that subordinate, who, after all, was responsible for those prisoners; but I suffered because, like the boy I was, I myself dreaded going to the adjutant for the key. I had felt, before, his rough and cutting tongue. Being quite a common fellow, with no merit except his savage valour, he made me feel his contempt and dislike from the first day I joined my battalion in garrison at the fort. It was only a fortnight before! I would have confronted him sword in hand, but I shrank from the mocking brutality of his sneers.

"I don't remember having been so miserable in my life before or since. The torment of my sensibility was so great that I wished the sergeant to fall dead at my feet, and the stupid soldiers who stared at me to turn into corpses; and even those wretches for whom my entreaties had procured a reprieve I wished dead also, because I could not face them without shame. A mephitic heat like a whiff of air from hell came out of that dark place in which they were confined. Those at the window who had heard what was going on jeered at me in very desperation: one of these fellows, gone mad no doubt, kept on urging me volubly to order the soldiers to fire through the window. His insane loquacity made my heart turn faint. And my feet were like lead. There was no higher officer to whom I could appeal. I had not even the firmness of spirit to simply go away.

"Benumbed by my remorse, I stood with my back to the window. You must not suppose that all this lasted a long time. How long could it have been? A minute? If you measured by mental suffering it was like a hundred years; a longer time than all my life has been since. No, certainly, it was not so much as a minute. The hoarse screaming of those miserable wretches died out in their dry throats, and then suddenly a voice spoke, a deep voice muttering calmly. It called upon me to turn round.

"That voice, senores, proceeded from the head of Gaspar Ruiz. Of his body I could see nothing. Some of his fellow-captives had clambered upon his back. He was holding them up. His eyes blinked without looking at me. That and the moving of his lips was all he seemed able to manage in his overloaded state. And when I turned round, this head, that seemed more than human size resting on its chin under a multitude of other heads, asked me whether I really desired to quench the thirst of the captives.

"I said, 'Yes, yes!' eagerly, and came up quite close to the window. I was like a child, and did not know what would happen. I was anxious to be comforted in my helplessness and remorse.

"'Have you the authority, Senor teniente, to release my wrists from their bonds?' Gaspar Ruiz's head asked me.

"His features expressed no anxiety, no hope; his heavy eyelids blinked upon his eyes that looked past me straight into the courtyard.

"As if in an ugly dream, I spoke, stammering: 'What do you mean? And how can I reach the bonds on your wrists?'

"'I will try what I can do,' he said; and then that large staring head moved at last, and all the wild faces piled up in that window disappeared, tumbling down. He had shaken his load off with one movement, so strong he was.

"And he had not only shaken it off, but he got free of the crush and vanished from my sight. For a moment there was no one at all to be seen at the window. He had swung about, butting and shouldering, clearing a space for himself in the only way he could do it with his hands tied behind his back.

"Finally, backing to the opening, he pushed out to me between the bars his wrists, lashed with many turns of rope. His hands, very swollen, with knotted veins, looked enormous and unwieldy. I saw his bent back. It was very broad. His voice was like the muttering of a bull.

"'Cut, Senor teniente. Cut!'

"I drew my sword, my new unblunted sword that had seen no service as yet, and severed the many turns of the hide rope. I did this without knowing the why and the wherefore of my action, but as it were compelled by my faith in that man. The sergeant made as if to cry out, but astonishment deprived him of his voice, and he remained standing with his mouth open as if overtaken by sudden imbecility.

"I sheathed my sword and faced the soldiers. An air of awestruck expectation had replaced their usual listless apathy. I heard the voice of Gaspar Ruiz shouting inside, but the words I could not make out plainly. I suppose that to see him with his arms free augmented the influence of his strength: I mean by this, the spiritual influence that with ignorant people attaches to an exceptional degree of bodily vigour. In fact, he was no more to be feared than before, on account of the numbness of his arms and hands, which lasted for some time.

"The sergeant had recovered his power of speech. 'By all the saints!' he cried, 'we shall have to get a cavalry man with a lasso to secure him again, if he is to be led to the place of execution. Nothing less than a good enlazador on a good horse can subdue him. Your worship was pleased to perform a very mad thing.'

"I had nothing to say. I was surprised myself, and I felt a childish curiosity to see what would happen next. But the sergeant was thinking of the difficulty of controlling Gaspar Ruiz when the time for making an example would come.

"'Or perhaps,' the sergeant pursued, vexedly, 'we shall be obliged to shoot him down as he dashes out when the door is opened.' He was going to give further vent to his anxieties as to the proper carrying out of the sentence; but he interrupted himself with a sudden exclamation, snatched a musket from a soldier, and stood watchful with his eyes fixed on the window."

4

"GASPAR RUIZ HAD CLAMBERED up on the sill, and sat down there with his feet against the thickness of the wall and his knees slightly bent. The window was not quite broad enough for the length of his legs. It appeared to my crestfallen perception that he meant to keep the window all to himself. He seemed to be taking up a comfortable position. Nobody inside dared to approach him now he could strike with his hands.

"'Por Dios!' I heard the sergeant muttering at my elbow, 'I shall shoot him through the head now, and get rid of that trouble. He is a condemned man.'

"At that I looked at him angrily. 'The general has not confirmed the sentence,' I said—though I knew well in my heart that these were but vain words. The sentence required no confirmation. 'You have no right to shoot him unless he tries to escape,' I added, firmly.

"'But sangre de Dios!' the sergeant yelled out, bringing his musket up to the shoulder, 'he is escaping now. Look!'

"But I, as if that Gaspar Ruiz had cast a spell upon me, struck the musket upward, and the bullet flew over the roofs somewhere. The sergeant dashed his arm to the ground and stared. He might have commanded the soldiers to fire, but he did not. And if he had he would not have been obeyed, I think, just then.

"With his feet against the thickness of the wall and his hairy hands grasping the iron bar, Gaspar sat still. It was an attitude. Nothing happened for a time. And suddenly it dawned upon us that he was straightening his bowed back and contracting his arms. His lips were twisted into a snarl. Next thing we perceived was that the bar of forged iron was being bent slowly by the mightiness of his pull. The sun was beating full upon his cramped, unquivering figure. A shower of sweat-drops burst out of his forehead. Watching the bar grow crooked, I saw a little blood ooze from under his finger-nails. Then he let go. For a moment he remained all huddled up, with a hanging head, looking drowsily into the upturned palms of his mighty hands. Indeed he seemed to have dozed off. Suddenly he flung himself backwards on the sill, and setting the soles of his bare feet against the other middle bar, he bent that one, too, but in the opposite direction from the first.

"Such was his strength, which in this case relieved my painful feelings. And the man seemed to have done nothing. Except for the change of position in order to use his feet, which made us all start by its swiftness, my recollection is that of immobility. But he had bent the bars wide apart. And now he could get out if he liked; but he dropped his legs inwards, and looking over his shoulder beckoned to the soldiers. 'Hand up the water,' he said. 'I will give them all a drink.'

"He was obeyed. For a moment I expected man and bucket to disappear, overwhelmed by the rush of eagerness; I thought they would pull him down with their teeth. There was a rush, but holding the bucket on his lap he repulsed the assault of those wretches by the mere swinging of his feet. They flew backwards at every kick, yelling with pain; and the soldiers laughed, gazing at the window.

"They all laughed, holding their sides, except the sergeant, who was gloomy and morose. He was afraid the prisoners would rise and break out—which would have been a bad example. But there was no fear of that, and I stood myself before the window with my drawn sword. When sufficiently tamed by the strength of Gaspar Ruiz they came up one by one, stretching their necks and presenting their lips to the edge of the bucket which the strong man tilted towards them from his knees with an extraordinary air of charity, gentleness, and compassion. That benevolent appearance was of course the effect of his care in not spilling the water and of his attitude as he sat on the sill; for, if a man lingered with his lips glued to the rim of the bucket after Gaspar Ruiz had said 'You have had enough,' there would be no tenderness or mercy in the shove of the foot which would send him groaning and doubled up far into the interior of the prison, where he would knock down two or three others before he fell himself. They came up to him again and again; it looked as if they meant to drink the well dry before going to their death; but the soldiers were so amused by Gaspar Ruiz's systematic proceedings that they carried the water up to the window cheerfully.

"When the adjutant came out after his siesta there was some trouble over this affair, I can assure you. And the worst of it was that the general whom we expected never came to the castle that day."

The guests of General Santierra unanimously expressed their regret that the man of such strength and patience had not been saved.

"He was not saved by my interference," said the General. "The prisoners were led to execution half an hour before sunset. Gaspar Ruiz, contrary to the sergeant's apprehensions, gave no trouble. There was no necessity to get a cavalry man with a lasso in order to subdue him, as if he were a wild bull of the campo. I believe he marched out with his arms free amongst the others who were bound. I did not see. I was not there. I had been put under arrest for interfering with the prisoner's guard. About dusk, sitting dismally in my quarters, I heard three volleys fired, and thought that I should never hear of Gaspar Ruiz again. He fell with the others. But we were to hear of him nevertheless, though the sergeant boasted that as he lay on his face expiring or dead in the heap of the slain, he had slashed his neck with a sword. He had done this, he said, to make sure of ridding the world of a dangerous traitor.

"I confess to you, senores, that I thought of that strong man with a sort of gratitude, and with some admiration. He had used his strength honourably. There dwelt, then, in his soul no fierceness corresponding to the vigour of his body."

5

Gaspar Ruiz, who could with ease bend apart the heavy iron bars of the prison, was led out with others to summary execution. "Every bullet has its billet," runs the proverb. All the merit of proverbs consists in the concise and picturesque expression. In the surprise of our minds is found their persuasiveness. In other words, we are struck and convinced by the shock.

What surprises us is the form, not the substance. Proverbs are art—cheap art. As a general rule they are not true; unless indeed they happen to be mere platitudes, as for instance the proverb, "Half a loaf is better than no bread," or "A miss is as good as a mile." Some proverbs are simply imbecile, others are immoral. That one evolved out of the naive heart of the great Russian people, "Man discharges the piece, but God carries the bullet," is piously atrocious, and at bitter variance with the accepted conception of a compassionate God. It would indeed be an inconsistent occupation for the Guardian of the poor, the innocent, and the helpless, to carry the bullet, for instance, into the heart of a father.

Gaspar Ruiz was childless, he had no wife, he had never been in love. He had hardly ever spoken to a woman, beyond his mother and the ancient negress of the household, whose wrinkled skin was the colour of cinders, and whose lean body was bent double from age. If some bullets from those muskets fired off at fifteen paces were specifically destined for the heart of Gaspar Ruiz, they all missed their billet. One, however, carried away a small piece of his ear, and another a fragment of flesh from his shoulder.

A red and unclouded sun setting into a purple ocean looked with a fiery stare upon the enormous wall of the Cordilleras, worthy witnesses of his glorious extinction. But it is inconceivable that it should have seen the ant-like men busy with their absurd and insignificant trials of killing and dying for reasons that, apart from being generally childish, were also imperfectly understood. It did light up, however, the backs of the firing party and the faces of the condemned men. Some of them had fallen on their knees, others remained standing, a few averted their heads from the levelled barrels of muskets. Gaspar Ruiz, upright, the burliest of them all, hung his big shock head. The low sun dazzled him a little, and he counted himself a dead man already.

He fell at the first discharge. He fell because he thought he was a dead man. He struck the ground heavily. The jar of the fall surprised him. "I am not dead apparently," he thought to himself, when he heard the execution platoon reloading its arms at the word of command. It was then that the hope of escape dawned upon him for the first time. He remained lying stretched out with rigid limbs under the weight of two bodies collapsed crosswise upon his back.

By the time the soldiers had fired a third volley into the slightly stirring heaps of the slain, the sun had gone out of sight, and almost immediately with the darkening of the ocean dusk fell upon the coasts of the young Republic. Above the gloom of the lowlands the snowy peaks of the Cordilleras remained luminous and crimson for a long time. The soldiers before marching back to the fort sat down to smoke.

The sergeant with a naked sword in his hand strolled away by himself along the heap of the dead. He was a humane man, and watched for any stir or twitch of limb in the merciful idea of plunging the point of his blade into any body giving the slightest sign of life. But none of the bodies afforded him an opportunity for the display of this charitable intention. Not a muscle twitched amongst them, not even the powerful muscles of Gaspar Ruiz, who, deluged with the blood of his neighbours and shamming death, strove to appear more lifeless than the others.

He was lying face down. The sergeant recognized him by his stature, and being himself a very small man, looked with envy and contempt at the prostration of so much strength. He had always disliked that particular soldier. Moved by an obscure animosity, he inflicted a long gash across the neck of Gaspar Ruiz, with some vague notion of making sure of that strong man's death, as if a powerful physique were more able to resist the bullets. For the sergeant had no doubt that Gaspar Ruiz had been shot through in many places. Then he passed on, and shortly afterwards marched off with his men, leaving the bodies to the care of crows and vultures.

Gaspar Ruiz had restrained a cry, though it had seemed to him that his head was cut off at a blow; and when darkness came, shaking off the dead, whose weight had oppressed him, he crawled away over the plain on his hands and knees. After drinking deeply, like a wounded beast, at a shallow stream, he assumed an upright posture, and staggered on light-headed and aimless, as if lost amongst the stars of the clear night. A small house seemed to rise out of the ground before him. He stumbled into the porch and struck at the door with his fist. There was not a gleam of light. Gaspar Ruiz might have thought that the inhabitants had fled from it, as from many others in the neighbourhood, had it not been for the shouts of abuse that answered his thumping. In his feverish and enfeebled state the angry screaming seemed to him part of a hallucination belonging to the weird, dreamlike feeling of his unexpected condemnation to death, of the thirst suffered, of the volleys fired at him within fifteen paces, of his head being cut off at a blow. "Open the door!" he cried. "Open in the name of God!"

An infuriated voice from within jeered at him: "Come in, come in. This house belongs to you. All this land belongs to you. Come and take it."

"For the love of God," Gaspar Ruiz murmured.

"Does not all the land belong to you patriots?" the voice on the other side of the door screamed on. "Are you not a patriot?"

Gaspar Ruiz did not know. "I am a wounded man," he said, apathetically.

All became still inside. Gaspar Ruiz lost the hope of being admitted, and lay down under the porch just outside the door. He was utterly careless of what was going to happen to him. All his consciousness seemed to be concentrated in his neck, where he felt a severe pain. His indifference as to his fate was genuine. The day was breaking when he awoke from a feverish doze; the door at which he had knocked in the dark stood wide open now, and a girl, steadying herself with her outspread arms, leaned over the threshold. Lying on his back, he stared up at her. Her face was pale and her eyes were very dark; her hair hung down black as ebony against her white cheeks; her lips were full and red. Beyond her he saw another head with long grey hair, and a thin old face with a pair of anxiously clasped hands under the chin.

6

"I KNEW THOSE PEOPLE BY SIGHT," General Santierra would tell his guests at the dining-table. "I mean the people with whom Gaspar Ruiz found shelter. The father was an old Spaniard, a man of property ruined by the revolution. His estates, his house in town, his money, everything he had in the world had been confiscated by proclamation, for he was a bitter foe of our independence. From a position of great dignity and influence on the Viceroy's Council he became of less importance than his own negro slaves made free by our glorious revolution. He had not even the means to flee the country, as other Spaniards had managed to do. It may be that, wandering ruined and houseless, and burdened with nothing but his life, which was left to him by the clemency of the Provisional Government, he had simply walked under that broken roof of old tiles. It was a lonely spot. There did not seem to be even a dog belonging to the place. But though the roof had holes, as if a cannon-ball or two had dropped through it, the wooden shutters were thick and tight-closed all the time.

"My way took me frequently along the path in front of that miserable rancho. I rode from the fort to the town almost every evening, to sigh at the window of a lady I was in love with, then. When one is young, you understand. . . . She was a good patriot, you may believe. Caballeros, credit me or not, political feeling ran so high in those days that I do not believe I could have been fascinated by the charms of a woman of Royalist opinions. . . ."

Murmurs of amused incredulity all round the table interrupted the General; and while they lasted he stroked his white beard gravely.

"Senores," he protested, "a Royalist was a monster to our overwrought feelings. I am telling you this in order not to be suspected of the slightest tenderness towards that old Royalist's daughter. Moreover, as you know, my affections were engaged elsewhere. But I could not help noticing her on rare occasions when with the front door open she stood in the porch.

"You must know that this old Royalist was as crazy as a man can be. His political misfortunes, his total downfall and ruin, had disordered his mind. To show his contempt for what we patriots could do, he affected to laugh at his imprisonment, at the confiscation of his lands, the burning of his houses, and at the misery to which he and his womenfolk were reduced. This habit of laughing had grown upon him, so that he would begin to laugh and shout directly he caught sight of any stranger. That was the form of his madness.

"I, of course, disregarded the noise of that madman with that feeling of superiority the success of our cause inspired in us Americans. I suppose I really despised him because he was an old Castilian, a Spaniard born, and a Royalist. Those were certainly no reasons to scorn a man; but for centuries Spaniards born had shown their contempt of us Americans, men as well descended as themselves, simply because we were what they called colonists. We had been kept in abasement and made to feel our inferiority in social intercourse. And now it was our turn. It was safe for us patriots to display the same sentiments; and I being a young patriot, son of a patriot, despised that old Spaniard, and despising him I naturally disregarded his abuse, though it was annoying to my feelings. Others perhaps would not have been so forbearing.

"He would begin with a great yell—'I see a patriot. Another of them!' long before I came abreast of the house. The tone of his senseless revilings, mingled with bursts of laughter, was sometimes piercingly shrill and sometimes grave. It was all very mad; but I felt it incumbent upon my dignity to check my horse to a walk without even glancing towards the house, as if that man's abusive clamour in the porch were less than the barking of a cur. Always I rode by preserving an expression of haughty indifference on my face.

"It was no doubt very dignified; but I should have done better if I had kept my eyes open. A military man in war time should never consider himself off duty; and especially so if the war is a revolutionary war, when the enemy is not at the door, but within your very house. At such times the heat of passionate convictions passing into hatred, removes the restraints of honour and humanity from many men and of delicacy and fear from some women. These last, when once they throw off the timidity and reserve of their sex, become by the vivacity of their intelligence and the violence of their merciless resentment more dangerous than so many armed giants."

The General's voice rose, but his big hand stroked his white beard twice with an effect of venerable calmness. "Si, Senores! Women are ready to rise to the heights of devotion unattainable by us men, or to sink into the depths of abasement which amazes our masculine prejudices. I am speaking now of exceptional women, you understand. . . ."

Here one of the guests observed that he had never met a woman yet who was not capable of turning out quite exceptional under circumstances that would engage her feelings strongly. "That sort of superiority in recklessness they have over us," he concluded, "makes of them the more interesting half of mankind."

The General, who bore the interruption with gravity, nodded courteous assent. "Si. Si. Under circumstances. . . . Precisely. They can do an infinite deal of mischief sometimes in quite unexpected ways. For who could have imagined that a young girl, daughter of a ruined Royalist whose life was held only by the contempt of his enemies, would have had the power to bring death and devastation upon two flourishing provinces and cause serious anxiety to the leaders of the revolution in the very hour of its success!" He paused to let the wonder of it penetrate our minds.

"Death and devastation," somebody murmured in surprise: "how shocking!"

The old General gave a glance in the direction of the murmur and went on. "Yes. That is, war—calamity. But the means by which she obtained the power to work this havoc on our southern frontier seem to me, who have seen her and spoken to her, still more shocking. That particular thing left on my mind a dreadful amazement which the further experience of life, of more than fifty years, has done nothing to diminish." He looked round as if to make sure of our attention, and, in a changed voice: "I am, as you know, a republican, son of a

Liberator," he declared. "My incomparable mother, God rest her soul, was a Frenchwoman, the daughter of an ardent republican. As a boy I fought for liberty; I've always believed in the equality of men; and as to their brotherhood, that, to my mind, is even more certain. Look at the fierce animosity they display in their differences. And what in the world do you know that is more bitterly fierce than brothers' quarrels?"

All absence of cynicism checked an inclination to smile at this view of human brotherhood. On the contrary, there was in the tone the melancholy natural to a man profoundly humane at heart who from duty, from conviction, and from necessity, had played his part in scenes of ruthless violence.

The General had seen much of fratricidal strife. "Certainly. There is no doubt of their brotherhood," he insisted. "All men are brothers, and as such know almost too much of each other. But"—and here in the old patriarchal head, white as silver, the black eyes humorously twinkled—"if we are all brothers, all the women are not our sisters."

One of the younger guests was heard murmuring his satisfaction at the fact. But the General continued, with deliberate earnestness: "They are so different! The tale of a king who took a beggar-maid for a partner of his throne may be pretty enough as we men look upon ourselves and upon love. But that a young girl, famous for her haughty beauty and, only a short time before, the admired of all at the balls in the Viceroy's palace, should take by the hand a guasso, a common peasant, is intolerable to our sentiment of women and their love. It is madness. Nevertheless it happened. But it must be said that in her case it was the madness of hate—not of love."

After presenting this excuse in a spirit of chivalrous justice, the General remained silent for a time. "I rode past the house every day almost," he began again, "and this was what was going on within. But how it was going on no mind of man can conceive. Her desperation must have been extreme, and Gaspar Ruiz was a docile fellow. He had been an obedient soldier. His strength was like an enormous stone lying on the ground, ready to be hurled this way or that by the hand that picks it up.

"It is clear that he would tell his story to the people who gave him the shelter he needed. And he needed assistance badly. His wound was not dangerous, but his life was forfeited. The old Royalist being wrapped up in his laughing madness, the two women arranged a hiding-place for the wounded man in one of the huts amongst the fruit trees at the back of the house. That hovel, an abundance of clear water while the fever was on him, and some words of pity were all they could give. I suppose he had a share of what food there was. And it would be but little: a handful of roasted corn, perhaps a dish of beans, or a piece of bread with a few figs. To such misery were those proud and once wealthy people reduced."

7

General Santierra was right in his surmise. Such was the exact nature of the assistance which Gaspar Ruiz, peasant son of peasants, received from the Royalist family whose daughter had opened the door of their miserable refuge to his extreme distress. Her sombre resolution ruled the madness of her father and the trembling bewilderment of her mother.

She had asked the strange man on the doorstep, "Who wounded you?"

"The soldiers, senora," Gaspar Ruiz had answered, in a faint voice.

"Patriots?"

"Si."

"What for?"

"Deserter," he gasped, leaning against the wall under the scrutiny of her black eyes. "I was left for dead over there."

She led him through the house out to a small hut of clay and reeds, lost in the long grass of the overgrown orchard. He sank on a heap of maize straw in a corner, and sighed profoundly.

"No one will look for you here," she said, looking down at him. "Nobody comes near us. We, too, have been left for dead—here."

He stirred uneasily on his heap of dirty straw, and the pain in his neck made him groan deliriously.

"I shall show Estaban some day that I am alive yet," he mumbled.

He accepted her assistance in silence, and the many days of pain went by. Her appearances in the hut brought him relief and became connected with the feverish dreams of angels which visited his couch; for Gaspar Ruiz was instructed in the mysteries of his religion, and had even been taught to read and write a little by the priest of his village. He waited for her with impatience, and saw her pass out of the dark hut and disappear in the brilliant sunshine with poignant regret. He discovered that, while he lay there feeling so very weak, he could, by closing his eyes, evoke her face with considerable distinctness. And this discovered faculty charmed the long, solitary hours of his convalescence. Later on, when he began to regain his strength, he would creep at dusk from his hut to the house and sit on the step of the garden door.

In one of the rooms the mad father paced to and fro, muttering to himself with short, abrupt laughs. In the passage, sitting on a stool, the mother sighed and moaned. The daughter, in rough threadbare clothing, and her white haggard face half hidden by a coarse manta, stood leaning against the side of the door. Gaspar Ruiz, with his elbows propped on his knees and his head resting in his hands, talked to the two women in an undertone.

The common misery of destitution would have made a bitter mockery of a marked insistence on social differences. Gaspar Ruiz understood this in his simplicity. From his captivity amongst the Royalists he could give them news of people they knew. He described their appearance; and when he related the story of the battle in which he was recaptured the two women lamented the blow to their cause and the ruin of their secret hopes.

He had no feeling either way. But he felt a great devotion for that young girl. In his desire to appear worthy of her condescension, he boasted a little of his bodily strength. He had nothing else to boast of. Because of that quality his comrades treated him with as great a deference, he explained, as though he had been a sergeant, both in camp and in battle.

"I could always get as many as I wanted to follow me anywhere, senorita. I ought to have been made an officer, because I can read and write."

Behind him the silent old lady fetched a moaning sigh from time to time; the distracted father muttered to himself, pacing the sala; and Gaspar Ruiz would raise his eyes now and then to look at the daughter of these people.

He would look at her with curiosity because she was alive, and also with that feeling of familiarity and awe with which he had contemplated in churches the inanimate and powerful statues of the saints, whose protection is invoked in dangers and difficulties. His difficulty was very great.

He could not remain hiding in an orchard for ever and ever. He knew also very well that before he had gone half a day's journey in any direction, he would be picked up by one of the cavalry patrols scouring the country, and brought into one or another of the camps where the patriot army destined for the liberation of Peru was collected. There he would in the end be recognized as Gaspar Ruiz—the deserter to the Royalists—and no doubt shot very effectually this time. There did not seem any place in the world for the innocent Gaspar Ruiz anywhere. And at this thought his simple soul surrendered itself to gloom and resentment as black as night.

They had made him a soldier forcibly. He did not mind being a soldier. And he had been a good soldier as he had been a good son, because of his docility and his strength. But now there was no use for either. They had taken him from his parents, and he could no longer be a soldier—not a good soldier at any rate. Nobody would listen to his explanations. What injustice it was! What injustice!

And in a mournful murmur he would go over the story of his capture and recapture for the twentieth time. Then, raising his eyes to the silent girl in the doorway, "Si, senorita," he would say with a deep sigh, "injustice has made this poor breath in my body quite worthless to me and to anybody else. And I do not care who robs me of it."

One evening, as he exhaled thus the plaint of his wounded soul, she condescended to say that, if she were a man, she would consider no life worthless which held the possibility of revenge.

She seemed to be speaking to herself. Her voice was low. He drank in the gentle, as if dreamy sound with a consciousness of peculiar delight of something warming his breast like a draught of generous wine.

"True, Senorita," he said, raising his face up to hers slowly: "there is Estaban, who must be shown that I am not dead after all."

The mutterings of the mad father had ceased long before; the sighing mother had withdrawn somewhere into one of the empty rooms. All was still within as well as without, in the moonlight bright as day on the wild orchard full of inky shadows. Gaspar Ruiz saw the dark eyes of Dona Erminia look down at him.

"Ah! The sergeant," she muttered, disdainfully.

"Why! He has wounded me with his sword," he protested, bewildered by the contempt that seemed to shine livid on her pale face.

She crushed him with her glance. The power of her will to be understood was so strong that it kindled in him the intelligence of unexpressed things.

"What else did you expect me to do?" he cried, as if suddenly driven to despair. "Have I the power to do more? Am I a general with an army at my back?—miserable sinner that I am to be despised by you at last."

8

"SENORES," related the General to his guests, "though my thoughts were of love then, and therefore enchanting, the sight of that house always affected me disagreeably, especially in the moonlight, when its close shutters and its air of lonely neglect appeared sinister. Still I went on using the bridle-path by the ravine, because it was a short cut. The mad Royalist howled and laughed at me every evening to his complete satisfaction; but after a time, as if wearied with my indifference, he ceased to appear in the porch. How they persuaded him to leave off I do not know. However, with Gaspar Ruiz in the house there would have been no difficulty in restraining him by force. It was now part of their policy in there to avoid anything which could provoke me. At least, so I suppose.

"Notwithstanding my infatuation with the brightest pair of eyes in Chile, I noticed the absence of the old man after a week or so. A few more days passed. I began to think that perhaps these Royalists had gone away somewhere else. But one evening, as I was hastening towards the city, I saw again somebody in the porch. It was not the madman; it was the girl. She stood holding on to one of the wooden columns, tall and white-faced, her big eyes sunk deep with privation and sorrow. I looked hard at her, and she met my stare with a strange, inquisitive look. Then, as I turned my head after riding past, she seemed to gather courage for the act, and absolutely beckoned me back.

"I obeyed, senores, almost without thinking, so great was my astonishment. It was greater still when I heard what she had to say. She began by thanking me for my forbearance of her father's infirmity, so that I felt ashamed of myself. I had meant to show disdain, not forbearance! Every word must have burnt her lips, but she never departed from a gentle and melancholy dignity which filled me with respect against my will. Senores, we are no match for women. But I could hardly believe my ears when she began her tale. Providence, she concluded, seemed to have preserved the life of that wronged soldier, who now trusted to my honour as a caballero and to my compassion for his sufferings.

"'Wronged man,' I observed, coldly. 'Well, I think so, too: and you have been harbouring an enemy of your cause.'

"'He was a poor Christian crying for help at our door in the name of God, senor,' she answered, simply.

"I began to admire her. 'Where is he now?' I asked, stiffly.

"But she would not answer that question. With extreme cunning, and an almost fiendish delicacy, she managed to remind me of my failure in saving the lives of the prisoners in the guardroom, without wounding my pride. She knew, of course, the whole story. Gaspar Ruiz, she said, entreated me to procure for him a safe-conduct from General San Martin himself. He had an important communication to make to the commander-in-chief.

"Por Dios, senores, she made me swallow all that, pretending to be only the mouthpiece of that poor man. Overcome by injustice, he expected to find, she said, as much generosity in me as had been shown to him by the Royalist family which had given him a refuge.

"Ha! It was well and nobly said to a youngster like me. I thought her great. Alas! she was only implacable.

"In the end I rode away very enthusiastic about the business, without demanding even to see Gaspar Ruiz, who I was confident was in the house.

"But on calm reflection I began to see some difficulties which I had not confidence enough in myself to encounter. It was not easy to approach a commander-in-chief with such a story. I feared failure. At last I thought it better to lay the matter before my general-of-division, Robles, a friend of my family, who had appointed me his aide-de-camp lately.

"He took it out of my hands at once without any ceremony.

"'In the house! of course he is in the house,' he said contemptuously. 'You ought to have gone sword in hand inside and demanded his surrender, instead of chatting with a Royalist girl in the porch. Those people should have been hunted out of that long ago. Who knows how many spies they have harboured right in the very midst of our camps? A safe-conduct from the Commander-in-Chief! The audacity of the fellow! Ha! ha! Now we shall catch him to-night, and then we shall find out, without any safe-conduct, what he has got to say, that is so very important. Ha! ha! ha!'

"General Robles, peace to his soul, was a short, thick man, with round, staring eyes, fierce and jovial. Seeing my distress he added:

"'Come, come, chico. I promise you his life if he does not resist. And that is not likely. We are not going to break up a good soldier if it can be helped. I tell you what! I am curious to see your strong man. Nothing but a general will do for the picaro—well, he shall have a general to talk to. Ha! ha! I shall go myself to the catching, and you are coming with me, of course.'

"And it was done that same night. Early in the evening the house and the orchard were surrounded quietly. Later on the General and I left a ball we were attending in town and rode out at an easy gallop. At some little distance from the house we pulled up. A mounted orderly held our horses. A low whistle warned the men watching all along the ravine, and we walked up to the porch softly. The barricaded house in the moonlight seemed empty.

"The General knocked at the door. After a time a woman's voice within asked who was there. My chief nudged me hard. I gasped.

"'It is I, Lieutenant Santierra,' I stammered out, as if choked. 'Open the door.'

"It came open slowly. The girl, holding a thin taper in her hand, seeing another man with me, began to back away before us slowly, shading the light with her hand. Her impassive white face looked ghostly. I followed behind General Robles. Her eyes were fixed on mine. I made a gesture of helplessness behind my chief's back, trying at the same time to give a reassuring expression to my face. None of us three uttered a sound.

"We found ourselves in a room with bare floor and walls. There was a rough table and a couple of stools in it, nothing else whatever. An old woman with her grey hair hanging loose wrung her hands when we appeared. A peal of loud laughter resounded through the empty house, very amazing and weird. At this the old woman tried to get past us.

"'Nobody to leave the room,' said General Robles to me.

"I swung the door to, heard the latch click, and the laughter became faint in our ears.

"Before another word could be spoken in that room I was amazed by hearing the sound of distant thunder.

"I had carried in with me into the house a vivid impression of a beautiful clear moonlight night, without a speck of cloud in the sky. I could not believe my ears. Sent early abroad for my education, I was not familiar with the most dreaded natural phenomenon of my native land. I saw, with inexpressible astonishment, a look of terror in my chief's eyes. Suddenly I felt giddy. The General staggered against me heavily; the girl seemed to reel in the middle of the room, the taper fell out of her hand and the light went out; a shrill cry of 'Misericordia!' from the old woman pierced my ears. In the pitchy darkness I heard the plaster off the walls falling on the floor. It is a mercy there was no ceiling. Holding on to the latch of the door, I heard the grinding of the roof-tiles cease above my head. The shock was over.

"'Out of the house! The door! Fly, Santierra, fly!' howled the General. You know, senores, in our country the bravest are not ashamed of the fear an earthquake strikes into all the senses of man. One never gets used to it. Repeated experience only augments the mastery of that nameless terror.

"It was my first earthquake, and I was the calmest of them all. I understood that the crash outside was caused by the porch, with its wooden pillars and tiled roof projection, falling down. The next shock would destroy the house, maybe. That rumble as of thunder was approaching again. The General was rushing round the room, to find the door perhaps. He made a noise as though he were trying to climb the walls, and I heard him distinctly invoke the names of several saints. 'Out, out, Santierra!' he yelled.

"The girl's voice was the only one I did not hear.

"'General,' I cried, I cannot move the door. We must be locked in.'

"I did not recognize his voice in the shout of malediction and despair he let out. Senores, I know many men in my country, especially in the provinces most subject to earthquakes, who will neither eat, sleep, pray, nor even sit down to cards with closed doors. The danger is not in the loss of time, but in this—that the movement of the walls may prevent a door being opened at all. This was what had happened to us. We were trapped, and we had no help to expect from anybody. There is no man in my country who will go into a house when the earth trembles. There never was—except one: Gaspar Ruiz.

"He had come out of whatever hole he had been hiding in outside, and had clambered over the timbers of the destroyed porch. Above the awful subterranean groan of coming destruction I heard a mighty voice shouting the word 'Erminia!' with the lungs of a giant. An earthquake is a great leveller of distinctions. I collected all my resolution against the terror of the scene. 'She is here,' I shouted back. A roar as of a furious wild beast answered me—while my head swam, my heart sank, and the sweat of anguish streamed like rain off my brow.

"He had the strength to pick up one of the heavy posts of the porch. Holding it under his armpit like a lance, but with both hands, he charged madly the rocking house with the force of a battering-ram, bursting open the door and rushing in, headlong, over our prostrate bodies. I and the General picking ourselves up, bolted out together, without looking round once till we got across the road. Then, clinging to each other, we beheld the house change suddenly into a heap of formless rubbish behind the back of a man, who staggered towards us bearing the form of a woman clasped in his arms. Her long black hair hung nearly to his feet. He laid her down reverently on the heaving earth, and the moonlight shone on her closed eyes.

"Senores, we mounted with difficulty. Our horses getting up plunged madly, held by the soldiers who had come running from all sides. Nobody thought of catching Gaspar Ruiz then. The eyes of men and animals shone with wild fear. My general approached Gaspar Ruiz, who stood motionless as a statue above the girl. He let himself be shaken by the shoulder without detaching his eyes from her face.

"'Que guape!' shouted the General in his ear. 'You are the bravest man living. You have saved my life. I am General Robles. Come to my quarters to-morrow if God gives us the grace to see another day.'

"He never stirred—as if deaf, without feeling, insensible.

"We rode away for the town, full of our relations, of our friends, of whose fate we hardly dared to think. The soldiers ran by the side of our horses. Everything was forgotten in the immensity of the catastrophe overtaking a whole country."

. . . .

Gaspar Ruiz saw the girl open her eyes. The raising of her eyelids seemed to recall him from a trance. They were alone; the cries of terror and distress from homeless people filled the plains of the coast remote and immense, coming like a whisper into their loneliness.

She rose swiftly to her feet, darting fearful glances on all sides. "What is it?" she cried out low, and peering into his face. "Where am I?"

He bowed his head sadly, without a word.

". . . Who are you?"

He knelt down slowly before her, and touched the hem of her coarse black baize skirt. "Your slave," he said.

She caught sight then of the heap of rubbish that had been the house, all misty in the cloud of dust. "Ah!" she cried, pressing her hand to her forehead.

"I carried you out from there," he whispered at her feet.

"And they?" she asked in a great sob.

He rose, and taking her by the arms, led her gently towards the shapeless ruin half overwhelmed by a landslide. "Come and listen," he said.

The serene moon saw them clambering over that heap of stones, joists and tiles, which was a grave. They pressed their ears to the interstices, listening for the sound of a groan, for a sigh of pain.

At last he said, "They died swiftly. You are alone."

She sat down on a piece of broken timber and put one arm across her face. He waited—then approaching his lips to her ear: "Let us go," he whispered.

"Never—never from here," she cried out, flinging her arms above her head.

He stooped over her, and her raised arms fell upon his shoulders. He lifted her up, steadied himself and began to walk, looking straight before him.

"What are you doing?" she asked, feebly.

"I am escaping from my enemies," he said, never once glancing at his light burden.

"With me?" she sighed, helplessly.

"Never without you," he said. "You are my strength."

He pressed her close to him. His face was grave and his footsteps steady. The conflagrations bursting out in the ruins of destroyed villages dotted the plain with red fires;

and the sounds of distant lamentations, the cries of Misericordia! Misericordia! made a desolate murmur in his ears. He walked on, solemn and collected, as if carrying something holy, fragile, and precious.

The earth rocked at times under his feet.

9

WITH MOVEMENTS of mechanical care and an air of abstraction old General Santierra lighted a long and thick cigar.

"It was a good many hours before we could send a party back to the ravine," he said to his guests. "We had found one-third of the town laid low, the rest shaken up; and the inhabitants, rich and poor, reduced to the same state of distraction by the universal disaster. The affected cheerfulness of some contrasted with the despair of others. In the general confusion a number of reckless thieves, without fear of God or man, became a danger to those who from the downfall of their homes had managed to save some valuables. Crying 'Misericordia' louder than any at every tremor, and beating their breast with one hand, these scoundrels robbed the poor victims with the other, not even stopping short of murder.

"General Robles' division was occupied entirely in guarding the destroyed quarters of the town from the depredations of these inhuman monsters. Taken up with my duties of orderly officer, it was only in the morning that I could assure myself of the safety of my own family. My mother and my sisters had escaped with their lives from that ballroom, where I had left them early in the evening. I remember those two beautiful young women—God rest their souls—as if I saw them this moment, in the garden of our destroyed house, pale but active, assisting some of our poor neighbours, in their soiled ball-dresses and with the dust of fallen walls on their hair. As to my mother, she had a stoical soul in her frail body. Half-covered by a costly shawl, she was lying on a rustic seat by the side of an ornamental basin whose fountain had ceased to play for ever on that night.

"I had hardly had time to embrace them all with transports of joy when my chief, coming along, dispatched me to the ravine with a few soldiers, to bring in my strong man, as he called him, and that pale girl.

"But there was no one for us to bring in. A landslide had covered the ruins of the house; and it was like a large mound of earth with only the ends of some timbers visible here and there—nothing more.

"Thus were the tribulations of the old Royalist couple ended. An enormous and unconsecrated grave had swallowed them up alive, in their unhappy obstinacy against the will of a people to be free. And their daughter was gone.

"That Gaspar Ruiz had carried her off I understood very well. But as the case was not foreseen, I had no instructions to pursue them. And certainly I had no desire to do so. I had grown mistrustful of my interference. It had never been successful, and had not even appeared creditable. He was gone. Well, let him go. And he had carried off the Royalist girl! Nothing better. Vaya con Dios. This was not the time to bother about a deserter who, justly or unjustly, ought to have been dead, and a girl for whom it would have been better to have never been born.

"So I marched my men back to the town.

"After a few days, order having been re-established, all the principal families, including my own, left for Santiago. We had a fine house there. At the same time the division of Robles was moved to new cantonments near the capital. This change suited very well the state of my domestic and amorous feelings.

"One night, rather late, I was called to my chief. I found General Robles in his quarters, at ease, with his uniform off, drinking neat brandy out of a tumbler—as a precaution, he used to say, against the sleeplessness induced by the bites of mosquitoes. He was a good soldier, and he taught me the art and practice of war. No doubt God has been merciful to his soul; for his motives were never other than patriotic, if his character was irascible. As to the use of mosquito nets, he considered it effeminate, shameful—unworthy of a soldier. I noticed at the first glance that his face, already very red, wore an expression of high good-humour.

"'Aha! Senor teniente,' he cried, loudly, as I saluted at the door. 'Behold! Your strong man has turned up again.'

"He extended to me a folded letter, which I saw was superscribed 'To the Commander-in-Chief of the Republican Armies.'

"'This,' General Robles went on in his loud voice, 'was thrust by a boy into the hand of a sentry at the Quartel General, while the fellow stood there thinking of his girl, no doubt—for before he could gather his wits together the boy had disappeared amongst the market people, and he protests he could not recognize him to save his life.'

"'My chief told me further that the soldier had given the letter to the sergeant of the guard, and that ultimately it had reached the hands of our generalissimo. His Excellency had deigned to take cognizance of it with his own eyes. After that he had referred the matter in confidence to General Robles.

"The letter, senores, I cannot now recollect textually. I saw the signature of Gaspar Ruiz. He was an audacious fellow. He had snatched a soul for himself out of a cataclysm, remember. And now it was that soul which had dictated the terms of his letter. Its tone was very independent. I remember it struck me at the time as noble—dignified. It was, no doubt, her letter. Now I shudder at the depth of its duplicity. Gaspar Ruiz was made to complain of the injustice of which he had been a victim. He invoked his previous record of fidelity and courage. Having been saved from death by the miraculous interposition of Providence, he could think of nothing but of retrieving his character. This, he wrote, he could not hope to do in the ranks as a discredited soldier still under suspicion. He had the means to give a striking proof of his fidelity. He had ended by proposing to the General-in-Chief a meeting at midnight in the middle of the Plaza before the Moneta. The signal would be to strike fire with flint and steel three times, which was not too conspicuous and yet distinctive enough for recognition.

"San Martin, the great Liberator, loved men of audacity and courage. Besides, he was just and compassionate. I told him as much of the man's story as I knew, and was ordered to accompany him on the appointed night. The signals were duly exchanged. It was midnight, and the whole town was dark and silent. Their two cloaked figures came together in the centre of the vast Plaza, and, keeping discreetly at a distance, I listened for an hour or more to the murmur of their voices. Then the General motioned me to approach; and as I did so I heard San Martin, who was courteous to gentle and simple alike, offer Gaspar Ruiz the hospitality of the headquarters for the night. But the soldier refused, saying that he would be not worthy of that honour till he had done something.

"'You cannot have a common deserter for your guest, Excellency,' he protested with a low laugh, and stepping backwards merged slowly into the night.

"The Commander-in-Chief observed to me, as we turned away: 'He had somebody with him, our friend Ruiz. I saw two figures for a moment. It was an unobtrusive companion.'

"I, too, had observed another figure join the vanishing form of Gaspar Ruiz. It had the appearance of a short fellow in a poncho and a big hat. And I wondered stupidly who it could be he had dared take into his confidence. I might have guessed it could be no one but that fatal girl—alas!

"Where he kept her concealed I do not know. He had—it was known afterwards—an uncle, his mother's brother, a small shopkeeper in Santiago. Perhaps it was there that she found a roof and food. Whatever she found, it was poor enough to exasperate her pride and keep up her anger and hate. It is certain she did not accompany him on the feat he undertook to accomplish first of all. It was nothing less than the destruction of a store of war material collected secretly by the Spanish authorities in the south, in a town called Linares. Gaspar Ruiz was entrusted with a small party only, but they proved themselves worthy of San Martin's confidence. The season was not propitious. They had to swim swollen rivers. They seemed, however, to have galloped night and day out-riding the news of their foray, and holding straight for the town, a hundred miles into the enemy's country, till at break of day they rode into it sword in hand, surprising the little garrison. It fled without making a stand, leaving most of its officers in Gaspar Ruiz' hands.

"A great explosion of gunpowder ended the conflagration of the magazines the raiders had set on fire without loss of time. In less than six hours they were riding away at the same mad speed, without the loss of a single man. Good as they were, such an exploit is not performed without a still better leadership.

"I was dining at the headquarters when Gaspar Ruiz himself brought the news of his success. And it was a great blow to the Royalist troops. For a proof he displayed to us the garrison's flag. He took it from under his poncho and flung it on the table. The man was transfigured; there was something exulting and menacing in the expression of his face. He stood behind General San Martin's chair and looked proudly at us all. He had a round blue cap edged with silver braid on his head, and we all could see a large white scar on the nape of his sunburnt neck.

"Somebody asked him what he had done with the captured Spanish officers.

"He shrugged his shoulders scornfully. 'What a question to ask! In a partisan war you do not burden yourself with prisoners. I let them go—and here are their sword-knots.'

"He flung a bunch of them on the table upon the flag. Then General Robles, whom I was attending there, spoke up in his loud, thick voice: 'You did! Then, my brave friend, you do not know yet how a war like ours ought to be conducted. You should have done—this.' And he passed the edge of his hand across his own throat.

"Alas, senores! It was only too true that on both sides this contest, in its nature so heroic, was stained by ferocity. The murmurs that arose at General Robles' words were by no means unanimous in tone. But the generous and brave San Martin praised the humane action, and pointed out to Ruiz a place on his right hand. Then rising with a full glass he proposed a toast: 'Caballeros and comrades-in-arms, let us drink the health of Captain Gaspar Ruiz.' And when we had emptied our glasses: 'I intend,' the Commander-in-Chief continued, 'to entrust him with the guardianship of our southern frontier, while we go afar to liberate our brethren in Peru. He whom the enemy could not stop from striking a blow at his very heart will know how to protect the peaceful populations we leave behind us to pursue our sacred task.' And he embraced the silent Gaspar Ruiz by his side.

"Later on, when we all rose from table, I approached the latest officer of the army with my congratulations. 'And, Captain Ruiz,' I added, 'perhaps you do not mind telling a man who has always believed in the uprightness of your character what became of Dona Erminia on that night?'

"At this friendly question his aspect changed. He looked at me from under his eyebrows with the heavy, dull glance of a guasso—of a peasant. 'Senor teniente,' he said, thickly, and as if very much cast down, 'do not ask me about the senorita, for I prefer not to think about her at all when I am amongst you."

"He looked, with a frown, all about the room, full of smoking and talking officers. Of course I did not insist.

"These, senores, were the last words I was to hear him utter for a long, long time. The very next day we embarked for our arduous expedition to Peru, and we only heard of Gaspar Ruiz' doings in the midst of battles of our own. He had been appointed military guardian of our southern province. He raised a partida. But his leniency to the conquered foe displeased the Civil Governor, who was a formal, uneasy man, full of suspicions. He forwarded reports against Gaspar Ruiz to the Supreme Government; one of them being that he had married publicly, with great pomp, a woman of Royalist tendencies. Quarrels were sure to arise between these two men of very different character. At last the Civil Governor began to complain of his inactivity and to hint at treachery, which, he wrote, would be not surprising in a man of such antecedents. Gaspar Ruiz heard of it. His rage flamed up, and the woman ever by his side knew how to feed it with perfidious words. I do not know whether really the Supreme Government ever did—as he complained afterwards—send orders for his arrest. It seems certain that the Civil Governor began to tamper with his officers, and that Gaspar Ruiz discovered the fact.

"One evening, when the Governor was giving a tertullia, Gaspar Ruiz, followed by six men he could trust, appeared riding through the town to the door of the Government House, and entered the sala armed, his hat on his head. As the Governor, displeased, advanced to meet him, he seized the wretched man round the body, carried him off from the midst of the appalled guests, as though he were a child, and flung him down the outer steps into the street. An angry hug from Gaspar Ruiz was enough to crush the life out of a giant; but in addition Gaspar Ruiz' horsemen fired their pistols at the body of the Governor as it lay motionless at the bottom of the stairs."

10

"AFTER THIS—AS he called it—act of justice, Ruiz crossed the Rio Blanco, followed by the greater part of his band, and entrenched himself upon a hill. A company of regular troops sent out foolishly against him was surrounded, and destroyed almost to a man. Other expeditions, though better organized, were equally unsuccessful.

"It was during these sanguinary skirmishes that his wife first began to appear on horseback at his right hand. Rendered proud and self-confident by his successes, Ruiz no longer charged at the head of his partida, but presumptuously, like a general directing the movements of an army, he remained in the rear, well mounted and motionless on an eminence, sending out his orders. She was seen repeatedly at his side, and for a long time was mistaken for a man. There was much talk then of a mysterious white-faced chief, to whom the defeats of our troops were ascribed. She rode like an Indian woman, astride, wearing a broad-rimmed man's hat and a dark poncho. Afterwards, in the day of their greatest prosperity, this poncho was embroidered in gold, and she wore then, also, the sword of poor Don Antonio de Leyva. This veteran Chilian officer, having the misfortune to be surrounded with his small force, and running short of ammunition, found his death at the hands of the Arauco Indians, the allies and auxiliaries of Gaspar Ruiz. This was the fatal affair long remembered afterwards as the 'Massacre of the Island.' The sword of the unhappy officer was presented to her by Peneleo, the Araucanian chief; for these Indians, struck by her aspect, the deathly pallor of her face, which no exposure to the weather seemed to affect, and her calm indifference under fire, looked upon her as a supernatural being, or at least as a witch. By this superstition the prestige and authority of Gaspar Ruiz amongst these ignorant people were greatly augmented. She must have savoured her vengeance to the full on that day when she buckled on the sword of Don Antonio de Leyva. It never left her side, unless she put on her woman's clothes—not that she would or could ever use it, but she loved to feel it beating upon her thigh as a perpetual reminder and symbol of the dishonour to the arms of the Republic. She was insatiable. Moreover, on the path she had led Gaspar Ruiz upon, there is no stopping. Escaped prisoners—and they were not many—used to relate how with a few whispered words she could change the expression of his face and revive his flagging animosity. They told how after every skirmish, after every raid, after every successful action, he would ride up to her and look into her face. Its haughty calm was never relaxed. Her embrace, senores, must have been as cold as the embrace of a statue. He tried to melt her icy heart in a stream of warm blood. Some English naval officers who visited him at that time noticed the strange character of his infatuation."

At the movement of surprise and curiosity in his audience General Santierra paused for a moment.

"Yes—English naval officers," he repeated. "Ruiz had consented to receive them to arrange for the liberation of some prisoners of your nationality. In the territory upon which he ranged, from sea coast to the Cordillera, there was a bay where the ships of that time, after rounding Cape Horn, used to resort for wood and water. There, decoying the crew on shore, he captured first the whaling brig Hersalia, and afterwards made himself master by surprise of two more ships, one English and one American.

"It was rumoured at the time that he dreamed of setting up a navy of his own. But that, of course, was impossible. Still, manning the brig with part of her own crew, and putting an officer and a good many men of his own on board, he sent her off to the Spanish Governor of the island of Chiloe with a report of his exploits, and a demand for assistance in the war against the rebels. The Governor could not do much for him; but he sent in return two light field-pieces, a letter of compliments, with a colonel's commission in the royal forces, and a great Spanish flag. This standard with much ceremony was hoisted over his house in the heart of the Arauco country. Surely on that day she may have smiled on her guasso husband with a less haughty reserve.

"The senior officer of the English squadron on our coast made representations to our Government as to these captures. But Gaspar Ruiz refused to treat with us. Then an English frigate proceeded to the bay, and her captain, doctor, and two lieutenants travelled inland under a safe-conduct. They were well received, and spent three days as guests of the partisan chief. A sort of military barbaric state was kept up at the residence. It was furnished with the loot of frontier towns. When first admitted to the principal sala, they saw his wife lying down (she was not in good health then), with Gaspar Ruiz sitting at the foot of the couch. His hat was lying on the floor, and his hands reposed on the hilt of his sword.

"During that first conversation he never removed his big hands from the sword-hilt, except once, to arrange the coverings about her, with gentle, careful touches. They noticed that whenever she spoke he would fix his eyes upon her in a kind of expectant, breathless attention, and seemingly forget the existence of the world and his own existence, too. In the course of the farewell banquet, at which she was present reclining on her couch, he burst forth into complaints of the treatment he had received. After General San Martin's departure he had been beset by spies, slandered by civil officials, his services ignored, his liberty and even his life threatened by the Chilian Government. He got up from the table, thundered execrations pacing the room wildly, then sat down on the couch at his wife's feet, his breast heaving, his eyes fixed on the floor. She reclined on her back, her head on the cushions, her eyes nearly closed.

"'And now I am an honoured Spanish officer,' he added in a calm voice.

"The captain of the English frigate then took the opportunity to inform him gently that Lima had fallen, and that by the terms of a convention the Spaniards were withdrawing from the whole continent.

"Gaspar Ruiz raised his head, and without hesitation, speaking with suppressed vehemence, declared that if not a single Spanish soldier were left in the whole of South America he would persist in carrying on the contest against Chile to the last drop of blood.

When he finished that mad tirade his wife's long white hand was raised, and she just caressed his knee with the tips of her fingers for a fraction of a second.

"For the rest of the officers' stay, which did not extend for more than half an hour after the banquet, that ferocious chieftain of a desperate partida overflowed with amiability and kindness. He had been hospitable before, but now it seemed as though he could not do enough for the comfort and safety of his visitors' journey back to their ship.

"Nothing, I have been told, could have presented a greater contrast to his late violence or the habitual taciturn reserve of his manner. Like a man elated beyond measure by an unexpected happiness, he overflowed with good-will, amiability, and attentions. He embraced the officers like brothers, almost with tears in his eyes. The released prisoners were presented each with a piece of gold. At the last moment, suddenly, he declared he could do no less than restore to the masters of the merchant vessels all their private property. This unexpected generosity caused some delay in the departure of the party, and their first march was very short.

"Late in the evening Gaspar Ruiz rode up with an escort, to their camp fires, bringing along with him a mule loaded with cases of wine. He had come, he said, to drink a stirrup cup with his English friends, whom he would never see again. He was mellow and joyous in his temper. He told stories of his own exploits, laughed like a boy, borrowed a guitar from the Englishmen's chief muleteer, and sitting cross-legged on his superfine poncho spread before the glow of the embers, sang a guasso love-song in a tender voice. Then his head dropped on his breast, his hands fell to the ground; the guitar rolled off his knees—and a great hush fell over the camp after the love-song of the implacable partisan who had made so many of our people weep for destroyed homes and for loves cut short.

"Before anybody could make a sound he sprang up from the ground and called for his horse.

"'Adios, my friends!' he cried. 'Go with God. I love you. And tell them well in Santiago that between Gaspar Ruiz, colonel of the King of Spain, and the republican carrion-crows of Chile there is war to the last breath—war! war! war!'

"With a great yell of 'War! war! war!' which his escort took up, they rode away, and the sound of hoofs and of voices died out in the distance between the slopes of the hills.

"The two young English officers were convinced that Ruiz was mad. How do you say that?—tile loose—eh? But the doctor, an observant Scotsman with much shrewdness and philosophy in his character, told me that it was a very curious case of possession. I met him many years afterwards, but he remembered the experience very well. He told me, too, that in his opinion that woman did not lead Gaspar Ruiz into the practice of sanguinary treachery by direct persuasion, but by the subtle way of awakening and keeping alive in his simple mind a burning sense of an irreparable wrong. Maybe, maybe. But I would say that she poured half of her vengeful soul into the strong clay of that man, as you may pour intoxication, madness, poison into an empty cup.

"If he wanted war he got it in earnest when our victorious army began to return from Peru. Systematic operations were planned against this blot on the honour and prosperity of our hardly won independence. General Robles commanded, with his well-known ruthless severity. Savage reprisals were exercised on both sides and no quarter was given in the field. Having won my promotion in the Peru campaign, I was a captain on the staff. Gaspar Ruiz found himself hard pressed; at the same time we heard by means of a fugitive priest who had been carried off from his village presbytery and galloped eighty miles into the hills to perform the christening ceremony, that a daughter was born to them. To celebrate the event, I suppose, Ruiz executed one or two brilliant forays clear away at the rear of our forces, and defeated the detachments sent out to cut off his retreat. General Robles nearly had a stroke of apoplexy from rage. He found another cause of insomnia than the bites of mosquitoes; but against this one, senores, tumblers of raw brandy had no more effect than so much water. He took to railing and storming at me about my strong man. And from our impatience to end this inglorious campaign I am afraid that all we young officers became reckless and apt to take undue risks on service.

"Nevertheless, slowly, inch by inch as it were, our columns were closing upon Gaspar Ruiz, though he had managed to raise all the Araucanian nation of wild Indians against us. Then a year or more later our Government became aware through its agents and spies that he had actually entered into alliance with Carreras, the so-called dictator of the so-called republic of Mendoza, on the other side of the mountains. Whether Gaspar Ruiz had a deep political intention, or whether he wished only to secure a safe retreat for his wife and child while he pursued remorselessly against us his war of surprises and massacres, I cannot tell. The alliance, however, was a fact. Defeated in his attempt to check our advance from the sea, he retreated with his usual swiftness, and preparing for another hard and hazardous tussle, began by sending his wife with the little girl across the Pequena range of mountains, on the frontier of Mendoza."

II

"NOW CARRERAS, under the guise of politics and liberalism, was a scoundrel of the deepest dye, and the unhappy state of Mendoza was the prey of thieves, robbers, traitors, and murderers, who formed his party. He was under a noble exterior a man without heart, pity, honour, or conscience. He aspired to nothing but tyranny, and though he would have made use of Gaspar Ruiz for his nefarious designs, yet he soon became aware that to propitiate the Chilian Government would answer his purpose better. I blush to say that he made proposals to our Government to deliver up on certain conditions the wife and child of the man who had trusted to his honour, and that this offer was accepted.

"While on her way to Mendoza over the Pequena Pass she was betrayed by her escort of Carreras' men, and given up to the officer in command of a Chilian fort on the upland at the foot of the main Cordillera range. This atrocious transaction might have cost me dear, for as a matter of fact I was a prisoner in Gaspar Ruiz' camp when he received the news. I had been captured during a reconnaissance, my escort of a few troopers being speared by the Indians of his bodyguard. I was saved from the same fate because he recognized my features just in time. No doubt my friends thought I was dead, and I would not have given much for my life at any time. But the strong man treated me very well, because, he said, I had always believed in his innocence and had tried to serve him when he was a victim of injustice.

"'And now,' was his speech to me, 'you shall see that I always speak the truth. You are safe.'

"I did not think I was very safe when I was called up to go to him one night. He paced up and down like a wild beast, exclaiming, 'Betrayed! Betrayed!'

"He walked up to me clenching his fists. 'I could cut your throat.'

"'Will that give your wife back to you?' I said as quietly as I could.

"'And the child!' he yelled out, as if mad. He fell into a chair and laughed in a frightful, boisterous manner. 'Oh, no, you are safe.'

"I assured him that his wife's life was safe, too; but I did not say what I was convinced of —that he would never see her again. He wanted war to the death, and the war could only end with his death.

"He gave me a strange, inexplicable look, and sat muttering blankly, 'In their hands. In their hands.'

"I kept as still as a mouse before a cat.

"Suddenly he jumped up. 'What am I doing here?' he cried; and opening the door, he yelled out orders to saddle and mount. 'What is it?' he stammered, coming up to me. 'The Pequena fort; a fort of palisades! Nothing. I would get her back if she were hidden in the very heart of the mountain.' He amazed me by adding, with an effort: 'I carried her off in my two arms while the earth trembled. And the child at least is mine. She at least is mine!'

"Those were bizarre words; but I had no time for wonder.

"'You shall go with me,' he said, violently. 'I may want to parley, and any other messenger from Ruiz, the outlaw, would have his throat cut.'

"This was true enough. Between him and the rest of incensed mankind there could be no communication, according to the customs of honourable warfare.

"In less than half an hour we were in the saddle, flying wildly through the night. He had only an escort of twenty men at his quarters, but would not wait for more. He sent, however, messengers to Peneleo, the Indian chief then ranging in the foothills, directing him to bring his warriors to the uplands and meet him at the lake called the Eye of Water, near whose shores the frontier fort of Pequena was built.

"We crossed the lowlands with that untired rapidity of movement which had made Gaspar Ruiz' raids so famous. We followed the lower valleys up to their precipitous heads. The ride was not without its dangers. A cornice road on a perpendicular wall of basalt wound itself around a buttressing rock, and at last we emerged from the gloom of a deep gorge upon the upland of Pequena.

"It was a plain of green wiry grass and thin flowering bushes; but high above our heads patches of snow hung in the folds and crevices of the great walls of rock. The little lake was as round as a staring eye. The garrison of the fort were just driving in their small herd of cattle when we appeared. Then the great wooden gates swung to, and that four-square enclosure of broad blackened stakes pointed at the top and barely hiding the grass roofs of the huts inside seemed deserted, empty, without a single soul.

"But when summoned to surrender, by a man who at Gaspar Ruiz' order rode fearlessly forward those inside answered by a volley which rolled him and his horse over. I heard Ruiz by my side grind his teeth. 'It does not matter,' he said. 'Now you go.'

"Torn and faded as its rags were, the vestiges of my uniform were recognized, and I was allowed to approach within speaking distance; and then I had to wait, because a voice clamouring through a loophole with joy and astonishment would not allow me to place a word. It was the voice of Major Pajol, an old friend. He, like my other comrades, had thought me killed a long time ago.

"'Put spurs to your horse, man!' he yelled, in the greatest excitement; 'we will swing the gate open for you.'

"I let the reins fall out of my hand and shook my head. 'I am on my honour,' I cried.

"'To him!' he shouted, with infinite disgust.

"'He promises you your life.'

"'Our life is our own. And do you, Santierra, advise us to surrender to that rastrero?'

"'No!' I shouted. 'But he wants his wife and child, and he can cut you off from water.'

"'Then she would be the first to suffer. You may tell him that. Look here—this is all nonsense: we shall dash out and capture you.'

"'You shall not catch me alive,' I said, firmly.

"'Imbecile!'

"'For God's sake,' I continued, hastily, 'do not open the gate.' And I pointed at the multitude of Peneleo's Indians who covered the shores of the lake.

"I had never seen so many of these savages together. Their lances seemed as numerous as stalks of grass. Their hoarse voices made a vast, inarticulate sound like the murmur of the sea.

"My friend Pajol was swearing to himself. 'Well, then—go to the devil!' he shouted, exasperated. But as I swung round he repented, for I heard him say hurriedly, 'Shoot the fool's horse before he gets away.'

"He had good marksmen. Two shots rang out, and in the very act of turning my horse staggered, fell and lay still as if struck by lightning. I had my feet out of the stirrups and rolled clear of him; but I did not attempt to rise. Neither dared they rush out to drag me in.

"The masses of Indians had begun to move upon the fort. They rode up in squadrons, trailing their long chusos; then dismounted out of musket-shot, and, throwing off their fur mantles, advanced naked to the attack, stamping their feet and shouting in cadence. A sheet of flame ran three times along the face of the fort without checking their steady march. They crowded right up to the very stakes, flourishing their broad knives. But this palisade was not fastened together with hide lashings in the usual way, but with long iron nails, which they could not cut. Dismayed at the failure of their usual method of forcing an entrance, the heathen, who had marched so steadily against the musketry fire, broke and fled under the volleys of the besieged.

"Directly they had passed me on their advance I got up and rejoined Gaspar Ruiz on a low ridge which jutted out upon the plain. The musketry of his own men had covered the attack, but now at a sign from him a trumpet sounded the 'Cease fire.' Together we looked in silence at the hopeless rout of the savages.

"'It must be a siege, then,' he muttered. And I detected him wringing his hands stealthily.

"But what sort of siege could it be? Without any need for me to repeat my friend Pajol's message, he dared not cut the water off from the besieged. They had plenty of meat. And, indeed, if they had been short he would have been too anxious to send food into the stockade had he been able. But, as a matter of fact, it was we on the plain who were beginning to feel the pinch of hunger.

"Peneleo, the Indian chief, sat by our fire folded in his ample mantle of guanaco skins. He was an athletic savage, with an enormous square shock head of hair resembling a straw beehive in shape and size, and with grave, surly, much-lined features. In his broken Spanish he repeated, growling like a bad-tempered wild beast, that if an opening ever so small were made in the stockade his men would march in and get the senora—not otherwise.

"Gaspar Ruiz, sitting opposite him, kept his eyes fixed on the fort night and day as it were, in awful silence and immobility. Meantime, by runners from the lowlands that arrived nearly every day, we heard of the defeat of one of his lieutenants in the Maipu valley. Scouts sent afar brought news of a column of infantry advancing through distant passes to the relief of the fort. They were slow, but we could trace their toilful progress up the lower valleys. I wondered why Ruiz did not march to attack and destroy this threatening force, in some wild gorge fit for an ambuscade, in accordance with his genius for guerilla warfare. But his genius seemed to have abandoned him to his despair.

"It was obvious to me that he could not tear himself away from the sight of the fort. I protest to you, senores, that I was moved almost to pity by the sight of this powerless strong man sitting on the ridge, indifferent to sun, to rain, to cold, to wind; with his hands clasped round his legs and his chin resting on his knees, gazing—gazing—gazing.

"And the fort he kept his eyes fastened on was as still and silent as himself. The garrison gave no sign of life. They did not even answer the desultory fire directed at the loopholes.

"One night, as I strolled past him, he, without changing his attitude, spoke to me unexpectedly. 'I have sent for a gun,' he said. 'I shall have time to get her back and retreat before your Robles manages to crawl up here.'

"He had sent for a gun to the plains.

"It was long in coming, but at last it came. It was a seven-pounder field gun. Dismounted and lashed crosswise to two long poles, it had been carried up the narrow paths between two mules with ease. His wild cry of exultation at daybreak when he saw the gun escort emerge from the valley rings in my ears now.

"But, senores, I have no words to depict his amazement, his fury, his despair and distraction, when he heard that the animal loaded with the gun-carriage had, during the last night march, somehow or other tumbled down a precipice. He broke into menaces of death and torture against the escort. I kept out of his way all that day, lying behind some bushes, and wondering what he would do now. Retreat was left for him, but he could not retreat.

"I saw below me his artillerist, Jorge, an old Spanish soldier, building up a sort of structure with heaped-up saddles. The gun, ready loaded, was lifted on to that, but in the act of firing the whole thing collapsed and the shot flew high above the stockade.

"Nothing more was attempted. One of the ammunition mules had been lost, too, and they had no more than six shots to fire; ample enough to batter down the gate providing the gun was well laid. This was impossible without it being properly mounted. There was no time nor means to construct a carriage. Already every moment I expected to hear Robles' bugle-calls echo amongst the crags.

"Peneleo, wandering about uneasily, draped in his skins, sat down for a moment near me growling his usual tale.

"'Make an entrada—a hole. If make a hole, bueno. If not make a hole, then vamos—we must go away.'

"After sunset I observed with surprise the Indians making preparations as if for another assault. Their lines stood ranged in the shadows of the mountains. On the plain in front of the fort gate I saw a group of men swaying about in the same place.

"I walked down the ridge disregarded. The moonlight in the clear air of the uplands was bright as day, but the intense shadows confused my sight, and I could not make out what they were doing. I heard the voice of Jorge, the artillerist, say in a queer, doubtful tone, 'It is loaded, senor.'

"Then another voice in that group pronounced firmly the words, 'Bring the riata here.' It was the voice of Gaspar Ruiz.

"A silence fell, in which the popping shots of the besieged garrison rang out sharply. They, too, had observed the group. But the distance was too great and in the spatter of spent musket-balls cutting up the ground, the group opened, closed, swayed, giving me a glimpse of busy stooping figures in its midst. I drew nearer, doubting whether this was a weird vision, a suggestive and insensate dream.

"A strangely stifled voice commanded, 'Haul the hitches tighter.'

"'Si, senor,' several other voices answered in tones of awed alacrity.

"Then the stifled voice said: 'Like this. I must be free to breathe.'

"Then there was a concerned noise of many men together. 'Help him up, hombres. Steady! Under the other arm.'

"That deadened voice ordered: 'Bueno! Stand away from me, men.'

"I pushed my way through the recoiling circle, and heard once more that same oppressed voice saying earnestly: 'Forget that I am a living man, Jorge. Forget me altogether, and think of what you have to do.'

"'Be without fear, senor. You are nothing to me but a gun-carriage, and I shall not waste a shot.'

"I heard the spluttering of a port-fire, and smelt the saltpetre of the match. I saw suddenly before me a nondescript shape on all fours like a beast, but with a man's head drooping below a tubular projection over the nape of the neck, and the gleam of a rounded mass of bronze on its back.

"In front of a silent semicircle of men it squatted alone, with Jorge behind it and a trumpeter motionless, his trumpet in his hand, by its side.

"Jorge, bent double, muttered, port-fire in hand: 'An inch to the left, senor. Too much. So. Now, if you let yourself down a little by letting your elbows bend, I will . . .'

"He leaped aside, lowering his port-fire, and a burst of flame darted out of the muzzle of the gun lashed on the man's back.

"Then Gaspar Ruiz lowered himself slowly. 'Good shot?' he asked.

"'Full on, senor.'

"'Then load again.'

"He lay there before me on his breast under the darkly glittering bronze of his monstrous burden, such as no love or strength of man had ever had to bear in the lamentable history of the world. His arms were spread out, and he resembled a prostrate penitent on the moonlit ground.

"Again I saw him raised to his hands and knees and the men stand away from him, and old Jorge stoop glancing along the gun.

"'Left a little. Right an inch. Por Dios, senor, stop this trembling. Where is your strength?'

"The old gunner's voice was cracked with emotion. He stepped aside, and quick as lightning brought the spark to the touch-hole.

"'Excellent!' he cried, tearfully; but Gaspar Ruiz lay for a long time silent, flattened on the ground.

"'I am tired,' he murmured at last. 'Will another shot do it?'

"'Without doubt,' said Jorge, bending down to his ear.

"'Then—load,' I heard him utter distinctly. 'Trumpeter!'

"'I am here, senor, ready for your word.'

"'Blow a blast at this word that shall be heard from one end of Chile to the other,' he said, in an extraordinarily strong voice. 'And you others stand ready to cut this accursed riata, for then will be the time for me to lead you in your rush. Now raise me up, and you, Jorge—be quick with your aim.'

"The rattle of musketry from the fort nearly drowned his voice. The palisade was wreathed in smoke and flame.

"'Exert your force forward against the recoil, mi amo,' said the old gunner, shakily. 'Dig your fingers into the ground. So. Now!'

"A cry of exultation escaped him after the shot. The trumpeter raised his trumpet nearly to his lips and waited. But no word came from the prostrate man. I fell on one knee, and heard all he had to say then.

"'Something broken,' he whispered, lifting his head a little, and turning his eyes towards me in his hopelessly crushed attitude.

"'The gate hangs only by the splinters,' yelled Jorge.

"Gaspar Ruiz tried to speak, but his voice died out in his throat, and I helped to roll the gun off his broken back. He was insensible.

"I kept my lips shut, of course. The signal for the Indians to attack was never given. Instead, the bugle-calls of the relieving force for which my ears had thirsted so long, burst out, terrifying like the call of the Last Day to our surprised enemies.

"A tornado, senores, a real hurricane of stampeded men, wild horses, mounted Indians, swept over me as I cowered on the ground by the side of Gaspar Ruiz, still stretched out on his face in the shape of a cross. Peneleo, galloping for life, jabbed at me with his long chuso in passing—for the sake of old acquaintance, I suppose. How I escaped the flying lead is more difficult to explain. Venturing to rise on my knees too soon some soldiers of the 17th Taltal regiment, in their hurry to get at something alive, nearly bayoneted me on the spot. They looked very disappointed, too, when, some officers galloping up drove them away with the flat of their swords.

"It was General Robles with his staff. He wanted badly to make some prisoners. He, too, seemed disappointed for a moment. 'What! Is it you?' he cried. But he dismounted at once to embrace me, for he was an old friend of my family. I pointed to the body at our feet, and said only these two words:

"'Gaspar Ruiz.'

"He threw his arms up in astonishment.

"'Aha! Your strong man! Always to the last with your strong man. No matter. He saved our lives when the earth trembled enough to make the bravest faint with fear. I was frightened out of my wits. But he—no! Que guape! Where's the hero who got the best of him? ha! ha! ha! What killed him, chico?'

"'His own strength, General,' I answered."

12

"BUT GASPAR RUIZ BREATHED YET. I had him carried in his poncho under the shelter of some bushes on the very ridge from which he had been gazing so fixedly at the fort while unseen death was hovering already over his head.

"Our troops had bivouacked round the fort. Towards daybreak I was not surprised to hear that I was designated to command the escort of a prisoner who was to be sent down at once to Santiago. Of course the prisoner was Gaspar Ruiz' wife.

"'I have named you out of regard for your feelings,' General Robles remarked. 'Though the woman really ought to be shot for all the harm she has done to the Republic.'

"And as I made a movement of shocked protest, he continued:

"'Now he is as well as dead, she is of no importance. Nobody will know what to do with her. However, the Government wants her.' He shrugged his shoulders. 'I suppose he must have buried large quantities of his loot in places that she alone knows of.'

"At dawn I saw her coming up the ridge, guarded by two soldiers, and carrying her child on her arm.

"I walked to meet her.

"'Is he living yet?' she asked, confronting me with that white, impassive face he used to look at in an adoring way.

"I bent my head, and led her round a clump of bushes without a word. His eyes were open. He breathed with difficulty, and uttered her name with a great effort.

"'Erminia!'

"She knelt at his head. The little girl, unconscious of him, and with her big eyes looking about, began to chatter suddenly, in a joyous, thin voice. She pointed a tiny finger at the rosy glow of sunrise behind the black shapes of the peaks. And while that child-talk, incomprehensible and sweet to the ear, lasted, those two, the dying man and the kneeling woman, remained silent, looking into each other's eyes, listening to the frail sound. Then the prattle stopped. The child laid its head against its mother's breast and was still.

"'It was for you,' he began. 'Forgive.' His voice failed him. Presently I heard a mutter and caught the pitiful words: 'Not strong enough.'

"She looked at him with an extraordinary intensity. He tried to smile, and in a humble tone, 'Forgive me,' he repeated. 'Leaving you . . .'

"She bent down, dry-eyed and in a steady voice: 'On all the earth I have loved nothing but you, Gaspar,' she said.

"His head made a movement. His eyes revived. 'At last!' he sighed out. Then, anxiously, 'But is this true . . . is this true?'

"'As true as that there is no mercy and justice in this world,' she answered him, passionately. She stooped over his face. He tried to raise his head, but it fell back, and when she kissed his lips he was already dead. His glazed eyes stared at the sky, on which pink clouds floated very high. But I noticed the eyelids of the child, pressed to its mother's breast, droop and close slowly. She had gone to sleep.

"The widow of Gaspar Ruiz, the strong man, allowed me to lead her away without shedding a tear.

"For travelling we had arranged for her a sidesaddle very much like a chair, with a board swung beneath to rest her feet on. And the first day she rode without uttering a word, and hardly for one moment turning her eyes away from the little girl, whom she held on her knees. At our first camp I saw her during the night walking about, rocking the child in her arms and gazing down at it by the light of the moon. After we had started on our second day's march she asked me how soon we should come to the first village of the inhabited country.

"I said we should be there about noon.

"'And will there be women there?' she inquired.

"I told her that it was a large village. 'There will be men and women there, senora,' I said, 'whose hearts shall be made glad by the news that all the unrest and war is over now.'

"'Yes, it is all over now,' she repeated. Then, after a time: 'Senor officer, what will your Government do with me?'

"'I do not know, senora,' I said. 'They will treat you well, no doubt. We republicans are not savages and take no vengeance on women.'

"She gave me a look at the word 'republicans' which I imagined full of undying hate. But an hour or so afterwards, as we drew up to let the baggage mules go first along a narrow path skirting a precipice, she looked at me with such a white, troubled face that I felt a great pity for her.

"'Senor officer,' she said, 'I am weak, I tremble. It is an insensate fear.' And indeed her lips did tremble while she tried to smile, glancing at the beginning of the narrow path which was not so dangerous after all. 'I am afraid I shall drop the child. Gaspar saved your life, you remember. . . . Take her from me.'

"I took the child out of her extended arms. 'Shut your eyes, senora, and trust to your mule,' I recommended.

"She did so, and with her pallor and her wasted, thin face she looked deathlike. At a turn of the path where a great crag of purple porphyry closes the view of the lowlands, I saw her open her eyes. I rode just behind her holding the little girl with my right arm. 'The child is all right,' I cried encouragingly.

"'Yes,' she answered, faintly; and then, to my intense terror, I saw her stand up on the foot-rest, staring horribly, and throw herself forward into the chasm on our right.

"I cannot describe to you the sudden and abject fear that came over me at that dreadful sight. It was a dread of the abyss, the dread of the crags which seemed to nod upon me. My head swam. I pressed the child to my side and sat my horse as still as a statue. I was speechless and cold all over. Her mule staggered, sidling close to the rock, and then went on.

My horse only pricked up his ears with a slight snort. My heart stood still, and from the depths of the precipice the stones rattling in the bed of the furious stream made me almost insane with their sound.

"Next moment we were round the turn and on a broad and grassy slope. And then I yelled. My men came running back to me in great alarm. It seems that at first I did nothing but shout, 'She has given the child into my hands! She has given the child into my hands!' The escort thought I had gone mad."

General Santierra ceased and got up from the table. "And that is all, senores," he concluded, with a courteous glance at his rising guests.

"But what became of the child. General?" we asked.

"Ah, the child, the child."

He walked to one of the windows opening on his beautiful garden, the refuge of his old days. Its fame was great in the land. Keeping us back with a raised arm, he called out, "Erminia, Erminia!" and waited. Then his cautioning arm dropped, and we crowded to the windows.

From a clump of trees a woman had come upon the broad walk bordered with flowers. We could hear the rustle of her starched petticoats and observed the ample spread of her old-fashioned black silk skirt. She looked up, and seeing all these eyes staring at her stopped, frowned, smiled, shook her finger at the General, who was laughing boisterously, and drawing the black lace on her head so as to partly conceal her haughty profile, passed out of our sight, walking with stiff dignity.

"You have beheld the guardian angel of the old man—and her to whom you owe all that is seemly and comfortable in my hospitality. Somehow, senores, though the flame of love has been kindled early in my breast, I have never married. And because of that perhaps the sparks of the sacred fire are not yet extinct here." He struck his broad chest. "Still alive, still alive," he said, with serio-comic emphasis. "But I shall not marry now. She is General Santierra's adopted daughter and heiress."

One of our fellow-guests, a young naval officer, described her afterwards as a "short, stout, old girl of forty or thereabouts." We had all noticed that her hair was turning grey, and that she had very fine black eyes.

"And," General Santierra continued, "neither would she ever hear of marrying any one. A real calamity! Good, patient, devoted to the old man. A simple soul. But I would not advise any of you to ask for her hand, for if she took yours into hers it would be only to crush your bones. Ah! she does not jest on that subject. And she is the own daughter of her father, the strong man who perished through his own strength: the strength of his body, of his simplicity—of his love!"

THE PLANTER OF MALATA

I

In the private editorial office of the principal newspaper in a great colonial city two men were talking. They were both young. The stouter of the two, fair, and with more of an urban look about him, was the editor and part-owner of the important newspaper.

The other's name was Renouard. That he was exercised in his mind about something was evident on his fine bronzed face. He was a lean, lounging, active man. The journalist continued the conversation.

"And so you were dining yesterday at old Dunster's."

He used the word old not in the endearing sense in which it is sometimes applied to intimates, but as a matter of sober fact. The Dunster in question was old. He had been an eminent colonial statesman, but had now retired from active politics after a tour in Europe and a lengthy stay in England, during which he had had a very good press indeed. The colony was proud of him.

"Yes. I dined there," said Renouard. "Young Dunster asked me just as I was going out of his office. It seemed to be like a sudden thought. And yet I can't help suspecting some purpose behind it. He was very pressing. He swore that his uncle would be very pleased to see me. Said his uncle had mentioned lately that the granting to me of the Malata concession was the last act of his official life."

"Very touching. The old boy sentimentalises over the past now and then."

"I really don't know why I accepted," continued the other. "Sentiment does not move me very easily. Old Dunster was civil to me of course, but he did not even inquire how I was getting on with my silk plants. Forgot there was such a thing probably. I must say there were more people there than I expected to meet. Quite a big party."

"I was asked," remarked the newspaper man. "Only I couldn't go. But when did you arrive from Malata?"

"I arrived yesterday at daylight. I am anchored out there in the bay—off Garden Point. I was in Dunster's office before he had finished reading his letters. Have you ever seen young Dunster reading his letters? I had a glimpse of him through the open door. He holds the paper in both hands, hunches his shoulders up to his ugly ears, and brings his long nose and his thick lips on to it like a sucking apparatus. A commercial monster."

"Here we don't consider him a monster," said the newspaper man looking at his visitor thoughtfully.

"Probably not. You are used to see his face and to see other faces. I don't know how it is that, when I come to town, the appearance of the people in the street strike me with such force. They seem so awfully expressive."

"And not charming."

"Well—no. Not as a rule. The effect is forcible without being clear. . . . I know that you think it's because of my solitary manner of life away there."

"Yes. I do think so. It is demoralising. You don't see any one for months at a stretch. You're leading an unhealthy life."

The other hardly smiled and murmured the admission that true enough it was a good eleven months since he had been in town last.

"You see," insisted the other. "Solitude works like a sort of poison. And then you perceive suggestions in faces—mysterious and forcible, that no sound man would be bothered with. Of course you do."

Geoffrey Renouard did not tell his journalist friend that the suggestions of his own face, the face of a friend, bothered him as much as the others. He detected a degrading quality in the touches of age which every day adds to a human countenance. They moved and disturbed him, like the signs of a horrible inward travail which was frightfully apparent to the fresh eye he had brought from his isolation in Malata, where he had settled after five strenuous years of adventure and exploration.

"It's a fact," he said, "that when I am at home in Malata I see no one consciously. I take the plantation boys for granted."

"Well, and we here take the people in the streets for granted. And that's sanity."

The visitor said nothing to this for fear of engaging a discussion. What he had come to seek in the editorial office was not controversy, but information. Yet somehow he hesitated to approach the subject. Solitary life makes a man reticent in respect of anything in the nature of gossip, which those to whom chatting about their kind is an everyday exercise regard as the commonest use of speech.

"You very busy?" he asked.

The Editor making red marks on a long slip of printed paper threw the pencil down.

"No. I am done. Social paragraphs. This office is the place where everything is known about everybody—including even a great deal of nobodies. Queer fellows drift in and out of this room. Waifs and strays from home, from up-country, from the Pacific. And, by the way, last time you were here you picked up one of that sort for your assistant—didn't you?"

"I engaged an assistant only to stop your preaching about the evils of solitude," said Renouard hastily; and the pressman laughed at the half-resentful tone. His laugh was not very loud, but his plump person shook all over. He was aware that his younger friend's deference to his advice was based only on an imperfect belief in his wisdom—or his sagacity. But it was he who had first helped Renouard in his plans of exploration: the five-years' programme of scientific adventure, of work, of danger and endurance, carried out with such distinction and rewarded modestly with the lease of Malata island by the frugal colonial government. And this reward, too, had been due to the journalist's advocacy with word and pen—for he was an influential man in the community. Doubting very much if Renouard really liked him, he was himself without great sympathy for a certain side of that man which he could not quite make out. He only felt it obscurely to be his real personality—the true—

and, perhaps, the absurd. As, for instance, in that case of the assistant. Renouard had given way to the arguments of his friend and backer—the argument against the unwholesome effect of solitude, the argument for the safety of companionship even if quarrelsome. Very well. In this docility he was sensible and even likeable. But what did he do next? Instead of taking counsel as to the choice with his old backer and friend, and a man, besides, knowing everybody employed and unemployed on the pavements of the town, this extraordinary Renouard suddenly and almost surreptitiously picked up a fellow—God knows who—and sailed away with him back to Malata in a hurry; a proceeding obviously rash and at the same time not quite straight. That was the sort of thing. The secretly unforgiving journalist laughed a little longer and then ceased to shake all over.

"Oh, yes. About that assistant of yours. . . ."

"What about him," said Renouard, after waiting a while, with a shadow of uneasiness on his face.

"Have you nothing to tell me of him?"

"Nothing except. . . ." Incipient grimness vanished out of Renouard's aspect and his voice, while he hesitated as if reflecting seriously before he changed his mind. "No. Nothing whatever."

"You haven't brought him along with you by chance—for a change."

The Planter of Malata stared, then shook his head, and finally murmured carelessly: "I think he's very well where he is. But I wish you could tell me why young Dunster insisted so much on my dining with his uncle last night. Everybody knows I am not a society man."

The Editor exclaimed at so much modesty. Didn't his friend know that he was their one and only explorer—that he was the man experimenting with the silk plant. . . .

"Still, that doesn't tell me why I was invited yesterday. For young Dunster never thought of this civility before. . . ."

"Our Willie," said the popular journalist, "never does anything without a purpose, that's a fact."

"And to his uncle's house too!"

"He lives there."

"Yes. But he might have given me a feed somewhere else. The extraordinary part is that the old man did not seem to have anything special to say. He smiled kindly on me once or twice, and that was all. It was quite a party, sixteen people."

The Editor then, after expressing his regret that he had not been able to come, wanted to know if the party had been entertaining.

Renouard regretted that his friend had not been there. Being a man whose business or at least whose profession was to know everything that went on in this part of the globe, he could probably have told him something of some people lately arrived from home, who were amongst the guests. Young Dunster (Willie), with his large shirt-front and streaks of white skin shining unpleasantly through the thin black hair plastered over the top of his head, bore down on him and introduced him to that party, as if he had been a trained dog or a child phenomenon. Decidedly, he said, he disliked Willie—one of these large oppressive men. . . .

A silence fell, and it was as if Renouard were not going to say anything more when, suddenly, he came out with the real object of his visit to the editorial room.

"They looked to me like people under a spell."

The Editor gazed at him appreciatively, thinking that, whether the effect of solitude or not, this was a proof of a sensitive perception of the expression of faces.

"You omitted to tell me their name, but I can make a guess. You mean Professor Moorsom, his daughter and sister—don't you?"

Renouard assented. Yes, a white-haired lady. But from his silence, with his eyes fixed, yet avoiding his friend, it was easy to guess that it was not in the white-haired lady that he was interested.

"Upon my word," he said, recovering his usual bearing. "It looks to me as if I had been asked there only for the daughter to talk to me."

He did not conceal that he had been greatly struck by her appearance. Nobody could have helped being impressed. She was different from everybody else in that house, and it was not only the effect of her London clothes. He did not take her down to dinner. Willie did that. It was afterwards, on the terrace. . . .

The evening was delightfully calm. He was sitting apart and alone, and wishing himself somewhere else—on board the schooner for choice, with the dinner-harness off. He hadn't exchanged forty words altogether during the evening with the other guests. He saw her suddenly all by herself coming towards him along the dimly lighted terrace, quite from a distance.

She was tall and supple, carrying nobly on her straight body a head of a character which to him appeared peculiar, something—well—pagan, crowned with a great wealth of hair. He had been about to rise, but her decided approach caused him to remain on the seat. He had not looked much at her that evening. He had not that freedom of gaze acquired by the habit of society and the frequent meetings with strangers. It was not shyness, but the reserve of a man not used to the world and to the practice of covert staring, with careless curiosity. All he had captured by his first, keen, instantly lowered, glance was the impression that her hair was magnificently red and her eyes very black. It was a troubling effect, but it had been evanescent; he had forgotten it almost till very unexpectedly he saw her coming down the terrace slow and eager, as if she were restraining herself, and with a rhythmic upward undulation of her whole figure. The light from an open window fell across her path, and suddenly all that mass of arranged hair appeared incandescent, chiselled and fluid, with the daring suggestion of a helmet of burnished copper and the flowing lines of molten metal. It kindled in him an astonished admiration. But he said nothing of it to his friend the Editor. Neither did he tell him that her approach woke up in his brain the image of love's infinite grace and the sense of the inexhaustible joy that lives in beauty. No! What he imparted to the Editor were no emotions, but mere facts conveyed in a deliberate voice and in uninspired words.

"That young lady came and sat down by me. She said: 'Are you French, Mr. Renouard?'"

He had breathed a whiff of perfume of which he said nothing either—of some perfume he did not know. Her voice was low and distinct. Her shoulders and her bare arms gleamed with an extraordinary splendour, and when she advanced her head into the light he saw the admirable contour of the face, the straight fine nose with delicate nostrils, the exquisite crimson brushstroke of the lips on this oval without colour. The expression of the eyes was lost in a shadowy mysterious play of jet and silver, stirring under the red coppery gold of the hair as though she had been a being made of ivory and precious metals changed into living tissue.

". . . I told her my people were living in Canada, but that I was brought up in England before coming out here. I can't imagine what interest she could have in my history."

"And you complain of her interest?"

The accent of the all-knowing journalist seemed to jar on the Planter of Malata.

"No!" he said, in a deadened voice that was almost sullen. But after a short silence he went on. "Very extraordinary. I told her I came out to wander at large in the world when I was nineteen, almost directly after I left school. It seems that her late brother was in the same school a couple of years before me. She wanted me to tell her what I did at first when I came out here; what other men found to do when they came out—where they went, what was likely to happen to them—as if I could guess and foretell from my experience the fates of men who come out here with a hundred different projects, for hundreds of different reasons —for no reason but restlessness—who come, and go, and disappear! Preposterous. She seemed to want to hear their histories. I told her that most of them were not worth telling."

The distinguished journalist leaning on his elbow, his head resting against the knuckles of his left hand, listened with great attention, but gave no sign of that surprise which Renouard, pausing, seemed to expect.

"You know something," the latter said brusquely. The all-knowing man moved his head slightly and said, "Yes. But go on."

"It's just this. There is no more to it. I found myself talking to her of my adventures, of my early days. It couldn't possibly have interested her. Really," he cried, "this is most extraordinary. Those people have something on their minds. We sat in the light of the window, and her father prowled about the terrace, with his hands behind his back and his head drooping. The white-haired lady came to the dining-room window twice—to look at us I am certain. The other guests began to go away—and still we sat there. Apparently these people are staying with the Dunsters. It was old Mrs. Dunster who put an end to the thing. The father and the aunt circled about as if they were afraid of interfering with the girl. Then she got up all at once, gave me her hand, and said she hoped she would see me again."

While he was speaking Renouard saw again the sway of her figure in a movement of grace and strength—felt the pressure of her hand—heard the last accents of the deep murmur that came from her throat so white in the light of the window, and remembered the black rays of her steady eyes passing off his face when she turned away. He remembered all this visually, and it was not exactly pleasurable. It was rather startling like the discovery of a new faculty in himself. There are faculties one would rather do without—such, for instance, as seeing through a stone wall or remembering a person with this uncanny vividness. And what about those two people belonging to her with their air of expectant solicitude! Really, those figures from home got in front of one. In fact, their persistence in getting between him and the solid forms of the everyday material world had driven Renouard to call on his friend at the office. He hoped that a little common, gossipy information would lay the ghost of that unexpected dinner-party. Of course the proper person to go to would have been young Dunster, but, he couldn't stand Willie Dunster—not at any price.

In the pause the Editor had changed his attitude, faced his desk, and smiled a faint knowing smile.

"Striking girl—eh?" he said.

The incongruity of the word was enough to make one jump out of the chair. Striking! That girl striking! Stri . . .! But Renouard restrained his feelings. His friend was not a person to give oneself away to. And, after all, this sort of speech was what he had come there to hear. As, however, he had made a movement he re-settled himself comfortably and said, with very creditable indifference, that yes—she was, rather. Especially amongst a lot of over-dressed frumps. There wasn't one woman under forty there.

"Is that the way to speak of the cream of our society; the 'top of the basket,' as the French say," the Editor remonstrated with mock indignation. "You aren't moderate in your expressions—you know."

"I express myself very little," interjected Renouard seriously.

"I will tell you what you are. You are a fellow that doesn't count the cost. Of course you are safe with me, but will you never learn. . . ."

"What struck me most," interrupted the other, "is that she should pick me out for such a long conversation."

"That's perhaps because you were the most remarkable of the men there."

Renouard shook his head.

"This shot doesn't seem to me to hit the mark," he said calmly. "Try again."

"Don't you believe me? Oh, you modest creature. Well, let me assure you that under ordinary circumstances it would have been a good shot. You are sufficiently remarkable. But you seem a pretty acute customer too. The circumstances are extraordinary. By Jove they are!"

He mused. After a time the Planter of Malata dropped a negligent—

"And you know them."

"And I know them," assented the all-knowing Editor, soberly, as though the occasion were too special for a display of professional vanity; a vanity so well known to Renouard that its absence augmented his wonder and almost made him uneasy as if portending bad news of some sort.

"You have met those people?" he asked.

"No. I was to have met them last night, but I had to send an apology to Willie in the morning. It was then that he had the bright idea to invite you to fill the place, from a muddled notion that you could be of use. Willie is stupid sometimes. For it is clear that you are the last man able to help."

"How on earth do I come to be mixed up in this—whatever it is?" Renouard's voice was slightly altered by nervous irritation. "I only arrived here yesterday morning."

2

HIS FRIEND the Editor turned to him squarely. "Willie took me into consultation, and since he seems to have let you in I may just as well tell you what is up. I shall try to be as short as I can. But in confidence—mind!"

He waited. Renouard, his uneasiness growing on him unreasonably, assented by a nod, and the other lost no time in beginning. Professor Moorsom—physicist and philosopher—fine head of white hair, to judge from the photographs—plenty of brains in the head too—all these famous books—surely even Renouard would know. . . .

Renouard muttered moodily that it wasn't his sort of reading, and his friend hastened to assure him earnestly that neither was it his sort—except as a matter of business and duty, for the literary page of that newspaper which was his property (and the pride of his life). The only literary newspaper in the Antipodes could not ignore the fashionable philosopher of the age. Not that anybody read Moorsom at the Antipodes, but everybody had heard of him—women, children, dock labourers, cabmen. The only person (besides himself) who had read Moorsom, as far as he knew, was old Dunster, who used to call himself a Moorsomian (or was it Moorsomite) years and years ago, long before Moorsom had worked himself up into the great swell he was now, in every way. . . Socially too. Quite the fashion in the highest world.

Renouard listened with profoundly concealed attention. "A charlatan," he muttered languidly.

"Well—no. I should say not. I shouldn't wonder though if most of his writing had been done with his tongue in his cheek. Of course. That's to be expected. I tell you what: the only really honest writing is to be found in newspapers and nowhere else—and don't you forget it."

The Editor paused with a basilisk stare till Renouard had conceded a casual: "I dare say," and only then went on to explain that old Dunster, during his European tour, had been made rather a lion of in London, where he stayed with the Moorsoms—he meant the father and the girl. The professor had been a widower for a long time.

"She doesn't look just a girl," muttered Renouard. The other agreed. Very likely not.

Had been playing the London hostess to tip-top people ever since she put her hair up, probably.

"I don't expect to see any girlish bloom on her when I do have the privilege," he continued. "Those people are staying with the Dunster's *incog.*, in a manner, you understand —something like royalties. They don't deceive anybody, but they want to be left to themselves. We have even kept them out of the paper—to oblige old Dunster. But we shall put your arrival in—our local celebrity."

"Heavens!"

"Yes. Mr. G. Renouard, the explorer, whose indomitable energy, etc., and who is now working for the prosperity of our country in another way on his Malata plantation . . . And, by the by, how's the silk plant—flourishing?"

"Yes."

"Did you bring any fibre?"

"Schooner-full."

"I see. To be transhipped to Liverpool for experimental manufacture, eh? Eminent capitalists at home very much interested, aren't they?"

"They are."

A silence fell. Then the Editor uttered slowly—"You will be a rich man some day."

Renouard's face did not betray his opinion of that confident prophecy. He didn't say anything till his friend suggested in the same meditative voice—

"You ought to interest Moorsom in the affair too—since Willie has let you in."

"A philosopher!"

"I suppose he isn't above making a bit of money. And he may be clever at it for all you know. I have a notion that he's a fairly practical old cove. . . . Anyhow," and here the tone of the speaker took on a tinge of respect, "he has made philosophy pay."

Renouard raised his eyes, repressed an impulse to jump up, and got out of the arm-chair slowly. "It isn't perhaps a bad idea," he said. "I'll have to call there in any case."

He wondered whether he had managed to keep his voice steady, its tone unconcerned enough; for his emotion was strong though it had nothing to do with the business aspect of this suggestion. He moved in the room in vague preparation for departure, when he heard a soft laugh. He spun about quickly with a frown, but the Editor was not laughing at him. He was chuckling across the big desk at the wall: a preliminary of some speech for which Renouard, recalled to himself, waited silent and mistrustful.

"No! You would never guess! No one would ever guess what these people are after. Willie's eyes bulged out when he came to me with the tale."

"They always do," remarked Renouard with disgust. "He's stupid."

"He was startled. And so was I after he told me. It's a search party. They are out looking for a man. Willie's soft heart's enlisted in the cause."

Renouard repeated: "Looking for a man."

He sat down suddenly as if on purpose to stare. "Did Willie come to you to borrow the lantern," he asked sarcastically, and got up again for no apparent reason.

"What lantern?" snapped the puzzled Editor, and his face darkened with suspicion. "You, Renouard, are always alluding to things that aren't clear to me. If you were in politics, I, as a party journalist, wouldn't trust you further than I could see you. Not an inch further. You are such a sophisticated beggar. Listen: the man is the man Miss Moorsom was engaged to for a year. He couldn't have been a nobody, anyhow. But he doesn't seem to have been very wise. Hard luck for the young lady."

He spoke with feeling. It was clear that what he had to tell appealed to his sentiment.

Yet, as an experienced man of the world, he marked his amused wonder. Young man of good family and connections, going everywhere, yet not merely a man about town, but with a foot in the two big F's.

Renouard lounging aimlessly in the room turned round: "And what the devil's that?" he asked faintly.

"Why Fashion and Finance," explained the Editor. "That's how I call it. There are the three R's at the bottom of the social edifice and the two F's on the top. See?"

"Ha! Ha! Excellent! Ha! Ha!" Renouard laughed with stony eyes.

"And you proceed from one set to the other in this democratic age," the Editor went on with unperturbed complacency. "That is if you are clever enough. The only danger is in being too clever. And I think something of the sort happened here. That swell I am speaking of got himself into a mess. Apparently a very ugly mess of a financial character. You will understand that Willie did not go into details with me. They were not imparted to him with very great abundance either. But a bad mess—something of the criminal order. Of course he was innocent. But he had to quit all the same."

"Ha! Ha!" Renouard laughed again abruptly, staring as before. "So there's one more big F in the tale."

"What do you mean?" inquired the Editor quickly, with an air as if his patent were being infringed.

"I mean—Fool."

"No. I wouldn't say that. I wouldn't say that."

"Well—let him be a scoundrel then. What the devil do I care."

"But hold on! You haven't heard the end of the story."

Renouard, his hat on his head already, sat down with the disdainful smile of a man who had discounted the moral of the story. Still he sat down and the Editor swung his revolving chair right round. He was full of unction.

"Imprudent, I should say. In many ways money is as dangerous to handle as gunpowder. You can't be too careful either as to who you are working with. Anyhow there was a mighty flashy burst up, a sensation, and—his familiar haunts knew him no more. But before he vanished he went to see Miss Moorsom. That very fact argues for his innocence—don't it? What was said between them no man knows—unless the professor had the confidence from his daughter. There couldn't have been much to say. There was nothing for it but to let him go—was there?—for the affair had got into the papers. And perhaps the kindest thing would have been to forget him. Anyway the easiest. Forgiveness would have been more difficult, I fancy, for a young lady of spirit and position drawn into an ugly affair like that. Any ordinary young lady, I mean. Well, the fellow asked nothing better than to be forgotten, only he didn't find it easy to do so himself, because he would write home now and then. Not to any of his friends though. He had no near relations. The professor had been his guardian. No, the poor devil wrote now and then to an old retired butler of his late father, somewhere in the country, forbidding him at the same time to let any one know of his whereabouts. So that worthy old ass would go up and dodge about the Moorsom's town house, perhaps waylay Miss Moorsom's maid, and then would write to 'Master Arthur' that the young lady looked well and happy, or some such cheerful intelligence. I dare say he wanted to be forgotten, but I shouldn't think he was much cheered by the news. What would you say?"

Renouard, his legs stretched out and his chin on his breast, said nothing. A sensation which was not curiosity, but rather a vague nervous anxiety, distinctly unpleasant, like a mysterious symptom of some malady, prevented him from getting up and going away.

"Mixed feelings," the Editor opined. "Many fellows out here receive news from home with mixed feelings. But what will his feelings be when he hears what I am going to tell you now? For we know he has not heard yet. Six months ago a city clerk, just a common drudge of finance, gets himself convicted of a common embezzlement or something of that kind. Then seeing he's in for a long sentence he thinks of making his conscience comfortable, and makes a clean breast of an old story of tampered with, or else suppressed, documents, a story which clears altogether the honesty of our ruined gentleman. That embezzling fellow was in a position to know, having been employed by the firm before the smash. There was no doubt about the character being cleared—but where the cleared man was nobody could tell. Another sensation in society. And then Miss Moorsom says: 'He will come back to claim me, and I'll marry him.' But he didn't come back. Between you and me I don't think he was much wanted—except by Miss Moorsom. I imagine she's used to have her own way. She grew impatient, and declared that if she knew where the man was she would go to him. But all that could be got out of the old butler was that the last envelope bore the postmark of our beautiful city; and that this was the only address of 'Master Arthur' that he ever had. That and no more. In fact the fellow was at his last gasp—with a bad heart. Miss Moorsom wasn't allowed to see him. She had gone herself into the country to learn what she could, but she had to stay downstairs while the old chap's wife went up to the invalid. She brought down the scrap of intelligence I've told you of. He was already too far gone to be cross-examined on it, and that very night he died. He didn't leave behind him much to go by, did he? Our Willie hinted to me that there had been pretty stormy days in the professor's house, but—here they are. I have a notion she isn't the kind of everyday young lady who may be permitted to gallop about the world all by herself—eh? Well, I think it rather fine of her, but I quite understand that the professor needed all his philosophy under the circumstances. She is his only child now—and brilliant—what? Willie positively spluttered trying to describe her to me; and I could see directly you came in that you had an uncommon experience."

Renouard, with an irritated gesture, tilted his hat more forward on his eyes, as though he were bored. The Editor went on with the remark that to be sure neither he (Renouard) nor yet Willie were much used to meet girls of that remarkable superiority. Willie when learning business with a firm in London, years before, had seen none but boarding-house society, he guessed. As to himself in the good old days, when he trod the glorious flags of Fleet Street, he neither had access to, nor yet would have cared for the swells. Nothing interested him then but parliamentary politics and the oratory of the House of Commons.

He paid to this not very distant past the tribute of a tender, reminiscent smile, and returned to his first idea that for a society girl her action was rather fine. All the same the professor could not be very pleased. The fellow if he was as pure as a lily now was just about as devoid of the goods of the earth. And there were misfortunes, however undeserved, which damaged a man's standing permanently. On the other hand, it was difficult to oppose cynically a noble impulse—not to speak of the great love at the root of it. Ah! Love! And then the lady was quite capable of going off by herself. She was of age, she had money of her own, plenty of pluck too. Moorsom must have concluded that it was more truly paternal, more prudent too, and generally safer all round to let himself be dragged into this chase. The aunt came along for the same reasons. It was given out at home as a trip round the world of the usual kind.

Renouard had risen and remained standing with his heart beating, and strangely affected by this tale, robbed as it was of all glamour by the prosaic personality of the narrator. The Editor added: "I've been asked to help in the search—you know."

Renouard muttered something about an appointment and went out into the street. His inborn sanity could not defend him from a misty creeping jealousy. He thought that obviously no man of that sort could be worthy of such a woman's devoted fidelity. Renouard, however, had lived long enough to reflect that a man's activities, his views, and even his ideas may be very inferior to his character; and moved by a delicate consideration for that splendid girl he tried to think out for the man a character of inward excellence and outward gifts—some extraordinary seduction. But in vain. Fresh from months of solitude and from days at sea, her splendour presented itself to him absolutely unconquerable in its perfection, unless by her own folly. It was easier to suspect her of this than to imagine in the man qualities which would be worthy of her. Easier and less degrading. Because folly may be generous—could be nothing else but generosity in her; whereas to imagine her subjugated by something common was intolerable.

Because of the force of the physical impression he had received from her personality (and such impressions are the real origins of the deepest movements of our soul) this conception of her was even inconceivable. But no Prince Charming has ever lived out of a fairy tale. He doesn't walk the worlds of Fashion and Finance—and with a stumbling gait at that. Generosity. Yes. It was her generosity. But this generosity was altogether regal in its splendour, almost absurd in its lavishness—or, perhaps, divine.

In the evening, on board his schooner, sitting on the rail, his arms folded on his breast and his eyes fixed on the deck, he let the darkness catch him unawares in the midst of a meditation on the mechanism of sentiment and the springs of passion. And all the time he had an abiding consciousness of her bodily presence. The effect on his senses had been so penetrating that in the middle of the night, rousing up suddenly, wide-eyed in the darkness of his cabin, he did not create a faint mental vision of her person for himself, but, more intimately affected, he scented distinctly the faint perfume she used, and could almost have sworn that he had been awakened by the soft rustle of her dress. He even sat up listening in the dark for a time, then sighed and lay down again, not agitated but, on the contrary, oppressed by the sensation of something that had happened to him and could not be undone.

3

In the afternoon he lounged into the editorial office, carrying with affected nonchalance that weight of the irremediable he had felt laid on him suddenly in the small hours of the night—that consciousness of something that could no longer be helped. His patronising friend informed him at once that he had made the acquaintance of the Moorsom party last night. At the Dunsters, of course. Dinner.

"Very quiet. Nobody there. It was much better for the business. I say . . ."

Renouard, his hand grasping the back of a chair, stared down at him dumbly.

"Phew! That's a stunning girl. . . Why do you want to sit on that chair? It's uncomfortable!"

"I wasn't going to sit on it." Renouard walked slowly to the window, glad to find in himself enough self-control to let go the chair instead of raising it on high and bringing it down on the Editor's head.

"Willie kept on gazing at her with tears in his boiled eyes. You should have seen him bending sentimentally over her at dinner."

"Don't," said Renouard in such an anguished tone that the Editor turned right round to look at his back.

"You push your dislike of young Dunster too far. It's positively morbid," he disapproved mildly. "We can't be all beautiful after thirty. . . . I talked a little, about you mostly, to the professor. He appeared to be interested in the silk plant—if only as a change from the great subject. Miss Moorsom didn't seem to mind when I confessed to her that I had taken you into the confidence of the thing. Our Willie approved too. Old Dunster with his white beard seemed to give me his blessing. All those people have a great opinion of you, simply because I told them that you've led every sort of life one can think of before you got struck on exploration. They want you to make suggestions. What do you think 'Master Arthur' is likely to have taken to?"

"Something easy," muttered Renouard without unclenching his teeth.

"Hunting man. Athlete. Don't be hard on the chap. He may be riding boundaries, or droving cattle, or humping his swag about the back-blocks away to the devil—somewhere. He may be even prospecting at the back of beyond—this very moment."

"Or lying dead drunk in a roadside pub. It's late enough in the day for that."

The Editor looked up instinctively. The clock was pointing at a quarter to five. "Yes, it is," he admitted. "But it needn't be. And he may have lit out into the Western Pacific all of a sudden—say in a trading schooner. Though I really don't see in what capacity. Still . . . "

"Or he may be passing at this very moment under this very window."

"Not he . . . and I wish you would get away from it to where one can see your face. I hate talking to a man's back. You stand there like a hermit on a sea-shore growling to yourself. I tell you what it is, Geoffrey, you don't like mankind."

"I don't make my living by talking about mankind's affairs," Renouard defended himself. But he came away obediently and sat down in the arm-chair. "How can you be so certain that your man isn't down there in the street?" he asked. "It's neither more nor less probable than every single one of your other suppositions."

Placated by Renouard's docility the Editor gazed at him for a while. "Aha! I'll tell you how. Learn then that we have begun the campaign. We have telegraphed his description to the police of every township up and down the land. And what's more we've ascertained definitely that he hasn't been in this town for the last three months at least. How much longer he's been away we can't tell."

"That's very curious."

"It's very simple. Miss Moorsom wrote to him, to the post office here directly she returned to London after her excursion into the country to see the old butler. Well—her letter is still lying there. It has not been called for. Ergo, this town is not his usual abode. Personally, I never thought it was. But he cannot fail to turn up some time or other. Our main hope lies just in the certitude that he must come to town sooner or later. Remember he doesn't know that the butler is dead, and he will want to inquire for a letter. Well, he'll find a note from Miss Moorsom."

Renouard, silent, thought that it was likely enough. His profound distaste for this conversation was betrayed by an air of weariness darkening his energetic sun-tanned features, and by the augmented dreaminess of his eyes. The Editor noted it as a further proof of that immoral detachment from mankind, of that callousness of sentiment fostered by the unhealthy conditions of solitude—according to his own favourite theory. Aloud he observed that as long as a man had not given up correspondence he could not be looked upon as lost. Fugitive criminals had been tracked in that way by justice, he reminded his friend; then suddenly changed the bearing of the subject somewhat by asking if Renouard had heard from his people lately, and if every member of his large tribe was well and happy.

"Yes, thanks."

The tone was curt, as if repelling a liberty. Renouard did not like being asked about his people, for whom he had a profound and remorseful affection. He had not seen a single human being to whom he was related, for many years, and he was extremely different from them all.

On the very morning of his arrival from his island he had gone to a set of pigeon-holes in Willie Dunster's outer office and had taken out from a compartment labelled "Malata" a very small accumulation of envelopes, a few addressed to himself, and one addressed to his assistant, all to the care of the firm, W. Dunster and Co. As opportunity offered, the firm used to send them on to Malata either by a man-of-war schooner going on a cruise, or by some trading craft proceeding that way. But for the last four months there had been no opportunity.

"You going to stay here some time?" asked the Editor, after a longish silence.

Renouard, perfunctorily, did see no reason why he should make a long stay.

"For health, for your mental health, my boy," rejoined the newspaper man. "To get used to human faces so that they don't hit you in the eye so hard when you walk about the streets. To get friendly with your kind. I suppose that assistant of yours can be trusted to look after things?"

"There's the half-caste too. The Portuguese. He knows what's to be done."

"Aha!" The Editor looked sharply at his friend. "What's his name?"

"Who's name?"

"The assistant's you picked up on the sly behind my back."

Renouard made a slight movement of impatience.

"I met him unexpectedly one evening. I thought he would do as well as another. He had come from up country and didn't seem happy in a town. He told me his name was Walter. I did not ask him for proofs, you know."

"I don't think you get on very well with him."

"Why? What makes you think so."

"I don't know. Something reluctant in your manner when he's in question."

"Really. My manner! I don't think he's a great subject for conversation, perhaps. Why not drop him?"

"Of course! You wouldn't confess to a mistake. Not you. Nevertheless I have my suspicions about it."

Renouard got up to go, but hesitated, looking down at the seated Editor.

"How funny," he said at last with the utmost seriousness, and was making for the door, when the voice of his friend stopped him.

"You know what has been said of you? That you couldn't get on with anybody you couldn't kick. Now, confess—is there any truth in the soft impeachment?"

"No," said Renouard. "Did you print that in your paper."

"No. I didn't quite believe it. But I will tell you what I believe. I believe that when your heart is set on some object you are a man that doesn't count the cost to yourself or others. And this shall get printed some day."

"Obituary notice?" Renouard dropped negligently.

"Certain—some day."

"Do you then regard yourself as immortal?"

"No, my boy. I am not immortal. But the voice of the press goes on for ever. . . . And it will say that this was the secret of your great success in a task where better men than you—meaning no offence—did fail repeatedly."

"Success," muttered Renouard, pulling-to the office door after him with considerable energy. And the letters of the word PRIVATE like a row of white eyes seemed to stare after his back sinking down the staircase of that temple of publicity.

Renouard had no doubt that all the means of publicity would be put at the service of love and used for the discovery of the loved man. He did not wish him dead. He did not wish him any harm. We are all equipped with a fund of humanity which is not exhausted without many and repeated provocations—and this man had done him no evil. But before Renouard had left old Dunster's house, at the conclusion of the call he made there that very afternoon, he had discovered in himself the desire that the search might last long. He never really flattered himself that it might fail. It seemed to him that there was no other course in this world for himself, for all mankind, but resignation. And he could not help thinking that Professor Moorsom had arrived at the same conclusion too.

Professor Moorsom, slight frame of middle height, a thoughtful keen head under the thick wavy hair, veiled dark eyes under straight eyebrows, and with an inward gaze which when disengaged and arriving at one seemed to issue from an obscure dream of books, from the limbo of meditation, showed himself extremely gracious to him. Renouard guessed in him a man whom an incurable habit of investigation and analysis had made gentle and indulgent; inapt for action, and more sensitive to the thoughts than to the events of existence. Withal not crushed, sub-ironic without a trace of acidity, and with a simple manner which put people at ease quickly. They had a long conversation on the terrace commanding an extended view of the town and the harbour.

The splendid immobility of the bay resting under his gaze, with its grey spurs and shining indentations, helped Renouard to regain his self-possession, which he had felt shaken, in coming out on the terrace, into the setting of the most powerful emotion of his life, when he had sat within a foot of Miss Moorsom with fire in his breast, a humming in his ears, and in a complete disorder of his mind. There was the very garden seat on which he had been enveloped in the radiant spell. And presently he was sitting on it again with the professor talking of her. Near by the patriarchal Dunster leaned forward in a wicker armchair, benign and a little deaf, his big hand to his ear with the innocent eagerness of his advanced age remembering the fires of life.

It was with a sort of apprehension that Renouard looked forward to seeing Miss Moorsom. And strangely enough it resembled the state of mind of a man who fears disenchantment more than sortilege. But he need not have been afraid. Directly he saw her in a distance at the other end of the terrace he shuddered to the roots of his hair. With her approach the power of speech left him for a time. Mrs. Dunster and her aunt were accompanying her. All these people sat down; it was an intimate circle into which Renouard felt himself cordially admitted; and the talk was of the great search which occupied all their minds. Discretion was expected by these people, but of reticence as to the object of the journey there could be no question. Nothing but ways and means and arrangements could be talked about.

By fixing his eyes obstinately on the ground, which gave him an air of reflective sadness, Renouard managed to recover his self-possession. He used it to keep his voice in a low key and to measure his words on the great subject. And he took care with a great inward effort to make them reasonable without giving them a discouraging complexion. For he did not want the quest to be given up, since it would mean her going away with her two attendant grey-heads to the other side of the world.

He was asked to come again, to come often and take part in the counsels of all these people captivated by the sentimental enterprise of a declared love. On taking Miss Moorsom's hand he looked up, would have liked to say something, but found himself voiceless, with his lips suddenly sealed. She returned the pressure of his fingers, and he left her with her eyes vaguely staring beyond him, an air of listening for an expected sound, and the faintest possible smile on her lips. A smile not for him, evidently, but the reflection of some deep and inscrutable thought.

4

He went on board his schooner. She lay white, and as if suspended, in the crepuscular atmosphere of sunset mingling with the ashy gleam of the vast anchorage. He tried to keep his thoughts as sober, as reasonable, as measured as his words had been, lest they should get away from him and cause some sort of moral disaster. What he was afraid of in the coming night was sleeplessness and the endless strain of that wearisome task. It had to be faced however. He lay on his back, sighing profoundly in the dark, and suddenly beheld his very own self, carrying a small bizarre lamp, reflected in a long mirror inside a room in an empty and unfurnished palace. In this startling image of himself he recognised somebody he had to follow—the frightened guide of his dream. He traversed endless galleries, no end of lofty halls, innumerable doors. He lost himself utterly—he found his way again. Room succeeded room. At last the lamp went out, and he stumbled against some object which, when he stooped for it, he found to be very cold and heavy to lift. The sickly white light of dawn showed him the head of a statue. Its marble hair was done in the bold lines of a helmet, on its lips the chisel had left a faint smile, and it resembled Miss Moorsom. While he was staring at it fixedly, the head began to grow light in his fingers, to diminish and crumble to pieces, and at last turned into a handful of dust, which was blown away by a puff of wind so chilly that he woke up with a desperate shiver and leaped headlong out of his bed-place. The day had really come. He sat down by the cabin table, and taking his head between his hands, did not stir for a very long time.

Very quiet, he set himself to review this dream. The lamp, of course, he connected with the search for a man. But on closer examination he perceived that the reflection of himself in the mirror was not really the true Renouard, but somebody else whose face he could not remember. In the deserted palace he recognised a sinister adaptation by his brain of the long corridors with many doors, in the great building in which his friend's newspaper was lodged on the first floor. The marble head with Miss Moorsom's face! Well! What other face could he have dreamed of? And her complexion was fairer than Parian marble, than the heads of angels. The wind at the end was the morning breeze entering through the open porthole and touching his face before the schooner could swing to the chilly gust.

Yes! And all this rational explanation of the fantastic made it only more mysterious and weird. There was something daemonic in that dream. It was one of those experiences which throw a man out of conformity with the established order of his kind and make him a creature of obscure suggestions.

Henceforth, without ever trying to resist, he went every afternoon to the house where she lived. He went there as passively as if in a dream. He could never make out how he had attained the footing of intimacy in the Dunster mansion above the bay—whether on the ground of personal merit or as the pioneer of the vegetable silk industry. It must have been the last, because he remembered distinctly, as distinctly as in a dream, hearing old Dunster once telling him that his next public task would be a careful survey of the Northern Districts to discover tracts suitable for the cultivation of the silk plant. The old man wagged his beard at him sagely. It was indeed as absurd as a dream.

Willie of course would be there in the evening. But he was more of a figure out of a nightmare, hovering about the circle of chairs in his dress-clothes like a gigantic, repulsive, and sentimental bat. "Do away with the beastly cocoons all over the world," he buzzed in his blurred, water-logged voice. He affected a great horror of insects of all kinds. One evening he appeared with a red flower in his button-hole. Nothing could have been more disgustingly fantastic. And he would also say to Renouard: "You may yet change the history of our country. For economic conditions do shape the history of nations. Eh? What?" And he would turn to Miss Moorsom for approval, lowering protectingly his spatulous nose and looking up with feeling from under his absurd eyebrows, which grew thin, in the manner of canebrakes, out of his spongy skin. For this large, bilious creature was an economist and a sentimentalist, facile to tears, and a member of the Cobden Club.

In order to see as little of him as possible Renouard began coming earlier so as to get away before his arrival, without curtailing too much the hours of secret contemplation for which he lived. He had given up trying to deceive himself. His resignation was without bounds. He accepted the immense misfortune of being in love with a woman who was in search of another man only to throw herself into his arms. With such desperate precision he defined in his thoughts the situation, the consciousness of which traversed like a sharp arrow the sudden silences of general conversation. The only thought before which he quailed was the thought that this could not last; that it must come to an end. He feared it instinctively as a sick man may fear death. For it seemed to him that it must be the death of him followed by a lightless, bottomless pit. But his resignation was not spared the torments of jealousy: the cruel, insensate, poignant, and imbecile jealousy, when it seems that a woman betrays us simply by this that she exists, that she breathes—and when the deep movements of her nerves or her soul become a matter of distracting suspicion, of killing doubt, of mortal anxiety.

In the peculiar condition of their sojourn Miss Moorsom went out very little. She accepted this seclusion at the Dunsters' mansion as in a hermitage, and lived there, watched over by a group of old people, with the lofty endurance of a condescending and strong-headed goddess. It was impossible to say if she suffered from anything in the world, and whether this was the insensibility of a great passion concentrated on itself, or a perfect restraint of manner, or the indifference of superiority so complete as to be sufficient to itself. But it was visible to Renouard that she took some pleasure in talking to him at times. Was it because he was the only person near her age? Was this, then, the secret of his admission to the circle?

He admired her voice as well poised as her movements, as her attitudes. He himself had always been a man of tranquil tones. But the power of fascination had torn him out of his very nature so completely that to preserve his habitual calmness from going to pieces had become a terrible effort.

He used to go from her on board the schooner exhausted, broken, shaken up, as though he had been put to the most exquisite torture. When he saw her approaching he always had a moment of hallucination. She was a misty and fair creature, fitted for invisible music, for the shadows of love, for the murmurs of waters. After a time (he could not be always staring at the ground) he would summon up all his resolution and look at her. There was a sparkle in the clear obscurity of her eyes; and when she turned them on him they seemed to give a new meaning to life. He would say to himself that another man would have found long before the happy release of madness, his wits burnt to cinders in that radiance. But no such luck for him. His wits had come unscathed through the furnaces of hot suns, of blazing deserts, of flaming angers against the weaknesses of men and the obstinate cruelties of hostile nature.

Being sane he had to be constantly on his guard against falling into adoring silences or breaking out into wild speeches. He had to keep watch on his eyes, his limbs, on the muscles of his face. Their conversations were such as they could be between these two people: she a young lady fresh from the thick twilight of four million people and the artificiality of several London seasons; he the man of definite conquering tasks, the familiar of wide horizons, and in his very repose holding aloof from these agglomerations of units in which one loses one's importance even to oneself. They had no common conversational small change. They had to use the great pieces of general ideas, but they exchanged them trivially. It was no serious commerce. Perhaps she had not much of that coin. Nothing significant came from her. It could not be said that she had received from the contacts of the external world impressions of a personal kind, different from other women. What was ravishing in her was her quietness and, in her grave attitudes, the unfailing brilliance of her femininity. He did not know what there was under that ivory forehead so splendidly shaped, so gloriously crowned. He could not tell what were her thoughts, her feelings. Her replies were reflective, always preceded by a short silence, while he hung on her lips anxiously. He felt himself in the presence of a mysterious being in whom spoke an unknown voice, like the voice of oracles, bringing everlasting unrest to the heart.

He was thankful enough to sit in silence with secretly clenched teeth, devoured by jealousy—and nobody could have guessed that his quiet deferential bearing to all these grey-heads was the supreme effort of stoicism, that the man was engaged in keeping a sinister watch on his tortures lest his strength should fail him. As before, when grappling with other forces of nature, he could find in himself all sorts of courage except the courage to run away.

It was perhaps from the lack of subjects they could have in common that Miss Moorsom made him so often speak of his own life. He did not shrink from talking about himself, for he was free from that exacerbated, timid vanity which seals so many vain-glorious lips. He talked to her in his restrained voice, gazing at the tip of her shoe, and thinking that the time was bound to come soon when her very inattention would get weary of him. And indeed on stealing a glance he would see her dazzling and perfect, her eyes vague, staring in mournful immobility, with a drooping head that made him think of a tragic Venus arising before him, not from the foam of the sea, but from a distant, still more formless, mysterious, and potent immensity of mankind.

5

One afternoon Renouard stepping out on the terrace found nobody there. It was for him, at the same time, a melancholy disappointment and a poignant relief.

The heat was great, the air was still, all the long windows of the house stood wide open. At the further end, grouped round a lady's work-table, several chairs disposed sociably suggested invisible occupants, a company of conversing shades. Renouard looked towards them with a sort of dread. A most elusive, faint sound of ghostly talk issuing from one of the rooms added to the illusion and stopped his already hesitating footsteps. He leaned over the balustrade of stone near a squat vase holding a tropical plant of a bizarre shape. Professor Moorsom coming up from the garden with a book under his arm and a white parasol held over his bare head, found him there and, closing the parasol, leaned over by his side with a remark on the increasing heat of the season. Renouard assented and changed his position a little; the other, after a short silence, administered unexpectedly a question which, like the blow of a club on the head, deprived Renouard of the power of speech and even thought, but, more cruel, left him quivering with apprehension, not of death but of everlasting torment. Yet the words were extremely simple.

"Something will have to be done soon. We can't remain in a state of suspended expectation for ever. Tell me what do you think of our chances?"

Renouard, speechless, produced a faint smile. The professor confessed in a jocular tone his impatience to complete the circuit of the globe and be done with it. It was impossible to remain quartered on the dear excellent Dunsters for an indefinite time. And then there were the lectures he had arranged to deliver in Paris. A serious matter.

That lectures by Professor Moorsom were a European event and that brilliant audiences would gather to hear them Renouard did not know. All he was aware of was the shock of this hint of departure. The menace of separation fell on his head like a thunderbolt. And he saw the absurdity of his emotion, for hadn't he lived all these days under the very cloud? The professor, his elbows spread out, looked down into the garden and went on unburdening his mind. Yes. The department of sentiment was directed by his daughter, and she had plenty of volunteered moral support; but he had to look after the practical side of life without assistance.

"I have the less hesitation in speaking to you about my anxiety, because I feel you are friendly to us and at the same time you are detached from all these sublimities—confound them."

"What do you mean?" murmured Renouard.

"I mean that you are capable of calm judgment. Here the atmosphere is simply detestable. Everybody has knuckled under to sentiment. Perhaps your deliberate opinion could influence . . ."

"You want Miss Moorsom to give it up?" The professor turned to the young man dismally.

"Heaven only knows what I want."

Renouard leaning his back against the balustrade folded his arms on his breast, appeared to meditate profoundly. His face, shaded softly by the broad brim of a planter's Panama hat, with the straight line of the nose level with the forehead, the eyes lost in the depth of the setting, and the chin well forward, had such a profile as may be seen amongst the bronzes of classical museums, pure under a crested helmet—recalled vaguely a Minerva's head.

"This is the most troublesome time I ever had in my life," exclaimed the professor testily.

"Surely the man must be worth it," muttered Renouard with a pang of jealousy traversing his breast like a self-inflicted stab.

Whether enervated by the heat or giving way to pent up irritation the professor surrendered himself to the mood of sincerity.

"He began by being a pleasantly dull boy. He developed into a pointlessly clever young man, without, I suspect, ever trying to understand anything. My daughter knew him from childhood. I am a busy man, and I confess that their engagement was a complete surprise to me. I wish their reasons for that step had been more naïve. But simplicity was out of fashion in their set. From a worldly point of view he seems to have been a mere baby. Of course, now, I am assured that he is the victim of his noble confidence in the rectitude of his kind. But that's mere idealising of a sad reality. For my part I will tell you that from the very beginning I had the gravest doubts of his dishonesty. Unfortunately my clever daughter hadn't. And now we behold the reaction. No. To be earnestly dishonest one must be really poor. This was only a manifestation of his extremely refined cleverness. The complicated simpleton. He had an awful awakening though."

In such words did Professor Moorsom give his "young friend" to understand the state of his feelings toward the lost man. It was evident that the father of Miss Moorsom wished him to remain lost. Perhaps the unprecedented heat of the season made him long for the cool spaces of the Pacific, the sweep of the ocean's free wind along the promenade decks, cumbered with long chairs, of a ship steaming towards the Californian coast. To Renouard the philosopher appeared simply the most treacherous of fathers. He was amazed. But he was not at the end of his discoveries.

"He may be dead," the professor murmured.

"Why? People don't die here sooner than in Europe. If he had gone to hide in Italy, for instance, you wouldn't think of saying that."

"Well! And suppose he has become morally disintegrated. You know he was not a strong personality," the professor suggested moodily. "My daughter's future is in question here."

Renouard thought that the love of such a woman was enough to pull any broken man together—to drag a man out of his grave. And he thought this with inward despair, which kept him silent as much almost as his astonishment. At last he managed to stammer out a generous—

"Oh! Don't let us even suppose. . ."

The professor struck in with a sadder accent than before—

"It's good to be young. And then you have been a man of action, and necessarily a believer in success. But I have been looking too long at life not to distrust its surprises. Age! Age! Here I stand before you a man full of doubts and hesitation—*spe lentus, timidus futuri.*"

He made a sign to Renouard not to interrupt, and in a lowered voice, as if afraid of being overheard, even there, in the solitude of the terrace—

"And the worst is that I am not even sure how far this sentimental pilgrimage is genuine. Yes. I doubt my own child. It's true that she's a woman. . . . "

Renouard detected with horror a tone of resentment, as if the professor had never forgiven his daughter for not dying instead of his son. The latter noticed the young man's stony stare.

"Ah! you don't understand. Yes, she's clever, open-minded, popular, and—well, charming. But you don't know what it is to have moved, breathed, existed, and even triumphed in the mere smother and froth of life—the brilliant froth. There thoughts, sentiments, opinions, feelings, actions too, are nothing but agitation in empty space—to amuse life—a sort of superior debauchery, exciting and fatiguing, meaning nothing, leading nowhere. She is the creature of that circle. And I ask myself if she is obeying the uneasiness of an instinct seeking its satisfaction, or is it a revulsion of feeling, or is she merely deceiving her own heart by this dangerous trifling with romantic images. And everything is possible—except sincerity, such as only stark, struggling humanity can know. No woman can stand that mode of life in which women rule, and remain a perfectly genuine, simple human being. Ah! There's some people coming out."

He moved off a pace, then turning his head: "Upon my word! I would be infinitely obliged to you if you could throw a little cold water. . . " and at a vaguely dismayed gesture of Renouard, he added: "Don't be afraid. You wouldn't be putting out a sacred fire."

Renouard could hardly find words for a protest: "I assure you that I never talk with Miss Moorsom—on—on—that. And if you, her father . . . "

"I envy you your innocence," sighed the professor. "A father is only an everyday person. Flat. Stale. Moreover, my child would naturally mistrust me. We belong to the same set. Whereas you carry with you the prestige of the unknown. You have proved yourself to be a force."

Thereupon the professor followed by Renouard joined the circle of all the inmates of the house assembled at the other end of the terrace about a tea-table; three white heads and that resplendent vision of woman's glory, the sight of which had the power to flutter his heart like a reminder of the mortality of his frame.

He avoided the seat by the side of Miss Moorsom. The others were talking together languidly. Unnoticed he looked at that woman so marvellous that centuries seemed to lie between them. He was oppressed and overcome at the thought of what she could give to some man who really would be a force! What a glorious struggle with this amazon. What noble burden for the victorious strength.

Dear old Mrs. Dunster was dispensing tea, looking from time to time with interest towards Miss Moorsom. The aged statesman having eaten a raw tomato and drunk a glass of milk (a habit of his early farming days, long before politics, when, pioneer of wheat-growing, he demonstrated the possibility of raising crops on ground looking barren enough to discourage a magician), smoothed his white beard, and struck lightly Renouard's knee with his big wrinkled hand.

"You had better come back to-night and dine with us quietly."

He liked this young man, a pioneer, too, in more than one direction. Mrs. Dunster added: "Do. It will be very quiet. I don't even know if Willie will be home for dinner." Renouard murmured his thanks, and left the terrace to go on board the schooner. While lingering in the drawing-room doorway he heard the resonant voice of old Dunster uttering oracularly—

". . . the leading man here some day. . . . Like me."

Renouard let the thin summer portière of the doorway fall behind him. The voice of Professor Moorsom said—

"I am told that he has made an enemy of almost every man who had to work with him."

"That's nothing. He did his work. . . . Like me."

"He never counted the cost they say. Not even of lives."

Renouard understood that they were talking of him. Before he could move away, Mrs. Dunster struck in placidly—

"Don't let yourself be shocked by the tales you may hear of him, my dear. Most of it is envy."

Then he heard Miss Moorsom's voice replying to the old lady—

"Oh! I am not easily deceived. I think I may say I have an instinct for truth."

He hastened away from that house with his heart full of dread.

6

On board the schooner, lying on the settee on his back with the knuckles of his hands pressed over his eyes, he made up his mind that he would not return to that house for dinner —that he would never go back there any more. He made up his mind some twenty times. The knowledge that he had only to go up on the quarter deck, utter quietly the words: "Man the windlass," and that the schooner springing into life would run a hundred miles out to sea before sunrise, deceived his struggling will. Nothing easier! Yet, in the end, this young man, almost ill-famed for his ruthless daring, the inflexible leader of two tragically successful expeditions, shrank from that act of savage energy, and began, instead, to hunt for excuses.

No! It was not for him to run away like an incurable who cuts his throat. He finished dressing and looked at his own impassive face in the saloon mirror scornfully. While being pulled on shore in the gig, he remembered suddenly the wild beauty of a waterfall seen when hardly more than a boy, years ago, in Menado. There was a legend of a governor-general of the Dutch East Indies, on official tour, committing suicide on that spot by leaping into the chasm. It was supposed that a painful disease had made him weary of life. But was there ever a visitation like his own, at the same time binding one to life and so cruelly mortal!

The dinner was indeed quiet. Willie, given half an hour's grace, failed to turn up, and his chair remained vacant by the side of Miss Moorsom. Renouard had the professor's sister on his left, dressed in an expensive gown becoming her age. That maiden lady in her wonderful preservation reminded Renouard somehow of a wax flower under glass. There were no traces of the dust of life's battles on her anywhere. She did not like him very much in the afternoons, in his white drill suit and planter's hat, which seemed to her an unduly Bohemian costume for calling in a house where there were ladies. But in the evening, lithe and elegant in his dress clothes and with his pleasant, slightly veiled voice, he always made her conquest afresh. He might have been anybody distinguished—the son of a duke. Falling under that charm probably (and also because her brother had given her a hint), she attempted to open her heart to Renouard, who was watching with all the power of his soul her niece across the table. She spoke to him as frankly as though that miserable mortal envelope, emptied of everything but hopeless passion, were indeed the son of a duke.

Inattentive, he heard her only in snatches, till the final confidential burst: ". . . glad if you would express an opinion. Look at her, so charming, such a great favourite, so generally admired! It would be too sad. We all hoped she would make a brilliant marriage with somebody very rich and of high position, have a house in London and in the country, and entertain us all splendidly. She's so eminently fitted for it. She has such hosts of distinguished friends! And then—this instead! . . . My heart really aches."

Her well-bred if anxious whisper was covered by the voice of professor Moorsom discoursing subtly down the short length of the dinner table on the Impermanency of the Measurable to his venerable disciple. It might have been a chapter in a new and popular book of Moorsomian philosophy. Patriarchal and delighted, old Dunster leaned forward a little, his eyes shining youthfully, two spots of colour at the roots of his white beard; and Renouard, glancing at the senile excitement, recalled the words heard on those subtle lips, adopted their scorn for his own, saw their truth before this man ready to be amused by the side of the grave. Yes! Intellectual debauchery in the froth of existence! Froth and fraud!

On the same side of the table Miss Moorsom never once looked towards her father, all her grace as if frozen, her red lips compressed, the faintest rosiness under her dazzling complexion, her black eyes burning motionless, and the very coppery gleams of light lying still on the waves and undulation of her hair. Renouard fancied himself overturning the table, smashing crystal and china, treading fruit and flowers under foot, seizing her in his arms, carrying her off in a tumult of shrieks from all these people, a silent frightened mortal, into some profound retreat as in the age of Cavern men. Suddenly everybody got up, and he hastened to rise too, finding himself out of breath and quite unsteady on his feet.

On the terrace the philosopher, after lighting a cigar, slipped his hand condescendingly under his "dear young friend's" arm. Renouard regarded him now with the profoundest mistrust. But the great man seemed really to have a liking for his young friend—one of those mysterious sympathies, disregarding the differences of age and position, which in this case might have been explained by the failure of philosophy to meet a very real worry of a practical kind.

After a turn or two and some casual talk the professor said suddenly: "My late son was in your school—do you know? I can imagine that had he lived and you had ever met you would have understood each other. He too was inclined to action."

He sighed, then, shaking off the mournful thought and with a nod at the dusky part of the terrace where the dress of his daughter made a luminous stain: "I really wish you would drop in that quarter a few sensible, discouraging words."

Renouard disengaged himself from that most perfidious of men under the pretence of astonishment, and stepping back a pace—

"Surely you are making fun of me, Professor Moorsom," he said with a low laugh, which was really a sound of rage.

"My dear young friend! It's no subject for jokes, to me. . . You don't seem to have any notion of your prestige," he added, walking away towards the chairs.

"Humbug!" thought Renouard, standing still and looking after him. "And yet! And yet! What if it were true?"

He advanced then towards Miss Moorsom. Posed on the seat on which they had first spoken to each other, it was her turn to watch him coming on. But many of the windows were not lighted that evening. It was dark over there. She appeared to him luminous in her clear dress, a figure without shape, a face without features, awaiting his approach, till he got quite near to her, sat down, and they had exchanged a few insignificant words. Gradually she came out like a magic painting of charm, fascination, and desire, glowing mysteriously on the dark background. Something imperceptible in the lines of her attitude, in the modulations of her voice, seemed to soften that suggestion of calm unconscious pride which enveloped her always like a mantle. He, sensitive like a bond slave to the moods of the master, was moved by the subtle relenting of her grace to an infinite tenderness. He fought down the impulse to seize her by the hand, lead her down into the garden away under the big trees, and throw himself at her feet uttering words of love. His emotion was so strong that he had to cough slightly, and not knowing what to talk to her about he began to tell her of his mother and sisters. All the family were coming to London to live there, for some little time at least.

"I hope you will go and tell them something of me. Something seen," he said pressingly.

By this miserable subterfuge, like a man about to part with his life, he hoped to make her remember him a little longer.

"Certainly," she said. "I'll be glad to call when I get back. But that 'when' may be a long time."

He heard a light sigh. A cruel jealous curiosity made him ask—

"Are you growing weary, Miss Moorsom?"

A silence fell on his low spoken question.

"Do you mean heart-weary?" sounded Miss Moorsom's voice. "You don't know me, I see."

"Ah! Never despair," he muttered.

"This, Mr. Renouard, is a work of reparation. I stand for truth here. I can't think of myself."

He could have taken her by the throat for every word seemed an insult to his passion; but he only said—

"I never doubted the—the—nobility of your purpose."

"And to hear the word weariness pronounced in this connection surprises me. And from a man too who, I understand, has never counted the cost."

"You are pleased to tease me," he said, directly he had recovered his voice and had mastered his anger. It was as if Professor Moorsom had dropped poison in his ear which was spreading now and tainting his passion, his very jealousy. He mistrusted every word that came from those lips on which his life hung. "How can you know anything of men who do not count the cost?" he asked in his gentlest tones.

"From hearsay—a little."

"Well, I assure you they are like the others, subject to suffering, victims of spells. . . ."

"One of them, at least, speaks very strangely."

She dismissed the subject after a short silence. "Mr. Renouard, I had a disappointment this morning. This mail brought me a letter from the widow of the old butler—you know. I expected to learn that she had heard from—from here. But no. No letter arrived home since we left."

Her voice was calm. His jealousy couldn't stand much more of this sort of talk; but he was glad that nothing had turned up to help the search; glad blindly, unreasonably—only because it would keep her longer in his sight—since she wouldn't give up.

"I am too near her," he thought, moving a little further on the seat. He was afraid in the revulsion of feeling of flinging himself on her hands, which were lying on her lap, and covering them with kisses. He was afraid. Nothing, nothing could shake that spell—not if she were ever so false, stupid, or degraded. She was fate itself. The extent of his misfortune plunged him in such a stupor that he failed at first to hear the sound of voices and footsteps inside the drawing-room. Willie had come home—and the Editor was with him.

They burst out on the terrace babbling noisily, and then pulling themselves together stood still, surprising—and as if themselves surprised.

❧ 7 ❧

THEY HAD BEEN FEASTING a poet from the bush, the latest discovery of the Editor. Such discoveries were the business, the vocation, the pride and delight of the only apostle of letters in the hemisphere, the solitary patron of culture, the Slave of the Lamp—as he subscribed himself at the bottom of the weekly literary page of his paper. He had had no difficulty in persuading the virtuous Willie (who had festive instincts) to help in the good work, and now they had left the poet lying asleep on the hearthrug of the editorial room and had rushed to the Dunster mansion wildly. The Editor had another discovery to announce. Swaying a little where he stood he opened his mouth very wide to shout the one word "Found!" Behind him Willie flung both his hands above his head and let them fall dramatically. Renouard saw the four white-headed people at the end of the terrace rise all together from their chairs with an effect of sudden panic.

"I tell you—he—is—found," the patron of letters shouted emphatically.

"What is this!" exclaimed Renouard in a choked voice. Miss Moorsom seized his wrist suddenly, and at that contact fire ran through all his veins, a hot stillness descended upon him in which he heard the blood—or the fire—beating in his ears. He made a movement as if to rise, but was restrained by the convulsive pressure on his wrist.

"No, no." Miss Moorsom's eyes stared black as night, searching the space before her. Far away the Editor strutted forward, Willie following with his ostentatious manner of carrying his bulky and oppressive carcass which, however, did not remain exactly perpendicular for two seconds together.

"The innocent Arthur . . . Yes. We've got him," the Editor became very business-like. "Yes, this letter has done it."

He plunged into an inside pocket for it, slapped the scrap of paper with his open palm. "From that old woman. William had it in his pocket since this morning when Miss Moorsom gave it to him to show me. Forgot all about it till an hour ago. Thought it was of no importance. Well, no! Not till it was properly read."

Renouard and Miss Moorsom emerged from the shadows side by side, a well-matched couple, animated yet statuesque in their calmness and in their pallor. She had let go his wrist. On catching sight of Renouard the Editor exclaimed:

"What—you here!" in a quite shrill voice.

There came a dead pause. All the faces had in them something dismayed and cruel.

"He's the very man we want," continued the Editor. "Excuse my excitement. You are the very man, Renouard. Didn't you tell me that your assistant called himself Walter? Yes? Thought so. But here's that old woman—the butler's wife—listen to this. She writes: All I can tell you, Miss, is that my poor husband directed his letters to the name of H. Walter."

Renouard's violent but repressed exclamation was lost in a general murmur and shuffle of feet. The Editor made a step forward, bowed with creditable steadiness.

"Miss Moorsom, allow me to congratulate you from the bottom of my heart on the happy —er—issue. . . "

"Wait," muttered Renouard irresolutely.

The Editor jumped on him in the manner of their old friendship. "Ah, you! You are a fine fellow too. With your solitary ways of life you will end by having no more discrimination than a savage. Fancy living with a gentleman for months and never guessing. A man, I am certain, accomplished, remarkable, out of the common, since he had been distinguished" (he bowed again) "by Miss Moorsom, whom we all admire."

She turned her back on him.

"I hope to goodness you haven't been leading him a dog's life, Geoffrey," the Editor addressed his friend in a whispered aside.

Renouard seized a chair violently, sat down, and propping his elbow on his knee leaned his head on his hand. Behind him the sister of the professor looked up to heaven and wrung her hands stealthily. Mrs. Dunster's hands were clasped forcibly under her chin, but she, dear soul, was looking sorrowfully at Willie. The model nephew! In this strange state! So very much flushed! The careful disposition of the thin hairs across Willie's bald spot was deplorably disarranged, and the spot itself was red and, as it were, steaming.

"What's the matter, Geoffrey?" The Editor seemed disconcerted by the silent attitudes round him, as though he had expected all these people to shout and dance. "You have him on the island—haven't you?"

"Oh, yes: I have him there," said Renouard, without looking up.

"Well, then!" The Editor looked helplessly around as if begging for response of some sort. But the only response that came was very unexpected. Annoyed at being left in the background, and also because very little drink made him nasty, the emotional Willie turned malignant all at once, and in a bibulous tone surprising in a man able to keep his balance so well—

"Aha! But you haven't got him here—not yet!" he sneered. "No! You haven't got him yet."

This outrageous exhibition was to the Editor like the lash to a jaded horse. He positively jumped.

"What of that? What do you mean? We—haven't—got—him—here. Of course he isn't here! But Geoffrey's schooner is here. She can be sent at once to fetch him here. No! Stay! There's a better plan. Why shouldn't you all sail over to Malata, professor? Save time! I am sure Miss Moorsom would prefer. . ."

With a gallant flourish of his arm he looked for Miss Moorsom. She had disappeared. He was taken aback somewhat.

"Ah! H'm. Yes. . . . Why not. A pleasure cruise, delightful ship, delightful season, delightful errand, del . . . No! There are no objections. Geoffrey, I understand, has indulged in a bungalow three sizes too large for him. He can put you all up. It will be a pleasure for him. It will be the greatest privilege. Any man would be proud of being an agent of this happy reunion. I am proud of the little part I've played. He will consider it the greatest honour. Geoff, my boy, you had better be stirring to-morrow bright and early about the preparations for the trip. It would be criminal to lose a single day."

He was as flushed as Willie, the excitement keeping up the effect of the festive dinner. For a time Renouard, silent, as if he had not heard a word of all that babble, did not stir. But when he got up it was to advance towards the Editor and give him such a hearty slap on the back that the plump little man reeled in his tracks and looked quite frightened for a moment.

"You are a heaven-born discoverer and a first-rate manager. . . He's right. It's the only way. You can't resist the claim of sentiment, and you must even risk the voyage to Malata. . . " Renouard's voice sank. "A lonely spot," he added, and fell into thought under all these eyes converging on him in the sudden silence. His slow glance passed over all the faces in succession, remaining arrested on Professor Moorsom, stony eyed, a smouldering cigar in his fingers, and with his sister standing by his side.

"I shall be infinitely gratified if you consent to come. But, of course, you will. We shall sail to-morrow evening then. And now let me leave you to your happiness."

He bowed, very grave, pointed suddenly his finger at Willie who was swaying about with a sleepy frown. . . . "Look at him. He's overcome with happiness. You had better put him to bed . . . " and disappeared while every head on the terrace was turned to Willie with varied expressions.

Renouard ran through the house. Avoiding the carriage road he fled down the steep short cut to the shore, where his gig was waiting. At his loud shout the sleeping Kanakas jumped up. He leaped in. "Shove off. Give way!" and the gig darted through the water. "Give way! Give way!" She flew past the wool-clippers sleeping at their anchors each with the open unwinking eye of the lamp in the rigging; she flew past the flagship of the Pacific squadron, a great mass all dark and silent, heavy with the slumbers of five hundred men, and where the invisible sentries heard his urgent "Give way! Give way!" in the night. The Kanakas, panting, rose off the thwarts at every stroke. Nothing could be fast enough for him! And he ran up the side of his schooner shaking the ladder noisily with his rush.

On deck he stumbled and stood still.

Wherefore this haste? To what end, since he knew well before he started that he had a pursuer from whom there was no escape.

As his foot touched the deck his will, his purpose he had been hurrying to save, died out within. It had been nothing less than getting the schooner under-way, letting her vanish silently in the night from amongst these sleeping ships. And now he was certain he could not do it. It was impossible! And he reflected that whether he lived or died such an act would lay him under a dark suspicion from which he shrank. No, there was nothing to be done.

He went down into the cabin and, before even unbuttoning his overcoat, took out of the drawer the letter addressed to his assistant; that letter which he had found in the pigeon-hole labelled "Malata" in young Dunster's outer office, where it had been waiting for three months some occasion for being forwarded. From the moment of dropping it in the drawer he had utterly forgotten its existence—till now, when the man's name had come out so clamorously. He glanced at the common envelope, noted the shaky and laborious handwriting: H. Walter, Esqre. Undoubtedly the very last letter the old butler had posted before his illness, and in answer clearly to one from "Master Arthur" instructing him to address in the future: "Care of Messrs. W. Dunster and Co." Renouard made as if to open the envelope, but paused, and, instead, tore the letter deliberately in two, in four, in eight. With his hand full of pieces of paper he returned on deck and scattered them overboard on the dark water, in which they vanished instantly.

He did it slowly, without hesitation or remorse. H. Walter, Esqre, in Malata. The innocent Arthur—What was his name? The man sought for by that woman who as she went by seemed to draw all the passion of the earth to her, without effort, not deigning to notice, naturally, as other women breathed the air. But Renouard was no longer jealous of her very existence. Whatever its meaning it was not for that man he had picked up casually on obscure impulse, to get rid of the tiresome expostulations of a so-called friend; a man of whom he really knew nothing—and now a dead man. In Malata. Oh, yes! He was there secure enough, untroubled in his grave. In Malata. To bury him was the last service Renouard had rendered to his assistant before leaving the island on this trip to town.

Like many men ready enough for arduous enterprises Renouard was inclined to evade the small complications of existence. This trait of his character was composed of a little indolence, some disdain, and a shrinking from contests with certain forms of vulgarity—like a man who would face a lion and go out of his way to avoid a toad. His intercourse with the meddlesome journalist was that merely outward intimacy without sympathy some young men get drawn into easily. It had amused him rather to keep that "friend" in the dark about the fate of his assistant. Renouard had never needed other company than his own, for there was in him something of the sensitiveness of a dreamer who is easily jarred. He had said to himself that the all-knowing one would only preach again about the evils of solitude and worry his head off in favour of some forlornly useless protégé of his. Also the inquisitiveness of the Editor had irritated him and had closed his lips in sheer disgust.

And now he contemplated the noose of consequences drawing tight around him.

It was the memory of that diplomatic reticence which on the terrace had stiffled his first cry which would have told them all that the man sought for was not to be met on earth any more. He shrank from the absurdity of hearing the all-knowing one, and not very sober at that, turning on him with righteous reproaches—

"You never told me. You gave me to understand that your assistant was alive, and now you say he's dead. Which is it? Were you lying then or are you lying now?" No! the thought of such a scene was not to be borne. He had sat down appalled, thinking: "What shall I do now?"

His courage had oozed out of him. Speaking the truth meant the Moorsoms going away at once—while it seemed to him that he would give the last shred of his rectitude to secure a day more of her company. He sat on—silent. Slowly, from confused sensations, from his talk with the professor, the manner of the girl herself, the intoxicating familiarity of her sudden hand-clasp, there had come to him a half glimmer of hope. The other man was dead. Then! . . . Madness, of course—but he could not give it up. He had listened to that confounded busybody arranging everything—while all these people stood around assenting, under the spell of that dead romance. He had listened scornful and silent. The glimmers of hope, of opportunity, passed before his eyes. He had only to sit still and say nothing. That and no more. And what was truth to him in the face of that great passion which had flung him prostrate in spirit at her adored feet!

And now it was done! Fatality had willed it! With the eyes of a mortal struck by the maddening thunderbolt of the gods, Renouard looked up to the sky, an immense black pall dusted over with gold, on which great shudders seemed to pass from the breath of life affirming its sway.

8

AT LAST, one morning, in a clear spot of a glassy horizon charged with heraldic masses of black vapours, the island grew out from the sea, showing here and there its naked members of basaltic rock through the rents of heavy foliage. Later, in the great spilling of all the riches of sunset, Malata stood out green and rosy before turning into a violet shadow in the autumnal light of the expiring day. Then came the night. In the faint airs the schooner crept on past a sturdy squat headland, and it was pitch dark when her headsails ran down, she turned short on her heel, and her anchor bit into the sandy bottom on the edge of the outer reef; for it was too dangerous then to attempt entering the little bay full of shoals. After the last solemn flutter of the mainsail the murmuring voices of the Moorsom party lingered, very frail, in the black stillness.

They were sitting aft, on chairs, and nobody made a move. Early in the day, when it had become evident that the wind was failing, Renouard, basing his advice on the shortcomings of his bachelor establishment, had urged on the ladies the advisability of not going ashore in the middle of the night. Now he approached them in a constrained manner (it was astonishing the constraint that had reigned between him and his guests all through the passage) and renewed his arguments. No one ashore would dream of his bringing any visitors with him. Nobody would even think of coming off. There was only one old canoe on the plantation. And landing in the schooner's boats would be awkward in the dark. There was the risk of getting aground on some shallow patches. It would be best to spend the rest of the night on board.

There was really no opposition. The professor smoking a pipe, and very comfortable in an ulster buttoned over his tropical clothes, was the first to speak from his long chair.

"Most excellent advice."

Next to him Miss Moorsom assented by a long silence. Then in a voice as of one coming out of a dream—

"And so this is Malata," she said. "I have often wondered . . ."

A shiver passed through Renouard. She had wondered! What about? Malata was himself. He and Malata were one. And she had wondered! She had . . .

The professor's sister leaned over towards Renouard. Through all these days at sea the man's—the found man's—existence had not been alluded to on board the schooner. That reticence was part of the general constraint lying upon them all. She, herself, certainly had not been exactly elated by this finding—poor Arthur, without money, without prospects. But she felt moved by the sentiment and romance of the situation.

"Isn't it wonderful," she whispered out of her white wrap, "to think of poor Arthur sleeping there, so near to our dear lovely Felicia, and not knowing the immense joy in store for him to-morrow."

There was such artificiality in the wax-flower lady that nothing in this speech touched Renouard. It was but the simple anxiety of his heart that he was voicing when he muttered gloomily—

"No one in the world knows what to-morrow may hold in store."

The mature lady had a recoil as though he had said something impolite. What a harsh thing to say—instead of finding something nice and appropriate. On board, where she never saw him in evening clothes, Renouard's resemblance to a duke's son was not so apparent to her. Nothing but his—ah—bohemianism remained. She rose with a sort of ostentation.

"It's late—and since we are going to sleep on board to-night . . ." she said. "But it does seem so cruel."

The professor started up eagerly, knocking the ashes out of his pipe. "Infinitely more sensible, my dear Emma."

Renouard waited behind Miss Moorsom's chair.

She got up slowly, moved one step forward, and paused looking at the shore. The blackness of the island blotted out the stars with its vague mass like a low thundercloud brooding over the waters and ready to burst into flame and crashes.

"And so—this is Malata," she repeated dreamily, moving towards the cabin door. The clear cloak hanging from her shoulders, the ivory face—for the night had put out nothing of her but the gleams of her hair—made her resemble a shining dream-woman uttering words of wistful inquiry. She disappeared without a sign, leaving Renouard penetrated to the very marrow by the sounds that came from her body like a mysterious resonance of an exquisite instrument.

He stood stock still. What was this accidental touch which had evoked the strange accent of her voice? He dared not answer that question. But he had to answer the question of what was to be done now. Had the moment of confession come? The thought was enough to make one's blood run cold.

It was as if those people had a premonition of something. In the taciturn days of the passage he had noticed their reserve even amongst themselves. The professor smoked his pipe moodily in retired spots. Renouard had caught Miss Moorsom's eyes resting on himself more than once, with a peculiar and grave expression. He fancied that she avoided all opportunities of conversation. The maiden lady seemed to nurse a grievance. And now what had he to do?

The lights on the deck had gone out one after the other. The schooner slept.

About an hour after Miss Moorsom had gone below without a sign or a word for him, Renouard got out of his hammock slung in the waist under the midship awning—for he had given up all the accommodation below to his guests. He got out with a sudden swift movement, flung off his sleeping jacket, rolled his pyjamas up his thighs, and stole forward, unseen by the one Kanaka of the anchor-watch. His white torso, naked like a stripped athlete's, glimmered, ghostly, in the deep shadows of the deck. Unnoticed he got out of the ship over the knight-heads, ran along the back rope, and seizing the dolphin-striker firmly with both hands, lowered himself into the sea without a splash.

He swam away, noiseless like a fish, and then struck boldly for the land, sustained, embraced, by the tepid water. The gentle, voluptuous heave of its breast swung him up and down slightly; sometimes a wavelet murmured in his ears; from time to time, lowering his feet, he felt for the bottom on a shallow patch to rest and correct his direction. He landed at the lower end of the bungalow garden, into the dead stillness of the island. There were no lights. The plantation seemed to sleep, as profoundly as the schooner. On the path a small shell cracked under his naked heel.

The faithful half-caste foreman going his rounds cocked his ears at the sharp sound. He gave one enormous start of fear at the sight of the swift white figure flying at him out of the night. He crouched in terror, and then sprang up and clicked his tongue in amazed recognition.

"Tse! Tse! The master!"

"Be quiet, Luiz, and listen to what I say."

Yes, it was the master, the strong master who was never known to raise his voice, the man blindly obeyed and never questioned. He talked low and rapidly in the quiet night, as if every minute were precious. On learning that three guests were coming to stay Luiz clicked his tongue rapidly. These clicks were the uniform, stenographic symbols of his emotions, and he could give them an infinite variety of meaning. He listened to the rest in a deep silence hardly affected by the low, "Yes, master," whenever Renouard paused.

"You understand?" the latter insisted. "No preparations are to be made till we land in the morning. And you are to say that Mr. Walter has gone off in a trading schooner on a round of the islands."

"Yes, master."

"No mistakes—mind!"

"No, master."

Renouard walked back towards the sea. Luiz, following him, proposed to call out half a dozen boys and man the canoe.

"Imbecile!"

"Tse! Tse! Tse!"

"Don't you understand that you haven't seen me?"

"Yes, master. But what a long swim. Suppose you drown."

"Then you can say of me and of Mr. Walter what you like. The dead don't mind."

Renouard entered the sea and heard a faint "Tse! Tse! Tse!" of concern from the half-caste, who had already lost sight of the master's dark head on the overshadowed water.

Renouard set his direction by a big star that, dipping on the horizon, seemed to look curiously into his face. On this swim back he felt the mournful fatigue of all that length of the traversed road, which brought him no nearer to his desire. It was as if his love had sapped the invisible supports of his strength. There came a moment when it seemed to him that he must have swum beyond the confines of life. He had a sensation of eternity close at hand, demanding no effort—offering its peace. It was easy to swim like this beyond the confines of life looking at a star. But the thought: "They will think I dared not face them and committed suicide," caused a revolt of his mind which carried him on. He returned on board, as he had left, unheard and unseen. He lay in his hammock utterly exhausted and with a confused feeling that he had been beyond the confines of life, somewhere near a star, and that it was very quiet there.

9

SHELTERED by the squat headland from the first morning sparkle of the sea the little bay breathed a delicious freshness. The party from the schooner landed at the bottom of the garden. They exchanged insignificant words in studiously casual tones. The professor's sister put up a long-handled eye-glass as if to scan the novel surroundings, but in reality searching for poor Arthur anxiously. Having never seen him otherwise than in his town clothes she had no idea what he would look like. It had been left to the professor to help his ladies out of the boat because Renouard, as if intent on giving directions, had stepped forward at once to meet the half-caste Luiz hurrying down the path. In the distance, in front of the dazzlingly sunlit bungalow, a row of dark-faced house-boys unequal in stature and varied in complexion preserved the immobility of a guard of honour.

Luiz had taken off his soft felt hat before coming within earshot. Renouard bent his head to his rapid talk of domestic arrangements he meant to make for the visitors; another bed in the master's room for the ladies and a cot for the gentleman to be hung in the room opposite where—where Mr. Walter—here he gave a scared look all round—Mr. Walter—had died.

"Very good," assented Renouard in an even undertone. "And remember what you have to say of him."

"Yes, master. Only"—he wriggled slightly and put one bare foot on the other for a moment in apologetic embarrassment—"only I—I—don't like to say it."

Renouard looked at him without anger, without any sort of expression. "Frightened of the dead? Eh? Well—all right. I will say it myself—I suppose once for all. . . ." Immediately he raised his voice very much.

"Send the boys down to bring up the luggage."

"Yes, master."

Renouard turned to his distinguished guests who, like a personally conducted party of tourists, had stopped and were looking about them.

"I am sorry," he began with an impassive face. "My man has just told me that Mr. Walter . . ." he managed to smile, but didn't correct himself . . . "has gone in a trading schooner on a short tour of the islands, to the westward."

This communication was received in profound silence.

Renouard forgot himself in the thought: "It's done!" But the sight of the string of boys marching up to the house with suit-cases and dressing-bags rescued him from that appalling abstraction.

"All I can do is to beg you to make yourselves at home . . . with what patience you may."

This was so obviously the only thing to do that everybody moved on at once. The professor walked alongside Renouard, behind the two ladies.

"Rather unexpected—this absence."

"Not exactly," muttered Renouard. "A trip has to be made every year to engage labour."

"I see . . . And he . . . How vexingly elusive the poor fellow has become! I'll begin to think that some wicked fairy is favouring this love tale with unpleasant attentions."

Renouard noticed that the party did not seem weighed down by this new disappointment. On the contrary they moved with a freer step. The professor's sister dropped her eye-glass to the end of its chain. Miss Moorsom took the lead. The professor, his lips unsealed, lingered in the open: but Renouard did not listen to that man's talk. He looked after that man's daughter—if indeed that creature of irresistible seductions were a daughter of mortals. The very intensity of his desire, as if his soul were streaming after her through his eyes, defeated his object of keeping hold of her as long as possible with, at least, one of his senses. Her moving outlines dissolved into a misty coloured shimmer of a woman made of flame and shadows, crossing the threshold of his house.

The days which followed were not exactly such as Renouard had feared—yet they were not better than his fears. They were accursed in all the moods they brought him. But the general aspect of things was quiet. The professor smoked innumerable pipes with the air of a worker on his holiday, always in movement and looking at things with that mysteriously sagacious aspect of men who are admittedly wiser than the rest of the world. His white head of hair—whiter than anything within the horizon except the broken water on the reefs—was glimpsed in every part of the plantation always on the move under the white parasol. And once he climbed the headland and appeared suddenly to those below, a white speck elevated in the blue, with a diminutive but statuesque effect.

Felicia Moorsom remained near the house. Sometimes she could be seen with a despairing expression scribbling rapidly in her lock-up dairy. But only for a moment. At the sound of Renouard's footsteps she would turn towards him her beautiful face, adorable in that calm which was like a wilful, like a cruel ignoring of her tremendous power. Whenever she sat on the verandah, on a chair more specially reserved for her use, Renouard would stroll up and sit on the steps near her, mostly silent, and often not trusting himself to turn his glance on her. She, very still with her eyes half-closed, looked down on his head—so that to a beholder (such as Professor Moorsom, for instance) she would appear to be turning over in her mind profound thoughts about that man sitting at her feet, his shoulders bowed a little, his hands listless—as if vanquished. And, indeed, the moral poison of falsehood has such a decomposing power that Renouard felt his old personality turn to dead dust. Often, in the evening, when they sat outside conversing languidly in the dark, he felt that he must rest his forehead on her feet and burst into tears.

The professor's sister suffered from some little strain caused by the unstability of her own feelings toward Renouard. She could not tell whether she really did dislike him or not. At times he appeared to her most fascinating; and, though he generally ended by saying something shockingly crude, she could not resist her inclination to talk with him—at least not always. One day when her niece had left them alone on the verandah she leaned forward in her chair—speckless, resplendent, and, in her way, almost as striking a personality as her niece, who did not resemble her in the least. "Dear Felicia has inherited her hair and the greatest part of her appearance from her mother," the maiden lady used to tell people.

She leaned forward then, confidentially.

"Oh! Mr. Renouard! Haven't you something comforting to say?"

He looked up, as surprised as if a voice from heaven had spoken with this perfect society intonation, and by the puzzled profundity of his blue eyes fluttered the wax-flower of refined womanhood. She continued. "For—I can speak to you openly on this tiresome subject—only think what a terrible strain this hope deferred must be for Felicia's heart—for her nerves."

"Why speak to me about it," he muttered feeling half choked suddenly.

"Why! As a friend—a well-wisher—the kindest of hosts. I am afraid we are really eating you out of house and home." She laughed a little. "Ah! When, when will this suspense be relieved! That poor lost Arthur! I confess that I am almost afraid of the great moment. It will be like seeing a ghost."

"Have you ever seen a ghost?" asked Renouard, in a dull voice.

She shifted her hands a little. Her pose was perfect in its ease and middle-aged grace.

"Not actually. Only in a photograph. But we have many friends who had the experience of apparitions."

"Ah! They see ghosts in London," mumbled Renouard, not looking at her.

"Frequently—in a certain very interesting set. But all sorts of people do. We have a friend, a very famous author—his ghost is a girl. One of my brother's intimates is a very great man of science. He is friendly with a ghost . . . Of a girl too," she added in a voice as if struck for the first time by the coincidence. "It is the photograph of that apparition which I have seen. Very sweet. Most interesting. A little cloudy naturally. . . . Mr. Renouard! I hope you are not a sceptic. It's so consoling to think. . ."

"Those plantation boys of mine see ghosts too," said Renouard grimly.

The sister of the philosopher sat up stiffly. What crudeness! It was always so with this strange young man.

"Mr. Renouard! How can you compare the superstitious fancies of your horrible savages with the manifestations . . . "

Words failed her. She broke off with a very faint primly angry smile. She was perhaps the more offended with him because of that flutter at the beginning of the conversation. And in a moment with perfect tact and dignity she got up from her chair and left him alone.

Renouard didn't even look up. It was not the displeasure of the lady which deprived him of his sleep that night. He was beginning to forget what simple, honest sleep was like. His hammock from the ship had been hung for him on a side verandah, and he spent his nights in it on his back, his hands folded on his chest, in a sort of half conscious, oppressed stupor. In the morning he watched with unseeing eyes the headland come out a shapeless inkblot against the thin light of the false dawn, pass through all the stages of daybreak to the deep purple of its outlined mass nimbed gloriously with the gold of the rising sun. He listened to the vague sounds of waking within the house: and suddenly he became aware of Luiz standing by the hammock—obviously troubled.

"What's the matter?"

"Tse! Tse! Tse!"

"Well, what now? Trouble with the boys?"

"No, master. The gentleman when I take him his bath water he speak to me. He ask me —he ask—when, when, I think Mr. Walter, he come back."

The half-caste's teeth chattered slightly. Renouard got out of the hammock.

"And he is here all the time—eh?"

Luiz nodded a scared affirmative, but at once protested, "I no see him. I never. Not I! The ignorant wild boys say they see . . . Something! Ough!"

He clapped his teeth on another short rattle, and stood there, shrunk, blighted, like a man in a freezing blast.

"And what did you say to the gentleman?"

"I say I don't know—and I clear out. I—I don't like to speak of him."

"All right. We shall try to lay that poor ghost," said Renouard gloomily, going off to a small hut near by to dress. He was saying to himself: "This fellow will end by giving me away. The last thing that I . . . No! That mustn't be." And feeling his hand being forced he discovered the whole extent of his cowardice.

10

THAT MORNING WANDERING about his plantation, more like a frightened soul than its creator and master, he dodged the white parasol bobbing up here and there like a buoy adrift on a sea of dark-green plants. The crop promised to be magnificent, and the fashionable philosopher of the age took other than a merely scientific interest in the experiment. His investments were judicious, but he had always some little money lying by, for experiments.

After lunch, being left alone with Renouard, he talked a little of cultivation and such matters. Then suddenly:

"By the way, is it true what my sister tells me, that your plantation boys have been disturbed by a ghost?"

Renouard, who since the ladies had left the table was not keeping such a strict watch on himself, came out of his abstraction with a start and a stiff smile.

"My foreman had some trouble with them during my absence. They funk working in a certain field on the slope of the hill."

"A ghost here!" exclaimed the amused professor. "Then our whole conception of the psychology of ghosts must be revised. This island has been uninhabited probably since the dawn of ages. How did a ghost come here. By air or water? And why did it leave its native haunts. Was it from misanthropy? Was he expelled from some community of spirits?"

Renouard essayed to respond in the same tone. The words died on his lips. Was it a man or a woman ghost, the professor inquired.

"I don't know." Renouard made an effort to appear at ease. He had, he said, a couple of Tahitian amongst his boys—a ghost-ridden race. They had started the scare. They had probably brought their ghost with them.

"Let us investigate the matter, Renouard," proposed the professor half in earnest. "We may make some interesting discoveries as to the state of primitive minds, at any rate."

This was too much. Renouard jumped up and leaving the room went out and walked about in front of the house. He would allow no one to force his hand. Presently the professor joined him outside. He carried his parasol, but had neither his book nor his pipe with him. Amiably serious he laid his hand on his "dear young friend's" arm.

"We are all of us a little strung up," he said. "For my part I have been like sister Anne in the story. But I cannot see anything coming. Anything that would be the least good for anybody—I mean."

Renouard had recovered sufficiently to murmur coldly his regret of this waste of time. For that was what, he supposed, the professor had in his mind.

"Time," mused Professor Moorsom. "I don't know that time can be wasted. But I will tell you, my dear friend, what this is: it is an awful waste of life. I mean for all of us. Even for my sister, who has got a headache and is gone to lie down."

He shook gently Renouard's arm. "Yes, for all of us! One may meditate on life endlessly, one may even have a poor opinion of it—but the fact remains that we have only one life to live. And it is short. Think of that, my young friend."

He released Renouard's arm and stepped out of the shade opening his parasol. It was clear that there was something more in his mind than mere anxiety about the date of his lectures for fashionable audiences. What did the man mean by his confounded platitudes? To Renouard, scared by Luiz in the morning (for he felt that nothing could be more fatal than to have his deception unveiled otherwise than by personal confession), this talk sounded like encouragement or a warning from that man who seemed to him to be very brazen and very subtle. It was like being bullied by the dead and cajoled by the living into a throw of dice for a supreme stake.

Renouard went away to some distance from the house and threw himself down in the shade of a tree. He lay there perfectly still with his forehead resting on his folded arms, light-headed and thinking. It seemed to him that he must be on fire, then that he had fallen into a cool whirlpool, a smooth funnel of water swirling about with nauseating rapidity. And then (it must have been a reminiscence of his boyhood) he was walking on the dangerous thin ice of a river, unable to turn back. . . . Suddenly it parted from shore to shore with a loud crack like the report of a gun.

With one leap he found himself on his feet. All was peace, stillness, sunshine. He walked away from there slowly. Had he been a gambler he would have perhaps been supported in a measure by the mere excitement. But he was not a gambler. He had always disdained that artificial manner of challenging the fates. The bungalow came into view, bright and pretty, and all about everything was peace, stillness, sunshine. . . .

While he was plodding towards it he had a disagreeable sense of the dead man's company at his elbow. The ghost! He seemed to be everywhere but in his grave. Could one ever shake him off? he wondered. At that moment Miss Moorsom came out on the verandah; and at once, as if by a mystery of radiating waves, she roused a great tumult in his heart, shook earth and sky together—but he plodded on. Then like a grave song-note in the storm her voice came to him ominously.

"Ah! Mr. Renouard. . . " He came up and smiled, but she was very serious. "I can't keep still any longer. Is there time to walk up this headland and back before dark?"

The shadows were lying lengthened on the ground; all was stillness and peace. "No," said Renouard, feeling suddenly as steady as a rock. "But I can show you a view from the central hill which your father has not seen. A view of reefs and of broken water without end, and of great wheeling clouds of sea-birds."

She came down the verandah steps at once and they moved off. "You go first," he proposed, "and I'll direct you. To the left."

She was wearing a short nankin skirt, a muslin blouse; he could see through the thin stuff the skin of her shoulders, of her arms. The noble delicacy of her neck caused him a sort of transport. "The path begins where these three palms are. The only palms on the island."

"I see."

She never turned her head. After a while she observed: "This path looks as if it had been made recently."

"Quite recently," he assented very low.

They went on climbing steadily without exchanging another word; and when they stood on the top she gazed a long time before her. The low evening mist veiled the further limit of the reefs. Above the enormous and melancholy confusion, as of a fleet of wrecked islands, the restless myriads of sea-birds rolled and unrolled dark ribbons on the sky, gathered in clouds, soared and stooped like a play of shadows, for they were too far for them to hear their cries.

Renouard broke the silence in low tones.

"They'll be settling for the night presently." She made no sound. Round them all was peace and declining sunshine. Near by, the topmost pinnacle of Malata, resembling the top of a buried tower, rose a rock, weather-worn, grey, weary of watching the monotonous centuries of the Pacific. Renouard leaned his shoulders against it. Felicia Moorsom faced him suddenly, her splendid black eyes full on his face as though she had made up her mind at last to destroy his wits once and for all. Dazzled, he lowered his eyelids slowly.

"Mr. Renouard! There is something strange in all this. Tell me where he is?"

He answered deliberately.

"On the other side of this rock. I buried him there myself."

She pressed her hands to her breast, struggled for her breath for a moment, then: "Ohhh! . . . You buried him! . . . What sort of man are you? . . . You dared not tell! . . . He is another of your victims? . . . You dared not confess that evening. . . . You must have killed him. What could he have done to you? . . . You fastened on him some atrocious quarrel and . . ."

Her vengeful aspect, her poignant cries left him as unmoved as the weary rock against which he leaned. He only raised his eyelids to look at her and lowered them slowly. Nothing more. It silenced her. And as if ashamed she made a gesture with her hand, putting away from her that thought. He spoke, quietly ironic at first.

"Ha! the legendary Renouard of sensitive idiots—the ruthless adventurer—the ogre with a future. That was a parrot cry, Miss Moorsom. I don't think that the greatest fool of them all ever dared hint such a stupid thing of me that I killed men for nothing. No, I had noticed this man in a hotel. He had come from up country I was told, and was doing nothing. I saw him sitting there lonely in a corner like a sick crow, and I went over one evening to talk to him. Just on impulse. He wasn't impressive. He was pitiful. My worst enemy could have told you he wasn't good enough to be one of Renouard's victims. It didn't take me long to judge that he was drugging himself. Not drinking. Drugs."

"Ah! It's now that you are trying to murder him," she cried.

"Really. Always the Renouard of shopkeepers' legend. Listen! I would never have been jealous of him. And yet I am jealous of the air you breathe, of the soil you tread on, of the world that sees you—moving free—not mine. But never mind. I rather liked him. For a certain reason I proposed he should come to be my assistant here. He said he believed this would save him. It did not save him from death. It came to him as it were from nothing—just a fall. A mere slip and tumble of ten feet into a ravine. But it seems he had been hurt before up-country—by a horse. He ailed and ailed. No, he was not a steel-tipped man. And his poor soul seemed to have been damaged too. It gave way very soon."

"This is tragic!" Felicia Moorsom whispered with feeling. Renouard's lips twitched, but his level voice continued mercilessly.

"That's the story. He rallied a little one night and said he wanted to tell me something. I, being a gentleman, he said, he could confide in me. I told him that he was mistaken. That there was a good deal of a plebeian in me, that he couldn't know. He seemed disappointed. He muttered something about his innocence and something that sounded like a curse on some woman, then turned to the wall and—just grew cold."

"On a woman," cried Miss Moorsom indignantly. "What woman?"

"I wonder!" said Renouard, raising his eyes and noting the crimson of her ear-lobes against the live whiteness of her complexion, the sombre, as if secret, night-splendour of her eyes under the writhing flames of her hair. "Some woman who wouldn't believe in that poor innocence of his. . . Yes. You probably. And now you will not believe in me—not even in me who must in truth be what I am—even to death. No! You won't. And yet, Felicia, a woman like you and a man like me do not often come together on this earth."

The flame of her glorious head scorched his face. He flung his hat far away, and his suddenly lowered eyelids brought out startlingly his resemblance to antique bronze, the profile of Pallas, still, austere, bowed a little in the shadow of the rock. "Oh! If you could only understand the truth that is in me!" he added.

She waited, as if too astounded to speak, till he looked up again, and then with unnatural force as if defending herself from some unspoken aspersion, "It's I who stand for truth here! Believe in you! In you, who by a heartless falsehood—and nothing else, nothing else, do you hear?—have brought me here, deceived, cheated, as in some abominable farce!" She sat down on a boulder, rested her chin in her hands, in the pose of simple grief—mourning for herself.

"It only wanted this. Why! Oh! Why is it that ugliness, ridicule, and baseness must fall across my path."

On that height, alone with the sky, they spoke to each other as if the earth had fallen away from under their feet.

"Are you grieving for your dignity? He was a mediocre soul and could have given you but an unworthy existence."

She did not even smile at those words, but, superb, as if lifting a corner of the veil, she turned on him slowly.

"And do you imagine I would have devoted myself to him for such a purpose! Don't you know that reparation was due to him from me? A sacred debt—a fine duty. To redeem him would not have been in my power—I know it. But he was blameless, and it was for me to come forward. Don't you see that in the eyes of the world nothing could have rehabilitated him so completely as his marriage with me? No word of evil could be whispered of him after I had given him my hand. As to giving myself up to anything less than the shaping of a man's destiny—if I thought I could do it I would abhor myself. . . ." She spoke with authority in her deep fascinating, unemotional voice. Renouard meditated, gloomy, as if over some sinister riddle of a beautiful sphinx met on the wild road of his life.

"Yes. Your father was right. You are one of these aristocrats . . ."

She drew herself up haughtily.

"What do you say? My father! . . . I an aristocrat."

"Oh! I don't mean that you are like the men and women of the time of armours, castles, and great deeds. Oh, no! They stood on the naked soil, had traditions to be faithful to, had their feet on this earth of passions and death which is not a hothouse. They would have been too plebeian for you since they had to lead, to suffer with, to understand the commonest humanity. No, you are merely of the topmost layer, disdainful and superior, the mere pure froth and bubble on the inscrutable depths which some day will toss you out of existence.

But you are you! You are you! You are the eternal love itself—only, O Divinity, it isn't your body, it is your soul that is made of foam."

She listened as if in a dream. He had succeeded so well in his effort to drive back the flood of his passion that his life itself seemed to run with it out of his body. At that moment he felt as one dead speaking. But the headlong wave returning with tenfold force flung him on her suddenly, with open arms and blazing eyes. She found herself like a feather in his grasp, helpless, unable to struggle, with her feet off the ground. But this contact with her, maddening like too much felicity, destroyed its own end. Fire ran through his veins, turned his passion to ashes, burnt him out and left him empty, without force—almost without desire. He let her go before she could cry out. And she was so used to the forms of repression enveloping, softening the crude impulses of old humanity that she no longer believed in their existence as if it were an exploded legend. She did not recognise what had happened to her. She came safe out of his arms, without a struggle, not even having felt afraid.

"What's the meaning of this?" she said, outraged but calm in a scornful way.

He got down on his knees in silence, bent low to her very feet, while she looked down at him, a little surprised, without animosity, as if merely curious to see what he would do. Then, while he remained bowed to the ground pressing the hem of her skirt to his lips, she made a slight movement. He got up.

"No," he said. "Were you ever so much mine what could I do with you without your consent? No. You don't conquer a wraith, cold mist, stuff of dreams, illusion. It must come to you and cling to your breast. And then! Oh! And then!"

All ecstasy, all expression went out of his face.

"Mr. Renouard," she said, "though you can have no claim on my consideration after having decoyed me here for the vile purpose, apparently, of gloating over me as your possible prey, I will tell you that I am not perhaps the extraordinary being you think I am. You may believe me. Here I stand for truth itself."

"What's that to me what you are?" he answered. "At a sign from you I would climb up to the seventh heaven to bring you down to earth for my own—and if I saw you steeped to the lips in vice, in crime, in mud, I would go after you, take you to my arms—wear you for an incomparable jewel on my breast. And that's love—true love—the gift and the curse of the gods. There is no other."

The truth vibrating in his voice made her recoil slightly, for she was not fit to hear it—not even a little—not even one single time in her life. It was revolting to her; and in her trouble, perhaps prompted by the suggestion of his name or to soften the harshness of expression, for she was obscurely moved, she spoke to him in French.

"*Assez! J'ai horreur de tout cela,*" she said.

He was white to his very lips, but he was trembling no more. The dice had been cast, and not even violence could alter the throw. She passed by him unbendingly, and he followed her down the path. After a time she heard him saying:

"And your dream is to influence a human destiny?"

"Yes!" she answered curtly, unabashed, with a woman's complete assurance.

"Then you may rest content. You have done it."

She shrugged her shoulders slightly. But just before reaching the end of the path she relented, stopped, and went back to him.

"I don't suppose you are very anxious for people to know how near you came to absolute turpitude. You may rest easy on that point. I shall speak to my father, of course, and we will agree to say that he has died—nothing more."

"Yes," said Renouard in a lifeless voice. "He is dead. His very ghost shall be done with presently."

She went on, but he remained standing stock still in the dusk. She had already reached the three palms when she heard behind her a loud peal of laughter, cynical and joyless, such as is heard in smoking-rooms at the end of a scandalous story. It made her feel positively faint for a moment.

II

Slowly a complete darkness enveloped Geoffrey Renouard. His resolution had failed him. Instead of following Felicia into the house, he had stopped under the three palms, and leaning against a smooth trunk had abandoned himself to a sense of an immense deception and the feeling of extreme fatigue. This walk up the hill and down again was like the supreme effort of an explorer trying to penetrate the interior of an unknown country, the secret of which is too well defended by its cruel and barren nature. Decoyed by a mirage, he had gone too far—so far that there was no going back. His strength was at an end. For the first time in his life he had to give up, and with a sort of despairing self-possession he tried to understand the cause of the defeat. He did not ascribe it to that absurd dead man.

The hesitating shadow of Luiz approached him unnoticed till it spoke timidly. Renouard started.

"Eh? What? Dinner waiting? You must say I beg to be excused. I can't come. But I shall see them to-morrow morning, at the landing place. Take your orders from the professor as to the sailing of the schooner. Go now."

Luiz, dumbfounded, retreated into the darkness. Renouard did not move, but hours afterwards, like the bitter fruit of his immobility, the words: "I had nothing to offer to her vanity," came from his lips in the silence of the island. And it was then only that he stirred, only to wear the night out in restless tramping up and down the various paths of the plantation. Luiz, whose sleep was made light by the consciousness of some impending change, heard footsteps passing by his hut, the firm tread of the master; and turning on his mats emitted a faint Tse! Tse! Tse! of deep concern.

Lights had been burning in the bungalow almost all through the night; and with the first sign of day began the bustle of departure. House boys walked processionally carrying suit-cases and dressing-bags down to the schooner's boat, which came to the landing place at the bottom of the garden. Just as the rising sun threw its golden nimbus around the purple shape of the headland, the Planter of Malata was perceived pacing bare-headed the curve of the little bay. He exchanged a few words with the sailing-master of the schooner, then remained by the boat, standing very upright, his eyes on the ground, waiting.

He had not long to wait. Into the cool, overshadowed garden the professor descended first, and came jauntily down the path in a lively cracking of small shells. With his closed parasol hooked on his forearm, and a book in his hand, he resembled a banal tourist more than was permissible to a man of his unique distinction. He waved the disengaged arm from a distance, but at close quarters, arrested before Renouard's immobility, he made no offer to shake hands. He seemed to appraise the aspect of the man with a sharp glance, and made up his mind.

"We are going back by Suez," he began almost boisterously. "I have been looking up the sailing lists. If the zephirs of your Pacific are only moderately propitious I think we are sure to catch the mail boat due in Marseilles on the 18th of March. This will suit me excellently. . . ." He lowered his tone. "My dear young friend, I'm deeply grateful to you."

Renouard's set lips moved.

"Why are you grateful to me?"

"Ah! Why? In the first place you might have made us miss the next boat, mightn't you? . . . I don't thank you for your hospitality. You can't be angry with me for saying that I am truly thankful to escape from it. But I am grateful to you for what you have done, and—for being what you are."

It was difficult to define the flavour of that speech, but Renouard received it with an austerely equivocal smile. The professor stepping into the boat opened his parasol and sat down in the stern-sheets waiting for the ladies. No sound of human voice broke the fresh silence of the morning while they walked the broad path, Miss Moorsom a little in advance of her aunt.

When she came abreast of him Renouard raised his head.

"Good-bye, Mr. Renouard," she said in a low voice, meaning to pass on; but there was such a look of entreaty in the blue gleam of his sunken eyes that after an imperceptible hesitation she laid her hand, which was ungloved, in his extended palm.

"Will you condescend to remember me?" he asked, while an emotion with which she was angry made her pale cheeks flush and her black eyes sparkle.

"This is a strange request for you to make," she said, exaggerating the coldness of her tone.

"Is it? Impudent perhaps. Yet I am not so guilty as you think; and bear in mind that to me you can never make reparation."

"Reparation? To you! It is you who can offer me no reparation for the offence against my feelings—and my person; for what reparation can be adequate for your odious and ridiculous plot so scornful in its implication, so humiliating to my pride. No! I don't want to remember you."

Unexpectedly, with a tightening grip, he pulled her nearer to him, and looking into her eyes with fearless despair—

"You'll have to. I shall haunt you," he said firmly.

Her hand was wrenched out of his grasp before he had time to release it. Felicia Moorsom stepped into the boat, sat down by the side of her father, and breathed tenderly on her crushed fingers.

The professor gave her a sidelong look—nothing more. But the professor's sister, yet on shore, had put up her long-handle double eye-glass to look at the scene. She dropped it with a faint rattle.

"I've never in my life heard anything so crude said to a lady," she murmured, passing before Renouard with a perfectly erect head. When, a moment afterwards, softening suddenly, she turned to throw a good-bye to that young man, she saw only his back in the distance moving towards the bungalow. She watched him go in—amazed—before she too left the soil of Malata.

Nobody disturbed Renouard in that room where he had shut himself in to breathe the evanescent perfume of her who for him was no more, till late in the afternoon when the half-caste was heard on the other side of the door.

He wanted the master to know that the trader *Janet* was just entering the cove.

Renouard's strong voice on his side of the door gave him most unexpected instructions. He was to pay off the boys with the cash in the office and arrange with the captain of the *Janet* to take every worker away from Malata, returning them to their respective homes. An order on the Dunster firm would be given to him in payment.

And again the silence of the bungalow remained unbroken till, next morning, the half-caste came to report that everything was done. The plantation boys were embarking now.

Through a crack in the door a hand thrust at him a piece of paper, and the door slammed to so sharply that Luiz stepped back. Then approaching cringingly the keyhole, in a propitiatory tone he asked:

"Do I go too, master?"

"Yes. You too. Everybody."

"Master stop here alone?"

Silence. And the half-caste's eyes grew wide with wonder. But he also, like those "ignorant savages," the plantation boys, was only too glad to leave an island haunted by the ghost of a white man. He backed away noiselessly from the mysterious silence in the closed room, and only in the very doorway of the bungalow allowed himself to give vent to his feelings by a deprecatory and pained—

"Tse! Tse! Tse!"

12

The Moorsoms did manage to catch the homeward mail boat all right, but had only twenty-four hours in town. Thus the sentimental Willie could not see very much of them. This did not prevent him afterwards from relating at great length, with manly tears in his eyes, how poor Miss Moorsom—the fashionable and clever beauty—found her betrothed in Malata only to see him die in her arms. Most people were deeply touched by the sad story. It was the talk of a good many days.

But the all-knowing Editor, Renouard's only friend and crony, wanted to know more than the rest of the world. From professional incontinence, perhaps, he thirsted for a full cup of harrowing detail. And when he noticed Renouard's schooner lying in port day after day he sought the sailing master to learn the reason. The man told him that such were his instructions. He had been ordered to lie there a month before returning to Malata. And the month was nearly up. "I will ask you to give me a passage," said the Editor.

He landed in the morning at the bottom of the garden and found peace, stillness, sunshine reigning everywhere, the doors and windows of the bungalow standing wide open, no sight of a human being anywhere, the plants growing rank and tall on the deserted fields. For hours the Editor and the schooner's crew, excited by the mystery, roamed over the island shouting Renouard's name; and at last set themselves in grim silence to explore systematically the uncleared bush and the deeper ravines in search of his corpse. What had happened? Had he been murdered by the boys? Or had he simply, capricious and secretive, abandoned his plantation taking the people with him. It was impossible to tell what had happened. At last, towards the decline of the day, the Editor and the sailing master discovered a track of sandals crossing a strip of sandy beach on the north shore of the bay. Following this track fearfully, they passed round the spur of the headland, and there on a large stone found the sandals, Renouard's white jacket, and the Malay sarong of chequered pattern which the planter of Malata was well known to wear when going to bathe. These things made a little heap, and the sailor remarked, after gazing at it in silence—

"Birds have been hovering over this for many a day."

"He's gone bathing and got drowned," cried the Editor in dismay.

"I doubt it, sir. If he had been drowned anywhere within a mile from the shore the body would have been washed out on the reefs. And our boats have found nothing so far."

Nothing was ever found—and Renouard's disappearance remained in the main inexplicable. For to whom could it have occurred that a man would set out calmly to swim beyond the confines of life—with a steady stroke—his eyes fixed on a star!

Next evening, from the receding schooner, the Editor looked back for the last time at the deserted island. A black cloud hung listlessly over the high rock on the middle hill; and under the mysterious silence of that shadow Malata lay mournful, with an air of anguish in the wild sunset, as if remembering the heart that was broken there.

THE SHADOW LINE

A Confession

I

I

ONLY THE YOUNG have such moments. I don't mean the very young. No. The very young have, properly speaking, no moments. It is the privilege of early youth to live in advance of its days in all the beautiful continuity of hope which knows no pauses and no introspection.

One closes behind one the little gate of mere boyishness—and enters an enchanted garden. Its very shades glow with promise. Every turn of the path has its seduction. And it isn't because it is an undiscovered country. One knows well enough that all mankind had streamed that way. It is the charm of universal experience from which one expects an uncommon or personal sensation—a bit of one's own.

One goes on recognizing the landmarks of the predecessors, excited, amused, taking the hard luck and the good luck together—the kicks and the half-pence, as the saying is—the picturesque common lot that holds so many possibilities for the deserving or perhaps for the lucky. Yes. One goes on. And the time, too, goes on—till one perceives ahead a shadow-line warning one that the region of early youth, too, must be left behind.

This is the period of life in which such moments of which I have spoken are likely to come. What moments? Why, the moments of boredom, of weariness, of dissatisfaction. Rash moments. I mean moments when the still young are inclined to commit rash actions, such as getting married suddenly or else throwing up a job for no reason.

This is not a marriage story. It wasn't so bad as that with me. My action, rash as it was, had more the character of divorce—almost of desertion. For no reason on which a sensible person could put a finger I threw up my job—chucked my berth—left the ship of which the worst that could be said was that she was a steamship and therefore, perhaps, not entitled to that blind loyalty which. . . . However, it's no use trying to put a gloss on what even at the time I myself half suspected to be a caprice.

It was in an Eastern port. She was an Eastern ship, inasmuch as then she belonged to that port. She traded among dark islands on a blue reef-scarred sea, with the Red Ensign over the taffrail and at her masthead a house-flag, also red, but with a green border and with a white crescent in it. For an Arab owned her, and a Syed at that. Hence the green border on the flag.

He was the head of a great House of Straits Arabs, but as loyal a subject of the complex British Empire as you could find east of the Suez Canal. World politics did not trouble him at all, but he had a great occult power amongst his own people.

It was all one to us who owned the ship. He had to employ white men in the shipping part of his business, and many of those he so employed had never set eyes on him from the first to the last day. I myself saw him but once, quite accidentally on a wharf—an old, dark little man blind in one eye, in a snowy robe and yellow slippers. He was having his hand severely kissed by a crowd of Malay pilgrims to whom he had done some favour, in the way of food and money. His alms-giving, I have heard, was most extensive, covering almost the whole Archipelago. For isn't it said that "The charitable man is the friend of Allah"?

Excellent (and picturesque) Arab owner, about whom one needed not to trouble one's head, a most excellent Scottish ship—for she was that from the keep up—excellent sea-boat, easy to keep clean, most handy in every way, and if it had not been for her internal propulsion, worthy of any man's love, I cherish to this day a profound respect for her memory. As to the kind of trade she was engaged in and the character of my shipmates, I could not have been happier if I had had the life and the men made to my order by a benevolent Enchanter.

And suddenly I left all this. I left it in that, to us, inconsequential manner in which a bird flies away from a comfortable branch. It was as though all unknowing I had heard a whisper or seen something. Well—perhaps! One day I was perfectly right and the next everything was gone—glamour, flavour, interest, contentment—everything. It was one of these moments, you know. The green sickness of late youth descended on me and carried me off. Carried me off that ship, I mean.

We were only four white men on board, with a large crew of Kalashes and two Malay petty officers. The Captain stared hard as if wondering what ailed me. But he was a sailor, and he, too, had been young at one time. Presently a smile came to lurk under his thick iron-gray moustache, and he observed that, of course, if I felt I must go he couldn't keep me by main force. And it was arranged that I should be paid off the next morning. As I was going out of his cabin he added suddenly, in a peculiar wistful tone, that he hoped I would find what I was so anxious to go and look for. A soft, cryptic utterance which seemed to reach deeper than any diamond-hard tool could have done. I do believe he understood my case.

But the second engineer attacked me differently. He was a sturdy young Scot, with a smooth face and light eyes. His honest red countenance emerged out of the engine-room companion and then the whole robust man, with shirt sleeves turned up, wiping slowly the massive fore-arms with a lump of cotton-waste. And his light eyes expressed bitter distaste, as though our friendship had turned to ashes. He said weightily: "Oh! Aye! I've been thinking it was about time for you to run away home and get married to some silly girl."

It was tacitly understood in the port that John Nieven was a fierce misogynist; and the absurd character of the sally convinced me that he meant to be nasty—very nasty—had meant to say the most crushing thing he could think of. My laugh sounded deprecatory. Nobody but a friend could be so angry as that. I became a little crestfallen. Our chief engineer also took a characteristic view of my action, but in a kindlier spirit.

He was young, too, but very thin, and with a mist of fluffy brown beard all round his haggard face. All day long, at sea or in harbour, he could be seen walking hastily up and down the after-deck, wearing an intense, spiritually rapt expression, which was caused by a perpetual consciousness of unpleasant physical sensations in his internal economy. For he was a confirmed dyspeptic. His view of my case was very simple. He said it was nothing but deranged liver. Of course! He suggested I should stay for another trip and meantime dose myself with a certain patent medicine in which his own belief was absolute. "I'll tell you what I'll do. I'll buy you two bottles, out of my own pocket. There. I can't say fairer than that, can I?"

I believe he would have perpetrated the atrocity (or generosity) at the merest sign of weakening on my part. By that time, however, I was more discontented, disgusted, and dogged than ever. The past eighteen months, so full of new and varied experience, appeared a dreary, prosaic waste of days. I felt—how shall I express it?—that there was no truth to be got out of them.

What truth? I should have been hard put to it to explain. Probably, if pressed, I would have burst into tears simply. I was young enough for that.

Next day the Captain and I transacted our business in the Harbour Office. It was a lofty, big, cool, white room, where the screened light of day glowed serenely. Everybody in it—the officials, the public—were in white. Only the heavy polished desks gleamed darkly in a central avenue, and some papers lying on them were blue. Enormous punkahs sent from on high a gentle draught through that immaculate interior and upon our perspiring heads.

The official behind the desk we approached grinned amiably and kept it up till, in answer to his perfunctory question, "Sign off and on again?" my Captain answered, "No! Signing off for good." And then his grin vanished in sudden solemnity. He did not look at me again till he handed me my papers with a sorrowful expression, as if they had been my passports for Hades.

While I was putting them away he murmured some question to the Captain, and I heard the latter answer good-humouredly:

"No. He leaves us to go home."

"Oh!" the other exclaimed, nodding mournfully over my sad condition.

I didn't know him outside the official building, but he leaned forward the desk to shake hands with me, compassionately, as one would with some poor devil going out to be hanged; and I am afraid I performed my part ungraciously, in the hardened manner of an impenitent criminal.

No homeward-bound mail-boat was due for three or four days. Being now a man without a ship, and having for a time broken my connection with the sea—become, in fact, a mere potential passenger—it would have been more appropriate perhaps if I had gone to stay at an hotel. There it was, too, within a stone's throw of the Harbour Office, low, but somehow palatial, displaying its white, pillared pavilions surrounded by trim grass plots. I would have felt a passenger indeed in there! I gave it a hostile glance and directed my steps toward the Officers' Sailors' Home.

I walked in the sunshine, disregarding it, and in the shade of the big trees on the esplanade without enjoying it. The heat of the tropical East descended through the leafy boughs, enveloping my thinly-clad body, clinging to my rebellious discontent, as if to rob it of its freedom.

The Officers' Home was a large bungalow with a wide verandah and a curiously suburban-looking little garden of bushes and a few trees between it and the street. That institution partook somewhat of the character of a residential club, but with a slightly Governmental flavour about it, because it was administered by the Harbour Office. Its manager was officially styled Chief Steward. He was an unhappy, wizened little man, who if put into a jockey's rig would have looked the part to perfection. But it was obvious that at some time or other in his life, in some capacity or other, he had been connected with the sea. Possibly in the comprehensive capacity of a failure.

I should have thought his employment a very easy one, but he used to affirm for some reason or other that his job would be the death of him some day. It was rather mysterious. Perhaps everything naturally was too much trouble for him. He certainly seemed to hate having people in the house.

On entering it I thought he must be feeling pleased. It was as still as a tomb. I could see no one in the living rooms; and the verandah, too, was empty, except for a man at the far end dozing prone in a long chair. At the noise of my footsteps he opened one horribly fish-like eye. He was a stranger to me. I retreated from there, and crossing the dining room—a very bare apartment with a motionless punkah hanging over the centre table—I knocked at a door labelled in black letters: "Chief Steward."

The answer to my knock being a vexed and doleful plaint: "Oh, dear! Oh, dear! What is it now?" I went in at once.

It was a strange room to find in the tropics. Twilight and stuffiness reigned in there. The fellow had hung enormously ample, dusty, cheap lace curtains over his windows, which were shut. Piles of cardboard boxes, such as milliners and dressmakers use in Europe, cumbered the corners; and by some means he had procured for himself the sort of furniture that might have come out of a respectable parlour in the East End of London—a horsehair sofa, arm-chairs of the same. I glimpsed grimy antimacassars scattered over that horrid upholstery, which was awe-inspiring, insomuch that one could not guess what mysterious accident, need, or fancy had collected it there. Its owner had taken off his tunic, and in white trousers and a thin, short-sleeved singlet prowled behind the chair-backs nursing his meagre elbows.

An exclamation of dismay escaped him when he heard that I had come for a stay; but he could not deny that there were plenty of vacant rooms.

"Very well. Can you give me the one I had before?"

He emitted a faint moan from behind a pile of cardboard boxes on the table, which might have contained gloves or handkerchiefs or neckties. I wonder what the fellow did keep in them? There was a smell of decaying coral, or Oriental dust of zoological speciments in that den of his. I could only see the top of his head and his unhappy eyes levelled at me over the barrier.

"It's only for a couple of days," I said, intending to cheer him up.

"Perhaps you would like to pay in advance?" he suggested eagerly.

"Certainly not!" I burst out directly I could speak. "Never heard of such a thing! This is the most infernal cheek. . . ."

He had seized his head in both hands—a gesture of despair which checked my indignation.

"Oh, dear! Oh, dear! Don't fly out like this. I am asking everybody."

"I don't believe it," I said bluntly.

"Well, I am going to. And if you gentlemen all agreed to pay in advance I could make Hamilton pay up, too. He's always turning up ashore dead broke, and even when he has some money he won't settle his bills. I don't know what to do with him. He swears at me and tells me I can't chuck a white man out into the street here. So if you only would. . . ."

I was amazed. Incredulous, too. I suspected the fellow of gratuitous impertinence. I told him with marked emphasis that I would see him and Hamilton hanged first, and requested him to conduct me to my room with no more of his nonsense. He produced then a key from somewhere and led the way out of his lair, giving me a vicious sidelong look in passing.

"Any one I know staying here?" I asked him before he left my room.

He had recovered his usual pained impatient tone, and said that Captain Giles was there, back from a Solo Sea trip. Two other guests were staying also. He paused. And, of course, Hamilton, he added.

"Oh, yes! Hamilton," I said, and the miserable creature took himself off with a final groan.

His impudence still rankled when I came into the dining room at tiffin time. He was there on duty overlooking the Chinamen servants. The tiffin was laid on one end only of the long table, and the punkah was stirring the hot air lazily—mostly above a barren waste of polished wood.

We were four around the cloth. The dozing stranger from the chair was one. Both his eyes were partly opened now, but they did not seem to see anything. He was supine. The dignified person next him, with short side whiskers and a carefully scraped chin, was, of course, Hamilton. I have never seen any one so full of dignity for the station in life Providence had been pleased to place him in. I had been told that he regarded me as a rank outsider. He raised not only his eyes, but his eyebrows as well, at the sound I made pulling back my chair.

Captain Giles was at the head of the table. I exchanged a few words of greeting with him and sat down on his left. Stout and pale, with a great shiny dome of a bald forehead and prominent brown eyes, he might have been anything but a seaman. You would not have been surprised to learn that he was an architect. To me (I know how absurd it is) he looked like a churchwarden. He had the appearance of a man from whom you would expect sound advice, moral sentiments, with perhaps a platitude or two thrown in on occasion, not from a desire to dazzle, but from honest conviction.

Though very well known and appreciated in the shipping world, he had no regular employment. He did not want it. He had his own peculiar position. He was an expert. An expert in—how shall I say it?—in intricate navigation. He was supposed to know more about remote and imperfectly charted parts of the Archipelago than any man living. His brain must have been a perfect warehouse of reefs, positions, bearings, images of headlands, shapes of obscure coasts, aspects of innumerable islands, desert and otherwise. Any ship, for instance, bound on a trip to Palawan or somewhere that way would have Captain Giles on board, either in temporary command or "to assist the master." It was said that he had a retaining fee from a wealthy firm of Chinese steamship owners, in view of such services. Besides, he was always ready to relieve any man who wished to take a spell ashore for a time. No owner was ever known to object to an arrangement of that sort. For it seemed to be the established opinion at the port that Captain Giles was as good as the best, if not a little better. But in Hamilton's view he was an "outsider." I believe that for Hamilton the generalisation "outsider" covered the whole lot of us; though I suppose that he made some distinctions in his mind.

I didn't try to make conversation with Captain Giles, whom I had not seen more than twice in my life. But, of course, he knew who I was. After a while, inclining his big shiny head my way, he addressed me first in his friendly fashion. He presumed from seeing me there, he said, that I had come ashore for a couple of days' leave.

He was a low-voiced man. I spoke a little louder, saying that: No—I had left the ship for good.

"A free man for a bit," was his comment.

"I suppose I may call myself that—since eleven o'clock," I said.

Hamilton had stopped eating at the sound of our voices. He laid down his knife and fork gently, got up, and muttering something about "this infernal heat cutting one's appetite," went out of the room. Almost immediately we heard him leave the house down the verandah steps.

On this Captain Giles remarked easily that the fellow had no doubt gone off to look after my old job. The Chief Steward, who had been leaning against the wall, brought his face of an unhappy goat nearer to the table and addressed us dolefully. His object was to unburden himself of his eternal grievance against Hamilton. The man kept him in hot water with the Harbour Office as to the state of his accounts. He wished to goodness he would get my job, though in truth what would it be? Temporary relief at best.

I said: "You needn't worry. He won't get my job. My successor is on board already."

He was surprised, and I believe his face fell a little at the news. Captain Giles gave a soft laugh. We got up and went out on the verandah, leaving the supine stranger to be dealt with by the Chinamen. The last thing I saw they had put a plate with a slice of pine-apple on it before him and stood back to watch what would happen. But the experiment seemed a failure. He sat insensible.

It was imparted to me in a low voice by Captain Giles that this was an officer of some Rajah's yacht which had come into our port to be dry-docked. Must have been "seeing life" last night, he added, wrinkling his nose in an intimate, confidential way which pleased me vastly. For Captain Giles had prestige. He was credited with wonderful adventures and with some mysterious tragedy in his life. And no man had a word to say against him. He continued:

"I remember him first coming ashore here some years ago. Seems only the other day. He was a nice boy. Oh! these nice boys!"

I could not help laughing aloud. He looked startled, then joined in the laugh. "No! No! I didn't mean that," he cried. "What I meant is that some of them do go soft mighty quick out here."

Jocularly I suggested the beastly heat as the first cause. But Captain Giles disclosed himself possessed of a deeper philosophy. Things out East were made easy for white men. That was all right. The difficulty was to go on keeping white, and some of these nice boys did not know how. He gave me a searching look, and in a benevolent, heavy-uncle manner asked point blank:

"Why did you throw up your berth?"

I became angry all of a sudden; for you can understand how exasperating such a question was to a man who didn't know. I said to myself that I ought to shut up that moralist; and to him aloud I said with challenging politeness:

"Why . . . ? Do you disapprove?"

He was too disconcerted to do more than mutter confusedly: "I! . . . In a general way. . ." and then gave me up. But he retired in good order, under the cover of a heavily humorous remark that he, too, was getting soft, and that this was his time for taking his little siesta—when he was on shore. "Very bad habit. Very bad habit."

There was a simplicity in the man which would have disarmed a touchiness even more youthful than mine. So when next day at tiffin he bent his head toward me and said that he had met my late Captain last evening, adding in an undertone: "He's very sorry you left. He had never had a mate that suited him so well," I answered him earnestly, without any affectation, that I certainly hadn't been so comfortable in any ship or with any commander in all my sea-going days.

"Well—then," he murmured.

"Haven't you heard, Captain Giles, that I intend to go home?"

"Yes," he said benevolently. "I have heard that sort of thing so often before."

"What of that?" I cried. I thought he was the most dull, unimaginative man I had ever met. I don't know what more I would have said, but the much-belated Hamilton came in just then and took his usual seat. So I dropped into a mumble.

"Anyhow, you shall see it done this time."

Hamilton, beautifully shaved, gave Captain Giles a curt nod, but didn't even condescend to raise his eyebrows at me; and when he spoke it was only to tell the Chief Steward that the food on his plate wasn't fit to be set before a gentleman. The individual addressed seemed much too unhappy to groan. He cast his eyes up to the punkah and that was all.

Captain Giles and I got up from the table, and the stranger next to Hamilton followed our example, manoeuvring himself to his feet with difficulty. He, poor fellow, not because he was hungry but I verily believe only to recover his self-respect, had tried to put some of that unworthy food into his mouth. But after dropping his fork twice and generally making a failure of it, he had sat still with an air of intense mortification combined with a ghastly glazed stare. Both Giles and I had avoided looking his way at table.

On the verandah he stopped short on purpose to address to us anxiously a long remark which I failed to understand completely. It sounded like some horrible unknown language. But when Captain Giles, after only an instant for reflection, assured him with homely friendliness, "Aye, to be sure. You are right there," he appeared very much gratified indeed, and went away (pretty straight, too) to seek a distant long chair.

"What was he trying to say?" I asked with disgust.

"I don't know. Mustn't be down too much on a fellow. He's feeling pretty wretched, you may be sure; and to-morrow he'll feel worse yet."

Judging by the man's appearance it seemed impossible. I wondered what sort of complicated debauch had reduced him to that unspeakable condition. Captain Giles' benevolence was spoiled by a curious air of complacency which I disliked. I said with a little laugh:

"Well, he will have you to look after him." He made a deprecatory gesture, sat down, and took up a paper. I did the same. The papers were old and uninteresting, filled up mostly with dreary stereotyped descriptions of Queen Victoria's first jubilee celebrations. Probably we should have quickly fallen into a tropical afternoon doze if it had not been for Hamilton's voice raised in the dining room. He was finishing his tiffin there. The big double doors stood wide open permanently, and he could not have had any idea how near to the doorway our chairs were placed. He was heard in a loud, supercilious tone answering some statement ventured by the Chief Steward.

"I am not going to be rushed into anything. They will be glad enough to get a gentleman I imagine. There is no hurry."

A loud whispering from the Steward succeeded and then again Hamilton was heard with even intenser scorn.

"What? That young ass who fancies himself for having been chief mate with Kent so long? . . . Preposterous."

Giles and I looked at each other. Kent being the name of my late commander, Captain Giles' whisper, "He's talking of you," seemed to me sheer waste of breath. The Chief Steward must have stuck to his point, whatever it was, because Hamilton was heard again more supercilious if possible, and also very emphatic:

"Rubbish, my good man! One doesn't *compete* with a rank outsider like that. There's plenty of time."

Then there were pushing of chairs, footsteps in the next room, and plaintive expostulations from the Steward, who was pursuing Hamilton, even out of doors through the main entrance.

"That's a very insulting sort of man," remarked Captain Giles—superfluously, I thought. "Very insulting. You haven't offended him in some way, have you?"

"Never spoke to him in my life," I said grumpily. "Can't imagine what he means by competing. He has been trying for my job after I left—and didn't get it. But that isn't exactly competition."

Captain Giles balanced his big benevolent head thoughtfully. "He didn't get it," he repeated very slowly. "No, not likely either, with Kent. Kent is no end sorry you left him. He gives you the name of a good seaman, too."

I flung away the paper I was still holding. I sat up, I slapped the table with my open palm. I wanted to know why he would keep harping on that, my absolutely private affair. It was exasperating, really.

Captain Giles silenced me by the perfect equanimity of his gaze. "Nothing to be annoyed about," he murmured reasonably, with an evident desire to soothe the childish irritation he had aroused. And he was really a man of an appearance so inoffensive that I tried to explain myself as much as I could. I told him that I did not want to hear any more about what was past and gone. It had been very nice while it lasted, but now it was done with I preferred not to talk about it or even think about it. I had made up my mind to go home.

He listened to the whole tirade in a particular lending-the-ear attitude, as if trying to detect a false note in it somewhere; then straightened himself up and appeared to ponder sagaciously over the matter.

"Yes. You told me you meant to go home. Anything in view there?"

Instead of telling him that it was none of his business I said sullenly:

"Nothing that I know of."

I had indeed considered that rather blank side of the situation I had created for myself by leaving suddenly my very satisfactory employment. And I was not very pleased with it. I had it on the tip of my tongue to say that common sense had nothing to do with my action, and that therefore it didn't deserve the interest Captain Giles seemed to be taking in it. But he was puffing at a short wooden pipe now, and looked so guileless, dense, and commonplace, that it seemed hardly worth while to puzzle him either with truth or sarcasm.

He blew a cloud of smoke, then surprised me by a very abrupt: "Paid your passage money yet?"

Overcome by the shameless pertinacity of a man to whom it was rather difficult to be rude, I replied with exaggerated meekness that I had not done so yet. I thought there would be plenty of time to do that to-morrow.

And I was about to turn away, withdrawing my privacy from his fatuous, objectless attempts to test what sort of stuff it was made of, when he laid down his pipe in an extremely significant manner, you know, as if a critical moment had come, and leaned sideways over the table between us.

"Oh! You haven't yet!" He dropped his voice mysteriously. "Well, then I think you ought to know that there's something going on here."

I had never in my life felt more detached from all earthly goings on. Freed from the sea for a time, I preserved the sailor's consciousness of complete independence from all land affairs. How could they concern me? I gazed at Captain Giles' animation with scorn rather than with curiosity.

To his obviously preparatory question whether our Steward had spoken to me that day I said he hadn't. And what's more he would have had precious little encouragement if he had tried to. I didn't want the fellow to speak to me at all.

Unrebuked by my petulance, Captain Giles, with an air of immense sagacity, began to tell me a minute tale about a Harbour Office peon. It was absolutely pointless. A peon was seen walking that morning on the verandah with a letter in his hand. It was in an official envelope. As the habit of these fellows is, he had shown it to the first white man he came across. That man was our friend in the arm-chair. He, as I knew, was not in a state to interest himself in any sublunary matters. He could only wave the peon away. The peon then wandered on along the verandah and came upon Captain Giles, who was there by an extraordinary chance. . . .

At this point he stopped with a profound look. The letter, he continued, was addressed to the Chief Steward. Now what could Captain Ellis, the Master Attendant, want to write to the Steward for? The fellow went every morning, anyhow, to the Harbour Office with his report, for orders or what not. He hadn't been back more than an hour before there was an office peon chasing him with a note. Now what was that for?

And he began to speculate. It was not for this—and it could not be for that. As to that other thing it was unthinkable.

The fatuousness of all this made me stare. If the man had not been somehow a sympathetic personality I would have resented it like an insult. As it was, I felt only sorry for him. Something remarkably earnest in his gaze prevented me from laughing in his face. Neither did I yawn at him. I just stared.

His tone became a shade more mysterious. Directly the fellow (meaning the Steward) got that note he rushed for his hat and bolted out of the house. But it wasn't because the note called him to the Harbour Office. He didn't go there. He was not absent long enough for that. He came darting back in no time, flung his hat away, and raced about the dining room moaning and slapping his forehead. All these exciting facts and manifestations had been observed by Captain Giles. He had, it seems, been meditating upon them ever since.

I began to pity him profoundly. And in a tone which I tried to make as little sarcastic as possible I said that I was glad he had found something to occupy his morning hours.

With his disarming simplicity he made me observe, as if it were a matter of some consequence, how strange it was that he should have spent the morning indoors at all. He generally was out before tiffin, visiting various offices, seeing his friends in the harbour, and so on. He had felt out of sorts somewhat on rising. Nothing much. Just enough to make him feel lazy.

All this with a sustained, holding stare which, in conjunction with the general inanity of the discourse, conveyed the impression of mild, dreary lunacy. And when he hitched his chair a little and dropped his voice to the low note of mystery, it flashed upon me that high professional reputation was not necessarily a guarantee of sound mind.

It never occurred to me then that I didn't know in what soundness of mind exactly consisted and what a delicate and, upon the whole, unimportant matter it was. With some idea of not hurting his feelings I blinked at him in an interested manner. But when he proceeded to ask me mysteriously whether I remembered what had passed just now between that Steward of ours and "that man Hamilton," I only grunted sourly assent and turned away my head.

"Aye. But do you remember every word?" he insisted tactfully.

"I don't know. It's none of my business," I snapped out, consigning, moreover, the Steward and Hamilton aloud to eternal perdition.

I meant to be very energetic and final, but Captain Giles continued to gaze at me thoughtfully. Nothing could stop him. He went on to point out that my personality was involved in that conversation. When I tried to preserve the semblance of unconcern he became positively cruel. I heard what the man had said? Yes? What did I think of it then?—he wanted to know.

Captain Giles' appearance excluding the suspicion of mere sly malice, I came to the conclusion that he was simply the most tactless idiot on earth. I almost despised myself for the weakness of attempting to enlighten his common understanding. I started to explain that I did not think anything whatever. Hamilton was not worth a thought. What such an offensive loafer . . . "Aye! that he is," interjected Captain Giles . . . thought or said was below any decent man's contempt, and I did not propose to take the slightest notice of it.

This attitude seemed to me so simple and obvious that I was really astonished at Giles giving no sign of assent. Such perfect stupidity was almost interesting.

"What would you like me to do?" I asked, laughing. "I can't start a row with him because of the opinion he has formed of me. Of course, I've heard of the contemptuous way he alludes to me. But he doesn't intrude his contempt on my notice. He has never expressed it in my hearing. For even just now he didn't know we could hear him. I should only make myself ridiculous."

That hopeless Giles went on puffing at his pipe moodily. All at once his face cleared, and he spoke.

"You missed my point."

"Have I? I am very glad to hear it," I said.

With increasing animation he stated again that I had missed his point. Entirely. And in a tone of growing self-conscious complacency he told me that few things escaped his attention, and he was rather used to think them out, and generally from his experience of life and men arrived at the right conclusion.

This bit of self-praise, of course, fitted excellently the laborious inanity of the whole conversation. The whole thing strengthened in me that obscure feeling of life being but a waste of days, which, half-unconsciously, had driven me out of a comfortable berth, away from men I liked, to flee from the menace of emptiness . . . and to find inanity at the first turn. Here was a man of recognized character and achievement disclosed as an absurd and dreary chatterer. And it was probably like this everywhere—from east to west, from the bottom to the top of the social scale.

A great discouragement fell on me. A spiritual drowsiness. Giles' voice was going on complacently; the very voice of the universal hollow conceit. And I was no longer angry with it. There was nothing original, nothing new, startling, informing, to expect from the world; no opportunities to find out something about oneself, no wisdom to acquire, no fun to enjoy. Everything was stupid and overrated, even as Captain Giles was. So be it.

The name of Hamilton suddenly caught my ear and roused me up.

"I thought we had done with him," I said, with the greatest possible distaste.

"Yes. But considering what we happened to hear just now I think you ought to do it."

"Ought to do it?" I sat up bewildered. "Do what?"

Captain Giles confronted me very much surprised.

"Why! Do what I have been advising you to try. You go and ask the Steward what was there in that letter from the Harbour Office. Ask him straight out."

I remained speechless for a time. Here was something unexpected and original enough to be altogether incomprehensible. I murmured, astounded:

"But I thought it was Hamilton that you . . ."

"Exactly. Don't you let him. You do what I tell you. You tackle that Steward. You'll make him jump, I bet," insisted Captain Giles, waving his smouldering pipe impressively at me. Then he took three rapid puffs at it.

His aspect of triumphant acuteness was indescribable. Yet the man remained a strangely sympathetic creature. Benevolence radiated from him ridiculously, mildly, impressively. It was irritating, too. But I pointed out coldly, as one who deals with the incomprehensible, that I didn't see any reason to expose myself to a snub from the fellow. He was a very unsatisfactory steward and a miserable wretch besides, but I would just as soon think of tweaking his nose.

"Tweaking his nose," said Captain Giles in a scandalized tone. "Much use it would be to you."

That remark was so irrelevant that one could make no answer to it. But the sense of the absurdity was beginning at last to exercise its well-known fascination. I felt I must not let the man talk to me any more. I got up, observing curtly that he was too much for me—that I couldn't make him out.

Before I had time to move away he spoke again in a changed tone of obstinacy and puffing nervously at his pipe.

"Well—he's a—no account cuss—anyhow. You just—ask him. That's all."

That new manner impressed me—or rather made me pause. But sanity asserting its sway at once I left the verandah after giving him a mirthless smile. In a few strides I found myself in the dining room, now cleared and empty. But during that short time various thoughts occurred to me, such as: that Giles had been making fun of me, expecting some amusement at my expense; that I probably looked silly and gullible; that I knew very little of life. . . .

The door facing me across the dining room flew open to my extreme surprise. It was the door inscribed with the word "Steward" and the man himself ran out of his stuffy, Philistinish lair in his absurd, hunted-animal manner, making for the garden door.

To this day I don't know what made me call after him. "I say! Wait a minute." Perhaps it was the sidelong glance he gave me; or possibly I was yet under the influence of Captain Giles' mysterious earnestness. Well, it was an impulse of some sort; an effect of that force somewhere within our lives which shapes them this way or that. For if these words had not escaped from my lips (my will had nothing to do with that) my existence would, to be sure, have been still a seaman's existence, but directed on now to me utterly inconceivable lines.

No. My will had nothing to do with it. Indeed, no sooner had I made that fateful noise than I became extremely sorry for it. Had the man stopped and faced me I would have had to retire in disorder. For I had no notion to carry out Captain Giles' idiotic joke, either at my own expense or at the expense of the Steward.

But here the old human instinct of the chase came into play. He pretended to be deaf, and I, without thinking a second about it, dashed along my own side of the dining table and cut him off at the very door.

"Why can't you answer when you are spoken to?" I asked roughly.

He leaned against the lintel of the door. He looked extremely wretched. Human nature is, I fear, not very nice right through. There are ugly spots in it. I found myself growing angry, and that, I believe, only because my quarry looked so woe-begone. Miserable beggar!

I went for him without more ado. "I understand there was an official communication to the Home from the Harbour Office this morning. Is that so?"

Instead of telling me to mind my own business, as he might have done, he began to whine with an undertone of impudence. He couldn't see me anywhere this morning. He couldn't be expected to run all over the town after me.

"Who wants you to?" I cried. And then my eyes became opened to the inwardness of things and speeches the triviality of which had been so baffling and tiresome.

I told him I wanted to know what was in that letter. My sternness of tone and behaviour was only half assumed. Curiosity can be a very fierce sentiment—at times.

He took refuge in a silly, muttering sulkiness. It was nothing to me, he mumbled. I had told him I was going home. And since I was going home he didn't see why he should. . . .

That was the line of his argument, and it was irrelevant enough to be almost insulting. Insulting to one's intelligence, I mean.

In that twilight region between youth and maturity, in which I had my being then, one is peculiarly sensitive to that kind of insult. I am afraid my behaviour to the Steward became very rough indeed. But it wasn't in him to face out anything or anybody. Drug habit or solitary tippling, perhaps. And when I forgot myself so far as to swear at him he broke down and began to shriek.

I don't mean to say that he made a great outcry. It was a cynical shrieking confession, only faint—piteously faint. It wasn't very coherent either, but sufficiently so to strike me dumb at first. I turned my eyes from him in righteous indignation, and perceived Captain Giles in the verandah doorway surveying quietly the scene, his own handiwork, if I may express it in that way. His smouldering black pipe was very noticeable in his big, paternal fist. So, too, was the glitter of his heavy gold watch-chain across the breast of his white tunic. He exhaled an atmosphere of virtuous sagacity serene enough for any innocent soul to fly to confidently. I flew to him.

"You would never believe it," I cried. "It was a notification that a master is wanted for some ship. There's a command apparently going about and this fellow puts the thing in his pocket."

The Steward screamed out in accents of loud despair: "You will be the death of me!"

The mighty slap he gave his wretched forehead was very loud, too. But when I turned to look at him he was no longer there. He had rushed away somewhere out of sight. This sudden disappearance made me laugh.

This was the end of the incident—for me. Captain Giles, however, staring at the place where the Steward had been, began to haul at his gorgeous gold chain till at last the watch came up from the deep pocket like solid truth from a well. Solemnly he lowered it down again and only then said:

"Just three o'clock. You will be in time—if you don't lose any, that is."

"In time for what?" I asked.

"Good Lord! For the Harbour Office. This must be looked into."

Strictly speaking, he was right. But I've never had much taste for investigation, for showing people up and all that no doubt ethically meritorious kind of work. And my view of the episode was purely ethical. If any one had to be the death of the Steward I didn't see why it shouldn't be Captain Giles himself, a man of age and standing, and a permanent resident. Whereas, I in comparison, felt myself a mere bird of passage in that port. In fact, it might have been said that I had already broken off my connection. I muttered that I didn't think—it was nothing to me. . . .

"Nothing!" repeated Captain Giles, giving some signs of quiet, deliberate indignation. "Kent warned me you were a peculiar young fellow. You will tell me next that a command is nothing to you—and after all the trouble I've taken, too!"

"The trouble!" I murmured, uncomprehending. What trouble? All I could remember was being mystified and bored by his conversation for a solid hour after tiffin. And he called that taking a lot of trouble.

He was looking at me with a self-complacency which would have been odious in any other man. All at once, as if a page of a book had been turned over disclosing a word which made plain all that had gone before, I perceived that this matter had also another than an ethical aspect.

And still I did not move. Captain Giles lost his patience a little. With an angry puff at his pipe he turned his back on my hesitation.

But it was not hesitation on my part. I had been, if I may express myself so, put out of gear mentally. But as soon as I had convinced myself that this stale, unprofitable world of my discontent contained such a thing as a command to be seized, I recovered my powers of locomotion.

It's a good step from the Officers' Home to the Harbour Office; but with the magic word "Command" in my head I found myself suddenly on the quay as if transported there in the twinkling of an eye, before a portal of dressed white stone above a flight of shallow white steps.

All this seemed to glide toward me swiftly. The whole great roadstead to the right was just a mere flicker of blue, and the dim cool hall swallowed me up out of the heat and glare of which I had not been aware till the very moment I passed in from it.

The broad inner staircase insinuated itself under my feet somehow. Command is a strong magic. The first human beings I perceived distinctly since I had parted with the indignant back of Captain Giles were the crew of the harbour steam-launch lounging on the spacious landing about the curtained archway of the shipping office.

It was there that my buoyancy abandoned me. The atmosphere of officialdom would kill anything that breathes the air of human endeavour, would extinguish hope and fear alike in the supremacy of paper and ink. I passed heavily under the curtain which the Malay coxswain of the harbour launch raised for me. There was nobody in the office except the clerks, writing in two industrious rows. But the head Shipping-Master hopped down from his elevation and hurried along on the thick mats to meet me in the broad central passage.

He had a Scottish name, but his complexion was of a rich olive hue, his short beard was jet black, and his eyes, also black, had a languishing expression. He asked confidentially:

"You want to see Him?"

All lightness of spirit and body having departed from me at the touch of officialdom, I looked at the scribe without animation and asked in my turn wearily:

"What do you think? Is it any use?"

"My goodness! He has asked for you twice today."

This emphatic He was the supreme authority, the Marine Superintendent, the Harbour-Master—a very great person in the eyes of every single quill-driver in the room. But that was nothing to the opinion he had of his own greatness.

Captain Ellis looked upon himself as a sort of divine (pagan) emanation, the deputy-Neptune for the circumambient seas. If he did not actually rule the waves, he pretended to rule the fate of the mortals whose lives were cast upon the waters.

This uplifting illusion made him inquisitorial and peremptory. And as his temperament was choleric there were fellows who were actually afraid of him. He was redoubtable, not in virtue of his office, but because of his unwarrantable assumptions. I had never had anything to do with him before.

I said: "Oh! He has asked for me twice. Then perhaps I had better go in."

"You must! You must!"

The Shipping-Master led the way with a mincing gait around the whole system of desks to a tall and important-looking door, which he opened with a deferential action of the arm.

He stepped right in (but without letting go of the handle) and, after gazing reverently down the room for a while, beckoned me in by a silent jerk of the head. Then he slipped out at once and shut the door after me most delicately.

Three lofty windows gave on the harbour. There was nothing in them but the dark-blue sparkling sea and the paler luminous blue of the sky. My eye caught in the depths and distances of these blue tones the white speck of some big ship just arrived and about to anchor in the outer roadstead. A ship from home—after perhaps ninety days at sea. There is something touching about a ship coming in from sea and folding her white wings for a rest.

The next thing I saw was the top-knot of silver hair surmounting Captain Ellis' smooth red face, which would have been apoplectic if it hadn't had such a fresh appearance.

Our deputy-Neptune had no beard on his chin, and there was no trident to be seen standing in a corner anywhere, like an umbrella. But his hand was holding a pen—the official pen, far mightier than the sword in making or marring the fortune of simple toiling men. He was looking over his shoulder at my advance.

When I had come well within range he saluted me by a nerve-shattering: "Where have you been all this time?"

As it was no concern of his I did not take the slightest notice of the shot. I said simply that I had heard there was a master needed for some vessel, and being a sailing-ship man I thought I would apply. . . .

He interrupted me. "Why! Hang it! *You* are the right man for that job—if there had been twenty others after it. But no fear of that. They are all afraid to catch hold. That's what's the matter."

He was very irritated. I said innocently: "Are they, sir. I wonder why?"

"Why!" he fumed. "Afraid of the sails. Afraid of a white crew. Too much trouble. Too much work. Too long out here. Easy life and deck-chairs more their mark. Here I sit with the Consul-General's cable before me, and the only man fit for the job not to be found anywhere. I began to think you were funking it, too. . . ."

"I haven't been long getting to the office," I remarked calmly.

"You have a good name out here, though," he growled savagely without looking at me.

"I am very glad to hear it from you, sir," I said.

"Yes. But you are not on the spot when you are wanted. You know you weren't. That steward of yours wouldn't dare to neglect a message from this office. Where the devil did you hide yourself for the best part of the day?"

I only smiled kindly down on him, and he seemed to recollect himself, and asked me to take a seat. He explained that the master of a British ship having died in Bangkok the Consul-General had cabled to him a request for a competent man to be sent out to take command.

Apparently, in his mind, I was the man from the first, though for the looks of the thing the notification addressed to the Sailors' Home was general. An agreement had already been prepared. He gave it to me to read, and when I handed it back to him with the remark that I accepted its terms, the deputy-Neptune signed it, stamped it with his own exalted hand, folded it in four (it was a sheet of blue foolscap) and presented it to me—a gift of extraordinary potency, for, as I put it in my pocket, my head swam a little.

"This is your appointment to the command," he said with a certain gravity. "An official appointment binding the owners to conditions which you have accepted. Now—when will you be ready to go?"

I said I would be ready that very day if necessary. He caught me at my word with great alacrity. The steamer Melita was leaving for Bangkok that evening about seven. He would request her captain officially to give me a passage and wait for me till ten o'clock.

Then he rose from his office chair, and I got up, too. My head swam, there was no doubt about it, and I felt a certain heaviness of limbs as if they had grown bigger since I had sat down on that chair. I made my bow.

A subtle change in Captain Ellis' manner became perceptible as though he had laid aside the trident of deputy-Neptune. In reality, it was only his official pen that he had dropped on getting up.

2

He shook hands with me: "Well, there you are, on your own, appointed officially under my responsibility."

He was actually walking with me to the door. What a distance off it seemed! I moved like a man in bonds. But we reached it at last. I opened it with the sensation of dealing with mere dream-stuff, and then at the last moment the fellowship of seamen asserted itself, stronger than the difference of age and station. It asserted itself in Captain Ellis' voice.

"Good-bye—and good luck to you," he said so heartily that I could only give him a grateful glance. Then I turned and went out, never to see him again in my life. I had not made three steps into the outer office when I heard behind my back a gruff, loud, authoritative voice, the voice of our deputy-Neptune.

It was addressing the head Shipping-Master who, having let me in, had, apparently, remained hovering in the middle distance ever since. "Mr. R., let the harbour launch have steam up to take the captain here on board the Melita at half-past nine to-night."

I was amazed at the startled alacrity of R's "Yes, sir." He ran before me out on the landing. My new dignity sat yet so lightly on me that I was not aware that it was I, the Captain, the object of this last graciousness. It seemed as if all of a sudden a pair of wings had grown on my shoulders. I merely skimmed along the polished floor.

But R. was impressed.

"I say!" he exclaimed on the landing, while the Malay crew of the steam-launch standing by looked stonily at the man for whom they were going to be kept on duty so late, away from their gambling, from their girls, or their pure domestic joys. "I say! His own launch. What have you done to him?"

His stare was full of respectful curiosity. I was quite confounded.

"Was it for me? I hadn't the slightest notion," I stammered out.

He nodded many times. "Yes. And the last person who had it before you was a Duke. So, there!"

I think he expected me to faint on the spot. But I was in too much of a hurry for emotional displays. My feelings were already in such a whirl that this staggering information did not seem to make the slightest difference. It merely fell into the seething cauldron of my brain, and I carried it off with me after a short but effusive passage of leave-taking with R.

The favour of the great throws an aureole round the fortunate object of its selection. That excellent man enquired whether he could do anything for me. He had known me only by sight, and he was well aware he would never see me again; I was, in common with the other seamen of the port, merely a subject for official writing, filling up of forms with all the artificial superiority of a man of pen and ink to the men who grapple with realities outside the consecrated walls of official buildings. What ghosts we must have been to him! Mere symbols to juggle with in books and heavy registers, without brains and muscles and perplexities; something hardly useful and decidedly inferior.

And he—the office hours being over—wanted to know if he could be of any use to me!

I ought—properly speaking—I ought to have been moved to tears. But I did not even think of it. It was merely another miraculous manifestation of that day of miracles. I parted from him as if he were a mere symbol. I floated down the staircase. I floated out of the official and imposing portal. I went on floating along.

I use that word rather than the word "flew," because I have a distinct impression that, though uplifted by my aroused youth, my movements were deliberate enough. To that mixed white, brown, and yellow portion of mankind, out abroad on their own affairs, I presented the appearance of a man walking rather sedately. And nothing in the way of abstraction could have equalled my deep detachment from the forms and colours of this world. It was, as it were, final.

And yet, suddenly, I recognized Hamilton. I recognized him without effort, without a shock, without a start. There he was, strolling toward the Harbour Office with his stiff, arrogant dignity. His red face made him noticeable at a distance. It flamed, over there, on the shady side of the street.

He had perceived me, too. Something (unconscious exuberance of spirits perhaps) moved me to wave my hand to him elaborately. This lapse from good taste happened before I was aware that I was capable of it.

The impact of my impudence stopped him short, much as a bullet might have done. I verily believe he staggered, though as far as I could see he didn't actually fall. I had gone past in a moment and did not turn my head. I had forgotten his existence.

The next ten minutes might have been ten seconds or ten centuries for all my consciousness had to do with it. People might have been falling dead around me, houses crumbling, guns firing, I wouldn't have known. I was thinking: "By Jove! I have got it." *It* being the command. It had come about in a way utterly unforeseen in my modest day-dreams.

I perceived that my imagination had been running in conventional channels and that my hopes had always been drab stuff. I had envisaged a command as a result of a slow course of promotion in the employ of some highly respectable firm. The reward of faithful service. Well, faithful service was all right. One would naturally give that for one's own sake, for the sake of the ship, for the love of the life of one's choice; not for the sake of the reward.

There is something distasteful in the notion of a reward.

And now here I had my command, absolutely in my pocket, in a way undeniable indeed, but most unexpected; beyond my imaginings, outside all reasonable expectations, and even notwithstanding the existence of some sort of obscure intrigue to keep it away from me. It is true that the intrigue was feeble, but it helped the feeling of wonder—as if I had been specially destined for that ship I did not know, by some power higher than the prosaic agencies of the commercial world.

A strange sense of exultation began to creep into me. If I had worked for that command ten years or more there would have been nothing of the kind. I was a little frightened.

"Let us be calm," I said to myself.

Outside the door of the Officers' Home the wretched Steward seemed to be waiting for me. There was a broad flight of a few steps, and he ran to and fro on the top of it as if chained there. A distressed cur. He looked as though his throat were too dry for him to bark.

I regret to say I stopped before going in. There had been a revolution in my moral nature. He waited open-mouthed, breathless, while I looked at him for half a minute.

"And you thought you could keep me out of it," I said scathingly.

"You said you were going home," he squeaked miserably. "You said so. You said so."

"I wonder what Captain Ellis will have to say to that excuse," I uttered slowly with a sinister meaning.

His lower jaw had been trembling all the time and his voice was like the bleating of a sick goat. "You have given me away? You have done for me?"

Neither his distress nor yet the sheer absurdity of it was able to disarm me. It was the first instance of harm being attempted to be done to me—at any rate, the first I had ever found out. And I was still young enough, still too much on this side of the shadow line, not to be surprised and indignant at such things.

I gazed at him inflexibly. Let the beggar suffer. He slapped his forehead and I passed in, pursued, into the dining room, by his screech: "I always said you'd be the death of me."

This clamour not only overtook me, but went ahead as it were on to the verandah and brought out Captain Giles.

He stood before me in the doorway in all the commonplace solidity of his wisdom. The gold chain glittered on his breast. He clutched a smouldering pipe.

I extended my hand to him warmly and he seemed surprised, but did respond heartily enough in the end, with a faint smile of superior knowledge which cut my thanks short as if with a knife. I don't think that more than one word came out. And even for that one, judging by the temperature of my face, I had blushed as if for a bad action. Assuming a detached tone, I wondered how on earth he had managed to spot the little underhand game that had been going on.

He murmured complacently that there were but few things done in the town that he could not see the inside of. And as to this house, he had been using it off and on for nearly ten years. Nothing that went on in it could escape his great experience. It had been no trouble to him. No trouble at all.

Then in his quiet, thick tone he wanted to know if I had complained formally of the Steward's action.

I said that I hadn't—though, indeed, it was not for want of opportunity. Captain Ellis had gone for me bald-headed in a most ridiculous fashion for being out of the way when wanted.

"Funny old gentleman," interjected Captain Giles. "What did you say to that?"

"I said simply that I came along the very moment I heard of his message. Nothing more. I didn't want to hurt the Steward. I would scorn to harm such an object. No. I made no complaint, but I believe he thinks I've done so. Let him think. He's got a fright he won't forget in a hurry, for Captain Ellis would kick him out into the middle of Asia. . . ."

"Wait a moment," said Captain Giles, leaving me suddenly. I sat down feeling very tired, mostly in my head. Before I could start a train of thought he stood again before me, murmuring the excuse that he had to go and put the fellow's mind at ease.

I looked up with surprise. But in reality I was indifferent. He explained that he had found the Steward lying face downward on the horsehair sofa. He was all right now.

"He would not have died of fright," I said contemptuously.

"No. But he might have taken an overdose out of one of them little bottles he keeps in his room," Captain Giles argued seriously. "The confounded fool has tried to poison himself once—a few years ago."

"Really," I said without emotion. "He doesn't seem very fit to live, anyhow."

"As to that, it may be said of a good many."

"Don't exaggerate like this!" I protested, laughing irritably. "But I wonder what this part of the world would do if you were to leave off looking after it, Captain Giles? Here you have got me a command and saved the Steward's life in one afternoon. Though why you should have taken all that interest in either of us is more than I can understand."

Captain Giles remained silent for a minute. Then gravely:

"He's not a bad steward really. He can find a good cook, at any rate. And, what's more, he can keep him when found. I remember the cooks we had here before his time! . . ."

I must have made a movement of impatience, because he interrupted himself with an apology for keeping me yarning there, while no doubt I needed all my time to get ready.

What I really needed was to be alone for a bit. I seized this opening hastily. My bedroom was a quiet refuge in an apparently uninhabited wing of the building. Having absolutely nothing to do (for I had not unpacked my things), I sat down on the bed and abandoned myself to the influences of the hour. To the unexpected influences. . . .

And first I wondered at my state of mind. Why was I not more surprised? Why? Here I was, invested with a command in the twinkling of an eye, not in the common course of human affairs, but more as if by enchantment. I ought to have been lost in astonishment. But I wasn't. I was very much like people in fairy tales. Nothing ever astonishes them. When a fully appointed gala coach is produced out of a pumpkin to take her to a ball, Cinderella does not exclaim. She gets in quietly and drives away to her high fortune.

Captain Ellis (a fierce sort of fairy) had produced a command out of a drawer almost as unexpectedly as in a fairy tale. But a command is an abstract idea, and it seemed a sort of "lesser marvel" till it flashed upon me that it involved the concrete existence of a ship.

A ship! My ship! She was mine, more absolutely mine for possession and care than anything in the world; an object of responsibility and devotion. She was there waiting for me, spell-bound, unable to move, to live, to get out into the world (till I came), like an enchanted princess. Her call had come to me as if from the clouds. I had never suspected her existence. I didn't know how she looked, I had barely heard her name, and yet we were indissolubly united for a certain portion of our future, to sink or swim together!

A sudden passion of anxious impatience rushed through my veins, gave me such a sense of the intensity of existence as I have never felt before or since. I discovered how much of a seaman I was, in heart, in mind, and, as it were, physically—a man exclusively of sea and ships; the sea the only world that counted, and the ships, the test of manliness, of temperament, of courage and fidelity—and of love.

I had an exquisite moment. It was unique also. Jumping up from my seat, I paced up and down my room for a long time. But when I came downstairs I behaved with sufficient composure. Only I couldn't eat anything at dinner.

Having declared my intention not to drive but to walk down to the quay, I must render the wretched Steward justice that he bestirred himself to find me some coolies for the luggage. They departed, carrying all my worldly possessions (except a little money I had in my pocket) slung from a long pole. Captain Giles volunteered to walk down with me.

We followed the sombre, shaded alley across the Esplanade. It was moderately cool there under the trees. Captain Giles remarked, with a sudden laugh: "I know who's jolly thankful at having seen the last of you."

I guessed that he meant the Steward. The fellow had borne himself to me in a sulkily frightened manner at the last. I expressed my wonder that he should have tried to do me a bad turn for no reason at all.

"Don't you see that what he wanted was to get rid of our friend Hamilton by dodging him in front of you for that job? That would have removed him for good. See?"

"Heavens!" I exclaimed, feeling humiliated somehow. "Can it be possible? What a fool he must be! That overbearing, impudent loafer! Why! He couldn't. . . . And yet he's nearly done it, I believe; for the Harbour Office was bound to send somebody."

"Aye. A fool like our Steward can be dangerous sometimes," declared Captain Giles sententiously. "Just because he is a fool," he added, imparting further instruction in his complacent low tones. "For," he continued in the manner of a set demonstration, "no sensible person would risk being kicked out of the only berth between himself and starvation just to get rid of a simple annoyance—a small worry. Would he now?"

"Well, no," I conceded, restraining a desire to laugh at that something mysteriously earnest in delivering the conclusions of his wisdom as though it were the product of prohibited operations. "But that fellow looks as if he were rather crazy. He must be."

"As to that, I believe everybody in the world is a little mad," he announced quietly.

"You make no exceptions?" I inquired, just to hear his manner.

"Why! Kent says that even of you."

"Does he?" I retorted, extremely embittered all at once against my former captain. "There's nothing of that in the written character from him which I've got in my pocket. Has he given you any instances of my lunacy?"

Captain Giles explained in a conciliating tone that it had been only a friendly remark in reference to my abrupt leaving the ship for no apparent reason.

I muttered grumpily: "Oh! leaving his ship," and mended my pace. He kept up by my side in the deep gloom of the avenue as if it were his conscientious duty to see me out of the colony as an undesirable character. He panted a little, which was rather pathetic in a way. But I was not moved. On the contrary. His discomfort gave me a sort of malicious pleasure.

Presently I relented, slowed down, and said:

"What I really wanted was to get a fresh grip. I felt it was time. Is that so very mad?"

He made no answer. We were issuing from the avenue. On the bridge over the canal a dark, irresolute figure seemed to be awaiting something or somebody.

It was a Malay policeman, barefooted, in his blue uniform. The silver band on his little round cap shone dimly in the light of the street lamp. He peered in our direction timidly.

Before we could come up to him he turned about and walked in front of us in the direction of the jetty. The distance was some hundred yards; and then I found my coolies squatting on their heels. They had kept the pole on their shoulders, and all my worldly goods, still tied to the pole, were resting on the ground between them. As far as the eye could reach along the quay there was not another soul abroad except the police peon, who saluted us.

It seems he had detained the coolies as suspicious characters, and had forbidden them the jetty. But at a sign from me he took off the embargo with alacrity. The two patient fellows, rising together with a faint grunt, trotted off along the planks, and I prepared to take my leave of Captain Giles, who stood there with an air as though his mission were drawing to a close. It could not be denied that he had done it all. And while I hesitated about an appropriate sentence he made himself heard:

"I expect you'll have your hands pretty full of tangled-up business."

I asked him what made him think so; and he answered that it was his general experience of the world. Ship a long time away from her port, owners inaccessible by cable, and the only man who could explain matters dead and buried.

"And you yourself new to the business in a way," he concluded in a sort of unanswerable tone.

"Don't insist," I said. "I know it only too well. I only wish you could impart to me some small portion of your experience before I go. As it can't be done in ten minutes I had better not begin to ask you. There's that harbour launch waiting for me, too. But I won't feel really at peace till I have that ship of mine out in the Indian Ocean."

He remarked casually that from Bangkok to the Indian Ocean was a pretty long step. And this murmur, like a dim flash from a dark lantern, showed me for a moment the broad belt of islands and reefs between that unknown ship, which was mine, and the freedom of the great waters of the globe.

But I felt no apprehension. I was familiar enough with the Archipelago by that time. Extreme patience and extreme care would see me through the region of broken land, of faint airs, and of dead water to where I would feel at last my command swing on the great swell and list over to the great breath of regular winds, that would give her the feeling of a large, more intense life. The road would be long. All roads are long that lead toward one's heart's desire. But this road my mind's eye could see on a chart, professionally, with all its complications and difficulties, yet simple enough in a way. One is a seaman or one is not. And I had no doubt of being one.

The only part I was a stranger to was the Gulf of Siam. And I mentioned this to Captain Giles. Not that I was concerned very much. It belonged to the same region the nature of which I knew, into whose very soul I seemed to have looked during the last months of that existence with which I had broken now, suddenly, as one parts with some enchanting company.

"The gulf . . . Ay! A funny piece of water—that," said Captain Giles.

Funny, in this connection, was a vague word. The whole thing sounded like an opinion uttered by a cautious person mindful of actions for slander.

I didn't inquire as to the nature of that funniness. There was really no time. But at the very last he volunteered a warning.

"Whatever you do keep to the east side of it. The west side is dangerous at this time of the year. Don't let anything tempt you over. You'll find nothing but trouble there."

Though I could hardly imagine what could tempt me to involve my ship amongst the currents and reefs of the Malay shore, I thanked him for the advice.

He gripped my extended arm warmly, and the end of our acquaintance came suddenly in the words: "Good-night."

That was all he said: "Good-night." Nothing more. I don't know what I intended to say, but surprise made me swallow it, whatever it was. I choked slightly, and then exclaimed with a sort of nervous haste: "Oh! Good-night, Captain Giles, good-night."

His movements were always deliberate, but his back had receded some distance along the deserted quay before I collected myself enough to follow his example and made a half turn in the direction of the jetty.

Only my movements were not deliberate. I hurried down to the steps, and leaped into the launch. Before I had fairly landed in her sternsheets the slim little craft darted away from the jetty with a sudden swirl of her propeller and the hard, rapid puffing of the exhaust in her vaguely gleaming brass funnel amidships.

The misty churning at her stern was the only sound in the world. The shore lay plunged in the silence of the deeper slumber. I watched the town recede still and soundless in the hot night, till the abrupt hail, "Steam-launch, ahoy!" made me spin round face forward. We were close to a white ghostly steamer. Lights shone on her decks, in her portholes. And the same voice shouted from her:

"Is that our passenger?"

"It is," I yelled.

Her crew had been obviously on the jump. I could hear them running about. The modern spirit of haste was loudly vocal in the orders to "Heave away on the cable"—to "Lower the sideladder," and in urgent requests to me to "Come along, sir! We have been delayed three hours for you. . . . Our time is seven o'clock, you know!"

I stepped on the deck. I said "No! I don't know." The spirit of modern hurry was embodied in a thin, long-armed, long-legged man, with a closely clipped gray beard. His meagre hand was hot and dry. He declared feverishly:

"I am hanged if I would have waited another five minutes Harbour-Master or no Harbour-Master."

"That's your own business," I said. "I didn't ask you to wait for me."

"I hope you don't expect any supper," he burst out. "This isn't a boarding-house afloat. You are the first passenger I ever had in my life and I hope to goodness you will be the last."

I made no answer to this hospitable communication; and, indeed, he didn't wait for any, bolting away on to his bridge to get his ship under way.

The three days he had me on board he did not depart from that half-hostile attitude. His ship having been delayed three hours on my account he couldn't forgive me for not being a more distinguished person. He was not exactly outspoken about it, but that feeling of annoyed wonder was peeping out perpetually in his talk.

He was absurd.

He was also a man of much experience, which he liked to trot out; but no greater contrast with Captain Giles could have been imagined. He would have amused me if I had wanted to be amused. But I did not want to be amused. I was like a lover looking forward to a meeting. Human hostility was nothing to me. I thought of my unknown ship. It was amusement enough, torment enough, occupation enough.

He perceived my state, for his wits were sufficiently sharp for that, and he poked sly fun at my preoccupation in the manner some nasty, cynical old men assume toward the dreams and illusions of youth. I, on my side, refrained from questioning him as to the appearance of my ship, though I knew that being in Bangkok every fortnight or so he must have known her by sight. I was not going to expose the ship, my ship! to some slighting reference.

He was the first really unsympathetic man I had ever come in contact with. My education was far from being finished, though I didn't know it. No! I didn't know it.

All I knew was that he disliked me and had some contempt for my person. Why? Apparently because his ship had been delayed three hours on my account. Who was I to have such a thing done for me? Such a thing had never been done for him. It was a sort of jealous indignation.

My expectation, mingled with fear, was wrought to its highest pitch. How slow had been the days of the passage and how soon they were over. One morning, early, we crossed the bar, and while the sun was rising splendidly over the flat spaces of the land we steamed up the innumerable bends, passed under the shadow of the great gilt pagoda, and reached the outskirts of the town.

There it was, spread largely on both banks, the Oriental capital which had as yet suffered no white conqueror; an expanse of brown houses of bamboo, of mats, of leaves, of a vegetable-matter style of architecture, sprung out of the brown soil on the banks of the muddy river. It was amazing to think that in those miles of human habitations there was not probably half a dozen pounds of nails. Some of those houses of sticks and grass, like the nests of an aquatic race, clung to the low shores. Others seemed to grow out of the water; others again floated in long anchored rows in the very middle of the stream. Here and there in the distance, above the crowded mob of low, brown roof ridges, towered great piles of masonry, King's Palace, temples, gorgeous and dilapidated, crumbling under the vertical sunlight, tremendous, overpowering, almost palpable, which seemed to enter one's breast with the breath of one's nostrils and soak into one's limbs through every pore of one's skin.

The ridiculous victim of jealousy had for some reason or other to stop his engines just then. The steamer drifted slowly up with the tide. Oblivious of my new surroundings I walked the deck, in anxious, deadened abstraction, a commingling of romantic reverie with a very practical survey of my qualifications. For the time was approaching for me to behold my command and to prove my worth in the ultimate test of my profession.

Suddenly I heard myself called by that imbecile. He was beckoning me to come up on his bridge.

I didn't care very much for that, but as it seemed that he had something particular to say I went up the ladder.

He laid his hand on my shoulder and gave me a slight turn, pointing with his other arm at the same time.

"There! That's your ship, Captain," he said.

I felt a thump in my breast—only one, as if my heart had then ceased to beat. There were ten or more ships moored along the bank, and the one he meant was partly hidden away from my sight by her next astern. He said: "We'll drift abreast her in a moment."

What was his tone? Mocking? Threatening? Or only indifferent? I could not tell. I suspected some malice in this unexpected manifestation of interest.

He left me, and I leaned over the rail of the bridge looking over the side. I dared not raise my eyes. Yet it had to be done—and, indeed, I could not have helped myself. I believe I trembled.

But directly my eyes had rested on my ship all my fear vanished. It went off swiftly, like a bad dream. Only that a dream leaves no shame behind it, and that I felt a momentary shame at my unworthy suspicions.

Yes, there she was. Her hull, her rigging filled my eye with a great content. That feeling of life-emptiness which had made me so restless for the last few months lost its bitter plausibility, its evil influence, dissolved in a flow of joyous emotion.

At first glance I saw that she was a high-class vessel, a harmonious creature in the lines of her fine body, in the proportioned tallness of her spars. Whatever her age and her history, she had preserved the stamp of her origin. She was one of those craft that, in virtue of their design and complete finish, will never look old. Amongst her companions moored to the bank, and all bigger than herself, she looked like a creature of high breed—an Arab steed in a string of cart-horses.

A voice behind me said in a nasty equivocal tone: "I hope you are satisfied with her, Captain." I did not even turn my head. It was the master of the steamer, and whatever he meant, whatever he thought of her, I knew that, like some rare women, she was one of those creatures whose mere existence is enough to awaken an unselfish delight. One feels that it is good to be in the world in which she has her being.

That illusion of life and character which charms one in men's finest handiwork radiated from her. An enormous bulk of teak-wood timber swung over her hatchway; lifeless matter, looking heavier and bigger than anything aboard of her. When they started lowering it the surge of the tackle sent a quiver through her from water-line to the trucks up the fine nerves of her rigging, as though she had shuddered at the weight. It seemed cruel to load her so. . . .

Half an hour later, putting my foot on her deck for the first time, I received the feeling of deep physical satisfaction. Nothing could equal the fullness of that moment, the ideal completeness of that emotional experience which had come to me without the preliminary toil and disenchantments of an obscure career.

My rapid glance ran over her, enveloped, appropriated the form concreting the abstract sentiment of my command. A lot of details perceptible to a seaman struck my eye, vividly in that instant. For the rest, I saw her disengaged from the material conditions of her being. The shore to which she was moored was as if it did not exist. What were to me all the countries of the globe? In all the parts of the world washed by navigable waters our relation to each other would be the same—and more intimate than there are words to express in the language. Apart from that, every scene and episode would be a mere passing show. The very gang of yellow coolies busy about the main hatch was less substantial than the stuff dreams are made of. For who on earth would dream of Chinamen? . . .

I went aft, ascended the poop, where, under the awning, gleamed the brasses of the yacht-like fittings, the polished surfaces of the rails, the glass of the skylights. Right aft two seamen, busy cleaning the steering gear, with the reflected ripples of light running playfully up their bent backs, went on with their work, unaware of me and of the almost affectionate glance I threw at them in passing toward the companion-way of the cabin.

The doors stood wide open, the slide was pushed right back. The half-turn of the staircase cut off the view of the lobby. A low humming ascended from below, but it stopped abruptly at the sound of my descending footsteps.

3

THE FIRST THING I saw down there was the upper part of a man's body projecting backward, as it were, from one of the doors at the foot of the stairs. His eyes looked at me very wide and still. In one hand he held a dinner plate, in the other a cloth.

"I am your new Captain," I said quietly.

In a moment, in the twinkling of an eye, he had got rid of the plate and the cloth and jumped to open the cabin door. As soon as I passed into the saloon he vanished, but only to reappear instantly, buttoning up a jacket he had put on with the swiftness of a "quick-change" artist.

"Where's the chief mate?" I asked.

"In the hold, I think, sir. I saw him go down the after-hatch ten minutes ago."

"Tell him I am on board."

The mahogany table under the skylight shone in the twilight like a dark pool of water. The sideboard, surmounted by a wide looking-glass in an ormulu frame, had a marble top. It bore a pair of silver-plated lamps and some other pieces—obviously a harbour display. The saloon itself was panelled in two kinds of wood in the excellent simple taste prevailing when the ship was built.

I sat down in the armchair at the head of the table—the captain's chair, with a small tell-tale compass swung above it—a mute reminder of unremitting vigilance.

A succession of men had sat in that chair. I became aware of that thought suddenly, vividly, as though each had left a little of himself between the four walls of these ornate bulkheads; as if a sort of composite soul, the soul of command, had whispered suddenly to mine of long days at sea and of anxious moments.

"You, too!" it seemed to say, "you, too, shall taste of that peace and that unrest in a searching intimacy with your own self—obscure as we were and as supreme in the face of all the winds and all the seas, in an immensity that receives no impress, preserves no memories, and keeps no reckoning of lives."

Deep within the tarnished ormulu frame, in the hot half-light sifted through the awning, I saw my own face propped between my hands. And I stared back at myself with the perfect detachment of distance, rather with curiosity than with any other feeling, except of some sympathy for this latest representative of what for all intents and purposes was a dynasty, continuous not in blood indeed, but in its experience, in its training, in its conception of duty, and in the blessed simplicity of its traditional point of view on life.

It struck me that this quietly staring man whom I was watching, both as if he were myself and somebody else, was not exactly a lonely figure. He had his place in a line of men whom he did not know, of whom he had never heard; but who were fashioned by the same influences, whose souls in relation to their humble life's work had no secrets for him.

Suddenly I perceived that there was another man in the saloon, standing a little on one side and looking intently at me. The chief mate. His long, red moustache determined the character of his physiognomy, which struck me as pugnacious in (strange to say) a ghastly sort of way.

How long had he been there looking at me, appraising me in my unguarded day-dreaming state? I would have been more disconcerted if, having the clock set in the top of the mirror-frame right in front of me, I had not noticed that its long hand had hardly moved at all.

I could not have been in that cabin more than two minutes altogether. Say three. . . . So he could not have been watching me more than a mere fraction of a minute, luckily. Still, I regretted the occurrence.

But I showed nothing of it as I rose leisurely (it had to be leisurely) and greeted him with perfect friendliness.

There was something reluctant and at the same time attentive in his bearing. His name was Burns. We left the cabin and went round the ship together. His face in the full light of day appeared very pale, meagre, even haggard. Somehow I had a delicacy as to looking too often at him; his eyes, on the contrary, remained fairly glued on my face. They were greenish and had an expectant expression.

He answered all my questions readily enough, but my ear seemed to catch a tone of unwillingness. The second officer, with three or four hands, was busy forward. The mate mentioned his name and I nodded to him in passing. He was very young. He struck me as rather a cub.

When we returned below, I sat down on one end of a deep, semi-circular, or, rather, semi-oval settee, upholstered in red plush. It extended right across the whole after-end of the cabin. Mr. Burns motioned to sit down, dropped into one of the swivel-chairs round the table, and kept his eyes on me as persistently as ever, and with that strange air as if all this were make-believe and he expected me to get up, burst into a laugh, slap him on the back, and vanish from the cabin.

There was an odd stress in the situation which began to make me uncomfortable. I tried to react against this vague feeling.

"It's only my inexperience," I thought.

In the face of that man, several years, I judged, older than myself, I became aware of what I had left already behind me—my youth. And that was indeed poor comfort. Youth is a fine thing, a mighty power—as long as one does not think of it. I felt I was becoming self-conscious. Almost against my will I assumed a moody gravity. I said: "I see you have kept her in very good order, Mr. Burns."

Directly I had uttered these words I asked myself angrily why the deuce did I want to say that? Mr. Burns in answer had only blinked at me. What on earth did he mean?

I fell back on a question which had been in my thoughts for a long time—the most natural question on the lips of any seaman whatever joining a ship. I voiced it (confound this self-consciousness) in a degaged cheerful tone: "I suppose she can travel—what?"

Now a question like this might have been answered normally, either in accents of apologetic sorrow or with a visibly suppressed pride, in a "I don't want to boast, but you shall see," sort of tone. There are sailors, too, who would have been roughly outspoken: "Lazy brute," or openly delighted: "She's a flyer." Two ways, if four manners.

But Mr. Burns found another way, a way of his own which had, at all events, the merit of saving his breath, if no other.

Again he did not say anything. He only frowned. And it was an angry frown. I waited. Nothing more came.

"What's the matter? . . . Can't you tell after being nearly two years in the ship?" I addressed him sharply.

He looked as startled for a moment as though he had discovered my presence only that very moment. But this passed off almost at once. He put on an air of indifference. But I suppose he thought it better to say something. He said that a ship needed, just like a man, the chance to show the best she could do, and that this ship had never had a chance since he had been on board of her. Not that he could remember. The last captain. . . . He paused.

"Has he been so very unlucky?" I asked with frank incredulity. Mr. Burns turned his eyes away from me. No, the late captain was not an unlucky man. One couldn't say that. But he had not seemed to want to make use of his luck.

Mr. Burns—man of enigmatic moods—made this statement with an inanimate face and staring wilfully at the rudder casing. The statement itself was obscurely suggestive. I asked quietly:

"Where did he die?"

"In this saloon. Just where you are sitting now," answered Mr. Burns.

I repressed a silly impulse to jump up; but upon the whole I was relieved to hear that he had not died in the bed which was now to be mine. I pointed out to the chief mate that what I really wanted to know was where he had buried his late captain.

Mr. Burns said that it was at the entrance to the gulf. A roomy grave; a sufficient answer. But the mate, overcoming visibly something within him—something like a curious reluctance to believe in my advent (as an irrevocable fact, at any rate), did not stop at that—though, indeed, he may have wished to do so.

As a compromise with his feelings, I believe, he addressed himself persistently to the rudder-casing, so that to me he had the appearance of a man talking in solitude, a little unconsciously, however.

His tale was that at seven bells in the forenoon watch he had all hands mustered on the quarterdeck and told them they had better go down to say good-bye to the captain.

Those words, as if grudged to an intruding personage, were enough for me to evoke vividly that strange ceremony: The bare-footed, bare-headed seamen crowding shyly into that cabin, a small mob pressed against that sideboard, uncomfortable rather than moved, shirts open on sunburnt chests, weather-beaten faces, and all staring at the dying man with the same grave and expectant expression.

"Was he conscious?" I asked.

"He didn't speak, but he moved his eyes to look at them," said the mate.

After waiting a moment, Mr. Burns motioned the crew to leave the cabin, but he detained the two eldest men to stay with the captain while he went on deck with his sextant to "take the sun." It was getting toward noon and he was anxious to obtain a good observation for latitude. When he returned below to put his sextant away he found that the two men had retreated out into the lobby. Through the open door he had a view of the captain lying easy against the pillows. He had "passed away" while Mr. Burns was taking this observation. As near noon as possible. He had hardly changed his position.

Mr. Burns sighed, glanced at me inquisitively, as much as to say, "Aren't you going yet?" and then turned his thoughts from his new captain back to the old, who, being dead, had no authority, was not in anybody's way, and was much easier to deal with.

Mr. Burns dealt with him at some length. He was a peculiar man—of sixty-five about—iron gray, hard-faced, obstinate, and uncommunicative. He used to keep the ship loafing at sea for inscrutable reasons. Would come on deck at night sometimes, take some sail off her, God only knows why or wherefore, then go below, shut himself up in his cabin, and play on the violin for hours—till daybreak perhaps. In fact, he spent most of his time day or night playing the violin. That was when the fit took him. Very loud, too.

It came to this, that Mr. Burns mustered his courage one day and remonstrated earnestly with the captain. Neither he nor the second mate could get a wink of sleep in their watches below for the noise. . . . And how could they be expected to keep awake while on duty? He pleaded. The answer of that stern man was that if he and the second mate didn't like the noise, they were welcome to pack up their traps and walk over the side. When this alternative was offered the ship happened to be 600 miles from the nearest land.

Mr. Burns at this point looked at me with an air of curiosity. I began to think that my predecessor was a remarkably peculiar old man.

But I had to hear stranger things yet. It came out that this stern, grim, wind-tanned, rough, sea-salted, taciturn sailor of sixty-five was not only an artist, but a lover as well. In Haiphong, when they got there after a course of most unprofitable peregrinations (during which the ship was nearly lost twice), he got himself, in Mr. Burns' own words, "mixed up" with some woman. Mr. Burns had had no personal knowledge of that affair, but positive evidence of it existed in the shape of a photograph taken in Haiphong. Mr. Burns found it in one of the drawers in the captain's room.

In due course I, too, saw that amazing human document (I even threw it overboard later). There he sat, with his hands reposing on his knees, bald, squat, gray, bristly, recalling a wild boar somehow; and by his side towered an awful mature, white female with rapacious nostrils and a cheaply ill-omened stare in her enormous eyes. She was disguised in some semi-oriental, vulgar, fancy costume. She resembled a low-class medium or one of those women who tell fortunes by cards for half a crown. And yet she was striking. A professional sorceress from the slums. It was incomprehensible. There was something awful in the thought that she was the last reflection of the world of passion for the fierce soul which seemed to look at one out of the sardonically savage face of that old seaman. However, I noticed that she was holding some musical instrument—guitar or mandoline—in her hand. Perhaps that was the secret of her sortilege.

For Mr. Burns that photograph explained why the unloaded ship had kept sweltering at anchor for three weeks in a pestilential hot harbour without air. They lay there and gasped. The captain, appearing now and then on short visits, mumbled to Mr. Burns unlikely tales about some letters he was waiting for.

Suddenly, after vanishing for a week, he came on board in the middle of the night and took the ship out to sea with the first break of dawn. Daylight showed him looking wild and ill. The mere getting clear of the land took two days, and somehow or other they bumped slightly on a reef. However, no leak developed, and the captain, growling "no matter," informed Mr. Burns that he had made up his mind to take the ship to Hong-Kong and drydock her there.

At this Mr. Burns was plunged into despair. For indeed, to beat up to Hong-Kong against a fierce monsoon, with a ship not sufficiently ballasted and with her supply of water not completed, was an insane project.

But the captain growled peremptorily, "Stick her at it," and Mr. Burns, dismayed and enraged, stuck her at it, and kept her at it, blowing away sails, straining the spars, exhausting the crew—nearly maddened by the absolute conviction that the attempt was impossible and was bound to end in some catastrophe.

Meantime the captain, shut up in his cabin and wedged in a corner of his settee against the crazy bounding of the ship, played the violin—or, at any rate, made continuous noise on it.

When he appeared on deck he would not speak and not always answer when spoken to. It was obvious that he was ill in some mysterious manner, and beginning to break up.

As the days went by the sounds of the violin became less and less loud, till at last only a feeble scratching would meet Mr. Burns' ear as he stood in the saloon listening outside the door of the captain's state-room.

One afternoon in perfect desperation he burst into that room and made such a scene, tearing his hair and shouting such horrid imprecations that he cowed the contemptuous spirit of the sick man. The water-tanks were low, they had not gained fifty miles in a fortnight. She would never reach Hong-Kong.

It was like fighting desperately toward destruction for the ship and the men. This was evident without argument. Mr. Burns, losing all restraint, put his face close to his captain's and fairly yelled: "You, sir, are going out of the world. But I can't wait till you are dead before I put the helm up. You must do it yourself. You must do it now!"

The man on the couch snarled in contempt. "So I am going out of the world—am I?"

"Yes, sir—you haven't many days left in it," said Mr. Burns calming down. "One can see it by your face."

"My face, eh? . . . Well, put up the helm and be damned to you."

Burns flew on deck, got the ship before the wind, then came down again composed, but resolute.

"I've shaped a course for Pulo Condor, sir," he said. "When we make it, if you are still with us, you'll tell me into what port you wish me to take the ship and I'll do it."

The old man gave him a look of savage spite, and said those atrocious words in deadly, slow tones.

"If I had my wish, neither the ship nor any of you would ever reach a port. And I hope you won't."

Mr. Burns was profoundly shocked. I believe he was positively frightened at the time. It seems, however, that he managed to produce such an effective laugh that it was the old man's turn to be frightened. He shrank within himself and turned his back on him.

"And his head was not gone then," Mr. Burns assured me excitedly. "He meant every word of it."

"Such was practically the late captain's last speech. No connected sentence passed his lips afterward. That night he used the last of his strength to throw his fiddle over the side. No one had actually seen him in the act, but after his death Mr. Burns couldn't find the thing anywhere. The empty case was very much in evidence, but the fiddle was clearly not in the ship. And where else could it have gone to but overboard?"

"Threw his violin overboard!" I exclaimed.

"He did," cried Mr. Burns excitedly. "And it's my belief he would have tried to take the ship down with him if it had been in human power. He never meant her to see home again.

He wouldn't write to his owners, he never wrote to his old wife, either—he wasn't going to. He had made up his mind to cut adrift from everything. That's what it was. He didn't care for business, or freights, or for making a passage—or anything. He meant to have gone wandering about the world till he lost her with all hands."

Mr. Burns looked like a man who had escaped great danger. For a little he would have exclaimed: "If it hadn't been for me!" And the transparent innocence of his indignant eyes was underlined quaintly by the arrogant pair of moustaches which he proceeded to twist, and as if extend, horizontally.

I might have smiled if I had not been busy with my own sensations, which were not those of Mr. Burns. I was already the man in command. My sensations could not be like those of any other man on board. In that community I stood, like a king in his country, in a class all by myself. I mean an hereditary king, not a mere elected head of a state. I was brought there to rule by an agency as remote from the people and as inscrutable almost to them as the Grace of God.

And like a member of a dynasty, feeling a semimystical bond with the dead, I was profoundly shocked by my immediate predecessor.

That man had been in all essentials but his age just such another man as myself. Yet the end of his life was a complete act of treason, the betrayal of a tradition which seemed to me as imperative as any guide on earth could be. It appeared that even at sea a man could become the victim of evil spirits. I felt on my face the breath of unknown powers that shape our destinies.

Not to let the silence last too long I asked Mr. Burns if he had written to his captain's wife. He shook his head. He had written to nobody.

In a moment he became sombre. He never thought of writing. It took him all his time to watch incessantly the loading of the ship by a rascally Chinese stevedore. In this Mr. Burns gave me the first glimpse of the real chief mate's soul which dwelt uneasily in his body.

He mused, then hastened on with gloomy force.

"Yes! The captain died as near noon as possible. I looked through his papers in the afternoon. I read the service over him at sunset and then I stuck the ship's head north and brought her in here. I—brought—her—in."

He struck the table with his fist.

"She would hardly have come in by herself," I observed. "But why didn't you make for Singapore instead?"

His eyes wavered. "The nearest port," he muttered sullenly.

I had framed the question in perfect innocence, but his answer (the difference in distance was insignificant) and his manner offered me a clue to the simple truth. He took the ship to a port where he expected to be confirmed in his temporary command from lack of a qualified master to put over his head. Whereas Singapore, he surmised justly, would be full of qualified men. But his naive reasoning forgot to take into account the telegraph cable reposing on the bottom of the very Gulf up which he had turned that ship which he imagined himself to have saved from destruction. Hence the bitter flavour of our interview. I tasted it more and more distinctly—and it was less and less to my taste.

"Look here, Mr. Burns," I began very firmly. "You may as well understand that I did not run after this command. It was pushed in my way. I've accepted it. I am here to take the ship home first of all, and you may be sure that I shall see to it that every one of you on board here does his duty to that end. This is all I have to say—for the present."

He was on his feet by this time, but instead of taking his dismissal he remained with trembling, indignant lips, and looking at me hard as though, really, after this, there was nothing for me to do in common decency but to vanish from his outraged sight. Like all very simple emotional states this was moving. I felt sorry for him—almost sympathetic, till (seeing that I did not vanish) he spoke in a tone of forced restraint.

"If I hadn't a wife and a child at home you may be sure, sir, I would have asked you to let me go the very minute you came on board."

I answered him with a matter-of-course calmness as though some remote third person were in question.

"And I, Mr. Burns, would not have let you go. You have signed the ship's articles as chief officer, and till they are terminated at the final port of discharge I shall expect you to attend to your duty and give me the benefit of your experience to the best of your ability."

Stony incredulity lingered in his eyes: but it broke down before my friendly attitude. With a slight upward toss of his arms (I got to know that gesture well afterward) he bolted out of the cabin.

We might have saved ourselves that little passage of harmless sparring. Before many days had elapsed it was Mr. Burns who was pleading with me anxiously not to leave him behind; while I could only return him but doubtful answers. The whole thing took on a somewhat tragic complexion.

And this horrible problem was only an extraneous episode, a mere complication in the general problem of how to get that ship—which was mine with her appurtenances and her men, with her body and her spirit now slumbering in that pestilential river—how to get her out to sea.

Mr. Burns, while still acting captain, had hastened to sign a charter-party which in an ideal world without guile would have been an excellent document. Directly I ran my eye over it I foresaw trouble ahead unless the people of the other part were quite exceptionally fair-minded and open to argument.

Mr. Burns, to whom I imparted my fears, chose to take great umbrage at them. He looked at me with that usual incredulous stare, and said bitterly:

"I suppose, sir, you want to make out I've acted like a fool?"

I told him, with my systematic kindliness which always seemed to augment his surprise, that I did not want to make out anything. I would leave that to the future.

And, sure enough, the future brought in a lot of trouble. There were days when I used to remember Captain Giles with nothing short of abhorrence. His confounded acuteness had let me in for this job; while his prophecy that I "would have my hands full" coming true, made it appear as if done on purpose to play an evil joke on my young innocence.

Yes. I had my hands full of complications which were most valuable as "experience." People have a great opinion of the advantages of experience. But in this connection experience means always something disagreeable as opposed to the charm and innocence of illusions.

I must say I was losing mine rapidly. But on these instructive complications I must not enlarge more than to say that they could all be resumed in the one word: Delay.

A mankind which has invented the proverb, "Time is money," will understand my vexation. The word "Delay" entered the secret chamber of my brain, resounded there like a tolling bell which maddens the ear, affected all my senses, took on a black colouring, a bitter taste, a deadly meaning.

"I am really sorry to see you worried like this. Indeed, I am. . . ."

It was the only humane speech I used to hear at that time. And it came from a doctor, appropriately enough.

A doctor is humane by definition. But that man was so in reality. His speech was not professional. I was not ill. But other people were, and that was the reason of his visiting the ship.

He was the doctor of our Legation and, of course, of the Consulate, too. He looked after the ship's health, which generally was poor, and trembling, as it were, on the verge of a break-up. Yes. The men ailed. And thus time was not only money, but life as well.

I had never seen such a steady ship's company. As the doctor remarked to me: "You seem to have a most respectable lot of seamen." Not only were they consistently sober, but they did not even want to go ashore. Care was taken to expose them as little as possible to the sun. They were employed on light work under the awnings. And the humane doctor commended me.

"Your arrangements appear to me to be very judicious, my dear Captain."

It is difficult to express how much that pronouncement comforted me. The doctor's round, full face framed in a light-coloured whisker was the perfection of a dignified amenity. He was the only human being in the world who seemed to take the slightest interest in me. He would generally sit in the cabin for half an hour or so at every visit.

I said to him one day:

"I suppose the only thing now is to take care of them as you are doing till I can get the ship to sea?"

He inclined his head, shutting his eyes under the large spectacles, and murmured:

"The sea . . . undoubtedly."

The first member of the crew fairly knocked over was the steward—the first man to whom I had spoken on board. He was taken ashore (with choleric symptoms) and died there at the end of a week. Then, while I was still under the startling impression of this first home-thrust of the climate, Mr. Burns gave up and went to bed in a raging fever without saying a word to anybody.

I believe he had partly fretted himself into that illness; the climate did the rest with the swiftness of an invisible monster ambushed in the air, in the water, in the mud of the river-bank. Mr. Burns was a predestined victim.

I discovered him lying on his back, glaring sullenly and radiating heat on one like a small furnace. He would hardly answer my questions, and only grumbled. Couldn't a man take an afternoon off duty with a bad headache—for once?

That evening, as I sat in the saloon after dinner, I could hear him muttering continuously in his room. Ransome, who was clearing the table, said to me:

"I am afraid, sir, I won't be able to give the mate all the attention he's likely to need. I will have to be forward in the galley a great part of my time."

Ransome was the cook. The mate had pointed him out to me the first day, standing on the deck, his arms crossed on his broad chest, gazing on the river.

Even at a distance his well-proportioned figure, something thoroughly sailor-like in his poise, made him noticeable. On nearer view the intelligent, quiet eyes, a well-bred face, the disciplined independence of his manner made up an attractive personality. When, in addition, Mr. Burns told me that he was the best seaman in the ship, I expressed my surprise that in his earliest prime and of such appearance he should sign on as cook on board a ship.

"It's his heart," Mr. Burns had said. "There's something wrong with it. He mustn't exert himself too much or he may drop dead suddenly."

And he was the only one the climate had not touched—perhaps because, carrying a deadly enemy in his breast, he had schooled himself into a systematic control of feelings and movements. When one was in the secret this was apparent in his manner. After the poor steward died, and as he could not be replaced by a white man in this Oriental port, Ransome had volunteered to do the double work.

"I can do it all right, sir, as long as I go about it quietly," he had assured me.

But obviously he couldn't be expected to take up sick-nursing in addition. Moreover, the doctor peremptorily ordered Mr. Burns ashore.

With a seaman on each side holding him up under the arms, the mate went over the gangway more sullen than ever. We built him up with pillows in the gharry, and he made an effort to say brokenly:

"Now—you've got—what you wanted—got me out of—the ship."

"You were never more mistaken in your life, Mr. Burns," I said quietly, duly smiling at him; and the trap drove off to a sort of sanatorium, a pavilion of bricks which the doctor had in the grounds of his residence.

I visited Mr. Burns regularly. After the first few days, when he didn't know anybody, he received me as if I had come either to gloat over an enemy or else to curry favour with a deeply wronged person. It was either one or the other, just as it happened according to his fantastic sickroom moods. Whichever it was, he managed to convey it to me even during the period when he appeared almost too weak to talk. I treated him to my invariable kindliness.

Then one day, suddenly, a surge of downright panic burst through all this craziness.

If I left him behind in this deadly place he would die. He felt it, he was certain of it. But I wouldn't have the heart to leave him ashore. He had a wife and child in Sydney.

He produced his wasted forearms from under the sheet which covered him and clasped his fleshless claws. He would die! He would die here. . . .

He absolutely managed to sit up, but only for a moment, and when he fell back I really thought that he would die there and then. I called to the Bengali dispenser, and hastened away from the room.

Next day he upset me thoroughly by renewing his entreaties. I returned an evasive answer, and left him the picture of ghastly despair. The day after I went in with reluctance, and he attacked me at once in a much stronger voice and with an abundance of argument which was quite startling. He presented his case with a sort of crazy vigour, and asked me finally how would I like to have a man's death on my conscience? He wanted me to promise that I would not sail without him.

I said that I really must consult the doctor first. He cried out at that. The doctor! Never! That would be a death sentence.

The effort had exhausted him. He closed his eyes, but went on rambling in a low voice. I had hated him from the start. The late captain had hated him, too. Had wished him dead. Had wished all hands dead. . . .

"What do you want to stand in with that wicked corpse for, sir? He'll have you, too," he ended, blinking his glazed eyes vacantly.

"Mr. Burns," I cried, very much discomposed, "what on earth are you talking about?"

He seemed to come to himself, though he was too weak to start.

"I don't know," he said languidly. "But don't ask that doctor, sir. You and I are sailors. Don't ask him, sir. Some day perhaps you will have a wife and child yourself."

And again he pleaded for the promise that I would not leave him behind. I had the firmness of mind not to give it to him. Afterward this sternness seemed criminal; for my mind was made up. That prostrated man, with hardly strength enough to breathe and ravaged by a passion of fear, was irresistible. And, besides, he had happened to hit on the right words. He and I were sailors. That was a claim, for I had no other family. As to the wife and child (some day) argument, it had no force. It sounded merely bizarre.

I could imagine no claim that would be stronger and more absorbing than the claim of that ship, of these men snared in the river by silly commercial complications, as if in some poisonous trap.

However, I had nearly fought my way out. Out to sea. The sea—which was pure, safe, and friendly. Three days more.

That thought sustained and carried me on my way back to the ship. In the saloon the doctor's voice greeted me, and his large form followed his voice, issuing out of the starboard spare cabin where the ship's medicine chest was kept securely lashed in the bed-place.

Finding that I was not on board he had gone in there, he said, to inspect the supply of drugs, bandages, and so on. Everything was completed and in order.

I thanked him; I had just been thinking of asking him to do that very thing, as in a couple of days, as he knew, we were going to sea, where all our troubles of every sort would be over at last.

He listened gravely and made no answer. But when I opened to him my mind as to Mr. Burns he sat down by my side, and, laying his hand on my knee amicably, begged me to think what it was I was exposing myself to.

The man was just strong enough to bear being moved and no more. But he couldn't stand a return of the fever. I had before me a passage of sixty days perhaps, beginning with intricate navigation and ending probably with a lot of bad weather. Could I run the risk of having to go through it single-handed, with no chief officer and with a second quite a youth? . . .

He might have added that it was my first command, too. He did probably think of that fact, for he checked himself. It was very present to my mind.

He advised me earnestly to cable to Singapore for a chief officer, even if I had to delay my sailing for a week.

"Never," I said. The very thought gave me the shivers. The hands seemed fairly fit, all of them, and this was the time to get them away. Once at sea I was not afraid of facing anything. The sea was now the only remedy for all my troubles.

The doctor's glasses were directed at me like two lamps searching the genuineness of my resolution. He opened his lips as if to argue further, but shut them again without saying anything. I had a vision so vivid of poor Burns in his exhaustion, helplessness, and anguish, that it moved me more than the reality I had come away from only an hour before. It was purged from the drawbacks of his personality, and I could not resist it.

"Look here," I said. "Unless you tell me officially that the man must not be moved I'll make arrangements to have him brought on board tomorrow, and shall take the ship out of the river next morning, even if I have to anchor outside the bar for a couple of days to get her ready for sea."

"Oh! I'll make all the arrangements myself," said the doctor at once. "I spoke as I did only as a friend—as a well-wisher, and that sort of thing."

He rose in his dignified simplicity and gave me a warm handshake, rather solemnly, I thought. But he was as good as his word. When Mr. Burns appeared at the gangway carried on a stretcher, the doctor himself walked by its side. The programme had been altered in so far that this transportation had been left to the last moment, on the very morning of our departure.

It was barely an hour after sunrise. The doctor waved his big arm to me from the shore and walked back at once to his trap, which had followed him empty to the river-side. Mr. Burns, carried across the quarter-deck, had the appearance of being absolutely lifeless.

Ransome went down to settle him in his cabin. I had to remain on deck to look after the ship, for the tug had got hold of our towrope already.

The splash of our shore-fasts falling in the water produced a complete change of feeling in me. It was like the imperfect relief of awakening from a nightmare. But when the ship's head swung down the river away from that town, Oriental and squalid, I missed the expected elation of that striven-for moment. What there was, undoubtedly, was a relaxation of tension which translated itself into a sense of weariness after an inglorious fight.

About midday we anchored a mile outside the bar. The afternoon was busy for all hands. Watching the work from the poop, where I remained all the time, I detected in it some of the languor of the six weeks spent in the steaming heat of the river. The first breeze would blow that away. Now the calm was complete. I judged that the second officer—a callow youth with an unpromising face—was not, to put it mildly, of that invaluable stuff from which a commander's right hand is made. But I was glad to catch along the main deck a few smiles on those seamen's faces at which I had hardly had time to have a good look as yet. Having thrown off the mortal coil of shore affairs, I felt myself familiar with them and yet a little strange, like a long-lost wanderer among his kin.

Ransome flitted continually to and fro between the galley and the cabin. It was a pleasure to look at him. The man positively had grace. He alone of all the crew had not had a day's illness in port. But with the knowledge of that uneasy heart within his breast I could detect the restraint he put on the natural sailor-like agility of his movements. It was as though he had something very fragile or very explosive to carry about his person and was all the time aware of it.

I had occasion to address him once or twice. He answered me in his pleasant, quiet voice and with a faint, slightly wistful smile. Mr. Burns appeared to be resting. He seemed fairly comfortable.

After sunset I came out on deck again to meet only a still void. The thin, featureless crust of the coast could not be distinguished. The darkness had risen around the ship like a mysterious emanation from the dumb and lonely waters. I leaned on the rail and turned my ear to the shadows of the night. Not a sound. My command might have been a planet flying vertiginously on its appointed path in a space of infinite silence. I clung to the rail as if my sense of balance were leaving me for good. How absurd. I failed nervously.

"On deck there!"

The immediate answer, "Yes, sir," broke the spell. The anchor-watch man ran up the poop ladder smartly. I told him to report at once the slightest sign of a breeze coming.

Going below I looked in on Mr. Burns. In fact, I could not avoid seeing him, for his door stood open. The man was so wasted that, in this white cabin, under a white sheet, and with his diminished head sunk in the white pillow, his red moustaches captured their eyes exclusively, like something artificial—a pair of moustaches from a shop exhibited there in the harsh light of the bulkhead-lamp without a shade.

While I stared with a sort of wonder he asserted himself by opening his eyes and even moving them in my direction. A minute stir.

"Dead calm, Mr. Burns," I said resignedly.

In an unexpectedly distinct voice Mr. Burns began a rambling speech. Its tone was very strange, not as if affected by his illness, but as if of a different nature. It sounded unearthly. As to the matter, I seemed to make out that it was the fault of the "old man"—the late captain—ambushed down there under the sea with some evil intention. It was a weird story.

I listened to the end; then stepping into the cabin I laid my hand on the mate's forehead.

It was cool. He was light-headed only from extreme weakness. Suddenly he seemed to become aware of me, and in his own voice—of course, very feeble—he asked regretfully:

"Is there no chance at all to get under way, sir?"

"What's the good of letting go our hold of the ground only to drift, Mr. Burns?" I answered.

He sighed and I left him to his immobility. His hold on life was as slender as his hold on sanity. I was oppressed by my lonely responsibilities. I went into my cabin to seek relief in a few hours' sleep, but almost before I closed my eyes the man on deck came down reporting a light breeze. Enough to get under way with, he said.

And it was no more than just enough. I ordered the windlass manned, the sails loosed, and the topsails set. But by the time I had cast the ship I could hardly feel any breath of wind. Nevertheless, I trimmed the yards and put everything on her. I was not going to give up the attempt.

II

I

WITH HER ANCHOR at the bow and clothed in canvas to her very trucks, my command seemed to stand as motionless as a model ship set on the gleams and shadows of polished marble. It was impossible to distinguish land from water in the enigmatical tranquillity of the immense forces of the world. A sudden impatience possessed me.

"Won't she answer the helm at all?" I said irritably to the man whose strong brown hands grasping the spokes of the wheel stood out lighted on the darkness; like a symbol of mankind's claim to the direction of its own fate.

He answered me.

"Yes, sir. She's coming-to slowly."

"Let her head come up to south."

"Aye, aye, sir."

I paced the poop. There was not a sound but that of my footsteps, till the man spoke again.

"She is at south now, sir."

I felt a slight tightness of the chest before I gave out the first course of my first command to the silent night, heavy with dew and sparkling with stars. There was a finality in the act committing me to the endless vigilance of my lonely task.

"Steady her head at that," I said at last. "The course is south."

"South, sir," echoed the man.

I sent below the second mate and his watch and remained in charge, walking the deck through the chill, somnolent hours that precede the dawn.

Slight puffs came and went, and whenever they were strong enough to wake up the black water the murmur alongside ran through my very heart in a delicate crescendo of delight and died away swiftly. I was bitterly tired. The very stars seemed weary of waiting for daybreak. It came at last with a mother-of-pearl sheen at the zenith, such as I had never seen before in the tropics, unglowing, almost gray, with a strange reminder of high latitudes.

The voice of the look-out man hailed from forward:

"Land on the port bow, sir."

"All right."

Leaning on the rail I never even raised my eyes.

The motion of the ship was imperceptible. Presently Ransome brought me the cup of morning coffee. After I had drunk it I looked ahead, and in the still streak of very bright pale orange light I saw the land profiled flatly as if cut out of black paper and seeming to float on the water as light as cork. But the rising sun turned it into mere dark vapour, a doubtful, massive shadow trembling in the hot glare.

The watch finished washing decks. I went below and stopped at Mr. Burns' door (he could not bear to have it shut), but hesitated to speak to him till he moved his eyes. I gave him the news.

"Sighted Cape Liant at daylight. About fifteen miles."

He moved his lips then, but I heard no sound till I put my ear down, and caught the peevish comment: "This is crawling. . . . No luck."

"Better luck than standing still, anyhow," I pointed out resignedly, and left him to whatever thoughts or fancies haunted his awful immobility.

Later that morning, when relieved by my second officer, I threw myself on my couch and for some three hours or so I really found oblivion. It was so perfect that on waking up I wondered where I was. Then came the immense relief of the thought: on board my ship! At sea! At sea!

Through the port-holes I beheld an unruffled, sun-smitten horizon. The horizon of a windless day. But its spaciousness alone was enough to give me a sense of a fortunate escape, a momentary exultation of freedom.

I stepped out into the saloon with my heart lighter than it had been for days. Ransome was at the sideboard preparing to lay the table for the first sea dinner of the passage. He turned his head, and something in his eyes checked my modest elation.

Instinctively I asked: "What is it now?" not expecting in the least the answer I got. It was given with that sort of contained serenity which was characteristic of the man.

"I am afraid we haven't left all sickness behind us, sir."

"We haven't! What's the matter?"

He told me then that two of our men had been taken bad with fever in the night. One of them was burning and the other was shivering, but he thought that it was pretty much the same thing. I thought so, too. I felt shocked by the news. "One burning, the other shivering, you say? No. We haven't left the sickness behind. Do they look very ill?"

"Middling bad, sir." Ransome's eyes gazed steadily into mine. We exchanged smiles. Ransome's a little wistful, as usual, mine no doubt grim enough, to correspond with my secret exasperation.

I asked:

"Was there any wind at all this morning?"

"Can hardly say that, sir. We've moved all the time though. The land ahead seems a little nearer."

That was it. A little nearer. Whereas if we had only had a little more wind, only a very little more, we might, we should, have been abreast of Liant by this time and increasing our distance from that contaminated shore. And it was not only the distance. It seemed to me that a stronger breeze would have blown away the contamination which clung to the ship. It obviously did cling to the ship. Two men. One burning, one shivering. I felt a distinct reluctance to go and look at them. What was the good? Poison is poison. Tropical fever is tropical fever. But that it should have stretched its claw after us over the sea seemed to me an extraordinary and unfair license. I could hardly believe that it could be anything worse than the last desperate pluck of the evil from which we were escaping into the clean breath of the sea. If only that breath had been a little stronger. However, there was the quinine against the fever. I went into the spare cabin where the medicine chest was kept to prepare two doses. I opened it full of faith as a man opens a miraculous shrine. The upper part was inhabited by a collection of bottles, all square-shouldered and as like each other as peas. Under that orderly array there were two drawers, stuffed as full of things as one could imagine—paper packages, bandages, cardboard boxes officially labelled. The lower of the two, in one of its compartments, contained our provision of quinine.

There were five bottles, all round and all of a size. One was about a third full. The other four remained still wrapped up in paper and sealed. But I did not expect to see an envelope lying on top of them. A square envelope, belonging, in fact, to the ship's stationery.

It lay so that I could see it was not closed down, and on picking it up and turning it over I perceived that it was addressed to myself. It contained a half-sheet of notepaper, which I unfolded with a queer sense of dealing with the uncanny, but without any excitement as people meet and do extraordinary things in a dream.

"My dear Captain," it began, but I ran to the signature. The writer was the doctor. The date was that of the day on which, returning from my visit to Mr. Burns in the hospital, I had found the excellent doctor waiting for me in the cabin; and when he told me that he had been putting in time inspecting the medicine chest for me. How bizarre! While expecting me to come in at any moment he had been amusing himself by writing me a letter, and then as I came in had hastened to stuff it into the medicine-chest drawer. A rather incredible proceeding. I turned to the text in wonder.

In a large, hurried, but legible hand the good, sympathetic man for some reason, either of kindness or more likely impelled by the irresistible desire to express his opinion, with which he didn't want to damp my hopes before, was warning me not to put my trust in the beneficial effects of a change from land to sea. "I didn't want to add to your worries by discouraging your hopes," he wrote. "I am afraid that, medically speaking, the end of your troubles is not yet." In short, he expected me to have to fight a probable return of tropical illness. Fortunately I had a good provision of quinine. I should put my trust in that, and administer it steadily, when the ship's health would certainly improve.

I crumpled up the letter and rammed it into my pocket. Ransome carried off two big doses to the men forward. As to myself, I did not go on deck as yet. I went instead to the door of Mr. Burns' room, and gave him that news, too.

It was impossible to say the effect it had on him. At first I thought that he was speechless. His head lay sunk in the pillow. He moved his lips enough, however, to assure me that he was getting much stronger; a statement shockingly untrue on the face of it.

That afternoon I took my watch as a matter of course. A great over-heated stillness enveloped the ship and seemed to hold her motionless in a flaming ambience composed in two shades of blue. Faint, hot puffs eddied nervelessly from her sails. And yet she moved. She must have. For, as the sun was setting, we had drawn abreast of Cape Liant and dropped it behind us: an ominous retreating shadow in the last gleams of twilight.

In the evening, under the crude glare of his lamp, Mr. Burns seemed to have come more to the surface of his bedding. It was as if a depressing hand had been lifted off him. He answered my few words by a comparatively long, connected speech. He asserted himself strongly. If he escaped being smothered by this stagnant heat, he said, he was confident that in a very few days he would be able to come up on deck and help me.

While he was speaking I trembled lest this effort of energy should leave him lifeless before my eyes. But I cannot deny that there was something comforting in his willingness. I made a suitable reply, but pointed out to him that the only thing that could really help us was wind—a fair wind.

He rolled his head impatiently on the pillow. And it was not comforting in the least to hear him begin to mutter crazily about the late captain, that old man buried in latitude 8 d 20′, right in our way—ambushed at the entrance of the Gulf.

"Are you still thinking of your late captain, Mr. Burns?" I said. "I imagine the dead feel no animosity against the living. They care nothing for them."

"You don't know that one," he breathed out feebly.

"No. I didn't know him, and he didn't know me. And so he can't have any grievance against me, anyway."

"Yes. But there's all the rest of us on board," he insisted.

I felt the inexpugnable strength of common sense being insidiously menaced by this gruesome, by this insane, delusion. And I said:

"You mustn't talk so much. You will tire yourself."

"And there is the ship herself," he persisted in a whisper.

"Now, not a word more," I said, stepping in and laying my hand on his cool forehead. It proved to me that this atrocious absurdity was rooted in the man himself and not in the disease, which, apparently, had emptied him of every power, mental and physical, except that one fixed idea.

I avoided giving Mr. Burns any opening for conversation for the next few days. I merely used to throw him a hasty, cheery word when passing his door. I believe that if he had had the strength he would have called out after me more than once. But he hadn't the strength. Ransome, however, observed to me one afternoon that the mate "seemed to be picking up wonderfully."

"Did he talk any nonsense to you of late?" I asked casually.

"No, sir." Ransome was startled by the direct question; but, after a pause, he added equably: "He told me this morning, sir, that he was sorry he had to bury our late captain right in the ship's way, as one may say, out of the Gulf."

"Isn't this nonsense enough for you?" I asked, looking confidently at the intelligent, quiet face on which the secret uneasiness in the man's breast had thrown a transparent veil of care.

Ransome didn't know. He had not given a thought to the matter. And with a faint smile he flitted away from me on his never-ending duties, with his usual guarded activity.

Two more days passed. We had advanced a little way—a very little way—into the larger space of the Gulf of Siam. Seizing eagerly upon the elation of the first command thrown into my lap, by the agency of Captain Giles, I had yet an uneasy feeling that such luck as this has got perhaps to be paid for in some way. I had held, professionally, a review of my chances. I was competent enough for that. At least, I thought so. I had a general sense of my preparedness which only a man pursuing a calling he loves can know. That feeling seemed to me the most natural thing in the world. As natural as breathing. I imagined I could not have lived without it.

I don't know what I expected. Perhaps nothing else than that special intensity of existence which is the quintessence of youthful aspirations. Whatever I expected I did not expect to be beset by hurricanes. I knew better than that. In the Gulf of Siam there are no hurricanes. But neither did I expect to find myself bound hand and foot to the hopeless extent which was revealed to me as the days went on.

Not that the evil spell held us always motionless. Mysterious currents drifted us here and there, with a stealthy power made manifest only by the changing vistas of the islands fringing the east shore of the Gulf. And there were winds, too, fitful and deceitful. They raised hopes only to dash them into the bitterest disappointment, promises of advance ending in lost ground, expiring in sighs, dying into dumb stillness in which the currents had it all their own way—their own inimical way.

The island of Koh-ring, a great, black, upheaved ridge amongst a lot of tiny islets, lying upon the glassy water like a triton amongst minnows, seemed to be the centre of the fatal circle. It seemed impossible to get away from it. Day after day it remained in sight. More than once, in a favourable breeze, I would take its bearings in the fast-ebbing twilight, thinking that it was for the last time. Vain hope. A night of fitful airs would undo the gains of temporary favour, and the rising sun would throw out the black relief of Koh-ring looking more barren, inhospitable, and grim than ever.

"It's like being bewitched, upon my word," I said once to Mr. Burns, from my usual position in the doorway.

He was sitting up in his bed-place. He was progressing toward the world of living men; if he could hardly have been said to have rejoined it yet. He nodded to me his frail and bony head in a wisely mysterious assent.

"Oh, yes, I know what you mean," I said. "But you cannot expect me to believe that a dead man has the power to put out of joint the meteorology of this part of the world. Though indeed it seems to have gone utterly wrong. The land and sea breezes have got broken up into small pieces. We cannot depend upon them for five minutes together."

"It won't be very long now before I can come up on deck," muttered Mr. Burns, "and then we shall see."

Whether he meant this for a promise to grapple with supernatural evil I couldn't tell. At any rate, it wasn't the kind of assistance I needed. On the other hand, I had been living on deck practically night and day so as to take advantage of every chance to get my ship a little more to the southward. The mate, I could see, was extremely weak yet, and not quite rid of his delusion, which to me appeared but a symptom of his disease. At all events, the hopefulness of an invalid was not to be discouraged. I said:

"You will be most welcome there, I am sure, Mr. Burns. If you go on improving at this rate you'll be presently one of the healthiest men in the ship."

This pleased him, but his extreme emaciation converted his self-satisfied smile into a ghastly exhibition of long teeth under the red moustache.

"Aren't the fellows improving, sir?" he asked soberly, with an extremely sensible expression of anxiety on his face.

I answered him only with a vague gesture and went away from the door. The fact was that disease played with us capriciously very much as the winds did. It would go from one man to another with a lighter or heavier touch, which always left its mark behind, staggering some, knocking others over for a time, leaving this one, returning to another, so that all of them had now an invalidish aspect and a hunted, apprehensive look in their eyes; while Ransome and I, the only two completely untouched, went amongst them assiduously distributing quinine. It was a double fight. The adverse weather held us in front and the disease pressed on our rear. I must say that the men were very good. The constant toil of trimming yards they faced willingly. But all spring was out of their limbs, and as I looked at them from the poop I could not keep from my mind the dreadful impression that they were moving in poisoned air.

Down below, in his cabin, Mr. Burns had advanced so far as not only to be able to sit up, but even to draw up his legs. Clasping them with bony arms, like an animated skeleton, he emitted deep, impatient sighs.

"The great thing to do, sir," he would tell me on every occasion, when I gave him the chance, "the great thing is to get the ship past 8 d 20′ of latitude. Once she's past that we're all right."

At first I used only to smile at him, though, God knows, I had not much heart left for smiles. But at last I lost my patience.

"Oh, yes. The latitude 8 d 20′. That's where you buried your late captain, isn't it?" Then with severity: "Don't you think, Mr. Burns, it's about time you dropped all that nonsense?"

He rolled at me his deep-sunken eyes in a glance of invincible obstinacy. But for the rest he only muttered, just loud enough for me to hear, something about "Not surprised . . . find . . . play us some beastly trick yet. . . ."

Such passages as this were not exactly wholesome for my resolution. The stress of adversity was beginning to tell on me. At the same time, I felt a contempt for that obscure weakness of my soul. I said to myself disdainfully that it should take much more than that to affect in the smallest degree my fortitude.

I didn't know then how soon and from what unexpected direction it would be attacked.

It was the very next day. The sun had risen clear of the southern shoulder of Koh-ring, which still hung, like an evil attendant, on our port quarter. It was intensely hateful to my sight. During the night we had been heading all round the compass, trimming the yards again and again, to what I fear must have been for the most part imaginary puffs of air. Then just about sunrise we got for an hour an inexplicable, steady breeze, right in our teeth. There was no sense in it. It fitted neither with the season of the year nor with the secular experience of seamen as recorded in books, nor with the aspect of the sky. Only purposeful malevolence could account for it. It sent us travelling at a great pace away from our proper course; and if we had been out on pleasure sailing bent it would have been a delightful breeze, with the awakened sparkle of the sea, with the sense of motion and a feeling of unwonted freshness. Then, all at once, as if disdaining to carry farther the sorry jest, it dropped and died out completely in less than five minutes. The ship's head swung where it listed; the stilled sea took on the polish of a steel plate in the calm.

I went below, not because I meant to take some rest, but simply because I couldn't bear to look at it just then. The indefatigable Ransome was busy in the saloon. It had become a regular practice with him to give me an informal health report in the morning. He turned away from the sideboard with his usual pleasant, quiet gaze. No shadow rested on his intelligent forehead.

"There are a good many of them middling bad this morning, sir," he said in a calm tone.

"What? All knocked out?"

"Only two actually in their bunks, sir, but—"

"It's the last night that has done for them. We have had to pull and haul all the blessed time."

"I heard, sir. I had a mind to come out and help only, you know. . . ."

"Certainly not. You mustn't. . . . The fellows lie at night about the decks, too. It isn't good for them."

Ransome assented. But men couldn't be looked after like children. Moreover, one could hardly blame them for trying for such coolness and such air as there was to be found on deck. He himself, of course, knew better.

He was, indeed, a reasonable man. Yet it would have been hard to say that the others were not. The last few days had been for us like the ordeal of the fiery furnace. One really couldn't quarrel with their common, imprudent humanity making the best of the moments of relief, when the night brought in the illusion of coolness and the starlight twinkled through the heavy, dew-laden air. Moreover, most of them were so weakened that hardly anything could be done without everybody that could totter mustering on the braces. No, it was no use remonstrating with them. But I fully believed that quinine was of very great use indeed.

I believed in it. I pinned my faith to it. It would save the men, the ship, break the spell by its medicinal virtue, make time of no account, the weather but a passing worry and, like a magic powder working against mysterious malefices, secure the first passage of my first command against the evil powers of calms and pestilence. I looked upon it as more precious than gold, and unlike gold, of which there ever hardly seems to be enough anywhere, the ship had a sufficient store of it. I went in to get it with the purpose of weighing out doses. I stretched my hand with the feeling of a man reaching for an unfailing panacea, took up a fresh bottle and unrolled the wrapper, noticing as I did so that the ends, both top and bottom, had come unsealed. . . .

But why record all the swift steps of the appalling discovery? You have guessed the truth already. There was the wrapper, the bottle, and the white powder inside, some sort of powder! But it wasn't quinine. One look at it was quite enough. I remember that at the very moment of picking up the bottle, before I even dealt with the wrapper, the weight of the object I had in my hand gave me an instant premonition. Quinine is as light as feathers; and my nerves must have been exasperated into an extraordinary sensibility. I let the bottle smash itself on the floor. The stuff, whatever it was, felt gritty under the sole of my shoe. I snatched up the next bottle and then the next. The weight alone told the tale. One after another they fell, breaking at my feet, not because I threw them down in my dismay, but slipping through my fingers as if this disclosure were too much for my strength.

It is a fact that the very greatness of a mental shock helps one to bear up against it by producing a sort of temporary insensibility. I came out of the state-room stunned, as if something heavy had dropped on my head. From the other side of the saloon, across the table, Ransome, with a duster in his hand, stared open-mouthed. I don't think that I looked wild. It is quite possible that I appeared to be in a hurry because I was instinctively hastening up on deck. An example this of training become instinct. The difficulties, the dangers, the problems of a ship at sea must be met on deck.

To this fact, as it were of nature, I responded instinctively; which may be taken as a proof that for a moment I must have been robbed of my reason.

I was certainly off my balance, a prey to impulse, for at the bottom of the stairs I turned and flung myself at the doorway of Mr. Burns' cabin. The wildness of his aspect checked my mental disorder. He was sitting up in his bunk, his body looking immensely long, his head drooping a little sideways, with affected complacency. He flourished, in his trembling hand, on the end of a forearm no thicker than a walking-stick, a shining pair of scissors which he tried before my very eyes to jab at his throat.

I was to a certain extent horrified; but it was rather a secondary sort of effect, not really strong enough to make me yell at him in some such manner as: "Stop!" . . . "Heavens!" . . . "What are you doing?"

In reality he was simply overtaxing his returning strength in a shaky attempt to clip off the thick growth of his red beard. A large towel was spread over his lap, and a shower of stiff hairs, like bits of copper wire, was descending on it at every snip of the scissors.

He turned to me his face grotesque beyond the fantasies of mad dreams, one cheek all bushy as if with a swollen flame, the other denuded and sunken, with the untouched long moustache on that side asserting itself, lonely and fierce. And while he stared thunderstruck, with the gaping scissors on his fingers, I shouted my discovery at him fiendishly, in six words, without comment.

2

I HEARD the clatter of the scissors escaping from his hand, noted the perilous heave of his whole person over the edge of the bunk after them, and then, returning to my first purpose, pursued my course on the deck. The sparkle of the sea filled my eyes. It was gorgeous and barren, monotonous and without hope under the empty curve of the sky. The sails hung motionless and slack, the very folds of their sagging surfaces moved no more than carved granite. The impetuosity of my advent made the man at the helm start slightly. A block aloft squeaked incomprehensibly, for what on earth could have made it do so? It was a whistling note like a bird's. For a long, long time I faced an empty world, steeped in an infinity of silence, through which the sunshine poured and flowed for some mysterious purpose. Then I heard Ransome's voice at my elbow.

"I have put Mr. Burns back to bed, sir."

"You have."

"Well, sir, he got out, all of a sudden, but when he let go the edge of his bunk he fell down. He isn't light-headed, though, it seems to me."

"No," I said dully, without looking at Ransome. He waited for a moment, then cautiously, as if not to give offence: "I don't think we need lose much of that stuff, sir," he said, "I can sweep it up, every bit of it almost, and then we could sift the glass out. I will go about it at once. It will not make the breakfast late, not ten minutes."

"Oh, yes," I said bitterly. "Let the breakfast wait, sweep up every bit of it, and then throw the damned lot overboard!"

The profound silence returned, and when I looked over my shoulder, Ransome—the intelligent, serene Ransome—had vanished from my side. The intense loneliness of the sea acted like poison on my brain. When I turned my eyes to the ship, I had a morbid vision of her as a floating grave. Who hasn't heard of ships found floating, haphazard, with their crews all dead? I looked at the seaman at the helm, I had an impulse to speak to him, and, indeed, his face took on an expectant cast as if he had guessed my intention. But in the end I went below, thinking I would be alone with the greatness of my trouble for a little while. But through his open door Mr. Burns saw me come down, and addressed me grumpily: "Well, sir?"

I went in. "It isn't well at all," I said.

Mr. Burns, reestablished in his bed-place, was concealing his hirsute cheek in the palm of his hand.

"That confounded fellow has taken away the scissors from me," were the next words he said.

The tension I was suffering from was so great that it was perhaps just as well that Mr. Burns had started on his grievance. He seemed very sore about it and grumbled, "Does he think I am mad, or what?"

"I don't think so, Mr. Burns," I said. I looked upon him at that moment as a model of self-possession. I even conceived on that account a sort of admiration for that man, who had (apart from the intense materiality of what was left of his beard) come as near to being a disembodied spirit as any man can do and live. I noticed the preternatural sharpness of the ridge of his nose, the deep cavities of his temples, and I envied him. He was so reduced that he would probably die very soon. Enviable man! So near extinction—while I had to bear within me a tumult of suffering vitality, doubt, confusion, self-reproach, and an indefinite reluctance to meet the horrid logic of the situation. I could not help muttering: "I feel as if I were going mad myself."

Mr. Burns glared spectrally, but otherwise was wonderfully composed.

"I always thought he would play us some deadly trick," he said, with a peculiar emphasis on the *he*.

It gave me a mental shock, but I had neither the mind, nor the heart, nor the spirit to argue with him. My form of sickness was indifference. The creeping paralysis of a hopeless outlook. So I only gazed at him. Mr. Burns broke into further speech.

"Eh! What! No! You won't believe it? Well, how do you account for this? How do you think it could have happened?"

"Happened?" I repeated dully. "Why, yes, how in the name of the infernal powers did this thing happen?"

Indeed, on thinking it out, it seemed incomprehensible that it should just be like this: the bottles emptied, refilled, rewrapped, and replaced. A sort of plot, a sinister attempt to deceive, a thing resembling sly vengeance, but for what? Or else a fiendish joke. But Mr. Burns was in possession of a theory. It was simple, and he uttered it solemnly in a hollow voice.

"I suppose they have given him about fifteen pounds in Haiphong for that little lot."

"Mr. Burns!" I cried.

He nodded grotesquely over his raised legs, like two broomsticks in the pyjamas, with enormous bare feet at the end.

"Why not? The stuff is pretty expensive in this part of the world, and they were very short of it in Tonkin. And what did he care? You have not known him. I have, and I have defied him. He feared neither God, nor devil, nor man, nor wind, nor sea, nor his own conscience. And I believe he hated everybody and everything. But I think he was afraid to die. I believe I am the only man who ever stood up to him. I faced him in that cabin where you live now, when he was sick, and I cowed him then. He thought I was going to twist his neck for him. If he had had his way we would have been beating up against the Nord-East monsoon, as long as he lived and afterward, too, for ages and ages. Acting the Flying Dutchman in the China Sea! Ha! Ha!"

"But why should he replace the bottles like this?" . . . I began.

"Why shouldn't he? Why should he want to throw the bottles away? They fit the drawer. They belong to the medicine chest."

"And they were wrapped up," I cried.

"Well, the wrappers were there. Did it from habit, I suppose, and as to refilling, there is always a lot of stuff they send in paper parcels that burst after a time. And then, who can tell? I suppose you didn't taste it, sir? But, of course, you are sure. . . ."

"No," I said. "I didn't taste it. It is all overboard now."

Behind me, a soft, cultivated voice said: "I have tasted it. It seemed a mixture of all sorts, sweetish, saltish, very horrible."

Ransome, stepping out of the pantry, had been listening for some time, as it was very excusable in him to do.

"A dirty trick," said Mr. Burns. "I always said he would."

The magnitude of my indignation was unbounded. And the kind, sympathetic doctor, too. The only sympathetic man I ever knew . . . instead of writing that warning letter, the very refinement of sympathy, why didn't the man make a proper inspection? But, as a matter of fact, it was hardly fair to blame the doctor. The fittings were in order and the medicine chest is an officially arranged affair. There was nothing really to arouse the slightest suspicion. The person I could never forgive was myself. Nothing should ever be taken for granted. The seed of everlasting remorse was sown in my breast.

"I feel it's all my fault," I exclaimed, "mine and nobody else's. That's how I feel. I shall never forgive myself."

"That's very foolish, sir," said Mr. Burns fiercely.

And after this effort he fell back exhausted on his bed. He closed his eyes, he panted; this affair, this abominable surprise had shaken him up, too. As I turned away I perceived Ransome looking at me blankly. He appreciated what it meant, but managed to produce his pleasant, wistful smile. Then he stepped back into his pantry, and I rushed up on deck again to see whether there was any wind, any breath under the sky, any stir of the air, any sign of hope. The deadly stillness met me again. Nothing was changed except that there was a different man at the wheel. He looked ill. His whole figure drooped, and he seemed rather to cling to the spokes than hold them with a controlling grip. I said to him:

"You are not fit to be here."

"I can manage, sir," he said feebly.

As a matter of fact, there was nothing for him to do. The ship had no steerage way. She lay with her head to the westward, the everlasting Koh-ring visible over the stern, with a few small islets, black spots in the great blaze, swimming before my troubled eyes. And but for those bits of land there was no speck on the sky, no speck on the water, no shape of vapour, no wisp of smoke, no sail, no boat, no stir of humanity, no sign of life, nothing!

The first question was, what to do? What could one do? The first thing to do obviously was to tell the men. I did it that very day. I wasn't going to let the knowledge simply get about. I would face them. They were assembled on the quarterdeck for the purpose. Just before I stepped out to speak to them I discovered that life could hold terrible moments. No confessed criminal had ever been so oppressed by his sense of guilt. This is why, perhaps, my face was set hard and my voice curt and unemotional while I made my declaration that I could do nothing more for the sick in the way of drugs. As to such care as could be given them they knew they had had it.

I would have held them justified in tearing me limb from limb. The silence which followed upon my words was almost harder to bear than the angriest uproar. I was crushed by the infinite depth of its reproach. But, as a matter of fact, I was mistaken. In a voice which

I had great difficulty in keeping firm, I went on: "I suppose, men, you have understood what I said, and you know what it means."

A voice or two were heard: "Yes, sir. . . . We understand."

They had kept silent simply because they thought that they were not called to say anything; and when I told them that I intended to run into Singapore and that the best chance for the ship and the men was in the efforts all of us, sick and well, must make to get her along out of this, I received the encouragement of a low assenting murmur and of a louder voice exclaiming: "Surely there is a way out of this blamed hole."

Here is an extract from the notes I wrote at the time.

"We have lost Koh-ring at last. For many days now I don't think I have been two hours below altogether. I remain on deck, of course, night and day, and the nights and the days wheel over us in succession, whether long or short, who can say? All sense of time is lost in the monotony of expectation, of hope, and of desire—which is only one: Get the ship to the southward! Get the ship to the southward! The effect is curiously mechanical; the sun climbs and descends, the night swings over our heads as if somebody below the horizon were turning a crank. It is the prettiest, the most aimless! . . . and all through that miserable performance I go on, tramping, tramping the deck. How many miles have I walked on the poop of that ship! A stubborn pilgrimage of sheer restlessness, diversified by short excursions below to look upon Mr. Burns. I don't know whether it is an illusion, but he seems to become more substantial from day to day. He doesn't say much, for, indeed, the situation doesn't lend itself to idle remarks. I notice this even with the men as I watch them moving or sitting about the decks. They don't talk to each other. It strikes me that if there exists an invisible ear catching the whispers of the earth, it will find this ship the most silent spot on it. . . .

"No, Mr. Burns has not much to say to me. He sits in his bunk with his beard gone, his moustaches flaming, and with an air of silent determination on his chalky physiognomy. Ransome tells me he devours all the food that is given him to the last scrap, but that, apparently, he sleeps very little. Even at night, when I go below to fill my pipe, I notice that, though dozing flat on his back, he still looks very determined. From the side glance he gives me when awake it seems as though he were annoyed at being interrupted in some arduous mental operation; and as I emerge on deck the ordered arrangement of the stars meets my eye, unclouded, infinitely wearisome. There they are: stars, sun, sea, light, darkness, space, great waters; the formidable Work of the Seven Days, into which mankind seems to have blundered unbidden. Or else decoyed. Even as I have been decoyed into this awful, this death-haunted command. . . ."

The only spot of light in the ship at night was that of the compass-lamps, lighting up the faces of the succeeding helmsmen; for the rest we were lost in the darkness, I walking the poop and the men lying about the decks. They were all so reduced by sickness that no watches could be kept. Those who were able to walk remained all the time on duty, lying about in the shadows of the main deck, till my voice raised for an order would bring them to their enfeebled feet, a tottering little group, moving patiently about the ship, with hardly a murmur, a whisper amongst them all. And every time I had to raise my voice it was with a pang of remorse and pity.

Then about four o'clock in the morning a light would gleam forward in the galley. The unfailing Ransome with the uneasy heart, immune, serene, and active, was getting ready for the early coffee for the men. Presently he would bring me a cup up on the poop, and it was then that I allowed myself to drop into my deck chair for a couple of hours of real sleep. No doubt I must have been snatching short dozes when leaning against the rail for a moment in sheer exhaustion; but, honestly, I was not aware of them, except in the painful form of convulsive starts that seemed to come on me even while I walked. From about five, however, until after seven I would sleep openly under the fading stars.

I would say to the helmsman: "Call me at need," and drop into that chair and close my eyes, feeling that there was no more sleep for me on earth. And then I would know nothing till, some time between seven and eight, I would feel a touch on my shoulder and look up at Ransome's face, with its faint, wistful smile and friendly, gray eyes, as though he were tenderly amused at my slumbers. Occasionally the second mate would come up and relieve me at early coffee time. But it didn't really matter. Generally it was a dead calm, or else faint airs so changing and fugitive that it really wasn't worth while to touch a brace for them. If the air steadied at all the seaman at the helm could be trusted for a warning shout: "Ship's all aback, sir!" which like a trumpet-call would make me spring a foot above the deck. Those were the words which it seemed to me would have made me spring up from eternal sleep. But this was not often. I have never met since such breathless sunrises. And if the second mate happened to be there (he had generally one day in three free of fever) I would find him sitting on the skylight half senseless, as it were, and with an idiotic gaze fastened on some object near by—a rope, a cleat, a belaying pin, a ringbolt.

That young man was rather troublesome. He remained cubbish in his sufferings. He seemed to have become completely imbecile; and when the return of fever drove him to his cabin below, the next thing would be that we would miss him from there. The first time it happened Ransome and I were very much alarmed. We started a quiet search and ultimately Ransome discovered him curled up in the sail-locker, which opened into the lobby by a sliding door. When remonstrated with, he muttered sulkily, "It's cool in there." That wasn't true. It was only dark there.

The fundamental defects of his face were not improved by its uniform livid hue. The disease disclosed its low type in a startling way. It was not so with many of the men. The wastage of ill-health seemed to idealise the general character of the features, bringing out the unsuspected nobility of some, the strength of others, and in one case revealing an essentially comic aspect. He was a short, gingery, active man with a nose and chin of the Punch type, and whom his shipmates called "Frenchy." I don't know why. He may have been a Frenchman, but I have never heard him utter a single word in French.

To see him coming aft to the wheel comforted one. The blue dungaree trousers turned up the calf, one leg a little higher than the other, the clean check shirt, the white canvas cap, evidently made by himself, made up a whole of peculiar smartness, and the persistent jauntiness of his gait, even, poor fellow, when he couldn't help tottering, told of his invincible spirit. There was also a man called Gambril. He was the only grizzled person in the ship. His face was of an austere type. But if I remember all their faces, wasting tragically before my eyes, most of their names have vanished from my memory.

The words that passed between us were few and puerile in regard of the situation. I had to force myself to look them in the face. I expected to meet reproachful glances. There were none. The expression of suffering in their eyes was indeed hard enough to bear. But that they couldn't help. For the rest, I ask myself whether it was the temper of their souls or the sympathy of their imagination that made them so wonderful, so worthy of my undying regard.

For myself, neither my soul was highly tempered, nor my imagination properly under control. There were moments when I felt, not only that I would go mad, but that I had gone mad already; so that I dared not open my lips for fear of betraying myself by some insane shriek. Luckily I had only orders to give, and an order has a steadying influence upon him who has to give it. Moreover, the seaman, the officer of the watch, in me was sufficiently sane. I was like a mad carpenter making a box. Were he ever so convinced that he was King of Jerusalem, the box he would make would be a sane box. What I feared was a shrill note escaping me involuntarily and upsetting my balance. Luckily, again, there was no necessity to raise one's voice. The brooding stillness of the world seemed sensitive to the slightest sound, like a whispering gallery. The conversational tone would almost carry a word from one end of the ship to the other. The terrible thing was that the only voice that I ever heard was my own. At night especially it reverberated very lonely amongst the planes of the unstirring sails.

Mr. Burns, still keeping to his bed with that air of secret determination, was moved to grumble at many things. Our interviews were short five-minute affairs, but fairly frequent. I was everlastingly diving down below to get a light, though I did not consume much tobacco at that time. The pipe was always going out; for in truth my mind was not composed enough to enable me to get a decent smoke. Likewise, for most of the time during the twenty-four hours I could have struck matches on deck and held them aloft till the flame burnt my fingers. But I always used to run below. It was a change. It was the only break in the incessant strain; and, of course, Mr. Burns through the open door could see me come in and go out every time.

With his knees gathered up under his chin and staring with his greenish eyes over them, he was a weird figure, and with my knowledge of the crazy notion in his head, not a very attractive one for me. Still, I had to speak to him now and then, and one day he complained that the ship was very silent. For hours and hours, he said, he was lying there, not hearing a sound, till he did not know what to do with himself.

"When Ransome happens to be forward in his galley everything's so still that one might think everybody in the ship was dead," he grumbled. "The only voice I do hear sometimes is yours, sir, and that isn't enough to cheer me up. What's the matter with the men? Isn't there one left that can sing out at the ropes?"

"Not one, Mr. Burns," I said. "There is no breath to spare on board this ship for that. Are you aware that there are times when I can't muster more than three hands to do anything?"

He asked swiftly but fearfully:

"Nobody dead yet, sir?"

"No."

"It wouldn't do," Mr. Burns declared forcibly. "Mustn't let him. If he gets hold of one he will get them all."

I cried out angrily at this. I believe I even swore at the disturbing effect of these words. They attacked all the self-possession that was left to me. In my endless vigil in the face of the enemy I had been haunted by gruesome images enough. I had had visions of a ship drifting in calms and swinging in light airs, with all her crew dying slowly about her decks. Such things had been known to happen.

Mr. Burns met my outburst by a mysterious silence.

"Look here," I said. "You don't believe yourself what you say. You can't. It's impossible. It isn't the sort of thing I have a right to expect from you. My position's bad enough without being worried with your silly fancies."

He remained unmoved. On account of the way in which the light fell on his head I could not be sure whether he had smiled faintly or not. I changed my tone.

"Listen," I said. "It's getting so desperate that I had thought for a moment, since we can't make our way south, whether I wouldn't try to steer west and make an attempt to reach the mailboat track. We could always get some quinine from her, at least. What do you think?"

He cried out: "No, no, no. Don't do that, sir. You mustn't for a moment give up facing that old ruffian. If you do he will get the upper hand of us."

I left him. He was impossible. It was like a case of possession. His protest, however, was essentially quite sound. As a matter of fact, my notion of heading out west on the chance of sighting a problematical steamer could not bear calm examination. On the side where we were we had enough wind, at least from time to time, to struggle on toward the south. Enough, at least, to keep hope alive. But suppose that I had used those capricious gusts of wind to sail away to the westward, into some region where there was not a breath of air for days on end, what then? Perhaps my appalling vision of a ship floating with a dead crew would become a reality for the discovery weeks afterward by some horror-stricken mariners.

That afternoon Ransome brought me up a cup of tea, and while waiting there, tray in hand, he remarked in the exactly right tone of sympathy:

"You are holding out well, sir."

"Yes," I said. "You and I seem to have been forgotten."

"Forgotten, sir?"

"Yes, by the fever-devil who has got on board this ship," I said.

Ransome gave me one of his attractive, intelligent, quick glances and went away with the tray. It occurred to me that I had been talking somewhat in Mr. Burns' manner. It annoyed me. Yet often in darker moments I forgot myself into an attitude toward our troubles more fit for a contest against a living enemy.

Yes. The fever-devil had not laid his hand yet either on Ransome or on me. But he might at any time. It was one of those thoughts one had to fight down, keep at arm's length at any cost. It was unbearable to contemplate the possibility of Ransome, the housekeeper of the ship, being laid low. And what would happen to my command if I got knocked over, with Mr. Burns too weak to stand without holding on to his bed-place and the second mate reduced to a state of permanent imbecility? It was impossible to imagine, or rather, it was only too easy to imagine.

I was alone on the poop. The ship having no steerage way, I had sent the helmsman away to sit down or lie down somewhere in the shade. The men's strength was so reduced that all unnecessary calls on it had to be avoided. It was the austere Gambril with the grizzly beard. He went away readily enough, but he was so weakened by repeated bouts of fever, poor fellow, that in order to get down the poop ladder he had to turn sideways and hang on with both hands to the brass rail. It was just simply heart-breaking to watch. Yet he was neither very much worse nor much better than most of the half-dozen miserable victims I could muster up on deck.

It was a terribly lifeless afternoon. For several days in succession low clouds had appeared in the distance, white masses with dark convolutions resting on the water, motionless, almost solid, and yet all the time changing their aspects subtly. Toward evening they vanished as a rule. But this day they awaited the setting sun, which glowed and smouldered sulkily amongst them before it sank down. The punctual and wearisome stars reappeared over our mastheads, but the air remained stagnant and oppressive.

The unfailing Ransome lighted the binnaclelamps and glided, all shadowy, up to me.

"Will you go down and try to eat something, sir?" he suggested.

His low voice startled me. I had been standing looking out over the rail, saying nothing, feeling nothing, not even the weariness of my limbs, overcome by the evil spell.

"Ransome," I asked abruptly, "how long have I been on deck? I am losing the notion of time."

"Twelve days, sir," he said, "and it's just a fortnight since we left the anchorage."

His equable voice sounded mournful somehow. He waited a bit, then added: "It's the first time that it looks as if we were to have some rain."

I noticed then the broad shadow on the horizon, extinguishing the low stars completely, while those overhead, when I looked up, seemed to shine down on us through a veil of smoke.

How it got there, how it had crept up so high, I couldn't say. It had an ominous appearance. The air did not stir. At a renewed invitation from Ransome I did go down into the cabin to—in his own words—"try and eat something." I don't know that the trial was very successful. I suppose at that period I did exist on food in the usual way; but the memory is now that in those days life was sustained on invincible anguish, as a sort of infernal stimulant exciting and consuming at the same time.

It's the only period of my life in which I attempted to keep a diary. No, not the only one. Years later, in conditions of moral isolation, I did put down on paper the thoughts and events of a score of days. But this was the first time. I don't remember how it came about or how the pocketbook and the pencil came into my hands. It's inconceivable that I should have looked for them on purpose. I suppose they saved me from the crazy trick of talking to myself.

Strangely enough, in both cases I took to that sort of thing in circumstances in which I did not expect, in colloquial phrase, "to come out of it." Neither could I expect the record to outlast me. This shows that it was purely a personal need for intimate relief and not a call of egotism.

Here I must give another sample of it, a few detached lines, now looking very ghostly to my own eyes, out of the part scribbled that very evening:

"THERE IS something going on in the sky like a decomposition; like a corruption of the air, which remains as still as ever. After all, mere clouds, which may or may not hold wind or rain. Strange that it should trouble me so. I feel as if all my sins had found me out. But I suppose the trouble is that the ship is still lying motionless, not under command; and that I have nothing to do to keep my imagination from running wild amongst the disastrous images of the worst that may befall us. What's going to happen? Probably nothing. Or anything. It may be a furious squall coming, butt end foremost. And on deck there are five men with the vitality and the strength of, say, two. We may have all our sails blown away. Every stitch of canvas has been on her since we broke ground at the mouth of the Mei-nam, fifteen days ago . . . or fifteen centuries. It seems to me that all my life before that momentous day is infinitely remote, a fading memory of light-hearted youth, something on the other side of a shadow. Yes, sails may very well be blown away. And that would be like a death sentence on the men. We haven't strength enough on board to bend another suit; incredible thought, but it is true. Or we may even get dismasted. Ships have been dismasted in squalls simply because they weren't handled quick enough, and we have no power to whirl the yards around. It's like being bound hand and foot preparatory to having one's throat cut. And what appals me most of all is that I shrink from going on deck to face it. It's due to the ship, it's due to the men who are there on deck—some of them, ready to put out the last remnant of their strength at a word from me. And I am shrinking from it. From the mere vision. My first command. Now I understand that strange sense of insecurity in my past. I always suspected that I might be no good. And here is proof positive. I am shirking it. I am no good."

AT THAT MOMENT, or, perhaps, the moment after, I became aware of Ransome standing in the cabin. Something in his expression startled me. It had a meaning which I could not make out. I exclaimed: "Somebody's dead."

It was his turn then to look startled.

"Dead? Not that I know of, sir. I have been in the forecastle only ten minutes ago and there was no dead man there then."

"You did give me a scare," I said.

His voice was extremely pleasant to listen to. He explained that he had come down below to close Mr. Burns' port in case it should come on to rain. "He did not know that I was in the cabin," he added.

"How does it look outside?" I asked him.

"Very black, indeed, sir. There is something in it for certain."

"In what quarter?"

"All round, sir."

I repeated idly: "All round. For certain," with my elbows on the table.

Ransome lingered in the cabin as if he had something to do there, but hesitated about doing it. I said suddenly:

"You think I ought to be on deck?"

He answered at once but without any particular emphasis or accent: "I do, sir."

I got to my feet briskly, and he made way for me to go out. As I passed through the lobby I heard Mr. Burns' voice saying:

"Shut the door of my room, will you, steward?" And Ransome's rather surprised: "Certainly, sir."

I thought that all my feelings had been dulled into complete indifference. But I found it as trying as ever to be on deck. The impenetrable blackness beset the ship so close that it seemed that by thrusting one's hand over the side one could touch some unearthly substance. There was in it an effect of inconceivable terror and of inexpressible mystery. The few stars overhead shed a dim light upon the ship alone, with no gleams of any kind upon the water, in detached shafts piercing an atmosphere which had turned to soot. It was something I had never seen before, giving no hint of the direction from which any change would come, the closing in of a menace from all sides.

There was still no man at the helm. The immobility of all things was perfect. If the air had turned black, the sea, for all I knew, might have turned solid. It was no good looking in any direction, watching for any sign, speculating upon the nearness of the moment. When the time came the blackness would overwhelm silently the bit of starlight falling upon the ship, and the end of all things would come without a sigh, stir, or murmur of any kind, and all our hearts would cease to beat like run-down clocks.

It was impossible to shake off that sense of finality. The quietness that came over me was like a foretaste of annihilation. It gave me a sort of comfort, as though my soul had become suddenly reconciled to an eternity of blind stillness.

The seaman's instinct alone survived whole in my moral dissolution. I descended the ladder to the quarter-deck. The starlight seemed to die out before reaching that spot, but when I asked quietly: "Are you there, men?" my eyes made out shadow forms starting up around me, very few, very indistinct; and a voice spoke: "All here, sir." Another amended anxiously:

"All that are any good for anything, sir."

Both voices were very quiet and unringing; without any special character of readiness or discouragement. Very matter-of-fact voices.

"We must try to haul this mainsail close up," I said.

The shadows swayed away from me without a word. Those men were the ghosts of themselves, and their weight on a rope could be no more than the weight of a bunch of ghosts. Indeed, if ever a sail was hauled up by sheer spiritual strength it must have been that sail, for, properly speaking, there was not muscle enough for the task in the whole ship let alone the miserable lot of us on deck. Of course, I took the lead in the work myself. They wandered feebly after me from rope to rope, stumbling and panting. They toiled like Titans. We were half-an-hour at it at least, and all the time the black universe made no sound. When the last leech-line was made fast, my eyes, accustomed to the darkness, made out the shapes of exhausted men drooping over the rails, collapsed on hatches. One hung over the after-capstan, sobbing for breath, and I stood amongst them like a tower of strength, impervious to disease and feeling only the sickness of my soul. I waited for some time fighting against the weight of my sins, against my sense of unworthiness, and then I said:

"Now, men, we'll go aft and square the mainyard. That's about all we can do for the ship; and for the rest she must take her chance."

3

As we all went up it occurred to me that there ought to be a man at the helm. I raised my voice not much above a whisper, and, noiselessly, an uncomplaining spirit in a fever-wasted body appeared in the light aft, the head with hollow eyes illuminated against the blackness which had swallowed up our world—and the universe. The bared forearm extended over the upper spokes seemed to shine with a light of its own.

I murmured to that luminous appearance:

"Keep the helm right amidships."

It answered in a tone of patient suffering:

"Right amidships, sir."

Then I descended to the quarter-deck. It was impossible to tell whence the blow would come. To look round the ship was to look into a bottomless, black pit. The eye lost itself in inconceivable depths.

I wanted to ascertain whether the ropes had been picked up off the deck. One could only do that by feeling with one's feet. In my cautious progress I came against a man in whom I recognized Ransome. He possessed an unimpaired physical solidity which was manifest to me at the contact. He was leaning against the quarter-deck capstan and kept silent. It was like a revelation. He was the collapsed figure sobbing for breath I had noticed before we went on the poop.

"You have been helping with the mainsail!" I exclaimed in a low tone.

"Yes, sir," sounded his quiet voice.

"Man! What were you thinking of? You mustn't do that sort of thing."

After a pause he assented: "I suppose I mustn't." Then after another short silence he added: "I am all right now," quickly, between the tell-tale gasps.

I could neither hear nor see anybody else; but when I spoke up, answering sad murmurs filled the quarter-deck, and its shadows seemed to shift here and there. I ordered all the halyards laid down on deck clear for running.

"I'll see to that, sir," volunteered Ransome in his natural, pleasant tone, which comforted one and aroused one's compassion, too, somehow.

That man ought to have been in his bed, resting, and my plain duty was to send him there. But perhaps he would not have obeyed me; I had not the strength of mind to try. All I said was:

"Go about it quietly, Ransome."

Returning on the poop I approached Gambril. His face, set with hollow shadows in the light, looked awful, finally silenced. I asked him how he felt, but hardly expected an answer. Therefore, I was astonished at his comparative loquacity.

"Them shakes leaves me as weak as a kitten, sir," he said, preserving finely that air of unconsciousness as to anything but his business a helmsman should never lose. "And before I can pick up my strength that there hot fit comes along and knocks me over again."

He sighed. There was no reproach in his tone, but the bare words were enough to give me a horrible pang of self-reproach. It held me dumb for a time. When the tormenting sensation had passed off I asked:

"Do you feel strong enough to prevent the rudder taking charge if she gets sternway on her? It wouldn't do to get something smashed about the steering-gear now. We've enough difficulties to cope with as it is."

He answered with just a shade of weariness that he was strong enough to hang on. He could promise me that she shouldn't take the wheel out of his hands. More he couldn't say.

At that moment Ransome appeared quite close to me, stepping out of the darkness into visibility suddenly, as if just created with his composed face and pleasant voice.

Every rope on deck, he said, was laid down clear for running, as far as one could make certain by feeling. It was impossible to see anything. Frenchy had stationed himself forward. He said he had a jump or two left in him yet.

Here a faint smile altered for an instant the clear, firm design of Ransome's lips. With his serious clear, gray eyes, his serene temperament—he was a priceless man altogether. Soul as firm as the muscles of his body.

He was the only man on board (except me, but I had to preserve my liberty of movement) who had a sufficiency of muscular strength to trust to. For a moment I thought I had better ask him to take the wheel. But the dreadful knowledge of the enemy he had to carry about him made me hesitate. In my ignorance of physiology it occurred to me that he might die suddenly, from excitement, at a critical moment.

While this gruesome fear restrained the ready words on the tip of my tongue, Ransome stepped back two paces and vanished from my sight.

At once an uneasiness possessed me, as if some support had been withdrawn. I moved forward, too, outside the circle of light, into the darkness that stood in front of me like a wall. In one stride I penetrated it. Such must have been the darkness before creation. It had closed behind me. I knew I was invisible to the man at the helm. Neither could I see anything. He was alone, I was alone, every man was alone where he stood. And every form was gone too, spar, sail, fittings, rails; everything was blotted out in the dreadful smoothness of that absolute night.

A flash of lightning would have been a relief—I mean physically. I would have prayed for it if it hadn't been for my shrinking apprehension of the thunder. In the tension of silence I was suffering from it seemed to me that the first crash must turn me into dust.

And thunder was, most likely, what would happen next. Stiff all over and hardly breathing, I waited with a horribly strained expectation. Nothing happened. It was maddening, but a dull, growing ache in the lower part of my face made me aware that I had been grinding my teeth madly enough, for God knows how long.

It's extraordinary I should not have heard myself doing it; but I hadn't. By an effort which absorbed all my faculties I managed to keep my jaw still. It required much attention, and while thus engaged I became bothered by curious, irregular sounds of faint tapping on the deck. They could be heard single, in pairs, in groups. While I wondered at this mysterious devilry, I received a slight blow under the left eye and felt an enormous tear run down my cheek. Raindrops. Enormous. Forerunners of something. Tap. Tap. Tap. . . .

I turned about, and, addressing Gambrel earnestly, entreated him to "hang on to the wheel." But I could hardly speak from emotion. The fatal moment had come. I held my breath. The tapping had stopped as unexpectedly as it had begun, and there was a renewed moment of intolerable suspense; something like an additional turn of the racking screw. I don't suppose I would have ever screamed, but I remember my conviction that there was nothing else for it but to scream.

Suddenly—how am I to convey it? Well, suddenly the darkness turned into water. This is the only suitable figure. A heavy shower, a downpour, comes along, making a noise. You hear its approach on the sea, in the air, too, I verily believe. But this was different. With no preliminary whisper or rustle, without a splash, and even without the ghost of impact, I became instantaneously soaked to the skin. Not a very difficult matter, since I was wearing only my sleeping suit. My hair got full of water in an instant, water streamed on my skin, it filled my nose, my ears, my eyes. In a fraction of a second I swallowed quite a lot of it.

As to Gambril, he was fairly choked. He coughed pitifully, the broken cough of a sick man; and I beheld him as one sees a fish in an aquarium by the light of an electric bulb, an elusive, phosphorescent shape. Only he did not glide away. But something else happened. Both binnaclelamps went out. I suppose the water forced itself into them, though I wouldn't have thought that possible, for they fitted into the cowl perfectly.

The last gleam of light in the universe had gone, pursued by a low exclamation of dismay from Gambril. I groped for him and seized his arm. How startlingly wasted it was.

"Never mind," I said. "You don't want the light. All you need to do is to keep the wind, when it comes, at the back of your head. You understand?"

"Aye, aye, sir. . . . But I should like to have a light," he added nervously.

All that time the ship lay as steady as a rock. The noise of the water pouring off the sails and spars, flowing over the break of the poop, had stopped short. The poop scuppers gurgled and sobbed for a little while longer, and then perfect silence, joined to perfect immobility, proclaimed the yet unbroken spell of our helplessness, poised on the edge of some violent issue, lurking in the dark.

I started forward restlessly. I did not need my sight to pace the poop of my ill-starred first command with perfect assurance. Every square foot of her decks was impressed indelibly on my brain, to the very grain and knots of the planks. Yet, all of a sudden, I fell clean over something, landing full length on my hands and face.

It was something big and alive. Not a dog—more like a sheep, rather. But there were no animals in the ship. How could an animal. . . . It was an added and fantastic horror which I could not resist. The hair of my head stirred even as I picked myself up, awfully scared; not as a man is scared while his judgment, his reason still try to resist, but completely, boundlessly, and, as it were, innocently scared—like a little child.

I could see It—that Thing! The darkness, of which so much had just turned into water, had thinned down a little. There It was! But I did not hit upon the notion of Mr. Burns issuing out of the companion on all fours till he attempted to stand up, and even then the idea of a bear crossed my mind first.

He growled like one when I seized him round the body. He had buttoned himself up into an enormous winter overcoat of some woolly material, the weight of which was too much for his reduced state. I could hardly feel the incredibly thin lath of his body, lost within the thick stuff, but his growl had depth and substance: Confounded dump ship with a craven, tiptoeing crowd. Why couldn't they stamp and go with a brace? Wasn't there one Godforsaken lubber in the lot fit to raise a yell on a rope?

"Skulking's no good, sir," he attacked me directly. "You can't slink past the old murderous ruffian. It isn't the way. You must go for him boldly—as I did. Boldness is what you want. Show him that you don't care for any of his damned tricks. Kick up a jolly old row."

"Good God, Mr. Burns," I said angrily. "What on earth are you up to? What do you mean by coming up on deck in this state?"

"Just that! Boldness. The only way to scare the old bullying rascal."

I pushed him, still growling, against the rail. "Hold on to it," I said roughly. I did not know what to do with him. I left him in a hurry, to go to Gambril, who had called faintly that he believed there was some wind aloft. Indeed, my own ears had caught a feeble flutter of wet canvas, high up overhead, the jingle of a slack chain sheet. . . .

These were eerie, disturbing, alarming sounds in the dead stillness of the air around me. All the instances I had heard of topmasts being whipped out of a ship while there was not wind enough on her deck to blow out a match rushed into my memory.

"I can't see the upper sails, sir," declared Gambril shakily.

"Don't move the helm. You'll be all right," I said confidently.

The poor man's nerves were gone. Mine were not in much better case. It was the moment of breaking strain and was relieved by the abrupt sensation of the ship moving forward as if of herself under my feet. I heard plainly the soughing of the wind aloft, the low cracks of the upper spars taking the strain, long before I could feel the least draught on my face turned aft, anxious and sightless like the face of a blind man.

Suddenly a louder-sounding note filled our ears, the darkness started streaming against our bodies, chilling them exceedingly. Both of us, Gambril and I, shivered violently in our clinging, soaked garments of thin cotton. I said to him:

"You are all right now, my man. All you've got to do is to keep the wind at the back of your head. Surely you are up to that. A child could steer this ship in smooth water."

He muttered: "Aye! A healthy child." And I felt ashamed of having been passed over by the fever which had been preying on every man's strength but mine, in order that my remorse might be the more bitter, the feeling of unworthiness more poignant, and the sense of responsibility heavier to bear.

The ship had gathered great way on her almost at once on the calm water. I felt her slipping through it with no other noise but a mysterious rustle alongside. Otherwise, she had no motion at all, neither lift nor roll. It was a disheartening steadiness which had lasted for eighteen days now; for never, never had we had wind enough in that time to raise the slightest run of the sea. The breeze freshened suddenly. I thought it was high time to get Mr. Burns off the deck. He worried me. I looked upon him as a lunatic who would be very likely to start roaming over the ship and break a limb or fall overboard.

I was truly glad to find he had remained holding on where I had left him, sensibly enough. He was, however, muttering to himself ominously.

This was discouraging. I remarked in a matter-of-fact tone:

"We have never had so much wind as this since we left the roads."

"There's some heart in it, too," he growled judiciously. It was a remark of a perfectly sane seaman. But he added immediately: "It was about time I should come on deck. I've been nursing my strength for this—just for this. Do you see it, sir?"

I said I did, and proceeded to hint that it would be advisable for him to go below now and take a rest.

His answer was an indignant "Go below! Not if I know it, sir."

Very cheerful! He was a horrible nuisance. And all at once he started to argue. I could feel his crazy excitement in the dark.

"You don't know how to go about it, sir. How could you? All this whispering and tiptoeing is no good. You can't hope to slink past a cunning, wide-awake, evil brute like he was. You never heard him talk. Enough to make your hair stand on end. No! No! He wasn't mad. He was no more mad than I am. He was just downright wicked. Wicked so as to frighten most people. I will tell you what he was. He was nothing less than a thief and a murderer at heart. And do you think he's any different now because he's dead? Not he! His carcass lies a hundred fathom under, but he's just the same . . . in latitude 8 d 20′ north."

He snorted defiantly. I noted with weary resignation that the breeze had got lighter while he raved. He was at it again.

"I ought to have thrown the beggar out of the ship over the rail like a dog. It was only on account of the men. . . . Fancy having to read the Burial Service over a brute like that! . . . 'Our departed brother' . . . I could have laughed. That was what he couldn't bear. I suppose I am the only man that ever stood up to laugh at him. When he got sick it used to scare that . . . brother. . . . Brother. . . . Departed. . . . Sooner call a shark brother."

The breeze had let go so suddenly that the way of the ship brought the wet sails heavily against the mast. The spell of deadly stillness had caught us up again. There seemed to be no escape.

"Hallo!" exclaimed Mr. Burns in a startled voice. "Calm again!"

I addressed him as though he had been sane.

"This is the sort of thing we've been having for seventeen days, Mr. Burns," I said with intense bitterness. "A puff, then a calm, and in a moment, you'll see, she'll be swinging on her heel with her head away from her course to the devil somewhere."

He caught at the word. "The old dodging Devil," he screamed piercingly and burst into such a loud laugh as I had never heard before. It was a provoking, mocking peal, with a hair-raising, screeching over-note of defiance. I stepped back, utterly confounded.

Instantly there was a stir on the quarter-deck; murmurs of dismay. A distressed voice cried out in the dark below us: "Who's that gone crazy, now?"

Perhaps they thought it was their captain? Rush is not the word that could be applied to the utmost speed the poor fellows were up to; but in an amazing short time every man in the ship able to walk upright had found his way on to that poop.

I shouted to them: "It's the mate. Lay hold of him a couple of you. . . ."

I expected this performance to end in a ghastly sort of fight. But Mr. Burns cut his derisive screeching dead short and turned upon them fiercely, yelling:

"Aha! Dog-gone ye! You've found your tongues—have ye? I thought you were dumb. Well, then—laugh! Laugh—I tell you. Now then—all together. One, two, three—laugh!"

A moment of silence ensued, of silence so profound that you could have heard a pin drop on the deck. Then Ransome's unperturbed voice uttered pleasantly the words:

"I think he has fainted, sir—" The little motionless knot of men stirred, with low murmurs of relief. "I've got him under the arms. Get hold of his legs, some one."

Yes. It was a relief. He was silenced for a time—for a time. I could not have stood another peal of that insane screeching. I was sure of it; and just then Gambril, the austere Gambril, treated us to another vocal performance. He began to sing out for relief. His voice wailed pitifully in the darkness: "Come aft somebody! I can't stand this. Here she'll be off again directly and I can't. . . ."

I dashed aft myself meeting on my way a hard gust of wind whose approach Gambril's ear had detected from afar and which filled the sails on the main in a series of muffled reports mingled with the low plaint of the spars. I was just in time to seize the wheel while Frenchy who had followed me caught up the collapsing Gambril. He hauled him out of the way, admonished him to lie still where he was, and then stepped up to relieve me, asking calmly:

"How am I to steer her, sir?"

"Dead before it for the present. I'll get you a light in a moment."

But going forward I met Ransome bringing up the spare binnacle lamp. That man noticed everything, attended to everything, shed comfort around him as he moved. As he passed me he remarked in a soothing tone that the stars were coming out. They were. The breeze was sweeping clear the sooty sky, breaking through the indolent silence of the sea.

The barrier of awful stillness which had encompassed us for so many days as though we had been accursed, was broken. I felt that. I let myself fall on to the skylight seat. A faint white ridge of foam, thin, very thin, broke alongside. The first for ages—for ages. I could have cheered, if it hadn't been for the sense of guilt which clung to all my thoughts secretly. Ransome stood before me.

"What about the mate," I asked anxiously. "Still unconscious?"

"Well, sir—it's funny," Ransome was evidently puzzled. "He hasn't spoken a word, and his eyes are shut. But it looks to me more like sound sleep than anything else."

I accepted this view as the least troublesome of any, or at any rate, least disturbing. Dead faint or deep slumber, Mr. Burns had to be left to himself for the present. Ransome remarked suddenly:

"I believe you want a coat, sir."

"I believe I do," I sighed out.

But I did not move. What I felt I wanted were new limbs. My arms and legs seemed utterly useless, fairly worn out. They didn't even ache. But I stood up all the same to put on the coat when Ransome brought it up. And when he suggested that he had better now "take Gambril forward," I said:

"All right. I'll help you to get him down on the main deck."

I found that I was quite able to help, too. We raised Gambril up between us. He tried to help himself along like a man but all the time he was inquiring piteously:

"You won't let me go when we come to the ladder? You won't let me go when we come to the ladder?"

The breeze kept on freshening and blew true, true to a hair. At daylight by careful manipulation of the helm we got the foreyards to run square by themselves (the water keeping smooth) and then went about hauling the ropes tight. Of the four men I had with me at night, I could see now only two. I didn't inquire as to the others. They had given in. For a time only I hoped.

Our various tasks forward occupied us for hours, the two men with me moved so slow and had to rest so often. One of them remarked that "every blamed thing in the ship felt about a hundred times heavier than its proper weight." This was the only complaint uttered. I don't know what we should have done without Ransome. He worked with us, silent, too, with a little smile frozen on his lips. From time to time I murmured to him: "Go steady"—"Take it easy, Ransome"—and received a quick glance in reply.

When we had done all we could do to make things safe, he disappeared into his galley.

Some time afterward, going forward for a look round, I caught sight of him through the open door. He sat upright on the locker in front of the stove, with his head leaning back against the bulkhead. His eyes were closed; his capable hands held open the front of his thin cotton shirt baring tragically his powerful chest, which heaved in painful and laboured gasps. He didn't hear me.

I retreated quietly and went straight on to the poop to relieve Frenchy, who by that time was beginning to look very sick. He gave me the course with great formality and tried to go off with a jaunty step, but reeled widely twice before getting out of my sight.

And then I remained all alone aft, steering my ship, which ran before the wind with a buoyant lift now and then, and even rolling a little. Presently Ransome appeared before me with a tray. The sight of food made me ravenous all at once. He took the wheel while I sat down of the after grating to eat my breakfast.

"This breeze seems to have done for our crowd," he murmured. "It just laid them low—all hands."

"Yes," I said. "I suppose you and I are the only two fit men in the ship."

"Frenchy says there's still a jump left in him. I don't know. It can't be much," continued Ransome with his wistful smile. "Good little man that. But suppose, sir, that this wind flies round when we are close to the land—what are we going to do with her?"

"If the wind shifts round heavily after we close in with the land she will either run ashore or get dismasted or both. We won't be able to do anything with her. She's running away with us now. All we can do is to steer her. She's a ship without a crew."

"Yes. All laid low," repeated Ransome quietly. "I do give them a look-in forward every now and then, but it's precious little I can do for them."

"I, and the ship, and every one on board of her, are very much indebted to you, Ransome," I said warmly.

He made as though he had not heard me, and steered in silence till I was ready to relieve him. He surrendered the wheel, picked up the tray, and for a parting shot informed me that Mr. Burns was awake and seemed to have a mind to come up on deck.

"I don't know how to prevent him, sir. I can't very well stop down below all the time."

It was clear that he couldn't. And sure enough Mr. Burns came on deck dragging himself painfully aft in his enormous overcoat. I beheld him with a natural dread. To have him around and raving about the wiles of a dead man while I had to steer a wildly rushing ship full of dying men was a rather dreadful prospect.

But his first remarks were quite sensible in meaning and tone. Apparently he had no recollection of the night scene. And if he had he didn't betray himself once. Neither did he talk very much. He sat on the skylight looking desperately ill at first, but that strong breeze, before which the last remnant of my crew had wilted down, seemed to blow a fresh stock of vigour into his frame with every gust. One could almost see the process.

By way of sanity test I alluded on purpose to the late captain. I was delighted to find that Mr. Burns did not display undue interest in the subject. He ran over the old tale of that savage ruffian's iniquities with a certain vindictive gusto and then concluded unexpectedly:

"I do believe, sir, that his brain began to go a year or more before he died."

A wonderful recovery. I could hardly spare it as much admiration as it deserved, for I had to give all my mind to the steering.

In comparison with the hopeless languour of the preceding days this was dizzy speed. Two ridges of foam streamed from the ship's bows; the wind sang in a strenuous note which under other circumstances would have expressed to me all the joy of life. Whenever the hauled-up mainsail started trying to slat and bang itself to pieces in its gear, Mr. Burns would look at me apprehensively.

"What would you have me to do, Mr. Burns? We can neither furl it nor set it. I only wish the old thing would thrash itself to pieces and be done with it. That beastly racket confuses me."

Mr. Burns wrung his hands, and cried out suddenly:

"How will you get the ship into harbour, sir, without men to handle her?"

And I couldn't tell him.

Well—it did get done about forty hours afterward. By the exorcising virtue of Mr. Burns' awful laugh, the malicious spectre had been laid, the evil spell broken, the curse removed. We were now in the hands of a kind and energetic Providence. It was rushing us on. . . .

I shall never forget the last night, dark, windy, and starry. I steered. Mr. Burns, after having obtained from me a solemn promise to give him a kick if anything happened, went frankly to sleep on the deck close to the binnacle. Convalescents need sleep. Ransome, his back propped against the mizzen-mast and a blanket over his legs, remained perfectly still, but I don't suppose he closed his eyes for a moment. That embodiment of jauntiness, Frenchy, still under the delusion that there was a "jump" left in him, had insisted on joining us; but mindful of discipline, had laid himself down as far on the forepart of the poop as he could get, alongside the bucket-rack.

And I steered, too tired for anxiety, too tired for connected thought. I had moments of grim exultation and then my heart would sink awfully at the thought of that forecastle at the other end of the dark deck, full of fever-stricken men—some of them dying. By my fault. But never mind. Remorse must wait. I had to steer.

In the small hours the breeze weakened, then failed altogether. About five it returned, gentle enough, enabling us to head for the roadstead. Daybreak found Mr. Burns sitting wedged up with coils of rope on the stern-grating, and from the depths of his overcoat steering the ship with very white bony hands; while Ransome and I rushed along the decks letting go all the sheets and halliards by the run. We dashed next up on to the forecastle head. The perspiration of labour and sheer nervousness simply poured off our heads as we toiled to get the anchors cock-billed. I dared not look at Ransome as we worked side by side. We exchanged curt words; I could hear him panting close to me and I avoided turning my eyes his way for fear of seeing him fall down and expire in the act of putting forth his strength—for what? Indeed for some distinct ideal.

The consummate seaman in him was aroused. He needed no directions. He knew what to do. Every effort, every movement was an act of consistent heroism. It was not for me to look at a man thus inspired.

At last all was ready and I heard him say:

"Hadn't I better go down and open the compressors now, sir?"

"Yes. Do," I said.

And even then I did not glance his way. After a time his voice came up from the main deck.

"When you like, sir. All clear on the windlass here."

I made a sign to Mr. Burns to put the helm down and let both anchors go one after another, leaving the ship to take as much cable as she wanted. She took the best part of them both before she brought up. The loose sails coming aback ceased their maddening racket above my head. A perfect stillness reigned in the ship. And while I stood forward feeling a little giddy in that sudden peace, I caught faintly a moan or two and the incoherent mutterings of the sick in the forecastle.

As we had a signal for medical assistance flying on the mizzen it is a fact that before the ship was fairly at rest three steam launches from various men-of-war were alongside; and at least five naval surgeons had clambered on board. They stood in a knot gazing up and down the empty main deck, then looked aloft—where not a man could be seen, either.

I went toward them—a solitary figure, in a blue and gray striped sleeping suit and a pipe-clayed cork helmet on its head. Their disgust was extreme. They had expected surgical cases. Each one had brought his carving tools with him. But they soon got over their little disappointment. In less than five minutes one of the steam launches was rushing shoreward to order a big boat and some hospital people for the removal of the crew. The big steam pinnace went off to her ship to bring over a few bluejackets to furl my sails for me.

One of the surgeons had remained on board. He came out of the forecastle looking impenetrable, and noticed my inquiring gaze.

"There's nobody dead in there, if that's what you want to know," he said deliberately. Then added in a tone of wonder: "The whole crew!"

"And very bad?"

"And very bad," he repeated. His eyes were roaming all over the ship. "Heavens! What's that?"

"That," I said, glancing aft, "is Mr. Burns, my chief officer."

Mr. Burns with his moribund head nodding on the stalk of his lean neck was a sight for any one to exclaim at. The surgeon asked:

"Is he going to the hospital, too?"

"Oh, no," I said jocosely. "Mr. Burns can't go on shore till the mainmast goes. I am very proud of him. He's my only convalescent."

"You look—" began the doctor staring at me. But I interrupted him angrily:

"I am not ill."

"No. . . . You look queer."

"Well, you see, I have been seventeen days on deck."

"Seventeen! . . . But you must have slept."

"I suppose I must have. I don't know. But I'm certain that I didn't sleep for the last forty hours."

"Phew! . . . You will be going ashore presently I suppose?"

"As soon as ever I can. There's no end of business waiting for me there."

The surgeon released my hand, which he had taken while we talked, pulled out his pocket-book, wrote in it rapidly, tore out the page and offered it to me.

"I strongly advise you to get this prescription made up for yourself ashore. Unless I am much mistaken you will need it this evening."

"What is it, then?" I asked with suspicion.

"Sleeping draught," answered the surgeon curtly; and moving with an air of interest toward Mr. Burns he engaged him in conversation.

As I went below to dress to go ashore, Ransome followed me. He begged my pardon; he wished, too, to be sent ashore and paid off.

I looked at him in surprise. He was waiting for my answer with an air of anxiety.

"You don't mean to leave the ship!" I cried out.

"I do really, sir. I want to go and be quiet somewhere. Anywhere. The hospital will do."

"But, Ransome," I said. "I hate the idea of parting with you."

"I must go," he broke in. "I have a right!" . . . He gasped and a look of almost savage determination passed over his face. For an instant he was another being. And I saw under the worth and the comeliness of the man the humble reality of things. Life was a boon to him—this precarious hard life, and he was thoroughly alarmed about himself.

"Of course I shall pay you off if you wish it," I hastened to say. "Only I must ask you to remain on board till this afternoon. I can't leave Mr. Burns absolutely by himself in the ship for hours."

He softened at once and assured me with a smile and in his natural pleasant voice that he understood that very well.

When I returned on deck everything was ready for the removal of the men. It was the last ordeal of that episode which had been maturing and tempering my character—though I did not know it.

It was awful. They passed under my eyes one after another—each of them an embodied reproach of the bitterest kind, till I felt a sort of revolt wake up in me. Poor Frenchy had gone suddenly under. He was carried past me insensible, his comic face horribly flushed and as if swollen, breathing stertorously. He looked more like Mr. Punch than ever; a disgracefully intoxicated Mr. Punch.

The austere Gambril, on the contrary, had improved temporarily. He insisted on walking on his own feet to the rail—of course with assistance on each side of him. But he gave way to a sudden panic at the moment of being swung over the side and began to wail pitifully:

"Don't let them drop me, sir. Don't let them drop me, sir!" While I kept on shouting to him in most soothing accents: "All right, Gambril. They won't! They won't!"

It was no doubt very ridiculous. The bluejackets on our deck were grinning quietly, while even Ransome himself (much to the fore in lending a hand) had to enlarge his wistful smile for a fleeting moment.

I left for the shore in the steam pinnace, and on looking back beheld Mr. Burns actually standing up by the taffrail, still in his enormous woolly overcoat. The bright sunlight brought out his weirdness amazingly. He looked like a frightful and elaborate scarecrow set up on the poop of a death-stricken ship, set up to keep the seabirds from the corpses.

Our story had got about already in town and everybody on shore was most kind. The Marine Office let me off the port dues, and as there happened to be a shipwrecked crew staying in the Home I had no difficulty in obtaining as many men as I wanted. But when I inquired if I could see Captain Ellis for a moment I was told in accents of pity for my ignorance that our deputy-Neptune had retired and gone home on a pension about three weeks after I left the port. So I suppose that my appointment was the last act, outside the daily routine, of his official life.

It is strange how on coming ashore I was struck by the springy step, the lively eyes, the strong vitality of every one I met. It impressed me enormously. And amongst those I met there was Captain Giles, of course. It would have been very extraordinary if I had not met him. A prolonged stroll in the business part of the town was the regular employment of all his mornings when he was ashore.

I caught the glitter of the gold watch-chain across his chest ever so far away. He radiated benevolence.

"What is it I hear?" he queried with a "kind uncle" smile, after shaking hands. "Twenty-one days from Bangkok?"

"Is this all you've heard?" I said. "You must come to tiffin with me. I want you to know exactly what you have let me in for."

He hesitated for almost a minute.

"Well—I will," he said condescendingly at last.

We turned into the hotel. I found to my surprise that I could eat quite a lot. Then over the cleared table-cloth I unfolded to Captain Giles the history of these twenty days in all its professional and emotional aspects, while he smoked patiently the big cigar I had given him.

Then he observed sagely:

"You must feel jolly well tired by this time."

"No," I said. "Not tired. But I'll tell you, Captain Giles, how I feel. I feel old. And I must be. All of you on shore look to me just a lot of skittish youngsters that have never known a care in the world."

He didn't smile. He looked insufferably exemplary. He declared:

"That will pass. But you do look older—it's a fact."

"Aha!" I said.

"No! No! The truth is that one must not make too much of anything in life, good or bad."

"Live at half-speed," I murmured perversely. "Not everybody can do that."

"You'll be glad enough presently if you can keep going even at that rate," he retorted with his air of conscious virtue. "And there's another thing: a man should stand up to his bad luck, to his mistakes, to his conscience and all that sort of thing. Why—what else would you have to fight against."

I kept silent. I don't know what he saw in my face but he asked abruptly:

"Why—you aren't faint-hearted?"

"God only knows, Captain Giles," was my sincere answer.

"That's all right," he said calmly. "You will learn soon how not to be faint-hearted. A man has got to learn everything—and that's what so many of them youngsters don't understand."

"Well, I am no longer a youngster."

"No," he conceded. "Are you leaving soon?"

"I am going on board directly," I said. "I shall pick up one of my anchors and heave in to half-cable on the other directly my new crew comes on board and I shall be off at daylight to-morrow!"

"You will," grunted Captain Giles approvingly, "that's the way. You'll do."

"What did you think? That I would want to take a week ashore for a rest?" I said, irritated by his tone. "There's no rest for me till she's out in the Indian Ocean and not much of it even then."

He puffed at his cigar moodily, as if transformed.

"Yes. That's what it amounts to," he said in a musing tone. It was as if a ponderous curtain had rolled up disclosing an unexpected Captain Giles. But it was only for a moment, just the time to let him add, "Precious little rest in life for anybody. Better not think of it."

We rose, left the hotel, and parted from each other in the street with a warm handshake, just as he began to interest me for the first time in our intercourse.

The first thing I saw when I got back to the ship was Ransome on the quarter-deck sitting quietly on his neatly lashed sea-chest.

I beckoned him to follow me into the saloon where I sat down to write a letter of recommendation for him to a man I knew on shore.

When finished I pushed it across the table. "It may be of some good to you when you leave the hospital."

He took it, put it in his pocket. His eyes were looking away from me—nowhere. His face was anxiously set.

"How are you feeling now?" I asked.

"I don't feel bad now, sir," he answered stiffly. "But I am afraid of its coming on. . . ." The wistful smile came back on his lips for a moment. "I—I am in a blue funk about my heart, sir."

I approached him with extended hand. His eyes not looking at me had a strained expression. He was like a man listening for a warning call.

"Won't you shake hands, Ransome?" I said gently.

He exclaimed, flushed up dusky red, gave my hand a hard wrench—and next moment, left alone in the cabin, I listened to him going up the companion stairs cautiously, step by step, in mortal fear of starting into sudden anger our common enemy it was his hard fate to carry consciously within his faithful breast.